HOOD'S TEXAS BRIGADE

CONFLICTING WORLDS
New Dimensions of the American Civil War

T. Michael Parrish, Series Editor

HOOD'S TEXAS BRIGADE

THE SOLDIERS AND FAMILIES OF THE CONFEDERACY'S MOST CELEBRATED UNIT

SUSANNAH J. URAL

Louisiana State University Press
Baton Rouge

Published by Louisiana State University Press
lsupress.org

Copyright © 2017 by Louisiana State University Press
All rights reserved. Except in the case of brief quotations used in articles or reviews, no part of this publication may be reproduced or transmitted in any format or by any means without written permission of Louisiana State University Press.

Louisiana Paperback Edition, 2022

Designer: Michelle A. Neustrom
Typefaces: Sentinel, text; Centrifuge, display

Cover images: (front) Courtesy Rosenberg Library, Galveston, Texas; *(spine)* Courtesy The American Civil War Museum, Richmond, Virginia.

Maps created by George Skoch

Library of Congress Cataloging-in-Publication Data

Names: Ural, Susannah J., author.
Title: Hood's Texas Brigade : the soldiers and families of the Confederacy's most celebrated unit / Susannah J. Ural.
Other titles: Conflicting worlds.
Description: Baton Rouge : Louisiana State University Press, [2017] | Series: Conflicting worlds : new dimensions of the American Civil War | Includes bibliographical references and index.
Identifiers: LCCN 2017019254| ISBN 978-0-8071-6759-5 (cloth : alk. paper) | ISBN 978-0-8071-6760-1 (pdf) | ISBN 978-0-8071-6761-8 (epub) | ISBN 978-0-8071-7822-5 (paperback)
Subjects: LCSH: Confederate States of America. Army. Texas Brigade. | Texas—History—Civil War, 1861–1865. | United States—History—Civil War, 1861–1865.
Classification: LCC E580.4.T4 U73 2017 | DDC 973.7/464—dc23
LC record available at https://lccn.loc.gov/2017019254

for Robby and Ras

CONTENTS

Acknowledgements / *ix*

INTRODUCTION / *1*

1
TO ARMS IN TEXAS
Mobilizing the First Thousand Texans for Virginia / *11*

2
THE RUSH TO VIRGINIA
The Organization of the Fourth and Fifth Texas Infantry / *30*

3
RECRUITS ON THE DRILL FIELD
Becoming Citizen-Soldiers / *42*

4
THE POTOMAC BLOCKADE
The Texas Brigade's First Assignment / *58*

5
SEEING THE ELEPHANT
Turning Scouts into Soldiers / *75*

6
SLIPPING THE BRIDLE
The Battles of Second Manassas and Antietam / *104*

7
THE COST OF REPUTATION
Emancipation, Suffolk, and Gettysburg | *136*

8
A LACK OF LEADERSHIP
The Battle of Chickamauga and the Hard Winter of 1863–64 | *183*

9
REUNION WITH LEE
From the Wilderness through Petersburg | *204*

10
DETERMINATION AND DEFEAT
The Final Defense of Richmond and Surrender at Appomattox | *231*

11
WAGING PEACE
Texas Brigade Veterans and Families in Reconstruction and Beyond | *250*

CONCLUSION | *281*

Notes | *283*

Selected Bibliography | *333*

Index | *363*

Illustrations follow page 168

ACKNOWLEDGMENTS

I started researching and writing about Hood's Texans in 2004, the year my son was born. He'll be in eighth grade by the time these words appear in print. In my defense, I published three other books in the meantime, but I always returned to this project, fascinated by the men and their families and determined to help readers understand the significance of Hood's Texas Brigade in a new way. The first draft of this manuscript felt flat. I scrapped much of it because I offered few new insights and failed to capture the complexities of my subjects. My second draft benefited from a rich narrative but still failed to explain what made this unit so successful on the battlefield and so loyal to each other and their cause. Like Goldilocks, my third attempt at the manuscript was just right, thanks in no small part to the Dale Center for the Study of War & Society at the University of Southern Mississippi awarding me the Blount Professorship in Military History in 2013. This provided me with the resources and time to rethink, reshape, and rewrite this book. It proved invaluable to this project, and I'm thankful to Maj. Gen. Buford "Buff" Blount and his wife, Anita, for establishing the professorship to support Southern Miss historians working in the field of war and society.

    I am indebted to a host of archivists, but several of you went above and beyond to help me track down materials: Louise Arnold-Friend, the late Art Bergeron, Jack Bobinger, John Coski, Peggy Fox Michaels, Julie Holcomb, David Keough, Barbara Kievit-Mason, Judy Pate, Richard J. Sommers, Cheryl Spencer, and John Versiluis. Thanks, too, to the National Park Service historians who helped me work in their collections or hiked battlefields with me (or both): Ted Alexander, Scott Hartwig, John Hennessy, Bobby Krick, Jim Ogden, Frank O'Reilly, and Don Pfanz. Other historians and researchers shared their Texas Brigade research, walked positions with me, and debated key issues for this book: Robert Alton, Keith Bohannon, Pete Carmichael, Tom Clemens, Andie Custer, Rich DiNardo (who, along with his wife, Rita, hosted me during several research trips to northern Virginia), Rick Eiserman, John Favors, Don Frasier, Chuck Grear, Rick McCaslin, Jeff Prushankin, Carol Reardon, Ron Smith, Mark Snell, David Ward, Beth White, and Alfred Young. I also want to thank Rand Dotson, Lee Sioles, Neal Novak, and Kate Barton at LSU Press, who have been a pleasure to work with, as well as series editor Mike Parrish, who has the patience of Job. Thanks, too, to copy editor Susan Murray for her superb work and confidentiality policy on authors' grammatical weaknesses (that *is* confidential, right?), and to the talented George Skoch, who designed the maps for this book.

A group of friends and scholars critiqued this manuscript in its third and final phase. Rick Eiserman, Gary Gallagher, Lesley Gordon, Will Greene, and Mike Parrish read it in its entirety and offered key corrections, suggestions, and support. Thank you all. My thanks also go to Tom Clemens, Scott Hartwig, John Hennessy, Bobby Krick, Wayne Motts, Dave Powell, Carol Reardon, Andy Slap, Frank Towers, and Jon Wells who advised me on sections tied to their areas of expertise. If errors remain after all this help, they are, clearly, my own.

My colleagues at Sam Houston State University in Huntsville, Texas, where I began this project, were essential for the success of the first phase of this work: the late Terry Bilhartz, Caroline Castillo Crimm, Kenneth E. Hendrickson III, Nancy Sears Leavell, and Charlann Morris. My University of Southern Mississippi colleagues were key to the final half of this project, offering invaluable advice and encouragement along the way. Special thanks go to Allison Abra, Shelia Garris McArn, Heather Stur, Cindy Warren, Andy Wiest, and Kyle Zelner. Dr. J. T. Johnson, Director of the Center for Research Support at Southern Miss, was invaluable as I created the concept for my Texas Brigade sample and then processed and interpreted that data.

Several of my current and former graduate students helped with the statistical information for this book. Allan Branstiter did yeoman's work entering data for the large Texas Brigade sample, and Stephanie Seal Walters applied her digital history skills to help me clean and interpret that information. My thanks go to Samantha Taylor and Tracy Barnett for their help with images for this book, and, very early on, to a former student and now Texas history teacher, Leslie Hegman Sproat. Leslie traveled with me as we traced Hood's Texans from battlefield to battlefield, allowing me to work in archives by day, and then she, my son, Robby, and I toured key Texas Brigade positions in the evening.

I owe a special thanks to Texas Brigade descendants and researchers who shared or helped me access and analyze privately held sources: Jerry Beetz; Glenn and Marla Carroll; Gary Chandler; Finney Mack Clay; Rick Featherston; Katherine A. H. Goldberg; Martha Hartzog; Kenn Harding, Tammy Tiner, and Laura Harding; Dolly S. Jeffus; Melinda Jane Laird Kilian and Melissa Ann Laird Lingwall; Elizabeth Leifeste; Weldon Nash Jr.; Ruth Peebles; Mary Lou Percy; Joanne Watson Percy; Jane Gillette Riggs; Jim and Marty Rogers; Jim and Karen Shadle; John Stevens; HenryEtta McKinley Wilson; and Dan Worrell.

My friend Rick Eiserman, who has been researching the Texas Brigade for decades, deserves special mention. We met when I was about a year into this work. Since then we've coauthored articles, hiked battlefields, shared research, and debated more issues about Hood's Texans than I can recall. Rick was also a tremendous help in the final stages of this work as I double-checked arguments and source material. I need to thank Carmen Eiserman, too, for humoring our obsession with this unit. Another longtime Texas Brigade researcher, Kevin Jones, gave me his entire collection around 2005 and remained available for questions as I worked. Thank you, Kevin. My individual thanks go to George and Nancy Lowe, too, for their tremendous support, including funding researchers to help with data entry and collection, for hosting me in their home during research trips to Austin, and supporting this project to the end.

Several organizations provided general funding or grants and fellowships to support my work: the Dale Center for the Study of War & Society, the Center for the Study of the Gulf South, and the History Department, all at the University of Southern Mississippi, sent me to conferences to receive key critiques of my work and on trips to conduct research that was essential to this project's completion and success. I work with an incredible group of historians whose support and scholarship pushes me to always do better. I also benefited from a research grant from the College of Arts & Letters at Southern Miss, as well as a General and Mrs. Matthew B. Ridgway Research Grant from the U.S. Army Heritage and Education Center, and an Ottis Lock Research Grant from the East Texas Historical Association. The Hood's Texas Brigade Association Reactivated presented graduate fellowships to two of my students to process data for the research samples tied to this book. My doctoral student Allan Branstiter and I were also fortunate to attend a digital history workshop cosponsored by the National Endowment of the Humanities and the Society for

Military History hosted by Northeastern University in 2014. Our thanks go to Abby Mullens and the team of faculty who taught us so much there, including Scott Nesbit, Jeff McClurken, and Micki Kaufman, and to the Dale Center at Southern Miss and the Southern Miss Research Foundation, who sponsored our trip. I also want to offer special thanks to Dale Center supporters Beverly Dale, Wayde Benson, Richard McCarthy, and Craig Howard, along with our other patrons, who are invaluable to the work Southern Miss history faculty and graduate students do in the field of war and society.

For my sisters in the field, who offered support and healthy critiques, thank you Karen Cox, Lorien Foote, Sarah Gardner, Caroline Janney, Anne Marshall, Megan Kate Nelson, Margaret Storey, Amy Murrell Taylor, and especially the three I had on speed-dial: Judy Giesberg, Lesley Gordon, and Anne Sarah Rubin. I'm fortunate to have you as colleagues in this field, but even more fortunate to have such friends and confidants. Thanks, too, to the women who have offered unfailing support for over two decades: Randi Tinkleman Downey, Lisa Kiniry, Valeri Pappas, Kelli Shonter, and Ann-Marie Vannucci. Special thanks also go to my unofficial therapist and kindred spirit Peggy Douglas Waterman, who, more than once, has patched me up and helped me back on track when life knocked me down.

Two more scholar friends require special mention for always being available to discuss this project with me. They raised an eyebrow (thankfully) at my weaker arguments and encouraged me to continue with others I was ready to abandon. Kurt Hackemer and Kyle Zelner have thought more about Hood's Texans than they ever cared to simply because I asked for their help. I owe you guys. Again.

In the end, though, it is my family who keeps me going. My mother-in-law, Sandra Rasberry, knew when to help me escape with gardening, when to ignore the fact that I'd let the garden go to weeds, and when to simply share her faith in me and this project. My other Rasberry, Ellis, Robinson, Street, Summerlin, and Morgan in-laws mastered the art of when to ask about the book and when to change the subject. Thank you all. My parents, William F. and Sue C. Ural, deserve the most credit for how I approached this project. They inspired my fascination with military history and service and offered insights into my mother's experiences as she raised two young boys while my father served as a flight surgeon during the Vietnam War. They insisted that they suffered little compared to what many spouses endured, especially with men engaged in heavy combat, but their memories of that time served as an early reminder that historians need to capture whole families' experiences to fully understand war. My father died in 2013, and we moved my mother here to Mississippi, where she lives next door and saves my neck on a regular basis by helping with my son, Robby, or grocery runs, the occasional meal, and those wonderful afternoons on the porch when we enjoy a cocktail and discuss the day and my writing. She proofread early drafts of this manuscript for clarity and was superb at gently noting sections that needed rewriting or simply to be cut. She's an old-school mother: high expectations blended with unwavering love, patience, and support. I would be lost without her.

I dedicate this book to my husband, John Rasberry, and son, Robby Bruce. We've been through a lot while writing this, but we've had a lot of laughs, too. Quick with a hug and a smile, Robby grew up with this book, and his notes of encouragement, tucked in my laptop or left on a mirror, meant the world to me. I've found truth in a comment an older woman shared one day when Robby was a baby and I looked like I hadn't slept in weeks: "The days drag, but the years fly." What a treasure you are, kiddo. My husband, John, better known to us as Ras, is a constant, steady force in my life who makes the hard days better and the good days great. It's not that we "complete" each other; we're strong, independent souls on our own. It's just that we choose each other, day after day, through the good and the bad, even when I make him want to tear his hair out or that time he made me so mad I just about rolled a paint roller through the wall. Reader, you may consider writing a book or building a dream house, but I advise against doing them simultaneously. We might drive each other nuts sometimes, but there's no other place I'd rather be than at Ras's side, laughing on the porch as the sun goes down.

# HOOD'S TEXAS BRIGADE

INTRODUCTION

Texas-born Robert Campbell was a seventeen-year-old student in Louisiana when the Civil War began. He and his classmates organized a volunteer Confederate company in the spring of 1861, and they elected Campbell their captain. But school administrators dissolved the unit, and Campbell's father, an East Texas judge and member of Texas's secession convention, refused to let his son serve elsewhere. He was too young, Judge Campbell argued, insisting that the war would not last and that Robert should not interrupt his studies. By the following spring, however, it was clear that the war would last a bit longer than expected. Judge Campbell allowed his son to enlist this time and complained that he had but one son old enough to serve.[1] Robert Campbell could have joined Texas units that would keep him closer to home, but like hundreds of his fellow Texans, he chose to serve in Virginia, where a unique group of Texas volunteers believed they could contribute most to Confederate victory and independence. These men comprised the core regiments of one of the most respected units on either side of the American Civil War—John Bell Hood's Texas Brigade.

In August 1862, Private Campbell was wounded twice in the leg at the Battle of Second Manassas. He rejoined the Fifth Texas in time for the Battle of Chickamauga in September 1863, where he was wounded again in the leg and arm. Unwilling to abandon his brigade, but too badly injured to continue traditional infantry service, Campbell secured an appointment as a courier in Texas Brigade headquarters. At the Battle of the Wilderness in May 1864, he was the last brigade courier on the field, at least ten others having been killed, wounded, or sent back for more ordnance. After his horse was killed in battle in September 1864, Campbell, unable to secure another mount and determined to serve with fellow Texans, returned to the ranks. At the Battle of

Darbytown Road in October, he suffered severe wounds to his head, knee, and lungs. Campbell traveled to Huntsville, Texas, to recover at his family home, where he wrote to the *Houston Tri-Weekly Telegraph* to assure his fellow East Texans that years of hard fighting and heavy casualties might have reduced his company to something resembling "a corporal's guard," but they were "still unconquered" and eager to continue the fight.[2] By the spring of 1865, Campbell was still not fully recovered, but he began recruiting duty in Houston. On April 4, he finally applied for a medical discharge, knowing his wounds were too severe for him to return to service as an infantryman in the Texas Brigade. Just before the war ended, however, Campbell was busy trying to raise a cavalry unit so he could rejoin the fight for Confederate independence.[3]

Robert Campbell's devotion to the Confederate nation and to his unit speaks to the unique characteristics of the Texas Brigade. Like the Campbells, the majority of Texas Brigade soldiers and their families made their way west in the antebellum period, usually living for a few years in one southern slave state before moving on to another, and finally settling in Texas. Over two-thirds of the Texans in the brigade came from middle-class households in 1860. Most of them were farmers, though there were a few blacksmiths, teachers, physicians, and a host of lawyers. They were a blend of middle-class urban professionals and skilled laborers, self-farmers, backcountry yeoman, and poor farmers. Although most of them came from rural communities, a good number of Hood's Texans also called Galveston, Houston, Austin, and Dallas home.[4]

What united them, however, were the middle-class status and traditions they had earned by 1860 and their conviction that Republican Party policies, especially the containment of slavery, posed a disastrous threat to their futures. They were certain, as one Corsicana, Texas, newspaper warned their community—which sent hundreds of men to the Texas Brigade—that the election of Abraham Lincoln would result in the invasion of the South by fanatical northerners who would free, enfranchise, and arm African Americans and confiscate and redistribute southern white property.[5] In an effort to highlight the social, economic, and political success Texas Brigade households sought to defend in 1861 and the cultural connections the majority of Texas Brigade soldiers shared, this study utilized the definitions of poor, middling, and wealthy households that historian Charles Brooks used in his sociocultural study of the Texas Regiments of Hood's Texas Brigade. Like Brooks, *Hood's Texas Brigade* defines the poor in 1860s Texas as those households with real and personal property estimated at less than $500. Middle-class households held $500 to $19,999 in property, while the wealthy had combined property holdings of $20,000 or more.⁶

"Middle class" is a term that can have diverse meanings in nineteenth-century America. Hood's Texans were more unified by their cultural habits than their occupations or income. The majority of the soldiers in this brigade were not poor farmers or laborers, nor were they elite planters. Most of them embodied a middle-class disdain for ostentatious behavior, as seen in the Fifth Texas's abuse of Lt. Col. Frank Schaller and his military finery and their celebration of Lt. Col. John C. Upton, a middle-class rancher known for his rough mannerisms and his gift for command. The soldiers and families of Hood's Texas Brigade celebrated an industrious work ethic and a Jacksonian notion of the self-made man. They appreciated practical, even-tempered commanders, and they expressed their faith in simple terms that lacked pretension. It was these middle-class values that shaped how they lived and died for four years of war and how they waged their own version of peace in the decades that followed.

Two-thirds of Texas Brigade officers came from households that owned slaves. This proved true for only one-third of the Texas privates in the brigade, but the middle-class status most of them enjoyed tied them economically, socially, and politically to the slaveholders in their communities.⁷ Hood's Texans' comments regarding slaves and race relations during the war reflected that background, as well as their tremendous faith in themselves and in Confederate victory. Their writings revealed a classic paternalistic faith that Texas Brigade soldiers and their families were respectable masters whose slaves were satisfied with their place in the social order, a position, Hood's Texans would argue, that was natural and preordained. They believed that elite white males were best positioned to run their communities and their nation. Although it was possible for nonelite white men to rise to that ruling status through their labors and education (indeed, Hood's Texans celebrated such success), they did not believe nineteenth-century African Americans could or should enjoy such opportunities.

As a result of these racial beliefs, most Texas Brigade accounts that reference the enslaved are brief paternalistic greetings in letters home. Significantly, when emancipation became a key issue in the war in January 1863, Hood's Texans, unlike many Confederates, did not worry. They remained confident in their ability to secure Confederate independence, and believed emancipation would never affect their world. Secession had been the first step in defending their rights as slave owners, and Confederate independence would secure these. That confidence was not rattled until late in the war, when Texas Brigade men were attacked by African American Union soldiers in the fall of 1864. Then, Hood's Texans responded brutally to this challenge to their racial superiority and the social order. After the war, they continued to support the idea of a society led by whites. Texas Brigade veterans and their families expressed frustration with what they saw as the disastrous results of black suffrage and Radical Republican policies, and Hood's Texans longed for the return to white rule, though they did not universally support a return to Democratic Party rule.[8]

While the men's wealth and slave-owning status reflected the norm among mid-nineteenth-century white Texans, their ideological dedication to the Confederacy sets the Texas Brigade apart from their fellow Confederates. The volunteers and families who comprised this unit never lost their determination to help win Confederate independence. These men could have served close to home, but they insisted on fighting more than a thousand miles from their families because that is where they believed they could help most. As desertions rates spiked and will on the home front sank, Texas Brigade soldiers are unique in the historiography for their determination to stay in the ranks despite exhaustion and to return again and again after wounds and capture to continue the fight. Their families reflected that same ideological devotion. As frustrated letters from home arrived in Confederate camps and petitions flooded into the Texas governor's office to exempt men from service or provide, as promised, for soldiers' families, these were not pouring in from Texas Brigade families. Like their men in uniform, these mothers, fathers, wives, and siblings had either the ideological determination or the wealth to sustain themselves and each other in hard times, and their faith in their Confederate nation remained strong through the bitter end.[9]

Part of this devotion was inspired by the men and their families' strong and early identification with the Confederacy. But their nationalism and identity was also tied to the brigade's reputation, their commanders, and to each other. The Texas Brigade was celebrated as an elite unit throughout the Confederate high command and the ranks beginning as early as 1862. Gen. Robert E. Lee, in whose Army of Northern Virginia the Texas Brigade fought, admitted that he relied on his Texas soldiers "in all tight places" and argued, "We must have more of them" following the Battle of Antietam.[10] In April 1864, when Confederate lieutenant general James Longstreet's First Corps reunited with Lee's Army of Northern Virginia, Lee declared Hood's Texans "the best fighting brigade in the corps."[11] Lee cheered the Texas Brigade's arrival at the Battle of the Wilderness a week later, declaring "Texans always move them" as he expressed his confidence that these men would turn the tide of battle, which they did.[12]

It was not just Lee, however, who noted the brigade's incredible talent. Confederate major general Gustavus A. Smith commented after the Battle of Eltham's Landing in the spring of 1862 that "the Texans won immortal honor for themselves, their State, and for their commander, General Hood.... I could talk a week and then not say half they deserve. If the regiments now organized in Texas, could be transported here, and armed to-morrow, properly led, they would end the war in three months."[13] A French observer on Union general George McClellan's staff celebrated the bravery and discipline of Hood's Texans when writing about the Battle of Gaines's Mill, and North Carolina colonel Dorsey Pender confided to his wife that "Hood's Texas Boys" were "the best material on the continent without a doubt."[14] Confederate president Jefferson Davis insisted years after the war that Hood's Texas Brigade "showed on many battlefields its willingness 'to live and die for Dixie,'" and he argued that their motto might have been "No steps backwards." Even fellow foot soldiers agreed with the praise. Reflecting after the war, Pvt. Alexander Hunter of the First Virginia Infantry referred to the Texas Brigade as "the pride and glory of the Army of Northern Virginia."[15]

The Texas Brigade's success was grounded in the men's strong self-identity as Confederates, in the mutual respect between the brigade's junior officers and their men, and in their constant desire to maintain their reputation not just as Texans but also as the best soldiers in Robert E. Lee's army and all the Confederacy.[16] Part of this confidence—or arrogance, depending on one's perspective—was tied to their self-identification not just as white southern men but as Texans in particular. They saw themselves as the self-made men celebrated by nineteenth-century Americans. They took pride in their place in a slave-owning patriarchal society that enjoyed tremendous economic growth in the 1850s, growth that Texas Brigade volunteers were determined to secure for their futures. Their identity as Texans also contained a violent element that led people to assume the men were natural-born scouts and sharpshooters, despite the fact that most of the volunteers came from middle-class families in established cotton-based communities fueled by enslaved labor. Still, a desire to sustain the fighting reputation of Texans enhanced their continued devotion to the Confederate war effort. When junior officers emerged who knew how to inspire and lead a determinedly independent unit of citizen-soldier volunteers like those of the Texas Brigade, the unit was well on its way to earning its elite status in Lee's army.[17]

T. Harry Williams once argued that a brigade history done well is the "story of a democracy at war."[18] That idea inspired this book, but with a twist on traditional unit histories. *Hood's Texas Brigade* is a study of communities at war: the community the men built in their companies, regiments, and brigade, as well as the communities and families from which they came. Thus, this is not a conventional military history of a unit. There are a host of good studies that have already done that for the Texas Brigade and for the battles and campaigns that shaped their service.[19] To be sure, combat is key to understanding these men, and thus an analysis of them and their commanders in battle is found in this book. But this study is more focused on the motivations of Texas Brigade soldiers and their families, and how these evolved over the course of the war. It seeks to understand why these men were determined to serve so far from home, to remain in the Texas Brigade and the Army of Northern Virginia when so many other soldiers were deserting, and how their families reflected similar determination and identification with the Confederate nation. It also analyzes their strong devotion to the Confederacy and the cost of that devotion, and reveals how determined these men were to maintain their unit bonds, waging the peace of Reconstruction as Hood's Texas Brigade, just as they had waged the war.

Hood's Texans remind historians of the value of community studies and unit histories, because the Texas Brigade does not fit trends seen in the larger historiography. This unit offers new insights into the complexity of the Confederate war experience. We know, for example, that most Confederate soldiers and civilians expressed outrage over about the Emancipation Proclamation and worried about the unrest it would cause on the southern home front, but Hood's Texans had the opposite reaction, never fearing emancipation until the very end of the war.[20] They similarly diverge from historians' findings on issues of Confederate desertion, nationalism, the will to fight, and postwar adjustment. Hood's Texans also challenge the recent significant scholarship on civilians and soldiers who failed to live up to their own or their contemporaries' expectations. While some soldiers and families wrestled with depression, divorce, and suicidal thoughts and struggled to adjust to the postwar world, few of Hood's Texans did.[21] Ever-confident in themselves and their success,

Texas Brigade veterans never believed Confederate defeat had anything to do with them. Even when they surrendered their colors at Appomattox Court House, they did so with swagger. One of their color-bearers tied a note to the staff that held their flag, reminding any reader that they might be surrendering the staff, but they had stolen it from Maine men five months earlier.[22]

Organized into eleven chapters, the majority of *Hood's Texas Brigade* charts the creation and evolution of this elite Confederate unit from their rush to volunteer in 1861 through their defeat in the spring of 1865. This is supplemented with an investigation of how Hood's Texans adapted to their postwar lives by maintaining their brigade ties even after returning home. This book is influenced by the belief, shared by the men themselves, that units like the Texas Brigade succeeded because their families shared the men's strong devotion to the Confederacy, to their volunteer officers, and to Robert E. Lee. With this fact in mind, home-front morale and opinion shape this book as much as they shaped the brigade during the war.

Chapters 1 and 2 highlight the extreme enthusiasm for the war that Texas Brigade volunteers shared in 1861, arguing that this dedication, which evolved but never disappeared within the brigade, was central to their development as an elite unit. The chapters introduce the original volunteers of Hood's Texas Brigade, who would later form the First Texas Infantry Regiment, as they raced to Virginia after the fall of Fort Sumter in April 1861, arriving shortly after the Battle of First Manassas. They, their families, and their communities funded their travel at their own risk, and without any promise that these volunteers would be allowed to serve in Virginia. This original group maintained their enthusiastic and semi-disciplined fighting style at high cost. They were soon joined by another group of volunteers who were a little less radical but no less determined to play a martial role in the defense of their new nation. These later citizen-soldiers became the Fourth and Fifth Texas Infantry Regiments that, combined with the First Texas Infantry, became the Texas Brigade in the late fall of 1861.

Chapters 3 and 4 detail the men's development as citizen soldiers, focusing on their early training and the challenges that evolved as brothers, cousins, and neighbors chafed under a strict military hierarchy that required leadership from some and the cooperative obedience of others. These chapters argue that while the soldiers of the Texas Brigade fairly terrorized their officers appointed from Richmond, the men's determination to select their junior officers and assert their rights as citizen-soldiers helped a core group of exemplary citizen-officers emerge. This was not universal; some good men were driven off. But the Texans revealed a gift for selecting superb combat commanders who knew how to motivate and lead the men while also maintaining order in camp, and this proved especially true of their beloved John Bell Hood. These chapters cover the late fall of 1861, when the Eighteenth Georgia Infantry Regiment joined the Texas Brigade, through the early spring of 1862 as the men served in their first military assignment on the Potomac Blockade and battled disease, which proved their deadliest opponent.

Chapters 5, 6, and 7 focus on the key battles and campaigns that tested the officers and men and made the Texas Brigade's reputation. Reflecting on their service from Gaines's Mill through Gettysburg, Confederate leaders Robert E. Lee, Thomas Jonathan "Stonewall" Jackson, Jefferson Davis, W. C. "Chase" Whiting, and Dorsey Pender—none of them Texans—all publicly recognized the Texas Brigade as one of the best units in the Army of Northern Virginia. These chapters argue that it was in these battles that the brigade proved to the Confederacy, to their opponents, and perhaps to themselves that their reputation—a good bit of it based on stereotypes the men knew were largely contrived—was grounded in their tremendous skill as soldiers and officers. It was also during this time that the men's close relationship developed with Confederate general Robert E. Lee. This association became one of the most important factors in sustaining the Texas Brigade's morale and reputation as one of the best units in Lee's army. By 1863, the men and families of the Texas Brigade saw Lee, his army, and the Confederacy as one and the same. His leadership and their central role in Confederate victories or near victories fed their loyalty to their nation and sustained their willingness to sacrifice everything for it. Also discussed is the changing leadership of the brigade from John Bell Hood to William Wofford to J. B. Robertson, as well as the departure of the Eighteenth Georgia and Hampton's Legion from the Texas Brigade, and the entrance of the Third Arkansas. These chapters argue that through all of the upheaval of March 1862 through August 1863, the constancy of superb junior officers, the overarching leadership of Lee, and the determination of their families at home sustained the Texas Brigade despite high casualty rates and battlefield defeats. Finally, chapter 7 also highlights the brigade's calm response to President Abraham Lincoln's announcement of the Emancipation Proclamation. Hood's Texans spoke little about slavery in 1861 and 1862 because they had every confidence in Confederate victory. To their minds, the North, and especially Republicans, threatened slavery, which was key to the antebellum success Texas Brigade families had enjoyed. But Hood's Texans knew Confederate independence would nullify this threat. They had absolute faith in their ability to secure this and the futures they desired.

Chapters 8, 9, and 10 examine the hardest period of the war that the Texas Brigade faced. Despite their victory at the Battle of Chickamauga, the period from October 1863 through April 1864 proved to be a desperate one for the Texas Brigade. For the first time in the war, desertion rates spiked. To be fair, they were increasing during this period through the entire Confederacy. But whereas Lee's army suffered a 15 percent desertion rate, of the more than 7,000 men who served in Hood's Texas Brigade, only 6 percent deserted in four years of war. But one-third of these desertions took place between November 1863 and April 1864. Chapter 8 argues that several factors caused this: the brigade lacked a true commander because J. B. Robertson faced charges of purposely demoralizing the men and a possible court-martial; the men were undersupplied and underfed and closer to home than they had been in the entire war (which increased desertion rates throughout the army); their separation from Robert E. Lee and the Army of Northern Virginia further demoralized the men and caused fractures in their faith that their sacrifices could ensure Confederate independence. Chapters 9 and 10 use return rates to demonstrate that as the Texas Brigade reunited with Lee's army, the men's faith in the Confederate war effort rebounded. These chapters also chart the key but costly role the Texas Brigade played in the remainder of the war and argue that, once again, strong leadership by junior officers, continued support from their families at home, and a renewed faith in the war sustained the brigade as a fighting unit through their final surrender in April 1865.

Chapter 11 focuses on the postwar period and argues that Hood's Texans waged the tumultuous peace of Reconstruction together as a unit, just as they had waged the war they nearly won and that they firmly believed they could have won. It follows Hood's Texans from the surrender at Appomattox Court House, Virginia, to their homes in Texas and Arkansas. The major contributions of this chapter lie with just how devastated Hood's Brigade was as they left Virginia. Despite the possibility of resuming the fight by connecting with Confederate commanders Joseph E. Johnston or E. Kirby Smith on the brigade's journey home, not one of the men who kept diaries or later wrote about that trip mentioned the possibility. That is because, by 1865, their entire faith in victory rested with Lee and the Army of Northern Virginia. Once that army was defeated, Hood's Texans saw no chance for victory.

This chapter also shows the connections that Hood's Texans maintained with each other, and how they used their reputation to help them start businesses and to lead their communities in postwar Texas. Utilizing a statistical study of the brigade that compares the wealth of Texas Brigade households and counties in Arkansas and Texas in 1860 with their wealth in 1870, I found that although Hood's Texans suffered along with the rest of the region, on average, Hood's Texans were doing better in 1870 than their friends and neighbors in their county of residence. By waging peace together as a unit, the brigade's veterans were more successful than their neighbors in rebuilding their lives, in reestablishing white leadership in their communities, and in placing firm limits on the social, political, and racial changes made possible during Reconstruction. This final chapter also looks at the brigade veterans' care of John Bell Hood's orphans, the early establishment of their veterans' organization, and their role in caring for each other that lasted well into the twentieth century. Indeed, rather than put the war behind them, Confederate service and their memories of their celebrated status in the Army of Northern Virginia under John Bell Hood and Robert E. Lee influenced much of their later years in obvious and in subtle ways. Although Hood's Texans took the lead within the state on the establishment of their veterans' organization and the construction of a Confederate home in Austin, their rhetoric, especially after 1880, was less radical than what surfaced in other Confederate organizations of the same period because they believed they had long since proven their skills as soldiers and their devotion to the Confederate cause.

TO ARMS IN TEXAS

Mobilizing the First Thousand Texans for Virginia

The men who became Hood's Texas Brigade sprinted toward war in 1861. While the average military-age male, North and South, enlisted with enthusiasm, only a select few rushed, at their own expense or that of their communities, to their nation's capital. Significantly, this early willingness to live, fight, and possibly die more than a thousand miles from home to secure Confederate independence did not diminish in the years that followed secession. An appreciation for the depth of this dedication to Confederate victory is key to understanding the Texas Brigade's development as an elite unit in the American Civil War. One of the best, and worst, representations of that nationalistic fervor was a South Carolinian by birth and Texan by choice named Louis Trezevant Wigfall. He would become the original commander of the Texas Brigade, and his political star was rising in the year of Abraham Lincoln's election.

The Texas senator had made an impression from the moment he entered Washington City. He always made an impression. He was known for his duels, his temper, and his drinking, but Wigfall usually landed on his feet, largely due to his gift for politics. He was a physically imposing man whose dark, wavy hair fell to a grizzled beard that complemented his bear-like reputation. He had a raw but effective debate style, punctuated by "blows like those of a sledge-hammer," a friend explained. "He was bitter in his words, his delivery was careless and slovenly to affection, but some of his sentences were models of classic force, and as clear-cut as the diamond."[1]

It was with a mix of dread and excitement that senators watched Wigfall rise to speak on March 22, 1860. He had grown weary of his colleagues' warnings against secession. "It is all twaddle and nonsense to talk about fighting and bloodshed in the event of dissolution of the Union," Wigfall grumbled.

"What would the effect [be] . . . ? Their spindles would cease to turn; their looms would cease to move. Their ships would be laid up at their wharves," he fairly shouted, glaring at the northern senators who represented the "their" in his speech. "You going to conquer us! Where are you going to get the money? The Union being dissolved, and your ships knocked out of the carrying trade, we can put our cotton, our rice, our tobacco, our sugar, and our molasses, upon any bottoms that will carry them the cheapest." Leaning forward, Wigfall stared at James Simmons, the senator from Rhode Island: "I would like to know what he is going to do with his calico. Who is going to buy it? We would not. Your only market is in the South. What are you going to ship abroad? Cotton is king. We have our cotton and England is obliged to buy it."[2]

Wigfall made secessionists look like moderates that election year, and he outraged the Southern Unionists struggling to find solutions to the tensions that were tearing the country apart. This included Texas governor Sam Houston, who described Wigfall as "beyond the pale of national Democracy," a man who reflected his roots in "the South Carolina nursery of disunion."[3] Try as they might, though, moderates could not silence Wigfall, whose complaints resonated with many Texans. In 1859, they had elected Unionist Sam Houston as their governor, but as the next presidential election loomed, a race that would include a Republican candidate, Texans grew wary.

In the midst of these concerns, a massive fire swept through the growing town of Dallas, Texas, while others broke out in nearby Denton and Pilot Point. Many locals concluded that it was due to the relentless heat—temperatures had reached 110 degrees the day of the fire in Dallas—combined with the shipment of new, highly unstable phosphorous matches that had arrived in stores across the state. But *Dallas Herald* editor Charles R. Pryor was not so sure. He contacted *Austin State Gazette* editor John F. Marshall and warned that "certain negroes" had been questioned and had admitted that the fires were actually part of an abolitionist scheme "to devastate, with fire and assassination, the whole of Northern Texas." "I write in haste," Pryor added; "we sleep on our arms, and the whole country is deeply excited."[4] He shared this news with newspaper editors in Bonham and Houston as well, and soon reports of the slave conspiracy had the entire state in arms, with vigilante groups executing dozens of suspected poor whites and blacks, seeing the radicals Wigfall had warned them about at every turn. As they watched the presidential election that November, Abraham Lincoln's victory symbolized the culmination of their worst fears.

Texans organized a secession convention and voted on February 1, 1861, to leave the Union. Delegates who opposed the vote, and even some who favored it, insisted that this decision had to be ratified by popular vote. Unionists hoped that areas like Galveston County, where merchants had close trading ties with the North and abroad, might insist upon staying in the Union. They looked for the same in Travis County, which included Austin, the state capital. Travis and the counties to its west marked the edge of the settled portions of the state. Their security was tied to the protection that the U.S. Army provided. But the statewide February election revealed that Texans favored secession three to one, and Texas left the Union. Families in the eastern counties that provided the core of the Texas Brigade rushed to organize for war.[5]

By May 22, though, news surfaced that the Confederate government was rejecting all volunteers from Texas. This war would be a short one, they explained, and the Texans might be needed for frontier defenses. In Round Rock, just north of Austin, John Walker would have applauded the Confederate Congress's decision. It would have been the only thing he praised about the new Confederacy. He had watched the rush to war with concern, worried that it ignored the safety of thousands of Texans left at home. In late April he grumbled that "Govner Clark has ishued his proclamation ordering of the melitia of texas to be enrolled forth with & ready for Cervis for the Confederacy under Jef Davis the Dictator of the South." Nowhere, though, could Walker find information, "not one word" on who would "protect the women & children of Texas from the Comanches or mexicans." Apparently, the women and children of Texas, Walker continued, were to be abandoned "for the perpos of protecting South Carolina in her nulifying course." Walker did not favor Lincoln any more than he did the Palmetto State. He was "mutch opposed to old Abe Lincoln and Black Republicanism[.] [A]ny sain man aught to be." But, in the end, "Charity always begins at home," and that is where Walker thought Texans belonged. And he saw sufficient threats in Texas with Native Americans and Mexicans in the West and a governor in Austin whose decisions surpassed the tyranny of "any King or Emperrer Dictator [or] Poetentate in the aniels of history."[6]

Back east in Navarro County, however, other Texans remained determined to find some way to serve in the coming war. Corsicana newspaper editor and lawyer James Rodgers Loughridge watched the secession movement quietly. He was known for his objectivity and reason, captured in the policy of his newspaper, the *Prairie Blade,* to "keep the people always advised as to the position and basis of every party, and leave the mind of the reader (unprejudiced by any private notions of our own,) to decide for itself." It was an unusual stance in a day when papers typically served as the voice of one particular party. The *Blade* promised to "ever be ready to strike for the liberties of the people, or arouse them to action, when the enemy is at hand—apprising them that 'in the time of peace they should prepare for war'—that the *price of liberty is eternal vigilance!*"[7]

Loughridge was a South Carolina native who had traveled west with his father in search of fresh land and a new life in the 1830s. The family had done well for itself, and by 1860, which had brought the Texas Troubles and the election of Abraham Lincoln, Loughridge was an upper-middle-class judge in his late thirties. His wife, Felicia, was in her early twenties, a well-read, thoughtful mother raising their two young daughters. Throughout the Civil War era, they shared a powerful ideological faith in the Confederacy and would turn to their Christian faith to sustain them through the challenges the war brought. The men he led would come to appreciate Loughridge's quiet, steady determination and fearless leadership in battle. His dedication to Confederate independence never wavered. As he explained in the first year of the war: "Our independence as a nation, and the protection of those we love, must be secured. Chains & cuffs have been forged for us!" Texans had to "carry the war into this Northern Africa. Humble our foes, & force them to grant our demands. A few years ago their warriors stood side by side with ours on the burnings sands of Mexico. Now they are called upon to devestate, steal, & in every way rob us of our property."[8] Loughridge and another equally determined Corsicana attorney, Clinton M. Winkler, an Indianan-turned-Texan, took out ads in the local papers in May 1861 calling for a company of mounted riflemen who would serve the Confederacy as a cavalry unit or, if that were not acceptable, then as infantry.[9]

Across the state, Texas counties raised companies, and the most enthusiastic of them prepared to dash to Virginia to defend the new Confederacy. The Marion Rifles drilled in Marshall, Texas, before leaving for New Orleans on May 11.[10] Three days later, the Lone Star Rifles of Galveston announced that they would soon depart for Montgomery, Alabama, before continuing on to Virginia. A few spaces were available, they told readers of the *Houston Weekly Telegraph*, and all a man needed to join was ten or fifteen dollars, though "none but number one men will be accepted."[11] By late June, the citizens of Seguin were boasting that their company, under the command of Captain Benton, was ready to march as soon as the necessary supplies were raised. Several hundred miles to the north, the *Centerville Times* reported that a company from Robertson County already had their men and supplies together. The sixty-four volunteers were "each armed with one of Colt's five shooting rifles," while the company had gathered "1000 pounds [of] lead, 10 kegs powder, 27,000 ball cartridges and 27,000 percussion caps" along with the necessary wagons and mule teams to transport their volunteers to the "seat of war." No one seemed to know exactly where that would be, but Texans wanted to be there.[12]

At the height of their enthusiasm, word surfaced again that none of these men would be accepted for service east of the Mississippi. It appeared that enough volunteers were available in the East to meet the military needs there. The Confederate government repeated its request that the Lone Star State drill for their own defense.[13] Texans listened, and then rejected that option. They had every confidence in their ability both to protect their state's western border and to serve throughout the nation with which they had so quickly come to identify. This included the men who would join the Texas Brigade who believed Virginia was the most effective place for them to defend southern rights while also protecting Texans' rights.

They were right to trust that they would be allowed to serve in the East. None other than Louis T. Wigfall and John Marshall, the young editor who had alerted the state to the "arsons" of 1860, were making their case in Virginia, and their requests built upon a host of arguments Davis had heard from Texans that spring. Representatives came as individuals or in pairs, each sent from local communities who ignored or were ignorant of the idea that there might be a proper chain of command for such appeals. The citizens of Galveston sent Judge L. A. Thompson, while T. S. Lubbock and George Goldthwaite represented volunteers in Houston. Capt. Philip A. Work and 1st Lt. J. J. Burroughs (later of the First Texas Infantry) argued on behalf of the Woodville Rifles of Tyler County. By late June, President Jefferson Davis, either convinced by their arguments or exhausted, approved not one, but two regiments of Texans for the battle that was sure to come. "Let Texas now 'arm and to horse': for the battlefield of Virginia," their friends in Corpus Christi cheered.[14]

From Cass County in the north to Goliad near the Gulf of Mexico, men continued their rush to arms, organized themselves into companies, and offered their services to the Confederacy. Many Cass County men would later become Company D of the First Texas Volunteer Infantry Regiment, while Goliad County offered Company A of the Fourth Texas. The Lone Star Rifles of Galveston would become Company L of the First, while Washington County men could be found in Companies E, F, and I of the Fifth Texas. Even Wigfall raised a unit. Much like the hyperbolic senator, his would be a one-thousand-man elite regiment in which no man would weigh less than 170 pounds, all would be at least six feet tall and thirty-six years old, and every soldier would carry an Enfield rifle, two revolvers (Navy Colts, no less), and a "six-pound bowie knife." Led by the daring Wigfall, it "would be the terror of the Abolition army."[15]

Most of the companies were not officially mustered into service as members of Texas regiments until they arrived in Virginia, but all summer long, Texas families presented their men with flags and speeches that highlighted their faith in the liberty that they believed their new Confederate nation would protect against the tyranny of the Union. The "Robertston Five Shooters" drilled "regularly six hours a day . . . to meet, with becoming bearing, the Northern fanatics who have sworn our extermination."[16] These early volunteers for Virginia drilled not to defend their immediate homes but to travel thousands of miles to defend their new nation. In Austin, Texans took pride in this, with the editors of the *Austin State Gazette* arguing: "In taking troops from Texas the Confederate government passes [over] . . . troops in the Confederate States already raised, drilled, and in camps ready in an hour's warning to respond to the requisitions made. . . . It takes these twenty [Texas] companies at [a] much heavier outlay than those of any other State. We know well the obstacles in the way of the President Davis." They were honored by Davis's faith in Texans' unique ability to help save their new nation.[17] It was July 1861, Texas had been part of the Confederacy for only five months, and their loyalty to it was firmly in place.

The Schadt siblings of Galveston offer a superb example of how swiftly Texas Brigade volunteers identified with the Confederacy. When Charles and William Schadt enlisted in 1861, they could not bring themselves to tell their sister in person. Instead, Caroline discovered their decision in a letter that began: "Beloved Sister . . . Don't be surprised. . . . William and myself are going to Virginia. . . . Ere you receive this letter we will be on our route."[18] In a startling moment, Caroline realized that her only two remaining siblings had just left for war.

In 1845, Carl and Caroline Schaeffer Schadt had immigrated to Galveston from Prussia with their six children. They were part of a wave of migrants, foreign and domestic, who poured into Texas to seize the promise that the Republic offered. Galveston, recruiters promised, enjoyed a strong economy and one of the finest natural harbors in the Gulf of Mexico. Texas, they insisted, was going to be the "Empire State of the South," and Galveston would be the next New York City.[19]

When the Schadts arrived, it seemed many of these predictions would come true. But the neat streets that crisscrossed the island belied the filth and disease that plagued the town. Nearly one in every two children born on the coast died before reaching adulthood. The seven-week "fever season" that swept through the "Queen City" every year took a heavy toll on the immigrants who were "strangers to our climate," one Galveston hospital reported. Indeed, 90 percent of the patients who came through the city's charity hospital were born abroad. But "Yellow Jack" and dysentery attacked natives, rich, and poor alike. In 1844, 400 people died of yellow fever; a decade later, 535 died during the "fever season." William Pitt Ballinger, who served as U.S. district attorney for the State of Texas in the early 1850s, could do nothing to stop the disease that killed four of his children one summer, just as the prominent German newspaper editor Ferdinand Flake had watched helplessly as five of his children faded away one summer after another. It was the same for the Schadts. The disease likely swept in quickly, stealing the lives of the parents, Carl and Caroline Schadt, along with three of their children, in a matter of days, leaving the promise of America to four-year-old Caroline, five-year-old William, and nine-year-old Charles.

When the Civil War began, the siblings remained close, and Charles's and William's departure created a daunting situation for eighteen-year-old Caroline. But, as Charles explained, they had to go. "Don't grieve about us," he advised. "You will never have any reason to be ashamed of your brothers, we go [to Virginia] to fight and expect to have enough of it. It is hard to part, but our Country requires us, and as Southern men we must meet the call of our gallant President." Just sixteen years in the country, and Charles Schadt was as southern, and now as Confederate, as any man in the ranks of the Lone Star Rifles. And Caroline could only read his admonitions and pray that her brothers' transition from "Galveston street parading," as William called it, to real soldiering would go as well as Charles promised.

Not far from Galveston's shores, another Texas family watched their son rush off to war. Thomas Fletcher did not support secession. As his neighbors raged against what they saw as federal transgressions in the 1850s, Fletcher had steadfastly defended Union. By the end of the decade, Tom Fletcher was quieter, but no less determined in his views. He had moved his family from

St. Landry Parish, Louisiana, where Fletcher had worked in earlier years as an overseer, and then to Jasper County, Texas. There, Fletcher believed, his family would be safe, farther from the large slave populations of Louisiana that might unleash terror on local whites when the inevitable war came. And war was "sure to come," Fletcher insisted. In 1859, he moved his family again, this time settling in Beaumont.

Theirs was a sizeable household by 1860. Fifty-three-year-old Thomas and his forty-two-year-old wife, Margaret, both originally from North Carolina, had five children. The oldest, William, was twenty-one years old, and the youngest, Alyeneth, was a girl of six. The Fletchers owned five slaves—two adults, and three children—on their farm that the county valued at $600, which, with Tom Fletcher's personal property estimated at $3,000, placed them solidly in the middling class. As much as his neighbors supported war to protect their freedoms, property, and principles, Thomas Fletcher was equally determined to avoid it. He had warned his eldest son, William, to tune out the fire-eaters who clamored for war. But William was deaf to such concerns. He had heard too many men insist that "I can arm my few negroes and run the whole company of Yanks out of the State," or boast that "one Southerner with his superior marksmanship could shoot down the D―― Bluebellies as fast as they would come in sight." William looked on his father's concerns as younger generations often "feel toward the old—that they may be good, but don't fit the age."[20]

In April 1861, a neighbor, William Rogers, came riding by and announced that Confederates had attacked Fort Sumter. The war had begun. Perched high above on the roof he was repairing, William Fletcher leaned into the pitched eave and pondered their best approach to ensure that they could join the fight. His father might be a Unionist, but "Bill" Fletcher favored secession. He hurried through his work, determined to get to Virginia to defend this new nation.

Fletcher decided to purchase a ticket on a flatcar with Rogers contributing half the fee, and once Fletcher arrived in Houston or, if need be, Galveston, he would enroll both men in Confederate service. Fletcher got off all right the next morning, but the flatcar only took him as far as Liberty. Refusing to quit, he jumped on a handcar and, arms pumping, traveled the remaining forty miles to Houston. The sun had nearly set as Fletcher made his way through the city streets, asking where men could enlist. It turned out that Houstonians lacked Fletcher's enthusiasm that April, but they promised him they would be recruiting men soon enough. Still concerned, and believing that he lacked the local connections needed to secure a spot when city leaders finally got around to calling for volunteers, Fletcher caught a few hours' sleep and then made his way another fifty miles to Galveston. But he found the same tempered pace at Galveston.

Undeterred, Bill Fletcher made his way back to Liberty, and it was there that he heard that a local rancher named King Bryan was organizing a company. Fletcher made his way to Bryan's sizable ranch. It seemed that he "preferred his home boys," but Fletcher managed to persuade him to save two slots for Bill Rogers and him. Bryan kept his promise. Later that summer, after more delays that convinced Rogers to join a different unit, Bill Fletcher would finally march off to war.

His father never approved of secession. Tom Fletcher reminded his eldest boy, "William, I have long years since seen this had to come and it is a foolish undertaking, as there is no earthly show for Southern success." He prophesized that their ports would be blocked, and "the North will not only have advantage of men and means, but the world to draw from." There was little chance for young Bill's success, let alone survival. "If you live to return," his father said, "you will see my predictions are right." But Tom Fletcher was pro-Union, not pro-North, and when the war came, he sided, however reluctantly, with his neighbors. "While I have opposed it," he said, "as it is here, I will say that you are doing the only honorable thing and that is defending your country."[21]

As Bill Fletcher said good-bye to his parents, Kindallis "King" Bryan continued to fill the ranks of his company in Liberty, Texas. As in thousands of other companies North and South, the leaders of the community recruited and initially commanded them. The ranks were filled with some strangers, but more often than not they also contained brothers, cousins, uncles, fathers, and neighbors who had known each other for years. In Bryan's unit, "The Invincibles," the rolls listed two of Bryan's nephews and several members of his household, including his stockmen, P. C. Buxton and William McCary.

Marching off with them was twenty-three-year-old Louisiana native and steamboat captain Watson Dugat Williams, who joined King Bryan's company as a second lieutenant. Between his own hard work and that of the eleven enslaved men and women he owned, the 1850s had been very successful for Williams. But a shadow hung over the Williams family in Liberty. Dugat's father, Judge Williams, had sided with Mexico in the Texas Revolution and abandoned his wife, Margaretta Dugat, and three children in Liberty. They eventually divorced, and although the scandal did not prove an obstacle to Williams's financial success, his father's decisions troubled him for years to come.[22]

Miles to the west in Seguin, southwest of the state capital at Austin, Andrew Erskine pondered his responsibilities as his neighbors rushed to volunteer just as the men of East Texas had done. Erskine was a bear of a man, with dark hair and eyes and the broad shoulders that reflected a lifetime of work. By the time he was in his teens, his family were leaders in Seguin and quite wealthy. Like many of their neighbors, they had carved their fortune from the land around them, surviving the challenges of climate and neighboring Comanche who considered the area as much their own as the Erskines did.

Andrew's father, Michael Erskine, was one of the founding members of their town. Like many Texans, the Erskines had made their way to Texas in fits and starts beginning in Virginia, where Michael married Agnes Haynes in 1817. In the early 1830s, they moved west to Alabama, then to Mississippi, until finally settling in the Lone Star State in 1839. They originally lived along Arenosa Creek in Jackson County, where the family survived the Linnville Raid, in which hundreds of Kiowa Comanche attacked their settlement. Just fourteen years old, Andrew Erskine helped his father defend their family and all they owned. The Erskines later moved to Seguin, where Andrew joined the Texas Rangers and fought with Jack Coffee Hays against the Comanche as each side struggled to secure the lands they so desperately wanted.

When Andrew Erskine returned to Seguin in the mid-1840s, his father had purchased a sizable ranch where he raised cotton and cattle, shipping the former down the Guadalupe River to market and driving the latter as far west as California—the first in his community to do so. In 1846, Andrew expanded his own holdings by purchasing the Magnolia Hotel from Joseph F. Johnson, who became his father-in-law the following year when Michael married twenty-one-year-old Ann Theresa Johnson. Little is known about her, but Joseph Johnson was as prominent in early Seguin as the Erskines. Both families helped organize the first college in town, and Johnson went on to become a key benefactor of the Female Academy in Seguin in 1853.

By the time war broke out, Seguin could boast multiple schools for all ages and both genders (though only for whites), two newspapers (one Democratic, one mostly Democratic), three hotels, two grocery stores, a Masonic Lodge, various men's and women's benevolent societies, a branch of the "Sons of Temperance" that one local paper described as "flourishing," but not quite sufficient to drive out the town's taverns, as well as "The Lyceum," their public library. Streets curved around sprawling live oaks, and the Magnolia Hotel's bell rang frequently, announcing the arrival of new guests before the stagecoach continued toward Mill Road and the Erskine family ferry that took passengers across the Guadalupe River.

In 1860, Andrew and Ann Theresa Johnson Erskine, both in their mid-thirties, had six sons ranging in age from eleven years to one month old. Together, though likely with the assistance of some of Michael Erskine's twenty-two slaves, Andrew and Ann ran a gristmill and the ferry, as well as a sawmill, cotton gin, stage stand, and inn. The Erksines enjoyed tremendous antebellum success, which may be why Andrew contacted a friend in Austin in the summer of 1861 to offer his services in organizing a group of volunteers. A former Texas Ranger who had been raised on the Texas frontier would bring useful skills to the Confederate army. His contact in Austin agreed, responding that "men of your stamp are needed in raising troops."

For unknown reasons, however, Andrew Erskine did not organize a company, nor did his wealthy father. Andrew may have reevaluated his responsibilities to his family versus those to his country. In addition to his business ventures, he also managed his father's cattle ranch and thousands of additional acres and investments that ranged from Texas to Virginia. The other likely factor was that Ann had just become pregnant with their seventh child. With so many properties to run, and the need for a new ferryboat for their primary business, Andrew Erskine likely decided that he had served his community for years on the frontier and as a Texas Ranger. Younger men were rushing into uniform, including Ann's brother, Ignatius Johnson. The country could spare the Erskines for now.

More than one thousand miles to the east, another leading white southerner in his mid-thirties contemplated war. James Benjamin Griffin was a wealthy South Carolina planter who personified the world from which he came. He owned sixty-one slaves, was a father to seven children under the age of thirteen, and his wife was weeks from delivering their eighth child. Griffin's marriage to Eliza "Leila" Harwood Burt had combined two of the wealthiest families of Edgefield, South Carolina. It was his second marriage and her first; Griffin's first wife had died during the birth of their second son.[23]

As the nation crept toward war, Griffin's senator, James Henry Hammond, had insisted that the North "dare not make war on cotton. Cotton is king," a line Louis T. Wigfall borrowed two years later. It was a powerful argument, and one Griffin had witnessed firsthand. In 1850, he and his father, who farmed neighboring land and likely shared their slave labor, were diversified in corn, wheat, oats, beans, and other food crops, with only a small section of their hundreds of acres dedicated to growing a few dozen bales of cotton each year. A decade later, Griffin had inherited all of his father's land, making him the head of an estate that produced more than 100 bales of cotton annually on 1,500 acres. Their food crops had significantly decreased as Griffin, like planters across the Deep South, shifted production to benefit from the nation—and Europe's—seemingly insatiable demand for cotton.[24]

If Griffin was representative of his class and their livelihood, his hometown symbolized the violent nature that contemporaries and modern readers alike had come to associate with the antebellum South. Edgefield, South Carolina, was one of the most violent, paternalistic, and wealthy counties in a state that boasted an abundance of such attributes. Charleston newspaper editor William Watts Ball insisted that mid-nineteenth-century Edgefield had "more dashing, brilliant, romantic figures, statesmen, orators, soldiers, adventurers and daredevils than any other county in South Carolina, if not of any rural county in America." Modern historians have tended to agree with him, observing, "The Edgefield tradition in South Carolina has stood for the syndrome of violence and extremism that, until recent times, was thought to epitomize the South Carolina spirit."[25]

Griffin may have lacked those violent tendencies, but he embraced his community's extremist mind-set that inspired their support of secession. As a brigadier general in the South Carolina militia, Griffin oversaw slave patrols in his region, which intensified following John Brown's failure to inspire a slave rebellion in western Virginia in the fall of 1859. The election of President Abraham Lincoln in 1860 led to further radicalism in an already explosive part of the country. South Carolina rejected proposals that it should wait for a gathering of governors so that the South could respond to Lincoln's election—which occurred without a single vote from the Deep South—as a unified group. Griffin's neighbor, Martin Witherspoon Gary, captured their position best when he insisted, "This Union must be deliberately, solemnly, fearlessly, and speedily dissolved" because "it fails to protect our property and persons."[26] On December 20, 1860, South Carolina left the Union.

Within ten weeks, six other Deep South states followed in South Carolina's footsteps. From Charleston to Galveston, southerners watched events with a mixed sense of relief and excitement as they mobilized for war. As Griffin saw it, the North, populated by "black hearted wretches," was "doing all in their power, to subjugate a Noble race of people," and, as a leader of his community, it was his duty to ensure that this never happened.[27] Griffin did not apply those words "subjugate" and "race" to the scores of African American slaves who lived in the twelve homes that comprised his slave quarters. A classic southern paternalist, he could conceive of the idea that some slaves might, at some point, try to escape to freedom, but Griffin did not imagine that his slaves would. They were well fed, clothed, and cared for. They worshiped, though segregated by race, in the same church with Griffin's family. And when one of them later ran away to Union lines during the war, Griffin was dumbfounded.

In the spring of 1861 he joined friend and fellow South Carolinian Wade Hampton's Legion that was composed of units of infantry, cavalry, and artillery. As a wealthy planter known for his fine stable of horses and his military experience, Griffin was a natural choice as one of Hampton's cavalry officers. That was how, in July 1861, Leila Griffin found herself, eight-and-a-half weeks pregnant, watching her husband ride off on his quest to save his new nation. Accompanying Griffin were his finest horses, two slaves, his best hunting dog, and trunks of clothing and supplies that would, Griffin assumed, provide comfort while far from his beloved Edgefield. In about a year, he and a number of the South Carolinians he led would be brigaded with Wigfall's Texans.

When Griffin arrived in Virginia, he would have found representatives from across the South. Among those who had traveled the farthest were the Texas volunteers who eventually mustered into service as the First Texas Volunteer Infantry Regiment. It is significant to note that these men were especially motivated to fight for the Confederacy, not just Texas. These were volunteers who, upon learning that the Confederate government was asking Texans to stay home to protect the new nation's far western border, determined to rush to Virginia anyway.

Eighty percent of the original captains of the First Texas were slaveholders. Of the original privates, though, 67 percent of the privates did not own slaves but came from the middling class with strong ties to slaveholders in their communities.[28] Among the original officers was Harvey Hannibal Black, who personified the hard-won successes of the 1850s that were key to the men's motivations for service. Like many of his neighbors in Jefferson, Texas, Black was not born in Texas but rather in the Upper South. Like few of his friends, however, Black was raised on a profitable Indiana farm where most of his family remained throughout the nineteenth century. Harvey and his brother Albert left Indiana in 1852, driving a herd of Merino and Saxony sheep to Texas. Within a few years, Harvey Black shifted his interests to beef, opening a packery in Shreveport, Louisiana, in 1856, and expanding his enterprise to Jefferson, Texas, the following year. "I will give liberal prices in cash for all good fat heavy beef cattle," Black advertised in the early fall of 1857. Local newspapers cheered Black's enterprise, grateful for guaranteed prices for their stock in a local market. Traditionally ranchers had to drive herds to river ports and then take them by steamboat to New Orleans, a journey that reduced cattle weight and prices. But the Yankee Harvey Black changed all that, and local business leaders celebrated him.

By the end of 1857, Harvey Black employed twenty-five skilled packers from Louisville, Kentucky, with plans to slaughter 3,000 cattle that winter. Within a year Harvey Black's beeves were declared "by competent judges" to be "equal to any grass fed beef in the United States." In early 1859, the citizens of Jefferson basked in the glow of Harvey Black's success. He symbolized the potential wealth that civic boosters sold to would-be emigrants back east. Local editors praised Black's business as "one of the most important investments that has ever taken place in our progressive city. It not only adds much to the future interest of Jefferson, but it will hereafter be a market for all the hogs and cattle that can be raised in Northern Texas." Harvey Black was a man on the rise.

By the time of Lincoln's election in 1860, Black was busy selling his enterprise to a New Orleans firm, along with the houses, shop, warehouse, tools, and 3,500 cattle on the numerous lots he owned in Jefferson. Perhaps he was feeling the aftershocks of the Panic of 1857. When the census taker came calling that year, he listed Black as a twenty-seven-year-old Kentucky-born stock raiser who boarded with the local butcher and owned just one slave. He listed no personal wealth or property holdings.[29] Little is known of the motives that inspired Harvey Black in early 1861. He left no known letters. But his actions indicate that he had become thoroughly Texan and southern in the last few years, and he shifted with equal ease into the role of Confederate. Indeed, Black was so quick in his response to secession that by the end of April, he joined the first company of the first regiment of Texans to depart the state. The Confederate government had not yet said they would accept the Texans' service. They would be, the *Houston Telegraph* mused, "on their own hook."[30] But that was fine with Harvey Black, elected captain of the Marion Rifles as the men made their way to New Orleans in May, where they mustered into Confederate service.

Hundreds of Texans gathered there, New Orleans being the first major city and rail hub on their journey to Virginia. These men may have been strongly motivated to defend their new nation, but they did not always agree on where they should fight. On May 21, just days after Harvey Black and his Marion Rifles mustered into service, dozens of men deserted another Texas-based company, the Palmer Guards.[31] The company's organization was troubled from the start. Albert Glassel Dickinson, a successful New Orleans businessman, had set out to fill its ranks with men from both Texas and Louisiana, and named the unit after a prominent New Orleans minister. Dickinson came from a wealthy Virginia family and, like many of his generation, moved to what was then the Southwest—the Mississippi and Louisiana area—to make his fortune. When the war broke out, he was doing very well in the Crescent City and had just married Susan Marshall Coleman in Vicksburg, Mississippi. Coleman was the great-niece of Chief Justice John Marshall and daughter of N. D. Coleman, president of the Vicksburg, Shreveport, and Texas Railroad and former Kentucky congressman. A. G. Dickinson had mastered the nineteenth-century art of marrying well.

Just two weeks after his wedding, Dickinson called for "patriotic persons" to go to Shreveport, Louisiana, or Jefferson, Texas, to enlist in his company, the Palmer Guards, for twelve months' Confederate service. "Let there be no hesitation," Dickinson encouraged. "For with or without money, if your hearts are proud and true, you will be equipped and properly cared for." He planned to leave Jefferson, Texas, with one batch of recruits by the second week of May, collecting the other half of the unit in Shreveport.[32] Dickinson had little success in Marion County, though, likely because the citizenry had already supplied nearly a company of men, including Harvey Black, to the Marion Rifles. Or, perhaps it was because he was an outsider to the area. Undeterred, Dickinson expanded his recruiting base and managed to attract men from the other areas in northwest Texas, and as far west as Washington County.[33] When he arrived in New Orleans, Dickinson added more Louisianans to the mix by recruiting in Algiers, just across the river from the Crescent City.

Two days after Dickinson's volunteers were mustered into Confederate service for twelve months, however, approximately 20 percent of the Palmer Guards deserted. The historical documentation is too limited to draw any decisive conclusions on what happened to the seventeen men who abandoned the Palmer Guards before they even left New Orleans. Still, it is significant to note this unusual exodus, a prophetic harbinger of the problems to come for the Palmer Guards. Eventually mustered in as Company C of the First Texas Infantry, this unit would suffer the highest percentage of desertions by officers and enlisted men in the Texas Brigade.[34] None of their original officers and only one of the original noncommissioned officers would remain in the unit after May 1862. To be clear, two of the original officers resigned and served elsewhere in Texas, another was killed in May 1862, and the last deserted. Of the noncommissioned officers, four Company C men would desert the unit by May 1862. Another was discharged for disability, and one more man resigned his commission in April 1862. Thus the Palmer Guards suffered leadership problems from their earliest days, and the men who chose to remain would need to find strong leaders to replace those who left.[35]

Following the original four companies of the First Texas—the Marion Rifles under Captain Black, Co. A; the Livingston Guards, Co. B; the Palmer Guards, Co. C; the Star Rifles, Co. D—came men like Frederick Bass, a Virginia-born graduate of the Virginia Military Institute, who had valuable skills to offer as communities prepared for war. Bass was president and professor of military tactics at Marshall University that spring, where he also led the local militia company, the Marshall Guards. The wealthy planters of Marshall and Harrison County were not as enthusiastic about war as Harvey Black and their neighbors to the north in Marion County. In the fall of 1860, Black's fellow farmers, ranchers, and businessmen voted overwhelmingly for the Democratic presidential candidate, John C. Breckinridge, and in the spring of 1861 Marion County supported secession to a man. Harrison County was more influenced by its planters' conservative outlook, Whig politics, and diversified national investments, not to mention blended northern and southern families. Harrison voted against secession that spring. But as his neighbors pondered politics, Frederick Bass suspected war would come despite the county's vote. He drilled his company, inspected uniforms and weapons, and prepared the young men for war. By the time they left Texas in May 1861, not too far behind the Marion Rifles, the Marshall Guards were the only company truly outfitted for war among these earliest of volunteers.[36]

As Captain Bass led his men out of Marshall County, they were outraged to see that the boat on which they planned to ride to New Orleans, the *Texas*, was already in use by a different company raised in Marion County, Dr. Albert Gallatin Cloptin's Star Rifles. There was room for men on board, but the *Texas* refused to stop at Swanson's Landing. In perfect democratic fashion, the outraged Marshall Guards "held an indignation meeting, and passed resolutions condemning the boat, and requesting their friends behind to withhold their patronage from her in future." Upon reaching Shreveport, though, the early scouts were told that the *Texas* would be happy to let the Marshall Guards board, and rested at dock until the rest of Bass's men arrived on another vessel, the *Fleta*. Continuing their tradition as citizen-soldiers, the Marshall Guards "appointed a committee to wait on the Captain of the *Texas,* for an explanation, which he gave to their satisfaction—the boat is therefore exonerated from all blame," explained the *Texas Republican* via reports from one of the Marshall Guards. With their honor restored and their citizenship respected, Bass and Clopton's men continued on toward New Orleans.[37]

James Hendrick, a private in Bass's company, was less than impressed when they finally arrived in New Orleans. Or perhaps he was just trying to reassure his mother. The city was "much larger tha[n] I expected," and they had a "pleasant time so far" but "two days is just as long as I care about staying here. I have got tired of it already." They were waiting on official orders from Richmond to muster them into Confederate service in Virginia, as well as more standard uniforms that one the townspeople had made for the Marshall Guards. With each day, the volunteers grew more impatient. "The company is talking about starting this evening on the cars from Virginia," Hendrick explained, for fear they might miss their chance to fight. As things turned out, the Marshall Guards spent a week in New Orleans, and then an additional week, waiting for their official muster in and uniforms, which likely took place as soon as Davis and Marshall reached their agreement. By the second week of July, they had arrived in Richmond.[38]

The men of that first rush to arms, who formed the original companies of the First Texas Volunteer Infantry Regiment, all organized in response to the Confederacy's first and second troop levies in April 1861. These Texans, especially the early units like Company C, would maintain a reputation throughout the war as "diehards." They were highly motivated and excellent in battle, but often difficult for officers to control. The men were often as determined to defend their own rights as citizens as they were the rights of the Confederacy. They were also strongly nationalistic, identifying as Texans but preferring to fight in Virginia, where they believed their service would be most effective.

Those delayed in New Orleans mustered into service and then moved on, usually by rail, to Virginia. Most of them rode northward through the junctions in Canton and Holly Springs, Mississippi, and then cut eastward through Tennessee. Andrew G. Dickinson chose a different route and led his company of Texans and Louisianans along the coast of the Gulf of Mexico, traveling to Pensacola, Florida, where he recruited more men before pushing northward through to one of the South's major production centers, Atlanta, Georgia.

Dickinson's eighty men were accompanied by his new bride, Sue Coleman Dickinson, who pledged that "she [had] enlisted for the war and will share the destinies of her gallant husband, whatever they may be." Not far behind Sue Dickinson was "a standard bearer, in the person of Mademoiselle Jennette Warde from New Orleans—dressed a la bloomer, or soldier fashion, and belted with revolver, bowie knife &c. She was sprightly, shared and seemed to enjoy a soldier fare." Her weaponry was standard for the Palmer Guards, and she may have joined up with some of the men from New Orleans, or perhaps Algiers. No further record of Warde has been found, but she symbolized the unorthodox enlistments and determination that hastened the most determined volunteers to Virginia that spring.[39]

Alexis T. Rainey's company was about a month behind Dickinson's Palmer Guards. Rainey was a successful lawyer and politician in his late thirties in 1861. He had represented Anderson County as a Democrat in the Texas state legislature in the late 1850s, and his constituents called on Rainey to represent them in the Texas secession convention in 1861, where he echoed the sentiments of his county and voted in favor of leaving the Union. He, too, busied himself by raising a company. They left Texas that June, and among those who remained behind was Rainey's "darling little wife." She was nearly nine months pregnant and just twenty-one years old.[40]

Despite the challenges involved in leaving Texas, Rainey remained optimistic. On July 5, 1861, one day after he and his family would have traditionally celebrated America's independence, Rainey arrived in Shreveport, Louisiana, with "91 men, the finest company I ever saw." He felt strong and healthy, though he worried about his wife, Ann. Still, A. T. Rainey's future seemed bright. Stopping just a few hours in Shreveport, the men headed to New Orleans, where "there is not a case of yellow fever." Rainey's optimism carried well beyond his immediate challenges and led him to promise that he would "be at home before Christmas—I don't think we will have much fighting to do."[41]

Fourth Corp. Robert Gaston and his brother, William, a first sergeant, were traveling with Captain Rainey in the "Texas Guards." Neither was as convinced of the ease of their journey as their commander had been, or at least as Rainey had portrayed things to his wife. William had been sick when they left Texas but returned to good health quickly. The trip to Shreveport, however, proved "very fatiguing. From 8 to 12 of the boys were sick all the way." Families all along the way provided the men with shelter, usually refusing payment for their kindness, and the town of Henderson had even thrown them a party.[42]

The boat journey was much better than marching, the Gaston boys admitted, especially since they only had to pay half price. In New Orleans, the Gaston brothers had time to enjoy the city's "many strange and curious sites," Robert explained. His only complaint was that they still did not know if the Texas Guards would be accepted into Confederate service in Virginia. Rainey had telegraphed Richmond, Robert told his parents, but they were still awaiting a response: "The Governor of La. wants us to join a regiment that they are making up here, but I do not think we will do it." Later that night, Captain Rainey received word that the Texans were wanted in Virginia. They mustered into service on July 11 and started for Richmond.

Six days out from New Orleans, Rainey was still beaming about his company, "ninety of the finest looking men I ever saw." They had mustered in with Dr. John M. Woodward's 84 men known as the "Reagan Guards," all from Anderson County, Texas. Rainey remained confident that he would see his family soon, promising "I can get a furlough next winter without any difficulty and come home to see my little wife and children." Another option, he admitted, was that, "if I can see proper at any time, I can resign my commission and leave the army entirely, but I have no idea of doing so as it would be acting in bad faith to the Company."[43]

This determined band of Texans organized in the fall of 1861 in Richmond, Virginia, as the Texas Battalion under the command of a man who shared their resolve and their fire: former senator-turned–brigadier general Louis Trezevant Wigfall.

THE RUSH TO VIRGINIA
The Organization of the Fourth and Fifth Texas Infantry

As the First Texas Battalion organized in Richmond, a second group of Texans waited at home. They hesitated to travel until they knew that the Confederate government would accept more volunteers from their westernmost state. President Jefferson Davis reminded the Lone Star sons that Texas would need defending, too, and others across Texas expressed fears for their security if so many men went east. Still, hundreds of Texans watched and waited for their opportunity to defend their nation, positive that they could best serve the Confederate cause in Virginia. Clearly, this group was a little less radical than the First Texans. The fact that they were determined to serve so far from home underscores their enthusiasm for the Confederate war effort. These were the men who eventually mustered into service as the Fourth and Fifth Texas Infantry Regiments and who secured the Texas Brigade's early fame at the Battles of Gaines's Mill and Second Manassas. They would also provide some of the best junior officers in the brigade, including James Hunter, "Howdy" Martin, J. R. Loughridge, Benjamin Franklin Carter, and John C. Upton. Their disciplined and determined mobilization foreshadowed the same qualities in their leadership, which proved key to the Texas Brigade's development as one of the best units in the war.

In the early summer of 1861, students from Austin College gathered around the courthouse in downtown Huntsville, Texas. The boys "harangued the people" walking by, "inciting them to greater enthusiasm and desire to go to the front."[1] Constable James T. Hunter watched them quietly. He was twenty-five years old, but a youth filled with loss made him seem much older. Shortly after his birth in Tennessee, Hunter's family moved to Texas. His father and his slaves drove cattle to the Trinity River, where they helped establish the town of Cincinnati and Hunter's Tavern in the late 1830s. Their new life proved profitable in the Republic of Texas, and it continued to be when Texas joined the Union in the 1840s. But in 1853, the Hunters' fortunes turned. An explosion during a steamboat race off the coast of Galveston killed George, James's father, that March.[2] His widow, Tamar, and the children tried to manage the family's business interests, but six months later, Tamar was still lobbying for control of her husband's estate. While the county court pondered her request, a stagecoach brought a gravely ill man to the family tavern. Tamar nursed him as well as she could until the man continued on his way, but when he died a few days later, word spread quickly that yellow fever was to blame. By late September, the fever had killed Tamar and cut a swath through Cincinnati. "The female heads of most all the families were down with the fever" after that, James Hunter recalled, "for all had visited and waited on Mother. Very soon almost everybody in town... had the fever... and almost every one died." Six months after burying his father, and one month after burying his mother, James helped two of his sisters bury their husbands along with two of their children. When the yellow fever epidemic faded with the first frost, Cincinnati was nearly a ghost town.[3]

James's brother-in-law, appointed administer of George Hunter's estate, sold off the rest of the family holdings the next spring, while James took charge of several hundred head of cattle his father had owned. He did not return to the college classes he had abandoned after his mother fell ill, and instead focused on supporting his two sisters, both "yellow fever widows." In the late 1850s, Hunter served with the Texas Rangers in the Cortina War and then moved to Huntsville, Texas, where he became deputy sheriff. By the time the Civil War broke out in 1861, he was constable of Huntsville and a respected member in the town's middling class.[4]

That was how Hunter came to be watching the college boys "harangue" the locals as he pondered a request that had arrived in the mail. Confederate leaders had just announced that they would accept 2,000 more Texans for service in Virginia, and Texas governor Edward Clark appointed Hunter to oversee the recruiting of men from Grimes, Montgomery, and Walker Counties. Wise to local politics and pecking orders, Hunter organized the call and recruitment but insisted that the more prominent Proctor Porter of Montgomery should command the company. As they began printing and signing enlistment papers, similar efforts echoed across the state as men rushed forward for a fight that would take them a thousand miles from home.

This later group of Texas volunteers may not have rushed off with the haste of the First Texans, but they had fought hard for their right to serve in Virginia. Earlier that spring, letters had poured into the governor's office with offers, suggestions, and the occasional demand that they be allowed to volunteer. On April 22, for example, B. F. Benton informed Governor Clark from San Augustine that he had taken the oath as a brigadier general of the Third Brigade of Texas Militia and was prepared to lead that unit in support of the state and the Confederacy as needed.[5] Three days later, Benjamin Franklin Carter sent Clark the muster roll of the Austin City Light Infantry, numbering 76 officers and men. All men had sworn an oath to the state and the Austin City Light Infantry and "now await your orders."[6] The next day, April 26, Robert M. "Mike" Powell reported similar progress in Hempstead, informing Clark that Powell had organized a mounted company of six-month volunteers, and he was prepared to fight through the end of the war.[7]

These men spent the late spring drilling. James Hunter's recruits from Grimes, Montgomery, and Walker Counties trained in earnest for days around Round Top and then Roan's Prairie. With plenty of shade and freshwater, as well as an open prairie to practice maneuvers, it was a superb spot for the men to train. But after a few weeks, the men grew bored and frustrated with their uncertain future. They shifted their focus to foot and horse racing, then to wrestling and boxing, but after two weeks of training and games, "we were disbanded, much to the dissatisfaction of the men, who daily anticipated orders to start for Virginia." With no arms and the appearance that they might not be needed at all, most of the men returned to their homes or enlisted in other units assured of more militant futures.

But then, in mid-June, the papers called on them to return. "Texas is wanted," Austin editor John Marshall explained, "if but for the moral effect of her fearful name. . . . Let every man demand constant drill and never weary of it until the battle is to be fought."[8] Marshall explained to the governor: "The President has agreed to let you send 20 companies of 100 men each to Richmond. . . . You can prepare as early as you can for the organization." Not all of the recruits were still available, but as news of Marshall's announcement spread, the volunteers of early summer raced to return to their camps of instruction.[9] Responding to the overwhelming volunteer mobilization, Clark established eleven military districts that could recruit units, muster in volunteer companies, and drill in assigned training camps until officials in Austin or Richmond decided where these men could best be used.

When Governor Clark published the names of units approved for service in Virginia, some of the companies were horrified to find themselves missing from the list. Captain Porter and Lieutenant Hunter's company was among those omitted, as was King Bryan's "Company Invincibles" from Liberty. In a panic, Proctor Porter jumped on a train to Austin while Hunter remained with the men, who were, ironically, prepared to mutiny if they were not permitted to fight in Virginia. Captain Bryan was a bit more patient but still frustrated. Why had Robert M. Powell's boys made the list while Bryan's had not, he asked? Powell's Waverly Confederates were not ready for service until "after my company had been accepted," and Bryan believed he was "right to feel that my application has not received that attention which I could have expected." Tempering his complaint a bit, Bryan hoped that, with Clark now aware of the situation, "should there be another vacancy in the other regiment[,]" Bryan's command would be selected.[10]

Clinton Winkler's Navarro Rifles were not overlooked, but he had his own complaints that summer. Despite their company name, his men had no weapons. In early July he traveled to Austin to see if he could get a better response to his request in person, but he failed. There simply were not enough weapons to arm all of the Texas volunteers. Before his company reached Camp Van Dorn, their camp of instruction, Winkler felt compelled to put the matter of their service to a vote. He explained to his citizen volunteers that he could secure weapons and equipment if they would go to Virginia, but they would likely receive nothing until they arrived. The men asked to hear what the other officers thought, who all displayed "an eagerness to go." Exercising the individual freedoms that citizen-soldiers were serving to protect, only about a dozen of the Navarro Rifles stayed, and they departed with no ill feelings expressed by those who headed to Richmond.[11]

These frustrated volunteers tried everything to arm their men, though one Henderson County attorney's efforts reflected skills that would serve him well throughout the war. William H. Martin served in the state senate from 1853 to 1858, and he knew that lodging complaints or threats with the governor was pointless. Instead, Martin applied the timeless art of patronage. After reporting that his company was ready for service "at a moment's notice," Martin asked for arms for his men while reminding Clark that if he could help them secure arms, the governor "shall have any thing that this section has or may have for you in votes or any thing else."[12]

Clark was in a difficult position. He needed to defend Texas's ample frontier and coastal border. He also needed to mobilize the state for a war that many insisted would be waged in distant Virginia. But what if the rumors of a pending Federal invasion were true? Clark had to prepare for that as well. After selecting John S. "Rip" Ford to handle the Rio Grande defenses and Henry McCulloch to cover the northwestern portion of the state, Clark sent a series of letters to the Mexican governors of Coahuila, Tamaulipas, and Nuevo Leon to buttress border security with good diplomacy. Clark also worked closely with Col. Earl Van Dorn, the Confederate commander of Texas. On the economic front, Clark appointed Galveston businessman Ebenezer B. Nichols to sell bonds and purchase the necessary arms for the coming war, and Clark advised the state legislature to raise taxes to cover all of these expenses.[13] None of this, however, concerned the Texas volunteers bound for Virginia. They had won their case and would soon be on their way.

In July 1861, they made their way to the staging areas at Camp Clark near San Marcos or Camp Van Dorn at Harrisburg, and by late July and early August, most of them had consolidated at Camp Van Dorn. As excited as they were to play a role in the fighting in Virginia, some of those at home were worried. The editors in Marshall explained, "we hate to see" units hurrying to fights outside the state. "Our own state may be left defenseless," they warned. Similar concerns surfaced in south Texas. "So general is the impression now that Texas is to be invaded," warned the editors, "that there is much reluctance to see twenty of our best companies with their guns leave the state. There is much feeling here [in Houston] as well as in San Antonio, and we but express a very common wish where we hope the troops will not be sent to Virginia."[14]

The *Colorado Citizen* warned their readers in Columbus that they had lost three staff members in the rush to volunteer. Ben Baker had volunteered with John Upton's company, and the paper's apprentice, Webb Sheppard, had gone to Virginia as well, while Tom Harris left to help with frontier defenses.[15] The *Houston Weekly Telegraph* lost three men, too, to the Bayou City Guards, which was also headed to Virginia. Those editors did not sound too worried: "Should the BCG's take a printing press from the enemy we expect to see a gazette issued by Sweeney, Walker, and Revely. Success to all of them. Their positions shall be open to them when they come back."[16]

Despite the concern for home-front defenses and how the daily needs of each community would be met, "the only topic of interest in camp" at Harrisburg "is when are we going to get on the 'route' to Virginia."[17] As they waited for orders to leave Texas, some officers continued to drill their men, while others took the opportunity to rest or visit nearby Houston. All of the men hoped their stay at Camp Van Dorn would be brief, and not just because of their enthusiasm. Their drinking supply came from surface water that "caused considerable sickness throughout the camp," the men explained. One volunteer joked, "Our guard duty consist[ed] of watching night and day two little ponds of brackish water, lest they should dry up and a frog should pollute them by swimming in them."[18] They managed to eventually get spring water brought in, which improved conditions considerably, but the area as a whole remained unhealthy.

Volunteers Patrick Penn and his cousin, Robert Sullivan, of Oso, Texas, had joined the Mustang Grays of Bexar County that summer, and they, too, were unimpressed with Harrisburg. It was, Penn declared, "undoubtedly the hottest country it has ever been my misfortune to inhabit." Houston was a bit better, he admitted, with its "nice buildings" and "great many pretty women . . . and ice cream." But Penn and the 1,200 volunteers who had converged on Harrisburg grew frustrated waiting on their clothes, tents, and other men to arrive. Penn's company did not even drill because "it is too warm down here to think of such a thing. We'll all melt."[19]

Robert Sullivan's biggest complaint was not the heat but rather the boredom. In five days, he grumbled, they had done "nothing at all," making the men "very impatient to leave." The "water is bad and it is very warm weather." Some relief came in the form of religion and politics. Several men took turns preaching each evening, including one who "made the most eloquent appeals against swearing" that Sullivan had ever heard. The politicians impressed him less. Gubernatorial candidate Francis Lubbock visited the men on August 4. "He proved conclusively to me," Sullivan frowned, "that he is hardly suitable to fill the Office of Governor, but he will get nearly all the votes here, mine shall be given to Chambers."[20]

Sullivan's and Penn's irritation was likely tied to the comforts they missed from home. The cousins came from two of the wealthiest families in Oso, Texas, with close familial ties to other prominent families in Fayette County. Sullivan was raised in Pontotoc, Mississippi, in the very northern reaches of the state; Penn grew up near Talladega, Alabama. Both families settled in southwest Fayette County, Texas, in the 1850s, establishing farms and ranches like many of their neighbors. In those days, Fayette County, located between Houston and San Antonio, seemed to stretch to the sky, with thousands of horses and cattle grazing the land year-round.[21] Ellen Crockett farmed in the area along with her husband and five young children when the war began. Religion was central to antebellum Oso, Crockett explained, where "large congregations assembled, sermons were preached, [and] souls were converted.

Hymns were sung and heaven came down our souls to greet."[22] The town boasted a post office, tannery, blacksmith shop, and mill, and, in 1859, the locals opened the Pine Springs School to educate area children.[23] Robert Sullivan's brother William was just six years old when the war began. Despite the community's efforts to educate and uplift their souls, William's best memory of his childhood was escaping to an old swimming hole near the school that, he grinned, "cost 16 school boys 16 whippings for drinking less than 16 quarts of booze."[24]

Both Patrick Penn and Robert Sullivan likely benefited from private tutors for their early education. Sullivan was twenty-one years old the summer the war began and the oldest of eight children raised in an elite slave-owning family. Patrick Penn enjoyed similar wealth on a farm where much of the labor was done by nearly two dozen slaves.[25] Patrick's sister Lizzie had married a Methodist clergyman, Quinn Menefee, before the war. At thirty years old, Quinn held off from volunteering in 1861, but the call to serve would intensify in the coming months. The Menefees were not as wealthy as the Penns or Sullivans, but they lived comfortably in the planter class with Quinn's older brother, T. W., a stock raiser and farmer.[26] Not far from the Menefees lived twenty-six-year-old Edward Crockett, Patrick Penn's cousin by marriage. Crockett ran a successful farm with his wife, Agnes, and their young baby. Like Quinn Menefee, Crockett stayed home in 1861. Before long, though, all four men would be fighting together in Virginia.[27]

The years before the war were comfortable, secure, and profitable, and families like these rushed to defend a way of life they had no intention of changing. But the war also inspired an overwhelming sense of duty and desire for adventure. As Penn explained later that fall from Virginia: "I hope this war will come to a speedy close. I want one more big battle to be fought and I want to be in it. I do not care about getting killed or wounded, but I should wish to be there. I would not come to this place and go home again without being in an engagement for anything in the world."[28] Sullivan was a bit more philosophical and took comfort in his strong Christian faith. "Were it not that I feel it my sacred duty to serve my country," he confessed, "I would greatly prefer being at home, but as it is now, I would not exchange the trials, hardships and disappointments of a soldier for the comforts, pleasures and luxuries of a home." Still, Sullivan did "not love this kind of life, by any means. It is not agreeable to any of my tastes or habits. But I believe that we are engaged in a great, a holy, cause. I feel conscious of the rectitude of my intentions and endeavor to be not only contented but happy."[29]

If an overwhelming sense of duty inspired Sullivan and Penn that summer, Lucy Morton Sullivan, Robert's mother, felt only grief. She was sick with worry over what the war would bring. Robert and Patrick had already left, and Patrick's brother Abe and her son Morton, were talking about volunteering as well. Sensing his mother's fears, Robert Sullivan struggled to find some way to comfort her. "Be resolved to look forward with pleasure to the time when all three of your children will return to your embrace," he wrote. "We are defending you, our Brothers & Sisters, our homes & our interests as much where we are as if we were in Texas.... Don't give way to gloomy feelings. If you love me, if you love your younger children, cheer up and resolve to be contented."[30]

The wealth that the Sullivans, Penns, Crocketts, and Menefees enjoyed in Oso, Texas, was more the exception than the rule among Texas Brigade volunteers. Two-thirds of the original privates who volunteered for service in Virginia did not own slaves or came from nonslaveholding families, though they benefited from the system through business dealings in their communities and the larger economic wealth that enslaved labor generated, especially in antebellum East Texas.[31] The Sullivans' wealth placed them in the top 5 percent of the free Texas population in 1860 who owned slaves, and the top 7 percent of the original privates in the Fourth Texas, which the cousins joined later that fall.[32] Indeed, the wealth that privates like Penn and Sullivan enjoyed was more in line with the original junior officers of the Fourth and Fifth Texas, where 56 percent of the original Fourth Texas captains and 88 percent of the original Fifth Texas captains were slaveholders.[33]

Samuel Tine Owen camped near Penn and Sullivan in Harrisburg. He was equally disgusted with their environs, declaring it "too low down and the people is just like hogs and dogs." He frowned that "the report of our drawing money hear is all a lye," but Owen, too, remained "devoted to the instruction of a pious father through the disaster which is just about to overthrow our country" and pledged "to my country I will prove true although I may find a soldiers grave."[34] Owen represented the socioeconomic norm of the volunteers at Harrisburg.[35] His father was a middle-class farmer in Henderson, Texas, with a combined wealth of nearly $1,300. There is no indication that the family owned slaves, but their finances had improved significantly since coming to Texas several years earlier. Like many of the men around him, Owen had a lot to fight for that summer. Despite the setbacks he faced in Harrisburg, he remained determined to do that fighting in Virginia.[36]

By August 17, some of the men had finally departed for Richmond, but Owen's company, the Sandy Point Mounted Rifles of Athens, remained. Their commander, Captain Martin, still had no weapons for his men, but they planned to leave in the next couple days regardless. Whereas some of the officers at Harrisburg like Capt. R. T. P. Allen were earning the men's disdain for their demands of incessant drilling and respect for military protocol, Martin won his Texans over by demanding little of them in the brutal heat. He also mocked martial protocol, further endearing himself to the citizen-soldiers he led, who often bristled at the hierarchy and discipline of military life. As one Houstonian observed: "Bill Martin himself is a good officer. He roughs it all the time, and says that what is good enough for the men is good enough for him."[37]

With his shaggy, long hair and quick smile, Martin earned the nickname "Howdy" for his preference of a waved greeting over a snappy salute. Tall and lanky, Martin was born outside of Texas, like many of the men in camp, but came west in later years. Also like many of the officers in camp, Martin enjoyed middle-class success in the years leading up to the war.[38] Born in Georgia and educated in Alabama, he arrived in Texas in 1850 where he set up a law practice in Athens before winning a seat in the Texas Senate, which he held until 1858. He recruited ranch hands and farm boys into the Sandy Point Mounted Rifles. With a gift for persuasion, Martin convinced them to stay even after the men learned they would be foot, rather than horse, soldiers. Martin was self-confident without bravado. He was friendly, engaging, and known for rowdy "sermons" where, as when they had first marched off to war, he leapt "on an old goods box under a hickory tree . . . long, angular, [and] with a voice like thunder. . . . [A]s he spoke he would shake his long hair and look like he was mad enough to eat a Yankee raw." One contemporary mused that "it seemed he never did anything like other people," and the men loved him for it. He was their entertainer and kindly uncle, a man who inspired and protected lonesome, raucous young men far from home. In their short time together, the Sandy Point Rifles had realized that Martin was the kind of officer they needed. Indeed, he would prove to be one of the best in the brigade.[39]

By August 19, five of the companies had already departed for Virginia, leaving behind men who "felt somewhat like he who trods along the banquet hall deserted." They spent their days "reading the handsomely bound book, or neat little bible. . . . Others lounged up and down the bayou and occasionally a squad was found enjoying a bath. But the majority of the men attended divine services," the *Houston Weekly Telegraph* reported.[40] The delay that kept them there was caused in part by Gen. Earl Van Dorn's desire to have President Davis's June levy countermanded. Van Dorn wanted to keep the volunteers in

Texas for the state's defense. His plans frustrated Reverend Nicholas Davis, who joined the men as their chaplain, but Robert Sullivan had already adapted to the hurry-up-and-wait pace that defined military life. He was learning about military rumors, where some heard that Van Dorn was hoping to keep the men at home, while others believed he was lobbying for arms.[41] Pvt. G. S. Boyton of the Navarro Rifles reported to their hometown newspaper that Van Dorn's efforts to keep the Texans for home defense made him so unpopular that had he achieved his goal, "mutiny . . . would have been the result." Boyton had "not heard a single officer who did not oppose these arrangement of Van Dorn's," though he assured readers at home that everything would soon be settled peacefully and the volunteers would soon be on their way to Virginia.[42]

When they did finally all leave, most of this second wave of Texas volunteers bound for Virginia walked and waded across Louisiana. It was a "werisome trip . . . through mud and water . . . a hundred and fifty miles nearly all the company has been sick mostly colds," Tine Owen reported. The usually verbose Joe Polley, a private in the Mustang Grays along with Pat Penn and Robert Sullivan, summarized it years later as "that horrible walk through the swamps of Louisiana." The men endured hunger, blisters, fevers, floodwaters, torrential downpours, and the deaths of several volunteers to accident and disease as they made their way east.[43]

When they finally reached Lafayette and New Iberia, locals provided wagons and food, which made the final leg of the Texans' journey to New Orleans much easier. It was a simple thing: loaning or giving wagons and sharing what little food the citizens had. But the Texans never forgot it. In mid-September, Ben Baker described both the resistance and the support they had received on the march, and his brother, coeditor of the *Colorado Citizen*, published Ben's letter for all of Columbus, Texas, to read. "We were treated with great hospitality in many places," Ben explained, "in others, very rudely. At New Iberia we were furnished dinner and supper the day of our arrival, and the people on the road leading to the city furnished us with wagons, carriages, buggies and every other means of transportation. I can not speak too much in praise of the French who live on the route from Niblett's Bluff to New Iberia." These Louisiana Confederates were "actuated by the most ardent spirit of patriotism, and wished us much good luck in whipping out the Abolitionists. They will long live in the memory of our company."[44]

From New Orleans, the trip was far easier. The men traveled largely by rail with brief stops at towns along the way where they changed trains and visited family in the area. The majority of the volunteers were not native-born Texans, and they relished the opportunity to visit old school friends, as Thomas Selman did, or family along the route. Pat Penn and Robert Sullivan visited Robert's sister Bettie and his brother Morton, who had been living at their aunt's near Tupelo, Mississippi, in the months before the war. Morton was determined to "join the army as soon as he carries Bettie home."[45] Despite the ease of rail travel, dangers remained a part of their journey. Robert Sullivan was horrified when "one of the soldiers, attempting to get on the car" of the train, "fell, and his foot and arm were run over and crushed all to pieces."[46] This was likely Pvt. E. W. "Ras" Cartwright from the Porter Guards. He was over six feet six inches tall, and the men enjoyed dressing the massive Cartwright as a captain and parading him along their route as the best representation of Texas officer material. As they approached Holly Springs, Mississippi, the men were enjoying Cartwright "playing captain, when the whistle sounded 'All aboard.' All ran to get in," Capt. James Hunter recalled. Cartwright "was very active and thought to put his hands on the bulkheads of the two cars, spring up, and catch the door." Pvt. Zack Landrum, whose family knew the Cartwrights in Montgomery County, described to his sister the horrifying sight as Ras Cartwright's sword caught under a car, throwing him onto the tracks. The train ran over "his right arm between the hand and elbow, crushing it all to pieces," Landrum explained, and rolled "down his right leg bruising the flesh very bad and running over his foot, crushing it all to pieces." The company doctor, Thomas May, stayed behind along with Ras's brother Jimmy, who was also a volunteer in the Porter Guards, but there was little they could do. Ras Cartwright died the next morning. He left behind a widowed mother in her early forties who would send a third son, Lemuel, to join the Porter Guards (then Company H of the Fourth Texas Infantry) in 1862. Throughout the war, she worked with two daughters and her remaining son to raise hogs and a variety of corn. Her James would be killed in battle in the spring of 1864, and combat wounds that fall required the amputation Lemuel's arm. No one knew this, of course, in the heady optimism of 1861, but Ras Cartwright's tragic death in Holly Springs foreshadowed a very long war for the Cartwrights.[47]

As the privates made their way to Virginia, a number of their elected officers worked on their leadership skills. In Camp Van Dorn, Lt. J. R. Loughridge observed that "I have made some warm friends among our boys" in the Navarro Rifles "by my attention to them when sick."[48] First Lt. Dugat Williams learned similar lessons with the Company Invincibles on the road to New Orleans and decided their miserable trip would be key to their future endurance in battle. "We traveled emphatically by 'mud and water,'" he told Laura Bryan, "but we got along very well and I think it has been an advantage to all of us, it seems to have hardened us all a little and made us better fitted and more capable of undergoing the fatigues through which we will have to pass in Virginia." When many of the men were welcomed into private homes in New Iberia, their captain, King Bryan, and Dugat Williams stayed with the baggage trains and let the men enjoy the shelter. The commanders "missed all the nice suppers that the other boys had," Williams complained, but it was another important example of sacrifice that the men respected and expected in their officers.[49]

Despite their miserable march, the Texans were learning invaluable lessons in war, leadership, and the power exchange between officers and men. These volunteers were not regulars. They were citizen-soldiers who expected a certain level of respect and empathy to be awarded them that was tied to their social status rather than their military rank. Men like J. R. Loughridge, King Bryan, Dugat Williams, James Hunter. and Howdy Martin were mastering skills in those dreary weeks at Camp Van Dorn, on that awful march across Louisiana, and along the rails to Virginia that would prove key to the Texans' future success.

RECRUITS ON THE DRILL FIELD
Becoming Citizen-Soldiers

In the fall of 1861, the second wave of 2,000 additional Texas volunteers poured into Richmond. Like the First Texas that had arrived earlier in the summer, these men would learn lessons in soldiering before their first military assignment in November. The painful process required that they relinquish many of their civilian freedoms. But the Texans clung to some of their rights, especially in the selection of their officers. As the fall and coming winter would show, the same qualities that made the men incredibly tough soldiers also made them incredibly stubborn and disobedient enlisted men. They tested, tortured, and rejected many of their officers that fall, especially those appointed in Richmond. But those who survived—literally and figuratively—proved that the Texans knew, for the most part, the kind of leaders they needed.

The Texans' arrival in Virginia was as haphazard as their departure from home had been, but Mark Smither reveled in the fact that "the Waverley Confederates were the first company of the two Regmts of Texan Volunteers to plant our Flag at the Confederate Camp in Richmond." Of course, those of the First Texas had arrived much earlier, but of the men of Camp Van Dorn, Smither and his Walker County friends could rightly claim the glory. Captain Hutchinson's Grimes County Grays arrived next, and then, as Smither sat writing to his mother, shouts and cheers rang out. It was September 12, and the rest of the Texans had arrived.[1]

All along the journey, the men had sparked citizens' curiosity about the Texans of lore, of the Alamo and the Mexican War, and of America's southwestern frontier. "We were a perfect curiosity," Smither assured his mother. "The people would come from every direction to see the boys from Texas.

[T]hey had great ideas of the Texans." Smither, like many of the men, enjoyed his fame: "When we came through Augusta, Georgia, they gave us a supper and the boys put on their best behavior and the Ladies were much surprised to see us so well behaved. I overheard one Lady say to another, 'Why aint they quiet! I expected to hear them yelling all the time and they are good looking too! I expected to see them with their hair down to their heels and yellow as an Indian!'"

The men were uncertain where they would go next. "There are a great many troops here but they are leaving daily for Manassas to join the army there," Smither wrote. "We are hourly expecting to hear news of a great battle, the pickett guards of both sides are in sight of each other. The next fight will be at Washington City." Smither did not know if Texans would be in that fight, but he promised his mother, "If we are[,] you need not be afraid of the Texas Boys not doing their duty."[2]

John Marquis Smither is an excellent example of the southern connections that ran through many of the Texas Brigade families. Some historians have theorized that Texans were the least Confederate of all secessionists because Texas was such a recent addition to the United States. It had "its own patriotic symbols," and because of its location on the fringe of the Confederacy, they theorize that the Lone Star State was less attached to the new nation than were other southern states. The theory has also been proposed that Texans "did not have the strong identification with the generation of 1776 that many Virginians felt."[3] On the contrary, Texas Brigade soldiers and their families, who were largely recruited from the eastern and central portions of the state, were tied by birth, childhood, and family connections throughout the South, and they were quick to reference the Founders in that first winter of the war when they pondered what had brought them to Virginia.

Mark Smither's father, Robert, was a Virginian. His mother, Elizabeth E. Calmes, was from South Carolina. The family lived in Tennessee and Mississippi before continuing on to Texas, where Mark Smither was born in 1844. Also like many southerners, Mark Smither lost a parent to disease before he reached adulthood. His father owned a mercantile and blacksmith shop, as well as a drugstore. In the early 1850s, the elder Smither was doing well enough financially to move his family from their log home into a new frame house on "Smither Hill" in Huntsville, where he was an active member of the Odd Fellows and the local Masonic order. But then Robert contracted yellow fever while returning home from a purchasing trip in New York City. He died before reaching Huntsville, leaving Elizabeth a wealthy widow with six children to raise. Despite this, Elizabeth Smither did well. She joined a similarly prominent Huntsville family by marring Erasmus Wynne in 1858. By the time of Lincoln's election, Elizabeth Smither Wynne had a total wealth, listed separately from that of her second husband, of nearly $70,000. That was just a bit less than Erasmus enjoyed, and the family lived a life of ease made possible by the labor of the fifty-three enslaved men, women, and children who worked on the Wynne properties.[4]

John Marquis "Mark" Smither was not the average private among the Texans in Virginia. Among the Fifth Texas Infantry, the regiment in which Smither would fight, his wealth placed him among only 6 percent of the original privates. His family's wealth was atypical in Texas, too. In 1860, only about 2 percent of white Texans had wealth that matched that of the Smither and Wynne families.[5] Thus, when he left for war in 1861, Mark Smither walked away from a very comfortable life that he could not imagine losing; indeed, he rarely pondered it. His early letters bore little mention of his motivations other than repeated references to adventure and boastful descriptions of southerners' perceptions of Texans. A few vague references to duty were mixed in, but Mark Smither was, in 1861, a man comfortable in the life his family had built and confident that he could preserve their fortunes and status well into the future.

As the men of Camp Van Dorn arrived in Richmond, the First Texas was camped about one hundred miles to the north at the rail hub known as Manassas Junction. Charles Schadt and the Lone Star Rifles of Galveston had arrived there at the end of August and were mustered into the First Texas Volunteer Infantry Regiment commanded by their old champion: Senator, now Colonel, Louis T. Wigfall. The regiment included 850 men in ten Texas companies and one company from Alabama, the Daniel Boone Rifles of Mobile led by Capt. Albert Covington.[6]

Wigfall trained the First Texans tirelessly. They awoke at 5:00 a.m. each morning for roll call and breakfast, followed by drill as companies at 7:00 a.m., and then battalion drill extended from 9:00 a.m. until noon. This resumed after lunch for another four hours. At 6:00 p.m. the men had dress parade for thirty minutes followed by supper. Tattoo sounded the end of the day, with a final roll call at 9:00 p.m. with all lights and fires to be out by 9:30 p.m. Their drill ground, Charles Schadt explained, "is very rugged and hilly. We have to march through woods, over fences, across ditches and gullies, and keep line as soon as on firm ground, or the devil is to pay. Col. Wigfall is very strict in his commands and any negligence of duty is 48 hours extra duty or drill with packed knapsack." Charles's brother William frowned at how different real soldiering was "from Galveston street parading and a little more work than fun."[7]

While training, and in discussions around fires, the men debated their commanders' skills and worth. Lt. Col. Hugh McLeod, Wigfall's second in command, was born in New York City during the War of 1812 but raised in Georgia. Graduating from West Point in 1835, he received his first assignment to Fort Jessup, Louisiana. While traveling there, McLeod linked up with a Georgia battalion heading to Texas to fight in the revolution against Mexico. He abruptly resigned his commission in the U.S. Army and fell in with the Georgians. Uncle Sam may not have approved, but Texans celebrated his leadership of Republic of Texas forces against the Caddos, Kickapoos, and Cherokee in the late 1830s. When the Civil War began, Governor Edward Clark asked McLeod to help organize the volunteers in southeast Texas, working out of Galveston. He was mustered into Confederate service as the original lieutenant colonel of the First Texas Battalion, just below Colonel Wigfall.[8]

McLeod was "not well liked by the whole regiment," Charles Schadt noted, "although none have any reason to hate the man, for he acts as a gentleman. It is the old grudge the boys have against him, which will wear away as far as our Company is concerned." It is not clear what that "old grudge" was, unless Schadt was referring to McLeod's role in the failed Santa Fe Expedition of 1841, but the men generally approved of their company officers, "especially Captain [Alfred C.] McKeen, who acts as a father to the boys and provides for our comfort to his full extent." The Texans saved their greatest respect for commanders who demonstrated skill in drill but also for those who provided for, respected, and protected the men.[9]

While the First Texans trained near Manassas, Confederate authorities in Richmond mustered the companies from Camp Van Dorn into Confederate service in Virginia "for the war" as the Fourth and Fifth Texas Volunteer Infantry Regiments. Day after day went by with some drill, but for the most part the men wandered in and out of Richmond (when they could secure passes to do so) and mingled with nearby camps. The Texans had enough supplies for the fall, but Charles Schadt worried about the approaching winter: "We will be in want of flannel, which you cannot buy for love or money." Unfortunately, Schadt grumbled, the merchants were "a regular thieving set of settlers."[10]

Tom Selman of the Lone Star Guards marveled at all the excitement in the Confederate capital. When a fight broke out in a Louisiana regiment, one of several acts of Louisiana violence he had already noted in his diary, Selman declared the Louisianans "a desperate set." Union prisoners from Manassas struck Selman as "hearty hard stout looking men," and he stared as a woman walked by, "a lieutenant dressed in mens clothes. She had on a ladies hat, black feathers, black velvet dress which came a little below her knees, tight stockings, men's gaiters. Her shirt was trimmed with red. She had on a five shooter." Selman was not impressed. "She looked perfectly disgusting. I think she is a base woman," though, clearly fascinated, he noted when he spotted her again the following day.[11]

All of the fresh recruits in Richmond wanted to outdo each other. President Jefferson Davis visited the Texans' camp and warned them that "the troops of other States have their reputation to gain; the sons of the defenders of the Alamo have theirs to maintain!"[12] General Wigfall, ever the fire-eater and perhaps sensing the public mood, encouraged such high expectations of his Texans. He insisted that "the boys . . . would maintain [their reputation] or die," and promised that "the brave Texans who had never yet on any field turned their backs upon an enemy . . . would sleep on the battle-field, either the repose of victors or the sleep of death." It was, the soldiers' families in Dallas read, "a scene sublime in its enthusiasm and we felt about six inches taller in hearing our Texas boys so praised and applauded."[13]

The commanders and civilians may have been pleased, but some of the men frowned at such bravado. Pvt. Irenus Watson Landingham of Company A of the Fifth Texas noted that their fierce fighting reputation did not always prove an asset. When about seventy of the Fifth Texans went into Richmond in late October, Landingham noticed that "Windows went down in a hurry" when locals "heard that Texan's is coming. . . . They say Texans have no feeling whatever, that they are just like brutes[.] We are even looked upon as a kind of savage set by the citizens here. Our *terribleness* is greatly overrated," Landingham observed, "and I am fearful will prove a disadvantage some day."[14]

Mark Smither agreed, explaining to his aunt: "It is strange what kind of people they had an idea we were[. T]hey thought we were a set of desperadoes that would kill a man if he looked hard at them, a band of lawless adventurers who respected neither god nor man."[15] Just as the locals watched the Texans curiously, so, too, did volunteers from other states. Andy Wollard of the Fourth Texas grew tired of all the strutting, the bold expectations of Texans, and perhaps of some of their own boasting. Spotting a man decked out in a sharp new uniform, Wollard asked what unit he belonged to. The private lifted his chin and said, "the Wild Tiger Rifles." When the man returned the question, Wollard stared through him "with all the view of a serpent" and drawled, "the prancing Hyenas."[16]

For all the excitement that Richmond offered the volunteers, Robert Sullivan found little that impressed him. "The nights are now very cool," he observed in late September, "and the soldiers are cheated to death here. Goods are 50 percent dearer than at Oso [Texas]. Hard little apples sell for 25 cents per dozen." Sullivan was shocked when he saw a soldier who had been discharged from a Louisiana regiment "for some misdemeanor" try to rob a man in Richmond. The Louisianan "was shot and instantly killed," Sullivan winced. At night, Penn and he found little comfort on "the roughest, rockiest place you ever saw." The ground was "so slanting that when we go to sleep we slide down, we then awake and slide up again, and so on continually through the night." Taking stock of his new condition as a citizen-soldier, Sullivan concluded that "a soldier's life is fraught with nothing but danger, disappointments and annoyances."[17]

William Campbell of the Waverly Confederates, now Company D of the Fifth Texas, agreed. "The life of a soldier is any thing but pleasant and I can assure you that I am heartily tired of it," he explained. "I left home expecting a rough life and to do my duty as a soldier—I think I have done so—so far. . . . [But t]hat trip across Louisiana cooled the ardor of many of the boys and most of them thought as I did, that they would never join another infantry company." Musing on the frustrations of an infantryman, Campbell promised his aunt: "I have often heard it said that every one was made for some particular purpose. It may be so But I have concluded that I never was made for walking. I have become so perfectly disgusted with it that if I ever get home *horse flesh* will be bound to suffer."[18]

In September, the First Texas moved to the Dumfries, Virginia, area to help with the Potomac River defenses. Setting up camp northeast of town, they helped man the batteries Confederates constructed to stop all Federal traffic on the river, a key access route to the Union capital.[19] The following month, the Fourth and Fifth Texas moved further outside of Richmond to Camp Bragg, where they were organized into companies and informed of their commanders. It was here that significant discord surfaced in the ranks. The Texans were allowed to elect company-level officers, but all colonels, lieutenant colonels, majors, and certain staff members, they learned, would be appointed by the

Davis administration. The men disliked this policy intensely and spent the next several weeks making that view clear to their appointed officers and officials in Richmond.

Reverend Nicholas Davis, chaplain of the Fourth Texas, captured their frustration best. The president and Confederate War Department, the reverend explained bitterly, in "their wisdom ... grasped the subject, and considered it in all its details, and were resolved no mishap should befall our arms by reason of neglect." Their wise council would "show our brave boys the nearest and easiest paths to victory and glory." The task at hand was too important "to permit incompetent men to have places in the army as officers." And so it was "intimated that at Richmond there would be found sitting in imperial state, an imposing board of military Savants, deeply skilled in all the mysteries of military science, and so deeply imbued with occult lore, that no one but a man of military requirements and personal ability might hope to pass the ordeal of their examination."[20]

Some of the appointed officers were non-Texans. Others were Texans but martinets who did not listen to the complaints of the men and failed to respect their status within their communities—both at home and the regimental community they built in war. No matter who was presented, the Texans made clear that they would have the final word on to whom and how they would submit their rights as volunteers.

Dugat Williams, a lieutenant in what had just officially become Company F of the Fifth Texas Infantry, watched all of the new regimental officers carefully and worked to understand his role as a company officer. On October 7, he looked around the encampment and saw "quite a considerable little army of Texans, all good and brave men and ready to go to battle at any time. Everything goes along smoothly and quietly enough and everybody is satisfied with everything," he smiled. But then he frowned as he recalled one key problem. It was "the individuals composing our regimental officers," Williams explained. Their colonel was J. J. Archer. A Marylander, Archer was rumored to be "a good, competent, and brave officer," Williams admitted, but "he is not a Texan and the whole Regiment has, on this and other accounts, made decided objections to him. They all say he is not the man to lead them into battle, that he is from a state too far North and too near Yankeedom for Texas to trust as their commanding officer." The men, Williams observed, "all know that Texans are claimed as the best Soldiers in the Army and they think the position of Colonel is too high for a Marylander to hold over Texans."[21] Personally, Williams hoped

Archer might work out, but Williams feared the Marylander had made such a bad impression on the regiment that he could never turn things around. As Fifth Texan Tacitus T. Clay explained, Archer "is a little fellow . . . and may possibly be a very efficient man if in the Command of Regulars, but I fear he is not the right type to control or *give satisfaction* to Texas volunteers and the dissatisfaction in and out of the ranks is very general and I think there is a movement on foot with our Captains to have him supplanted."[22]

If Archer had problems, his lieutenant colonel was doomed from the start. He was Frank Schaller, born Franz Emil Schaller in the German state of Saxony. His grandfather, a major in Napoleon I's French Imperial Cavalry, died on the retreat from Moscow. Schaller's father was also an officer in the French army but left France in 1830 after the July Revolution. Franz Schaller was educated at l'Academie Militaire de Dresden and graduated from the University of Jena with a gift for the humanities and modern languages. He served briefly as an aide-de-camp in the Crimean War before emigrating to the United States, in part to prove his disapproving father wrong. Franz Schaller Americanized his name to "Frank" and taught at an Episcopal Military School in Maryland in the late 1850s and then at a military academy in Hillsborough, North Carolina, until 1861. On paper, he had superb credentials. In person, he was everything the Texans despised. As one Schaller descendent explained, Frank Schaller was "short, slim, and high-strung. He disguised his boyish features behind a French-inspired mustache and goatee. He had the obstinate propensity for going against the obvious direction wherein his true abilities lay. . . . Shy and lacking essential social skills, he nevertheless strove to be a leader of men."

Schaller's first effort at Confederate command was in the Polish Brigade, which failed miserably, though not from any of his own doing. By late September, he still had enough of President Davis's support to receive a new commission. Schaller was thrilled. "To-day, I have been appointed a Lieutenant Colonel . . . and will in a few days be ordered to duty with the 5th Texas Regiment," he told to his fiancée. "My gratification . . . I need not allude to. . . . I have not as yet seen my regiment but it is camped near Richmond. I shall call on the Colonel to-morrow and hope he is a pleasing man." As Schaller pondered his appearance, he decided a new uniform was in order, resplendent with gold stars and braiding that ran from his hat to his boots. Even his mare received shiny new accouterments with brass and gold piping.[23]

It was early October when Schaller rode into the Fifth Texans' camp. This is the regiment whose favorite officer would, in about sixth months, don a red shirt while carrying a frying pan and six-shooter into battle. Their most celebrated commanders had shaggy long hair and worn boots that gave the impression of self-made men. But here was Schaller, with his gold lace and stars, sounding and looking like anything but a Texan. Dugat Williams was stunned. "I hardly know how to begin to say anything about him. He is a man so little worthy of remark that I deem it a waste of paper and ink as well as time and trouble to make the slightest mention whatever of him. . . . He is a foreigner—Dutch-Polander, and speaks English not even so well as Isaac Black," Williams fumed. "He is a small, very dried-up specimen of human nature and his enormous mustache almost entirely covers his intellectual and Dutch looking face and would sooner be taken for the driver of a dray than the Lieut. col. of the Gentlemen composing the Regiment of Texas volunteers. I wish you could see him. I know you would fully agree with me in saying that he is totally unfit to occupy the position which he now holds."[24]

Reverend Davis thought little better of Schaller, and the rest of the unit agreed. "*What is it?* Is it a man, a fish, or a bird?" one asked. "Of course it is a man," another answered. "Don't you see his legs?" "Well," came the reply, "*that thing* may be a man, but we don't call them men in Texas."[25] Camp resounded that night with jeers and laughter as the men clarified their right to select officers suited to their skills and temperament. The last the Fifth Texans saw of Schaller was his back side, riding out of camp astride his horse, her mane sheared off and her tail naked and "sleek as an opossum's."[26]

Hardly any of the appointees won their acceptance. Dugat Williams had nothing better to say about his new major than he did about Schaller. The man's "name is Quattlebaum—just think, will you—Q-U-A-T-T-L-E-B-A-U-M—why, the name is enough to convince anybody in the world that—that—that—well, that he won't do. Quattlebaum. What a name. He ought to leave off the 'tlebaum' and change his name to Quat—it is much easier to say Quat than to pronounce all those jaw breaking sounds together." Pryor Bryan, their company commander's nephew, agreed that Quattlebaum just "won't do," and "every man in the Regiment" agreed because he is "incompetent and inexperienced," Williams explained. Schaller and Quattlebaum were simply not the right sort, the Texans declared.[27]

One might conclude that the main problem was that the appointees were non-Texans, but that would ignore the Fourth Texans' response to their regimental officers. R. T. P. Allen was a Marylander by birth but had settled in

Bastrop, Texas, where he ran a military academy before the war. Like Captain Key at Camp Van Dorn, Allen had commanded a camp of instruction, Camp Clark, where the men gathered in Texas before leaving for Virginia. While there, Allen earned a reputation as a martinet who was too quick to discipline and too slow to respect the rights of volunteers, who nicknamed him "Rarin', Tearin', Pitchin'" Allen. Simply put, Reverend Davis explained, Allen "did not suit their views of a commander." The men disliked Allen so much that they refused to accept his leadership. By late September, officers were "figuring about to get the President to recall the appointment of Allen," though Davis observed wisely that some of their resistance may have been inspired "to get some position for themselves." On September 30, Allen resigned, but that still was not enough for several of the men, who forced Allen onto his horse, without a bridle, and chased him with switches "out of the regimental grounds amid the hoots and jeers of the boys.... That colonel was never seen again," Fourth Texas Pvt. Mark Womack smiled.[28]

The Fourth Texans' lieutenant colonel did not fare much better. This was John Marshall, the newspaper editor and confidant of President Davis who had rushed to Richmond just a few months earlier to secure Davis's call for 2,000 additional Texas volunteers in Richmond. Marshall had been hailed as a hero in the Texas press and by most of the volunteers who later made up the Fourth and Fifth Texas. But when he was appointed rather than chosen by the men as their leader and repeatedly made basic command errors during drill that revealed his inexperience, the men made their disgust clear.

"He made a perfect fool of himself," Thomas Selman laughed, "giving wrong orders such as order arms from a present [arms,] fix bayonets when they were already fixed. The boys would not obey a single order that was wrong. When the parade was dismissed, every company left the ground whooping & yelling & repeating Marshall's commands & crying aloud Marshall's tactics." Marshall tried again two days later. This time he made "only one mistake." The newspaper editor turned officer had been practicing, but it was too late. "Not a soldier obeyed the command . . . but all laughed at him as usual," Selman explained. While the soldiers were initially grateful to Marshall for securing their positions in Virginia, now he embodied the Texas volunteers' frustrations with soldiering and their determination that only a man of their choosing would lead them.

The Fourth Texas did not force Marshall out of camp, but they would eventually petition him for his resignation in the spring of 1862. This happened about the same time that the Fourth Texans in Company C petitioned their own captain, William P. Townsend, for his resignation along with their Lt. Decimus et Ultimus Barziza (whose parents were clearly exhausted by the birth of their "tenth and last" child). Pvt. William Foster confided to his sister that when Townsend received the petition, "he called in all the officers, burnt the petition, without even looking at it, and said he would still be our captain."[29] Despite their repeated petitions, Townsend remained. Indeed, just days after Colonel Allen was forced out of camp, Townsend confided in a letter to his wife: "Our company is in the main doing well. Some discontent but nothing of the moment. The discontented are the worthless ones—they would be dissatisfied anywhere."[30]

Townsend's dismissal of the men's complaints is wise to consider when pondering the Texans' reactions to their federally appointed officers, as well as their rejection of junior officers that the men had accepted back in Texas. Certainly the complaints were not universal, but they were substantial enough to create unrest in camp. "I can urge nothing against Capt. T. more than little seeming partiality and indifference," William Foster explained about the petition, but "44 members, a majority, I think, of those now encamped, signed and presented it.... [N]either Bob [William's brother] nor I signed either." In November 1861, about a month after Townsend dismissed the grumblers while writing to his wife, Bob Foster, William's brother, explained to their parents that the situation continued. Townsend "is not so popular with his men as he used to be. 5 or 6 of his men, Lou Wells among the number, has gotten a transfer from this company to another [Texas company], on account of not being pleased with Capt. Townsend."[31]

Like the Fosters, Val Giles refused to sign the petition against his commander, John Marshall, in the spring of 1862. As he explained, "my father was an iron-clad Andrew Jackson Democrat, a political and personal friend of Colonel Marshall. I had known him from my early boyhood and as he had been very kind to me, in the regiment I refused to sign the petition when presented for my signature." Upon looking at the list of names, Giles felt "lonesome, for it was almost a complete muster roll of the whole regiment." When the leaders of the petition presented it to Marshall, however, he responded just as Captain Townsend had a few months earlier. Marshall "looked sideways at the committee, read the head lines, tossed the manuscript to his cook, saying 'Here Mose, this will do for kindling.' He then drew his martial cloak around him, bowed to the honorable committee and strolled in his tent, and that was the last of that."³²

But that was not the last of it. The men came to respect Townsend's bravery in battle and accepted him as well as Lieutenant Barziza.³³ Marshall, though, retained the image of a man who "does well enough to manage a paper and do the mere work of political machinery, but has no military talent whatever," Pvt. Joseph Polly explained. Marshall "cannot make himself heard from one end of the regiment even when on drill and how far could he be heard on a battle field[?] Great dissatisfaction exists in the regiment against him. I hope he will have sense enough to resign ere we are called into battle." That was March 1862. By mid-June the men would draft another petition, and if denied again, they pledged to resign. "If their resignations are accepted the men will stack arms and rebel sooner than serve under Marshall with new officers and if they do not accept the resignations we can stack arms all the same," Polley promised.³⁴ At that point, though, the spring campaign season had already started, and they were just ten days from the battle that would first secure the Texans' fame within the Confederate army and take Marshall from their ranks.

And so it was that the Texans, with the exception of a few officers, had the final word on most of their commanders. In the case of men like Allen and Schaller, they literally drove them from camp. Others were simply worn down by the Texans' stubborn disapproval. The Fifth Texas, Val Giles mused, was the worst of all. "They fired colonels, lieutenant colonels and majors faster than Mr. Davis and the Secretary of War could send them out. The troops were in open rebellion against all comers." They allowed Colonel Archer to remain until he was promoted out of the ranks, and the men generally accepted their doctor-turned–lieutenant colonel Jerome Bonaparte Robertson. But they wore Major Quattlebaum down, playing "on his name with verse and song." After several months Quattlebaum resigned his commission, declaring "that if he had to associate with devils he would wait till he went to hell, where he could select his own company."³⁵

The Fourth Texas may have been less cantankerous, but they, too, drove off men like Howell G. Thomas. He was a highly respected Richmond surgeon who had trained in Paris and taught at a Virginia medical school while editing a medical journal. He was a superb addition to their unit at a time when, even before heavy fighting began, the diseases that tore through their ranks required a skilled physician. But Thomas was an outsider appointed by federal authorities, and the men insisted that, as free men, their opinions must be respected. After a few miserable weeks Thomas resigned, declaring that "his connection with the Texans was the most unpleasant [time] of his life."[36]

As amusing as these accounts may be, they are significant to understanding the Texans' later success. Their internal rebellions against appointed officers, as well as commanders they deemed unsuitable to the position, speak to the Texans' understanding, first, of their rights as nineteenth-century American citizens, and, second, to the timeless power exchange between officers and citizen-soldiers.[37] In the weeks before their departure from Texas, local newspapers informed readers that the Davis administration would appoint regimental officers, and there had been no public outcry in response to this; certainly nothing like the anger expressed by Texans in Richmond weeks later. On July 3, the editors of the *Houston Telegraph* reported, "Officers of the companies will be elected by the company but the field officers will be appointed by the President, and no man can get one of these appointments until he has passed a most thorough examination by the military boards." The editors endorsed this approach, explaining: "This we believe is right. The best blood of the South is in our army and must not be trusted to incompetent men even if popularity of each men shall secure their election."[38] Similar reports appeared in Austin and in Dallas.[39]

The Texas volunteers' rejection of their officers reflected their development and thinking as citizen-soldiers. It was tied to their almost instinctive beliefs in nineteenth-century American concepts of citizenship and rights, and their responses embodied the timeless power exchange between officers and men. The Texans would follow only those they trusted could lead and care for them. They would relinquish some of their freedoms only to those they deemed worthy of such submission, which is key to understanding the Texas Brigade's development as a unit.[40]

They certainly had a wealth of events with which to assess their commanders in the first winter of the war. It was early October when the companies of the Fourth and Fifth Texas Infantry Regiments left their camps near Rockett's Landing on the James River and established "Camp Bragg," though they more often called it "Camp Texas," about four miles east of Richmond. They drilled there until October 22, when Confederate secretary of war Judah P. Benjamin assigned the Fourth and Fifth Texas Infantry to join the First Texas at Dumfries, Virginia, which made them all part of the Fifth Brigade under the command of their old friend, Louis T. Wigfall. They were attached to Maj. Gen. E. Kirby Smith's Fourth Division, of the Potomac District in the Department of Northern Virginia, Joseph E. Johnston commanding. In late November, as the Confederate high command struggled to organize their host of defenders, the Texans were transferred to the Fourth Division under Maj. Gen. James Longstreet, and shortly after that, the Eighteenth Georgia joined the brigade.[41]

As this process took place and the Fourth and Fifth Texas prepared to move to Dumfries, they received a message from General Wigfall urging them to move with all haste because "the enemy was threatening his position."[42] Chaplain Davis of the Fourth Texas marveled as the speed with which the men responded: "A general bustle, every one working for himself and every one doing his own talking. Here comes the teams [of] horses in a long trot the waggons rattling—chains jingling, drivers hollowing & whips poping." Even Davis grabbed a rifle and cartridges and fell into line. The men were accustomed to long marches, but rushing down rural roads and fields in the middle of the night was a challenge. "We had traversed the swamps of Louisiana when they stood at high water-mark, but we had day light to travel in. Now we had to sight for the course, and guess at the bottom. And, if I were allowed to guess, judging from my own feeling, the 'soundings' were not so amusing," the chaplain recalled. "We had been in service just long enough for the company officers to feel considerable pride in keeping their lines well 'dressed,' and it is unnecessary for me to say that they had a good time of it that night.... We had moved 18 miles during the night and were present, if not ready, for a fight."[43] But the threat had vanished, if it had even been there at all.

These false alarms became a habit of Wigfall's. Pvt. Joseph B. "Joe" Polley—brigade veteran, historian, and wordsmith—later explained that "General Wigfall's imagination was too often quickened by deep potations to be reliable. The colder the night and the more metallic the rustling of the pine tops above his quarters, the more plainly he could hear the rattling of oars in the oar-locks of boats transporting Federal troops across the Potomac."[44] Wigfall's weakness for alcohol, particularly applejack, became well known among the officers and men. Many of them appreciated his skills as a politician but came to dislike him as a commander.

Thomas Jewett Goree was an aide to James Longstreet and had two brothers serving in the Fifth Texas (a third would join them in 1863). Reflecting on the Confederate officer corps around Richmond in the late fall of 1861, Goree confided: "I like Genl Wigfall as a man, but on account of his habits I very much regret that [brothers] Langston and Edwin are in his brigade. I hope, though, that when he assumes the responsibility of three or four regiments, he will see the necessity of reformation."[45] Wigfall never reformed, and it troubled the men. Pvt. James Hendrick of Marshall, Texas, confided to his family that "many of the [Texas] battalion are dissatisfied with Colonel Wigfall. He keeps them too close. He has been drinking a great deal lately. I have seen him so drunk that he could hardly stand up."[46]

Joe Polley agreed. Wigfall saw "a Yankee in every shadow, hears one approaching in every breeze that rustles and clinks together the ice-incrusted boughs of the pine trees under which the cabin selected for brigade headquarters stands, and no sooner sees or hears one than he takes alarm and orders the long roll sounded by the drummer he keeps close at hand for just such emergencies." That roll, Polley explained in the January cold of 1862, "is not the spasmodic rat-a-tat you are accustomed to hear when a company of home guards are drilling in the vicinity of your prairie home, but is a continuous, ear-splitting tat-tat-tat." It signaled, he explained, that "danger is too imminent to permit of a moment's delay, and its effect on sleeping soldiers is always startling, and often ludicrous in the extreme. . . . The first time I heard it, it awoke me from the profoundest slumber of my life so suddenly, and scared me so badly, that for two minutes I looked under my bed for my gun and out of doors for my pantaloons."[47]

Fifty years later, an aging Polley showed a little more empathy for Wigfall and declared that "to a certain extent" the general's actions were excusable. "The 1st Texas had run him half-crazy with its unwillingness to submit to the rigorous discipline he would have enforced, and, in addition, but previous to the arrival of the 4th and 5th, had manufactured more than one false alarm just to see what he would do," Polley recalled.[48] Pvt. E. O. Perry, of Company E of the First Texas, confirmed this in December 1861, noting his brigadier's drunken threats to "have all the 12 months volunteers sent home," though Wigfall never actually did.[49]

They were hard lessons, but the Texans were learning that the men they had respected in civilian life did not always make the best officers. Their journey from Texas to Virginia had revealed some of this and gave junior officers the opportunity to enhance their skills as leaders. Different challenges emerged, however, in Richmond. Here the men wrestled with outsiders appointed by the Davis administration and some fellow Texans who could not earn the men's respect. In some cases, the men learned that they were wrong about officers like Townsend and Barziza, and they gradually accepted their leadership. Frustrations over men like John Marshall, however, never eased. The Texans clarified that he was an honorable man and a brave one, but they were never satisfied with him as a regimental commander or with the idea of placing their lives in his hands, and they would continue to voice these complaints.

THE POTOMAC BLOCKADE
The Texas Brigade's First Assignment

In late November 1861, as the Texas volunteers in Virginia came together near Dumfries, they mastered the fundamentals of their first military assignment. They excelled at scouting across the river to terrorize Federal troops on the opposite shore in Maryland. They learned, if grudgingly, the unpleasant tasks of soldiering, including picket duty in the freezing cold, building shore batteries and other defenses, as well as washing, cooking, and building winter quarters. The greatest impact of their winter along the Potomac, however, was how their shared experiences bonded the men and their officers. When they emerged that spring, they were still more scouts than soldiers, and they certainly were not yet the disciplined, organized, hardened combat infantrymen they would become. That first winter forged the Texas Brigade.

The first meeting of the Georgians and the Texans was not initially a smooth one. Capt. James Lemon, the commander of Company A of the Eighteenth Georgia recalled that the men were all proud of their state heritage, and none "were willing to show deference to the other, so there we stood, in two groups, giving each other 'the look.'" Tensions increased for a few moments until, Lemon recalled, "a few of the boys from both Georgia and Texas, being by nature less proud and more gregarious, walked through the 'firing-line' and cheerfully shook hands and exchanged pleasantries. This seemed to have a charmed effect and soon we realized our prideful folly and were soon amongst each other, clasping hands and chattering away like long-separated chums," a bond that would increase as they came to share the challenges of camp and combat.[1]

The Georgians were highly motivated volunteers who, like Company K's second lieutenant Thomas Dowtin, looked forward to "nobly defending my country's dearest rights."[2] Another man in Company A believed: "We did not bring this war upon ourselves but the black hearted abolitionist forced it upon us. They have made laws contrary to the old constitution" that southerners "as lovers of our rights could not submit to." Specifically referencing the decisions of "free state legislatures" "in regard to fugitive slaves," the Georgian willingly "suffer[ed] privations in defending our selfs, our homes, our liberties, our all."[3] Much of their time that winter, however, was focused on defending their position along Telegraph Road and helping to construct the Cockpit Point batteries.

In December, Eighteenth Georgia privates A. F. Burnett and W. W. White of Company A started the *Spirit of '61*, a camp newspaper designed to entertain the men amid the tedium of camp life. The editors promised their paper would be "so full of variety, novelty and usefulness as to always find a willing ear." It included a few references to their ideological and political motivations, but the paper was mostly a place to laugh, advertise, and display a gift for writing. One soldier contributed a story about "Adventures in the Adirondac and Racquet River region," while another submitted a poem about, "the ugliest pocket book... ever made." The paper included a notice about the opening of a bakery business in camp with a "full and complete stock of Ginger Cakes," which, James Lemon later recalled, was such a success that "men were soon standing in a long file in the cold outside our rude log establishment, eager to put down five cents for their fresh hot ginger cake and cup of hot coffee." The profits, in addition to keeping the store running, went toward covering emergency expenses among the men.[4]

There is disagreement on the exact location of the Texas Brigade's camps that winter, but they were generally positioned between Telegraph Road and the Potomac River, and from Quantico Creek to Neabsco Creek to the north. Most antebellum Americans traveling south from Washington City took a three-and-a-half-hour trip down the Potomac from the U.S. capital to Aquia Creek, where they then got on the Richmond, Fredericksburg, and Potomac Railroad to Richmond, a journey of about seventy-five miles or five-and-a-half hours.[5] To complete the first leg of that journey and reach Aquia Creek, travelers in 1861 had to pass Dumfries and the batteries Confederates constructed along the Potomac that fall. The Texans and Georgians spent their first winter of the war, along with host of other southern volunteers, as part of that Potomac River line, helping to blockade Federal travel on the river to partially isolate the U.S. capital, and to study and threaten Federal positions held by Union general Daniel Sickles's Excelsior Brigade and Col. Abram Duryée's Fifth New York Zouaves directly across the Potomac in Maryland.

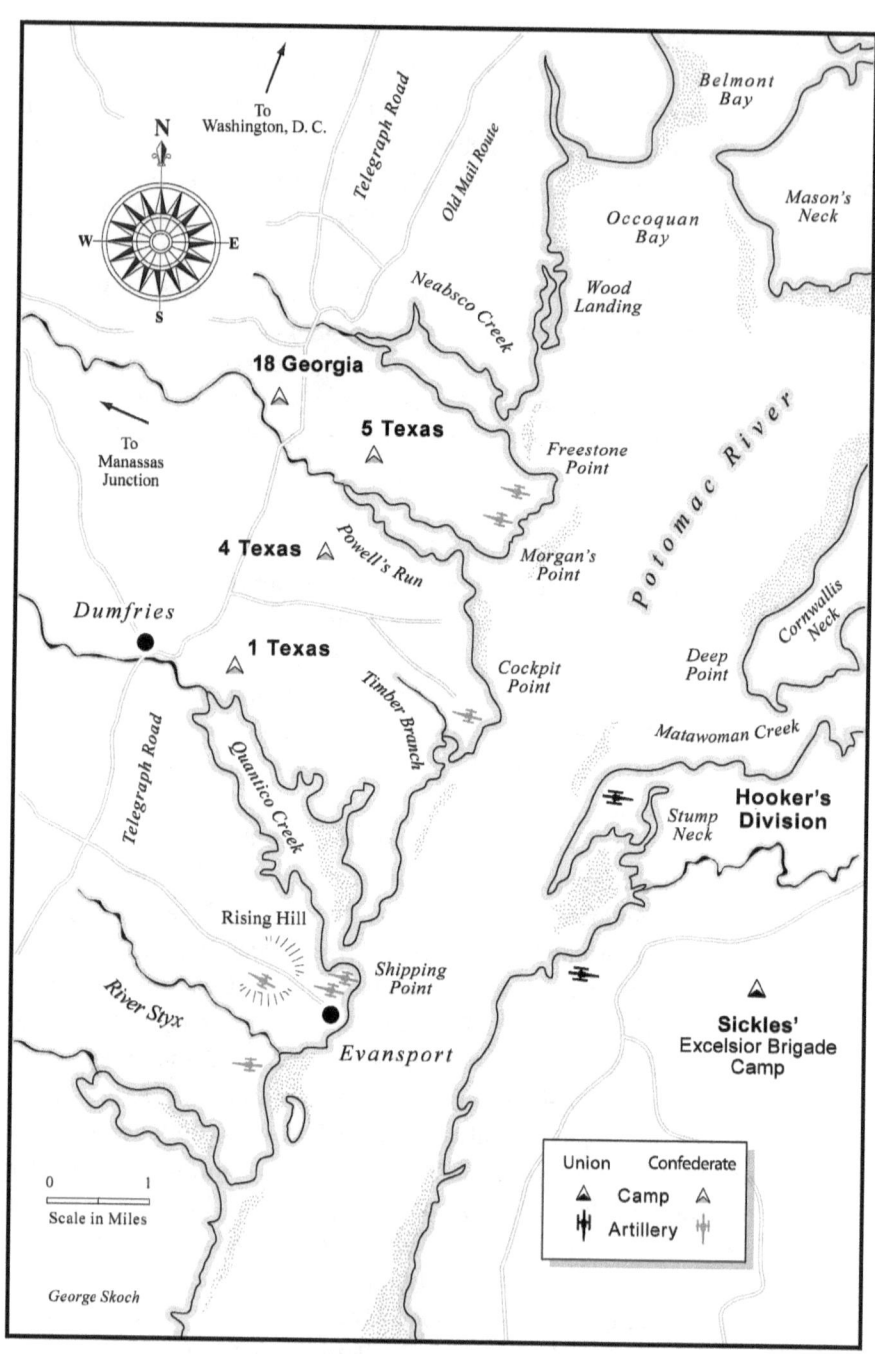

The Potomac Blockade, Winter 1861–1862

While the First Texas most likely camped along Quantico Creek, they could reach both the Evansport and Shipping Point batteries, and, on occasion, Cockpit Point battery farther north.[6] The Fifth Texas was most likely the northernmost unit and established their camp where Powell's Run crossed Telegraph Road. Their colonel, James J. Archer, was a native Marylander who watched his home state from the opposite side of the river that winter with horror. "Our Maryland is throttled," he wrote his brother from camp. "Every day I see her cross the Potomac—the armed heel of the disgusting despot trampling upon her bosom—And I can see no chance to relieve or avenge her."[7] Located between Powell's Run and Neabsco Creek, the Fifth Texas was about three miles from Dumfries and two miles east, Archer reported, of Freestone Point.[8] This allowed them to race to Telegraph Road if a threat came over land from the north, or hurry to the river if Federals attempted to move up or down the Potomac or cross over from Maryland.

The Fourth Texas camped between the First and Fifth Texas between Telegraph Road, Powell's Run, and Timber Branch and did frequent picket duty at Cockpit Point, located south of the Fifth Texans at Freestone Point and north of the First Texans near Possum Nose and Shipping Point. The Eighteenth Georgia was most likely camped across Telegraph Road north of Powell's Run, though none of these positions are precise, and archeological evidence has placed artifacts from all of these units in various locations in this vicinity. There may have been a Louisiana regiment or several companies camped with the Texans at this point, but records are unclear on this point.[9] With so many volunteers rushing to Richmond that summer and early fall, it is possible that Louisianans were with the Texas regiments for a brief period, and General Order 15 specifically refers to three Texas regiments and one regiment of Louisianans forming the Fifth Brigade under Wigfall, all part of Gen. E. Kirby Smith's Fourth Division in the Department of Northern Virginia. There was also an Alabama company attached to the First Texas, Company K, through the spring of 1862, when it transferred out of the unit and a fresh company of Texans took its place and its name.[10]

During this first winter of war, homesickness, loneliness, bone-chilling cold, and Federal attacks were key threats for the men, but disease remained their biggest concern. In early October 1861, the men's families in Seguin, Texas, opened their local paper, the *Southern Confederacy,* and learned that "the hospitals in Richmond are full to over flowing with sick soldiers—typhoid fever and the measles being the two epidemics. Deaths are frequent, verifying the well-established idea that 'disease in an army kills more than bullets,'" editors explained.¹¹ Newspapers across Texas carried similar reports on the boys in Richmond. At the end of October, Houstonians read the account of a Texas volunteer who signed himself "Wanderer," in which he warned: "A great many deaths occur here among the soldiers daily. I passed this morning fifty new made graves, in each of which some soldier 'slept his last sleep.' Four have died in our regiment this week—though we have been comparatively fortunate. Our company hasn't lost a man." Still, the dangers around him were frighteningly real. "We deplore weekly the death of friends in other companies," Wanderer explained. "We would much rather die amid the booming of cannon and the roar of battle, than to be wasted gradually away by loathsome disease."¹²

In early December, the Fourth Texas's Presbyterian chaplain, Nicholas Davis, made a plea for the home front to rally and alleviate the men's suffering. Those able to make the move to Evansport, near Dumfries on the Potomac River, were fine, Davis assured readers. They are "in grand glee" to push "Onward to the Potomac . . . singing and hallowing, laughing and talking, and setting fire to the brush arbors over their mess fires and tables. And to lend a charm to the scene" of the destruction of their temporary fall camps outside Richmond, "our brass band is performing Dixie with a kind of enchantment."

But the sick, Davis informed families at home, "cannot go with us." More than 300 men from the Fourth Texas had to be left behind in Richmond area hospitals and homes. Davis urged the Texas state legislature to do more to care for our "sick boys," who would, he reminded readers, "repay you if the cost be their blood. They are here 'to do or die' for you."¹³ James Jones's family and neighbors in Austin were frightened to learn that the Fourth Texan was battling both measles and pneumonia. They took comfort, though, in Jones's promise that Richmond women visited the men regularly, reading from the Bible and sharing "everything that was good to eat." But "six of our company have died" from the same combination of diseases Jones battled. "All of my mess were sick with five exceptions," he confessed to his parents.¹⁴

These reports and Davis's plea inspired action on the home front. By January, units like the "Tom Green Rifles," officially known as Company B of the Fourth Texas, received a shipment of blankets, clothes, and other necessities valued at more than four thousand dollars from the "citizens and ladies of Travis county," and a host of supplies poured in for the men and units from other counties as well.¹⁵ It would take nearly another year, hundreds of wounded men, and an act of Congress, however, before Texas Hospital opened in Richmond.¹⁶

Still, disease devastated the ranks that winter. Mark Smither mourned the loss of "five as brave spirits as ever lived" from his company that January. "They left home with high hopes and a resolve to defend their countrys honor and now they rest, two in Oakwood cemetery at Richmond and three on the hills above the banks of the beautiful Neabsco. But thank God the health of our Regiment is visibly improving."[17] Smither had just turned eighteen and boasted that he left Texas at 118 pounds but had gained thirty more since then.

It was odd how accounts of sickness were balanced by other men insisting they had never felt healthier. The latter may have resulted from their food rations, which First Texas captain A. T. Rainey insisted as early as August 1861 was better than the men received at home. Despite this, he worried about his men's health: "There is a great deal of sickness such as measles, typhoid fever, chills and fever—I have now fifty men on the sick list, but most of them are recovering and will soon be ready for duty again."[18] As rain, sleet, and snow set in, suffering increased as food rations were cut that winter when supplies could not reach their camps.[19]

Col. J. J. Archer, commander of the Fifth Texas, was pleased with his junior officers, "almost all intelligent gentlemen," but he could not say the same for the men in the ranks, though he insisted that it was through no fault of their own: "The men if they were well, would be all that I ask but unfortunately, owing, I believe, to their marching through the Louisiana Swamps during the bilious season, and to the measles which they took after arriving at Richmond, and the seven night march from Brook's Station and insufficient clothing, two thirds of my regiment is sick."[20]

Similar concerns surfaced in the ranks. Fourth Texan William Tannehill had nursed two of his messmates, sick with measles, along with a "good many" of the regiment, through much of October. Despite this, Tannehill reported being in "as good health . . . as I ever was in my life and as fleshy if I can only escape the measles."[21] He did, but he contracted typhoid fever instead. For eight weeks, Tannehill could not leave his Richmond hospital bed, "which has worn me completely out leaving nothing more than skin and bone." The hospital food, he reported, was not very good, but the ladies of Richmond and the attending physicians were excellent. Tannehill's only major complaint was about the "religious men who do not know anything about nursing the sick."[22]

The Texans and Georgians all agreed that disease rates were dropping, if slowly, by January 1862, but they marveled at how many men had died. The Eighteenth Georgia lost their regimental surgeon just before Christmas 1861.[23] First Texas's Col. Hugh McLeod succumbed to pneumonia on January 2, 1862.[24] He may have been unpopular when he took command of the unit without the men's vote, but from that point forward, E. O. Perry insisted, McLeod had "rendered himself very popular, and at the time of his death was beloved by the whole regiment. He was very kind to his men."[25]

Ike Turner of Company K of the Fifth Texas suffered the most losses of any unit in the brigade, with thirty of his men, about one-third of the company, dying from typhoid fever alone.[26] Spread by bacteria and transmitted through feces that spread into men's food and drinking water, typhoid was particularly devastating because in the mid-nineteenth century, no one knew how it spread or how to prevent it. There were rules on how camps were laid out, but there was little enforcement of cleanliness and little understanding of why it mattered. Some men believed ventilating their tents could help ward off typhoid, while a North Carolina surgeon in camp investigated possible causes in exposure or diet.[27] Volunteers boasted that winter of their improved cooking and housekeeping skills, but men paid little attention to keeping their messes clean or to sanitary food preparation.[28] As measles spread through their ranks, men would unknowingly contaminate their messmates in the seven to ten days they carried the disease before showing signs of it. Those who recovered from typhoid often remained carriers, inadvertently sharing it while handling food and other means of contact. Sick men soiled their blankets in tents and messes, or barely made it outside before emptying their bowls. Winter rains washed that waste downhill through camp to the Neabsco and the other creeks and rivers that the Texans and Georgians used all winter for drinking and cooking, cleaning soiled clothing and bedding, and, on rare occasions, bathing.[29]

The Texas Brigade along the "Potomac Blockade" officially received orders in December 1861 to build permanent winter quarters, though they did not actually move into these until January 1862. The one exception to this was the Eighteenth Georgia. William Shockley's Company C began construction on their cabins on November 25, and three days later Thomas Dowtin reported that Company K had made excellent progress on their homes.[30] George Maddox praised Company G's progress on November 29, 1861, boasting of their "excellent stick and dirt chimney." He worried, though, that they were "too hasty as we have received no order from our Gen (Wigfall) for any such proceedings, but our Col [William T. Wofford], I suppose took it for granted that here we will remain."[31] Just as Cols. John Bell Hood and James J. Archer learned to wait to confirm orders before sending their men out on General

Wigfall's midnight runs, Colonel Wofford appears to have decided that the health of his men required independent action and issued winter-quarter construction orders on his own.[32]

Dugat Williams and his compatriots built a semi-permanent structure of "pine logs, hogpen fashion, twelve by sixteen feet." This style was replicated through much of their company, with the men constructing "one door in each house but no window." They planned to add "a long fireplace where we can have a hot fire these cold days. Each company will be allowed ten houses which will give sufficient room," he believed. Williams marveled at the "little village" they would have when finished, as well as the home construction skills that would help them after the war. Hesitating, he corrected himself. No, "I have learned at least how to build a cheap house," but it would suffice.[33] Nearby, the Eighteenth Georgians were surprised by how many trees their project had required, noting that the "beautiful grove that once flourished upon the ground upon which we are now encamped is utterly distroyed."[34]

At home in Huntsville, Texas, Mark Smither's family likely took pride as they read his assurances that the Texans were respectful of locals' property when soldiers supplemented their rations and construction with nearby goods. "The Texas boys... are given up to be the finest set of men in the army," he promised. But "the other Regiments are feared by the inhabitants while ours have the utmost confidence of the people[. T]hey take our sick to their houses and treat them as their own sons[.] We never commit any depredations on them while the Georgians and Mississippi Regiments in the Brigade steal their hogs and poultry on every occasion," Smither frowned.[35]

The Georgians disagreed. Second Cpl. William Shockley promised that when the men did steal things, like some pumpkins that had gone missing one morning, Colonel Wofford made them pay the property owners for the items. "The Texians," on the other hand, "go out occasionly and kill a hog or any thing they come across but our Colonel will not allow his men to do such tricks," Shockley insisted.[36]

Local civilian C. W. C. Dunnington, however, insisted the volunteers were all scoundrels, especially the First Texans and Eighteenth Georgians. When Dunnington rode out to check on his rental properties along the Potomac River that winter, he found "every plank taken from the stable, the office removed, the kitchen and servants' house all gone but the brick chimneys, the shed portion of the dwelling entirely gone, the window-sash and doors and the weather-boarding torn off and carried away, the fencing gone, and what

I expected to be my future home a complete wreck." Dunnington rode to the Cockpit Point batteries and found men "erecting winter quarters out of my houses" with members of the Eighteenth Georgia and First Texas, which he specifically named, using portions of Dunnington's property to construct their messes. "We have no courts of justice, or I would prosecute the ruffians.... The country around here is treated more like an enemy's country than the homes of loyal citizens. What right has a colonel or captain, without my leave, to take my property!" Dunnington asked. "I shall never be able to rebuild, and the whole place will have to be deserted.... I give up all hope of saving any of my property except the soil, and I have a wife and seven children to provide with bread."[37] Whether a matter of miscommunication or appropriation, the Texans and Georgians saw abandoned properties as an acceptable source of free building supplies that proved key to their success in constructing "quite a village."[38]

Quarters were officially laid out by company according to army regulations, but the exact size and design of each structure, or mess, as the soldiers learned to call them, was up to the bunk mates who built them. W. D. Prichard of Company I in the First Texas Infantry explained that there were only two main regulations for the men to follow. There had to be a street of about eighty feet between each company and the houses were built in a straight line.[39] After that, the men could design things as they liked.

Mark Smither's mess was "a very nice little log cabin about 14 by 16 feet," while over in the Eighteenth Georgians' camp, William Shockley and the men of Company C built cabins 24 feet long by 12 feet wide that would house a dozen men in one mess.[40] In the Fourth Texas, Joe Polley and his messmates had a bit more trouble constructing their winter home. "All things considered," he explained, "our winter quarters are quite comfortable. They may lack symmetrical proportions, furniture, and now and then doors and roofs, but we have expended so much muscular energy upon them, and have taxed our combined architectural abilities so enormously, that we are both proud of them and glad to be relieved from further strain of mind."[41]

In Company B of the Fifth Texas, Val Giles believed their cabins were of an architectural style that "would have puzzled an expert. Some were on the hill, some under the hill, some above the ground, some underground. A few were large, but mostly they were small. Mess Number 2 had a high house, while Mess Number 5 had a low house. Number 3 had his chimney inside, while Number 7 had his on the outside." Some had no doors, while others placed doors "by the jamb or in the gable end. Windows might be under the bed or above the fireplace. The materials, as can well be imagined, were of the crudest. The Texans did not like digging, or any work of a menial sort, but they got the shanties up somehow," Giles smiled.[42]

Beyond disease, homesickness, and adjusting to the discipline of military life, the key military threats the Confederates faced that winter at Dumfries came in short but frequent bursts. They had two objectives: defending a land invasion from northern Virginia and blockading the Potomac River, especially at its narrowest point between Quantico and Neabsco Creeks, the stretch of land the Texas Brigade defended. General Whiting planned to respond to a land invasion by having his forces "harass and delay the enemy all along the Telegraph road by ambuscade and bush fighting," with a small defensive force entrenched along the south side of the Quantico that could fall back to a stronger force, where Whiting would "make my stand along Powell's Run in the dense woods and heights."[43] He kept the Eighteenth Georgia busy "straining every nerve in putting up fortifications and digging trenches" while separate details "fell[ed] trees on the road toward Washington" to hinder any invader's attempt to bring artillery to bear on the Confederates position.[44]

From the Potomac, however, Whiting had a constant fear of bombardment from Federal batteries on the Maryland shore and of a possible land invasion, and part of this was due to misinformation. In October 1861, the Confederate War Department received information from "an intelligent soldier" sent to spy on the Federals that they numbered nearly 15,000 supported by eighty artillery pieces positioned at several batteries. The true numbers were closer to 8,000 men and eighteen guns, but Confederate commanders did not realize this as they worked to defend their position rather than plan an attack across the river.[45]

Federal forces under Union general Joseph Hooker used aerial observation balloons that winter, which further convinced Confederates that they had to defend the blockade while also preparing for a Federal offensive.[46] It worried Johnston that he could not shift forces in secret because the "infernal balloon" would spot their movements.[47] Johnston hoped to have Centerville strengthened soon and would then send a brigade to Whiting.[48] When reinforcements did finally arrive, they were unarmed. "What are they sending me unarmed and new regiments for?" Whiting thundered at Samuel Cooper, Confederate adjutant and inspector general. "Don't want them. They will only be in my way. Can't feed them nor use them. I want re-enforcements, not recruits. . . . They can do no good here, and will only seriously embarrass all operations."[49]

As much as Confederates prepared, however, the Federals never launched an offensive. Just as Confederates overestimated the strength of their opponents, Federal commander Gen. George B. McClellan believed Confederates across the Potomac numbered 150,000, with 18,000 of those men entrenched at Dumfries. Also like the Confederates, he assumed that Johnston could launch an offensive at any moment, and McClellan urged the U.S. Navy to do more along the Potomac River in support of his position.[50] Navy commanders in the area, however, had explained in October that as "long as the [Confederate] batteries stand at Shipping Point and Evansport the navigation of the Potomac will be effectively closed. To attempt to reduce them with the vessels under my command would be vanity."[51] This realization had inspired McClellan to send Joseph Hooker to the Maryland side of the river, but McClellan never approved any Federal invasion plan. As a result of this impasse, the Confederates and the Federals along the Potomac spent much of that winter engaged in small attacks and raids on each other's positions.

As part of those operations, Texans and Georgians made daily or near-daily scouting trips across the river to infiltrate Federal lines.[52] Union forces, for their part, lobbed shells across the river that pestered the Confederate defenders but caused little significant damage. E. O. Perry reported that Confederate gunners often "commenced throwing bombs" whenever they saw the Federal observation balloon rise high above. Federals would respond with counterfire, but "they did not injure us." The scouting raids had the greatest effect, the volunteers told their families at home, instilling pride and a sense of action in the often bored and frustrated Confederates. "Twenty men from this regiment and twenty from the 4th and 5th Texas also have been detailed as scouts. They cross the Occoquan every day or two," E. O. Perry explained. "They go within 7 or 8 miles from Alexandria... [but] report that no Yankees are to be seen."[53] James Hendrick, in the same company with Perry, marveled that they could "see and hear Yankees talk sometimes on the other side" of the river, something nearly every soldier in the brigade commented on that winter.[54]

Both highly motivated ideologically and, in the case of some, seeking a fight, the First Texans developed a reputation for leading the most aggressive and occasionally unsanctioned raids. As brigade historian Joe Polley recalled, the First Texas had also, on more than one occasion, created a false alarm to torment their ever-alert and ever-intoxicated commander. "One night," Polley smiled, "grown tired of inaction and longing for excitement, the boys of the

First took French leave of their officers, and went in a body across the Potomac, and there waked up not only General Sickles and the Union troops then under his command, but spread consternation on the streets of Washington city by the report circulated by themselves that they were the advance guard of the Confederate army." Gen. Daniel Sickles rushed to organize his forces to respond, but by then, the Texans had already returned to their camps across the Potomac. In the days that followed, Polley reported, "the question with Wigfall and the equally ignorant officers of the 1st Texas was, Who was it that kicked up such a row among our friends, the enemy?"[55]

One of the Texans most famous fights came on January 28, 1862. A party of nine First Texans from Captain Bass's Company E, raised in Marshall, Texas, crossed the Potomac and, after scouting all day, stopped at a home in Colchester to spend the night before returning to camp.[56] After a local tipped Federals off to the party's location, about fifty Union troopers and infantry surrounded the home shortly before midnight. After a brief but intense firefight where the outnumbered Texans managed to defend their position, both sides claimed victory. Union brigadier general Samuel P. Heintzleman published an account celebrating the Thirty-Seventh New Yorkers' great victory, having lost one man killed, four wounded, and claiming to have killed all but one of the Texans, whom they captured. Papers in Washington, Baltimore, and New York cheered their exploit, which southern papers equally condemned. "Next to being the most unmitigated cowards in Christendom, they are certainly the most contemptible liars," William Ochiltree thundered, whose son, Tom, served in the company that had participated in the fight. The Texans, he reported, suffered no deaths, only one minor wound, and they, too, declared the episode a resounding success, a claim that General Whiting confirmed by Special Order at the end of January. The wounded soldier, J. B. Spratting, was actually seriously wounded and died about a week after the fight, but the Texans remained confident in the overwhelming success of their mission.[57]

Skirmishes like this one, which dominated their last few months on the Potomac Line, made little impact on either side. But it bolstered the men's confidence in themselves and gave expression to their strong ideological loyalty to the Confederacy and their dedication to victory. They took pride in their ability to hold their positions under enemy fire, to construct camps that offered them shelter from winter's cold, to remain steadfast despite overwhelming bouts of homesickness and devastating disease, and to master the fundamentals of drill and discipline that were key to their future success.

The men of the Texas Brigade learned invaluable skills along the Potomac. They had battled disease, climate, the loss of their civilian freedoms, and they understood more than ever before what made a good commander. The trying winter turned them from green volunteers into soldiers. They remained untested in battle, but they were prepared for the 1862 campaign season. They also retained the strong motivation for service that had inspired their enlistments the previous spring and summer. Indeed, their determination was so strong that it set them apart from many of the Confederates in the rank-and-file. As early as December 1861, Maj. Gen. T. H. Holmes, commander of the Aquia District, warned Adjutant and Inspector General Samuel Cooper that "the inhibition of trade, the absence of necessaries, such as salt, coffee, &c, and the heavy stress on the women and children incident to the absence of the men on militia and volunteer duty, are beginning to tell to the prejudice of our cause among the non-slave holders."[58] To be clear, Holmes advised military action, not the termination of enlistments, to solidify the men's support, but his warning echoed throughout the Confederate high command that winter and into the early spring of 1862.

Officers encouraged their twelve-month volunteers to reenlist, for patriotic reasons, to earn the fifty-dollar bounty and to receive a furlough home to visit family and friends. But Confederate forces did not respond well or quickly to any of this, and Confederate leaders admitted that their efforts "failed . . . to recruit the strength of our armies." Enthusiasm for the war had waned, citizen-soldiers resented military discipline and hierarchy, and the lack of action that winter convinced many men that Federal forces were not an imminent threat.[59] Recruiting trips on average did not do well, and twelve-month volunteers were slow to reenlist for three years or the war. This led the Confederate Congress to authorize the conscription of white males between the ages of eighteen and thirty-five, with certain exemptions. In the end, many Confederates in Virginia reenlisted because they feared they could be drafted if they went back home, but in late February and early March, it was not at all clear that many men would reenlist.[60]

In Texas Brigade camps, however, the experience was quite different. Recruiters brought just over 1,000 new men into the First, Fourth, and Fifth Texas Infantry Regiments in the spring of 1862. The recruiters' quota was set at 1,500 men, but they still succeeded in replacing the majority of the men lost to disease that winter through inspiration, the fifty-dollar bounty, or a desire to avoid the public shame of the draft and the opportunity to select their unit of service. The latter-most options let men serve with family, friends, and neighbors rather than be forced to live and fight among strangers.⁶¹

Within the ranks, the First Texans, in particular, revealed that their enthusiasm for the war had not faded. They bristled at the idea that a mere fifty dollars could secure their loyalty. Eugene Perry, like many of the Texas volunteers in Virginia, had soured on General Wigfall, but his reputation soared when he spoke out against a congressional bill that would secure the reenlistments of the twelve-month volunteers with a furlough and quick cash. Rumors swirled through camp that Wigfall "rebuk[ed] the Senate . . . saying that it was an insult to the 12 month volunteers and that it was treated [as] such by this Regiment [the First Texas]. He says to the Senate, disband them, let them go home," Perry told his family. Wigfall had insisted: "They are gentlemen. It was patriotism that brought them here and patriotism will bring them back. For god's sake, do not try and handl[e] them, force them to come back with the pitiful sum of fifty dollars." Perry searched for a copy of the speech, promising that if it were true, "there will be no one like Gen Wigfall with this regiment, although he stands low on the scales now."⁶²

At home, most of the Texas Brigade families supported the idea that their men should stay in Virginia. One of the few exceptions to this was Mintie Price, the daughter of the largest slaveholder in San Augustine County, Texas. Her husband, Frank, was a newspaper editor in San Augustine, and he joined the company his partner, Benjamin F. Benton, had organized in 1861. When they mustered into service as Company K of the First Texas, Frank was a first lieutenant and a firm believer in the role he needed to play in securing Confederate independence. Mintie, however, was not so sure. In January 1862 she advised him that he risked his health by staying and could make little difference because neither army seemed inclined to fight. Disgusted with inflation and limited supplies, Mintie hoped Frank would return home soon.⁶³

In February, however, Mintie Price was horrified when she opened a letter and discovered that Frank planned to reenlist. "You must not think of such a thing until you come home and see us," she insisted, "and then if the War continues I will let you go back."⁶⁴ But Lieutenant Price remained with the First Texas that spring. His thinking was in line with that of a fellow lieutenant in the Fourth Texas, James Rodgers Loughridge. In mid-January, trying to explain his absence to his young daughters, Mary, then four, and Ella, just two years old, Loughridge promised that he wanted "to come & see you both but Pa is helping to clear out a pretty piece of land for you & Ma & Grand Ma &

Uncle Jackson to live on."[65] When writing to his mother, Loughridge spoke more eloquently, pledging: "I do not desire to go home until my Country is free & independent. Mother I would far prefer to die than to live in a land overrun by base foes.... No mortal living has dearer and more loved ties to bind him to his house than I do. Yet I will give them all up & my life, too, before I will live in a land that is not independent."[66]

Mary Felicia Loughridge also hoped her husband could "get a furlough this spring or summer I am so anxious to see you and hear you call my name." But the similarities ended here. Felicia Loughridge, like most Texas Brigade families, matched her husband's dedication to the war effort that spring. She "could not possibly give you up so long for any other cause than the war. How proud of my noble patriotic husband and how much I love him is not in the power of pen and ink to tell."[67]

Similar dedication to the Confederate war effort surfaced that month in the Goree family in Polk County, Texas. At the same time southern military planners were worrying about the slow rates of reenlistments, Sarah Kittrell Goree, a fifty-three-year-old widow, read a letter from her eldest son, Thomas Jewett Goree. He served as an aide on Gen. James Longstreet's staff and was the patriarch of the family after his father's death. Two of his brothers, twenty-two-year-old Langston and nineteen-year-old Edwin, were already serving in Hood's Texas Brigade. Sarah Goree spent much of that spring watching her crops and worrying as East Texas languished in a painfully long drought.

Sitting at Raven Hill Plantation, which she bought from close friend Governor Sam Houston after her husband died, Sarah read Thomas's letter carefully. He called on her to let his brother, Robert, enlist as well, despite the fact that her wealth and prominence within the community could likely help him avoid such service. "I know it will be hard to do without him, and that you will feel the want of his presence at home very much, but it is a sacrifice you will have to make, and probably the sooner the better," Thomas explained.[68] Sarah Goree would still have her youngest son, Pleasant, or "Scrap," as he was known in the family, at home to help run the plantation.[69] Thomas also insisted that Robert serve in a unit that would keep him close to Texas so he could aid their mother if needed. But Robert must volunteer, Thomas insisted. Their country needed more men, and the cause justified the sacrifice, he argued. Sarah Goree agreed, and sent her fourth son into Confederate service on March 25. She would rely on Scrap, or her brother, or, as Thomas had advised, "some one who is not able to stand the hardships of a campaign" and could remain at home.[70]

Other Texas Brigade families followed patterns similar to the Gorees in March and April 1862, sending sons and cousins to join family already in the ranks in Virginia, or joining the Texas Brigade for the first time. John (26), William (24), Andrew (18), and Joseph Knight (19) all enlisted in Company H of the First Texas Infantry on March 20, 1862, leaving their fourteen-year-old brother, Thomas, at home to help their father run their middle-class family farm in Garden Valley, Texas.[71] In Seguin, Thomas Johnson enlisted his brothers-in-law Andrew and Alexander Erskine, ages thirty-one and thirty-six respectively.[72] The Bayou City Guards, Company A of the Fifth Texas, received fifty-five fresh recruits in the spring of 1862. They included seventeen-year-old Robert Campbell whose father "cheerfully gave his son to this country's cause, lamenting that he had but one old enough to go."[73]

This dedication to the war effort was not the norm in Texas, or across the rest of the Confederacy. Southern war planners were reluctant to pass conscription legislation that challenged American traditions—which Confederates argued they seceded to uphold—of relying on a *volunteer* force of citizen-soldiers in times of conflict. Texas leaders, like their counterparts in Richmond, hoped to inspire enlistments through calls in newspapers across the state, but volunteerism remained low in the Lone Star State.[74] The *Texas State Gazette* (Austin) assured its readers that Texans would volunteer; a state full of patriots would never need to be drafted.[75] The *Houston Tri-Weekly Telegraph* agreed, while the *Texas Republican* (Marshall) editors thundered: "What, has it come to this? That the Northern Government can raise a vast army of 600,000 men—the major part of whom fight for pay . . . and that we refuse, or are laggard to . . . drive back the myrmidon hosts of the tyrant."[76] Despite editors' efforts, volunteer rates remained flat in Texas and across the South that spring. This reflected divided opinions on both conscription and how to best wage the war.[77] The majority of twelve-month volunteers did eventually reenlist, but soldiers of the Texas Brigade stood out that spring for their continued enthusiasm for the war effort and their ability to recruit replacements for the hundreds of men lost to disease or declared unfit for military service, like William Barron, who received a discharge in December 1861 on grounds of "insanity," and whose sibling and fellow volunteer, Jasper, was detached to "go to Texas with his crazy brother."[78]

G. R. Thornwell, one of the South Carolinians of Wade Hampton's Legion that would soon join the Texas Brigade, captured the determination in the ranks that spring. When he heard rumors of peace, Thornwell claimed: "I don't want to make peace until we have exterminated the whole Yankee race, then I will be satisfied. I want to pay them off for keeping me out here this winter."[79] That determination was matched in the Federal ranks across the river among the Fifth New York, whose soldiers had called all winter for an attack on the Confederates across the river and carved on the walls of Pohic Church and other spots along the Occoquan their pledge for "Death to all Texians."[80]

This sweeping enthusiasm set the Texas Brigade apart from many soldiers in the Confederate army. Only highly dedicated men volunteered for a unit that took them so far from home. When they arrived in Virginia, that dedication emerged in their determination to scout, skirmish, and harass Federal positions along the Potomac Line. There were exceptions to this, of course. William Gaffney was one of dozens of fresh recruits to enlist in the Bayou City Guards in the spring of 1862, but he was among the few who deserted before he could be mustered into the company.[81] And not all families rushed to serve like the Gorees. That spring, at the same time Thomas Goree advised his mother to allow his brother, Robert, to enlist, Fifth Texas private Tine Owen, while encouraging others at home to enlist, discouraged his father from serving: "I think I am enough to leave that house and I think that if they will all turn out one from each house that will do.... I think that we can whip the Yankey with one from each famlay."[82] Despite this, John Owen joined the Twentieth Texas Cavalry later that year, leaving his wife, Asenath, to run their middle-class farm and raise five children still at home, ranging from sixteen-year old Sarah to two-year old Elizabeth.[83]

Amid a nation craving action, though not always willing to commit to it themselves, the soldiers and families of the Texas Brigade stood out from their fellow southerners in the spring of 1862. At times disruptive and disobedient, there was no doubt among Confederates in Johnston's Army of the Potomac that the Texans ranked among their best fighters. As Lt. Col. James Griffin observed, whose unit would soon join the Texas Brigade, "Those Texians are number one men... as gallant and brave as any thing."[84] Despite a brutal death toll to disease and the knowledge that loved ones who died would likely never be returned home for burial, Texas families continued to send men to their regiments in Virginia. Similarly, Texas volunteers overwhelmingly remained in the ranks, eagerly anticipating the 1862 campaign season. Only then would they know if the "gallant and brave" Texans had the order and discipline to be an effective combat unit.

SEEING THE ELEPHANT
Turning Scouts into Soldiers

The Texas Brigade anticipated the 1862 campaign season eagerly. As Tine Owen told his parents, "something has to be done an i dont car how soon for i am agiting mity hiard of doing nothing." The men could hear "fitting all around us and we cant git a fite but i think when we do have a fite it will cout." Owen asked his family to encourage "all of the boys to com with Mr. Burras [who returned to Henderson County to recruit replacements] for we hav the fastis Regiment that is on the River an i want a large company."¹

There had been earlier battles and skirmishes, but the vast majority of forces encamped in Virginia had not been tested in a major battle. The campaign season of 1862, and especially the Battles of Gaines's Mill, Second Manassas, and Antietam, would challenge the Texas Brigade with brutal fighting and astonishingly high casualties. The men would emerge from those battles, however, as one of the best units in the Confederacy with a continued focus on southern independence. This was fueled by their role in key victories, the continued support of their families at home, and the superb leadership of company, regimental, and brigade commanders. The men's strong motivations wavered on occasion that year, but they remained dedicated to their place in the fight for Confederate independence.

That season began at the end of February 1862, as Confederate camps along the Potomac bustled with activity. The rank-and-file were not sure where they were going, but orders came down to prepare to "retreat back from this place," Mark Smither explained. He frowned at the thought of abandoning "my *bower*, the *large and commodious* 'Aiken head House,'" that he and his messmates had built two months earlier, and pledged to "consign [it] . . . to the flames so that no Yankees can shelter their heads under my roof."² Smither's messmates Bernard Carrington and Ewing Barney, both battling the mumps, were evacuated with the rest of the sick men from their camp. Smither had heard they would be transferred to Fredericksburg, but no one seemed sure of anything. His friend Albert Sevy from the Fourth Texas walked over for a visit on February 27 and confirmed similar commotion in his camp. "Look out shortly to hear either of a fight or a footrace," Smither promised his mother. "I would not be surprised if it was a simultaneous falling back along the whole line of the Army of the Potomac. I don't know whether it is a feint to draw the enemy out or not for everything is kept with the most profound secrecy." Whatever came, Smither promised they would "try and show the Confederacy that if the Tennessee boys at Fort Donelson have forgotten how to fight the Texas boys in Northern Va. haven't," referring to the Federal capture of Forts Henry and Donelson in Tennessee earlier that month.[3] Despite serving on Gen. James Longstreet's staff, T. J. Goree did not know much more than Smither, but he shared his determination and disgust. "We once boasted that one Southerner could whip three Yankees in a fair fight, but the result of [Donelson] does not prove it. . . . You will never, I hope, hear of any such disgraceful conduct in this army," he fumed.[4]

Lieutenant Loughridge in the Fourth Texas did not know exactly what was planned either. Despite admitting that "a gloom surrounds many of us" regarding Tennessee, Loughridge took comfort in his faith and shared Smither's and Goree's determination. He warned his wife, Felicia, to "never look for me to submit to live under Yankee rule," and while he feared that Memphis or New Orleans could fall, which would greatly limit communication between the Texans and their families, he advised her to "Put your trust in God & live happy. Fear not for me—Our Heavenly Father reigns supreme" and would, Loughridge believed, help secure their independence.[5]

On March 8, the Texas Brigade waited to depart the Dumfries area in air filled with smoke. They had been busy burning batteries and supplies to prevent them from getting into Federal hands, and were finally ready to depart. Confederate general Joseph E. Johnston ordered the withdrawal because he feared he was not in the best position to stop a Federal offensive that spring. He directed the Confederate Army of the Potomac about forty miles to the south to a position behind the Rappahannock River. It was a better location, but the retreat was disorganized, valuable supplies were abandoned, and it did little to bolster morale when Confederates were already upset about losses in Tennessee. Jefferson Davis was not pleased with Johnston's decision either, and Davis was especially incensed about the wastefulness. General Whiting's division, in which the Texas Brigade marched, was cited, in particular, for the destruction of "tents, ammunition, [and] public property," and Davis demanded that the general explain himself. Whiting responded by declaring that such claims were slander. Yes, he said, a few old, worn-out tents were left behind, as were a few cartridges of ammunition, but they had taken with them everything of military use.[6]

Col. James J. Archer, commanding the Texas Brigade since Louis T. Wigfall had been elected to the Confederate senate in February, agreed. He admitted that they did leave some ammunition behind, but that was due to a limited number of wagons that had to travel on terrible roads and be hauled by teams that were not at full strength due to limited rations in their last weeks on the Potomac.[7] It seemed, though, that a good deal was left behind. Confederates destroyed what they could not take with them, to which even the Federals across the river could attest. It seemed like "everything burnable was set on fire, guns spiked, gunpowder blown up; and soon dense volumes of smoke arose from all the camps.... For over two hours, loud explosions were heard in the direction of this burning property, indicating that magazines and barracks were sharing the same fate," a Massachusetts chaplain recalled.[8]

When the First Massachusetts entered the Confederates' empty camps, including those of the Texas Brigade, they found far more abandoned than Whiting or Archer reported. The rebels "must have left in great haste as they left most everything behind them," one Massachusetts soldier explained. From ammunition to camp tools, "everything was left but what a soldier could carry."[9] Charles Perkins, another soldier in the unit, agreed. In addition to finding a wealth of camp supplies, Perkins noted that Federals seized several of the batteries' guns that Confederates had tried, but failed, to destroy. He marveled at the Texans' camp where men like John Smither had fulfilled their pledge to burn their mess before leaving. Perkins boasted of how much the Federals captured, including "plenty of old letters" that revealed "miserable spelling generally," though other men noted "delicate missives on gilt-edged paper" and "verbose documents ... on the prevailing sentiment, 'Death to the Yankees!'" Several of the Massachusetts men frowned at how chaotically the Confederates had lived. "Houses seem to have been built anywhere," Perkins observed.[10] Massachusetts chaplain Warren Cudworth, however, was impressed by how well supplied the Texans' messes were. They "were built of logs, with floors and roofs of board, some having glazed windows; and one actually [had] green blinds." The cabins were supplied with good quality and numerous cooking utensils, but Cudworth could not get over the "houses, beds, and ever thing else ... [that] were filthy to the first degree."[11]

The Texans could not have left in too much haste, though, because they had time to construct a careful ruse. Not far from a coffin storehouse, Confederates constructed a graveyard of sorts where they buried tents, cooking supplies, and tools that they could not take with them. At first, the Massachusetts men ignored the cemetery, but then they became curious. It was bordered with signs that threatened damnation to anyone who disturbed the dead, when other burial plots in the area had none of these. The area was also too neat compared to the rest of the camp. The boldest among them risked their souls, discovered the trick, and "complimented [the Texans] for the success of their first sacrilegious experiment, and recommended to try again."[12]

Federals took pride in the fact that Confederates had fallen back, and that the Potomac Blockade had ended, but when Johnston established a new line south of the Rappahannock, it forced Union general George McClellan to revise his plans for a spring offensive. He proposed, and President Lincoln reluctantly approved, a complex amphibious landing at the tip of a strip of land between the James and York Rivers. That would leave the Union capital thinly defended, but McClellan was certain of victory. In mid-March, as the First Massachusetts was exploring the Confederates' abandoned camps near Dumfries, Federal ships began carrying McClellan's army to the peninsula.

It was also around this time, on March 12 specifically, that John Bell Hood took command of the Texas Brigade.[13] Though Colonel Archer had led the unit in General Wigfall's absence and had seniority, Archer suspected the command went to Hood because "Politics & politicians govern these matters ... and Maryland has no delegation in congress." Despite his disappointment, Archer went immediately to Hood's tent to congratulate the Kentuckian-turned-Texan.[14] The two men had developed a strong friendship over the winter, and even when General Whiting offered Archer command of a different brigade, he turned down the opportunity. "I would rather command my own regiment which I knew would stand by me," Archer explained privately, "than take without rank or staff the command of a brigade of regiments I knew nothing about & which might fail me in battle—The Texans will always stand by me." Archer later reversed that decision when the temptation of his own brigade became too great, but a shared respect between him and his men had developed that winter.[15]

Hood's West Point training and appointment by President Davis, without the input of the men, could have easily worked against him with the Texans. Instead, they declared him "a very clever looking man" (a favorite nineteenth-century compliment) and noted how much time he spent caring for them, listening to them, and visiting with them in camp. As Fourth Texan Josiah Duke explained to his grandmother: "We are well pleased with Hood.... [H]e is a Texian himself and a good soldier and has the appearance of a brave man and that is just what Texians want is a man that will lead them on to victories or death."[16] Clinton Winkler, commander of Company I of the Fourth Texas, insisted that the men "found him able and ready to give all necessary instruction, not only in drilling them for the field, but also in the forms and technicalities of the clothing, commissary, ordnance and transportation departments" that were, the men had learned, key to their success as well.[17]

Hood had worked all winter to show that he valued his volunteers as men and as citizen-soldiers. He understood their importance within their home communities, and how they had to relinquish that civilian authority to military hierarchy. Hood sensed that their complaints were at times the normal grumblings of soldiers but at other times genuine frustrations that should be heard. He made a concerted effort to earn their loyalty and to help them become successful soldiers, junior officers, and a successful unit. In that first winter of the war, Hood later explained, "I lost no opportunity whenever the officers or men came to my quarters, or whenever I chanced to be in conversation with them, to arouse their pride, to impress upon them that" they would be the best, which was exactly what the Fourth Texas, and later the whole brigade, wanted to hear. Hood also insisted that "their conduct in camp should be such as not to require punishment, and, when thrown near or within towns, should one of their comrades be led to commit some breach of military discipline, they should, themselves, take him in charge, and not allow his misconduct to bring discredit upon the regiment." The men could, Hood helped them realize, reclaim some of their civilian authority by policing each other.[18]

Hood also spoke to the leadership style that made men like Allen, Schaller, and others so repugnant to the Texans. When issuing orders, those officers failed to explain why the order was necessary; orders were to be obeyed and followed. Hood believed this approach would never work. Take, for example, he offered, "the usual and important regulation, prohibiting lights or noise in quarters after ten o'clock at night," which "would be regarded by young recruits as unnecessary, and even arbitrary, unless the officer in command illustrated to them the necessity thereof." Hood insisted that officers had to help their men understand that "an Army in time of active operations must have sleep at night, in order to march and fight the following day; and that for this reason no soldier should be allowed to keep awake, say, six of his comrades in the same tent, nor be permitted to create a disturbance, which would deprive his neighbors of rest, and render them unfit for duty the ensuing morning." From the start, likely learned from his years in the Old Army in Texas, Hood demonstrated basic, timeless skills in military leadership.

The men, in turn, respected him as they did no other commander throughout the war. Joe Polley argued that Hood's successful leadership, where so many other appointees had failed, was due to his ability to lead volunteers rather than regulars. "Never did I see or know a man to rise higher and more quickly in the estimation of others than did Col. Hood. Well versed in human nature and thoroughly understanding the peculiarities of Texans character," Hood knew "full well that volunteers would not submit to the same restriction that would be imposed on regulars." Hood "tempered his conduct... as to win our favor at once." He knew not to "draw the reins of true military discipline very tight at first—issuing few orders and those quite lenient for sometime but gradually increasing," Polley explained.[19]

Eighteenth Georgian Milton Barrett observed the same thing in the Texans and in Hood. Some days, though, as much as he admired them, Barrett was not sure the Texans were worth the trouble. "I am mutch *better pleas with gen Hood than i was at firs* but the Texas regements is the most disapated foot soldiers in servis and it takes the tites dissipland to keep them rite.... [W]e are in a texans brigade and when we are in rome we have to do like rome," Barrett explained. But he "had as soon fought by the side of a Texan as any for tha ar brave and fought like tigers but tha are like a spiret horse." They were a talented yet trying unit, as their commanders well knew.[20]

In March, Hood led the men south of the Rappahannock River near Fredericksburg. In the first days of April, they were embarrassed by an early test of their discipline and skill as soldiers. On the evening of April 3, scouts rushed into camp reporting that Union general Dan Sickles and his Excelsior Brigade of New Yorkers, one of their nemeses from the previous winter across the Potomac, were advancing on Stafford Court House, Virginia. The Texans and Georgians left camp around 10:00 p.m. and marched through the night but became lost. When the Fourth Texans spotted their commander, John Marshall, asleep in his saddle, they blamed him for the mistake and left him on the side of the road. Too far from camp to return for the night, the men bivouacked south of Dumfries and shivered as a late spring snow fell around them. As they marched back to the Rappahannock, word arrived that Sickles and his men had damaged much of Stafford, breaking into homes and slave cabins, stealing food and destroying what they did not take. Angry and embarrassed, several men from the Texas Brigade broke rank and sneaked off to taverns in Falmouth where they drowned their frustrations. Provost marshals arrested a few, others slipped back through the lines, and the Texas Brigade settled back into camp awaiting the opportunity to reclaim their honor.[21]

McClellan's landings on the peninsula forced Johnston to revise his defensive plans for Richmond. He was not certain if McClellan's men were the main force or a ruse, so Johnston relied on the spring rains, which turned country roads into thick, soupy rivers, to buy Confederates time to plan their next move. They were aided by McClellan's propensity to believe reports, once again, that estimated Confederates at numbers much higher than were actually in the area. As Johnston and President Davis's military advisor, Robert E. Lee, had predicted, McClellan's army, which began landing at Fort Monroe in mid-March, stalled south of Yorktown. They were held off by weather and the belief that the only Confederates in the area, led by Confederate major general John Magruder, numbered higher than the 17,000 men he actually had. Magruder's men had dug fortifications behind Warwick River and Yorktown, and he did a superb job of shifting his men and limited artillery into different, visible positions to make McClellan's observers think the Confederate positions were well defended.[22]

While Magruder delayed on the peninsula, the Texans remained near Fredericksburg. Their only action was the failed Stafford Court House defense, and they were impatient for action. They continued to train and continued to be frustrated by officers like John Marshall, who had, Fourth Texan Thomas Selman observed, "exposed his ignorance . . . but that was such a common thing that no one wondered at it."[23]

On April 8, orders rang through camp for the men to prepare to march, and they began their journey to Yorktown, which Confederate planners had concluded was, indeed, the location of the main Federal threat. Shortly after departing Fredericksburg, the Texans and Georgians halted at a fairly deep and wide creek. Tom Selman watched as Hood rode forward and called "the boys to pitch in," but they hesitated. Hood swung down from his horse and "asked them if they would follow him & in he went."[24] First Texan Robert Gaston was impressed, watching one man after another follow their commander's lead. Hood was, Gaston promised his parents, "a very good appointment" for the brigade, and this account has been cited as an example of the men's admiration for Hood's willingness to sacrifice and lead.[25] The ever-realistic Tom Selman, however, was not impressed. "The Genl. had on water proof boots & India ruber pants," Selman explained. He admired Hood as their commander, but he liked keeping dry, too, as "we had several to wade before we struck camp, and I am on guard."[26]

Years later, Val Giles recalled the same feeling. Hood "stalked majestically through the cold ice water which was more than half leg-deep to him, and General Hood was over six feet tall." Giles noted, however, that he would not enjoy the protection of Hood's waterproof boots that rose to mid-thigh: "With a shivering whoop two first companies plunged into the cold stream, which came to the middle of some of the shorties... [and] the enthusiasm... was pretty well oozed out by the time [Giles's Fifth Texas,] Company B reached the crossing. Glancing down the stream, I discovered an old footlog spanning the creek, so I made a flank movement in that direction." Furious at Giles's decision to break ranks, Lt. J. T. Hunter, whom Hood had left to direct the remainder of the men across, spurred his horse and intercepted Giles "when I was about half way across it. I tried to avoid him, but he gave me a shove... I lost my balance and landed six feet below where the water was five feet deep. Man, gun, knapsack, and accouterment all went under." A roar of laughter went up from the ranks as Giles "crawled up the slippery bank as wet as a drowned rat and mad as a wet hen." That moment, Giles explained, happened "before we volunteers had learned that we could not play in an officer's back yard or 'halloa down his rain barrel.' The volunteers of the early sixties were hard to manage at best, and when we were commanded by former playmates it was a trying ordeal for the officers."[27] The men of the Texas Brigade were still watching Hood and their commanders, not entirely certain of who would earn their loyalty.

They traveled by foot and rail over the next eleven days on their "long weary march" to Yorktown. While there, they were used, once again, as scouts and sharpshooters, losing several men to skilled New England riflemen. Mark Smither took solace in their opportunity to use "our fine Enfield rifles... [to] show the 'Green Mountaineers' what the 'Lone Star boys' can do."[28] The Texans and Georgians helped push back several Federal assaults on their lines, and they waited for the big fight everyone anticipated.

They also continued to watch Hood, becoming more impressed with the day-to-day care he showed the men while maintaining discipline in camp. At Yorktown, the enlisted men of Hood's old regiment decided to present a gift that publicly recognized their faith in their new brigade commander. With the brigade gathered around him, 1st Sgt. J. M. Bookman stepped forward and explained that they purchased the horse not "to court your favor, but simply because we, as freemen and Texans, claim the ability to discern and the right to reward merit wherever it may be found. In you, sir, we recognize the soldier and gentleman. In you, sir, we have found a leader whom we are proud to follow—a commander whom it is a pleasure to obey.... In a word, General, 'you stand by us and we will stand by you.'"[29] The men had learned enough about military life to know they would never elect their regimental commanders. But they insisted that they could and would recognize the man who would lead them to victory. As Pvt. Val Giles explained, "It has always been a question among us whether Hood made the Texas Brigade or the Texas Brigade made Hood."[30]

By the first week of May, facing increased pressure, Johnston ordered the Confederates to withdraw northward toward Richmond. In a testimony to the Texas Brigade's reputation in the army, Whiting's division served as the rear guard that covered the Confederate retreat, with Hood's Texas Brigade in the southernmost position. When they reached Williamsburg, Whiting's division continued past their fellow Confederates to address a threat farther north on the Pamunkey River, where Union brigadier general William Franklin's division threatened to move between Confederate forces and Richmond.[31]

On May 7, rushing through rain and mud, Hood's Texas Brigade led the attack to stop Franklin. Advancing quietly toward Federal picket lines, with the Fourth and Fifth Texas first, followed by the First Texas in line behind the Fourth Texas and the Eighteenth Georgia behind the Fifth Texas, and Col. Wade Hampton's South Carolina Legion to their right, Hood led from the front and insisted that the men not load their weapons for fear that one would fire and reveal their advance. The Federals had the same idea, however, and surprised Hood with a line of skirmishers who rose from behind a steep hill in his path. He was nearly killed by a Federal corporal until Fourth Texas private John Deal, who had decided that morning to ignore Hood's order, shot the man and saved his commander's life. With a nod to Deal, Hood recovered from his momentary surprise and led the attack through about a mile of woods, driving Federals from their defenses until they reached the protective fire of Union gunboats on the Pamunkey.[32]

The battle was neither major nor decisive, though the Confederates succeeded in protecting their supply lines and artillery train. Eltham's Landing's key significance for the Texans and Georgians, however, was in testing their ability to fight as a unit when discipline and volley fire was valued over the individual skills of scouts. They succeeded brilliantly. President Davis insisted that the Texas Brigade "saved the rear of our army and the whole of our baggage train," and Gen. G. W. Smith commended the Texas Brigade for winning "immortal honors for themselves, their State, and their commander, General Hood." While he praised all of the units engaged that day for their disciplined action, Smith argued that the "brunt of the contest was borne by the Texans, and to them is due the largest share of the honors of the day at Eltham."[33] Within the ranks, Hood was pleased with the men. They fought as a disciplined unit, and despite intense resistance, when it became clear that they had to stop the advance due to the fire from Union gunboats, A. T. Rainey's First Texans, in the lead as always, promptly obeyed the order to halt.[34]

Their glory, however, came at a price. Maj. Harvey Black, the enterprising beef packer from Marshall, Texas, was mortally wounded in the assault. Despite his northern roots, Black was a favorite among the men. Years later, First Texan George Todd insisted that Black was their "working responsible commander" that first year, because Wigfall was "brave but ignorant of tactics and very dissipated" and McLeod was "a good officer but too old." The men buried Black at a nearby plantation, with an Episcopal service, in a private family cemetery.[35]

The summer heat had settled on Galveston, Texas, by the time word of the battle and its casualties reached Texas Brigade families at home. Caroline Schadt finally heard from her brother William, who was "so oppressed by grief at the loss of our only and dear brother" that it took him ten days to write. He promised that "Charley" was killed instantly, "shot in the head," and the siblings took comfort knowing that William and his fellow soldiers buried Charles "decently and respectfully." They placed him under the shade of an apple tree, carved his name and age into the trunk, and then took time to carve, letter by letter and word by word, "the cause he fell under." William tried to add what details he could to the letter, knowing they would be important to Caroline. "The fight was near Williamsburg and called the Battle of West Point [also known as Eltham's Landing]," he explained. Not knowing any way forward but through faith, William implored Caroline to turn "to God to nerve you . . . he is the only one to comfort us in our hardest trials . . . the only one we can put our trust in . . . the only comfort that we can receive." William found similar strength in his faith, as well as "the spirit of revenge" that "God . . . has nerved me with. . . . [W]oe be to the hated Yankee foe that ever I meet." Charles, William, and Caroline had arrived with their parents and three additional siblings in the 1850s. Yellow fever took most of them before the war, and now Charles lay buried somewhere in Virginia. Just William and Caroline Schadt remained.[36]

The Texas Brigade suffered forty men killed or wounded at Eltham's Landing, and most of those were in Colonel Rainey's First Texas.[37] The brigade inflicted far more casualties, though, and were charged in northern papers with atrocities against several Federals. On May 14, the *New York Times* reported that one soldier "was found sitting against a tree, with his throat cut, the evidence of his having been wounded before the foul deed was done being plainly visible. Another was brought in with his head crushed in, probably with the heel of a boot." One Union volunteer claimed that he was nearly killed by "some long-haired troops . . . with threatening gestures," until he cried, "I expected humane treatment from Texans." Pausing, one of the Confederates agreed to let the wounded man live and carried him to an officer for questioning.[38]

The level of truth in the story is hard to measure, but Texans' letters did refer to the brutal freedom that scouts enjoyed in their raids and the bounties that enraged Federals placed on them in retaliation. Mark Smither had boasted the previous month that two men in Fourth Texas captain John Hutcheson's Company G sneaked into a Federal guardhouse and killed an orderly sergeant before he could draw his pistol. Federals offered a thousand-dollar reward for each, and four thousand dollars for Madison Monroe Templeman of Fifth Texas captain John C. Cleveland's Company H, Smither reported. Scouts "have fine times," he insisted, and prove that "Infantry has a great many advantages over Cavalry."[39] If the accounts of Texas brutalities proved true, it appears that even as the Texas Brigade's reputation for disciplined fighting grew, the fierce skills they had enhanced over the previous winter remained in use.

On May 12 and 13, Confederate forces retreated into a defensive position around Richmond. The Texas Brigade camped on Pine Island, where they stayed through the end of the month. They were not heavily involved in the Battle of Seven Pines on May 31 and June 1, but they received a new army commander when General Johnston was wounded at that fight and replaced by Gen. Robert E. Lee. For the next few weeks, the Texans were used, along with other Confederate units, as scouts and sharpshooters as both armies continued to watch each other, as they had for weeks. The anticipation reminded Tom Selman of hunting, waiting "with his gun primed listening to the music of the hounds as they bring the deer to the spot where he has selected to fall him to the earth."

The Fourth Texas private was a realist. Selman was determined to continue the fight for Confederate independence, but as he looked at the months ahead he predicted a "fatal blow ... as has never yet been struck on the American continent. I dread it; we all ought as a nation to dread it." He was not "afraid of losing my own life alone, but the sacrifice will be so great that even if we are victorious we are bound to feel its effect." Still, Selman saw no way but through: "We have fallen back & retreated until 'forbearance has ceased to be a virtue,' & our backs are now against the wall. . . . In short, die or defend the city of Richmond. . . . Come it must & come it will before many days & I am of the opinion the sooner it comes the better it will be."[40]

As the men dealt with the short bursts of fighting around Richmond and awaited the larger fight they knew would come, fresh recruits and respected veterans joined their ranks. Many of the fresh recruits were not entirely new to the Texas Brigade. Brothers, sons, nephews, cousins, and brothers-in-law volunteered between February and April 1862, when veterans like Dugat Williams returned home to inspire more men to join their ranks. In addition to receiving an enlistment bounty, men could avoid what many saw as a shameful draft. Plus, volunteers could join companies of their own choosing, and they often chose service with family and neighbors.

Some of these men were young, like Williams's nineteen-year-old cousin, Beasley Dugat. The eldest of six children, Beasley came from a middle-class farming family in Chambers, Texas, with a host of extended family throughout the area. This included his cousin Albert Germilia Dugat, also nineteen, who had enlisted the previous summer with Dugat Williams. Despite his youth, sixteen-year-old Kindallis "Dallis" Bryan also joined Company F and looked forward to serving under his uncle, Capt. King Bryan. Crow Brashear had enlisted with his brother Charlie in the summer of 1861, but Crow had been discharged for chronic rheumatism in November 1861. Undaunted, he enlisted again in the Fifth Texas in March 1862, despite the fact that the majority of 1862 volunteers from western states chose to serve in units that remained closer to home.[41] A few recruits, like R. R. Harriot, were less enthusiastic and disappeared in New Orleans as Williams and his new volunteers made their way to Virginia. "I suppose he got tired of soldiering and wanted to splurge around in the city a while. I don't think he will ever join us," Williams complained.⁴²

Other recruits arriving that spring were notably older than Dallis Bryan and Beasley Dugat, including thirty-six-year-old Andrew Erskine and his thirty-year-old brother, Alexander. Their arrival was a bit of a homecoming for Andrew, who was born in Virginia, and Alexander, a graduate of the University of Virginia. They arrived with their nephews, also new recruits, M. Erskine Miller and William Ehringhaus, along with about two dozen volunteers and Thomas Ignatius "Ig" Johnson, who was married to Andrew Erskine's wife, Ann, and an original member of Company D of the Fourth Texas who had returned home to recruit replacements. The Erskine and Johnson men came from the leading families of Seguin, Texas, and Andrew, in particular, is representative of the older volunteers of 1862.⁴³

He had remained home in 1861, but now Andrew Erskine felt called to serve. It could not have been an easier decision than they had faced a year earlier. The family celebrated when Ann gave birth in January 1862, but six weeks later their son Powell, not yet two years old, wandered into the Guadalupe River and drowned. Despite their family's emotional turmoil, a sense of duty and a determination that he would never be drafted drove Andrew Erskine into the Confederate army that spring. As he and the new recruits traveled toward Virginia, he tried to help Ann understand his decision: "You know I left you and my sweet darling boys and my comfortable home because I deemed it my duty, and because I thought that the public expected me to go. I was too proud to remain at home when everybody in the country able to bear arms had left to go in defense of the bleeding and suffering country."

Ann Erskine appears to have been less enthusiastic about Andrew's service, since he continued to defend his decision to serve with her brother. "I am acting as all good patriots should act and that although it may seem to you hard that I should leave you and my little boys alone, remember that no one could say hereafter to my children, 'Your father did not aid in gaining the independence of the Southern Confederacy,'" he argued.⁴⁴

The men had a cheerful reunion outside Richmond when the new recruits arrived in camp. Dugat Williams was a little surprised at how happy he was to be back with Company F and by how much he had missed his Fifth Texans. "When I'm in the Company," he observed, "I feel more at home than any other place except *at home.*"⁴⁵ Their reunion was brief, however, before Beasley Dugat became seriously ill. He was carried to a Richmond hospital, but there was little doctors could do. He died on May 27 having never seen a single battle.⁴⁶

Company F's mood grew darker still when word arrived that Pryor Bryan, their jovial messmate whom Williams didn't "think we could get along without," had died one day after Beasley Dugat. Bryan had been sick on their retreat from Yorktown, and his compatriots had had to leave him at a private home. By the time communications opened enough for their captain, King Bryan, to send a wagon for his nephew, Pryor Bryan was dead. As had been the case with First Texan William Schadt, it took about a month for Dugat Williams to find a way to talk with Laura about her brother's and his cousin's deaths. He knew Captain Bryan had sent word home immediately, and Williams took comfort in his fellow soldiers and in Laura's steadfast support, but he barely managed a sentence on the tragic losses. Williams could not and would not, he insisted, "speak of their death."⁴⁷

Similar incidents occurred throughout camp that spring, causing Eighteenth Georgian Milton Barrett to frown as he pondered their situation: "Our troops is in bad condishion for marching. the exposure and fatig we have had scince we have left our winter quarters has cose a grate deal of sickness a mong soldiers and a grate many recruits have jest come and the most of them is sick."⁴⁸ Andrew Erskine observed the same when he arrived in Virginia in early June: "I never saw such muddy roads in my life and our company has been encamped where the mud is from ankle to knee deep. The consequence is that a great many of the boys are sick."⁴⁹

Other troubles in camp came from the units that held officer elections that spring, primarily the First Texas and in Wade Hampton's South Carolina Legion, which officially joined the Texas Brigade at the end of June.⁵⁰ Hampton's eight infantry companies had the respect of many of the Texans and Georgians from their shared service along the Potomac. "As infantry," Joe Polley claimed, "the Legion had grit, a staying quality and a dash that was admirable."⁵¹ They included wealthy planter James B. Griffin from Edgefield, South Carolina, whose wife, Leila, gave birth to their eighth child, James Hampton, shortly after Griffin left for Virginia.⁵²

The officer elections troubled the First Texans and South Carolinians that spring. Among the First Texans, all but Company G through L had enlisted for one year, as had all but Company H of the Carolinians. All other companies of the Fourth and Fifth Texas had enlisted "for the war," while the Eighteenth

Georgians had all enlisted for three years.⁵³ Company-grade officer elections were held throughout the war, but these were tied to replacing officers who died in combat or due to disease. The conscription bill passed by Congress in the spring of 1862, however, gave the right to hold elections of company and regimental officers to twelve-month volunteers who reenlisted. For this reason, the First Texas and Hampton's Legion suffered through tremendous upheaval in May and June 1862, just as the campaigns that year intensified.⁵⁴

The problem, Lt. Col. James Griffin explained to his wife, Leila, at home in Edgefield, South Carolina, was "that a good many of the old officers will be turned out, and *worse* ones put in their stead. As a general rule—the officers who have discharged their duties properly—are not popular with their men—and those who have allowed most privileges, and have been least efficient, are the men who will be elected."⁵⁵ First Texas private E. O. Perry was similarly frustrated. "This regiment has completely played out. It is in a manner disorganized. Tis a regiment without a head, and our company (as is the case with most of the companies in our regiment) has played out," Perry explained. "Captain [Frederick] Bass having been defeated for Colonel (by 24 votes) has taken up his head quarters in Richmond it seems he has left the company entirely, cares nothing for it." Perry decided to run for captain himself, as did two other men, but Captain Bass returned to camp and tossed his name into the mix as well. "I do not think that he acted altogether right," Perry fumed, when Bass was reelected.⁵⁶

By late May, the elections were over and nearly every company in the First Texas had elected new officers. Captain Bass remained with Company E, but all of their lieutenants lost reelection and went home to Texas, and the men elected E. O. Perry's brother Clint to replace one of them. It is not clear that the elections did any lasting damage. Although a number of men who failed re-election returned to Texas, Bass remained a strong and respected commander with the regiment through the end of the war and briefly commanded the brigade. A. C. Oliver was a private in Company D whom the men elected as their second lieutenant that spring, and he, too, would continue to fight and receive subsequent promotions by election later in the war.⁵⁷ In other cases, however, some truly talented officers, such as James Griffin, lost their positions. The Texas Brigade suffered from this turmoil in their command structure when they needed to focus on the fighting at hand. But the election process was also part of the citizen-soldier tradition, inefficient though it was, that many of the men demanded as enfranchised members of a democracy.⁵⁸

On June 11, about the time of elections in Hampton's Legion, Robert E. Lee sent the Texans and Georgians of Hood's Brigade on a ruse to make Federals think he was shifting his focus to support Stonewall Jackson's operations in the Shenandoah Valley. The brigade traveled by rail to Staunton, which they reached on June 17, but they had only one day in the area before orders directed them to return to Richmond, a round-trip of more than one hundred miles. As exhausting as the journey was, it succeeded in convincing Lincoln to keep 30,000 men between Jackson and Washington City rather than sending them to support McClellan.[59]

By the end of June, Lee was working to push McClellan off the peninsula. The Confederates stumbled at Beaver Dam Creek on June 26, but Lee tried again the next day, June 27, at a place called Gaines's Mill near New Cold Harbor, Virginia. For the first time, and quite possibly the last, Confederate forces outnumbered their aggressor. The Union army straddled the Chickahominy River, with one-third of its men on the northern banks with their backs to the water. Lee focused on this portion, which was Union general Fitz John Porter's Fifth Corps. Lee isolated Porter with a numerical advantage of 60,000 Confederates attacking 34,000 Union defenders. Porter's position was not quite as foolish as it sounds. He protected the rest of the Army of the Potomac until they could fully abandon their attack on the Confederate capital. Lee did not realize his advantage in numbers or the fact that McClellan was falling back, but Lee did sense that the Federals were vulnerable.

On the morning of June 27, Lee had his army in position and ordered six divisions forward. The men and their commanders were still relatively new, however, and challenging terrain disrupted their lines on the western and central portions of the battlefield. Stonewall Jackson compounded the problem by showing unusual fatigue. To make matters worse, Lee's sense of the battlefield was about 90 degrees off from the way the forces were actually laid out. Lee shifted his lines when he finally realized the situation, but it cost additional valuable time. All of this allowed Porter to thwart uncoordinated Confederate attacks. By late afternoon, nearly 100,000 men were engaged, but Confederate victory was far from assured. When Whiting's division, in which Hood's men served, entered the New Cold Harbor area around Gaines's Mill, Lee, Whiting, and Hood had a brief conference. Lee made it clear that he needed the division—his smallest; it included only two brigades—to break Porter's line. Fourth Texas lieutenant Decimus et Ultimus Barziza observed that it felt like Lee was rushing them forward "as if the fate of mankind depended on our coming."[60]

In that spot, the Union Fifth Corps men were at the top of a hill where, as the ground sloped downward, a strip of trees gave way to a steep embankment protected by tiers of Federal infantry who benefited from the moat-like barrier of Boatswain's Creek that flowed below them. It was these defenses that Hood's men were asked to breech. The impact of the battle began as soon as they approached New Cold Harbor, felt most powerfully by the solid shot that came bouncing through their lines. Bennett Wood of the Fourth Texas saw one round coming and fell to the ground, but his quick reaction left one of the three Smilie brothers in the ranks exposed. The lead ball tore James Smilie's head from his shoulders.[61]

Hood stood before his old command, as he had promised the Fourth Texas he would, to lead them into battle. This may not have been a wise decision. As division commander, he was likely needed elsewhere. But the brigade, and the Fourth Texas in particular, loved him for it, and Hood's presence helped calm the men as remnants of earlier attacks straggled past the Texans and, in some cases, ran back through their lines. Lieutenant Barziza had "never dreamed of such confusion.... Men deserted their colors, Colonels lost their commands, and God only knows how far off were a rout and panic," as the noise of battle and smoke from their powder filled the air.[62]

Despite all of this, Whiting, Hood, and Col. Evander M. Law (who commanded the other brigade in Whiting's division) managed to keep the men moving forward. They approached the battlefield with Hampton's Legion on their far left, followed by the Fifth Texas, First Texas, and Fourth Texas on the right, with the Eighteenth Georgia coming up behind them. When Hood received a request from Gen. Richard Ewell for support to their left, Hood sent Hampton's Legion, the Fifth Texas, and the First Texas across a farm lane on the edge of a wood line. Observing the challenging terrain around them, he realized that if he moved the Fourth Texas behind Evander Law's brigade, directly on his right, he could get them clear of the woods, get some momentum going for them, and also connect Law's position with portions of Gen. James Longstreet's forces, creating a more solid line for their attack. The Eighteenth Georgia followed the Fourth Texas when Hood did this. Both units were exposed to fire without the protection of the woods, but it kept them from getting mired among the trees.

To their left, past Law's brigade, the Fifth Texas had to advance through a maze of terrified Confederates retreating from earlier charges who "would implore us not to go as it was certain death," Robert Brantley recalled.[63] Robert Campbell, the seventeen-year-old from Huntsville, Texas, who had just

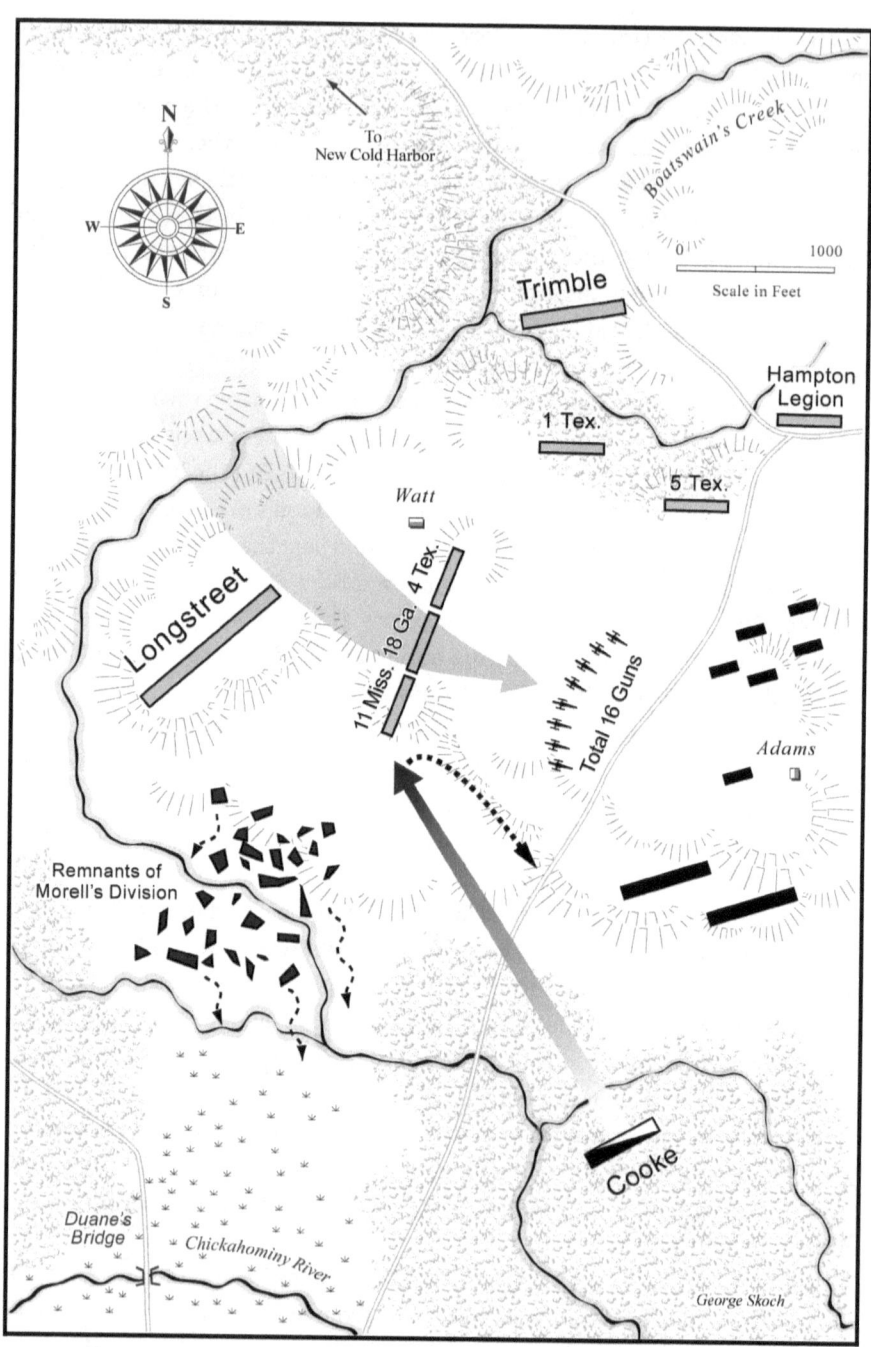

Battle of Gaines's Mill, June 27, 1862

joined Company A of the Fifth Texas, watched with fascination as their Lt. Col. John C. Upton walked among Company K, which had been placed before their position as skirmishers. He wore "an old pair of pants, a dilapidated pair of cavalry boots, and an old cotton shirt, a slouch black hat—a huge sabre, with a pair of six shooters—looking less like an officer than any of his men." The Texas cattleman walked calmly along their line, circling his saber over his head and yelling above the noise, "My brave boys, give it to them." When one of General Ewell's staff officers rode up and begged Upton's men, "Don't run my boys, give it to them—stand my men, for Gods sake stand—or the day is lost," Upton turned on the man in fury. Campbell grinned as Upton roared, "Leave here, you damn coward, these are my men, these are Texans, and they *don't know* how to run."[64]

To Campbell and the Fifth Texas's right, Law's advance stalled as they ran into Confederates from earlier attacks who refused to retreat, but who would not advance either. To their right, the Fourth Texas and Eighteenth Georgia continued into the space between Law's brigade and Longstreet's forces until Hood had his officers dress their lines before the final advance. Hood paused and rode out before the men to address the brigade, or at least this portion of it, looking at his old Fourth Texans whom he had promised to lead into battle.

Joe Polley insisted that the moment reminded him of Hood's old boast that he "could double-quick the 4th Texas to the gates of Hell and never break their line." Pat Penn, a fellow private in Company F with Polley, felt similar relief. Penn believed that if Colonel Marshall led the Fourth Texas into battle, "we will be whipped for sure. He will be sure to get us into confusion." Not a man approved of Marshall as their commander, Penn insisted, but "most of them think . . . he would do very well for Lieut. Col. if Hood was the Col. but without him I do not know what [Marshall] would be."[65] Lt. J. R. Loughridge, who watched his men in Company I, would have agreed. Marshall reminded him of "a Don Quixote with his horse, Rocinante." Marshall was a fellow newspaperman, but he belonged, Loughridge insisted, back in Austin editing the *Star Gazette* because "he has no latent talent for military matters."[66]

The Eighteenth Georgia was about one hundred yards behind the Fourth Texas and was fuming at being held in reserve. With their Col. William Wofford sick, regimental command had fallen to Lt. Col. Solon Z. Ruff. He struggled to assure the men that they would be used, and to maintain control of his own rage because he was not entirely sure that was true. When he had protested their position, Hood had scowled: "Never mind that, Colonel, and see to your troops & have them ready. When I send for you, follow me, and with dispatch." When the order finally came, Ruff spurred his horse, wheeled around and cried, "Up boys! Now is your time!" With a rush, the Eighteenth Georgia surged forward and fell into position about forty yards to the right rear of the Fourth Texas.[67]

It was 6:00 p.m. as they stood in the field near the Parson house, several hundred yards north of Boatswain's Creek. Hood ordered the men to hold their fire until he gave the order, to use the colors as their guide, to move steadily and without panic. He stepped forward, his sword raised in one hand and his hat in the other and with a yell of "Forward! Guide right!" Hood led the Fourth Texas, with their rifles on their right shoulders, into the fray.[68]

They had barely advanced when a ball tore through Colonel Marshall's neck. He fell from his horse, killed instantly.[69] Still the men kept formation, in part because Hood was with the Fourth to fill this command vacuum and perhaps because the men had learned not to rely on Marshall on military matters. The intensity of the fire stunned William Hamby. It fell "upon us like drops of rain from a passing cloud, and as we advanced their messengers of death grew thicker until they came in teeming showers.... At every step forward our comrades were falling around us."[70]

The Fourth Texas and Eighteenth Georgia moved forward, controlled and steady, through the field and into the woods that slowed their advance. As they passed Law's brigade, which had stalled again under the devastating fire and casualties, the Georgians began to "bleat at them like sheep." Law used the moment to rally his men, and they rejoined the assault.[71] Despite the obstacles, their pace quickened as the ground sloped steadily downward toward Boatswain's Creek. Men stepped around and tripped over the dead and wounded from the previous Confederate assaults. Hood's order to hold their fire until they were on top of the Federals kept the Confederates' attack swift and steady. Fourth Texas lieutenant colonel Bradfute Warwick gave in to instincts at one point and ordered the regiment to halt and return the Federals' fire. The Eighteenth Georgia saw this and was about to do the same when James Lemon saw Hood "instantly among them yelling 'Don't stop! Forward! Trail-Arms!" About fifty yards before them, Lemon could see the "first line of Yankees, as they furiously fired & reloaded. With blackened faces like demons from the infernal regions, they tore cartridges in clenched white teeth, while rammers flew up & down the barrel of their pieces," he recalled. Hood regained order, and the men rushed into and across the creek, constantly under fire, and with a confidence that terrified the first line of Union men on the opposite slope, who broke and ran over the rows of defenders behind them. As artillery and musket fire roared around them, Hood's order to "Fix Bayonets!" echoed down the line as officers repeated the command. Suddenly, Lemon understood the purpose behind Hood's unusual earlier command to trail arms, which allowed the men to place their bayonets efficiently and continue to follow the next order to charge up the hill. "I have always felt Hood was a genius for having the wisdom to know this in a very short time, as it saved precious moments & preserved our momentum," the Georgian explained.[72]

Lieutenant Barziza recalled, "We flew toward the breastworks, cleared them, and slaughtered the retreating devils as they scampered up the hill." Some men were fortunate to cross where the creek was shallow and narrow, but William Hamby remembered having to scramble up a twenty-foot embankment. Rushing through the abandoned Federal defenses, Hamby and his compatriots "fired into their retreating ranks as they ran up the hill, and, reloading as fast as we could, we followed them over their second fortifications, when their entire line gave way in disorder, but continued to fire as they retreated."[73]

When they broke through the wood line on the northern side of Boatswain's Creek, Hood's and Law's men were looking into fourteen Federal artillery pieces. Exhausted, the Confederates took cover where they could and caught their breath for a moment. A number of them gathered near Hood, who stood calmly in an orchard assessing their situation. His steady cool inspired William Morris, who marveled at Hood's confidence as he stood, "resting on one foot, his arm raised above his head, his hand grasping the limb of a tree, looking as unconcerned as if we were on dress parade." Morris decided that "if he could stand it, I would, too."[74]

Nearby, Andrew Erskine "was so much exhausted" that he, too, paused in the orchard "to blow" and missed the final assault as "my regiment and company got out of my sight very soon. I remained in the orchard for a short time, but the shower of grape was so terrific that I fell back a short distance to some large trees in a creek bottom." Failing to find the Fourth Texas, Erskine linked up with some North Carolinians and fought with them for the rest of the battle.[75]

Fourth Texan Val Giles had fallen closer to the orchard, wounded by canister from the Federal artillery pieces. He could not move and winced as "a terrific fire of grape, canister, and Minie balls" flew all around him. As more Confederates crested the hill and rushed toward the orchard, one man noticed the badly wounded Giles and "in passing grabbed me by the collar of my coat and unceremoniously snaked me along for a few yards and landed me behind a big apple tree. He handled me without gloves and hurt me fearfully, and in return for that act of humanity I cursed him. He made no reply, but hurried on with the great wave of victorious soldiers."[76]

They were not long in the orchard when the Texans, Georgians, and some Mississippians from Law's brigade pushed forward again, largely without officers, as they rushed to take the Federal guns. Barziza estimated that two-thirds of their officers and one-half of their men were killed or wounded, but still they rushed, "yelling, shouting, firing, running straight up to the death-dealing machines." It helped that the terrain offered them some protection, but they had three hundred yards clear, and the Federals gunners fired "a long, blazing flame" from the cannon that shook the ground and filled the air with smoke.

Suddenly, William Hamby of the Fourth Texas felt "the ground begin to tremble like an earthquake and heard a noise like the rumbling of distant thunder." In the next instant one of the men of the Eighteenth Georgia cried, "Cavalry!" Confederates stared with disbelief as Federal troopers loped toward them. It was Gen. Philip St. George Cooke, trying to buy the Federal artillerymen time to limber their guns and escape. Some Texans joined the Georgians and some of the Eleventh Mississippi, who were on the far right on the advance. They managed to organize themselves and fire a deadly volley into the line of advancing troopers. As Eighteenth Georgia lieutenant James Lemon recalled, "the left wing of our regt. continued towards the guns, [and] we on the right flank, about three companies, A, B, and C, refused our line to the right so as not to be flanked and in an instant, formed to 'receive cavalry.'" Despite their inexperience and exhaustion, and helped by the troopers' inexperience, the Confederates formed two lines, with the first kneeling and placing the butts of their rifles, with bayonets still fixed, "against the right knee. The rifle was thus angled upward and outward, toward the advancing enemy. The rear rank was standing behind them and ready to fire," Lemon recalled. They waited until the troopers "came within about 50 yards from our lines, and then we poured into them a volley which hit them like a whirlwind. Men seemed to fairly fly from their saddles in every sort of wild position."[77]

Chaos followed. Horses panicked and bolted, some dragging their riders behind them while others carried empty saddles and disappeared into the smoke and twilight. One trooper maintained control of his mount and slashed his saber at Pat Penn, who shoved his bayonet forward. It "got fast in him and he jerked the gun from my hands and rode on with the bayonet sticking him and the gun still hanging to him. I do not know how far he went before he fell.... I tell you," Penn marveled, "it was no time to watch a wounded yankee then. I turned round and found a gun lying just behind me like mine" that he used for the rest of the fight. He had not been scared, Penn insisted, but he admitted to his sister Lizzie, whose husband, Quinn, fought nearby, "the fight satisfied me. I am not half as anxious to meet the yankees now as I was before."[78]

While this went on to their right, portions of the Fourth Texas continued their advance on the increasingly panicked Federal gunners, with help from some of the Georgians and Mississippians. They were pouring a relentless fire into the artillery crews, so much so that the Federals could not sufficiently load and fire their guns. They fled with five of their guns, but the southerners captured the other nine, and Tom Rawls of the Eleventh Mississippi climbed up on one to celebrate, but, as his friends recalled, "his rear becoming painfully hot he was compelled to retire in quick order."[79]

East of the Fourth, Fifth, and First Texas had waged their own bloody struggle. It was less disciplined than the advance Hood directed, with the men firing as they descended toward Boatswain's Creek. They were also broken up by the swampy terrain that clung to their feet and claimed Robert Campbell's shoe. But this advance was just as determined and just as overwhelming, and soon the Federal defenders, like their comrades to their west, broke and ran. After a pause in the fight during which the Confederates rifled through captured Federal tents and possessions, they started to receive fire again. Upton reorganized the men, and they regained control of their section of the field and captured nearly 450 men of the Fourth New Jersey who were cut off from the rest of their force in the final stages of the battle. Robert Campbell felt some sympathy for his enemies, except one. A "young and boyish" Irishman started to debate the Texan on the causes of the war, explaining, "You are all brave fellows, but you are fighting against the stars and stripes, and my little man, you will all fail." Campbell was angry enough to take the man's canteen, but he shared his tobacco with some of the others. "Now that they were in our power, I sympathized for them," he explained.[80]

Hood's brigade and Whiting's division, as a whole, had secured victory for Lee's army, but the cost of success surprised them. All of the field officers of the Fourth Texas were killed or wounded. Hood searched the battlefield with his soldiers the night of June 27, looking for wounded and calling for stretchers. He loaned his own horse to Jake Smilie, who had located the bodies of his two dead brothers. Jim, decapitated early in the advance, was the first to fall, and Jake wanted him buried with William. Isolated lights spotted the dark battlefield as men stumbled over corpses and wounded, calling out for and responding to calls from friends and family. Hood ordered litter bearers about as they struggled to save the wounded. The next morning, he was stunned by the small number who turned out for roll. "Is this the 4th Tex[as?]," Hood asked. A quiet voice called from the ranks, "This is all that remains."[81]

Whiting's division had broken the Federal line, and the role Hood's brigade played in that success made them famous. Support from Law's brigade had been vital as well, but Hood was key to their success, and everyone from privates to statesmen celebrated the brigade. Years later, Confederate postmaster and Texan John Reagan insisted that Lee's relationship with the Texas Brigade was forged at Gaines's Mill: "After that on different occasions, General Lee urged me to aid him in getting a division of Texans ready for his command, remarking that with such a force he would . . . break any line of battle on earth in an open field." In a desperate moment, Lee, still new to army command, had asked John Bell Hood and his men, who were better known for scouting and ill-discipline, to take a well-defended position that had stopped determined Confederates attacks all day. Lee never forgot what they had done to save his army and the capital. Reviewing the ground after the battle, Stonewall Jackson, never effusive with praise, declared their attack an "almost matchless display of daring and valor" and insisted that the men who made it were "soldiers indeed!" Hood was proud of his men, too, and insisted "too much cannot, or ever will, be said in their praise." Additional accolades rolled in from President Davis and Senator Wigfall, and the Texas Brigade's reputation spread rapidly through newspapers across the South.[82]

Families back home stood a little taller as they read all that their men had accomplished.[83] One account out of Galveston insisted that near the end of the fight a bugler in the Fifth Texas paused to fill his canteen and stumbled upon twenty-five terrified Federals. Having no weapon, he "told them to throw down their guns or else he would blow his horn and the Texians would kill every one of them," editors boasted. "The word Texas seemed to be the *open sesame* by which all their courage oozed out."[84]

In Charleston, South Carolinians read about the bravery of Hampton's Legion and Fourth Texan Bradfute Warwick, who had fought with Garibaldi in Italy. At Gaines's Mill, Warwick carried their flag after seeing three color-bearers go down until he, too, was mortally wounded.[85] Residents of Macon,

Georgia, read that Hood's Texas Brigade—to which "the 18th Georgia belongs," editors reminded their readers—fell "like an avalanche on McClellan's flank" as the Confederates earned themselves "glorious laurels."[86] As far north as Cincinnati, Ohio, and Philadelphia, Pennsylvania—two border cities with divided loyalties—editors reported that it was difficult to decide which Confederate unit was right in their claim to have captured the guns in the final fighting at Gaines's Mill. Hood's brigade and other units who made such claims, the editors smiled, "all enjoy the joke, and laugh right heartily over the dangers of capture, never counting one danger, but only desiring new occasions to distinguish themselves."[87]

Families at home were also learning what such honors cost. Six weeks after the battle, the *San Antonio Semi-Weekly* filled two full front-page columns with the names of Texans killed, wounded, or missing at Gaines's Mill.[88] Their somber tributes were likely of little comfort to the families, though. In mid-August, the affable Howdy Martin, who went into the battle with a Dragoon six-shooter in each hand, sat down to write a painful letter to William Edwards's wife, Roxey. He had been wounded in the battle and died on July 15. Martin assured Roxey that her husband gave "his life for his country's cause," and of Martin's hope that "your neighbors and friends will assist & protect you ... and his dear child" as they struggled to find a way without William. An 1862 volunteer, he had said good-bye to Roxey just four months earlier.[89]

Joe Polley shared Martin's sorrow as he sent word home that his sister's husband, Connally Findlay Henderson, had died in the fight, too. "He fell with his face to the foe ... while pressing bravely onward in one of the most desperate and one of the most successful charges that History ever has recorded or ever will mention," Polley promised. He had Henderson "buried on the field where he fell, feeling assured ... that no place was more fitting for a soldier's grave than the field he had helped by his valor to win."[90] The words may have brought some comfort in the years that followed, and Susan Henderson would not want for much materially. Her husband had been a wealthy merchant in Bexar County when he enlisted that spring, and she had a good bit of her own wealth, too.[91] Still, her loss was just as real and lasting. Susan Henderson was pregnant with a child she named Conley when their daughter arrived in December.[92]

Robert Sullivan was killed in the attack as well. Either Patrick Penn was unable to talk about his cousin's death, or it was mentioned in a letter that no longer exists. Robert's mother, however, could not stop talking about him. For years after the war, she noted his loss each June in her diary: "My dear Robert ... O it seems so long. He was such a noble boy." In 1862, however, neither she nor the Penns could imagine how many more sons from Fayette County would die with Hood's Texas Brigade in Virginia before the war would end.[93]

Texas Brigade families waited with worry and dread throughout the summer of 1862 for news from Virginia. In early July, Cecelia Morse paced her home near Houston and held out hope that her husband would come home. Henry Morse had enlisted with his brother, George, that March in Company A of the Fifth Texas. Henry turned twenty-two that year and likely kept a close eye on his sixteen-year-old brother, George, in the fight. They would not have been far from Robert Campbell as they watched Colonel Upton swing his saber and carry his frying pan into their first big fight. Living at the Morse family plantation, Cecelia reminded herself constantly that "Providence rules all things and to him we trust ourselves and them." Still, rumors of a battle were sifting into town, and she worried "what fate our loved ones share.... Oh how I long for a letter just one more." In mid-July, she heard early reports of high casualties and braced herself for the worst. "Were I to lose Henry what in the world would I do," Cecelia Morse asked. "I could not bear to live on Ma and Pa [Morse] and not in some way remunerate them." Lonely, scared, and with sleep proving elusive, she sewed late into the night and watched their six-month-old baby rest: "How much I wish his Father could see him every day he grows more like him." A letter arrived at the end of the month, but it was dated June 12, before the Battle of Gaines's Mill. George had been sick since they arrived, Henry was depressed because he had received no letters from home, and he was thinking of getting a transfer to a company in Texas. But Cecelia still had no idea if her husband and brother-in-law were alive or dead. Finally, in August, another letter arrived. They had both survived. "God has been merciful to us so far he has spared our friends how greatful we ought to be to him for his goodness to us," Cecelia prayed. But she could not help adding, "I long to get another letter from [Henry] so bad." Families at home were learning how frustrating and painful the home front could be, even in relatively peaceful Texas.[94]

Andrew Erskine wrote to Ann the day after Gaines's Mill, knowing she would be worried as soon as word of it reached Texas. He tried to describe the fight, but a week later, he was writing again and still struggling to process what he had seen. "I never had a clear conception of the horrors of war until that night and the morning. On going round on the battlefield with a candle searching for my friends, I could hear on all sides the dreadful groans of the wounded and their heart-piercing cries for water and assistance. Friends and foes all together," Erskine explained. Come morning, he awoke "on the field and [saw] the mutilated condition of men and horses. Oh! The awful scene.... May I never see any more such in life." Walking among the wealth of blankets, jackets, guns, ammunition, and other supplies the Federals had abandoned, Erskine found some personal letters that contained "a picture of a little boy that reminded me of our dear lost Powell." Andrew carried the daguerreotype with him, and as July crept into August, he found himself looking at the photo and remembering "my sweet angel boy as I saw him when I found him in the river.... Doubtless some poor father who had been killed in battle that day had the picture of his dear little boy to look upon and remind him of his own happy home before this dreadful war, with all its horrors, came upon him. Oh! the horrors of this dreadful war."[95]

Ann would have felt tremendous relief after reading Andrew's first letter, but he still had not been able to find his brother "Zan" (Alexander) or their nephew Erskine Miller. Word finally arrived that they had both received wounds but would recover, and Zan's was only minor. Ann likely marveled at all their heartache that summer. Andrew's father, Michael Erskine, had also died, though from the normal dangers of life, regardless of a war. "Oh, my God, how little did I think I would hear such sad and distressing news," Andrew moaned. There had been so much heartache that summer. Crops were suffering from a drought, and Ann struggled to keep up with her own family business as well as her father-in-law's. Andrew did not know how she and his sisters would manage everything with so many of the men gone. He offered advice, just as the men who enlisted in the year before had tried to do. "You're right in stopping everything to push ahead with the [new ferry]boat as that is of the greatest importance, but I would try and get the pasture fence fixed also, as it will be of great value to you this winter in saving the lives of many of our livestock." He was stunned that delays were being caused by a man who promised to get the wood and have it milled, declaring, "Josh Erk[el] has acted like a dog." He hoped some other neighbors would help, but Ann, who had an excellent head for business and management, would struggle on with help from their eldest sons. Twelve-year-old Blucher was in charge of breaking, branding, and selling horses, and ten-year-old Eddie managed their hogs. The ferry, though, remained their biggest worry. It was their primary source of income and key to his family's stability in Andrew's absence.[96]

The Erskines were hardly the only family suffering in Guadalupe County. It seemed that nearly everyone had been affected by Gaines's Mill. "Poor Tom Holloman was killed, also Alonzo Millett, Parson Butler's son and old Mr. David's son, and two or three more not known. Young Austin Jones is supposed to be dead but can't be found," Andrew explained.[97] This was true, of course, of Texas Brigade communities that stretched from Texas to Georgia and South Carolina, and through the soldiers' extended families throughout the South. The total brigade losses in the fight were 86 killed, 481 wounded, and 4 missing, and the Fourth Texas was especially hard hit.[98] They went into the battle, William Townsend told his wife, Almira, with fewer than 500 men, and 257 fell killed or wounded or were still missing: "Col. Marshall, Lt. Col Warwick, and Major Key were shot down in 5 minutes after getting under fire.... Three of our Capts. were k[illed], and another badly w[ounded], a 5th slightly w[ounded], and another saved only by the hilt of his sword." Townsend had been promoted to major of the Fourth Texas, and Lt. Benjamin Franklin Carter would be his captain. They would both answer to Colonel Key. But Carter was terribly sick, and Key was recovering from his wound, so day-to-day operations fell on Townsend. Smiling a bit, the wealthy, forty-year-old Townsend reminded Almira that this was a terrible thing: "You know how lazy I am and you know that I am bored to death—For no blind horse in a tread which has more unceasing routine of duties than a commander of a volunteer regt." With so much work to do, Townsend could not even find time to read the paper, "and you know I fail to read the paper for no small cause." Still, he would remain. Not "for the plaudits of my fellow man but because I hate Yankees."[99] Similar upheaval spread through the brigade as wounded officers like A. T. Rainey and J. R. Loughridge went home on wound furloughs and new men assumed temporary command.

The Texas Brigade played a small role in the remaining Seven Days Battles. As McClellan's army retreated, Confederates around Richmond struggled through the aftermath of the campaign that had nearly conquered their capital. Roadsides, private homes, and hospitals were overwhelmed with dead and wounded. "Misery, suffering, and distress was all that met the eye," twenty-year-old Angelina Smith recalled. The daughter of a middle-class Richmond family, she would later marry an officer in the Fourth Texas, Clinton Winkler, and she spent much of the war as a volunteer nurse. She remembered the men who, "so torn by shot and shell" overwhelmed area hospitals in June and July 1862. Tobacco warehouses were transformed into temporary facilities for the wounded, where ambulances dropped off "frightful wrecks of men... helpless, thirsty, tired, battered with the conflict, bearing in their bodies the bullets which had stricken them down, all awaiting their turn for treatment by the surgeons, busy day and night with their ghastly work," Smith recalled. "The basement of every church, every tobacco factory, every empty building, and even every box car along the railroad tracks, was full of wounded men."[100] Try as they might, the living simply could not keep up with the dead.

Thomas Selman, wounded in the fight, spent the middle of July in a sick camp for the Fourth Texas. As he made his way to the camp with Willis Landrum from Company H, the two men noted that their dead were buried along their entire route. "One of our boys died last night by the name of Hicks," Selman noted in his diary on July 11. "He is still lying here & no prospect of getting a coffin to bury him." Hicks's body continued to lie in camp, and by July 12, he "was decomposing so fast that it was almost impossible to be about it. [Hicks] was wrapped up in a blanket & interred about one hundred & fifty yds. from camp." Disgusted and depressed, Selman concluded that "our government" simply did not care about its soldiers. "The poor fellow was treated more like a dog than a human."[101]

It was true that Richmond was simply overwhelmed by the demands of war that July, but southerners were also incredibly inspired by their victories in the east. As news of Union victories in Tennessee and Louisiana poured in, Hood's Texans took tremendous pride in the role they had played at Gaines's Mill in saving their nation's capital, and perhaps their nation itself. This had been their first true test as combat infantrymen, where discipline and volley fire, rather than scouting and sharpshooting, were central to success. Newspapers across the South celebrated the Texas Brigade as they also celebrated Robert E. Lee's army.[102] The war had proven to be more difficult and deadly than many of them had expected, but the men of Hood's Texas Brigade were more confident in their officers and in themselves than they had ever been before. That faith in victory would carry them through the remainder of the year, where bloody fighting had yet to be done.

SLIPPING THE BRIDLE
The Battles of Second Manassas and Antietam

The Battles of Second Manassas and Antietam would be the two costliest of the war for the Texas Brigade. But they enhanced the brigade's reputation within Lee's army and the Confederate nation. The battles also strengthened the pride and purpose Hood's men saw in their service in Virginia, as well as their faith in their commanders. Ordnance officer E. Porter Alexander would later argue that after Second Manassas, Lee's men "acquired that magnificent morale which made them equal to twice their numbers, & which they never lost even to the surrender at Appomattox."[1] Desertion rates that later plagued Lee's army call the universality of this comment into question, but it was certainly true for Hood's Texas Brigade.

Throughout July and early August, Texans continued to serve as scouts and engaged in smaller battles like Freeman's Ford. They did not see major action, however, until the Battle of Second Manassas at the end of that month. Lee had sent Jackson northward in early August to delay the threat of a new federal force under Gen. John Pope. As McClellan's army left the peninsula, Lee shifted his full attention to Pope and hastened to link with Stonewall Jackson's command, which included the Texas Brigade. On the afternoon of August 26, the Texas Brigade left Waterloo Bridge near Jeffersonton, Virginia. They covered nearly twenty-five miles in as many hours, slept briefly, and then pushed on to Thoroughfare Gap, where units from two Confederate divisions, including the Texas Brigade, helped secure that route through the Bull Run Mountains. This allowed Longstreet's command to rush to the aid of Jackson's wing of Lee's army about seven miles north of Manassas Junction on August 29.[2]

Hood, who had been promoted to division command to replace the ill "Chase" Whiting, deployed the Texas Brigade—which Hood also still officially commanded, though it was led by staff officer Capt. W. H. Sellers—on the south side of the Warrenton Pike and Evander Law's brigade along its north side. Longstreet's command came into position to the right of the Texans, while Jackson's wing was on their left. Near the end of the day, Longstreet ordered the Texans, along with the rest of Hood's division and a brigade under Nathan G. "Shanks" Evans, to test the strength of the Federals in front of them. Law's brigade was well in advance of the Texans, with Evans behind them, and just as they were all moving forward, Federals attacked their position.³

Ironically, General Pope had spotted movement in their area and was convinced that the Confederates were retreating after the intense fighting that day with Jackson's forces. Rushing to strike, Federal commanders believed they were attacking weary units protected by a rear guard. Instead, Hood's men responded with a brutal counterassault. The Second U.S. sharpshooters broke quickly before Law's brigade, but the Confederates slowed a bit as Union brigadier general Abner Doubleday deployed his three regiments to stop the assault.⁴

The Texas Brigade rushed up the Warrenton Pike with the First Texas, commanded by Lt. Col. P. A. Work in A. T. Rainey's absence, pushing toward the Seventy-Sixth New York and Fifty-Sixth Pennsylvania. To Work's right was the Fourth Texas, under Lt. Col. B. F. Carter (to whom Major Townsend had happily relinquished command and returned to his newspaper). To the right of the Fourth Texas came Col. William T. Wofford's Eighteenth Georgia and then the Hampton Legion led by newly elected Col. Martin Gary, followed by Col. Jerome Bonaparte Robertson leading the Fifth Texas. The Legion and Robertson's men were slowed a bit as they pushed through some wooded ground.⁵

The Texas Brigade's line extended well beyond that of the Federals in front of them, but as darkness fell, it was difficult for either side to apply their advantages. At one point a Federal brigade was ordered to advance through the brigade in front of it. Confusion swept the ranks, and the strengthened Federal position caused the southern advance to stall. As Evans's men advanced behind Law's brigade, the Confederates on the north side of the turnpike surged forward again. South of the road, the First Texas regained their momentum and pushed back the overlapped brigades of Abner Doubleday and Col. Timothy Sullivan. By this point, the Eighteenth Georgia and Fourth Texas were struggling through the woods, too, but managed to continue their advance. Joining with men of the First Texas, their fire intensified on the

Twenty-Fourth and Seventy-Sixth New Yorkers, who finally broke and began to fall back.

Confusion still dominated the fighting. Both sides were yelling to stop shooting, insisting that their comrades were firing on their own men. In some cases they were; in others the cry simply caused a momentary pause until soldiers identified, as best they could, their proper targets. A Federal major tried to rally some men only to discover he was shouting orders at, and was promptly captured by, members of the Second Mississippi of Law's brigade. A color-bearer from the Twenty-Fourth New York rushed up to some men, frantically trying to stop them from shooting fellow Yankees. At the last moment, the man pulled back, realizing his mistake, and hesitated briefly before J. J. O'Neill. The Eighteenth Georgia sergeant was seventeen when the war began, still living with his parents in Acworth, Georgia, where his wealthy father operated a mill and commanded the local militia company. In the darkness at Manassas, Sergeant O'Neill spotted the "stars and stripes . . . and grasped the flag, tore it from the staff." After the battle, O'Neill sent the Twenty-Fourth New York's flag to Governor Joseph E. Brown, where it hung at Milledgeville, Georgia, until reclaimed by William Tecumseh Sherman's men in 1864. Between the darkness, smoke, and woods, Fourth Texan Val Giles insisted, "I couldn't have told my best friend from a bluecoat five steps off." It was, wrote Eighteenth Georgia Chaplain Penfield Doll, a "desperate hand to hand fight" that left the ground "baptized in blood."[6]

Around 8:00 p.m. the fighting slowed and then stopped. Hood pulled together his brigade as best he could, as did Law, in the valley of Young's Branch, near the western base of Dogan Ridge. They were still astonishingly close to the Federals, with Hood's "line . . . in the midst of the enemy," he explained. For the next few hours, officers tried to bring order to their units, but the lines were "so intermingled that commanders of both armies gave orders . . . in some instances, to the troops of their opponents," Hood recalled. He rode to tell Lee and Longstreet that he did not see how commanders in his area could reorient their men to prepare for a morning assault, and suggested that they fall back. In the early morning hours of August 30, Confederates along the base of Dogan Ridge quietly made their way back to their original positions along the Warrenton Turnpike and collapsed for a few hours' sleep in the fields south of the road.[7] Law positioned his men on Hood's left along the turnpike, with Evans's men behind Hood's, all of them less than a mile west of Groveton. Throughout the night, additional commands from Longstreet's wing arrived and settled in around them. Hood suffered fewer than 100 casualties in the late night fight of August 29, and he had fulfilled his orders to measure the strength of the Federals in the area. But most of the men had seen enough fighting to know that the main battle was yet to come.[8]

Hood's men did not engage in much of the fighting on August 30. They waited and listened until around 4:00 p.m. as the second-largest attack Lee's army ever launched raged nearby. "Next to disappointment," Val Giles explained, "I hate suspense worse. The idea of waiting there" along Warrenton Pike "I thought would kill me.... [T]he suspense of a battle was worse than the action." As the battle raged to their north, Longstreet's men did their best to occupy their minds as they rested around the Cundiffe farm. Giles noticed as he looked around him that "Some were reading novels and newspapers, some playing cards and betting great rolls of Confederate money on their hands, regardless of the cannon balls which occasionally came tearing through the treetops. Some were scuffling like schoolboys, and others talking of home and friends and days gone by." Most of the men were in good spirits, their confidence buoyed by the successes they had enjoyed that summer and by their growing faith in their commanders.[9]

Hood's Texas Brigade led the attack on the late afternoon on August 30. Philip Work anchored the First Texas's left on the Warrenton Pike, followed to their right by the Fourth Texas, Eighteenth Georgia, Hampton's Legion, and finally the Fifth Texas in a line extending about seven hundred yards. They would have to cross challenging terrain with knolls, strips of woods, creeks, and ravines separating units and braking up lines. The men stepped forward with precision, maintaining a smooth, quick pace. They were so rapid, however, that after about one hundred yards, their line started to separate. Colonel Work, who was to keep his left on the turnpike, received word that the right of his First Texas had separated from the Fourth Texas. He halted his men, waiting for Col. B. F. Carter to bring his men up with Work. It turned out, though, that Carter was about 150 yards in front of him. They had, Fourth Texan Alexander Erskine explained, "started at a rapid rate & double quicked it all the time towards the batteries."[10] Work got his regiment moving again and raced at a double-quick to catch up, but the First Texas would remain largely separate from the rest of the brigade for the rest of the day, as would the Fourth Texas.[11]

To their right, the Eighteenth Georgia, Hampton's Legion, and the Fifth Texas remained together as a group and continued a similarly swift pace. Indeed, they moved so quickly that they were nearly on top of the skirmishers

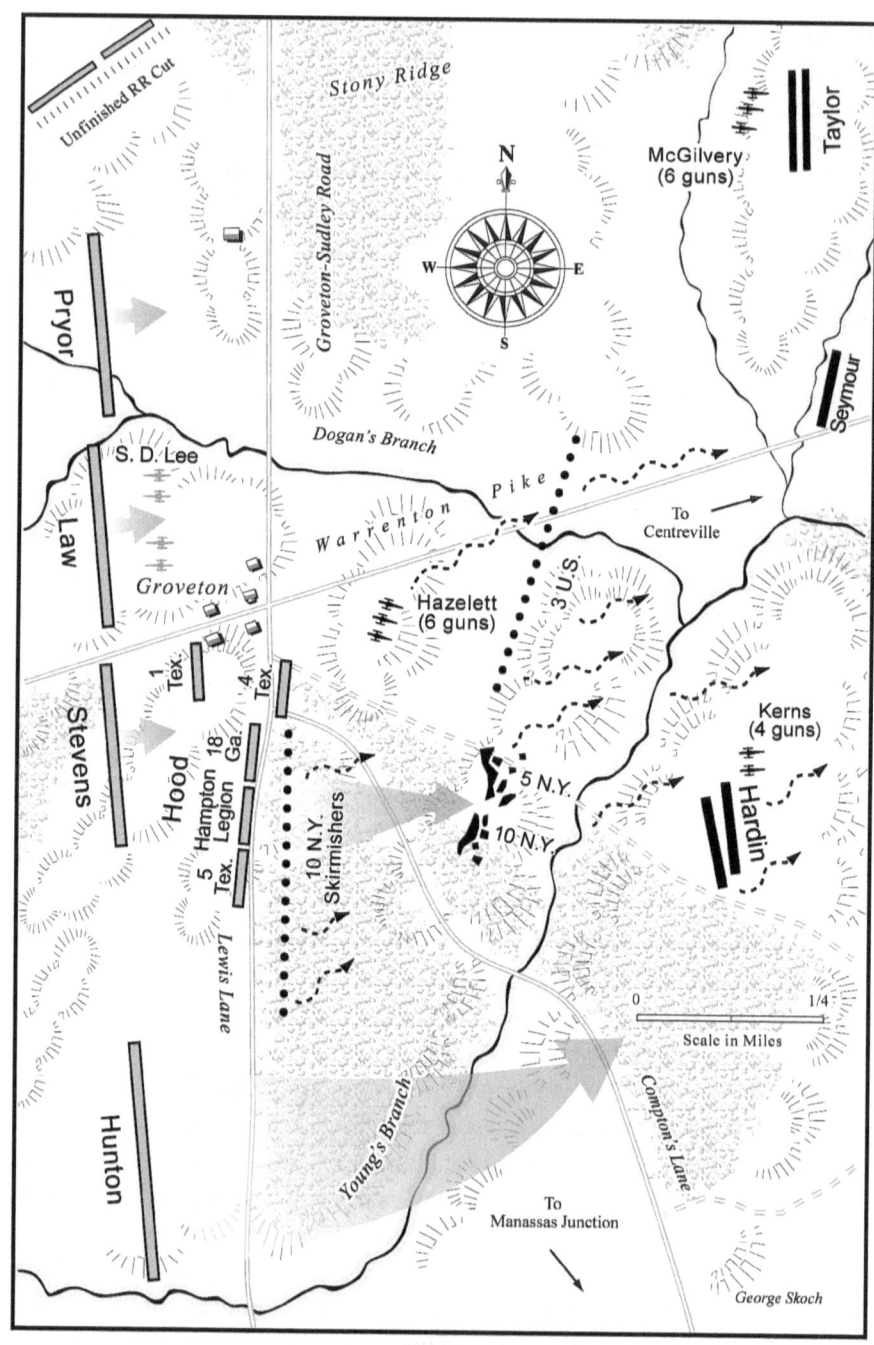

Battle of Second Manassas, August 30, 1862

of the Tenth New York before the men had time to fire. Surprised by an attack from a section of the field that Union commanders were positive was no threat—Pope had already wired Washington early that morning to report that Confederates were retreating—the skirmishers fell back toward the Fifth and Tenth New York.[12]

The Fifth New York, better known as Duryee's Zouaves, was still forming into lines as the Tenth New York poured through their position. This was followed quickly by a volley from the Fifth Texas. One Federal recalled that balls sounded "like hail. It was a continual hiss, snap, whiz" and then a "sluck," as balls hit their human targets.[13] The fight intensified as Confederates arced around the New Yorkers like an archer's bow with the Fifth Texas on their left, Hampton's Legion in the middle, and the Eighteenth Georgia wrapping around the New Yorkers' right. The Confederates loaded and fired as they advanced, putting constant, deadly pressure on the New Yorkers.[14] "This regiment of Zouaves had been wanting to fight the 5th Texas for a long time, and fortune favored their desire in accidentally placing us in front of them," Fifth Texan Pleasant Watson insisted, recalling the Fifth New York's promise of "Death to all Texians" during their raids on each other during the Potomac Blockade.

The Zouaves tried to stand their ground, but men were falling faster than they could reload. "Their left companies soon gave way, and when our Regt. got within a few yds of them their whole line broke and they fled, loading and firing as they retreated. Our boys followed them up closely . . . and by the time they got back to their support we had killed nearly all of them. I do not think that 20 escaped," Watson declared. "So much for the 5th New York."[15]

The New Yorkers raced down the slope toward Young's Branch. As they went, the Fifth Texans, Georgians, and Hampton's South Carolinians raced after them. Fifth Texan Robert Campbell recalled that "so much confusion attended their crossing that we made the branch run blood—and after crossing the branch we continued to bring them to the ground. . . . [A]s soon as we had got them started—we followed right upon their heels—and would shoot into a crowd at the distance of ten paces."[16] Nearly fifty years later, that was the scene Eighteenth Georgia private Joe Smith remembered the most, that moment "when we struck those New York Zuaves red britches fellers & left the ground red with them."[17]

A few lucky Federals escaped. When Fifth New Yorker George Mitchell's captain was killed, "the only commissioned officer we had in the company," Mitchell moved to replace him. Seconds later a ball tore through his haversack with such force that it knocked Mitchell to the ground. He scrambled to his feet but could barely stand. With balls flying and men falling everywhere, Mitchell used his rifle as an awkward crutch and made his way to the rear. When he finally had a moment to check his wound, he braced himself and peeled back pieces of his haversack, torn pants, and underclothes from his side and was stunned to realize the ball had never entered his body. All he found was a red spot the size of his hand that turned a blackish blue in the days to follow. "I never in all my life had anything to hurt me so much as that did," he wrote to his parents.[18] Mitchell was the exception that day. The fight on the ridge west of Young's Branch lasted about ten minutes. In those brief moments, the Fifth New York suffered nearly 300 casualties, of whom 120 died.[19]

As Federal lines collapsed, Gen. Irvin McDowell scrambled to buy time until more Union forces could come up. He found Capt. Mark Kerns's battery and a brigade of Pennsylvania Reserves under Col. Martin Hardin. McDowell ordered them to the northern slope of a knoll west of Chinn Ridge. They would have to buy the Federals time to organize a defense of Henry Hill, which was the key to victory at Manassas. Kerns's and Hardin's men watched nervously as the Texas Brigade approached. The Fourth Texas was still relatively untouched by this point and reconnected with the Eighteenth Georgia, Hampton's Legion, and the Fifth Texas as they rushed down toward Young's Branch, without orders, and then up toward the Pennsylvanians. Canister poured from Kerns's guns, but most of it went over the Confederates' heads. Enough hit their target, though, that the Fifth Texas shifted a bit to the right for the protection of a slip of woods, and in doing so, managed to move around to the left of the Eleventh Pennsylvania's line. Hardin worked to adjust their front, but the Confederate fire was too constant. Having held two of his four regiments in reserve, he rushed his second line forward, but his men still struggled. Then Colonel Hardin fell wounded.[20]

Leaderless and overwhelmed, the Pennsylvanians fell back. This allowed the Texas Brigade to focus on Kerns's guns. The slope shielded their approach from much of the canister that blasted from the barrels. More than two dozen artillery horses were dead or dying or racing from the field, and when the infantry broke—with Hood's men within fifty yards—the artillerymen did, too, knowing they could not save their guns without the horses.[21] The only man who remained was Captain Kerns, steadily working the guns by himself, a task that usually required ten men. Fourth Texan Joe Polley recalled that as they closed on Kerns, he was preparing to fire one last round when the Texans shot him. Impressed by the man's courage, the Confederates offered to carry him to a field hospital, but Kerns refused. "I have promised to drive you back, or die under my guns, and I have kept my word," he answered. Major Carter was so impressed by Kerns's action that he left his overcoat for the artilleryman's burial under a large oak near Young's Branch. In the days that followed, Carter sent a letter to Kerns's family with details on his final moments, along with a watch and other items the Fourth Texans found on his body.[22]

Hood moved his brigade forward from Kerns's batteries on the knoll and down to a ravine that offered shelter from a fresh Federal battery and brigade on Chinn Ridge. Here they caught their breath and refilled their canteens. Spotting a stretch of woods to his right, Hood ordered the Eighteenth Georgia, Hampton's Legion, and the Fifth Texas into the trees to ensure that the enemy could not advance unnoticed on their position and to protect them from artillery fired coming from north of the Warrenton Turnpike. This left the Fourth Texas feeling exposed. Having already suffered significant casualties in the fight for Kerns's knoll, Carter ordered his men back over the hill, past Kerns's guns, and into the shelter of Young's Branch. They reconnected with the First Texas here and remained in this position for the rest of the battle.[23]

The rest of the brigade, however, played an active role in the remainder of the fight. They linked with "Shanks" Evans's brigade and with three additional brigades from Gen. James Kemper's division. In a desperate struggle under rifle and artillery fire, they finally took Chinn Ridge. Hood ordered his forces to stop there, but then the remainder of Longstreet's wing moved past them as they continued on toward Henry Hill. Still engaged mentally if not physically, the Fifth Texas "slipped the bridle," as Hood later explained, and raced off with them. The "Bloody Fifth," as they would be known after this fight, chased after the Federals and helped fellow Confederates push Pope's army across Bull Run. "Had there been a Joshua to stay the setting sun, we might have made captives of almost the entire army," Fifth Texan Rufus King Felder promised.[24]

Colonel Robertson was wounded in the battle, as was King Bryan of Liberty County. Worse still, the Fifth Texans' beloved Col. John Upton was killed, shot through the left eye in the fight against Duryee's Zouaves. As at Gaines's Mill, the men struggled to comprehend their losses amid the rush of victory. Fourth Texas captain Edward Cunningham promised Upton's mother, who was also Cunningham's aunt, that Upton's loss was felt "by his immediate friends and by the entire brigade," noting that "he was decidedly the most useful officer in the Brigade" and that "his place" among Hood's Texans "cannot be filled."

Cunningham took comfort, and hoped Ann Upton would too, knowing that John Upton died "struggling for the independence of his country and . . . upon a victorious battlefield."[25]

Second Manassas was one of the Army of Northern Virginia's greatest victories, and perhaps James Longstreet's finest hour. But the Texas Brigade lost 628 men killed, wounded, or missing, the most they would lose in any battle in the war. They had fought bravely, but their aggression was often uncontrolled, resulting in uncoordinated advances that created problems for the timing of Longstreet's attacks and left Hood's men too far forward and unsupported. This was caused in part by the unusual command structure that had Hood leading the division at Manassas, and his poor decision to place his inexperienced adjutant-general, Capt. W. H. Sellers, in temporary command of the brigade rather than the more experienced Col. W. T. Wofford of the Eighteenth Georgia or Col. J. B. Robertson of the Fifth Texas. The battle was a great Confederate victory, but extremely costly for the Texas Brigade.[26]

The "Bloody Fifth" suffered the most, losing 261 men. Few regiments on either side lost more. Rufus King Felder, walking over the battlefield, found the sight "horrifying in the extreme," he confessed to his sister. "You could see corps[es] mangled in every conceivable way & hear the moans of the wounded in every direction. The only consolation," he added bitterly, "was that you could see five times as many Yanks as Rebels."[27] Pleasant Watson was wounded in the struggle for Chinn Ridge. Fire from a battery struck his arm and side "and knocked me senseless." His arm was cut nearly to the bone and was missing a good chunk of flesh above the elbow. At a field hospital he found several men from his company and learned about the fate of others. "Newton Mullins and Charley Moncrief, two *noble* young men were killed dead while bearing the colors. Jinnie Petty was shot in the bowels and mortally wounded. Sam Dean was wounded in the thigh and breast, severely. [Fifth Sgt. J. C.] Buster was wounded in the leg, bone broken & was amputated, Julien Hutchinson in knee, severely," Watson scribbled into his diary.[28]

The "Jinnie Petty" to whom Watson referred was his first sergeant, Virginius Petty, one of the most dedicated men in Company E, who had promised "to go naked and eat dirt" before he fell out of line of march, let alone a battle. His messmate W. H. McCalister did not bother to try to convince Petty's family that his death was swift, as so many death letters promised. "He suffered a great deal before he died," McCalister admitted, but Petty's "last injunction was to tell his friends that he died for a good cause and that he was perfectly willing to die for he had served his country faithfully."[29]

Compared to their losses at Gaines's Mill, the Fourth Texas suffered relatively few casualties. But among them was Ann Erskine's brother, Ig Johnson. "Oh my dear wife, how can I break to you and your poor mother and the children the dreadful intelligence I must convey.... Poor Ig is dead," Andrew Erskine began. In the fight to take Kerns's battery, a piece of shell or some canister tore through 2nd Lt. Thomas Ignacious "Ig" Johnson's thigh, cutting his femoral artery. "He was just ahead of me," Erskine explained, as they pushed up the knoll under heavy fire, about thirty yards from Kerns's guns. "I saw him turn around and sit down. I saw blood on his thigh and I asked him if he was badly hurt. He replied, 'Yes, pretty badly.'" But Erskine had to keep going, "knowing the strict orders against stopping behind with anyone."

After they captured the battery and the fighting died down, Andrew and Alexander Erskine found Ig Johnson. He had bled to death. They "gave him as decent a burial as it was possible to do on the battlefield... on the spot where he fell and I got two stones and cut his name on them to mark his grave, so if I live through this awful war, I may be able to find his grave and carry home his remains so they can be interred by the side of his father and sisters," Andrew explained.

Ig's death left Andrew Erskine "lonely and sorrow-stricken" and "little fit... for anything." He prayed "that these defeats will satisfy the wretches that they cannot subdue us and they will listen to some terms of peace. Oh! how dreadful it is that so many of our kind friends and relations have to lose their lives by the wicked war." Clearly shaken, the Erskine brothers were discussing how Andrew might return to Texas. Alexander "thinks I might get out of the service, as I enlisted before the passage of the conscription law," and Andrew had decided it was his "duty to return home since the death of my poor father, and assist in winding up his business." Andrew was "truly tired" and "would hail with delight" the opportunity to reunite with Ann, the children, and all of their family. "But I am afraid I will have to remain in the service until the war is over, as it is very difficult to get discharged now on any account."[30]

In the darkness that followed their fight at Manassas, General Hood checked on his beloved Fourth Texas and promised, as he had earlier that evening, that "he could never tell how highly he appreciated our gallant conduct." Days later, the praise remained with Alexander Erskine, despite the fact that he had buried his brother-in-law the day after the battle and helped with a mass grave for other Texans. Hood said that "we did too much more than was ever asked of us," Erskine recalled with pride. Despite all of their suffering, they still believed in Hood, in Lee, and in the Confederacy.[31]

Andrew and Alexander Erskine, determined but never enthusiastic volunteers, continued on with the Fourth Texas, in part from a sense of duty, and partly because they wanted their families to continue to enjoy the lifestyle they had made in Texas. The Johnsons and Erskines had built a successful farming, ranching, and business enterprise through their own hard, dangerous, and determined effort and that of dozens of enslaved men and women. Alexander and Andrew firmly believed that the advantages they had secured in the antebellum period would be destroyed if the North won the war. Those sentiments threaded through the entire brigade. The 1850s had been incredibly lucrative for the vast majority of these men and their families. Despite all of the hardships the war had brought, they remained convinced that Union threatened more than the war itself.

After his defeat on the plains of Manassas, John Pope led his men back to Washington, where they reunited with George McClellan's equally demoralized force returning from the Peninsula campaign. With morale at a low that President Lincoln had not seen in nearly a year, he reluctantly returned McClellan to command of all of the Army of the Potomac and called on him to do what he did best: rebuild the army, remind men of why they should believe in themselves and their cause, and prepare for the battles that loomed in their immediate future.

While Federals recovered in Washington, General Lee's army invaded Maryland. He wanted to ride the high morale their series of victories had inspired and take the war to the Union. He might also convince the North that their war could not be won. Within the ranks, the Texas Brigade reflected that optimism, despite the sadness that shadowed them from the hard year of fighting. Andrew Erskine still spoke of the loss of Ig Johnson and enclosed a lock of his hair in a letter to Ann, but he insisted their invasion of Maryland would secure the victory that would send him home. "We will whip the Yankees so badly in their own country that they will be glad to acknowledge our independence very soon. I believe we will have possession of Baltimore and Washington City in less than a month," he wrote from Frederick, Maryland.[32] His brother Alexander agreed. "I shall remember with pride," he promised his wife, Bettie, "that I belonged to the great army that fought before Richmond so gloriously, that made twice memorable Manassas['s] bloody plains & entered Maryland for its liberation."[33]

At the same time the Erskine brothers invaded Maryland, Ann Erskine was distracted by other battles at home. It rained almost every day of the first week of September, so there were more delays with the construction of their new ferryboat. "Gosh" Erkel was working on it again, but he was running low on lumber. Andrew trusted that Albert Berkley Moore would pay Ann the money he owed the family, but Ann doubted it. "I reckon Mr. Moore has never thought of me but once since you left, at least he has never sent me any money," she frowned. Andrew was also sure someone would help fix the pasture, but Ann could find no one, though she promised to keep trying. He repeatedly reminded her to save the grass as winter fodder. Yes, "I know how important it is, to save the grass," Ann sighed. The good news was that all of the rain would assure more grass, and she had not yet sold their mules but had a buyer who Ann thought would pay two hundred dollars for them.

Ann Erskine did not mind the work and was accustomed to helping run all of their properties. Despite the large number of slaves Andrew's father and Ann's family owned, she relied on hired help and often struggled to hire anyone or buy anything at a decent price. It was this lack of support while Andrew was gone that angered her. "I think it is hard for you all to leave your homes and fight for such a lot of skinflints as are left here," Ann frowned. "There is no price too high for them to ask for anything; coffee is $3.00 per pound, every thing else at the same rates. I cannot hire a hand for any price." Her biggest worry, though, was their ferry. The new boat was not yet ready, their profits were down almost 50 percent from July to August, and "some one has told such dreadful tales about the boat that nearly all the travel is on the other road," Ann fumed. A week-long rain had opened September, but Ann's worries so overwhelmed her that she closed her letter on September 9 complaining, "We have no rain yet to do much good." Then, in her rush to get the letter out with a man headed for Richmond, she forgot to include her usual comments about their sons. Clearly, 1862 was proving to be a trial. She gave birth to one son in January, buried another son in February, and buried her father-in-law in May. Andrew had been gone not quite six months, and Ann was tired, but she remained his "ever devoted wife," determined to keep things together at home. One can only imagine her heartbreak when shortly after she mailed this hasty letter, news arrived that her brother Ig was dead.[34]

Marching into Maryland, the men in the ranks shared the Erskine brothers' faith in a massive victory that could send them all home. Joe Polley promised his parents, "One more fight and I think the war will be over." He knew his mother would mourn the loss of Ig Johnson, whom the Polleys knew, but Joe promised that "all our boys in Camp are well and hearty." He did not know "how those in Richmond are," but Hood's Texas Brigade was, in Joe Polley's eyes, ready to win the war.[35]

Some of the men, like Dugat Williams, could not quite muster the bold claims of Polley or the Erskines, but then, Williams rarely did. On occasion he paused to consider "our cause" and Confederate independence, but most of his letters reported on friends and family in camp, asked about the same at home, and hoped he would see "my dear Laura" soon. As he camped outside Frederick, Maryland, the Fifth Texas officer spent more time describing the casualties at Second Manassas than the fight itself. These included his cousin Albert Dugat, one of the men from Liberty whom Williams had recruited six months earlier. The losses clearly hurt, yet Williams could see no other way but forward.[36]

As the Texas Brigade entered Maryland, Hood was not at their head. As the fighting ended at Second Manassas, several of Hood's scouts had captured some Federal ambulances. Hood's division received orders to move with Longstreet's wing into Maryland, and as they departed, General Nathan "Shanks" Evans demanded that Hood relinquish the ambulances for Evans's brigade. Hood did not mind sharing the wagons, he explained, but he refused to give them to Evans when his brigade "was in no manner entitled to them." Evans complained to General Longstreet, who placed Hood under arrest and ordered him to Culpeper Courthouse, Virginia, for a court-martial to hear the case. When General Lee heard of the incident, he refused to let one of his best division commanders leave the army in the middle of a campaign. He would not, however, undermine Longstreet's authority entirely. Lee ordered Hood to ride in the dishonored position at the rear of his division, much to the Texas Brigade's outrage.[37]

They crossed the Potomac River at White's Ford on September 6, continued on through Buckeystown, and on toward Frederick on September 7. There they paused for two days a few miles south of town.[38] The men slept, washed themselves and their tattered uniforms, and helped destroy the Baltimore and Ohio Railroad bridge. On September 10, the citizens of Frederick turned out to watch Longstreet's men, but the community showed little enthusiasm for Lee's army or his cause. Rufus Felder warned his family that any sense of the "southern feeling" of Maryland was "a mistake. There are some trusted men there, but the majority are Union," though he could not help but admire the beauty of the area and "plentiful fruit."[39] Unlike Virginia, the war had hardly touched Maryland, and Frederick's citizens showed little interest in joining the Confederacy.[40]

During the campaign, Lee divided his army and targeted weakly defended Federal garrisons and supplies in the area. He sent Longstreet's wing, along with D. H. Hill's division, toward Hagerstown, Maryland. They were to guard against any Federal approach from northeastern Maryland or southern Pennsylvania and to keep lines and communications open between Lee's forces and the Shenandoah Valley. By September 11, Hood's Texans were marching along the National Road toward the Catoctin Mountains, and they reached Hagerstown two days later. They set up camp five miles south of the Pennsylvania border, ready to help when Lee pushed farther north.[41]

That same day, September 13, alarming reports came into Lee's headquarters from Confederate Cavalry commander major general J. E. B. Stuart, and Confederate major general D. H. Hill. Both men shared information that indicated that Gen. George McClellan was pushing northward at an alarming clip with an army of about 85,000 men.[42] Lee ordered Longstreet to Boonsboro to support D. H. Hill's forces. Lee hoped to delay McClellan and the Army of the Potomac long enough to bring the Army of Northern Virginia together. Realizing the danger they faced, Longstreet pushed the men at a furious pace, covering thirteen miles at a forced march.[43]

As their footfalls and equipment thumped and clanked in unison, the men of the Texas Brigade became increasingly angry about Hood's arrest. Their frustration boiled over on September 14 as they hurried toward the sound of the guns and passed "our beloved General [Hood] riding, with bowed head, in the rear of the men who trusted him," Joe Polley explained. The moment "emphasized the outrage, and forced an appeal to supreme authority" as they spotted General Lee. As the Texans passed him they chanted, "Give us Hood! Give us Hood!" Once again, the men would insist on selecting their commander. Acknowledging their complaints, Lee raised his hat and promised, "You shall have him, gentlemen."[44]

Lee sent for Hood and promised to release him and return him to his command if Hood would "merely say that you regret this occurrence" with General Evans. But Hood refused. "Had I been ordered to turn them over for the general use of the army, I would have cheerfully acquiesced," Hood explained, but that was not the case. Evans insisted on them for his South Carolinians alone. Lee looked at Hood, wondering if the Kentuckian-turned-Texan could hear the enemy's guns as well as Lee could. He asked again, and once again Hood could not find a way to honestly express regret. With a sigh, Lee said, "Well, I will suspend your arrest till the impending battle is decided." With that, Hood swung onto his horse and loped to the front of his command. All down the line his men shouted, "Hurrah for General Lee! Hurray for General Hood! Go to hell Evans!"[45]

Hood's division reached Boonsboro about midafternoon on September 14. With Hill's forces engaged, Longstreet ordered Hood to take his men to Turner's Gap, the northernmost of three key passes through South Mountain. Confederates hoped to delay McClellan and the Army of the Potomac by defending those gaps, which would allow the Army of Northern Virginia to gather at Sharpsburg. Hood's division reached Turner's Gap about 4:30 p.m. The situation was grim. Union general Joseph Hooker's First Corps was forming to attack, and only Robert E. Rodes's brigade was in place to hold Hooker back north of the National Road. Longstreet originally ordered Evans's brigade and Hood's division (two brigades) into line to strengthen their defense of Turner's Gap. Within thirty minutes, though, Longstreet learned of an even greater threat just to their south at Fox's Gap. Leaving Evans's men in place, Longstreet ordered Hood's division to move to their right to block the Federals who were about to break at Fox's Gap and gain access to the Confederate rear. Beyond the tension and his men's exhaustion, Hood had to deal with extremely vague orders to simply "go to the right" to find the exact location of Fox's Gap. Stumbling southward, Hood's men reached Confederate brigadier general Thomas F. Drayton's brigade just as it had broken and scattered. Hood knew his men would not be able to stop this Union force for long, but, combined with the efforts at Turner's and Crampton's Gaps, they stabilized the situation and helped buy the rest of their army time to organize.[46]

Late in the evening of September 14, Hood's men fell back and served as the rear guard for Lee's army as it pushed in a northwesterly direction along the National Road toward Boonsboro and then cut southwest toward Sharpsburg. They crossed Antietam Creek at Middle Bridge about noon on September 15 and then rested for a few hours on the south side of Boonsboro Pike. That evening, Hood's men marched north of Sharpsburg out the Hagerstown Pike to help guard the army's left flank. They then settled on the left side of the road, just north and behind a small white meetinghouse known as Dunker Church. The men stacked arms just inside the West Woods and laid down to rest.[47]

The Texas Brigade waited in the West Woods from late on September 15 through the late afternoon of September 16. During that twenty-four-hour period, they slept and tried to find food, but the only thing nearby was a 20-acre cornfield across Hagerstown Pike. There was also little water among the hickory and oak trees around the church. In the last three days, they had lived on green corn and watermelons pilfered along their route and whatever small food items they had purchased, received, or "borrowed" while moving through Frederick and other towns. Hungry enough to stomach a few more ears, several of the men gathered some corn from across the road, and then they spent most of September 16 resting despite intermittent artillery.

A man walking through their position that afternoon would have run into Dugat Williams, Rufus Felder, and the Goree brothers of the Fifth Texas on the far right of the Texas Brigade's position. To their south was Law's brigade. Just north of the Fifth Texas were Joe Polley, Mark Smither, Val Giles, and "Howdy" Martin of the Fourth Texas. North of them were the First Texas, Eighteenth Georgia, and Hampton's Legion, in that order, moving south to north. Their line ran along Hagerstown Pike down to the Dunker Church, until a lane called Smoketown Road intersected the pike. About seven hundred yards north of that intersection lay the cornfield of David R. Miller. Confederate colonel Stephen D. Lee's artillery battery, deployed nearby along a ridge running southeast from the Dunker Church, thundered an occasional response to Federal guns in the woods just east and north of the corn. Here the men slept and grumbled along with their stomachs until late afternoon, when Lee learned that Joseph Hooker has crossed Antietam Creek at Upper Bridge and across fords near the mill of Samuel Pry. Lee ordered Hood to take his division and make contact with Hooker to get a better sense of what the Federals planned to do.[48]

Georgian William Wofford, commanding the Texas Brigade, and Col. Evander Law moved their brigades out of the protection of the woods near sunset and marched about seven hundred yards north of the Dunker Church. They formed the men into line facing northeast, with Law's brigade on the right along the southern edge of the cornfield and later moving up Smoketown Road, where it curved to the north, while the Texas Brigade was on their left across the plowed section of Miller's field anchored on the Hagerstown Pike. As they waited to advance, Stephen D. Lee's guns to south of Smoketown Road continued to exchange fire with the Federal artillery to the north and east.[49]

Capt. "Howdy" Martin's Company K of the Fourth Texas served as skirmishers and moved slowly through the corn several hundred yards in front of the division. They met some resistance from the skirmishers of the Thirteenth Pennsylvania Reserves, but Martin's men stopped the Pennsylvanians advance until they ran low on ammunition and fell back, while Captain Ike

Turner led the Fifth Texas forward to take their place.[50] Neither side could make much progress in the darkness, though, and when it began to rain around 9:00 p.m., the fighting tapered off. Hood's men pulled back into the West Woods with a few captured members of the Pennsylvania reserves, including a couple drummer boys "who were trying to 'put on a brave face,' but who were clearly terrified," Eighteenth Georgia lieutenant James Lemon recalled. Just before all of the Texans had withdrawn, Fifth Texas captain Ike Turner paused, wondering if Federals were advancing toward them in the darkness. Ordering eleven men forward—one from each company—they crept through the East Woods, moving quietly over soft ground that had little underbrush. When the Texans could nearly touch the Pennsylvanians, who let them get that close because they thought they were Federals, "the ball opened and . . . there was about the hottest fight of the war for about fifteen minutes, considering the number engaged," John Stevens recalled. Neither side gained the advantage, though, and the Texans fell back to the West Woods.[51]

Throughout the night of September 16, Hood searched for the wagons carrying rations for his men, despite the fact that he was as exhausted as they were. Meanwhile, commanders like P.A. Work of the First Texas ordered two men from each of his twelve companies to gather and roast corn for the regiment.[52] It is well that he did, because the wagons contained only flour and would not reach Hood's men until about 5:30 a.m. on September 17.[53] When the wagons arrived, the men grumbled about their poor rations while they mixed the flour with some water, worked it into dough, and wrapped it around their ramrods or laid it on bark near a fire. As it baked, they listened to the fighting east of their position where the divisions of Confederate brigadier generals Alexander Lawton and David R. "Neighbor" Jones tried to stop the advance of Joe Hooker's First Corps. Despite their relative safety from that fight, Fourth Texan W. E. Barry recalled hunching over his breakfast as stray Federal artillery "shells were bursting over our devoted heads and clipping the limbs of the trees, and scattering them at our feet." Nearby, Jim Polk was holding his ramrod and dough over the fire when a shell exploded nearby, knocking Polk back and breaking the leg of a man not far from him. They were still cooking when one of Lawton's couriers rushed into camp, and the men heard the call "To Arms!" Some men glowered as they left their dough, others ate off their ramrods while they hurried into line.[54]

Hood's 2,000-man division formed up and marched by the right flank, crossing Hagerstown Pike in front of the Dunker Church as Lawton's men fell back around them along with their wounded commander, carried on a litter. Years later, replaying the scene in his mind and knowing what awaited them, Hood marveled at all his men had been through that year, yet they remained "indomitable amid every trial," he observed.[55] Jim Polk remembered the moment as well, noting that "our ranks were so reduced that regiments looked like companies and brigades like regiments."[56] Still, the men were so anxious to engage in battle that accounts have them firing on Federals immediately after clearing the West Woods, before they had formally formed into line and advanced. It reinforced the image, W. T. Hill later admitted, that Hood's Texans sometimes "fought too fast," but it also reinforced the determination Hood sensed.[57]

Hood's division moved toward Miller's field from Smoketown Road. W. T. Hill noticed that the units they were coming up to support, Lawton's men, had lost so many soldiers that Hill could make out their position from the formation of dead men lying in the field rather than the living who were falling back. Before Hill and the rest of Wofford's brigade, a ridge of ground immediately south of the cornfield hid them from the two 12-pound Napoleons of Battery B, Fourth U.S. artillery near David Miller's barn. As Hood's men advanced, however, four more Federal guns would come up, bringing the total to six.[58]

Wofford's and Law's brigades faced north and extended about one-quarter mile to the east just north of Smoketown Road. On the far left, anchored on Hagerstown Pike, were the 77 men of Wade Hampton's Legion under the command of Lt. Col. Martin Gary.[59] To his right was the Eighteenth Georgia, Wofford's old regiment led by Lt. Col. Solon Ruff. To their right were the First Texas under Lt. Col. P. A. Work, Lt. Col. B. F. Carter's Fourth Texas, and finally the Fifth Texas, their ranks so depleted a few weeks earlier at Second Manassas that they were led by a captain, Georgia-born Ike Turner. Though one of the youngest officers on the field, Turner was respected in the ranks for his daring leadership and his quiet constancy. Indeed, amid all the upheaval of officer selections, rejections, and elections between 1861 and 1862, Company K remained loyal to their youthful captain who had helped organize the company.[60]

A collection of outnumbered Federal units opposed the Texas Brigade early that morning, though by the end of the fight, Hood's men would be facing a much larger force. The original opposing units included the Second and Sixth Wisconsin, an undersized brigade under Walter Phelps Jr., the Ninetieth Pennsylvania, and Capt. James Thompson's battery. Law's brigade was opposite Union brigadier general James B. Ricketts's division, which was at that

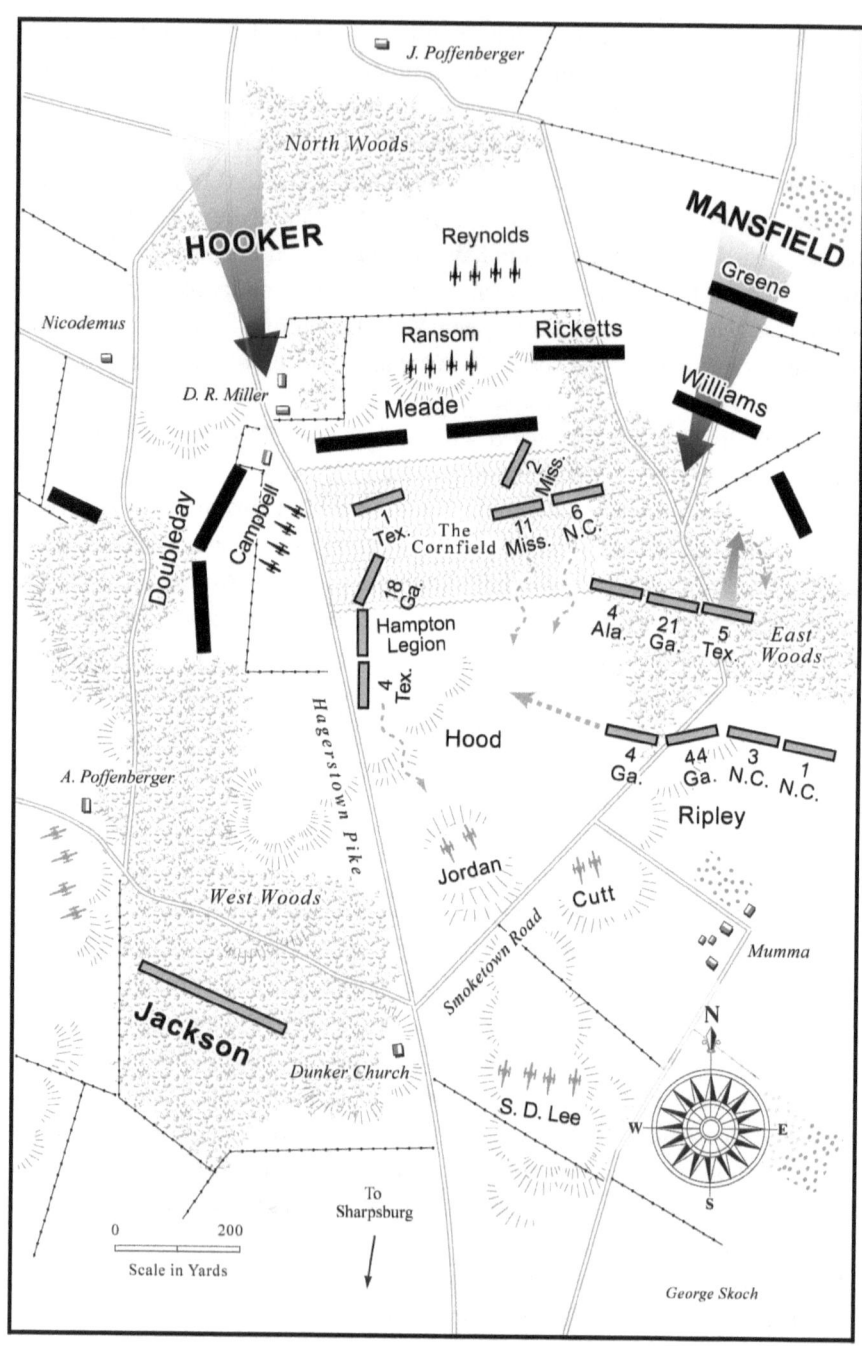

Battle of Antietam, September 17, 1862

moment pushing south through rows of corn and the East Woods. It helped Hood's division that their Federal opponents had been fighting for nearly ninety minutes by this point, while the Confederates were fresh, if hungry. They had barely formed into line when Hood ordered his division forward.[61]

On the left, Hampton's Legion and the Eighteenth Georgia fired a withering volley into the advancing line of John Gibbon's brigade, specifically the Second and Sixth Wisconsin and the Second U.S. Sharpshooters coming down the pike. It cut "like a scythe running through the line," Rufus Dawes recalled, commanding the Sixth Wisconsin. "Two out of every three of the men who went to the front of the line were shot." The Federals who could still move "raced for life" back to the cornfield, where the stalks, surprisingly intact despite all of the fighting, offered some cover.[62] Hood assessed the situation on the right of his line and ordered Ike Turner to shift his Fifth Texans to the far right of the division in the East Woods and assist Law with that Federal threat. Hood also ordered the Fourth Texas to lay down momentarily, though two of Carter's companies failed to hear the order and continued forward. The left of the brigade continued to pour withering fire into the Wisconsin volunteers and U.S. Sharpshooters. Eighteenth Georgian James Lemon watched as the Federals opposite him "shuddered & broke."[63] The Georgians and South Carolinians drove Gibbon and Phelps's men back through the corn until Federal reinforcements began arriving. It was the Seventh Wisconsin and the Nineteenth Indiana, followed by two regiments from Third Brigade commander Marsena Patrick, attacking from a ledge just north of the West Woods. These men slowed the Confederate advance, while fire from Battery B of the Fourth U.S. artillery brought it to a halt.[64]

The Federal artillerymen's double loads of canister tore through the Texas Brigade's left flank. Hood ordered Lieutenant Colonel Carter, who had not quite reached the cornfield, to shift the Fourth Texas to the far left to offer some support. They rushed past Hampton's Legion and fell in with Carter's front running parallel along the pike. The air was so "full of shot and shell," J. M. Polk noted in Company I, that "it seemed almost impossible for a rat to live in such a place." Men sought any kind of cover, even outcroppings of rocks, but there was little they could do but return fire as rapidly as possible. "I didn't take time to load my gun," Polk explained, "for there were plenty of loaded guns lying on the ground by the side of the dead and wounded men, and they were not all Confederates: the Blue and the Gray were all mixed up." Fourth Texan Haywood Brahan also found some cover behind fence rails along the east side of the Hagerstown Pike, and noted wryly that here they enjoyed "the full benefit of Federal minnie bullets from our front, as well as grape and canister from the Federal batteries that swept the Turnpike."[65]

Meanwhile, Hampton's Legion and the Eighteenth Georgia, moving to Carter's right, also shifted part of their line to the left to return fire into the West Woods but also to continue their assault on Battery B. The Eighteenth Georgia surged forward, and James Lemon staggered as the Napoleons "blew large gaps in our lines." The Georgians concentrated their fire on the gunners, hoping to silence the crews at a distance of less than seventy yards. They advanced again, but another blast from the battery tore through the ranks and Lemon saw his wife's brothers, William and Marcus Davenport, cut down together, "united in death as in life."[66]

The Eighteenth Georgia made three separate assaults on Battery B, but the Federal artillery fire "produced great destruction," tearing through the Eighteenth Georgia and the infantrymen of Hampton's Legion. The forces were so close together that the guns, firing double loads of canister, destroyed "whole ranks" and left corpses "piled on top of each other."[67] Opposite Gibbon's right and trying to maintain some sense of order in Hampton's Legion, Lt. Col. Martin Gary looked for their flag, knowing that when the men could no longer hear commands they could at least stay somewhat formed around their regimental colors. Gary marveled at the astonishing rate at which it dropped and rose again. "Herod Wilson, of Company F, the bearer of the colors ... [was] shot down," Gary observed. "They were raised by James Estes, of Company E, and he was shot down. They were then taken up by D. P. Poppenheim, of Company A, and he, too, was shot down. Maj. J. H. Dingle Jr., then caught them and began to advance with them, exclaiming, 'Legion, follow your colors!'" until Dingle fell along the turnpike, not fifty yards from the Federal line. Gary then picked up the colors himself until another man volunteered to carry them forward as Gary worked to direct his men's fire.[68]

While the three left regiments were engaged along the turnpike, Work's First Texans continued to advance. Their right was left exposed by several factors: when the Fifth Texas shifted toward Law's right, when Hood ordered the Fourth Texas to the Hagerstown Pike, and by Law's axis of advance. That vulnerability was amplified when the First Texas noticed portions of Abner Doubleday's division began retreating. Sensing weakness, the Texans rushed forward despite Work's shouts to hold the line. With discipline never their strong suit, the First Texas raced on until they came to a fence along the northern edge of the cornfield. There they stumbled into about 600 men of Lt. Col. Robert Anderson's brigade of Pennsylvania Reserves, supported by Dunbar Ransom's battery.[69]

Anderson's men were lying on the ground, with some concealed by fence rails they had stacked before them. Armed with smoothbores and firing buck and ball, they could just make out the Texans' legs beneath the smoke and their flag. At first Anderson thought it was a U.S. flag. When he realized they were Confederates, the Texans were just thirty yards away. The Pennsylvanians fired a volley, and a collective groan came up from Work's men as they stumbled backward. It may have been here that Company I's Capt. W. A. Bedell fell when a ball tore through his face. It broke his cheek bone, continued under his right eye, and exited behind his right ear. Moments later, a second ball cut through his shoulder, but the pain was so much less than the first that Bedell declared this a flesh wound. A third round nearly killed him but flew high and left a hole in his hat.[70]

Texans were on the ground all around Bedell, but the officers and men still able to fight rallied and organized. What the First Texas lacked in discipline, they made up for in determination and courage. Having formed, they lunged forward once more, and then again, but they could not break the Pennsylvanians. Compounding the problem was that in their ill-advised dash after Doubleday's men, the First Texas advanced at least 150 yards ahead of the rest of their division. They were fighting almost within Federal lines, and their lines of sight were almost nonexistent. The corn stalks all around them stood about seven feet high, making it impossible to see (or be seen) beyond a few feet. All of this contributed to the astonishingly high casualties the First Texas suffered, and Lieutenant Colonel Work's difficulty maintaining command and control.[71]

Work called desperately for reinforcements. Capt. John Woodward of Company G and Acting Adj. J. Winkfield Shropshire were both sent to request support, as was Pvt. Amos G. Hanks of Company F, and finally Private Hicks, but reinforcements never came. Work later discovered that Shropshire and Hanks were killed, while Hicks was hit so badly that his leg would require amputation. Work was struggling to bring his men together for a disciplined withdrawal when Maj. Matt Dale approached and reported that nearly half the regiment was down and they needed to withdraw before they lost the rest. He had to cup his hand around his mouth and shout into Work's ear to be heard, and just after completing his warning, Dale fell, killed instantly at Work's side.[72]

Concluding that his men could no longer advance or defend an attack, and worried that their line of retreat could be cut off, Work ordered them to fall back. What was left of the First Texas made their way back through David Miller's field, still under heavy fire. The Federal rounds, Work noticed, "when striking the hillside ground raised puffs of dust, just as in the beginning of a shower do large drops of rain on a dusty road." He stumbled to the ground when a round hit and bent the scabbard of his dress sword, which then caught between his legs. Scrambling to his feet, Work continued on with his men.[73]

Somewhere along their withdrawal, they realized that they had left their regimental colors, a gift from the brigade's first commander's wife. Made from her wedding dress, the First Texans called it Mrs. Wigfall's flag. Work had seen it when they started falling back, but the color-bearer, like others before him, was wounded or possibly killed. The corn made it impossible to know for sure, though the men later learned that John Hanson, James Day, Charles H. Kingsley, and James K. Malone were all wounded while carrying the colors; all would survive. Significantly, they were all 1861 volunteers, and all but Hanson suffered discipline problems within the regiment. Both Kingsley and Day were returned to the ranks after promotions in 1863, and that same year James Malone was arrested by local authorities in Richmond. Their blend of ill-discipline and uncommon courage while trying to raise the regimental colors at Antietam captured the character of the First Texas.[74]

Years later, William Barry spoke of seeing the flag after it and he were captured by the Ninth Pennsylvania Reserves. He learned that thirteen men lay dead around and on it when the Pennsylvanians found the First Texas colors, and from the description of the scene, Barry was certain one of them was Robert Gaston. He had enlisted with his brother William in Company H of the First Texas in 1861, the same year Robert, writing from Richmond, insisted that "the South ought never to allow Virginia [to be] overrun" and encouraged his parents to "tell all those who want to fight to come on & they will undoubtedly get a showing."[75]

Once Work realized their colors were missing, he considered sending a man back for it, but they had no idea where it was, and advancing Federals were within forty yards on his left and rear. He insisted that they would have to continue without it.[76] Finally, they reached a swale and farm lane that offered some cover, likely their original position along Smoketown Road. Here Work reorganized his men, along with other stragglers who had sought cover from the intense fight. Hood found them there and led them back to the

Dunker Church and into the West Woods. They reunited with Ruff's Georgians, Gary's South Carolinians, and Carter's Fourth Texas who had all pulled back about the same time the First Texas did. These men made their way into the West Woods.[77]

Meanwhile, Ike Turner's Fifth Texas and Law's brigade continued their fight in the East Woods. Captain Turner called for reinforcements when increased Federal fire indicated that Maj. Gen. Joseph K. F. Mansfield's Twelfth Corps had advanced to strengthen the Union lines. Some of D. H. Hill's men, from Samuel Garland's old brigade, arrived, though these men of D. K. McRae's brigade were actually sent to help strengthen A. H. Colquitt's right flank on the western side of the East Woods. McRae would later report that "confusion ensued" because of "conflicting orders" and a cry to cease firing because they were shooting their own men. In the midst of this, a Federal force appeared on their right, and shouts went down the line that they were flanked. Suddenly, the men broke and ran.[78]

From the Fifth Texas's perspective, however, these men were here to support them, and instead McRae's brigade had barely fired a volley before they broke and ran. Mark Smither was stunned, and Ike Turner was furious. He "called out to our men to fire at them as they ran out and then as the men prepared to do so, laughingly countermanded the order," Smither recalled.[79] Turner realized with disgust that his men were out of ammunition, support was not coming, and Federals were less than 100 feet away. Having noted that the rest of his division had already pulled back, he "deemed it prudent to fall back also."[80]

It was about 8:30 a.m. when Turner's men moved back toward the West Woods. The rest of Hood's division had pulled back an hour earlier. Federals and Confederates would engage in similarly brutal fights for the rest of the day, but Hood's men, what was left of them, would not reengage. As Hood brought his division together and checked on his old brigade, he was stunned by how few of them had made it back from their morning fight. It had seemed to last hours, but it was really only about thirty minutes in length. Hood would not know for sure until his officers filed reports, along with the surgeons, but looking at his men, lying quietly among the oaks and hickory, some asking about friends, many not talking at all, Hood knew their losses were staggering, especially when combined with their previous battles that year.

As the men formed for muster and surgeons filed reports, Hood discovered that B. F. Carter and Ike Turner had lost nearly half their regiments—killed, wounded, or missing—while Solon Ruff's Georgians suffered nearly 60 percent casualties, and Martin Gary's South Carolinians lost almost 80 percent. But it was the First Texas losses that stunned everyone.

Of the 211 men P. A. Work had led across the Hagerstown Pike and through Miller's fields, 182 of them were killed, wounded, or missing. No one remained from Company F, and Company A had just one survivor. Company C could offer the macabre boast of two soldiers, and Company E had three. Company M had the best survival rate, if one could call it that: eleven of its members survived the fight. With over 86 percent casualties, the First Texas had suffered the highest percentage of losses of any regiment in a single battle in the entire war. While the rest of the regiments of Hood's Brigade lost fewer men, the brigade still reported 64 percent overall losses. When General Lee asked Hood that night what happened to his "splendid division," Hood nearly shook with anger and sorrow. My men "are lying on the field where you sent them, sir," he replied. "My division has been almost wiped out."[81]

In the days and weeks after Antietam, the brigade's families in Texas, Georgia, and South Carolina heard about the battle in newspapers before they got specifics about their loved ones. Cecelia Morse confessed that "every battle has so much terror attached to it that I dread to hear," but then admitted that by mid-October, she had learned from "Mr. Edey"—likely Arthur Edey, the *Houston Tri-Weekly Telegraph* editor who served as an agent for the Fifth Texas at the Texas Depot in Richmond—that her husband, Henry, and his brother William were well when he had last heard from the Fifth Texas. But Cecelia had not heard from Henry directly since he was in Frederick City, Maryland, marching toward Sharpsburg.[82]

In Oso, Texas, Lizzie Penn Menefee was still mourning her cousin Robert Sullivan, killed at Gaines's Mill, when word arrived that her husband, Quin, had been badly wounded. Patrick Penn struggled to give his sister all the details he had, but he had been too sick to fight at Antietam, and everything he knew was secondhand. He assured her that Quin was alive, but he had been captured, and Patrick was sure that surgeons had amputated his right leg. It was too badly broken to save. He promised Lizzie, though, that Quin was in good hands and with fellow Texans. Still, Pat was upset that he was not with him. The rest of Patrick Penn's letter revealed just how deadly and confusing the battle had been. Ed Crockett, married to Quin's niece, was missing. "Taken prisoner or killed, no one knows which. He was one of the best men that God ever created. He was loved by every man in the Company," Penn wrote. "Our

Company [F] had over 30 men when the fight commenced. 22 were wounded and missing."[83]

Of the four friends and cousins from Oso who enlisted in 1861 and 1862, Robert Sullivan was dead, Ed Crockett was missing, and Quin Menefee was badly wounded. They reflected the diversity of motivations and suffering in the ranks. Robert was a quiet thinker who pondered religion and politics, and was often disgusted that camp life was so intellectually empty. Patrick was less reflective and struggled with his faith. He promised his sister Lizzie that he had "been trying to be a better man... but I believe it only makes me worse. I wish I was a Christian but I cannot make myself one and I do not know how to approach the Mercy Seat in such a way that God will help me." Still, he had promised that spring, "I will try to get no worse."[84]

Quin, the Methodist minister, had the strongest faith and the maturity of a thirty-year-old husband and father. He had postponed enlisting until March 1862, and he struggled at first to adjust. Robert had teased Lizzie that when her husband arrived in camp that spring "he had been complaining for sometime, but is about and now able for duty. He is weary of soldiering and sometimes deprecates the secession of the South, but I tell him, it is his secession from his wife and children and molasses that hurts him."[85]

Quin Menefee slowly adjusted to camp life, and at the request of Lt. J. D. Roberdeau, Menefee had preached to the Fifth Texas that summer. His religious devotion gave him comfort after Robert's death and may have been part of his increased determination to stay in ranks that summer. Some of the men suggested that Menefee apply for a chaplaincy, but he refused. "I prefer serving my country and my God in the double capacity of soldier and preacher," Menefee explained to Lizzie.[86]

After Gaines's Mill, Robert's death, and a summer of marching and small battles, Quin Menefee seems to have hardened as a soldier. In early August, in his last letter home before he was so badly wounded at Antietam, Menefee wrote a long letter to his young son, Willie. Quin promised that the next battle "cannot come too soon for me, for I am anxious to have the last yankee killed whose mean heart would prompt him to come down to our own loved South on a mission of murder." He warned Willie, "I may be killed or die of disease before I see you all again, but thank God I feel that I will fall (if fall I must) in a righteous cause, and that is better than all things else." For now, at least, it looked like Quin Menefee would survive his Antietam wound and amputation. Even better, he was coming home.[87]

For other families, though, Antietam proved far more destructive. Josh Kindred, the soldier who stayed behind with the wounded at Antietam whom Patrick Penn mentioned in his letter, was one of six brothers in Company F of the Fourth Texas. Their father, Alexander Kindred, had been the postmaster in Gonzales, Texas, until just before the war began. At the age of fifty-one, he joined a local militia force for home defense in 1861, and that same spring, his twenty-one-year-old son, Elisha, joined the Mustang Grays, who later became Company F. As was the case with many of the men in the ranks, the 1850s had been good to the Kindreds. When the decade began, Alexander and Sarah Kindred were living in Alabama with $1,000 in land and eight children between the ages of twenty and two.[88] Ten years later, Alexander was a wealthy merchant in Gonzales with a combined declared wealth of $11,500. Elisha was living on the farm next door, where he helped his widowed aunt, Lucy Threadgill Kindred, who estimated her personal and real estate wealth at $10,500. Between the two of them, Alexander and his sister-in-law, Lucy Kindred, owned fifteen slaves to help work their properties.[89]

Only Elisha joined the Fourth Texas in the summer of 1861, but by March 1862, brothers Joshua (32), John (28), Joseph (20), and James (16) had joined Elisha, who was promoted to second lieutenant on September 11. Six days later, in their desperate fight along the Hagerstown Pike, Joseph and James were wounded, John was killed, and Joshua remained behind to help care for them and other Texans like Quin Menefee. Joseph never recovered, dying of his wounds, though there was so much suffering that the army was not sure exactly when he died. The youngest, James, was given a furlough to return home to Texas to recover. He never rejoined Company F. But Joshua returned to the Texas Brigade after he was exchanged, and he and Elisha, later promoted to captain, would continue on in Company F as well.[90]

Andrew and Alexander Erskine were likely standing near the Kindred brothers in that fight along Hagerstown Pike. Though wounded in the left arm and twice in his side, Alexander struggled most with his brother's death. "Oh! how desolate is my sad heart at the loss of that brother twice endeared by the hardships and perils we have passed through together," he told Ann. "But if my heart is so sad, what must yours be, my sister, deprived of a husband and a friend." Alexander tried to explain what happened, but everything had been so chaotic: "Our dear one suffered no pain in death for he was shot through the temples ... in making a terrible charge on the enemy." Alexander had been too wounded to recover Andrew's body, but he assured Ann that Maj.

Moses George had promised to bury Andrew. "I cannot comfort you, but can only commend you to the tender mercies of our Heavenly Father," Alexander wrote, praying that God "would have mercy on you and your little children."[91] The year 1862 had proved tragic for her family. Andrew's father died in May, and Ann's brother was killed in August. And now, with Andrew's death, Ann was a thirty-two-year-old widow with a ferry, an inn, a cotton gin, a gristmill, a farm, and a ranch to run with six sons ranging from thirteen years to nine months old and a widowed mother to help care for.

Like Alexander Erskine, First Texas captain William Gaston struggled to explain Antietam to his parents. His brother, 1st Lt. Robert Gaston, was missing, and even two months later, William still had no answers. "I have been inquiring and hunting for him ever since he was lost. I can hear nothing from him," William told their father. "I feel that he was slain although I cannot give him up yet. There is some chance for him to be alive yet. He may have been badly wounded and still in the hands of the enemy. There have been some of my boys sent back from Maryland that I thought was killed. They saw nothing of Robert but say he may be there somewhere as our boys were scattered all over Maryland," William added hopefully. "I have felt miserable since he has been gone. . . . I hope you all will not think hard of me for not giving you all the particulars of his fate when it was out of my power. . . . We were overpowered by the Enemy and compelled to give up the battlefield leaving behind our killed and wounded with some prisoners & were not permitted to go on the field after the fight." Their father was planning a trip to Maryland to continue the search for Robert, and William tried to convince him of its futility: "If Robert can be found I will find him before I come. If killed, we will have to give him up for a time."[92]

Robert's death broke some of William's determination that he needed to fight for the Confederacy in Virginia. "I intend to come home this winter if I can. I may have to resign to do so but I think I have tried it long enough to satisfy me," he told his father. In the end, William remained in uniform, but he and Alexander Erskine transferred to Texas, where they could continue the fight but be closer to their families and homes. They remained devoted to Confederate independence, but the year 1862 broke their willingness to make sacrifices on the level that service in the Texas Brigade required.

Accounts from countless units recognized the bravery of the Texans at Antietam, and they were accurate, but the other truth was that the brigade was nearly destroyed that year. As Henry Travis, a private in Company H of the

Fourth Texas, explained, "There has been a heap of hard fighting down here," referring to the summer battles of Gaines's Mill, Second Manassas, and Antietam. "The Texas Brigade has been cut up pretty bad. The Texas Brigade has got a brave name here for fighting," of which Travis was proud. The problem, though, was that "It will not do it any good if it gets in another fight or two, for it will all be killed up," he explained to his sister. "The Texas boys go ahead in the fight."[93]

There was something about Travis's final comment that resonated throughout the army. The Texas Brigade had earned a reputation as one of the best units in Lee's army, and in the fall of 1862, he was calling for more of them. Four days after the Battle of Antietam, Lee contacted Texas senator Louis T. Wigfall about the "new Texas Regiment" the senator had promised to recruit. "I need them much," Lee explained. "I rely upon those we have in all tight places and fear I have to call upon them too often—They have fought grandly, nobly, and we must have more of them—Please make every possible exertion to get them in and send them on to me—You must help us in this matter," Lee implored. "With a few more such regiments as those which Hood now has, as an example of daring and bravery I could feel much more confident of the results of the campaign."[94] Wigfall, with his usual enthusiasm, assured Lee that he would soon have more Texans. He had "no doubt the Regts are now on their way here." In truth, there were no new regiments to join the Texas Brigade that fall and few would respond to the recruiting drive the following spring of 1863.[95]

In the three major battles of 1862, the Texas Brigade suffered 1,786 casualties.[96] This reflected one of the unusual facts about this unit. Whereas most Civil War soldiers died of disease rather than in combat, the opposite was true about the Texas Brigade. The majority of their deaths occurred on the battlefield or as a result of battle-related wounds. Shocked by the brutality of the fighting in 1862, some of the survivors who were officers and could secure transfers to other units returned home. But the vast majority of the officers and enlisted men remained steadfast in the beliefs that led them to Virginia in 1861 and 1862. When they were exchanged from Federal prisons, they made their way back to the Texas Brigade, not to their homes. Similarly, the majority of wounded men recovering at home in 1862 would return next spring for the 1863 campaign season. They were getting a bit tired of their reputation for "belicosity," as W. P. Townsend described it. The men, he confided to his wife, often raised a brow and complained that their next assignment would be "to charge a fleet of Yankee gunboats." But they were also incredibly proud of what they had contributed toward building an independent Confederacy. "Our regiment has gained quite a reputation in the Army," Townsend grinned, "so much so that every man and officer has '4 Texas' written in his cap." In that letter written shortly before the Battle of Second Manassas, Townsend included a description of their fight at Gaines's Mill so his wife, Elmira, could share it with their children, and he promised to send a copy of Hood's official report for her to read to their young son Tom.[97]

Despite all of the casualties, and even defeats like Antietam, Hood's Texans still very much believed that their best hopes for the future lay in protecting the lives and the laws that the Confederacy promised to preserve. William Townsend captured that sentiment in mid-October 1862 while recovering from his Antietam wound. Looking at his amputated leg, he confessed to Almira: "I will (I am afraid) have to leave the service. This is a bitter pill to me." Townsend had fought as a second lieutenant under Col. Jefferson Davis in the Mississippi Rifles in the Mexican War. An early and ardent secessionist, he had much to defend against the North's push for the expansion of free territory. With a combined wealth of nearly $40,000 in 1860 and the owner of almost thirty enslaved men, women, and children, any threat to the survival and expansion of slavery was a serious concern to the Townsends. Like most southern whites, they did not believe northern efforts to limit the expansion of slavery had anything to do with morality. They saw it as a power struggle; a strategy to check the decades-long political strength of the Democratic Party, which was grounded in the South. Townsend reflected those strong beliefs that ran through the Texas Brigade, and he never wavered in his devotion to Confederate independence. "I shall try to get some place in which I can serve the Country—no one labored harder to bring on this war than I did—and no one regrets more to leave the service," he mourned.[98]

Determined but exhausted, Hood's Texas Brigade marched back to Virginia with the rest of Lee's army in late September 1862. Lee's men were too weak and too few in number to stay in Maryland, especially with their backs to the swollen Potomac River. They buried what dead they could, but some of their dead remained exposed in territory under Federal control. These included men from the Fourth Texas, Fourteenth Georgia, and Hampton's Legion, who had fallen in piles along the Hagerstown Pike. They would have been on the minds of the Texas Brigade as they marched toward Martinsburg. Those Confederates were also on the minds of the Union men left behind in Sharpsburg.

One of those soldiers was Hugh Perkins, a private in the Seventh Wisconsin, who spent the weeks after Antietam calmly working his mind through the destruction he had seen, that he had been a part of, and marveling at how little it bothered him. As he looked at the Confederate corpses laying in the sun, Perkins grimaced. "There is so many and they smell so. . . . They're all black now as nigers, and the bubbles coming out of their mouth as if they was boiling inside. They will turn black in two hours after they die. Some say it is on acct. of not having salt, and some say it is the gun powder, and the whiskey that they drink," Perkins explained to his friend, Herbert Frisbie, back home in Waushara County, Wisconsin.[99]

Like many of the men he had killed, Perkins came from a middle-class farming family. Also like many of the Texans, the Perkins clan had made their way westward in the 1850s. His Vermont-born father and Scottish-born mother, Chapman and Margaret Perkins, lived in Leon, Wisconsin, when the war began and were raising five children the year Lincoln was elected. When their oldest son, Hugh, enlisted in 1861, he expected some of the challenges of a soldier's life, but he admitted that he had "seen . . . a good deal more than I expected to." So many "comrades and tentmates have fell on each side of me," but somehow he had survived. The battles of 1862 had hardened him, Perkins explained to Frisbie. "I have had over one hundred good fair shots at the gray backs, and I have got so that I can shoot just as cool and deliberate at them as I can at a prairie chicken or pidgeon. I know of three that I have made bite the dust, besides a great many others that I am pretty sure I hit," he boasted. "It has got so that it does not excight me any more to be in action than to be in a corn field hoeing, or digging potatoes.[100]

Fighting in Company I on September 17, Perkins was about seventy-five or one hundred yards west of the Hagerstown Pike, close to the eastern edge of the West Woods. It was Perkins and the Seventh Wisconsin, along with other Union forces, that devastated the Texas Brigade's exposed left flank, pouring fire into the Fourth Texas, Hampton's Legion, and the Eighteenth Georgia. The fighting became so intense that Perkins insisted the Wisconsin men took no prisoners: "The command was given to cease firing, but it was of no use. The boys had been fooled too much by the gray backs to let one slip," Perkins scowled. "They would stick up their hands and hullow and the next minute fall dead. There was not a man ever reached the woods, and strange to say there was not a man wounded on either side," he noted, looking at the ground where

Andrew Erskine and the Davenport brothers had fallen. "They was all killed instantly."[101]

Five days later, Perkins was still processing that fight. "We were brought up in the rear of a brigade of Rebels, and laid in the woods and fired 20 rounds before we was discovered.... piling them in heaps as they lay behind a stone fence. After they discovered our position they threw down their arms and broke for the woods (what was left of them). Then we had fun picking them off," he noted. "We killed every one of them; even a wounded man could not be seen creeping off without being plugged by a minnie. They refused to surrender to us, but they had to to our minnie balls."[102]

The intensity of the fight became especially clear when the Wisconsin private helped to bury the Union dead. "It was an awful sight," Perkins explained. "When we fought them their whole line of battle behind the stone breastwork was covered with dead so thick that you could lay them all lengthways the whole length and they would all touch one another." The fire from Hood's men had been equally intense. Perkins found some of the Union dead "setting up in the verry act of loading, with their cartridges in their mouth and gun still in their hands."[103] He was proud that "Gen. McClellan calls us the iron brigade," but he noted the same thing the Texas Brigade had observed: "By gaining this name, Herbert, we have lost from the brigade seventeen hundred and fifty men."[104] Burying his fellow soldiers sickened Perkins. "It was an awful job. It made me feel bad to see our poor boys laying dead," he mourned. "But the Rebs didn't have no more effect on me than so many sheep."[105] So they left the Confederates in the open. For elite units like Gibbon's brigade and Hood's Texans, the Battle of Antietam only hardened their dedication to their causes. Indeed, as Capt. William A. Bedell recovered from the lead ball that broke his cheek bone and exited behind his ear, he looked forward to returning to the fight. As soon as he was exchanged, Bedell told his widowed mother, he would rejoin the First Texas with "fresh ardor," and he did. Despite an earlier wound at Malvern Hill and receiving another wound in 1864 at the Battle of the Wilderness, Bedell always rejoined First Texas, where he remained through the end of the war.[106]

THE COST OF REPUTATION
Emancipation, Suffolk, and Gettysburg

As the Texas Brigade marched toward Virginia, they worried about the men they had left behind and fumed about their defeat. They had seen plenty of death, and they, too, had prioritized the burial of their own dead on the fields they had held. They could likely picture in their minds everything Perkins had described about their dead comrades left behind. Worse, though, they were positive the entire defeat had been avoidable. Fifth Texas commander Ike Turner asked for support four times and received none.[1] William Wofford lodged similar complaints, arguing that the men "deserved a better fate than to have been, as they were, sacrificed for the want of proper support."[2] General Hood agreed. "I am thoroughly of the opinion," he explained, that "had General McLaws arrived by 8:30 a.m. our victory on the left would have been as thorough, quick, and complete as upon the plains of Manassas on August 30."[3] Lieutenant Colonel Work, commanding the First Texas, was the most cutting of all. "If required to carry strong positions in a few more engagements, and, after carrying them, hold them unaided and alone," Work warned, "this regiment must soon become annihilated and extinct without having accomplished any material or permanent good."[4]

Lee's pleas for more Texas units and the admiration of other soldiers and commanders within the army assured them they were right. Years later, the men smiled at the story of the British observer, Col. Garnet Wolseley, frowning as the "Ragged First" Texas marched past in their retreat from Sharpsburg. Most of the men were barefoot, and they limped from the cuts and scrapes on the soles of their feet. Briar scratches covered their lower legs, and the cuffs of their pants and sleeves were shredded. Men like Capt. D. K. Rice of the First Texas had tossed their blankets away because they were "completely riddled; four different balls struck it, and as it was folded, they made over 70 holes through it, making it worthless."⁵ But Lee loved them. "Never mind their raggedness," he had told Colonel Wolseley. "The enemy never sees the backs of my Texans."⁶

Lee's loyalty and admiration for the Texas Brigade inspired a tattered determination that fall. As frustrated as they were by the lack of support they received at Sharpsburg, it is significant to note that none of that shook their faith in Lee, Longstreet, Hood, or Confederate victory. Indeed, their confidence in victory while retreating from Maryland underscored their incredible faith in themselves and their commanders. After listing their casualties and admitting that "I think it must be my turn to catch it next, I have had so many narrow escapes," D. K. Rice boasted to his uncle, "The enemy has lost something over 40,000 prisoners in the last thirty days. Is it not glorious?" Rice observed that "Everyone here believes we will be in Maryland again soon—very soon."⁷ The Texas Brigade was certain that failures at Antietam had nothing to do with them. Indeed, most Confederates did not see the battle as a major defeat.

Lee's army arrived in Martinsburg, Virginia, on September 19 and rested there until September 27, when they shifted to Winchester. They remained there for the next four weeks, enjoying some rest, getting resupplied, and continuing to crow about the victories they knew would soon be theirs. Tom Goree declared in mid-October that Lee's army "will soon be in better fighting condition than at any time since the battles around Richmond."⁸ Part of his optimism came from word that new uniforms and shoes—their first issue since early July—were coming into Lee's army. It would be several more weeks, however, before these reached the Texas Brigade, and they were desperately needed.

The brigade tried to bathe and wash their clothes when possible, but most of them were wearing the only items they owned, which were covered with lice.⁹ Rations were terrible as well. The often cranky Tom Selman was especially disgusted by the "poor beef with little salt, flour & no shortening." When General Hood paused during a visit to camp and "took great pains in telling me how to work my dough," Selman was not impressed. "I listened . . . carefully, but thought at the same time that I knew more about the business than the general. He asked us if we got enough to eat. All of us told him we did not except old [F. M.] Ramsey who said we got plenty. He only said so to bring himself up in notice," Selman frowned. "If it had [not] been for him our rations would have been increased."¹⁰

In fairness to Private Ramsey, there was not much Hood could do about their rations. Lee purchased or seized flour and wheat in the Shenandoah Valley, and in late September Quarter Master Gen. Abraham C. Myers's department had shipped seven thousand pairs of shoes to Lee's army and another ten thousand would soon be shipped to Virginia from warehouses in Tennessee.[11] Despite this, in mid-November, 2,000 men in Lee's army were still without shoes, and another 3,000 wore some semblance of footwear that would not last through Christmas.[12]

When the inspector-general for the Army of Northern Virginia, Col. Edwin J. Harvie, walked through the camps of Hood's two brigades in November, he confirmed all of this. The men "badly clothed and shod." One-third of the Texas Brigade was without shoes. The Fifth Texas and Hampton's Legion received a positive report on the condition of their weapons, though each unit was about forty to fifty guns short. The First Texas received just the opposite. Harvie declared them in "very bad order," as was the camp as a whole. He blamed this on "inexcusable neglect on the part of its officers." Harvie suggested implementing a fine that each man had to pay for lost weaponry, but Hood ignored him.[13]

Hood knew his citizen-soldiers never had particularly tidy camps, but the biggest issue was the continued lack of supplies. Tom Selman reported "the meanest rations . . . we ever had in the way of flour" as late as November 23. "It was the blackest I ever saw & had worms in it an inch long." Col. J. C. G. Key of the Fourth Texas ordered the men to wash their clothes, but no one complied. "We knew [it] was very necessary," Selman admitted, "yet we thought it was very impertinent when we only had one suit which was on our backs & not a pound of soap in the regt. Besides, [there was] quite a stiff breeze blowing from the north [so] the order was contemptably violated." At drill the next morning, Colonel Key "insisted that his order should be strictly obeyed," at least on "the first warm day that came."[14]

Despite these challenges, the Texans in Lee's army still believed in their commanders. At Antietam, Thomas J. Goree told his mother, "Hood's Texas Brigade sustained a heavier loss than any other," and once again, "it was always in front and in the thickest of the fight." He took tremendous pride in the role his brothers, Langston and Ed, played in that battle and in the brigade's reputation in Lee's army. Goree was almost certain Hood would be promoted and insisted: "No man deserves it more. He is one of the finest young officers I ever saw . . . and had we many more of the like sort at Sharpsburg, we would have whipped the Yankees worse than they were ever whipped before."[15]

Still, some men like Fifth Texan Rufus King Felder worried that the Texas Brigade had "been in so many fights and ha[d] suffered so much they would be willing never to go in another fight." He heard rumors that the brigade might be sent home for the winter on furlough, but he suspected they were untrue. "I think another big battle is pending and we have gained too great a reputation to be sent off," he explained.[16] Despite their sacrifices, Waters Berryman still preferred fighting in Virginia. With Lee's army, he explained, "I have killed more Yankees here in a week than" other Texas soldiers in the Trans-Mississippi West "will kill during the war where they are." He admitted to his mother that "It looks bad to kill up one another, but those words 'Rights and Liberty' must be sustained no matter how much blood it cost."[17]

Worn down and undersupplied, Hood's Texas Brigade rested for much of the rest of 1862 and into early 1863. After spending October in Winchester, they moved toward Culpeper and eventually Fredericksburg, Virginia, in late November. They had a few hard marches and several call to arms in the night, but most of those proved to be false alarms. The brigade was in line of the Battle of Fredericksburg on December 13, 1862, but they never engaged in the fight.

While Confederate supply slowly improved in 1863, three significant changes affected the brigade that winter. The first was the organization of the Army of Northern Virginia in November. Longstreet's and Jackson's wings officially became the First and Second Corps, respectively. Hood, now a major general, had two more brigades added to his division. Within the Texas Brigade, the Eighteenth Georgia and the infantry companies of Wade Hampton's much-reduced Legion were shifted out of the brigade as Lee's army was reorganized along state lines (for the most part). The Texans were sorry to see the Georgians and South Carolinians go, but they were replaced with an equally hard-fighting unit, the Third Arkansas Infantry. The Arkansans, the only other unit of men in Lee's army from west of the Mississippi, would remain with the Texas Brigade through the end of the war and were key to helping the unit rebuild and strengthen their ranks. Commanded by Col. Van H. Manning, the Third Arkansas earned a good reputation for their fighting at Antietam, and the men grew to respect each other, even to the point where the Texans nicknamed the Razorbacks the "Third Texas."

The second major change came with a command shift in the brigade. When William Wofford left the unit with his Eighteenth Georgians, Brig. Gen. Jerome Bonaparte Robertson of the Fifth Texas replaced him. Robertson's promotion to brigade command proved a mixed blessing. In some ways, he helped them deal with the problem of supply because he was such a strong advocate for his men. Tom Selman, who rarely had a kind word for his commanders, noted that somehow Robertson ensured that their food rations improved.[18] He also became known throughout the brigade for his tendency to defend men who stole food when supplies ran low. It was against orders, but their hunger, in his opinion, overrode such matters. The men praised Robertson, a surgeon by training, for his dedication to their care, even if they did see it as a bit motherly, which led to Robertson's nickname as "Aunt Pollie" and "Old Bob." They enjoyed their reputation in Lee's army for ensuring that they were well supplied, regardless of whether it was from need or simple desire.[19]

While he cared for his men, Robertson struggled with mastering the more martial skills of his job, and this proved problematic in a unit that expected much from their commanders. He found it difficult to maintain a level of discipline that satisfied him, and he ruffled feathers when he tried to assert his authority through drill. Indeed, that destroyed Tom Selman's early appreciation for Robertson. In early December, the Fourth Texan shook his head when Robertson "took the brigade this morning & marched it round the whole encampment just to show them a line of battle which he had timed out. The boys all cussed a good deal but had to stand it." The next day, Robertson took them around again, frustrating the men who insisted that they were well past the need of mastering drill and discipline.[20]

Years later, brigade historian Joseph Polley tried to explain the difference between Hood and their other commanders. Discussing one of their last commanders, John Gregg, and Robertson, Polley explained, "Each of these was brave and capable and his memory is yet cherished in the hearts of the soldiers he commanded; but neither had the personal magnetism of Hood, nor the swinging dash and reckless yet cool disregard of danger, which, from the outset, won the love and admiration of a brigade composed of boys just flowering into manhood." Neither of them, Polley continued, "made as just an estimate as Hood, of Texas character, nor felt and acted in such accord with it."[21]

The differences between Hood's leadership style and Robertson's were never so clear as when the brigade was returning to Richmond after they were ordered to join Lee's army near Ashland in March 1863. Their orders had been canceled after a tiring march, and the men were frustrated at the wasted journey. They spent the night in the woods and then resumed their march back to Richmond in a snowstorm. As evening fell and they approached the capital, the brigade "disintegrated," Joe Polley explained. "Every man of it, save the small minority of teetotalers," made "a flank movement" and went "in search of warming liquid refreshments." When Robertson looked back to check his column, he was horrified by how many men had left the unit. "Where in the hell is the Texas Brigade?" he shouted, and was about to give orders for the men to be rounded up and arrested, when Hood rode over. He may have been a West Pointer, Polley explained, but Hood was "fairly well acquainted with the Texas and Arkansas temperament and taste. 'Never mind, General—never mind,'" Hood advised Robertson. "You'll get them back in the morning, or at any rate in time to lead them into the next fight."[22]

A third factor that winter that proved especially helpful to the Texans' care in quarters were the fund-raising efforts of their families at home, Richmonders nearby, and Fourth Texas chaplain Nicholas Davis. In November, Davis published a plea titled "Texans Barefooted" in the *Richmond Whig* asking locals to help provide shoes and socks for the Texans, whose own families could not always get clothing and other items to their men. The brigade would continue to fight for Virginians, but would Virginia accept that aid while allowing soldiers to suffer, Davis asked? Well aware of the shortages that plagued the entire army, and that most Virginians had their own men to care for, Davis kept his request low. He asked for just "one hundred pairs of shoes and five hundred pairs of socks." Considering Colonel Harvie's report, the brigade needed about three times that number, but the response from Richmond was impressive. The shoes and socks arrived along with nearly five hundred dollars, more than two dozen rugs, nearly 150 pairs of pants, more than one hundred shirts, almost as many gloves, and a host of smaller items.[23] The Texans would repay the favor to Virginians in Fredericksburg after the December battle devastated their town, donating six thousand dollars raised in their ranks, including four hundred dollars that came from the Hood's Minstrels shows performed in camp.[24] This was a well-known theatrical group the men formed in camp during the first winter of the war. Their talents were so celebrated in Lee's army that soldiers constructed a wooden theater for performances (and for church services on Sundays) that winter of 1862–63 that featured soldiers, actors visiting from Richmond, and the famous Mollie Bailey, who performed with her husband, Third Arkansan Gus Bailey, as well as her sister, Pauline Kirkland. The Baileys, who owned a circus before and after the war, were comforting fixtures in camp, and Mollie Bailey, who was rumored to also serve as a Confederate spy, was remembered fondly by the men well into the postwar period for her ability to elevate performances "to the rank of first class entertainment."[25]

The Baileys, Chaplain Davis, Arthur Edey, and others worked tirelessly that winter of 1862–63 to care for the men of the brigade. Their efforts were aided by the opening of Texas Hospital in Richmond on December 29, 1862, in the old tobacco buildings of T & S Hardgrove. Two Texans, Drs. R. W. Lunday and J. G. Allen, ran the facility, and Lunday, in particular, was well known to Texas soldiers in Lee's army from his work in other hospitals in Richmond. Texas Hospital could care for 300 to 350 men, which could prove critical to keeping the men together with supporting friends and family from their unit when there was a large influx of wounded after a battle.

The downside to this, though, was unforeseen by those who called for the hospital's construction and helped to fund it. For much of 1862, most of the sick and wounded men of the Texas Brigade had been treated at the St. Frances de Sales hospital in Richmond. After the Battle of Antietam, 80 percent of the wounded cared for there by the Catholic sisters were Texas Brigade soldiers, and Chaplain Davis appears to have made this possible. He played a key role in adding a ward to the St. Frances de Sales hospital specifically for the care of Texas soldiers, and he was joined in this effort by Confederate First Lady Varina Davis, the local YMCA, and Richmond volunteers like Angelina Smith. The downside to the opening of large facilities like Texas Hospital was that men would no longer receive the specialized attention and experienced care of Sister Julian and her staff.[26]

Right around the time Texas Brigade Hospital opened in December 1862, Robertson's men began constructing winter quarters near Fredericksburg. As they celebrated Christmas, Mark Smither looked around the Fifth Texas camp and noted significant improvement in the men's conditions: "Our whole army are remarkably healthy and are in better condition than they have ever been." They were "all pretty well clad, tolerably well fed, and . . . cheered up with the idea that our country is doing everything she can for us." Smither's faith in his nation matched his faith in his commander. "I think our company is blessed with the best Company and Regimental officers there is in the service," the Fifth Texan insisted.[27]

In early January 1863, having returned from recruiting duty in Liberty, Texas, and his engagement to Laura Bryan, Dugat Williams rejoined the Texas Brigade. His confidence matched that of Mark Smither. "The health of the Company and the whole Regiment is by far better than it has ever been," Williams boasted. "All have become inured to the hardships and privations (and starvation) of camp life and are beginning to fatten upon it." After speaking with a few Texans about Robertson's new role as their commander, Williams declared Robertson "quite a favorite in the Brigade."[28] Later that month, Williams revised his opinion, explaining that a number of the men did not openly complain but felt that Robertson was "by no means a choice" they would have made for themselves, echoing their complaints of the previous spring. The men were ready, though, for the next campaign season.[29]

Williams did not often speak of his ideological motivations, but the burial mounds of the dead of Fredericksburg near their camp inspired reflection. There lay buried "the ignorant enemy, believing what has been told them, that they would by a conquest of the South get homesteads, these have indeed got them but of much smaller dimensions than their hopeful minds ever anticipated," Williams argued. The fraternization across the Rappahannock had dwindled, but Williams noted that some of the officers and men still rowed out in skiffs to trade newspapers and chat. During these discussions, he explained, "The more intelligent ones very freely confess they are tired of the war and express a hope that they may never have to meet us on the field again." The Federal soldiers "acknowledge we cannot be subjugated and say they are willing to let the contest drop where it is. How quick this war would be ended if left to the decision of the men of the two armies," Williams added. He was unwilling to surrender, but the Fifth Texas captain had seen enough death and suffering to match the Federal soldiers' desire to strike a compromise: "Even if our men could claim an unjust boundary I believe for the sake of avoiding another battle and for many other considerations they would willingly yield."[30]

Part of the Texas Brigade's optimism that spring, ironically, was tied to Abraham Lincoln's announcement of the Emancipation Proclamation. Despite the number of slave owners among the officer corps and in the ranks, there was astonishingly little grumbling about this decision. Emancipation would eventually create chaos on the southern home front as slaves abandoned crops in the fields and enlisted to fight in combat roles in the Union army and navy. But the Texans and Arkansans were not worried about Lincoln's proclamation in the spring of 1863.

Their comments on slavery after Lincoln's announcement were similar to what they had said since the war began. They asked their families to "say hello to the Negroes" or inquired about a particular enslaved man or woman. Texas Brigade soldiers would note when one of the slaves they brought to camp became sick or died, or how much they helped in camp with cooking or laundry. Some of the letters from home mentioned hiring out slaves or the buying or selling of men and women at home.³¹ But the Texas Brigade and their families expressed surprisingly little concern about the possible effects of Lincoln's proclamation.

The men were so confident in themselves as a unit, in their commanders, and in Confederate victory that they were certain they would win the war before emancipation had any direct impact on their lives. Indeed, if anything, Lincoln's proclamation increased their confidence in the spring of 1863. In late February, Waters Berryman captured these sentiments in the First Texas camp near Fredericksburg. His mother, Helena Dill Berryman, was a fifty-eight-year-old widow whose two sons were fighting in the "Ragged First." She remained at home in Cherokee County, Texas, running their farm with the labor of eight slaves and the help of her nearby daughter, who had a family of her own. Rather than voice concern about how emancipation might affect Helena, Waters Berryman observed that spring that "There seems to be a good prospect for peace now, as some of the western states are cutting up at Old Abe's Emancipation Proclamation. Indiana and Illinois are talking about succeeding [sic] and sending peace delegates to meet in Richmond." He assured his mother that "the opinion of our leading men here [is] that there will be peace in less than six months."³²

Dugat Williams made a similar observation that spring. While traveling back to Virginia from his recruiting assignment, he spoke with several Union prisoners who were part of a group of sixty men captured at the Battle of Murfreesboro. He noted that they "appear to dislike Lincoln's emancipation proclamation very much and say they had no idea when they joined their army that they were waging the war for the freedom of the black." Williams explained that several of the men told him that "they were still willing to fight for the Union" but had no great desire "to fight for the subjugation of the South or the emancipation of the negroes."³³

Later that spring, Williams's confidence grew. "The spring campaign has opened early and in all probability we are to have a hard one but the army was never in better condition and it will suit us as well as the enemy. Gen'l [Joseph] Hooker may try another 'on to Richmond' but if he does it will only be to get whipped and then Mr. Lincoln will have to hunt up another commander," Williams promised. "The people [in Texas] need not fear for the army here. The enemy have never, nor can never make much off us if the army in the West can hold out as well as the one here, then there is no danger.... [O]ur prospects are brightening every day and before a great many months will pass we may all be at home again enjoying all the pleasures of peace and independence," he predicted.[34]

Confident in their ability to win—as long as the rest of the Confederacy did their part—the Texas Brigade broke camp in early April and marched toward Suffolk, Virginia. Their force included Hood's division and Gen. George Pickett's division of Longstreet's First Corps. They were ordered south to forage for the Army of Northern Virginia, and to coordinate with Confederates in southern Virginia and upper North Carolina to draw Federal forces away from the rest of Lee's army.[35] For the next four weeks, Hood's and Pickett's divisions, along with that of S. G. French, put pressure on the strong Federal defenses at Suffolk. The Texas Brigade engaged in sharpshooting and small raids, keeping the Federals in their defenses while Confederates gathered fodder and supplies in the surrounding area.

Confederate casualties were not numerous, but decades later Samuel H. Emerson of the Third Arkansas and Waters Berryman still remembered the small-scale but intense fighting that dominated their experiences in Suffolk.[36] The biggest loss to the brigade that spring was the death of Fifth Texas captain Ike Turner, shot down while leading one of the Texans' many attacks at Suffolk. He was, Mark Smither declared, "the most gallant man in our Brigade," still celebrated for his command of the Fifth Texas at Antietam. Turner was shot "as usual . . . exposing himself most recklessly," Smither noted, while defending a Confederate fort on the river.[37] As Turner's family mourned at Turnwold Plantation in Georgia, they may have taken comfort in Hood's promise, after visiting Turner on his deathbed, that "he would as soon have lost any man in his division" but Turner.[38] He was, John Stevens insisted of his captain, "one of the bravest men in the brigade."[39]

Confederates focused on foraging while they kept Federals within their defenses at Suffolk through the end of April. It did not endear them to local farmers, but Hood's and Pickett's divisions gathered "immense quantities of corn and fodder and all sorts of forage for horses," Dugat Williams observed. Pvt. Ransom Swinney insisted that they "got more corn than he ever saw before" in his life. Others agreed and smiled as they tallied the bacon they collected and cured at nearly 3 million pounds.[40] General Longstreet promised Secretary of War James Seddon that it would "require another month to haul out the supplies of that portion of the country" around Suffolk.

John Stevens was especially pleased when they came across locals who preferred to sell to the U.S. Army. "We found a citizen who had 120,000 pounds of nice bacon which he had put up for the northern army under contract," Stevens explained, and they discovered another "100,000 pounds more in a corn crib covered with corn." These contractors "expect to get the greenbacks for it in a few days," but it was all going to the Confederate army.[41] Mark Smither shared Steven's enthusiasm for their success at Suffolk. "We staid down there a month," he told his mother, and laid "siege to the place and lick[ed] about 50,000 Yanks hemmed in the town scared nearly to death when there was only 15,000 of us." All the while, "we got all the forage out of the country."[42] Smither's numbers were off, but he captured the men's enthusiasm.

On April 30, Longstreet received orders to return to Richmond as quickly as possible, and from there he was to join the rest of Lee's army.[43] Longstreet had to gather all of his foragers first, and some of them were in North Carolina when the orders went out, but his two divisions marched northward late in the day on May 3. They were too late to help with the Battle of Chancellorsville but rushed toward Richmond with the Texas Brigade serving as rear guard for Hood's division. On May 7, with the battle over, Lee sent word for Longstreet to continue on, but he could slow his pace. His men passed through Richmond the next day and moved on until they established a camp near Sommerville and Raccoon fords on the Rapidan River about a week later.[44]

The men were still in good health and, for once, very well supplied, but the Texas Brigade was worried about the Federal siege of Vicksburg, Mississippi. Strategically, it would be a major loss for the Confederacy if the river port fell. For the men of the brigade, it would be a personal loss as well, because it would further reduce communications between Virginia and Texas. Still, this would not discourage the Texas Brigade, Capt. Dugat Williams promised, and "our devotion will not be changed."[45]

On May 29, the brigade received orders to cook rations and to prepare to move at dawn. Morning came and no movement was made, but Williams and the Texans were ready for the next "grand advance" that he was certain "is about to be commenced." Williams hoped they might engage with Union major general Joseph Hooker's army at Manassas because "we have a habit of whipping them and . . . we take pride in doing it upon the historical fields of the world." He assured Laura that the "'Army of the Potomac' is not apt to whip us anywhere. . . . So long as our Army can muster 80 thousand effective men, twice that number of Yankees cannot whip us." The men's health was not "first rate" in Company F, but most of that, Williams complained, was due to "colds and *laziness*."[46]

In the Fourth Texas, Mark Smither agreed. They were heartbroken over the loss of Gen. Thomas J. "Stonewall" Jackson, who died of pneumonia following the amputation of his arm in early May: "He was more generally loved by our army here than any man we had. Lee has our universal respect and confidence, but Jackson had the entire devotion of the whole army." Still, Smither boasted, they had commanders whose aggressive natures matched the brigade's. "As for our old 'warhorse' Longstreet," he told his mother, Elizabeth Wynne, "all that can be said of him and Hood is that they will fight at the drop of a hat and drop it themselves." There were rumors that they might be mounted, and the Texans, who preferred to ride ten miles than to walk a step, watched with a mixture of anticipation and jealousy when the Third Arkansas briefly received horses. It did not last, though. Hood's old brigade would remain an infantry unit, and they were expecting "no childs play this summer," Mark Smither promised. Lee's army was "determined to deal hard and heavy knocks until we conquer a peace."[47]

Elizabeth Smither Wynne likely read Mark's letter with concern. He was her oldest son, and she had just buried her second husband in March. In her mid-forties, Elizabeth Wynne had been briefly widowed until she married Erasmus Wynne in 1858. Though she enjoyed wealth in her first marriage, her connection to the prominent Wynne family placed her among the wealthiest residents of East Texas. When Mark's letter reached her Huntsville home in 1863, she still had plenty of resources, including the many slaves the family owned. But thirteen nieces, nephews, children, and stepchildren relied on her, and Eliza Wynne relied on Fourth Texan Mark Smither. His confidence may have brought her comfort, but it is likely that she shuddered as she contemplated another campaign season for the Army of Northern Virginia.[48] Seeming to sense this, Mark's next letter, written on the Rapidan on May 30, assured Eliza, "our regt is in better health than I've ever known it our ranks are fuller now than they have been at any time since the day before the ever memorable battle of Sharpsburg or 'Antietam' as the Yanks call it. [T]his mornings report shows an aggregate present of 516."[49]

On June 3, Lee's army advanced toward the Shenandoah Valley. Longstreet's First Corps brought up the rear, moving toward Culpeper Courthouse and then continued north and east of the Blue Ridge Mountains. In mid-June they entered the Shenandoah Valley after briefly guarding Snicker's Gap. After Confederate lieutenant generals Richard Ewell's Second Corps and A. P. Hill's Third Corps had passed (Lee reorganized his army into three corps after the death of "Stonewall" Jackson), Longstreet led his men out of Virginia.⁵⁰ The Texas Brigade reunited with Lee's army in time to cross the Potomac River at Williamsport on June 26.

Years later, Pvt. Val Giles of the Fourth Texas still smiled at their optimism that summer, which was aided by the whisky issued each man received when the Confederates crossed the Potomac. "It was chain lightning," he recalled, "and it knocked out many a valiant soldier, especially those who happily accepted the rations of their abstaining friends." They never did learn where Hood got the whiskey, "but every man in the Regiment was a know-nothing after he got his gill," Giles recalled. "We ate breakfast in the State of Virginia, dinner in the State of Maryland, supper in the State of Pennsylvania, and slept in the State of Intoxication—four states in twenty-four hours."⁵¹

Giles remembered, too, the man he was walking with when he crossed into the Keystone State. He had stepped out of line to wait for Company K's Capt. Howdy Martin, strolling at the "head of his company, his long cavalry saber thrown over his shoulder, squirrel-gun fashion." Giles grinned and asked Martin to join him in capturing the "State of Pennsylvania," which Martin readily agreed to do. That moment signified to Giles the tight bonds between the citizen volunteer officers and men in the brigade, a relationship that was key to their past and future success. "Arm in arm," Giles explained, "a Captain and a 4th Sergeant invaded the United States." Decades after the war, Giles insisted that "such familiarity as that between a captain and a noncommissioned officer would appear ridiculous in the eyes of strict disciplinarians, but Captain Martin was a man we all loved and could approach."⁵²

The men continued through Maryland and pushed on to the rolling hills of south central Pennsylvania. They camped at Greencastle that night, confident about the fight that awaited them. First Lt. James Rodgers Loughridge had recovered from his Gaines's Mill wound and rejoined Company I of the Fourth Texas that spring. The long march from Virginia caused his left hip and knee to ache, but he was determined to participate in the coming battle. "When I see the ruin & desolation brought on . . . good people . . . I feel almost mad," he told his wife, Felicia. Federal soldiers "drive women & children out in the cold without food [and] often try to dispoil them not only of these but of their honor," Loughridge fumed. Marching northward in mid-June, he prayed, "May God arm us with superhuman strength to strike these witches from the earth."⁵³

British lieutenant colonel Arthur J. L. Fremantle, an observer accompanying General Lee's army, noticed this optimism and determination among

Hood's men. His division, Fremantle noted, were "a queer lot to look at. They carry less than any other troops; many of them have only got an old piece of carpet or rug as baggage; many have discarded their shoes in the mud; all are ragged and dirty, but full of good-humour and confidence in themselves and in their general, Hood."[54]

Marching with that queer lot, Mark Smither wrestled with his unfamiliar role of invader. "I wish I could describe to you my feelings," he told Eliza Smither. "At first it was a feeling of exultation and then looking on every side of me as far as the eye could reach and seeing nothing but unfriendly looks from the whitehaired sirs down to the child. I confess it made me feel very badly." Smither was fascinated to find that the Texan and Arkansans' reputation had preceded them, noting, "we passed a crowd of people who enquired of me what troops were passing and on receiving the answer of 'Texas Brigade' one turned around to the rest and remarked 'they are the ones that have killed so many of our soldiers'!"[55] James Hendrick of the First Texas did not worry too much about the families they saw. He focused only on ending the war. "This is not like the Maryland trip," he promised his parents. "We are in the North and are going to stay in the North until this war is ended."[56]

The Texans and Arkansans made camp on June 30 at Greenwood, Pennsylvania, on the Chambersburg Pike, about sixteen miles west of Gettysburg. When the battle began on July 1, Confederate lieutenant general James Longstreet and his First Corps, which included John Bell Hood's division and the Texas Brigade, had not yet arrived on the field. Around 5:00 p.m., they left Greencastle and marched down the Chambersburg Pike behind Maj. Gen. Lafayette McLaws's division on an exhausting twelve- to thirteen-mile march of starts and stops without any rest. At 1:00 a.m., Hood's division reached the fields on the western bank of Marsh Creek; McLaws's men had collapsed an hour earlier on its eastern bank. Hood's division joined them, sleeping with their weapons, about 3.5 miles from Lee's headquarters on Seminary Ridge.[57]

Hood's division had two hours' rest, and then they were on the move again. They drank from Marsh Creek and made their way over rolling hills to the western edge of Herr Ridge. Arriving there around 8:00 a.m., the men stacked arms and rested in the fields where McLaws's division joined them about an hour later. Nearly 14,500 men slept, played cards, wrote letters home, and noted the evidence of a nearby battle. Pvt. A. C. Sims shuddered at "the bloody shirts, the men who had been wounded in the previous day's battle" who walked past the resting Texans, likely to a nearby Confederate field hospital.

Sims joined the Texas Brigade just a few months earlier in April. His twin brother, Albert Hubert Sims, had volunteered for Confederate service in the Thirteenth Texas Infantry Regiment the previous fall, even though both boys were underage at the time. A. C. had begged his brother to "wait until spring," promising that "I would go with him anywhere he might wish, but he would not consent." A. C. believed that if his brother entered the camps that winter, he would die of disease before he could be of any service to their country. Tragically, he was right. And so, in the spring of 1863, A. C. "was so crazed with grief for him who had been my constant associate from infancy that I resolved to go to that then seeming far off land Virginia to fight the battle of my Country." He could have fought in the West like his brother, but Sims sought service in the Texas Brigade, far from home.

By July, Sims's journey to Virginia had taken him to the gentle hills of Pennsylvania, which now rumbled with cannon and musket fire. Most of the Texans and Arkansans around him were veterans of several bloody fights, and the young Sims observed with concern the "bloody shirts" walking through their lines from the fighting on July 1. "What effect they had on the old soldiers, I know not," Sims recalled, "but to me, who had never seen the like, it was no pleasing sight to behold."[58]

Lee's plan for the second day at Gettysburg was for Longstreet's First Corps to attack the Federal left flank and roll up their line, while A. P. Hill and Third Corps kept pressure on the Federal center, preventing Union major general George Gordon Meade from supporting either flank while Hill remained ready to support Longstreet's success. On the Federal right, where their line curved around Culp's Hill in a fishhook, Richard Ewell's Second Corps was ordered to direct a series of diversionary attacks that he would act on with a full assault if possible. With this plan, Lee hoped to push Meade's army off the high ground and win the Battle of Gettysburg.

But by late morning, Longstreet was still not in position. Lee, growing frustrated, ordered the Georgian to get McLaws's and Hood's divisions into position. Lee wanted First Corps to hit the Federal left flank by attacking up Emmitsburg Road, rolling up the Union line. But Longstreet did not like the plan, fearing the Federals were too strong there for the attack to be successful. He asked for one more delay. He wanted to have Hood's division at full strength when it went into the fight. Lee agreed that they could wait for Brig. Gen. Evander Law's Alabama brigade, which was rushing in from New Guilford as the generals spoke. When Law arrived at noon, Longstreet ordered Hood and McLaws to Emmitsburg Road.

This was easier said than done. General Lee ordered Longstreet to conceal their movements as they made their way forward. Capt. S. R. Johnston was traveling with them to help them do this as either an official guide, as Hood and Longstreet later claimed, or in an unofficial capacity, as Johnston argued, as someone who had recently scouted the area. Johnston was a captain of engineers, served on Lee's staff, and was respected for his reconnaissance work earlier in the war. He reported on the morning of July 2 that there were no Federals on Little Round Top, which is why Lee directed Longstreet to position his men perpendicular to Emmitsburg Road in the area known today as the Peach Orchard. Either Johnston did a poor job scouting the area or he was confused about which sections of the Union line he actually saw.[59]

It was shortly after noon when Longstreet ordered his two divisions southward from their resting spot on the western slope of Herr Ridge. Staying close to tributaries of Marsh Creek, they marched through low, rolling fields to Black Horse Tavern Road. When the head of the column reached Fairfield Road, McLaws's division continued southward for another quarter mile until they reached a rise, where they hesitated. McLaws knew that Federal signalmen could not miss seeing their column if they continued forward. Hood's division likely came to a halt on Black Horse Tavern Road well before the Fairfield Road intersection.[60]

Longstreet and McLaws decided to reverse their route. They could have ordered a simple about-face of the entire command, but this would have placed Hood's division at the front of the column, and Lee had ordered McLaws's to lead the attack. Instead, Hood's men waited until McLaws's division worked its way back to Black Horse Tavern, and then both units used farm lanes as they traveled eastward to the protection of Herr's Ridge.

Once over the ridge, Hood's division marched southward in the protected valley of Willoughby Run. As they reached the Pitzer School House on the Millerstown Road, Sims, Smither, Williams, and their fellow Texans paused as McLaws's men, ahead of Hood's division, stopped when Longstreet and McLaws discovered that there was no way they could follow Lee's original order to attack up Emmitsburg Road. Union major general Dan Sickles had deployed, without permission, his Third Corps in an advanced position along the road. One division took up a battle line along Emmitsburg Road, and a second ran in a line from the Peach Orchard, through Mr. Rose's Wheatfield, and ended in a massive cluster of boulders and ledges on Houck's Ridge. The situation differed greatly from that which existed when Lee first gave his orders. This caused further delays as Longstreet revised the plan of attack and ordered Hood's division to extend McLaws's line to the south. Hood's men were now in position to strike the unexpected, and they hoped undermanned, Union forces on Houck's Ridge and Little Round Top.

As Longstreet modified the plan, Hood's division waited on the western slope of Warfield Ridge, a southeastern extension of Seminary Ridge. Colonel Van Manning's Third Arkansas rested on the far left of the front rank of Hood's divisional line, their position about two hundred yards west of Emmitsburg Road. To their right, the First Texas shifted into line by the right flank on the crest of Warfield Ridge, extended by the Fourth Texas, and then the Fifth Texas. The men welcomed the protection the trees and rolling ground provided from Federal artillery fire.[61] Looking over the ground before them, the men saw fields scattered with boulders and the occasional stone walls and wooden fence rails. Recognizing the incredibly difficult task that lay before them, Hood made several requests to approach the position from a different direction. He had sent Texas scouts to find an alternate route, which involved swinging around Round Top and using the country lane his men had found. Two Texans in particular, First Texas privates Leslie Thompson and John B. Elliott, spent much of their time slipping in and out of Union lines during the campaign. Before the war they had been students at the nearby college, Mount St. Mary's, in Emmitsburg, and they knew the area well.[62] But the information they gathered did not convince Longstreet. He had tried alternatives with Lee, though not as well reconnoitered as what Hood proposed, and all were denied. "We must obey the orders of General Lee," Longstreet insisted.

As Hood's old brigade waited along with the rest of his division, each man went through a quiet ritual of preparing for what would come. Some prayed while others teased the few new recruits who had joined the Texas Brigade that spring. To the Texans' right were General Law's parched Alabamans who had raced to catch up with Hood's division. A colonel had ordered a squad to gather their fellow soldiers' canteens to fill before the advance started, but they did not return before their division advanced.

It was about 4:00 p.m. when Confederate batteries opened. Capt. James Reilly's and Capt. Alexander C. Latham's guns, posted on the same line with the Texas Brigade, offered the men some protection, as did the Confederate First Corps Reserve Artillery battalion under E. Porter Alexander. Most of these, though, were focused on the Federal artillery in the Peach Orchard and along Emmitsburg Road, knowing that these Union guns could deliver oblique fire on Hood's men once they advanced.

The Texas Brigade waited anxiously in the woods along Warfield Ridge as Federal artillery careened through their lines. Samuel Emerson watched with horror as a single cannonball tore through Company H of the Third Arkansas, killing Capt. Lafayette Allen and two other men.[63] In the Fourth Texas, John West, facing his first battle, stared as solid shot "struck the ground about 50 or 60 feet from the line and passed by on a bound over us, scattering dust and dirt over our company." This was followed quickly by another ball that "passed about an equal distance beyond us, tearing up the earth." A third shot "hit our line about 8 feet in front of me knocking off one soldier's head and cutting another in 2 bespattering us with blood."[64]

A twenty-nine-year-old father of two, John West waited two years to see action in the Confederate army. He had joined Company E of the Fourth Texas Infantry in 1861, but President Jefferson Davis appointed West, then headmaster of the Waco and Trinity River Classical School, as the district attorney for the Confederacy's Western District. When West left that position to join a unit in Texas, Davis again had him transferred back to heading legal matters in the Western District. In April 1863, however, 3rd Lt. Tom Selman arrived in Waco on recruiting duty for the Fourth Texas. "Being more determined than ever to see a fight, and to remain in the ranks, if necessary, until the close of the war," West rejoined the Fourth Texas and said good-bye to his wife, Eliza, and two young children.[65]

Standing near West in the woods on Warfield Ridge, Capt. Decimus et Ultimus Barziza spread General Robertson's order for the men to lie down. This offered a bit more protection, but anticipation of the fight to come was, Barziza argued, often more difficult than the attack itself. "It is very trying upon the men to remain still and in ranks under a severe cannonading," he recalled. "One has time to reflect upon the danger, and there being no wild excitement as in a charge, [because here] he is more reminded of the utter helplessness of his present condition." With each passing shell, Barziza noticed that the men tried "to sink themselves into the earth. Nearly every face is overspread with a serious, thoughtful air, and what thoughts, vivid and burning, come trooping up from the inner chambers of memory, the soldier can only realize."[66]

Between 4:00 and 4:30 p.m., as Hood rode before the Fourth Texas, the entire brigade rose and reformed into lines. Private West watched as Hood "took his hat, held it above him in his right hand, [and] rose to his full height in his stirrups." A cheer went up and rippled down the line. "Forward! Steady, Forward!" Hood shouted, and his division stepped from the tree line and advanced.

On the far left of the Texas Brigade, Col. Van Manning stepped out with the Third Arkansas. Within a minute or two, the Arkansans had crossed Emmitsburg Road and continued at a swift pace. Officers tried to keep its right flank connected with Colonel Work's First Texas, but it continued to edge in front of them. The haste of Manning's and Work's men was likely fueled by the artillery fire from their left and the Federal skirmishers and Second U.S. Sharpshooters in front of them. The veteran soldiers knew that the faster they moved, the less exposed they were to artillery fire and the more difficult it was for artillerymen to target them. Swift movement also reduced the amount of time that skirmishers and sharpshooters could obstruct their advance. The other factor, though, was that Law's Alabamians were pushing forward at quick clip, and the Fourth and Fifth Texas were hurrying to keep pace with them. At a double-quick, Hood's division raced through toward the woods before them.

That swift movement created a serious concern for Manning. He had orders to keep his left on Emmitsburg Road, and his right connected with the First Texas. Just shy of his twenty-fourth birthday, Van Manning was a North Carolinian by birth who had settled in Arkansas in 1859 after a period in Mississippi. Well-liked by his men, Manning watched that July day as his line stretched to the breaking point. He could stay connected with P. A. Work's Texans or the road, but his Arkansans could not do both.[67] Manning and Robertson decided to keep the Arkansans' right flank connected with the rest of the brigade. The high ground before them was more important. Only when that was clear could they follow Lee's original plan to roll the Federals up Emmitsburg Road.[68]

The trouble, though, was that the entire Confederate advance was breaking apart. The Third Arkansas and First Texas—receiving the fire from Federal artillery in the Peach Orchard as well as fire from the sharpshooters in front of them and from the four guns from the Fourth New York artillery atop Devil's Den—were rushing for the cover of Rose Woods in front of them. The Fourth and Fifth Texas, meanwhile, faced the Second U.S. Sharpshooters and struggled to keep pace with the Alabamians.[69] As Col. J. C. G. Key's Fourth Texas and Col. Robert M. "Mike" Powell's Fifth Texas returned the sharpshooters' fire and drove them back, they kept the brigade's right attached to Law's left, which caused further separation in the middle of the Robertson's brigade between First Texas and Fourth Texas.[70]

Brig. Gen. Evander M. Law was aware of the issue, but his focus at that moment was on the Federal guns atop Devil's Den that "had been playing on our line from the moment the advance began," reported Col. William F. Perry of the Forty-Fourth Alabama. Law decided to pull the Forty-Fourth and Forty-Eighth Alabama out of line from the far right of his brigade and shifted them west, behind the Fourth and Fifth Texas.[71] This did not plug the gap in the Texas Brigade, but it did allow these Alabamians to aid the assault on Devil's Den. It also meant that the Texas Brigade would fight divided for the remainder of July 2, and it weakened the division's assault on Little Round Top. The Third Arkansas and First Texas, with support from the Forty-Fourth and Forty-Eighth Alabama on their right, would focus their assault on the Federal forces at Devil's Den. The Fourth and Fifth Texas linked with rest of Law's Alabamians—the Fourth, Forty-Seventh, and Fifteenth Alabama—for the attack on the Round Tops.[72]

Hood's leadership was desperately needed as these movements took place, but he was unable to help. A shell exploded over Hood's head and tore into his arm just minutes after his division launched their attack. As Hood was carried from the field with his left arm broken from above the elbow down to his wrist, he worried about "the inevitable fate of my brave fellow-soldiers, who formed one of the grandest divisions of that world-renowned army." Law took command of the division, but there is no record of him communicating with brigade commanders until the day's fighting had ended. This absence of leadership was already proving problematic as Hood's division shifted and separated early in their advance.[73]

As the Third Arkansas and First Texas had covered the ground between Warfield Ridge and Rose Woods—about eight hundred to one thousand yards—First Texas private Thomas McCarty recalled a man going down "at every report" of a cannon, not to mention the impact of the Federal sharpshooters posted behind a stone wall before them. This included the Berryman brothers' friend, Mort Murphy, who was killed just twenty yards into the advance.[74]

The Third Arkansas and First Texas likely did not know of Hood's wounding. Instead, they kept pushing the Federal sharpshooters back past the Bushman and Slyder farms, stone walls, homes, and outbuildings, and navigated around the large rocks and boulders that littered the ground. Like many of the men, A. C. Sims fell when his foot slipped on a loose rock, but he jumped up again. When a round knocked his rifle from his hands, Sims just "picked up another that lay before us." When he got that weapon "choked with a ball," he "threw it down and picked up another."[75]

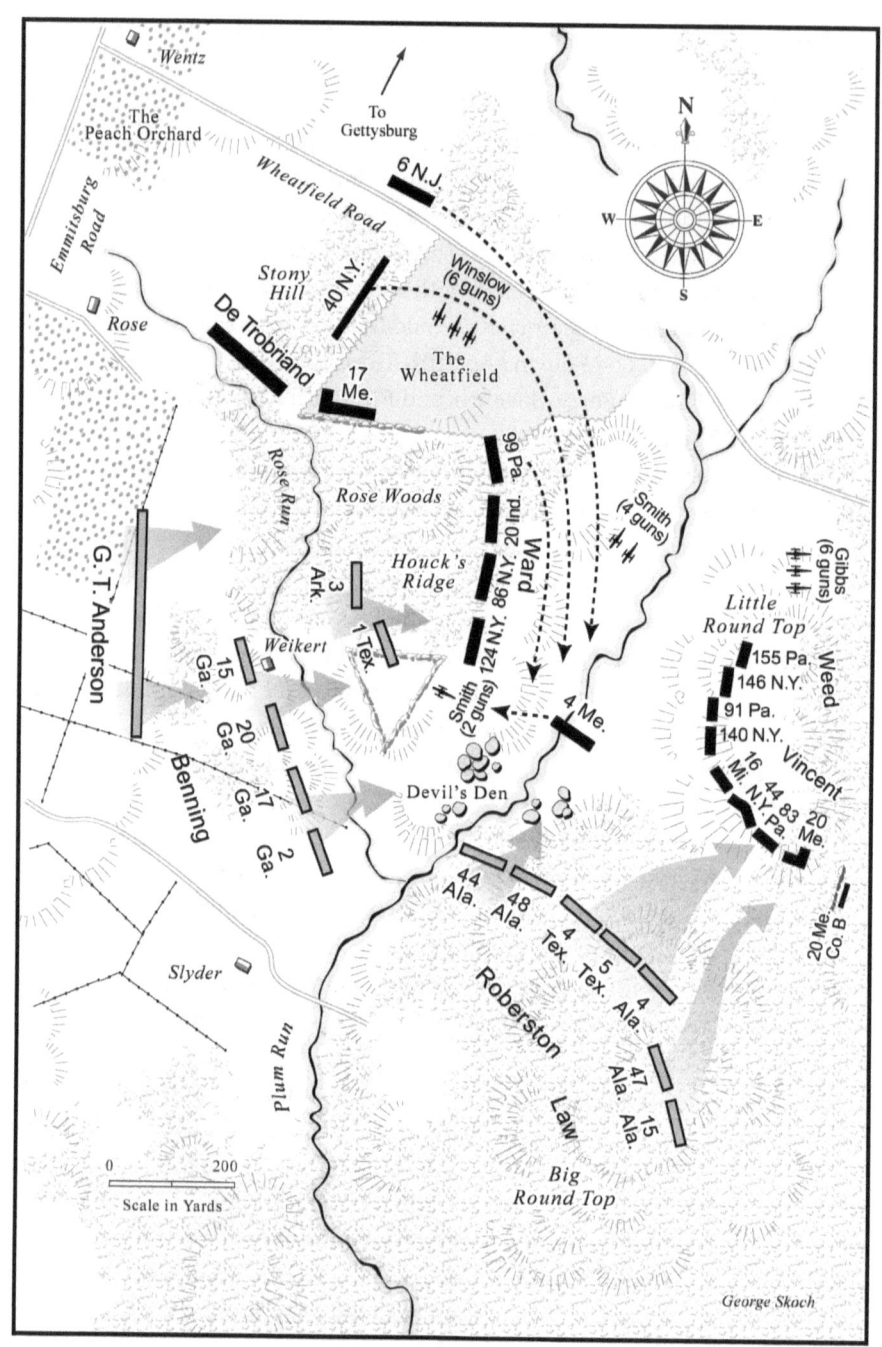

Battle of Gettysburg, July 2, 1863

The units creating such problems for the Arkansans and First Texans were the four guns of Capt. James Smith's Fourth New York Light Artillery and members of the 124th New York. Hidden by Rose Woods and the defilade of Houck's Ridge were the rest of Brig. Gen. John Henry Hobart Ward's Second Brigade of Maj. Gen. David G. Birney's division of Maj. Gen. Daniel Sickles Third Corps. Running in a south-to-north line along Houck's Ridge, this included the Fourth Maine, 124th New York, Eighty-Sixth New York, Twentieth Indiana, and the Ninety-Ninth Pennsylvania. James Smith's Fourth New York Light Artillery supported these infantry regiments with four Parrott guns on Ward's left flank near Devil's Den's largest boulders. Smith's remaining two guns were farther to their left and rear, left to help hold the gorge behind Houck's Ridge and because there was not enough room for them atop Devil's Den.

As Manning's and Work's men entered Rose Woods, they found some cover amid the trees and in the low ground. The sharpshooters had fallen back, and Hood's men were too close and too low, for now, for the fire of Smith's guns to reach them. They caught their breath in the low ground west of Houck's Ridge, below Ward's position. It is likely that a company or two of Work's First Texas joined Manning's men in the woods while the rest of Work's men looked up the steep, rocky, triangular-shaped meadow before them and prepared to make the final push for the crest.

As they surged forward through Rose Woods, Manning noticed that his Arkansans were receiving fire on their left flank. This was the Seventeenth Maine from Col. Philip Regis de Trobriand's brigade in Mr. Rose's Wheatfield. The Union infantrymen had taken shelter behind a stone wall that ran along the northern edge of the Rose Woods, and their skirmishers tormented the Arkansans. Manning ordered one company to shift to the left and respond to this fire, but the "smoke was so thick, and the roar of the muskets so loud," Arkansas private John Wilkerson recalled, that "we did not hear the command."[76]

At the northern edge of Rose Woods, Sgt. Frank Whittemore and the Seventeenth Maine waited for their skirmishers to rush back and clear their lines. He shuddered at the "fearful yell through the woods" but took some comfort in the cover of the stone wall. Then, with an officer's shout to fire, the Seventeenth Maine "opened upon them so furiously" that the Third Arkansas "began to skedaddle again but were finally rallied and turning round began to pour in to us a terrible fire." The fighting continued like this, with the Arkansans and First Texans advancing and then falling back, but slowly they were making progress.[77]

On the southern edge of Rose Woods, P. A. Work extended his line to the left to help Manning as much as Work could while also protecting his own right flank. His regimental front, Work explained, was "twice its legitimate length, guarding well my left, and advanced to the ledge of rocks from which we had previously been dislodged by the enemy's movement on my flank." It was this thin line that he ordered to advance into the triangular field, while the 124th New York fired down from the protection of a stone wall along the crest of the hill.

General Ward had ordered his men "not to fire until they could plainly see the enemy."[78] The delayed volleys of the Twentieth Indiana and the Eighty-Sixth New York, which Ward had ordered forward to a slight rise and in advance of the 124th New York, tore through Manning's men in Rose Woods. Similar delayed but effective close-range fire poured into Work's men from the 124th New York defending the triangular field. Below them, Pvt. Wilson Barbee of the First Texas refused to duck or find any useful cover. He was a courier on General Hood's staff, and after Hood was wounded and carried away, Barbee had lacked clear orders. He had decided to ride his horse down the slope and joined the rest of the First Texas. When his horse was shot from under him, Barbee continued on foot, picking up a dropped musket and cartridge box. Many of the First Texans, Waters Berryman observed, were "sheltering ourselves behind a big rock on the side of the mountain," but Barbee chose a different approach. He positioned himself on a large boulder, firing at Ward's men until a round pierced his right leg. Barbee fell from the boulder, climbed back up, and began shooting again. Within moments, he was hit in the other leg and again knocked down. But Barbee crawled up again, laying prone on the rock, before being hit once more, falling to the ground on his back, and crying for and cursing the men around him for failing to help him back on the rock.[79]

Colonel Work's ammunition was running low. The men of the First Texas resorted to taking cartridges and rounds from the dead and wounded men around them. Officers had long stopped trying to lead their companies and fought in the ranks with the enlisted men.[80] Above them, Col. A. Van Horne Ellis of the 124th New York was equally desperate. His unit, nicknamed the "Orange Blossoms" for the county where they were raised, had only fought in one previous battle, at Chancellorsville eight weeks earlier. Maj. James Cromwell urged Ellis to order a charge down the hill to break the Texans before they had a chance to overrun Smith's guns and seize Houck's Ridge. Ellis initially thought such a plan futile, but, finally, he agreed and mounted his horse declaring, "The men must see us today." The call went down the line to fix bayonets, and with a shout, Ellis, Cromwell, and the Orange Blossoms dashed down the steep, rocky slope. It was "a scene of butchery," one recalled, as soldiers fired at each other from a distance of just twenty-five yards. But the charge worked. The First Texas fell back, but they inflicted significant casualties on the New Yorkers. Cromwell was hit, reeled in his saddle, and fell to the ground dead, but still the New Yorkers pushed down the hill and into the Texans.[81]

It was a stunningly brave and effective charge, and it nearly turned the tide of the fight for Devil's Den. But then Brig. Gen. Henry L. "Rock" Benning's brigade, comprised of the Fifteenth, Twentieth, Seventeenth, and Second Georgia, came up in support of Work's and Manning's men. Benning was a forty-nine-year-old lawyer who had never warmed to army discipline and hierarchy, much like many of the First Texans before him. Also like the Texans, Benning's men adored him.

When a round killed Ellis and he fell to the ground, the Orange Blossoms' charge broke. They knew they could not defeat the Texans and Georgians, and with both commanders down, retreat seemed their best option. Confederates rushed forward with the help of the Forty-Fourth and Forty-Eighth Alabama, the two units Law had earlier shifted to the left of the Fourth Texas, who were advancing on the Texans right toward Ward's left and rear. Reinforced by the Georgians, the First Texas surged "forward toward the top of the hill at full speed," recalled First Texas private James O. Bradfield. Together they swept on the Federals before them in "one of the wildest, fiercest struggles of the war." Finally, Bradfield noticed the Federals falling back and then fleeing down the slope behind them. The combined pressure of the Texans, Arkansans, and Alabamians, supported by four fresh regiments of Georgians, proved too much for the Union defenders atop Houck's Ridge and Devil's Den.[82]

Smith pleaded that the New Yorkers and the Ninety-Ninth Pennsylvania stay and help defend his guns, but they were exhausted from their charge, led by a captain, and down to fewer than 100 men. Smith realized that he could not hold his position, nor could he pull his guns away—the limbers were in the valley behind him, the ground being so rough that his men had had to pull the heavy guns up by hand when horses could not. Defeated, Smith ordered his men to take their sponges, primers, rammers, and what ammunition was left and abandon his Parrotts. The exhausted Confederates struggled toward Smith's guns, and all of them later claimed credit for seizing them and celebrated their success in taking "the mountain." A. C. Sims, however, insisted that he was sure he heard General Benning tell the Georgians, "Ah, boys, those Texans had captured this battery before you were in a quarter of a mile of here."[83]

While enjoying their success, the men looked to the east and realized that they were not on top of the mountain they had seen when their attack began. Just past Smith's guns, which were temporarily useless without ammunition and the tools needed to fire them, the ground dropped into a valley and then rose quickly again. Smoke covered this second "mountain" where an equally desperate fight raged for Little Round Top.

The Confederates looking out from Devil's Den saw the final struggle as portions of the Forty-Fourth and Forty-Eighth Alabama shifted away from the fighting on Houck's Ridge to join the Fourth and Fifth Texas, and the rest of Law's brigade—the Fourth, Forty-Seventh, and Fifteenth Alabama—as they attacked Little Round Top. These units had advanced rapidly from the start of the attack, but they were slowed by Federal sharpshooters and the incredibly difficult terrain that covered the western slope of Big Round Top. Third Cpl. Zack Landrum of the Fourth Texas made his way past "rocks as large as a meeting house" while Union artillery and rifle fire hit men throughout the advancing line. Landrum felt like there were about "100 Guns firing on us."[84]

The Texans took whatever cover they could find behind boulders and trees, including Val Giles and his friend Pvt. John Griffith, who had already been wounded at Gaines's Mill and Antietam. They "pre-empted a moss-covered boulder about the size of a 500-pound cotton bale" for protection, but Giles was certain that some of the rounds coming in were from their own artillery on Warfield Ridge. "Nothing demoralizes troops quicker than to be fired into by their friends," he frowned.[85]

Running past trees and boulders, Zach Landrum stumbled to the ground. A round had cut through his left thigh, exited, and then smacked into his right thigh, severely bruising it.[86] Nearby, both Col. John C. G. Key and Lt. Col. Benjamin Franklin Carter of the Fourth Texas were badly injured. In the Fifth Texas, Lt. Col. King Bryan tried to maintain order in his ranks as he walked down the line in fire that "showered like hail upon us." As they advanced from the slopes of Big Round Top to Little Round Top, the men tried to move as a unit but steep, boulder-strewn hill slowed them, and fire from the Sixteenth Michigan and Forty-Fourth New York nearly stopped them. "Confusion reigned everywhere," Val Giles recalled. "Nearly all of our field officers were gone.... Colonel [R. M.] Powell of the 5th Texas was riddled with bullets

... and Colonel B. F. Carter of [the Fourth Texas] lay dying at the foot of the mountain." Still, the Texans kept up their pressure.

The Texans fell back to the base of Little Round Top, and King Bryan took a moment to organize the Fifth Texas. They were scattered in clumps behind the rocks that offered some protection below the steep incline of the "second heights," as Bryan called Little Round Top. When he concluded that reinforcements were not coming, and the men were as organized as he could get them, Bryan looked for Colonel Powell, expecting an order to rush once more up Little Round Top. But Bryan could not find him. Deciding that Powell must have been hit, Bryan moved toward the center of the regiment to assume command and found Powell lying on the ground. Reaching for him, a ball tore through Bryan's left arm. With both men down, command of the Fifth Texas devolved upon Maj. J. C. Rogers.[87]

Through the smoke and fire, Val Giles could hear Rogers shouting inspiration to the men, "a 4th of July speech" that was two days early, trying to keep them steady. "Order and discipline were gone" by this point, Giles recalled. Rogers and a captain from the Fourth Alabama were the only men Giles could see standing, the rest of them having "settled down behind rocks, logs, and trees," some at the base of Little Round Top while others took slightly better cover in the tree line at the western edge of Big Round Top. When a courier rode up, he shouted General Law's "compliments," along with an order "to hold this place at all hazards." Rogers, a Milam County lawyer, shouted, "Compliments, hell! Who wants any compliments in such a damned place as this? Go back and ask General Law if he expects me to hold the world in check with the 5th Texas Regiment."[88]

The Texans and Alabamians fell back into the trees of Big Round Top, reorganized, and then surged up Little Round Top in three, possibly four, separate assaults. Fifth Sgt. J. D. Caddell, fighting in Lt. J. R. Loughridge's Company I of the Fourth Texas, managed to get close to the Federal defenders before he, too, fell when a Minié ball passed through his leg.[89]

Opposite the Texans, Federal soldiers had barely formed into line to defend Little Round Top when the Confederate assaults up the heights began. Far out on the rocky ledge, 1st Lt. Charles H. Salter of Company B of the Sixteenth Michigan watched "a long line of rebels coming over and down a range of hills opposite us. If we had been 5 minutes later, the enemy would have gained the ridge we were on, and turned our left flank."[90] First Lt. Ziba B. Graham, also in the Sixteenth Michigan, insisted that the fighting "raged for fully half an hour."[91] Just to their left, William Brown fought with the Forty-Fourth New York. In a "dreadful hail of Bullets," he fired all thirty-five rounds in his cartridge box as "men were killed right by my side, one directly not over 4 feet from me."[92]

W. H. Clarke had already been hit once on Little Round Top when he and men from Company I of the 140th New York were ordered forward. They had rushed up as Union general Strong Vincent was rallying the Sixteenth Michigan, which was breaking under the tremendous pressure of Law's and Robertson's men. Vincent fell mortally wounded, as did Irish-born Col. Patrick O'Rourke of the 140th New York.[93]

The struggle for the Round Tops, Val Giles argued, was one of the Texas Brigade's most desperate fights of the war: "There seemed to be a viciousness in the very air we breathed." As darkness fell, Giles could hear "Yankee officers on the crest of the ridge in front of us cursing the men by platoons, and the men telling him to go to a country not very far away from us just at that time." Similar shouts came from Confederate lines as commanders struggled to direct their own men. "If that old Satanic dragon has ever been on earth since he offered our Saviour the world if He would serve him, he was certainly at Gettysburg that night," Giles insisted. "There was not a man there that cared a snap for the golden rule, or that could have remembered one line of the Lord's Prayer."[94]

The Fourth and Fifth Texas spent the night of July 2 in the woods near Plum Run at the base of Big Round Top, while the Third Arkansas and the First Texas settled on the heights of Houck's Ridge near Devil's Den. Federals made several attempts to reclaim the ridge but were repeatedly repulsed. At one point during the night Work reported that "a terrific artillery fire was concentrated against the hill occupied by this (the First Texas) regiment., and many were killed and wounded, some losing their heads, and others so horribly mutilated and mangled that their identity could scarcely be established." About 2:00 a.m., Work was finally able to get the Texans down the hill to a stonewall about one hundred yards from Devil's Den.[95] Despite an exhausting day that had continued into the night, several men from each company had to serve picket duty, and A. C. Sims was one of the unlucky few selected for that assignment. For two hours, he stood on alert between the two armies, listening "to the cries and groans of the wounded and dying, and their pleading for water." A man nearby called to Sims, begging him to bring some water. "No one will hurt you. My leg is shot off or I would come to you. I'll give you a dollar. . . .

I'll give you all the money I have," he pleaded, but Sims remained silent in the darkness. Just eighteen years old and still stunned by the experiences of his first battle, Sims had no water to share, and he refused to leave his post "for anything." Determined to do his duty, but exhausted by the "excitement, heat of battle, and suffocating smoke," Sims finally resorted to rubbing tobacco in his eyes to stay awake.[96]

The following day was fairly quiet for the Texas Brigade, positioned on the far right of the Confederate line and a good distance from the failed Pickett-Pettigrew-Trimble charge. But late that afternoon, Union brigadier general Judson Kilpatrick ordered one of his cavalry brigades, commanded by Brig. Gen. Elon J. Farnsworth, on a nearly impossible and suicidal assault on the Texans' position. Farnsworth's First Vermont and First West Virginia loped toward the First Texas, located near the Bushman farm in the low ground east of Warfield Ridge. The Texans were positioned in a lane lined with rock fences, and several men felt the ground tremble as the troopers approached.[97] Confederate skirmishers fired and then fell back, diving over the stone wall and into the protected lane. There they "lay as still as a panther ready to leap upon its prey," Waters Berryman boasted. When the Federals were within fifty yards of the wall, the First Texas poured a "murderous fire upon them," and the cavalrymen "scattered in every direction."

Thomas McCarty and men from Company L were near Berryman. They had taken down and then reassembled a rail fence at a 40-degree angle with the stone wall that ran along their right for three hundred yards. In moments the troopers were on top of the Texans, racing "through us cutting right & left" and "the firing for a few minutes was front, rear, & towards the flanks."[98] Not far from McCarty, Pvt. James Hendrick and other men in Company E fired desperately, and those who did not have weapons resorted to knocking troopers from their horses with rocks. The Berryman brothers experienced the same thing, noting that "all the boys had fired off their pieces and the Yanks would not give them time to load so the boys were using the butts of their guns. Moore killed one with a rock." One of the troopers had just slashed his saber into a Texan's head when Newt Berryman "ran up and blew [the trooper's] brains out."[99]

As the cavalrymen retreated, those who had fallen or been wounded were captured. The failed assault would become controversial for Kilpatrick, who had to explain his failed attack that led to Farnsworth's death. For the First Texans, however, it was "one of the most laughable scenes I ever experienced,"

Waters Berryman declared. Sudden and brief, the attack resulted in few casualties and left them with "horses, blankets, rations, and all of their accoutrements to be enjoyed by the victorious 1st Texas." After such a desperate fight the day before, Berryman experienced an almost manic release and celebrated their loot, which included Navy Colts and enough horses that the men "were about to mount ourselves, but 'the order was countermanded,'" Berryman smiled.[100]

Despite Berryman's confidence, Robert E. Lee knew the Army of Northern Virginia could not hold their ground. They had suffered extremely heavy losses, were low on ammunition, and had no fresh troops. He ordered a retreat to Virginia. The Texas Brigade had suffered nearly 600 casualties in a fight they started with 1,100 men; this amounted to 54.3 percent losses. Perhaps even more astonishing was the impact on the brigade's chain of command. In addition to division commander Hood, who fell near the start of the advance, brigade commander General Robertson was also wounded, along with Third Arkansas colonel Van Manning; Fourth Texas commanders J. C. G. Key and B. F. Carter; and Fifth Texas commanders Mike Powell and King Bryan.[101]

As they marched south and reentered Virginia, the Texas Brigade had mixed emotions about Gettysburg. Lt. James Rodgers Loughridge struggled to put the battle into words. He had ended the second day's fighting at Gettysburg as commander in the Fourth Texas Infantry because they lost so many officers, all for ground they gave up a day later. "Tis true we drove the enemy from a part of the high mountains that he occupied and retained the same for as long as we wished yet we finally had to fall back leaving the Yankees to take possession of our ground," he told his wife, Felicia. The rage and confidence that he expressed in June had shifted into a dark depression. "How terrible is this war upon the people of our land," Loughridge shuddered. "Had a Prophet arose 4 years ago & told of these horrors" to "the people North & South . . . that in a short time they would butcher each other up in cold blood no one would have believed him." He could only pray that, "God Almighty, the God of Hosts the mighty God of Battle is at the helm. & at the proper time will speak peace to this murderous storm that now makes all eyes sick with horror!"[102]

Pvt. Waters Berryman shared Loughridge's sentiments, telling his family that "Old Lee made a great blunder in butting his brains out as it were against the rocks of the Blue Ridge." Confederates "whipped them off the hills," but, he argued, "we lost more lives than necessary." Lee knew "his men would go where ever they were ordered and he knew if we routed them off of the hills they would be ruined." But in these same letters, Berryman and Loughridge also showed a continued faith in Lee and in Confederate victory, sentiments that echoed throughout the Texas Brigade. "Although we have met with disaster in the West the gallant soldier of Virginia seems more determined, more desperate than ever," Berryman insisted.[103] Loughridge agreed. "Our soldiers amid all their sufferings are confident of ultimate success," he told Felicia, and "many think that even the North will now prove to be a better friend to us than England" and "will this winter acknowledge independence & afterward try to heal the breach that this conflict of deadly arms has made."[104]

John West shared similar sentiments with his wife. "Our cause looks a little gloomy now, but I have no fears of the final result," he explained. The Confederate defeats at Gettysburg and Vicksburg would lengthen the war, and he admitted that "perhaps it would be better if I were on your side of the Mississippi." But, no, he shook his head. "I believe I am where I ought to be.... Every able-bodied man ought to be where he can strike the hardest blow for his country," and John West, like so many around him, believed that was with Robert E. Lee in Virginia.[105]

At home, Texas Brigade families echoed this blend of frustration, determination, and optimism. "You cannot tell the intense anxiety and uneasiness of those left at home," Charlotte Wigfall wrote in July, wife of the brigade's first commander. "We have all been watching with painful interest the course of our Army since it crossed the border, and although late accounts have cast a gloom upon us, we all feel assured that Lee will yet do something to make them tremble as much as they are now exulting over our misfortunes." Still, she advised her daughter, Louise, that "we are not dismayed, but believe that all will yet be right. The most sickening feature is the prolongation of the war. Groaning, however, will do neither you nor me any good, so a truce to it."[106]

In mid-August, the *Houston Tri-Weekly Telegraph* declared that, despite the July setback, the Army of Northern Virginia remained strong. Under the heading "Meade Left in a Lurch," Texas Brigade families cheered news that General Lee had all of his men and material back across the Potomac with few additional losses after the Battle of Gettysburg. He "not merely carries off the spoils of his Pennsylvania invasion, but the laurels of the campaign, subsequent to his defeat at Gettysburg, belong also to him."[107]

This optimism and continued determination was even shared among the wounded. The ball that tore through Zach Landrum's thigh was originally treated by the brigade's surgeons, who included the father of First Texas commander P. A. Work. After that, Landrum was transferred with the rest of the wounded by ambulance to Richmond on a tortuously painful journey. Riding with five other men from Company H of the Fourth Texas, Landrum "had a rough time coming down on a turnpike across the mountain" on roads "made of rock thrown in the road and beat down" in "wagons stopping and then having to trot to catch up and keep closed up, with a sore leg is anything but pleasant." Recovering in Richmond, Landrum heard rumors that Texas, Arkansas, and Louisiana were going to secede from the Confederacy and "place themselves under the protection of France." He hoped they would. "I think when a nation can't protect the states that form it they ought to protect themselves in the best way they can. I would much rather the French (if it does come to the worst) should rule us than any nation on the Globe." Still, even Landrum was not willing to quit. "I am anxious that the war should close but I am not willing to go under old Abe's Rule—We will fight until all are killed or we will have our Independence," he promised.[108]

Another wounded Texan who traveled south was one of the Fourth Texas's favorite officers, Lt. Col. Benjamin Franklin Carter. Shot had torn through his face, hand, and leg. His journey in an ambulance was so painful that Carter chose to be left on the side of the road rather than continue. Brought to Chambersburg, Pennsylvania, the townspeople looked with horror at the Confederate wounded. They were "filthy, bloody, with wounds undressed and swarming with vermin, and almost famished for food and water, they presented such a sight as I hope I may never see again," Chambersburg resident Jacob Hoke remembered.[109]

The Confederates went to homes, hospitals, and churches in the area. The names and units of the wounded circulated in town, and when Rev. Dr. Samuel Reed Fisher and his wife, Naomi, heard of Carter's arrival, they rushed to visit him. Naomi's son from her first marriage was Capt. Mark Kerns, who died beneath his guns at the Battle of Second Manassas. It was she who had received Kerns's effects that Carter insisted be sent to the captain's family, and Naomi Fisher also knew that Carter had had his men bury Kerns properly, wrapped in Carter's own coat. After being transferred to a nearby hospital, it became clear that Carter was dying. His one request was that someone give him "a Christian burial," but most of the local churches were refusing to accept Confederate dead. In the end, a Methodist Church in Chambersburg finally agreed to bury the former Austin mayor, perhaps for the mercy he had shown Naomi Fisher's son a year earlier.[110]

Pvt. John Lewis Tarkington of Company H, Fifth Texas, was wounded in the leg at Gettysburg and, like Carter, left behind when he "fell by the way," too sick to continue on the retreat with Lee's army. Tarkington lay in a workshop for three days in a small Maryland town, too sick to leave or even sit up. Locals found him and eventually took him to the home of a Mr. Keller. "They carried me into a room and stripped off my filthy rags, put me into a tub of warm water and with soap and towels, they not only bathed but gave me a good scrubbing." The Marylanders placed Tarkington, dressed in clean clothes, in the "first real bed I had seen since I left my mother's home." Attended to by a physician and Keller's family, Tarkington slowly recovered. When he announced that he would return to his unit, Keller suggested that Tarkington remain until the war ended, and then make the journey home to Liberty, Texas. But the private insisted, thinking that he had likely been "given up for dead" by the Fifth Texas for so long that he might get a discharge. Instead, Tarkington noted, upon rejoining Company H, "I got a darned ol musket and carried it until the war closed."[111]

As other Texas Brigade wounded rested at Texas Hospital in Richmond, those in camp discussed the likelihood that they would be engaged in more battles that summer. Nearly all of them agreed that they would, and John West, now a veteran, theorized that there would certainly be an engagement in the next few weeks. J. R. Loughridge mourned the loss of men like J. Q. Harris, the Navarro County schoolteacher who fell at Loughridge's side at Gettysburg. They were both out with the skirmishers well in advance of the Fourth Texas and wound up fighting closer to Devil's Den than with the rest of their regiment at Little Round Top. Harris was shot through the head as they had pushed forward, and Loughridge missed his "brave and noble friend." But he was happy to tell Felicia that the rest of their wounded were recovering nicely. J. D. Caddell is "fast getting well," and the men all cheered when they heard from John Bell Hood, who "sent us word that he would be out about the 15th [of August]."[112] J. R. Loughridge was tired of the fighting and tired of losing friends, but he believed the only way to end the war to his satisfaction and that of his family was through Confederate independence. Perhaps the next battle, the Texans mused, would secure their nation and send them home.

Mark Smither exemplified that confidence in late July 1863. He boasted that he and Company D of the Fifth Texas were "ahead as usual" at Gettysburg. "It is given up fact that it is the best fighting the best looking and [has] more gentlemen in it than any other company in the Regt.," he wrote. Smither had caught their original captain, Robert M. Powell, as he fell and later placed his close and wounded friend, 2nd Lt. Campbell Wood, on an equally wounded horse that carried Wood to a field hospital in a Gettysburg barn. There Wood sent for their old regimental surgeon, Robert H. Breckinridge, promoted to medical inspector for the entire Army of Northern Virginia, who had promised to care for the Fifth Texas men if they ever needed him. As Mark Smither marched south with Lee's army, he likely thought of Colonel Powell, Lt. Colonel Bryan, his dear friend Campbell Wood, and their captain, William T. Hill, also seriously wounded. But after listing all of their casualties and the deaths of friends and admitting that he was not sure if his letter would reach his mother across the Mississippi, Smither paused and smiled. "Do you remember this Day!" he asked? "Today, two years ago, you gave me your blessing and told me to go and serve my country!"[113]

The summer of 1863 inflicted devastating losses on the Texas Brigade and the Army of Northern Virginia, but it did little to dampen the men's morale. They did not see Gettysburg as a turning point in the war, nor did their defeat in Pennsylvania diminish their faith in Lee and in themselves. With the fall of Vicksburg, the chances of recruiting replacements had all but disappeared, and the continued dwindling of their ranks would become an issue. From this point forward, the men who remained in the brigade, or who returned to it from hospitals and as exchanged prisoners east of the Mississippi, were all that was left to keep the Texas Brigade in the field. Despite these hardships, Hood's Texans remained sure of themselves, their commanders, and their cause.

Arthur B. Allison, ca. 1860s. Company C, 5th Texas Infantry.
Archival Collection of Pearce Museum at Navarro College, Corsicana, Texas.

Possibly Harvey H. Black, ca. 1850s–1860s. Company A, 1st Texas Infantry.
Courtesy Weldon Nash, Jr. Dallas, Texas. Private Collection.

Andrew N. Erskine, ca. 1860s. Company D, 4th Texas Infantry.
Courtesy descendants Melinda Jane Laird Kilian (Austin, Texas) and Melissa Ann Laird Lingwall (Cedar Hill, Texas). Private Collections.

Ann Johnston Erskine, postwar. Her husband, brother, brother-in-law, and nephew served in Company D, 4th Texas Infantry.
Courtesy of descendants Melinda Jane Laird Kilian (Austin, Texa) and Melissa Ann Laird Lingwall (Cedar Hill, Texas). Private Collections.

Rufus King Felder and cousin Miers Felder. Company E, 5th Texas Infantry.
Courtesy of Historical Research Center, Texas Heritage Museum, Hill College, Hillsboro, Texas.

First Texas Infantry in Camp near Quantico, Virginia.
Courtesy of Rosenberg Library, Miscellaneous Photographs, Galveston, Texas.

Val Giles, 1868. Company B, 4th Texas Infantry.
By J. H. Fitzgibbon, Prints and Photographs Collection, di_08349, The Dolph Briscoe Center for American History, The University of Texas at Austin.

Goree Brothers, 1910. Pleasant K. "Scrap," Edwin K., and Robert D. Goree. Pleasant K. and Edwin K. Goree served in Company H, 5th Texas Infantry with their brother Langston. Robert served in Walker's Texas Division in the western theater. Courtesy of Historical Research Center, Texas Heritage Museum, Hill College, Hillsboro, Texas.

Thomas Jewett Goree, ca. 1860s. The eldest of the Goree brothers, T. J. served as an aide-de-camp on General James Longstreet's staff. Courtesy of SHSU Special Collections, Newton Gresham Library, Sam Houston State University, Huntsville, Texas.

A. B. Green, ca. 1860s. Company K, 5th Texas Infantry.
Courtesy of Polk County Memorial Museum, Livingston, Texas.

William T. Hill, postwar. Company D, 5th Texas Infantry.
Last commander of the 5th Texas.
Courtesy of Historical Research Center, Texas Heritage Museum, Hill College, Hillsboro, Texas.

Brigadier General John Bell Hood, 1862. He only commanded the brigade for six months, but Hood was the men's favorite commander. Courtesy of The American Civil War Museum, Richmond, Virginia.

Willis Landrum with wife Ann Elizabeth "Lizzie" Harris Landrum
and daughter Nancy Lula Landrum, ca 1870–1880.
Courtesy of Landrum descendants Mary Lou Percy, Georgetown, Texas,
and Joanne Watson Percy, Georgetown, Texas. Private Collections.

Felicia Martin Loughridge, ca. 1880s–1890s. Her husband, J. R. Loughridge, served
as 1st Lieutenant and later Captain of Company I, 4th Texas Infantry.
Courtesy of Pearce Museum at Navarro College. Corsicana, Texas.

James Rodgers Loughridge, ca. 1861–1865.
1st Lieutenant and later Captain of Company I, 4th Texas Infantry.
Courtesy of Pearce Museum at Navarro College. Corsicana, Texas.

Mary and Ella Loughridge, ca. 1860s–1870s.
Daughters of Felicia and James Rodgers Loughridge, Company I, 4th Texas Infantry.
Courtesy of Pearce Museum at Navarro College. Corsicana, Texas.

Van Manning, ca. 1860s–1880s. Commander, 3rd Arkansas Infantry.
Library of Congress.

William H. "Howdy" Martin, postwar, from painting. Original Captain, Company K,
4th Texas Infantry. Martin commanded the 4th Texas at the end of the war.
Courtesy of descendant Martha Hartzog from her family archives, Austin, Texas.
Private Collection of Martha Hartzog, Austin, Texas.

Joseph B. Polley, postwar. Original Private, Company F,
4th Texas Infantry, later Regimental Quatermaster-Sergeant.
Courtesy of Historical Research Center, Texas Heritage Museum, Hill College, Hillsboro, Texas.

Thomas J. Selman, ca. 1860s.
Original Private and later Captain, Company E, 4th Texas Infantry.
Courtesy of Historical Research Center, Texas Heritage Museum, Hill College, Hillsboro, Texas.

Lucy Morton Sullivan, postwar. Her son, Private Robert Anderson Sullivan, served in Company F, Fourth Texas Infantry with his close friend and cousin by marriage Patrick Penn, as well as Penn's brother, Abraham C. Penn, and Penn's brother-in-law, Quin Menefee, along with Sullivan's cousin Ed Crockett. Courtesy of Sullivan descendant, Jane Gillette Riggs, Baytown, Texas. Private Collection.

Robert Anderson Sullivan, ca. 1860s. Original Private, Company F, Fourth Texas Infantry. Courtesy of Sullivan descendant Jane Gillette Riggs, Baytown, Texas. Private Collection.

Louis T. Wigfall, ca. 1860s–1870s. Original commander of the Texas Brigade. Library of Congress.

Maude Jeannie Fuller Young, ca. 1860s–1870s. She was a nurse, fundraiser, and writer for the Confederate cause and especially Hood's Texas Brigade while her son (he enlisted January 1, 1865) and brother served in Company A, 5th Texas Infantry. Hood's Texans named her "Mother of Hood's Texas Brigade Association" at their first reunion in 1872.
Courtesy of The Dolph Briscoe Center for American History, University of Texas at Austin.

A LACK OF LEADERSHIP

The Battle of Chickamauga and the Hard Winter of 1863–64

In the fall of 1863, Hood's Texas Brigade was sent with much of James Longstreet's First Corps to support Braxton Bragg's efforts in East Tennessee. When they clashed with Federals at the Battle of Chickamauga, the Texas Brigade fought well but, once again, suffered significant casualties. They lost more still, for little gain, in the fighting at Knoxville in November. Morale in the unit would sag this winter, but it had little to do with those battles or with their families at home. Rather, the brigade suffered unusual fractures in their leadership from Gen. J. B. Robertson down to company commanders. This was compounded by supply problems that left the men insufficiently clothed, fed, and sheltered during a cold winter in the Tennessee mountains. These issues inspired a sense among the brigade that they were undervalued and unappreciated so far from their beloved Lee and his Army of Northern Virginia. The result was a spike in disciplinary issues and in desertions that were not fully resolved until Longstreet's corps returned to Virginia in April 1864. Once reunited with Lee, the Texas Brigade resumed its faith in itself and its focus on the war. Desertion dropped back down to their regular wartime levels (much lower than average for the army), men on French, or unapproved, leave returned to the ranks, and the brigade's rolls swelled as exchanged prisoners and the sick and wounded returned from hospitals and furloughs. By the time the campaign season of 1864 began, the Texas Brigade would number nearly 800 combat-ready men with a total of 1,300 soldiers on the rolls. The brigade was as confident as ever in their central role in securing Confederate independence. First, though, came the hardships in Tennessee.

In late August 1863, Confederate planners approved James Longstreet's proposal to move the divisions of John Bell Hood and Lafayette McLaws and Col. E. P. Alexander's artillery battalion by rail to east Tennessee. There they would help Confederate general Braxton Bragg deliver devastating blows to Union forces under Gen. William S. Rosecrans. Longstreet hoped to roll Federal forces back to the Ohio River, which would relieve pressure on the rest of Lee's army in Virginia, crush Union morale, and encourage Confederate confidence before both armies went into winter quarters.[1]

In the second week of September, the Texas Brigade left their position along the Rappahannock River and marched toward Richmond. They rode by rail through the Carolinas and Georgia, and during the week-long journey they reinforced their reputation as good, but ill-disciplined, soldiers. Longstreet's men, packed into freight cars, improved ventilation by destroying the cars' wooden walls. When passenger cars pulled to a side rail to let the military trains pass, Hood's men snatched hats off the heads of men leaning out their windows to cheer and wish the soldiers well.[2] During a twenty-four-hour layover in Wilmington, North Carolina, many of the men rested or visited extended family in the area. Others, however, found the taverns of Paddy Hollow and created such a disturbance that three members of the town guard were called out. One nearly had his skull cracked, another suffered multiple stab wounds, and the third, a man named Harker who was in his fifties, was badly beaten.[3] Locals were upset, as were the citizens of Raleigh when Benning's brigade created an even greater ruckus when they came through town. But officers were more focused on keeping to their schedule—and they were already behind—than pacifying locals on the home front, so Longstreet's corps rattled on through South Carolina and into Georgia.

The Texas Brigade was the first unit of Lee's army to arrive at Ringgold, Georgia, on September 18. They marched with Bushrod Johnson's Provisional Division until Hood caught up with the men along banks of Chickamauga Creek near Reed's Bridge later that day. The men knew not to cheer when they were so close to Federal lines, but "every hat was lifted" as Hood passed his old brigade. He was followed by some members of Terry's Texas Rangers, and a number of Hood's men stepped out of line to briefly greet friends and neighbors in the ranks. The rest of Terry's men were a few miles away, but several of Robertson's men noted seeing members of the Eighth Texas Cavalry shortly after seeing Hood. The Texas units were "kindred spirits," Joe Polley claimed, and all the men—including the Arkansans—enjoyed seeing members of their home state during their service in Tennessee. Similar, though brief reunions with friends in the Seventh Texas Infantry were also enjoyed later at the battle.[4]

Hood's arrival at Chickamauga placed him in temporary command of Longstreet's First Corps, because Longstreet had not yet arrived. Lafayette

McLaws had seniority over Hood, but McLaws was delayed, too. In addition to this unexpected change in the command structure, Hood had little time to get to know his fellow commanders in the Confederate Army of Tennessee, nor did they get to know him. This was troubling, as it would affect cooperation and communication in the coming battle. This situation was compounded by further disruptions in Hood's old division. They would fight under the leadership of Evander Law at Chickamauga, while Col. James L. Sheffield took command of Law's old brigade. But Sheffield would have to fight without a staff because Hood took his staff with him, as did Law, and Sheffield could not reasonably take the remaining regimental officers from his old Forty-Eighth Alabama.

Within the Texas Brigade, however, things remained relatively stable. Jerome B. Robertson had recovered from his Gettysburg wound and was in command of the brigade, and Van Manning had reunited with the Third Arkansas. The Fourth Texas was led by Maj. J. C. Rogers, who took command at Gettysburg after Lt. Col. B. F. Carter was mortally wounded. Similarly, Lt. Col. J. P. Bane led the Fifth Texas after the Gettysburg wounding and capture of Col. Mike Powell, and while Lt. Col. King Bryan was recovering from his Gettysburg wound.

The First Texas, however, suffered a late command change when Phillip Work became too ill to continue to lead his men. He left for Selma, Alabama, on September 18, and while recovering, he decided not to rejoin his unit. Work was frustrated that the official commander of the First Texas, Col. A. T. Rainey, had still not sufficiently recovered from his Gaines's Mill wound to resume leadership of the regiment, though Rainey had recently been assigned to military duties in Houston, Texas. In November 1863, Work had still not recovered and decided to resign his commission in part for his health but also to "be relieved of an unpleasant position" under Rainey's official, if absent, leadership. By the summer of 1864, Work would be fighting with a Texas cavalry regiment in the Trans-Mississippi West.[5] Work's departure placed Capt. R. J. Harding in command of the First Texas. Harding had attended the Virginia Military Institute, was an original first sergeant of Company B, and was later elected by the men as their first lieutenant and elected again as their captain. Clearly Harding had the men's respect and he knew them well, and he had been a successful company commander. But he had never led a regiment, and they were about to enter the second-bloodiest battle of the American Civil War.[6]

These changes created a challenging situation for the Texas Brigade at Chickamauga. They would fight in a corps and division with an entirely new command structure, and in an army with whom they had no connections or

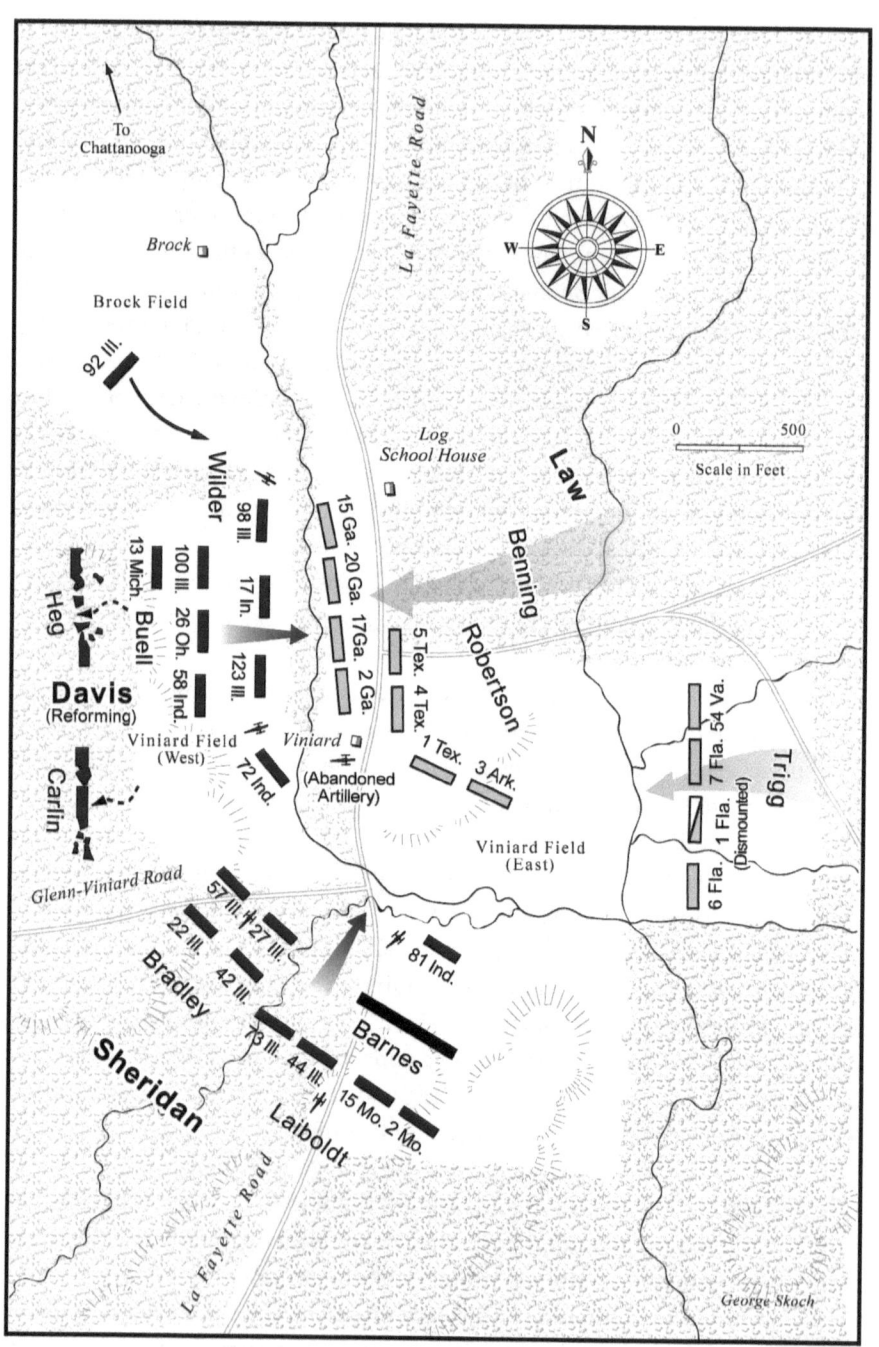

Battle of Chickamauga, September 19, 1863

familiarity. The Texas regiments would be led by men with combat and command experience but little familiarity with regimental command. One thing that worked to their advantage, however, was the number of their wounded and captured men from previous fights who had rejoined the brigade. Hood's Texans would go into the battle of Chickamauga with about 1,300 men.[7]

As the sun set on September 18, the Texas Brigade slept on their arms in the fields east of the La Fayette–Chattanooga Road near Dalton's Ford. They were so close to Union lines that the men could hear Federals cutting trees and preparing defenses for the next day's fight. Several units exchanged fire throughout that cold evening, and a few members of the brigade were wounded. Among them was one of the Perry brothers in the First Texas. A Federal round cut through Eugene Perry's cap box and into his hip, driving several caps into his body that proved incredibly painful. Between the cold, the orders prohibiting fires in camp, and the intermittent exchanges between Federals and Confederates, few of the men slept that night.[8]

The Battle of Chickamauga started on the right of the Confederate line, continued toward the middle, and spread finally to the Confederate left, where the Texas Brigade was deployed in the woods northeast of the Viniard farm and the Viniard-Alexander Road. Around 3:00 p.m., Hood ordered Bushrod Johnson to advance and push back the threat created by the attack of Union colonel Hans Heg's brigade. Desperate fighting raged for about an hour, when Hood ordered Robertson and Law to move their brigades up to replace Johnson's exhausted men, who were falling back. The Texas Brigade advanced through the woods, moving at an angle toward the southwest, straddling the Viniard-Alexander Road. They were hit with artillery fire as they moved forward, but the trees all around them offered some cover. Livestock had cleared most of the undergrowth, which eased the men's movement and would have improved visibility if the day's fighting had not left so much smoke in the air.

The Texas Brigade had barely entered the eastern field of the Viniard farm and was about two hundred yards east of La Fayette Road when fire poured into their left flank. Robertson gave Manning permission to shift two companies in response, but the pressure from the Thirty-Eighth Illinois and 101st Ohio soon required the entire regiment to focus their attention on this threat. As the brigade surged farther west, Robertson released his right flank from Sheffield's brigade; there was no way to support Manning and keep the division connected. Law's division would fight the rest of the day as two separate forces. Fortunately for Robertson, Gen. Henry Benning's Georgia brigade would advance to support him.[9]

As the Texas Brigade continued driving the Federals back, they could see the Viniard house and several outbuildings in the distance across La Fayette Road. Illinois soldiers poured fire into the advancing Confederates, but Robertson's men came on, using trees and terrain for limited cover and keeping up a steady fire. Their line would surge forward, and then Federal fire would stall the Confederate advance until, once again, the Texans and Arkansans recovered and pushed the Federals back, "stubbornly contesting every inch of ground," Robertson reported. He paused to dress his men in the cover of a ravine east of La Fayette Road and then continued the advance, driving the Federals before them as they raced up a small hill.

As the Texans and Arkansans crested the rise, infantry fire from their front, and grape and canister from Federal batteries on their right, tore into the brigade from a distance of just two hundred yards. Maj. J. C. Rogers, leading the Fifth Texas, was hit and collapsed amid an "incessant shower of grape and canister," Capt. Tacitus T. Clay reported, and "Volleys of Musketry" that "exceeded anything" Fifth Texas lieutenant B. I. Franklin had "ever heard."[10] In the Fourth Texas, Lt. Col. J. P. Bane was wounded, too, and command fell to Capt. Robert H. Bassett, but he soon fell, too, as did Lts. J. M. Bookman and Allen G. Killingsworth, and color sergeant Ed Francis. Command went to Capt. James T. Hunter, the Huntsville constable who had helped organize Company H, then known as the Porter Guards, in 1861. Nearby, Capt. R. J. Harding worked to maintain control of the "Ragged First," but they, too, suffered debilitating casualties, and the few officers who entered the battle were suffering as much as the men. At least twice, Hunter reported, enemy lines made contact, and the men resorted to clubbing each other with their muskets and stabbing with bayonets. Still, the Texas Brigade clung to their position at the Viniard farm, which they retained as Federals fell back about a mile to the west.[11]

Captain Estep and the Eighth Indiana battery had worked feverishly to save their guns, but the Texas Brigade's "musketry fire became so heavy, terrible, and galling," Estep explained. P. L. Hubbard, one of the Indiana artillerymen was working a gun in the dooryard of the Viniard house as Confederate artillery hammered their position in addition to the infantry fire. A shell burst overhead, killing five of the artillery horses for his gun. It was immediately after that, Hubbard explained, that the Texas Brigade came rushing toward them and he and the Eighth Indiana went "running to the rear," dragging their gun with them.[12]

The Texas Brigade was well in advance of the main Confederate line. They had lost dozens of men in each regiment, including a number of officers, and they were still losing men to persistent Federal artillery fire to their front from Union colonel John T. Wilder's brigade. Realizing that they could not hold the position without reinforcements, Robertson requested artillery support for the third time that afternoon, but none came. Benning's Georgians, however, advanced behind and beside the Texans just as they had at Gettysburg, and this added pressure proved too much for the weakening Federals. Sgt. W. R. Houghton in the Second Georgia watched as "the Yankee line in the field began to give way. As they ran back" Houghton and the Georgians, along with a number of Texans, continued to shoot down the Federals in a "horrible slaughter." Despite this, Benning and Robertson could not hold their position without more support. Robertson was furious at the thought of giving up all they had gained, but he refused to sacrifice men for nothing. He ordered his men back, with Benning's Georgians on their right, into the woods east of La Fayette Road.[13]

The night of September 19 was painfully cold as temperatures dropped low enough for a light frost to cover the ground. The Texas Brigade, like most of the units that fought around the Viniard farm, settled in disorganized lines a few hundred yards into the woods along a ridge line that ran parallel to La Fayette Road. Commanders forbade the men from building fires—they were too close to the Federals—and there were no rations to distribute. But at least their proximity to Chickamauga Creek provided freshwater. The Texans and Arkansans got what sleep they could before the battle resumed in the morning.[14]

On September 20, Robertson's men shifted to their right and took a position a couple hundred yards behind Sheffield's brigade, with "Rock" Benning's brigade on Robertson's right. Their confidence grew as word spread down the line that their corps commander, Gen. James Longstreet, had arrived on the field. Around 11:00 a.m., Hood's divisions moved forward, advancing across La Fayette Road. As the Texas Brigade passed the Brotherton House on their right, they continued across wooded, rolling ground for about eight hundred yards before turning north and marching another seven hundred yards while suffering under the efforts of determined Federal artillerymen. When intense fire opened on their right front, the brigade shifted their focus to meet the threat. Company and regimental commanders directed the men as they rushed toward the Federals on a small hill and drove them back. But the retreating Union infantry reorganized in a fortified position on the next ridgeline and stopped the Texas Brigade's advance. Still, things were going well for Confederates overall. Union general William Rosecrans had shifted a Federal division north down his line and accidentally left the spot they vacated wide open, just as Longstreet ordered Confederates into that same position. Federals tried to close the gap, but they failed to do so before eight brigades rushed forward and took advantage of the vacuum in their front.

For Hood's Texans, however, much of their fight on September 20 was defined by frustration and uncharacteristic failures in command. Steady Federal fired to their immediate front stalled their advance, and Texans and Arkansans, especially in the center and left of the brigade, suddenly realized that they were being hit with volleys from their flanks and rear. Robertson's men were well in advance of the rest of the Confederates around them, but the bigger issue was that Capt. John Cleveland, now in command of the Fifth Texas, had noted that Benning's Georgians had fallen back on his right. Assuming the whole division was withdrawing, Cleveland directed the Fifth Texans to fall back, too, until he realized that the rest of the Texas Brigade was still fighting. Before he could rush the "Bloody Fifth" back into line, the Fourth Texas came under tremendous fire from the Seventy-Fourth and Tenth Indiana. Compounding this were the Federal batteries not one hundred yards to their northwest that made "our position a veritable hell on earth," Val Giles insisted. Cleveland's men managed to advance and pour a volley into the Indianans on their right that temporarily stopped that threat.[15]

On the left of their line, however, the Third Arkansas came under intense fire that several of the men were certain came from fellow Confederates. The new uniforms the Texans and Arkansans had been issued in August were particularly dark, and some of the men later theorized that it caused them to be mistaken for Federals. Miles Smith in the Fourth Texas swore this was the case and insisted that errors like that made Chickamauga "the most demoralizing fight to me of the war." It is certainly possible that this was the case, but most of the fire was actually coming from the Twenty-First Ohio. It caused the brigade to, once again, falter in its coordination, leading Van Manning to frown at the "deranged condition of the line." Capt. Jim Hunter watched the left of the Texas Brigade give way and heard men shouting that "they were flanked." The Texas Brigade fell back in disorder to the relative security of some timber. Officers tried to dress their lines, but regiments were being led by lieutenants and captains, they had suffered serious casualties, and many of the men, from Robertson down to the privates, were positive they were being fired on by fellow Confederates. Compounding the issue was Col. Charles G. Harker's brigade of Union general Thomas Wood's division, which had just shifted into a solid line of resistance on the Texas Brigade's front. Robertson was willing to advance again with support, but there was none. Confederates all around them were already engaged in their own rapid advance or broken up from fighting earlier in the day. It was, Val Giles insisted, the "meanest, most unsatisfactory place . . . in the whole war. With my messmate, brave George W. Nichols, dead in the old road ten feet in front of me, J. K. P. Jones, a gallant boy of my company, dead twenty feet behind me," and a "poor Yankee dead at my feet," Giles felt "like the whole world was coming to an end then and there."[16] Unable to hold this forward position and under pressure on multiple fronts, Robertson ordered his brigade to wait in the timber until he received further orders.[17]

John Bell Hood had watched his old command fall back, and galloped over to help their officers launch a counterattack. While Hood and Robertson spoke, a ball slammed into Hood's left leg, tearing muscle and shattering bone. Several of the Texans raced to help him, while Hood continued to give orders and urge his division commanders to continue their pressure on the Federal line. Hood noted the irony that despite commanding five divisions that day, it was men from his old brigade who were closest to him and offered immediate care. He had enjoyed few things as much as his "long and constant service with this noble brigade." "If a ditch was to be leaped, or a fortified position to be carried," Hood boasted, "General Lee knew no better troops upon which to rely."[18] That frustrating fight at Chickamauga was the last time the Texas Brigade would serve on the same battlefield with their favorite commander and namesake.

Rosecrans's error and the Confederates' ability to capitalize on it led to success for Bragg's army, but Chickamauga did not feel like a victory to the Texas Brigade. They had fought bravely, but their advances lacked coordination and were not supported, which required them to fall back and give up ground for which they had sacrificed greatly. The brigade seethed about all that had gone wrong. Looking down the line, they could not help but notice how many experienced officers and enlisted men had fallen around the Viniard farm and in Dyer's field. With the Mississippi River closed, it would be almost impossible to recruit replacements for their dwindling brigade. Hood's wounding marked the climax of an incredibly disappointing two-day battle that had come at great cost and, at least from what the Texans and Arkansans could see, had brought little advantage.

Despite his September victory in Tennessee, Braxton Bragg failed to race after Rosecrans's army, and the Federals escaped to Chattanooga. Confederates laid siege to the city, and the Texas Brigade helped construct extensive defenses around their lines over the next month and helped to man them. They enjoyed a negotiated peace, Joe Polley explained, after coming to terms with the Union forces opposite them to not waste powder. No one would fall back, but there was no need for killing that would achieve nothing.[19] Waters Berryman insisted that things were not quite that friendly, but he, too, admitted that the Texans continued their habit of modifying orders they found excessive. With picket lines just one hundred yards apart, the men were not allowed to fire their weapons unless Union forces attacked, Berryman explained. In addition, "no communication what so ever [is] to be held with the enemy—death is the penalty, but some of the boys trade papers with them." Instead, both armies seemed to just sit and watch each other. "I know the Yankees will not attack us," Berryman explained to his mother, "and it would be foolish for General Bragg to attack them in fortifications almost impregnable."[20]

As they sat in their lines, the men reflected on all they had lost. About 1,300 men had journeyed to Georgia and 570 of them, or about 45 percent, had been killed, wounded, or went missing. Dugat Williams told his fiancée, Laura, that Confederates had gained a "great victory" at Chickamauga, but "I lost another cousin in this battle. Out of four that were members of Company F, I am the only one left."[21] When Confederate president Jefferson Davis traveled to Chattanooga, he visited the Texas Brigade in camp. Waters Berryman watched the formal, gaunt Mississippian and noted that when Davis "took a long look at our old Regiment, there were only about 90 men out in time to see him." When the president rode in front of their flag, all eyes looked at the colors, "riddled with minnieballs." Their "thinned ranks told the tale too well [of] where we had been," Berryman noted. Davis watched the men but remained silent. They may have been relieved that Davis spared them the boastful speeches of 1862.[22]

As frustrated as the men were that fall, they remained proud of themselves. The Texas Brigade heard rumors that General Hood was getting well and celebrated when they heard he might rejoin them soon. "He said he would fight Yankees as long as he lived," Berryman smiled. "We miss the Old General very much." The men had similar praise for the Fourth Texas's Capt. J. R. Loughridge, promoted after Capt. C. M. Winkler was wounded at Gettysburg. Berryman declared that Loughridge "went in with a yell and killed as many Yankees as anybody" at Chickamauga. He was "such a common looking man," Berryman smiled, but "he is as brave as Caesar himself."[23] Indeed, Captain Loughridge had fought so well that Texas Brigade commissary officer Maj. Tilford A. Hamilton insisted that "no braver man came from the Prairies of Texas to fight the Battles of his country.... It is sufficient to say that he fully deserves the title given him by the brave boys of the Texas Brigade, 'Marshall Ney.'"[24]

Their pride, however, was offset by sorrow. In the Third Arkansas, John Staples reflected quietly on all they had survived, including the Minié ball that had come so close it left a hole in his coat. He and his brother William had enlisted together in Union County, Arkansas, in the summer of 1861, sons of a wealthy Eldorado Hills farmer, Jethro Staples, who remained home with his wife, Elizabeth, and their other five children. William became so sick in the first fall of the war that he was sent home on a medical discharge, but he reenlisted in the spring of 1862, determined to fight in Virginia alongside his brother. It was not clear what made him ill, but by the following August, William was back in the hospital, and he died later that month. One year later, almost to the day of William's death, word arrived that their mother, Elizabeth, had died, too. William prayed that he would be "so luckey as to live to See this horreble war come to a close & get home," but even then, he added, home would never be the same.[25]

Death occupied C. S. Worsham's thoughts as well that fall as he sat amid his fellow Fourth Texans. "Our little Regt.," he noted, had suffered "a sad reduction indeed" since 1861. He heard rumors that the Texas Brigade might be furloughed, but he said nothing else on the matter, perhaps concluding that the likelihood was so slim it was not worth discussing. "Texas has been as a land of dreams for the last five months," Worsham confessed, "for during that time no news has reached me from its shores." Like Staples and Loughridge and many of the men, Worsham found strength and comfort in his faith. And for him, this was a new experience. "Ma," he explained, "I am a different boy now to what I was when I left you. I have been Baptized by our Chaplain and am trying to be a Christian Soldier Boy. Oh may *all my brothers* strive to do the same for their *Mother's sake.*"[26]

Like John Staples, "Sam" Worsham had buried his brother Ned, a fellow soldier in the Fourth Texas, in 1862. The sad truth was that such stories had become ordinary. Fifth Texas lieutenant B. I. Franklin's letters to his wife, Mary, were starting to sound as cold as the casualty reports published in the papers. Perhaps, though, he was trying to get accurate information to the families at home about the men in his company. "We lost some of our bravest and best men" at Chickamauga, he told Mary. "John Kilby killed dead on the field John Short mortally wounded died on the 21st Wm Crabtree Thigh amputated since dead Junius Graves leg amputated since dead Wounded James Holmes severely knee cap marked by pieces of shell W. A. Holmes slightly in thigh Ben Baldwin slight in Head Tooley slighting in thigh, Davis slight in thigh, Holt slighting in shoulder Spence slightly Hood slightly in hip," Franklin listed.

He was worried about what all of this would do to the men's families. Franklin thought of Elvira Short, a forty-eight-year-old widow at home in Washington County. "One of her sons [twenty-four-year-old William was] wounded & left in the hands of the enemy at Gettysburg and the other [seventeen-year-old John was] killed here. John was a brave boy and died like a man fighting for his country so of the others," Franklin told his wife, knowing she would share that with Elvira Short. "[Junius] Graves as good a young man as I know brave & noble," had fallen, too. "I Grieve for his Mother & sister & brother," Franklin explained and added the name of John Kilby, who "leaves a blind sister the other a wife & children dependent on them for support." The direct link between the battlefield and the home front was painfully obvious. Despite this, their letters did not yet indicate that the brigade had reached a breaking point. Instead, they were working to sustain each other in camp and at home.[27]

The Texas Brigade remained around Chattanooga until late October, when they participated in the Battle of Wauhatchie, another fight defined by confusion and misdirection. The lowest point of the battle was when most of the Fourth Texas heard they were flanked, once again, and this time the regiment broke and ran. Years later, Joe Polley, in writing his history of the brigade, explained that, "deeming it braver to live than to die, and moved by thoughts of home and its loved ones—the officers and privates of the gallant and hitherto invincible 4th Texas stood not upon the order of their going, but went with a celerity and unanimity truly remarkable." The regiment "disappeared bodily, stampeded *nolens volens* [like it or not], and plunged recklessly into the umbrageous and shadowy depths behind them, their flight hastened by the loud huzzaing of the triumphant Yankees, and the echoing volleys they poured into the treetops, high above the heads of their retreating antagonists."[28] The moment highlighted the brigade's weakening foundation, and it launched the first major attack on Robertson's leadership of the unit. He insisted that "my brigade did not 'abandon its position.' It came out under orders" and accomplished its objective, but this was not entirely true. The incident, and Longstreet's and Micah Jenkins's criticisms of Robertson, indicated the beginning of the end of his time with the Texas Brigade.[29]

On November 3, Longstreet's corps was ordered east to Knoxville. Bragg's plan was to use "Old Pete" as a diversion to draw Federal forces from Chattanooga to help defend Union general Ambrose Burnside's men at Knoxville. After Longstreet won there, Bragg theorized, he would return to help Bragg finish their siege. Mix-ups with their travel caused delays, and Longstreet struggled to command his men with few supplies, a diminished staff, no quartermaster, and inadequate maps. As at Chattanooga, the Texas Brigade's time at Knoxville was defined by frustrations and failures. They remained there even after Bragg was forced by Ulysses S. Grant to withdraw from Chattanooga and into northern Georgia. Longstreet finally admitted that he could not hold Knoxville, and he, too, fell back in early December. The Texas Brigade did some of their heaviest fighting in weeks covering the Confederates' withdrawal across the Holston River. Once the rebels were safely marching eastward, rumors spread through the ranks that they were headed back to Robert E. Lee and the Army of Northern Virginia. Joe Polley insisted years later that the men began to sing, "Carry Me Back to Ole Virginy" and relished the fact that their luck was turning. But it was not. They would spend the rest of the winter between Knoxville and Morristown, Tennessee, participating in small engagements with Union forces that accomplished little while the men starved, froze, and wondered how everything had gone so terribly wrong.[30]

If there was a time when the Texas Brigade faltered as one of the Confederacy's best units, it was over the winter of 1863–64. None of the faith they had in Lee was ever granted to their commanders in Tennessee, Braxton Bragg and Joseph E. Johnston. The Texas Brigade had lost faith in the Army of Tennessee and any contributions toward victory that they might make in Tennessee, and this fractured the determination that had defined and sustained them since 1861.

This can best be seen in the discipline problems and spike in desertions that defined the Texas Brigade between November 1863 through March 1864. Most of the discipline problems in the Texas Brigade were tied to the issue of insufficient rations and uniforms, blankets, and other fundamental supplies. During inspections in February 1864, multiple Texas Brigade companies had their discipline reported as "Not Good," their military appearance listed as "Shabby," and their uniforms ranked as "Very Inferior." Most of the companies had less than 50 percent of their "assigned for duty" men actually in camp for the muster.[31]

Of course, the Texas Brigade had never been celebrated for their orderly camps or their discipline off the battlefield. What was troubling, though, that discipline was reaching an all-time low; they were dangerously undersupplied; and desertion, for the first time, was an issue in the Texas Brigade. Of the 102 courts-martial involving Texas Brigade soldiers throughout the war, 20 percent of those took place between October 1863 and April 1864. Most men who received a severe sentence, including death, had it commuted or were assigned hard labor, but the spike in charges indicated a fissure in the once strong foundation of the brigade.[32]

Part of this was likely caused by an uncharacteristic lack of leadership in the brigade that winter. From late 1862 through late 1863, Jerome Bonaparte Robertson commanded the Texas Brigade. While not their most talented or aggressive field commander, Robertson earned the loyalty of the men through his attentiveness to their needs and his leadership in two of their biggest and most challenging battles: Gettysburg and Chickamauga. In East Tennessee, however, Robertson earned the ire of his division commander, Micah Jenkins, as well as their corps commander, James Longstreet.

In mid-December 1863, Jenkins officially charged Robertson with "conduct highly prejudicial to good order and military discipline," inspired in part by the brigade's failures at the Battle of Wauhatchie but largely derived from Robertson's open complaints about the lack of supply and care for his men. The court-martial investigated these charges carefully. The panel of officers included future Texas Brigade commander John Gregg, whom Hood's Texans had rescued from the Chickamauga battlefield after Gregg had been wounded and abandoned. The officers found Robertson innocent of improper motives, but they faulted his "conduct" and recommended a reprimand, which resulted in Robertson's removal from command of the Texas Brigade and transfer to the Trans-Mississippi West. With Robertson gone, John Gregg was selected as the Texans' new commander, but at the time of his appointment he was still recovering from a neck wound from Chickamauga. That left the Texas Brigade with a commander under charges from December 1863 through February 1864 and under the command of Fifth Texas colonel King Bryan for nearly a month until John Gregg arrived on March 7.[33]

The Fourth and Fifth Texas drafted a petition rejecting Gregg and requesting that Robertson be returned to brigade command. Whereas Gregg was "acceptable to us," Robertson had their full confidence, having been "at all times willing to sacrifice himself for us and our glorious cause." Additionally, the men noted, Robertson had been removed "without a hearing" and without their input. The Third Arkansas also submitted a petition that demonstrated similar loyalty to Robertson. All of their efforts were rejected, however, and there was nothing the men could do. Robertson departed for Texas in the spring of 1864.[34]

Terrible supply problems contributed to the moral and discipline issues that plagued Longstreet's men that winter. As early as mid-October 1863, Joe Polley had to start borrowing money to supplement his food. The men had "been doing eight days on three days half rations—have had to buy nearly everything we ate and . . . now my funds are run out," Polley complained. "The troops of this army are never paid off more often than three times a year and then only two months pay at one time—Some of the troops have eight or ten months pay due them."[35] By the time winter set in, the men struggled to survive on a diet of too little meat that was often sticky or slimy, and sometimes sparkled with an ominous bluish hue. First Texan O. T. Hanks insisted that if "a quarter [of the meat] was thrown against a wall it would stick." This was supplemented with flour that looked fine but proved anything but. It was "sour," so much so that when baked, the biscuits, Hanks explained, "wound nauseate the stomack like ipecac—sometimes would produce vomiting. We could not eat them." For quite some time that winter, West recalled, the men lived on "three or four ears [of corn] for man per day; that we shelled, parched, and ate . . . and received nothing else. Parched corn, a pipe of good tobacco, clear water, was the menu for several days."[36]

Dugat Williams marveled at their isolation. It seemed like the Texas Brigade, once so loved by Confederates, had been cut off from the world. "East Tennessee is a very much out of the way place," he thought. "This portion of it has no Rail Road Communication with the balance of the world at all. . . . We seldom see a newspaper here. I have seen but one since we left Chattanooga and it was six weeks old and contained nothing interesting but the President's message, so we are a long ways behind hand in the little events that have been transpiring in Virginia."[37] Rumors abounded that General Robertson might get them all transferred to Texas, and, for the first time, support for returning to Texas to continue the fight grew in the brigade. Some of the most dedicated soldiers in the brigade, including officers like Fifth Texan Dugat Williams, admitted that they all "earnestly hope[d]" it would happen, but he warned Laura that "it seems hardly reasonable that such good fortune is in store for us." John West frowned at the rumors, too. "I do not believe it," he said.[38] Despondent, Williams told Laura: "We are camped in a miserable, hilly mountainous, no account country. At present our bivouac is in a deep pass in a range of mountains through which the East Tennessee and Virginia Railroad passes. I have never learned the name of these mountains and I'm inclined to think they were never named on account of their ugliness."[39]

The isolation the men felt in Tennessee contributed to the shortage in clothing, shoes, blankets, and food that plagued the brigade. John West promised his wife that the "Waco boys are all well," but he worried about their physical condition. They were, "like all the rest, nearly all barefooted and half clad. Many of our best men have been killed and we begin to look like a remnant." Robert Campbell of the Fifth Texas insisted that it was "common site to see barefooted men, men with no pants and some without coats. I for one was without shoes and had but one leg to my pants." Sgt. D. H. Hamilton kept the split sections of his shoes together by tying the pieces to his feet. Eventually he and some others developed a system of cutting wet rawhide in the rough shape of a foot, which they loosely laced together. Malachiah Reeves received rawhides like these from home that winter. Thrilled with gift, he stepped in the center, "pulled it up around my foot and ankle, hairy side in, cut holes for laces, cut from the outer edge and pulled the thong tight enough to hold firmly. Made a good comfortable shoe while it lasted, better than being barefooted!" Reeves smiled. This footwear became popularly known in camp as "Longstreet's Moccasins," and Hamilton declared them a luxury compared to the alternative. In the summer of 1865, Robert Campbell reflected on their hardships that winter in the "snows, rains, and troubles" and declared their campaign in East Tennessee "one of the hardest of this war."[40]

The Texans and Arkansans were not alone in this suffering. Lee's army in Virginia endured similar shortages that winter. Rail lines across the region were damaged from excessive use and washouts from winter rains, and there were not enough mechanics and laborers to repair them (many of these men were serving in the army). There were thousands of tons of forage for the armies in neighboring states, but the weaknesses within the Confederate transportation system and the usual problems of winter travel made it nearly impossible to get those supplies to the men in Tennessee and Virginia before March.[41]

Texas Brigade letters and diaries from this period of November 1863 through March 1864 reveal a powerful sense of rejection and abandonment. This was something the unit, so often celebrated by Confederates, had never experienced. Years later, John West insisted that despite their sufferings, "I heard but little murmuring and *saw* no signs of revolt." The spike in Texas Brigade desertions that winter indicates otherwise. Desertion had been a growing problem for some time throughout the Confederate ranks, but never before for the Texas Brigade. Following the Gettysburg Campaign, Robert E. Lee warned

Confederate president Jefferson Davis that "the number of desertions from this army is so great, and still continues to such an extent, that unless some cessation of them can be caused, I fear success in the field will be seriously endangered." By late February 1864, as Longstreet's First Corps gathered in ranks for their bimonthly muster and inspection, the brigade could not quite muster 784 officers and men present for duty that winter. Robertson explained that there were technically 1,086 men on the rolls, but many of them were "not fit to march."[42] It was not just the Texas Brigade that suffered. Their division had only 5,931 present for duty with 8,729 men absent, and Longstreet's entire corps could muster only 25,514 men with just over that number (27,307) absent.[43] This continued into the spring of 1864, when Robert E. Lee expressed alarm that the Army of Northern Virginia had nearly 6,000 men absent without leave or officially listed as deserters. Over one-third of the men deserted in 1863 and 1864.[44]

In a representative sample of the more than 7,000 men who served in Hood's Brigade from 1861 through 1865, however, only 6 percent deserted during the war. Of those men, 34 percent abandoned the ranks between November 1863 and April 1864.[45] Most deserters in the Army of Northern Virginia came from poor, non-slaveholding families, and one in five was in his forties or older. Also, those who joined the army in 1861 and 1862 were less likely to desert than those who joined in 1863 or later. Indeed, one in every four of those later enlistees deserted.[46] But among Hood's Texans the opposite proved true. These deserters of the cold winter of 1863–64 had enlisted, overwhelmingly, in 1861. Only one in every two Texas Brigade deserters was an 1862 recruit, and throughout the war, only 4 percent of those Texas Brigade volunteers who deserted were 1863 or 1864 recruits.[47] These later enlistees were just as ideologically motivated and tied to the men in the unit as the volunteers of 1861. They chose to serve in a unit that fought far from their homes and was known to suffer high casualty rates. Such convictions had kept and would continue to keep the brigade's desertion rates low, but the spike in these numbers during their winter in East Tennessee indicated a significant problem for commanders.[48]

Officers in the Texas Brigade were well aware of the problems that winter. Tom Goree, serving on Longstreet's staff while three of his four brothers served with the Fifth Texas, told his mother that February: "The Texas Brigade is not in the condition I would desire to have it. The morale of it is bad. They have got it into their head to go across the Mississippi, and many have gone without leave. I hope, however, soon to see a great improvement." Goree declared, "Shame upon the men who have gone to Texas for easy service, and have deserted their brave comrades here." He was "very much mortified, as well as surprised, to hear that Willie Darby, who had obtained a furlough to go to Alabama, has signified his intention of trying to get to Texas and remaining there. When officers act this way, what must be expected of the privates!"[49]

When John Gregg was sufficiently recovered from his Chickamauga wound to take command of the Texas Brigade, he, too, was shocked by its condition. Gregg confided to a friend in Texas: "You know, when I took command of [the Texas Brigade], Genl. Robertson had been absent a long time. Col. [King] Bryan, not even having the first officer of a regiment could not reasonably exercise the influence which a brigade commander might. And the consequence was that I found the brigade a little body of malcontents, some of them deserting every day or two—having, I suppose present for duty about 500 muskets."[50]

Letters and diaries offer few clues to the desertions than those noted above. Their departure could have been inspired by frustration with the lack of furloughs for the Texans and Arkansans. Desertions may have been inspired by their relative proximity to Texas compared to when they were in Virginia.[51] It was also influenced by the poor leadership they suffered through that winter, from Braxton Bragg's failures to J. B. Robertson's court-martial while commander of the Texas Brigade, all of which was compounded by harsh environmental conditions and poor logistical support.

Significantly, the men were not likely as worried about their families as soldiers serving in other Deep South states. Unlike Mississippi, for example, Texas was still relatively untouched by Union forces, and most Texas Brigade families were economically stable at this time. Hood's men had stopped advising their wives on how to handle matters at home, and women like Felicia Loughridge had developed a habit of assuring her husband that he was missed, but all was well. "I am very well satisfied at Mothers her and brother are just as kind to me as they can be," she wrote J. R. Loughridge a week after Chickamauga. "Our corn is not sold yet nor the boat timber no one seems to be in a hurry though for what we owe them." Determined to do what she could for him, Felicia promised, "I intend making up a box of clothes and sending [it] to you if I have to sell some of our cows to get the money."[52]

Many of the women in Milam County, Texas, were doing about as well as Felicia Loughridge to their north. Men in that area had volunteered with J. C. Rogers in the Milam County Grays in 1861, which mustered in as Company

G of the Fifth Texas Infantry. Rogers had suffered a severe wound in his side during the Battle of Chickamauga, but it would be weeks before anyone at home knew that. The wives and families of Milam County, Susan Turnham McCown explained years later, heard little from their men in the Texas Brigade throughout the war. "Letters from east of the Mississippi . . . were very rare, and when we heard of some great battle it might be months before we could learn whether any one from Milam had met a soldier's death. . . . For four long years we waited and watched and prayed," she sighed. While remembering the challenges, McCown also noted that she rarely suffered for food or clothing. Her neighbor had a loom, and McCown's slaves continued to raise cotton in her husband's absence.[53] They carded the cotton, wove it on Mrs. Westbrook's loom, and clothed their families while sending any surplus to the army. "We always had plenty to eat," McCown said, "as both corn and wheat were raised and thousands of cattle roamed over the county and we had plenty of hogs in the post oaks."[54]

The McCowns were not particularly poor, but they were not exceptionally wealthy either. They were a solidly middle-class farm family, and others like them across Texas experienced similar hardships in 1863 that they were largely able to resolve on their own or with their communities' help. In Henderson County, for example, community leaders distributed the five thousand dollars that the Texas state legislature allocated to their area (as they did for counties throughout the state in 1863) to purchase and distribute cotton and wool cards to aid soldiers' families in supplying their own needs. They also worked animal hides at the local tanyards, and Leila Ione Reeves and her family sent these to men like her father, First Texan Malachiah Reeves.[55]

Counties across the state slowly distributed cotton cards—which straightened the cotton before it was woven into cloth—and other financial assistance to those in need in their communities in 1863, giving preference to soldiers' wives and orphans. Some of these funds came from the state, but in Seguin, Texas, the local courts had raised property taxes in 1862 and created the "Soldiers' Aid Society of Guadalupe County" to distribute the "war tax fund" to indigent soldiers' families. The Guadalupe Manufacturing Company was created to help meet these needs as well. By November 1863, more than four thousand dollars had been raised in proceeds from sales and allocated to the county treasury to provide for soldiers' families.[56]

In Corsicana, the Navarro County Court distributed both local funds totaling seven thousand dollars and those allocated by the legislature in Austin.⁵⁷ Clearly, a growing need was pressuring county leaders, but Texans were largely meeting those needs in late 1863. Not far from the Navarro County courthouse, New York–born attorney Jacob Eliot continued to buy and sell land and direct the slaughtering of hogs to meet his 2,000–pound quota demanded by the Confederate government. He was not pleased with the quality of salt in the area, but his business generally continued as usual that winter. Indeed, over a year after the Emancipation Proclamation, Eliot was still purchasing and selling enslaved men and women with little thought to the idea that such practices could become illegal in less than two years.⁵⁸

Clearly it was not worries at home that troubled the brigade. It was a lack of leadership, supply, and support, and these issues declined sharply when Longstreet's corps returned to Virginia in March 1864. Indeed, by the Battle of the Wilderness in May, John Gregg led an entirely revitalized unit. He boasted that, contrary to Robertson's insistence that the Texas Brigade "would never . . . carry more than five hundred (500) muskets into a fight . . . at the Wilderness we had 714 muskets." Gregg added, "Besides the muskets, there were perhaps officers enough to make the number 800." Resupplied with new uniforms and shoes that March and reunited with Lee and the Army of Northern Virginia, the men, while understrength, were ready and in good spirits for the fight to come.⁵⁹

Another sign of the continued dedication of Texas Brigade soldiers to the Confederate war effort in Virginia was the influx of 300 men into the ranks that spring. Some of these were soldiers who took unauthorized leave, were on furloughs, or were recuperating from wounds with family in the eastern theater. Scrap Goree, for example, visited family in North Carolina that spring, and his brother Thomas Jewett insisted that it did Scrap a world of good. He "remained up there some ten days or two weeks, and I have never seen any one as much delighted with a visit, and with the kind treatment received from his relatives, as he was," T. J. Goree told their mother.⁶⁰ Dugat Williams supported this, too, when he noted in mid-February 1864 that "the army recruited considerably this winter by the returning furloughed men who were slightly wounded at Chickamauga."⁶¹ Indeed, just over 320 men returned to the Texas Brigade after recovering from earlier 1862 and 1863 wounds to participate in the campaign season of 1864. Only four new recruits joined the brigade that spring, and the only unit allowed to send a man home on recruiting duty, the Third Arkansas, enlisted all of them. Resupplied, fed, reunited with Lee and the Army of Northern Virginia, and led by a strong commander once again, the Texas Brigade's faith in Confederate victory surged in April 1864. The men were so dedicated, that of the 1,360 men on the Texas Brigade's rolls in 1864, 307 of those wounded in combat that year would return to the brigade to fight again in 1864. Indeed, 85 of those men were wounded a second time and returned to fight yet again. By the last year of the war, the Texas Brigade was the size of an understrength regiment. It had lost key commanders to death and others to demands at home, like J. R. Loughridge, who was elected by his fellow citizens to represent Navarro County in the state legislature. For those who remained, however, their faith in their commanders, in their army, in themselves, and in Confederate independence was as strong as ever as they marched toward a place called the Wilderness to clash with their old foe under a new commander.

REUNION WITH LEE
From the Wilderness through Petersburg

A new commander led the Union forces opposite Robert E. Lee and the Army of Northern Virginia in the spring 1864. Officially, Gen. Ulysses S. Grant led all Union forces, but he rode in the field with Gen. George G. Meade's Army of the Potomac and directed their action. Grant made his reputation in the West, beginning with successful operations in Tennessee in 1862. He won control of the Mississippi River with his campaigns in the Magnolia State in 1862 and 1863, which split the Confederacy into two sections.

When he arrived in the East in 1864, no one knew quite what to expect from Grant, but he did not particularly concern the men of Hood's Texas Brigade. Like much of Lee's army, they were confident that year would bring the last battles of the war and secure Confederate victory. Indeed, the men were eager to start fighting; the sooner they won, the sooner they would go home.¹ They had no way of knowing, however, that 1864 would bring their most brutal fighting of the war. If they suffered fewer casualties, it was only because there were so few of them left to fall.

The Texas Brigade, like units on both sides, struggled to sustain recruiting success in 1864, but they also remained selective about who they allowed into their elite brigade. As Fifth Texas lieutenant Dugat Williams explained after the battle of Antietam: "Unless they are the very best men, the best soldiers, I do not wish them to come. Our little Brigade has made itself known here and unless the new Regiments were fully our equals I would not want them," he explained. A recruiting officer for the Fifth Texas in spring of 1862 and 1863, Williams insisted, "I do not hesitate to say ours is the best—decidedly the best, Brigade ever upon Virginia soil," and they would only take "*good* men." With the brigade cut off from Texas and Arkansas once Federals controlled the Mississippi River, its ability to send recruiters home to enlist "good men" faded. In 1864, the Texans and Arkansans would have to rely upon the steady determination that had sustained them from the war's start.

The Texas Brigade also found strength in 1864 in the leadership of the company and regimental commanders who continued to be key to the Texas Brigade's success. The battles of 1863, followed by the intense fighting in 1864, created frequent turnover among their junior volunteer officers, but time and again, these men proved their ability to keep leading their men as disciplined units in the field.

Finally, and perhaps most importantly, the Texas Brigade's reunion with Robert E. Lee proved key to the men's renewed faith in Confederate independence and the role they wanted to play in that victory. During the incredibly difficult winter of 1863 and 1864, the Texans and Arkansans had felt adrift so far from Lee, the Army of Northern Virginia, and from Virginia, which they saw as the decisive epicenter of the war. Shortly after their return to Virginia, the men received fresh uniforms, and Longstreet's First Corps gathered to be reviewed by Lee. It was "an imposing affair," Fourth Texas lieutenant colonel C. M. Winkler told his new bride, Angelina V. Smith, a Richmonder who had been nursing Texas Brigade soldiers and other Confederates in Richmond for years. Winkler joked that "General Lee's army say they can cope with Grant without the 1st army corps, though they confess they feel more comfortable to know we are about." Lee disagreed. He knew the essential role Longstreet's men would play in the coming campaign, and the Texans in particular. The Texas Brigade, Lee told the men at the review, was "the best fighting brigade in the corps," and he was grateful to have them back.[2] Reunited with Lee in Virginia and under the direction of the talented John Gregg, the Texas Brigade, once again, had no doubt that Confederates would win the war in 1864 and that they were key to that success.

In April and May, Texas Brigade soldiers milled about their camps with full bellies and new uniforms, talking about the fighting to come. Their Tennessee struggles were behind them, and they anticipated hard but successful battles now that they had returned to Virginia and Lee. As James Manahan explained, "Winter has come and passed, bringing with it the coldest weather ever experienced by the soldiers in this Army and taking everything into consideration we have made the hardest campaign we have ever went through." The brigade had endured "long marches over frozen grounds and nearly all of the men barefooted, myself included" and done it all on "hard corn issued to us for rations," Manahan explained to twenty-year-old Williametta "Willie" Thomason in Waco, Texas. The daughter of a local merchant, Thomason would later marry Manahan, who assured her that "notwithstanding all this" suffering, "the men are still in fine spirits and as sanguine of success as they were when the war began. We all know that the darkest hour of our nation's troubles is now upon us but we put our trust in the God of battles and our own right army."[3]

About one hundred miles southeast of Willie Thomason, Sarah Goree sensed that optimism, too, at her Raven Hill plantation in Walker County. Her eldest son, Tom, explained in April 1864 that "There is pretty general rejoicing ... that we are back again in the noble old Army of Northern Virginia." She likely read the news with relief, trusting her son that he and his brothers in the Fifth Texas were in the best of dangerous situations. They all felt "great confidence in the result" of the coming campaign, Tom Goree promised, insisting that the "army is in fine spirits and in splendid condition." He smiled at the opportunities 1864 offered now that Longstreet's First Corps had rejoined Lee's army: "We ag[ain] constitute a part of the greatest of all armies under the leadership of the greatest living chieftain, and if we can succeed in inflicting on Grant a crushing defeat, it will do much towards bringing about a speedy peace."[4]

When the war began, two of Sarah Goree's sons, Langston ("Lang") and Edwin King ("Ed"), volunteered in Company G of the Fifth Texas. They joined brother Tom, already in Virginia in July 1861, where he served as an unofficial aide to Gen. James Longstreet. In 1862, her son Robert, at Tom's insistence, volunteered, too, though he joined the Sixth Texas Cavalry to serve closer to home and their widowed mother. Ed and Lang visited Sarah over the winter of 1863, and Lang remained with her in Walker County with a lingering hand wound from Second Manassas that had resulted in his medical discharge from the Texas Brigade.

Sarah Goree likely felt relieved to have him home, especially since her youngest son, Pleasant Kittrell "Scrap" Goree, had left Texas the previous summer of 1863. He turned eighteen just before the Battle of Gettysburg and decided that the best place to help secure Confederate independence was not in Texas, or in the West with Robert, but with his brothers in Lee's Army of Northern Virginia. Scrap Goree was one of the last recruits to join the Texas Brigade. Nearly 90 percent of the men who served in the unit during the war volunteered in 1861 or 1862. New recruits barely boosted the brigade's numbers in 1863 with an increase of just 4 percent of their total strength, and by 1864, fewer than a dozen men arrived in Virginia to replace the previous year's losses.[5] The fall of Vicksburg was the biggest challenge to the brigade's ability to recruit more men. That was certainly the case with Tom Green Rifles members Thomas Cater, E. B. Millican, and W. B. Burditt. They went home on furloughs or leave in late 1862, and when they tried to return to Virginia, they could not get across the Mississippi. They were listed as absent without leave until word arrived that the men were not avoiding service. Still determined to fight, all three served in Texas units west of the Mississippi for the remainder of the war.[6]

The recruiting concern by 1864 was the threat of Federal operations in Texas. Over the last year, increasing numbers of white southerners had been relocating their families and their slaves to Texas, which was relatively untouched by the war. By the fall of 1863, however, Union forces under Gen. Nathaniel T. Banks attacked both the eastern coastline at Sabine Pass and the southern coast at Brownsville. Defeated at Sabine, Banks shifted operations to the southwest corner of Texas. Federals took Brownsville and Corpus Christi and severely limited trade with Mexico across the Rio Grande. When these forces shifted their focus to Louisiana in early 1864, Texans reclaimed much of their lost territory in the south, but it was not clear at the time what might happen to Texas Brigade families in Arkansas and in the Lone Star State. This may have discouraged men from considering service far from home in 1864, though the primary issue remained Federal control of the Mississippi, which kept recruits from reaching Virginia and the Confederate high command from sending Texas Brigade men to their home states to recruit or rest.

The battle began on May 5 after Union forces had crossed the Rapidan River. They marched down Germanna Plank Road on May 4 and 5, hoping to outflank Lee's army. Lee let Grant advance and used the densely thicketed area called the Wilderness of Spotsylvania to Confederates' advantage, allowing the terrain to create obstacles for the Federals and reduce their numerical superiority. For much of May 5, Confederate general Richard S. Ewell's Second Corp and Union major general Gouverneur K. Warren's Fifth Corps battled along the Orange Turnpike, while to their south, Confederate general A. P. Hill's Third Corps fought elements of the Union Second and Sixth Corps along the Orange Plank Road. The battle ground to a standstill, and the exhausted troops used the night of May 5 to bring in reinforcements and rest.[7]

The next morning, Winfield Scott Hancock's Second Corps broke the quiet dawn with an attack up the Orange Plank Road, rolling Hill's corps back. Hill refused to order his exhausted men to construct any defenses over the night of May 5. Many of the men had simply collapsed and slept where they were when the fighting stopped, lying in completely disorganized lines and, in most cases, with no pickets to alert their units to any threat. Using that chaos to his advantage, Hancock's corps cut through Hill's position and had nearly broken the Confederate line when James Longstreet arrived with his First Corps.[8]

They had rushed in from Mechanicsville, an area so isolated that Lee's Old Warhorse had had difficulty making good time to rejoin Lee. Despite that, Longstreet's men made excellent time, leaving Mechanicsville on the afternoon of May 4 and marching with little or no stops for more than twenty-four hours. They slept for several hours and then were on the move again around 3:00 a.m. on May 5. Still, Hill, Lee, and the Confederates in the Wilderness spent much of that morning wondering where the First Corps was and if they could hold their position long enough for Longstreet to arrive.[9]

In the predawn darkness of May 6, his men rushed toward the sound of the guns. Most of them had had only a few hours' rest in the last forty-eight hours and had used up the last of their rations the previous day. Still, the veterans sensed the desperation of the moment from their officers' shouts and the thundering battle to the east. Longstreet's men covered the last two miles of their march at a double-quick, racing toward Hill's fractured line.

The Texas Brigade, in Gen. Charles W. Field's division, moved along the north side of the Plank Road behind Gen. G. T. Anderson's brigade. Gen. Joseph B. Kershaw's division loped alongside Field's men to the south. As Longstreet's men approached the overgrown fields of Catharine Tapp's farm, Hill's retreating corps moving through Longstreet's column slowed their progress, but the advancing Confederates kept their formation and pressed on. Years later, Evander Law still marveled at their discipline that morning: "In perfect order, ranks well closed, and no stragglers, those splendid troops came on, regardless of the confusion on every side, pushing their steady way onward like 'a river in the sea' of confused and troubled human waves around them."[10]

Longstreet arrived about thirty minutes before his men, and Lee was visibly relieved as he shook the Georgian's hand. "I never was so glad to see you," Lee said. "Hancock has broken my line." The chaos of the ground around them likely shocked Longstreet as much as it stunned Fourth Texan Joe Polley when the Texas Brigade arrived on the scene. Hill's rout created a "scene of utter, and apparently irremediable confusion, such as we had never witnessed before in Lee's army," Polley explained. Plank Road "was crowded with standing and moving wagons, horses and mules, and threading their way through this tangled mass, each with his face to the rear, were hundreds of men of Wilcox's and Heth's divisions [of Hill's corps], which were being driving from their lines" as Hancock's Federals raced to close the distance between themselves and the fractured Confederate line.[11]

When Lee saw Confederates coming toward him, he called out, "Who are you, my boys?" To the answer, "Texas boys," Lee waved his hat and yelled, "Hurrah for Texas! Hurrah for Texas!" Overwhelmed by their army commander's uncharacteristic exuberance, shouts rang from their lines as the Texans and Arkansans answered Lee. Officers regained their attention, and the brigade moved as a column behind Lt. Col. William T. Poague's guns to their left. They then faced right to form a line of battle. Looking toward the sun, the veterans studied the ground before them.

Catharine Tapp's cabin stood in a rare piece of open ground surrounded by dense woods of oaks and chestnuts choked by nearly impenetrable underbrush. The forty-acre field north of Plank Road was littered with saplings that had inched their way into the overgrown field. No one had farmed the land for several years. Tapp, a fifty-nine-year-old widow with just $120 to her name, reflected the economic downturn that had troubled that area of Virginia. She rented or paid for her small 30-by-20-foot cabin by sharecropping. The house sheltered her son, three daughters, four-year-old granddaughter, and a white laborer in his mid-twenties named Jackson Lewis. Several milk cows and pigs wandered about the home and outbuildings, and plum, cherry, and apple trees spotted the area around the cabin.[12]

It is unclear if Catharine Tapp was on the property when the battle began the day before, but the granddaughter, Phenie Tapp, was. Years later she recalled the family rushing from their home because, she was told, "a lot of very bad men in blue were going to get a whipping." The four-year-old assumed that the men had likely been throwing pebbles in the spring on the property; that was what she got whippings for, at least. Rushing westward with the few items they managed to grab, Phenie noted, "Large drops hit the road and dust spurted up the way it does when the first raindrops fall, before the ground gets wet." The Tapp family managed to avoid getting hit by the lead dropping around them, continuing their westward race down Plank Road to a neighbor's home.[13]

Several hundred yards west of the Tapp cabin, Poague's men had constructed quick breastworks of confiscated fence rails during the night of May 5. These offered some shelter to the artillerymen and the infantry who

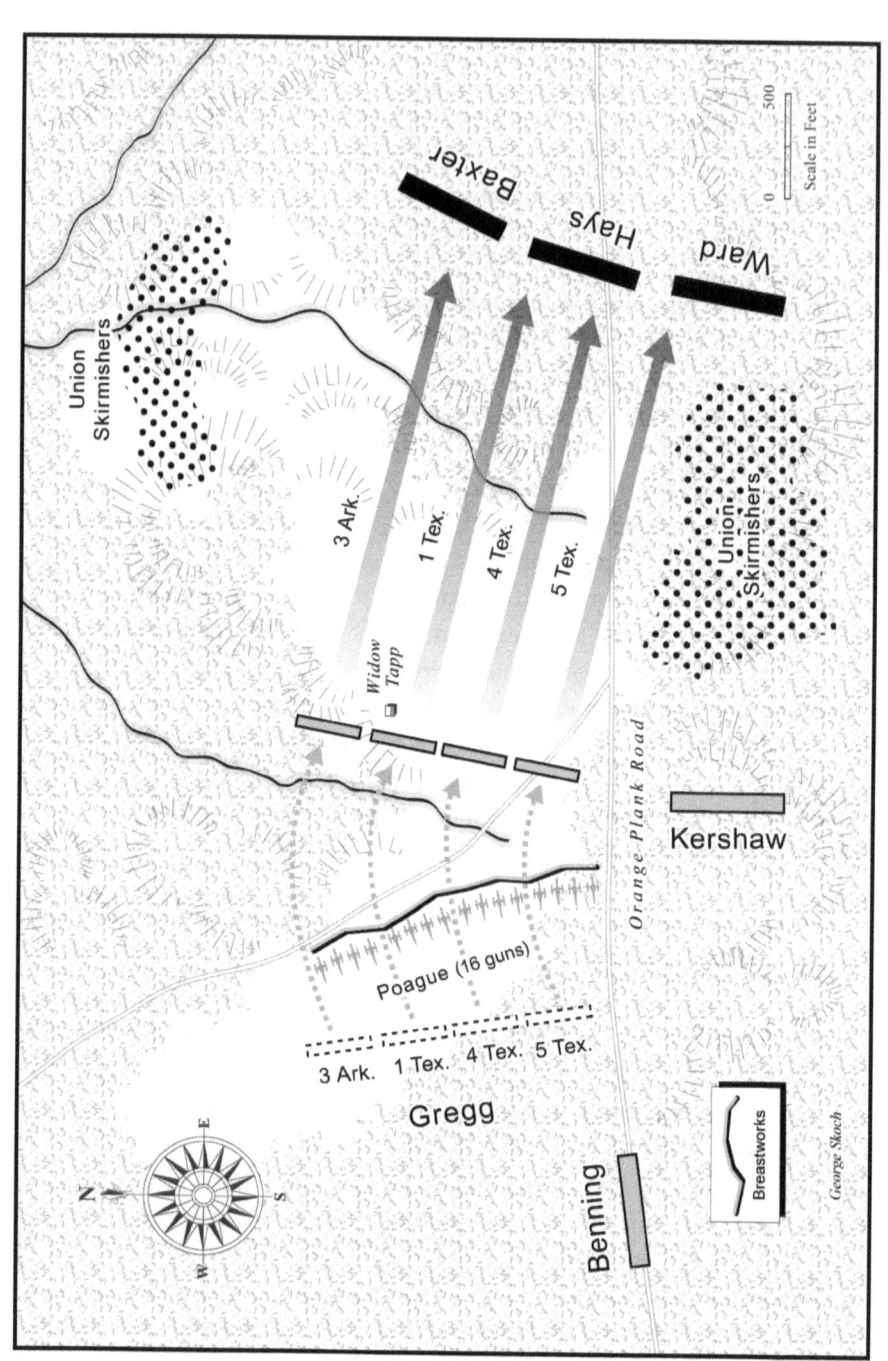

Battle of the Wilderness, May 6, 1864

organized behind his guns. Poague had four batteries manned by North Carolinians, Virginians, and, on the far left, the Madison Light Artillery recruited out of Canton, Mississippi. His nine Napoleons and the canister they fired were Poague's most valuable tools that day, with most of the fighting taking place at close range in the field before him. His men also had two ten-pounder Parrott rifles and two three-inch rifles. Without a need for any distance, Poague would load these with canister, too, despite the damage that would do to their rifling.[14]

On Poague's right, Yankee skirmishers had come dangerously close to taking his guns, but Kershaw's men had arrived just in time. Organizing as best they could by company, because the dense woods kept them from coordinating at the regimental or brigade level, Kershaw's South Carolina and Mississippi infantrymen checked the Federal advance on the south side of Plank Road. This bought the Texas Brigade and the rest of Field's division time to form in the Tapp field to Kershaw's left.[15]

Poague's men also gave the Texas Brigade the time they needed to reorder their lines before advancing. The gunners waited for as many of their own men to clear the ground before them and across the Plank Road, and then all four batteries, including one gun in the road, opened fire. Thousands of small iron balls cut through the air before them, likely hitting a few of their own men before halting the advance of Alexander Hay's old brigade, now commanded by Elijah Walker of the Fourth Maine. Poague's men "worked with almost superhuman energy" as "muzzles belched their withering blast" into Walker's men and the additional skirmishers trying to push forward from the north and south. In a moment filled with astonishing examples of Confederate talent and determination, Poague's men ranked among the best. They skillfully delayed the Second Corps' advance, allowing Field's division to organize behind the guns, all the while supporting Kershaw's men on Poague's right.[16]

Behind the busy artillerymen, the Texans and Arkansans prepared to move forward. Ramrods rattled as they responded to the order to load and cap their weapons. The Third Arkansas stood on the far left, followed by the First, Fourth, and finally the Fifth Texas with its right anchored on Plank Road. The right half of the line enjoyed some protection from the woods that extended eastward from their rear. Longstreet rode among them, advising the men to "keep cool, we will straighten this out in a short time, keep cool," referring to the need to get his units into position despite the threat to their front and the distraction of Hill's broken corps. Benning's Georgia brigade fell in behind the Texans and Arkansans, while Col. William F. Perry led Evander Law's old Alabama brigade into their position behind the Georgians. All three brigades were largely invisible, protected by the slight rise where Poague's guns stood, to the Federals advancing from the east.

Longstreet's plan was to send one brigade in after another, sensing that this was the best strategy for the tightly packed terrain. The Texas Brigade would advance first, and as General Gregg rode before the men, he recalled what Lee had told him when Gregg first arrived on the scene. "We *must* drive these people back," Lee had said. "The Texans always *drive* them." Sensing his brigade's eagerness to start the advance, Gregg shouted, "Men, the eye of Genl. Lee is on you," and the Texans and Arkansans responded with cheers. Lee, riding nearby, came forward, and waved his hat, and shouts again came from the ranks. He was, Gregg observed, "very much excited and tears were coming from his eyes." With a shout of "Forward!" the Texans and Arkansans advanced with a yell. Their lines wrapped around Poague's guns, returning to formation after clearing the artillery line.

Then, suddenly, several of the men noticed that Lee was advancing with them. Dozens of them would later recount the story, and many claimed to have personally taken the reins of Lee's horse, Traveller, to lead their commander back. Nearby, Capt. William A. Bedell watched as Lee "followed us some distance into the enemy's fire."[17] Wounded at Malvern Hill and Antietam, Bedell was one of the original recruits of Company L of the First Texas, organized in Galveston County, and he, along with several others, implored Lee to stop. Cpl. W. G. Lockhart and Capt. A. C. Jones in the Third Arkansas and Pvt. J. G. Wheeler in the Fourth Texas heard Lee insist, "I want to lead the Texas Brigade in this charge." Gregg and his men, however, refused to risk losing Lee. "Go back, go back," the men insisted. "We won't go forward until you go back," they warned.[18] Samuel "Tom" Blessing, advancing with the First Texas, heard one man warn, "You will get killed dad[d]y."[19] Watching from the Fifth Texas ranks, Leonard Gee wept at Lee's faith in the Texas Brigade and their sacrificial loyalty to him. "I would charge hell itself for that old man," Gee swore. Groce Lawrence in the Fourth Texas watched as their chieftain finally turned toward the rear. "Go back, General Lee, go back! We have whipped them before, and damn 'em, we can whip 'em again!" With a friendly kick at Traveller, Lawrence hollered, "Get out of the Wilderness with General Lee, you old loony." Moments later, as Gregg's men rushed forward, Corporal Lawrence fell dead in Widow Tapp's field, as would hundreds of his fellow Texans and Arkansans.[20]

With a last look at Lee behind them, Gregg ordered the Texas Brigade forward. Joe Polley in the Fourth Texas felt like they were entirely alone, racing forward and taking heavy fire from skirmishers on their right flank. "The storm of battle became terrific," he recalled. Tom Blessing, on Polley's left, thought they drove the Federals "nearly a half mile" until "our ranks became so decimated that we were compelled to fall back." In the Fifth Texas, lead cut into Col. King Bryan's right wrist and Acting Maj. J. J. McBride fell to the ground when a ball tore through both of his legs. Pvt. Pryor Choate fell, too, grasping his side, and nearby, Octave Copal, one of the March 1863 recruits, grabbed his arm where a ball destroyed so much bone and muscle that amputation would be his only option.

In the Fourth Texas, Pvt. William E. Lewis and Sgt. William H. Lewis from Waverly, Texas, were killed as well. Both men came from elite planter families in Walker County and were likely related. They were messmates of Mark Smither, and he was especially close to William E. Lewis, a "general favorite" in the regiment and loved by Smither "as if he were a brother." *Huntsville Item* newspaperman, Canadian-born R. H. Giffin, who was an original recruit who had rejoined the Fifth Texas after a wound at Second Manassas, also fell dead. So did John Alversen and James Shaw, men whose lives were the direct opposite of the wealthy Lewises. Both 1862 recruits, Alversen and Shaw were "two poor, hardworking men" whose families eked out a living along the Trinity River in northern Walker County, a life that would likely become harder with their absence.[21]

When exactly these men fell is unclear. It could have been in their initial surge into the Tapp field, or after Gregg reformed his line and ordered the men to advance in a second charge that Blessing estimated drove the Federals back another six or eight hundred yards. Dead, dying, and wounded men lay all around the Texans and Arkansans. Realizing that they had pushed the Federals as far as they could, Gregg, wounded himself, withdrew his men as Benning's Georgians pushed forward behind them. Benning's brigade kept pressure on the Federals, driving them back with the help of the Alabama brigade that came up behind the Georgians. Lee had called to their colonel, William Perry, "God bless the Alabamians." Looking at Perry's men, Lee challenged, "All I ask of you is to keep up with the Texans." With a shout, they had rushed forward to reinforce the Georgians' weakening position. For the Federals opposite them, the pressure was too much. Wadsworth's division, one witness insisted, was "driven back, and badly scattered" while other Federals watched Union soldiers retreating toward the Lacy house. The Iron Brigade, which had destroyed much of the Texas Brigade at Antietam, had also suffered too many losses to hold their line. Working in concert with Kershaw's division on their right, the Texas, Georgia, and Alabama Brigades had done what Lee asked. Hancock's advance, which seemed destined to destroy Lee's army that morning, had been stopped and pushed back.

The Texans' and Arkansans' role in the fight in the Wilderness on May 6 became legendary. The "Lee to the Rear" scene, though repeated with other units later that spring, would be forever linked with the Texas Brigade. Their success in the Wilderness was not possible without the support of Kershaw's division, Poague's artillerymen, and Benning's and Perry's brigades, but the Texans became the most celebrated unit on the field that morning. Their fight and Lee's praise of them inspired poetry, paintings, songs, novels, and memorials. The brigade played a more individually decisive role at Gaines's Mill, but the desperation of the situation in the Wilderness and Lee's repeated insistence that the Texans could save their position, that other troops need only "keep up with the Texans," and that the Texans were "the best fighting brigade" in Longstreet's corps, sealed the brigade's place in history.

But that fame came at a heavy cost. The Texas Brigade lost two-thirds of their force in the Battle of the Wilderness. John Gregg was proud that they had "contributed greatly to save the fight, small as our number were," but he mourned that they were now the size of "a small regiment." On the night of May 6, Tom Blessing and many of the men walked Widow Tapp's field, trying to help the wounded and bury their fallen comrades. Blessing found Fred Cole among the dead. He was just eighteen years old when he enlisted with the First Texas in 1861. Lt. W. P. Randall was dead, too. An original second corporal in Company L, Randall was wounded at Second Manassas and captured at Chickamauga, but he had always found his way back to his men. Blessing continued searching for wounded men and then listed the killed, injured, and missing in a carefully detailed letter to his sister, who had it published in the *Galveston Weekly News*. It may have been here that Caroline Schadt learned that her last remaining sibling, William, had been "severely" wounded and likely captured.

The Texas dead were gathered and buried in a mass grave along Orange Plank Road. The living, likely including Tom Blessing and perhaps Dugat Williams, lined the large burial pit with blankets and coats. A number of men who had been with the brigade since the beginning were laid to rest, including E. O.

Perry, the determined if often frustrated volunteer of 1861. He had joined the First Texas with three brothers, but Howard and Clinton were killed at Antietam. E. O. Perry and his brother Bose were wounded at Sharpsburg as well, and E. O. suffered an additional wound at Chickamauga before he fell at the Wilderness. On May 6, nearly three years after they had gone to war, Bose Perry was the only brother who remained.[22] He was likely with the group who buried their family and friends, nailing a large sign that read "Texas Dead" to a tree along the road before the remnants of the Texas Brigade marched south with Lee's army.

Sarah Goree's son Ed was among those who fell in Catharine Tapp's field on May 6, or possibly where portions of the Fourth and Fifth Texas crossed to the south side of Plank Road. Litter bearers walked past him several times but assumed he was dead and prioritized their efforts on the wounded. Ed Goree laid there throughout the night, his leg too shattered to move. On the morning of May 7, he terrified a burial squad when they grasped what they assumed was a dead man and Ed suddenly awoke. One of the soldiers lifted him onto a horse behind another man, and they made their way to a field hospital. But Ed fainted from blood loss and the pain of his wound, and he fell to the ground. Assumed dead for a second time, soldiers abandoned Ed Goree once more. Finally, after more hours lying in the rain, another group of soldiers found Ed and took him to a hospital.

It was there that Tom Goree found his brother. Tom got the brigade's favorite surgeon, Dr. Breckenridge, to evaluate the situation, but Breckenridge could only repeat what Tom already feared. "Your brother is going to die, Major," Breckenridge explained, despite Ed's insistence that they were all wrong. In July, Tom Goree decided he needed to make sure their mother understood just how badly injured Ed was and that she be prepared for the worst. Ed was hit just below the knee, Tom explained, "in the fleshy part of the leg, the ball striking the bone, and ranging downwards. It remained in the leg several weeks before it could be found & cut out. The bone was not thought to be injured." Then, for unknown reasons, Ed developed "an inflammation of the knee joint, from which he has suffered terribly for five or six weeks." There were moments of relief, but then "the least motion or jar would produce a recurrence of it." Tom and the doctors worried that Ed was not getting better. The wound would not start "granulating & filling up & discharging healthy matter as it should do," Tom explained. Instead, it "discharged rather thin pus, of a greenish color & mixed with blood, until nearly all the muscles of the calf of the leg seemed to be destroyed." Breckenridge and other doctors studied Ed Goree's situation and were "*very uneasy* about him ever since the inflammation of the knee joint," Tom explained.

Tom watched doctors drain about a quart of pus from Ed's leg and dreaded convincing his brother to agree to the amputation, especially when doctors gave him only two chances in a hundred to recover. At Tom's request, ministers visited with Ed, and they talked with him about dying, as did Tom. He explained all of this in a letter to his uncle, in which he enclosed the separate letter for Sarah Goree to ensure she would not be alone when she read the painful details.[23]

As the Gorees wrestled with their personal tragedy from the Battle of the Wilderness, the fighting continued at a relentless pace. On May 7, Lee's army hurried toward Spotsylvania Court House, traveling through the night on a rough road that ran parallel to and a couple miles apart from their Federal opponents. Confederates succeeded in reaching the small town first and hurried to construct defenses on May 8. The First Corps—now commanded by Gen. Richard Anderson who replaced Longstreet, also wounded at the Wilderness— took their position on the strategically valued Laurel Hill. For the next two weeks, the armies attacked each other from their defenses at Spotsylvania. Most of that time was defined by small raids, deadly accurate sharpshooting, and artillery exchanges, but there were also several fierce assaults. The heaviest fighting for the Texas Brigade took place on May 10, when 40,000 Federal soldiers attacked Anderson's and Ewell's positions.

Field's division stopped the first two Federal attacks, but their third assault nearly broke the Confederate line. The Texas Brigade's ranks were so thin that the men were standing about five feet apart, and they were armed with a surplus of weapons that they had taken from dead and wounded Federals who fell before their defenses in the previous two attacks. Miles Smith, standing with the Fourth Texas, insisted that most of the men had two Enfields each and a musket whose buckshot would be effective as the Federals closed on them. The Texans and Arkansans watched closely, anticipating an assault after Federal artillery had hammered the Confederate defenses.

Sam Bailey, a twenty-five-year-old farmer from Harris County, watched for the attack, too, standing near Mark Smither in the center left of the Confederate line. Both were Fifth Texas men: Bailey had joined Company A, the Bayou City Guards, in 1861 about the same time Smither had joined Company D, recruited out of the counties north of Houston. Bailey carried wounds from

Gaines's Mill, Second Manassas, and Gettysburg, and had been captured at Manassas. The loss of a thumb at Gettysburg kept him from effectively loading a weapon, and lingering problems from a wound to his hip suffered at Gaines's Mill had forced Bailey into Chimborazo Hospital in April 1864. Despite his ailments, Sam Bailey had rejoined Company A by the Battle of Spotsylvania Court House.[24]

Mark Smither officially served in Company D, but their regiment was so small that he and Bailey sat side by side in their trenches. They developed a system where Smither loaded Bailey's gun and his own, and then both men would rise slowly and fire before squatting down behind their defenses. On Smither's other side sat twenty-three-year-old John J. Pridgen, an 1862 volunteer in Company C from Centerville, Texas. Pridgen had been skirmishing in front of their position, then fell back to the Texans' defenses next to Smither. He was passing Bailey his loaded gun when an artillery shell crashed through their position. It tore off Bailey's head, drove one of their guns into Pridgen's torso up to the barrel, and knocked Smither unconscious and buried him in dirt and debris. When he awoke he was "stunned" by the destruction and the randomness of his survival.[25]

Shortly after Pridgen and Bailey were killed, Federal soldiers launched a strong late-afternoon assault. As they neared the Confederate defenses, the Union men increased their pace, racing forward with bayonets fixed in a line of soldiers five men deep. Most of the Texas Brigade held the Federals back, but a gully cut through their defenses where the First Texas stood, and the Ragged First could not stop the Federals as they poured into their lines, shouting "Surrender!" or, as Tom Blessing heard, "No Quarter!" They came so fast that "before we knew it they had run in to the works . . . and killed and wounded two or three with the bayonet." With fists, knives, and rifle butts, the First Texans fought desperately while the Third Arkansas fired into the Federal attackers from the left—and likely the First Texans, too—while the Fourth and Fifth Texans fired from the right. Finally, unable to hold the breach they had made, the Federals fell back, continuing to suffer casualties from Confederate artillery and infantry fire. Two days later, Federals attacked the Texas Brigade's position twice more but were again repulsed.

The fighting at the Spotsylvania continued until May 20, including several large-scale attacks, but the heavy engagements were over for the Texas Brigade. They would continue to lose men to sharpshooters who were so accurate and determined that First Texan O. T. Hanks insisted that they cut an oak with a sixteen-inch diameter in half. Despite their exhaustion and the tremendous casualties they had suffered, the Texas Brigade remained confident of victory. Later historians would see Grant's emergence and determination at the Wilderness and Spotsylvania Court House as a key turning point of the war, but to Lee's men, they were two moments where Confederates refused to let Grant and the Federals achieve their goals.

Tom Blessing captured that sentiment in May when he expressed his surprise and "profound gratitude to Almighty God, for his preserving care over me." He marveled at the number of "my comrades who have fallen on every side, killed and mangled by the missiles of our ruthless invaders," yet "I have been spared, and am to day as sound as when the battles began. This I can ascribe," Blessing insisted, "not to 'good luck,' but only to the mercy of God." Still, he counted these battles as successes, limited though they were, and Dugat Williams shared Blessing's optimism. "The victory so far is decidedly in our favor" at the Wilderness and Spotsylvania, "though the enemy of course claim all advantages," Williams told his sister Eugenia on May 18. "The news from all quarters is very cheering indeed. The army is in the finest condition and spirits and anxious for Grant to make another attack. A perfect enthusiasm prevails in the army and the men are so confident of a decisive victory that they exhibit a delight in fight," Williams boasted.[26]

Blessing also saw their experiences in May as a statement of the strength of the Texas Brigade. For the last four weeks, he argued, their "powers of endurance have been put to the test, by hard battles, long marches, &c., but within the past 26 days we have endured more hardships than we ever did before in a period three times its length. By day we fought the enemy and at night we either marched all night or were kept awake by alarms and demonstrations." Blessing shook his head and explained: "What made it worse was that it rained about one-third of the time. I have been so sleepy that I actually fell asleep walking along, and was only prevented from falling to the ground by those around me whom I fell against. At one time for the space of five days we did not dare take off our accoutrements." The majority of that time, Blessing noted, "we were kept in the ditches which were only prevented from filling with water by continually bailing out—that is it was not a constant rain, but from one to three heavy thunder showers daily. In those five days I do not think that I slept over ten hours, all put together, and that was only taken by snatches of a few minutes at a time."

Blessing insisted that the Federals had lost "at least ten to our one." He noticed "on several occasions" that Federals "refused to charge on our works when ordered to do so." Blessing was positive that Lee's Army would defeat Grant in Virginia. Then, "if Johnston can only whip Sherman in Georgia, I think this campaign will end the war, and I pray God that it may, so that we may have peace once more." He took comfort in reports of Confederate victories west of the Mississippi and hoped "the enemy may see their folly, and bring this dreadful war to a close."[27]

While confident, the men were also exhausted. The Texas Brigade was fortunate to see little action in the fighting along the North Anna River in late May. On June 3, they helped repel the Federal assaults at the Battle of Cold Harbor, but at little personal cost. Joe Polley watched that bloody day as Federals advanced toward his position with the Fourth Texas "in four lines, about fifty yards apart." Moving across open ground toward the well-protected Confederates, the Union attackers "presented the fairest of targets for . . . Texas and Arkansas marksmanship. . . . Men could not live in the fire poured on them from front and flanks, and although in the first rush a few came within seventy yards of our lines, they halted . . . and fled," Polley explained.[28]

The armies remained here for over a week, and the Federals' disaster at Cold Harbor inspired even more confidence among the Confederates. Although the Confederates suffered fewer losses than their federal opponents that early summer of 1864, they suffered far more than Williams was either willing to admit or realized. Also troubling was the fact that Confederates could not replace these losses. Still, the optimism that Williams and other men in the Texas Brigade displayed is telling of the mood in the ranks. Decades after the war, Samuel Emerson of the Third Arkansas still emphasized the overwhelming Federal losses that the spring offensives had cost Grant. "Gen. Grant says he lost in the campaign from the wilderness to Cold Harbor . . . 39,000 men but careful examination of the figures show that his real loss was near 100,000 about twice as many as Gen. Lee had in his army."[29]

Other Third Arkansans expressed similar optimism and determination that year. In January 1864, while still in East Tennessee, George Butler, a chaplain in Company I, admitted to his sister that "I am very anxious to see the close of this dreadful war. But peace," he insisted, "is not so dear, nor is life so sweet, as to be purchased at the sacrifice of liberty."[30] Six months later, writing about a week after the Battle of Cold Harbor, Butler explained, "Our men are in good spirits and never more confident of success." Like Williams and Emerson, Butler cited the high Federal casualties and compared them to Confederate losses, and he credited Lee for much of their success. "Our soldiers have fought well since the commencement of these fights. Gen. Lee, by the blessing of God, has not been driven from any position he has taken. If he has repeatedly left a line that he had established, it was only when the enemy refused to come out and fight him," Butler insisted. "Our loss has been very small in comparison with that of the enemy," he added. "They have lost four or five times as many men as we have. Thousands of them were left unburied on the field of battle. The inhumanity of Gen. Grant to his own men, well, wounded, and killed is beyond question."[31] Nicholas Denson, also in the Third Arkansas, showed similar determination as he insisted that his Spotsylvania wounds were healed and hurried to rejoin his regiment that summer.[32]

By mid-June, temporarily abandoning his target of Richmond, Virginia, Grant focused his attention on the rail hub of Petersburg, twenty miles south of the capital. Taking Petersburg, he theorized, would help isolate Richmond and finally destroy it and the Confederacy. The Army of the Potomac abandoned their trenches north of Richmond on June 12 and 13. The Texas Brigade and the rest of the Army of Northern Virginia hurried after the Federals once Lee was certain Grant had abandoned the capital. On their march south, Longstreet's First Corps, still commanded by Richard H. Anderson while "Old Pete" recovered, crossed the Chickahominy and James Rivers and marched down the Petersburg Turnpike on June 16. The following day, while in position in the trenches near Bermuda Hundred, Anderson's corps suffered under incessant fire from Federal artillery, sharpshooters, and skirmishers. Several brigades from Gen. George Pickett's division were ordered to silence this threat, and the Texas Brigade, without orders, joined them. The men "leaped from their trenches" as one spontaneous force led "first [by] the men, then the officers and flagbearers," Robert Lowery explained. Between their speed and the suddenness of their movement, the Confederate attackers soon drove the Federals from their position.[33]

Bermuda Hundred was a small assault in which the Texas Brigade suffered few deaths, and most of those wounded returned to the ranks later that month or by August.[34] After that fight, they settled into line east of Petersburg and south of the Appomattox River with the rest of Field's division to the right of Kershaw's division. Here their biggest threat, Robert Lowery insisted, was "skirmishing and cannonading." Those two words appeared repeatedly in his diary for much of July, along with the occasional report of "sharpshooting." This proved "costly and demoralizing," Lowery explained. "To lift one's head above the trench in daylight was to commit suicide," the Arkansan claimed. Joe Polley agreed that the pressure was constant, and not just from the enemy.

From late June through the end of July, Polley wrote, "the Texas Brigade stayed on guard under a hot, almost blistering sun, and with [the only] shade made by blankets and tent-cloths." There was so little rain that dust covered every surface and permeated their clothing. With the opposing armies just yards from each other, C. M. Winkler explained that "one third of the officers and men are on duty every night," and those off duty could barely sleep, Polley grumbled, for the "unceasing volley" that came from each side as a matter of routine.

On July 27, Union general Winfield Scott Hancock's Second Corps, which had proved such a threat at the Wilderness, moved with cover provided by Gen. Philip Sheridan's cavalry northward to the James River. Lee responded by sending Anderson's First Corps and Wilcox's division after the Federals to protect Richmond. The Texas Brigade slipped quietly from the Petersburg defenses along with the rest of Field's division on the night of July 28. Traveling by foot and by train, they crossed the James River as the sun was setting on July 29 and took their position near Fussell's Mill at Deep Bottom, south of the Confederate capital.

Over the next several months, the Texas Brigade would shift in a slow, northeasterly arch in one battle after another as they defended Richmond. They clashed with Federals at Second Deep Bottom in mid-August, Chaffin's Bluff (or New Market Heights) in late September, and at Darbytown Road on October 7 and 13. In late October, the Texas Brigade engaged again at Williamsburg Road, and they participated in one last battle of 1864 at New Market Road on December 10. They would remain east of Richmond through the spring of 1865, struggling to defend the capital that had been a second home to many of them since the first winter of the war.[35]

Most of these battles were fairly small engagements, but the fighting at New Market Heights on September 29 stood out to the Texans for their successful role in helping to save Richmond. It also marked their first direct encounter with Union African American soldiers. The Federal attacks on Richmond were planned by Union major general Benjamin F. Butler and part of Grant's Fifth Offensive in the Richmond-Petersburg Campaign. Two of Butler's Union corps struck thinly defended Confederate positions along the James River, while Maj. Gen. George Gordon Meade threatened Confederates southwest of Petersburg. Butler's operations southeast of Richmond were a serious concern. New Market Heights comprised Richmond's first line of defense, and when Federals punctured these and captured Fort Harrison as well, Lee had to scramble to protect the Confederate capital. He organized a new defensive line and held the city, but he failed to drive the Federals back. The Texas Brigade played a key role in helping Lee stop the Union advance and stabilize the situation around Richmond.

The Federal advance toward New Market Heights began at dawn on September 29 as Butler's two corps crossed the James River and advanced toward the Confederates lines. The Texas Brigade was part of a small force tasked with stopping the Federal attack, but Gregg's men enjoyed a superb, if thinly defended, position behind Confederate works constructed just south of New Market Road. The men stood along parapets and trenches that connected their left with a brigade of mostly Virginia cavalry, and on the Texans' right, the Richmond Howitzers manned an artillery position. Two lines of abatis protected the Texans' and Arkansans' front, while the low parapets allowed the defenders to cover the Federal approach with sweeping fire.[36]

Col. Samuel Duncan's Third Brigade of U.S. Colored Troops (USCT) led the attack in two battle lines with the Fourth USCT in front, followed by the Sixth USCT. The Confederate defenders remained quiet for much of Duncan's advance, confident in the strength of their position and holding their fire until it would be most effective. Fog covered the ground, which allowed the men to hear each other before they could actually see the threat before them. Duncan's soldiers crossed a creek before the Confederate defenses, dressed their lines, and continued their advance in good order. When they hit the abatis, the first row of felled trees and cumbersome branches slowed the attackers. It was becoming clear just how badly this initial attack would fail. Even after determined Union soldiers got through those defenses, they still had to wrestle through a second line of chevaux-de-frise made of logs or beams with sharpened spikes sticking out at regular intervals. Duncan's white officers tried to lead the men through, as did many of the black sergeants, but those who continued forward still had to cross marshy terrain before reaching the final Confederate position. But few of Duncan's soldiers pushed this point. The ground between the creek and the defenses, Sixth USCT lieutenant Nathan Edgerton recalled, was "thickly covered with our dead and wounded."[37]

Under the direct command of Col. Frederick Bass while John Gregg helped organize the larger Confederate defenses on the heights, the Texas Brigade fired into the USCTs from the front and on both banks. Supported by artillery fire, it did not matter that the Confederates were outnumbered. Their works held and what Federals were able to do so fell back.[38] Standing with his fellow First Texans, Samuel S. Watson marveled at the Federal soldiers' determination that morning: "Thim Bloody Negroes of Grants made a charge on us and a charge it was they came rite up till you could See the white of thare eyes the boys litterley coverd the ground with Dead Nigs. Dont think that I am braging for it is so."[39] Robert E. Fitzgerald, an original volunteer in Company I of the Fifth Texas, insisted that the Texans and Arkansans "scorn[ed] the use of the breast works" when they realized that it was African American men attacking them. Fitzgerald argued that the USCTs were forced to advance, "goaded by the bayonets of the white troops in the rear" until the Federals "were slaughtered like sheep."[40]

In the Fourth Texas, Joe Polley had watched Duncan's advance but could only initially make out a "moving black wall a hundred feet away" through the dense fog. Once the Federal soldiers became entangled in the abatis, however, the Texas Brigade, Polley quipped, "engaged in slaughtering negroes for breakfast." In a short five minutes, citing the *New York Herald,* Polley and several members of the Texas Brigade boasted that they "killed one-hundred and ninety-four non-commissioned officers and privates, and twenty-three commissioned officers ... which is very creditable work," Polley insisted, "for a brigade numbering scarcely six hundred, all told." Some of the Federals who tried to surrender were killed, but Polley spoke of capturing a number of USCTs who had "played possum" until their units fell back: "Given the choice of going to the Libby [Prison] or saying 'master' to their receptive captors, most of the poor devils chose the latter alternative, and while I remained with the regiment I had a likely young negro always at my beck and call."[41]

Samuel Emerson in the Third Arkansas recalled seeing the USCTs ordered "by their officers to lay down upon the ground in the edge of our abitis, hoping thereby to shield themselves but we were ordered to mount the work," Emerson explained, "which we did shooting," and, as Fitzgerald had said, "slaughtering them like sheep." More than "200 negroes were buried in front of the brigade," Emerson recalled, while "our loss was very light" and even resulted in the capture of two Federal flags.[42]

Years later, D. H. Hamilton of the First Texas pondered the possibility "that Grant wanted to humiliate us and also give the Niggers some glory," during the assault on the morning of September 29. "Whatever his purpose was, the effect of it was like flaunting a red flag before a mad bull. No man in our Brigade would have retreated from, or surrendered to Niggers," Hamilton frowned. "When they charged up within good range the fun began. Every man made his shots count. Only a few of them escaped. We killed in our front about a million

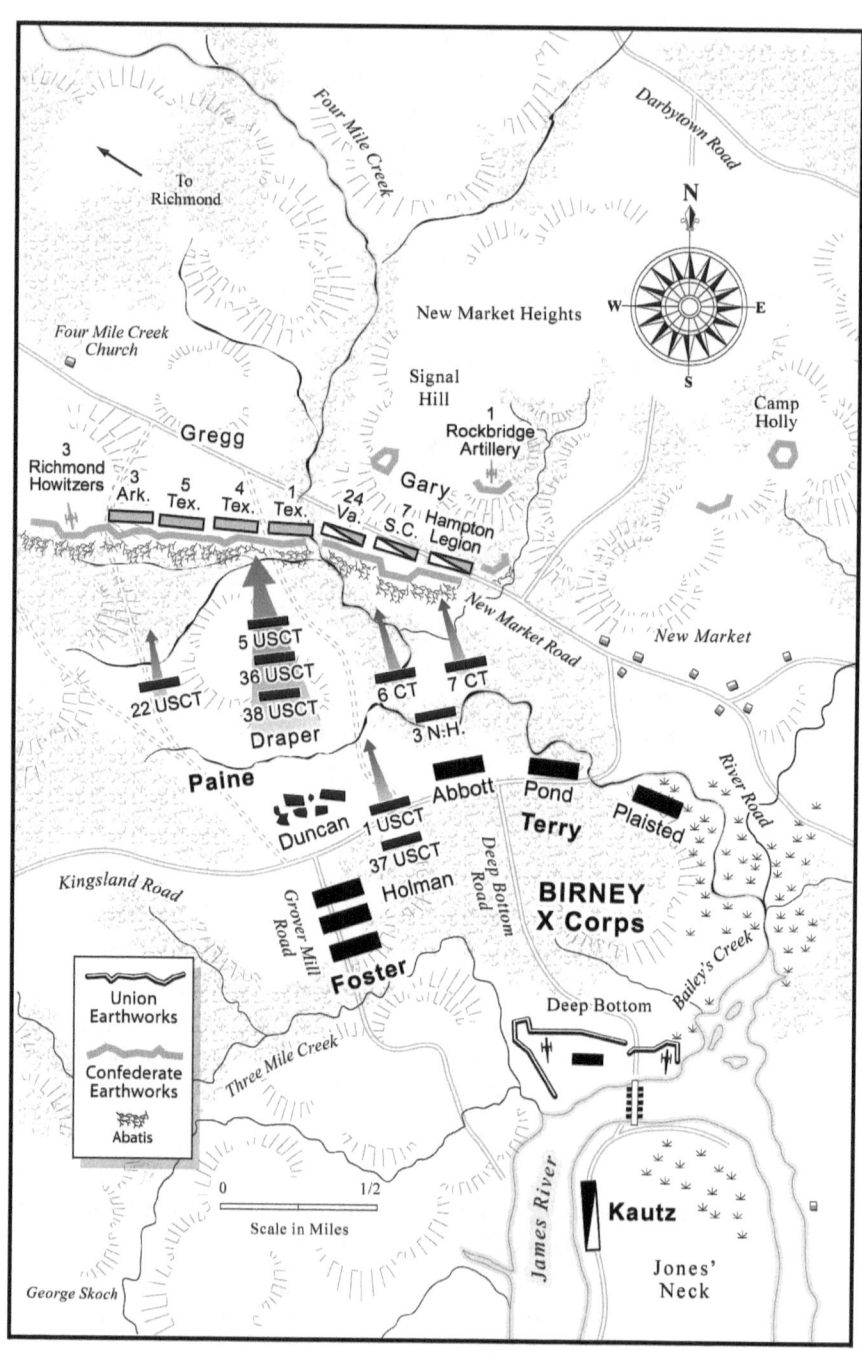

Battle of New Market Heights, September 29, 1864

dollars worth of niggers, at current prices."⁴³ Almost fifty years later, Third Arkansas lieutenant James D. Pickens recalled the slaughter as well, noting that a section of the creek was nearly dammed with dead Union soldiers. Still, he was one of the few men to insist on noting that "in my opinion, no troops up to that time had fought us with more bravery than did those negroes."⁴⁴

Later that morning, Alonzo G. Draper's Fifth, Thirty-Sixth, and Thirty-Eighth USCTs launched a second assault on New Market Heights, moving in behind Duncan's men. Despite support from the Twenty-Second USCT, Draper's brigade endured a "half hour of terrible suspense," he noted, amid the same debilitating Confederate artillery and infantry fire, boggy ground, and nearly impenetrable defenses that Duncan's men had faced. Lt. Joseph Scroggs of the Fifth USCT marveled at the men's determination in such an overwhelming situation. He noticed "a Sergeant who had received three different wounds crying because the battalion would not go farther" and insisted "no man dare hereafter say aught in my presence against the bravery and soldierly qualities of the colored soldiers."⁴⁵

Gradually, Draper realized the Confederate fire was slowing, and he ordered his men forward. The USCTs struggled through the abatis and the frise, over the parapets, and finally seized New Market Heights. Despite their deadly defense, the Texans and Arkansans had had to fall back. Butler's offensives were threatening too many positions, and Confederates could not hold New Market Heights while also securing Fort Harrison as well as Fort Gilmer, which was closer to Richmond. If it fell, all might be lost. Gregg ordered Bass to abandon the heights, and Fort Harrison fell into Federal hands as well. But the Texans and Arkansans helped save Fort Gilmer on Varina Road. In doing so, they bought time for more Confederates to come up to defend the position, which in turn stopped the Federal advance and saved Richmond.⁴⁶

The Texans and Arkansans spoke of the slaughter of the USCTs on September 29 with remarkable viciousness. This was likely because the Federal attack at New Market Heights symbolized the worst fears of a slave society: armed black men asserting their rights and killing southern whites with northern endorsement and support. The Texans' and Arkansans' brutal response revealed the limits of paternalism and their determination to maintain their antebellum racial order. Brief comments on this issue of African American troops had emerged in the fighting around Petersburg when men like Rufus King Felder complained, "It is very humiliating to know that we have to fight & expose our lives to this mixed horde of black & white demons." The war, Felder insisted, was and should remain a "white folks fight."[47] But nothing stirred such a powerful response as the fight at New Market Heights.

Hood's Texans believed enslaved labor was key to the wealth their families and their communities enjoyed in the 1850s, whether they owned slaves or benefited from ties to the wealthier members of their communities who did. Ending slavery threatened their economic future, as well as the racial order of their society. Furthermore, they had been certain since before the war began that northerners were determined to check southern power by limiting the expansion of slavery. Louis T. Wigfall captured their support in the late 1850s because he spoke to so many of those fears, and New Market Heights symbolized the fruition of these concerns. Armed African American men, endorsed as soldiers by their nation, were attacking southern whites. Worse still, Bass's men had to relinquish their position to the USCTs to secure the larger threat to Richmond. The Texans' and Arkansans' comments about New Market Heights reveal exhausted and frustrated men. After all the Texas Brigade and their families had sacrificed, the attack of the USCTs indicated a real possibility that the Confederates' world might change. Up until this point, they did not fear emancipation because they knew the Confederacy would not lose. Now, angry and concerned, they would not abandon the war, but they witnessed a paradigm shift at New Market Heights, and it worried them.

The last significant battle for the Texas Brigade came about a week later on October 7, 1864. Lee had launched a Confederate offensive along Darbytown Road outside Richmond to reclaim much of the territory they had lost around Fort Harrison. Lee directed the action personally, placing Field's division (which included the Texas Brigade) on the left and Robert Hoke's division on the right, with orders to assault the Federal lines along New Market and Darbytown Roads. This difficult assignment would be made easier by a Confederate attack into the Federal right flank led by Martin Gary's brigade of cavalry supported by Evander Law's old Alabama Brigade, now commanded by Col. Pinckney Bowles.

Opposite them was a Union cavalry division directed by Brig. Gen. August Valentine Kautz. Skirmishers exchanged fire in the early-morning hours of October 7, and Confederates probed Federal lines, looking for the best position for their attack. Their probes fooled several Federal troopers into believing that they had enjoyed a small, quick victory where they pushed the Confederates back. In several sections of his line, Kautz's defenses were quite strong with obstacles in well-placed positions that would slow the Confederate assault. In other sections, however, the Federal defenses were dangerously thin. The probes that morning, especially from the Confederate left wing, clarified how Confederates might best tweak their plans before they launched their full attack around 8:00 a.m. It began on the Confederate left, as Martin Gary's cavalrymen and the Alabama Brigade captured the Federals' attention with an aggressive assault on the Federal flank. Union troopers and artillerymen held as long as they could, but fractured lines and exhausted ammunition supplies forced them to retreat after an intense fight of about sixty minutes.[48]

About 9:00 a.m., Field's division advanced on the Union center. The Texas Brigade had arrived in line earlier that morning, the first to fall in. As General Lee oversaw their movement and awaited reports from Gary's and Bowles's attacks, Lee asked about the men forming in front of him. Were they ready to advance? "None but the Texas Brigade, General," answered one of his aides. Lee nodded, "The Texas Brigade is always ready." Standing nearby, Capt. W. T. Hill of the Fifth Texas smiled at the compliment. "His tone was not loud," Hill recalled, "but in the still, frosty air of the early morning, every member of my company could distinctly hear his words."[49] Once more, the men were inspired by Lee's faith in them, and his comments spread swiftly down the line. They waited for the rest of Field's division to form, and then four of his five brigades stepped off, moving into swampy ground with the Texas Brigade on the far right. Their left connected with Anderson's Georgians, followed by Bratton's South Carolinians. Bowles's Alabamians formed on Field's division's far left, and Dudley DuBose, who commanded Benning's old brigade, brought up the rear as the reserve unit.[50]

Moving at a steady pace over open ground, the division proceeded with the efficiency one would expect from veterans. The problem, though, was that they were receiving heavy fire, and not all of Field's brigades kept pace. While Bratton's South Carolinians and Gregg's Texas Brigade moved forward, Anderson's Georgia Brigade fell behind. Bowles's Alabamians were slow that morning as well. As a result, only two of Field's brigades, totaling about 2,000 men, actually bore the brunt of the Federal infantrymen's fierce resistance, who numbered closer to 3,000 men. Worse still for Gregg's men, many of those Union soldiers opposite him were armed with Spencer carbines that could, in experienced hands, fire one round every three to four seconds.[51]

Equally problematic was the ground the Texas Brigade had to cover. In an assault that was eerily similar to that made by Duncan's USCTs on September 29, Field's men advanced over largely open ground until they came

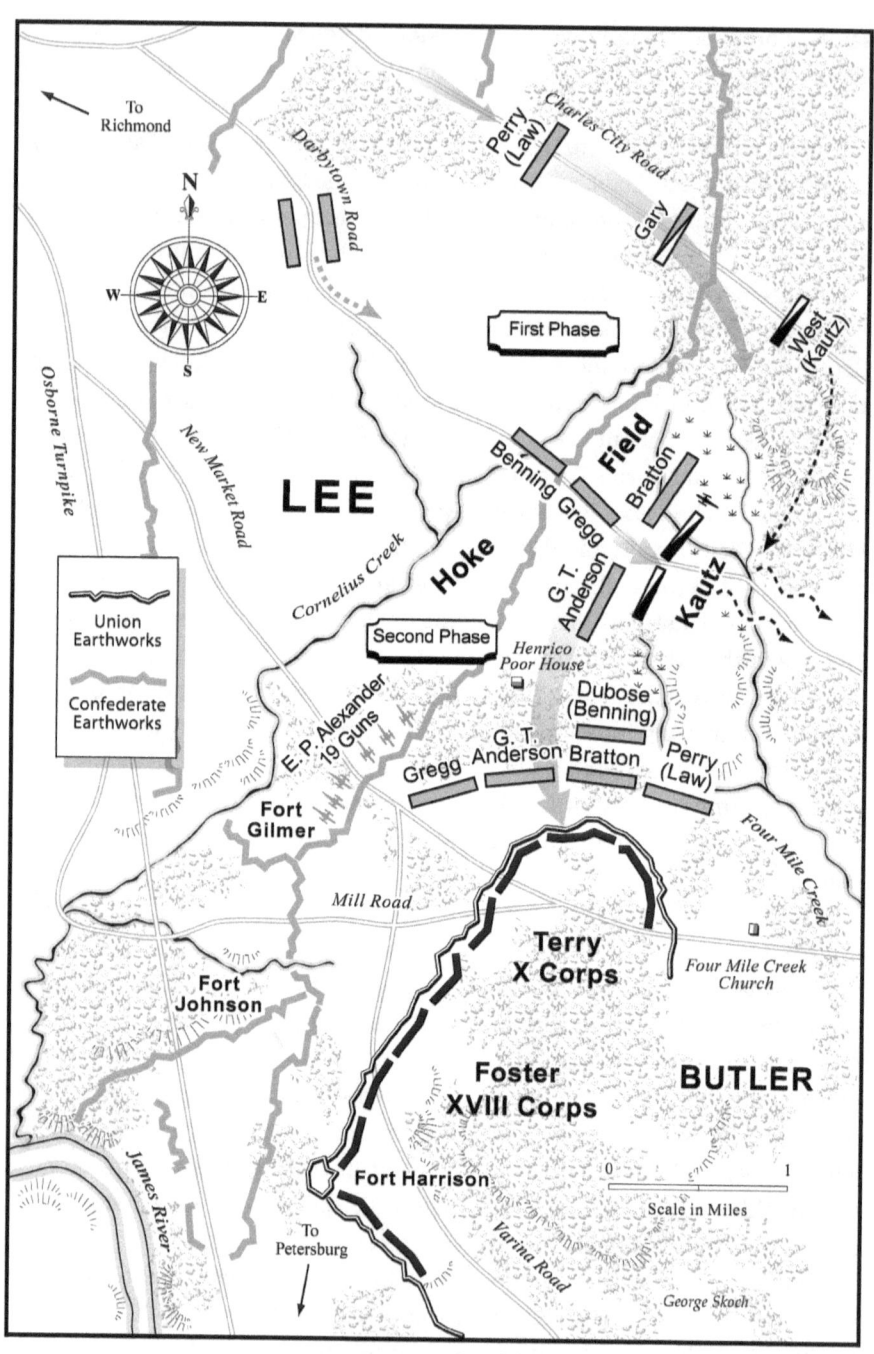

Battle of Darbytown Road, October 7, 1864

into close range of the Union defenders. The abatis tore their already ragged uniforms and scraped their eyes, faces, and limbs. Many of the men advanced so aggressively that by the time they realized they had to fall back, it was too late. They were trapped in the abatis under the Federals' withering fire. Some threw their hands up to surrender, but others refused to give up. John Gregg was trying to bring order to the chaos when a ball tore through his neck, and he fell to the ground.

Command of the Texas Brigade fell to Col. Frederick Bass of the First Texas, but he was wounded, too. Leadership then evolved to C. M. Winkler of the Fourth Texas. The Texas Brigade had never before lost a brigade commander in the middle of battle. Colonel Winkler looked at the few men who remained standing around him and ordered a color-bearer to a swale in the ground, directing the brigade to form around him. After most of the Texans and Arkansans had fallen in, Winkler ordered them to withdraw under a withering fire that left no opportunity for the men to take Gregg with them.[52] Horrified at the thought of leaving their commander, Lt. John Shotwell and Pvt. Charles Settle of the Fifth Texas, along with several other men, crawled forward, rolled Gregg onto a blanket and pulled and dragged him back toward their lines, still under fire.[53] Around noon, Lee finally called off the Confederate attack, and his army fell back across Cornelius Creek.

It is unclear exactly how many casualties the Texas Brigade suffered at Darbytown Road. Robert Campbell in the Fifth Texas claimed 200 of the 450 men in the brigade fell, though they actually entered the fight with closer to 650 men. Campbell laid among the bleeding and dead with severe wounds to his head, knee, and lungs. Other wounded men included similarly devoted members of the brigade like Fourth Texas quarter master sergeant Joe Polley, who was so badly injured that his foot required amputation. Pvt. John Pinkney "Pink" O'Rear, an original recruit of the First Texas, had survived every battle to date without a wound. But he, too, fell at Darbytown Road when a lead ball cut through his leg, shattering the bone just below his knee. He was captured and had his leg amputated in a Federal hospital near Petersburg. Years later, O'Rear said that, despite all he had endured since the war began, it was in that hospital that he "saw the horrible side of war. Although I was kindly treated I suffered much and the groans of the wounded were never out of my ears day or night." When O'Rear was finally released as a Federal prisoner at the end of the war, it took him five months to make the journey home to Cass County, Texas.[54]

W. T. Hill tallied 53 casualties in his regiment at Darbytown Road. It appeared that the Bloody Fifth earned their name again that month. Dugat Williams looked at the survivors of Company F and realized that of the thirteen men he led down Darbytown Road, only four escaped without a wound. Williams's fellow officer Lieutenant McKinnon had been injured again while his men moved forward, his second wound that year, and Williams's close friend Peter Mallory had fallen, mortally wounded, near Williams's side.[55]

On the day after the battle, John Gregg's body was taken into Richmond, where it lay in state in the Confederate House of Representatives, surrounded by Confederate and Texas flags. "All day Saturday," Angelina Winkler recalled, members of the Texas Brigade, the Texas delegation in congress, members of Jefferson Davis's cabinet and staff, and local citizens streamed by to mourn and pay their respects. The funeral that followed on October 9 "was the saddest I ever witnessed." Gregg's wife was unable to reach Richmond in time for the service, so Hood's Texans escorted their commander's body to a vault at Hollywood Cemetery to await her decision on burial. "Never were sadder faces than those who turned away after the last rite was ended, and wearily made their way back to the city,—out to the fortifications beyond,—still prepared to endure," Winkler noted.[56]

The battles of 1864 nearly destroyed the Texas Brigade. That winter they would have to face the depressing news that they would not be granted furloughs home to rest and recruit and that their ranks had thinned to a point that they might be consolidated with other units. Such action would eliminate the unit and their identity as Lee's best brigade, and possibly the best unit the Confederacy had. Their determination to fight this, to continue to fight for their beloved commander, and their steadfast faith in victory would carry them through the last winter of the war.

DETERMINATION & DEFEAT
The Final Defense of Richmond and Surrender at Appomattox

In September 1864, Pvt. Darius Rachal was desperate to reunite with Company F of the Fifth Texas Infantry. Early that year he had returned to Liberty on a furlough of indulgence, likely for a family emergency. The Rachals were prominent ranchers and farmers in Liberty County, and though his parents, Cyriaque and Anais, were not wealthy enough to be considered elite, they were comfortably ranked in the community's middling class. Darius tried to rejoin the Texas Brigade in September 1864, but travel across the Mississippi was impossible. Determined to serve in some way, he joined Confederate forces under E. Kirby Smith's command in Louisiana, where he fought for the remainder of the war. When Rachal surrendered, however, he insisted on identifying with another unit in another army and signed his parole "D. C. Rachal, Co. F, 5th Texas Inf."[1]

Rachal's determination to continue to fight in late 1864, and his stubborn identification with the Texas Brigade in Virginia, reflected a dedication to the Confederate war effort and to each other that sustained the brigade in the last months of the war. Despite everything they faced—death, wounds, sickness, capture and imprisonment, threats of consolidation, fracturing supply lines, and denied furloughs home—Hood's Texas Brigade continued their fight in Lee's army.[2] Superb junior volunteer officers played a key role in that determination. They supported the men, adapted to logistical limitations at the company and regimental levels, and advocated for the brigade with the high command. The Texas Brigade certainly felt the frustration and exhaustion that permeated Confederate ranks the previous winter. They stayed and fought, however, because of the loyalty they felt toward each other, toward their brigade and their reputation as Texans, and toward their commander, Robert E. Lee, and their nation. That loyalty echoed back to their families at home, who reflected their men's faith in Confederate independence despite diminishing opportunities for their success.

One of the best examples of this was in the number of men who, like Private Rachal, fought to return to the brigade after wounds, disease, and capture took them from the ranks in 1863 and 1864. The Texas Brigade suffered 706 casualties at the Battle of Gettysburg, or 60 percent of the brigade. They suffered another 410 casualties two months later at the Battle of Chickamauga. Over 30 percent of the men wounded in those battles recovered sufficiently to return to the Texas Brigade in time for the 1864 campaign season. Ten of the men returned from wounds at both Gettysburg and Chickamauga. Other men returned from other battles in 1863, from sick furloughs, and from assignments outside the army, which brought a total of about 320 men who returned to the Texas Brigade to fight in 1864. Even that year, of the 1,360 men on the Texas Brigade's rolls in 1864, 307 of those wounded returned to combat later that year. Indeed, 85 of those men were wounded a second time and returned to fight again. Three of them returned after a third, and one, Lt. R. J. McKinnon, one of Private Rachal's officers, returned three times after three wounds in 1864. He suffered his fourth wound at the Battle of Williamsburg Road on October 27, 1864, and was hospitalized that winter.[3]

These returnees were key to the Texas Brigade's ability to remain in the field as a functioning unit, especially since only four recruits joined the brigade in 1864. But it still kept the brigade at about 500 men, the equivalent of an undersized regiment, for most of the fighting that year. Doctors could not keep up with the devastating casualties. In May alone, Virginia hospitals treated more than 48,000 soldiers, one-third more from any other month that year. In May, June, and July doctors treated more than 102,000 soldiers, and the overwhelmed medical department began shipping patients to Danville and Farmville, Virginia, while others went to hospitals in North Carolina or Tennessee. Recovery rates were improving, but physicians could not keep up with the losses. This, combined with complaints about denied furloughs home and the threat of consolidation, created fractures in the Texas Brigade's morale.[4]

Rufus King Felder, an original private of Company E of the Fifth Texas Infantry, noted these issues in the early fall of 1864. He did not see an end to the fighting, and, depressed, tired, and underfed, he could not help reflecting on all the friends he had lost "whose bones & bodys, yet scarce decayed, are still exposed to the gaze of man & at the sight of which, the very angels weep."[5] The only positive thing Felder noted was that now that the Texas Brigade was near

Richmond, they were doing less fighting. As early as the fall of 1862, shortly after Antietam, Felder had told his sister, when she "hoped the Texians thirst for Yankee blood had been partly quenched," that it had indeed. "I can speak for the three [Texas] reg. in Va," Felder wrote. "Their thirst has not only been partially quenched, they have been in so many fights and have suffered so much they would be willing never to go in another fight."[6] But after two years of sadness, of seeing friends die and of learning of deaths at home, of hunger and exhaustion, Felder still refused to quit.

Part of Felder's determination may have been tied to all his family stood to lose if Republican power grew and emancipation became the law of the land. Rufus Felder's grandfather Gabriel Felder moved to Texas in the early 1850s. He purchased and had cleared 2,500 acres in Washington County in 1851. Rufus Felder, his widowed mother, and his siblings followed Gabriel to Texas three years later, as had Rufus's cousin Miers. By 1860, the Felders ranked among the wealthiest and largest slave-owning families in one of the wealthiest counties in Texas.[7] Rufus also, however, saw himself and Miers, who also served in the Fifth Texas, as a Confederates fighting for a noble cause—a cause he refused to abandon. Felder desperately wanted to go home, but not before Confederate independence was secured and with the knowledge that he had played a key role in that victory. As he explained to his sister in September 1864, "All that I want on this earth to make me happy is independence & a safe return to our once happy home." He had been in every battle the brigade had fought, and he remained after Miers left on a wound furlough following the Battle of Second Manassas. There is no doubt that Rufus Felder was frustrated and exhausted in late 1864. But, like many of the men around him, he refused to consider surrender and he refused to leave his unit.[8]

Not far from Felder, twenty-six-year-old William Terry reflected similar determination. He rose through the ranks partly through talent and partly through his service in a hard-fighting unit. That fighting reputation, however, had come at a heavy cost. By the fall of 1864, Company G was a quarter of its original size. The fighting had nerved the men to much of the loss, but Terry, like Felder, counted when each man fell, listing their names in letters home and mourning their absence. Despite the losses, Terry insisted: "We are fixed here now so that half of our force can hold Richmond against any force they can bring against us. We have the best fortifications in the confederate states and we are satisfied here that the Yankees can do nothing."[9] Terry made similar claims in a letter to his father a week earlier and boasted that "all of the company that is here is well and in good spirits," and "keeping old Grant back." Terry promised, "You need not fear but what we can keep all the Yankees back that they can send."[10]

Even captured Texas Brigade soldiers remained determined that fall. Fourth Texas sergeant Sidney E. Mosely, recovering in the prisoners' ward of Hampton Hospital in Hampton, Virginia, had been wounded at Gaines's Mill, the Wilderness, and again at Darbytown Road, where he was finally captured and had a leg amputated by a Union surgeon. Of all men, Mosely certainly had reason to lose faith in the war. But he remained confident of Confederate victory and the justness of their cause. That winter, Dr. Alfred Mercer, an English-born abolitionist practicing medicine in Syracuse, New York, had asked a colleague, Dr. John Newel Tilden, "if among your reb prisoners any one is willing to write me I should be glad to hear from him or them, and learn what they expect to gain for liberty or humanity, or what greater worldly prosperity they expect from our division of the Union." Fourth Texan Moseley pledged to "reply with as much brevity as possible," and then went on for more than twenty handwritten pages of biting sarcasm, countering each of Mercer's claims about the nobility of the Union cause.[11]

"I am a one-legged Confederate Soldier," Moseley began, "having but recently lost my leg in battling against the insolent invader of our country. I am also sorely afflicted with the itch, the sore eye, the Yankees and various other miserable and disagreeable things, too numerous to enumerate." After defending state sovereignty and slavery, and pointing to northern "nullification" of the Fugitive Slave Law, Moseley declared: "We glory in the Knowledge that we are eternally and irrevocably separated from all such ranting, fanatical and Puritanical abolitionists as you seem to be. When the war is ended,—which, I think, will soon be . . . we hope to have nothing more to do with you." Mercer's insistence that he had no animosity toward Confederates only infuriated the Texas sergeant: "You have no hatred for us, nevertheless you invade and devastate our country, murder our people, burn our houses, barns, mills, and provisions, and our towns and cities, and perform numerous other little delicate, amiable and charitable deeds."[12]

Dr. Mercer had theorized that older southerners "will most likely die still hating" the Union flag, but he "believe[d] the young and middle aged will yet learn to love it." Moseley fumed, "The old men of our country will most certainly die, hating the old flag; and can you blame them, when its followers have created so much suffering and misery in our land." The doctor was "entirely wrong when you think the young and middle aged will ever love it. None of us will ever have any reverence or love for it."[13]

The trouble, though, was that the Confederacy was running out of men to wage the battle Moseley continued from his hospital bed. General Lee called all available men back to the ranks in early October. He ordered officers to review their rolls and recall any men on detached duty, any nearly recovered soldier on sick leave, and any man who might possibly perform active service in the army. Any men incapable of active service, Lee ordered, were to remain with the army rather than be sent to Richmond or the Carolinas on sick or wound furloughs. They could serve as couriers, hospital attendants, or foragers and replace healthy men currently in those positions.[14]

In Richmond, the Confederate Congress reacted to the dwindling Confederate ranks by passing a Consolidation Bill. This would require understrength companies and regiments to combine and reassign junior officer and staff positions to fill essential holes in the ranks.[15] It hurt army morale, especially in units that took pride in their long service to the Confederate cause, but Lee believed it was essential to his army's and the Confederacy's survival.[16] Lee's First Corps commander, Lt. Gen. James Longstreet, opposed the idea and warned Lee that the policy threatened units' "prestige" and "esprit de corps ... the two most important elements in military organizations."[17]

The Texas Brigade was exactly the kind of unit Longstreet described. All fall, the Texans and Arkansans had hoped they would be granted leave to go home for the winter, recruit fresh troops to fill their ranks, and return, strengthened, for the campaign season of 1865. Col. Frederick S. Bass, commanding the Texas Brigade briefly that winter (and symbolizing the understrength nature of the unit through his rank more officially suited for regimental command), submitted their recruiting plan to Confederate secretary of war James Seddon in December. Rufus Felder took pride in all they were doing to make their case, writing to his mother: "We have been using every exertion in our power to have the brigade transferred or furloughed to Texas this winter. We have drawn up a memorial to that effect, signed by all the officers & men of the brigade and presented it to the President." But Felder was also a realist, adding, "Many are confident that we will go home this winter, but I must confess that I think our chances are very slim."[18]

First Texan Seaborn Dominey shared Felder's hopes but was even more frustrated. His wife, Caroline, had been running their small farm and caring for their infant daughter since he left for war almost three years earlier. In

November, he confessed to her: "There is some talk of consolidating the army this winter. If they do, I don't know what they will do with us as there is not enough for a regiment. The men say if they consolidate them, they will run away to join in the Service in Texas. Some of the best soldiers in the Brigade is using such language."[19]

By December, he was still worried and explained that if their proposal was rejected and men deserted, "It is not because they are tired of fighting but they know they have not had the chance to visit their homes that other troops have." Significantly, he revealed that some men were losing faith in their ability to make a difference in Virginia: "Some of the best soldiers in the Brigade says they are going to come home but they don't intend to quit the war. The Brigade is too small to enter another campaign as it is. I think something will have to be done with us before Spring."[20]

Dominey made a similar comment to his sister, Elisa Davis. She had just praised his determination, but the private was not feeling as resolute as he had six months or even a week earlier: "You say that you glory in my spunk. I am not so patriotic as I once was and I don't think you will blame me for not being so when you hear my cause." He was frustrated that they were by the lack of support they received after all the Texas Brigade had sacrificed: "Here we are out off from our homes where we can't get anything like clothing and I think other soldiers get as much clothing from the Government as we do. I have around three pair of pants, two shirts, one pair of drawers, two pair of shoes, one jacket, no blanket, no socks, nor hat. You certainly think I am not to blame ... for I have picked up stuff often off the Battlefield to supply me." If they did not get permission to go home that winter, he thought that "fully one half will come home without leave & they are all good soldiers, the best we got. They do not want to get out of service but they have been away from their families as long as they are going to without seeing their families & to speak the truth, I don't blame them."[21]

On January 15, 1865, Secretary of War Seddon informed the Texas Brigade that, with another campaign season approaching, the Confederacy could not risk them leaving for Texas and being unable to return. Lee recognized that "No brigade has done nobler service, or gained more credit for its State, than this. Though I should be much gratified at every indulgence shown to this brigade," he could not give them this.[22]

Officially, the Texas Brigade accepted the news and understood the needs that kept them in Virginia. Privately, however, officers were worried. They knew Seaborn Dominey's frustrations were shared throughout the unit. Without a recruiting furlough, the brigade would remain too small, which seemed to guarantee that they would be consolidated with other units and lose the unique identification as the Texas Brigade that was so important to them. Texas Brigade quartermaster major J. H. Littlefield confided to his wife in Texas, "We all fear consolidation; do not know what effect that will have." He insisted that, despite an invitation to transfer to Texas to serve on the staff of Brig. Gen. Jerome Robertson (former commander of the Texas Brigade), Littlefield knew he must remain in Virginia: "I should like to go very much, but will do nothing unworthy of past life, my wife, and my boys, to get home. An honored grave would be a richer legacy to them than a few years in disgrace and remorse."

Littlefield shifted to more positive matters, but his mood swayed between determined optimism and grave concern. "Have no fears; all will be well to those who put their trust in Him," he promised. "Think of our own comparative situation to the poor houseless and homeless wanderers in Georgia. This is a dark hour. All is gloom away from the 'lines around Richmond'; all is confidence here. We have plenty to eat, such as it is. Tomorrow, molasses and sugar will be issued in lieu of meat. Feed us, and this army can never be conquered," though he did not expand on how an army was to fight on a diet that substituted sugars for protein. Littlefield struggled to accept their fate. "I am fearful that consolidation will make many attempt to escape the army," he explained, but he knew it was "a great military and financial necessity; to us it will be, seemingly hard, but other States pride themselves on their brigades as much as we do the 'Texas Brigade.'"[23]

Despite frustrations like these, the vast majority of the Texas Brigade remained with the army, including men like Seaborn Dominey. There had been a few desertions that year, but most occurred in the late summer and were not reactions to the denied furlough request or consolidation fears either. Pvt. Asbury Lawson joined Company C of the Fifth Texas Infantry in the summer of 1861, was wounded at Gettysburg, exchanged, and returned to the ranks in April 1864. After a brief hospital stay in May, Lawson deserted to Federal forces in September.[24] Pvt. Edwin Searle had shown signs of trouble from the start. He joined Company C of the First Texas Infantry in the summer of 1861 and quickly was promoted to third corporal, but was reduced back down to private in February 1862. By January 1863, though, he was a second sergeant, and that April the men elected him as their first sergeant. Wounded at Chickamauga, Searle rejoined the Texas Brigade by the end of 1863 only to desert them in January 1864. After being captured and arrested, Searle was returned to the ranks to fight, where he deserted again on July 26, and this time, he took the Federal Loyalty Oath and joined the Third Delaware Infantry.[25]

Henry Bradley followed a similar path in late September 1864. An original member of Company F of the First Texas, Bradley fought with the Texas Brigade through nearly every major battle until he was wounded at Chickamauga in September 1863. After returning to the ranks in January 1864, he deserted that fall and took the Federal Loyalty Oath on September 20.[26] Other deserters like Joseph Chiles and Charles Mixon had received pardons by President Davis in the summer of 1864. Their joy at their salvation, however, was cut short when Chiles was captured at Chaffin's Farm in September, and Mixon was killed the following month at Darbytown Road.[27] Despite these examples, desertion in the Texas Brigade did not increase due to fears over consolidation or their denied furlough request. The 1864 deserters were men who enlisted predominantly in 1861 and 1862, voluntarily joining units they knew would take them more than one thousand miles from their homes. But they did not represent the core who remained in December 1864, frustrated though they were, and who would stay until the end.

The Texas Brigade decided to accept their denied furloughs, but they fought consolidation.[28] The men met and selected Maj. William "Howdy" Martin of the Fourth Texas, one of their favorite officers, to go directly to President Davis to make a case that the Texas Brigade, despite its reduced size, should remain an independent unit. Not many units had been consolidated by that point in the war, but some had, including the famous Stonewall Brigade. As part of Maj. Gen. Edward "Allegheny" Johnson's division that was largely destroyed at the Battle of Spotsylvania Court House in May 1864, the Stonewall Brigade and the remnants of Johnson's old division were combined to form a brigade under Col. William Terry, while two other brigades shifted elsewhere in Lee's army.[29]

The men were unwilling to accept such a fate, and their selection of Major Martin to make their case was a wise one. By this point in the war, Martin had become the personification of a Texas Brigade officer. He led his men in battle and cared for them in camp, often defending those who found themselves in the guardhouse for one offense or another. One account may be apocryphal, but its frequent repetition after the war speaks to how Martin was remembered as a volunteer officer. The story related that on one occasion, Martin went before President Davis's cabinet to argue that a Texan's death sentence be commuted, and he was so convincing that he "moved the members... to tears" and saved the man's life.

Major Martin had not risen through the ranks rapidly. Beloved by his men, he was a strict disciplinarian when it came to fighting, but Company K's camp was never the tidiest, and when half of his men failed to appear for drill, Howdy himself would defend their absence. Martin was the Fourth Texans' leader, confessor, mentor, and advisor; a man who inspired, protected, and consoled hard-fighting men far from home. He was their first choice as the man best able to plead their case to President Davis.[30]

Likely with help from either Postmaster General John Reagan or Texas Confederate senator Louis T. Wigfall, Martin received an appointment to meet with President Davis. As fate had it, General Lee was in Davis's office that day. Martin's fellow Texans watched him leave camp in "an old blue coat which once belonged to a Union soldier" where the coat tails had been removed to make it a short jacket or roundabout. Despite the modifications, Martin's shirt showed through a split in the back and "the Howdy Martin hair" poked through a hole in his hat. The major's appearance might not have been to code, but he made his case masterfully when he stood before the president and his commanding general. Holding his weathered hat in his hands, Martin explained that the men selected him "to protest against the order of your Excellency to consolidate the Texas regiments." Such a plan "would break the hearts of our men." For four years they had fought. "The bones of their comrades are bleaching upon many battlefields in the South," Martin reminded Davis and Lee, and the dead were mourned by the soldiers who continued to fight and others who "returned to their homes broken down in health forever." All that they asked, Martin explained, was that the Texas Brigade maintain its identity as a separate fighting unit.[31] In the silence that followed Martin's plea, Lee looked at Davis and offered an informal but powerful endorsement: "I want to say I never ordered that brigade to hold a place, that they did not hold it." Davis nodded and promised Martin that "as long as there is a man to carry that battle flag, you shall remain a brigade."[32] "Howdy" Martin had saved his men again.

As an additional response to the consolidation crisis, the Texas Brigade, like other elite units in Lee's army, drafted a series of resolutions that winter to ensure that their commanding officers, their representatives in Congress, and the families at home understood their determination to win the war. Gathering in late January, the leaders of the group included Lt. Haywood

Brahan, Pvt. William H. Burges, and Lt. Col. Clinton M. Winkler, who began the war as a company commander, and now found himself commanding the brigade. They came together in Camp Texas outside Richmond, part of the winter entrenchments of Lee's Army of Northern Virginia. All down the line, soldiers hunched in the defenses, coughing and shivering in the frozen ground and "spitting snow" that had given way to "dark, cold, sleety" rain by the end of January 1865. Mother Nature, one soldier declared, had created "too much mud between the two armies for either to make a serious advance," leaving "the troops" with "as much as they can do to keep from freezing."[33]

Despite the miserable weather, the men clustered around Brahan, Burges, and Winkler. For some of them, the approaching spring marked their fourth year of fighting. But they would continue, the men insisted, for a fifth, sixth, or more, if that was what Confederate victory required. They had come together to formally state this as the citizen-soldiers they were, ever aware of their constitutional rights and obligations.

Burges, who served in the same company with Brahan, proposed that they should select five men from each of the four regiments that comprised the brigade. These representatives would draft resolutions that expressed the sentiments of their units. Then they would combine these into one, clear, bold proclamation that would be submitted to the Confederate Congress, President Jefferson Davis, and General Lee, and for printing in newspapers across the South.

While the selected men departed to draft their resolutions, the rest of the brigade "was agreeably and pleasantly entertained by eloquent and patriotic speeches" by Lt. Col. Winkler and Pvt. T. D. Williams, whose equal billing with Winkler unconsciously symbolized the egalitarian streak that ran through the brigade. When the regimental representatives returned, they tweaked and revised their document until it received unanimous support.

It captured their worries about "the clouds of gloom and despondency that have recently gathered in the sky of our young nation," and their relief that these were "happily being dispelled by returning confidence." They clarified that the Texas Brigade had never embraced such despair and remained determined "to maintain, at all hazards, and to the last extremity, the rights and liberties which a merciful God has been pleased to bestow upon us, and even to contend for a perpetual separation from the hated and despised foe, who have murdered our grey-haired fathers, insulted our women and children, and turned out thousands of helpless families to starve—after robbing them and burning their houses—leaving them destitute of all except their honor."[34]

The men of the Texas Brigade, they explained, had "considered well the causes and consequences" of their actions when they went to war in 1861. They had "gone boldly forward, now for nearly four years, and our determination has not abated." Surely, "no one can now be so blind and stupid," they argued, "as not to agree with us, that the warning was the inspiration, and that then was the auspicious time to strike for our rights.... [W]e will rid ourselves of the tyranny the enemy would thrust upon us, or die in the attempt."[35]

The Texans clarified their faith in victory, as well as their faith in their leaders. They reminded readers of their numerous battlefield successes and their faith that there were more victories to come. As they awaited the spring campaign season, they mocked the "heterogeneous mass" that was the Union army, "the Babel of modern times, in which is represented the African, shoulder to shoulder with his brother, the Yankee, who sells himself for a bounty and deserts and sells himself again—the man with the brogue so rich—the avaricious Hessian, and the dungeons of Europe." In contrast, the Texans explained, the Confederate Army fought "to be free and independent of those who would kill eight millions of whites or enslave them in order to give a pretended freedom to half that number of African negroes." Fear not, they advised their readers. "Our final triumph is certain and inevitable, and our subjugation is an impossibility."[36]

The only major problem, they warned, was on the home front. Significantly, of all the resolutions listed, the soldiers' faith in victory and their concern about demoralization at home received the majority of the Texans' and Arkansans' comments. They could not, they explained, "be indifferent lookers on at those in our own country, who would divide and distract the counsels of the nation and tear down the present able and patriotic Administration; and, at the same time, give aid and comfort to the enemy." They warned the "politicians and demagogue newspaper editors, men in and out of positions, croakers, and *those who would fire from the rear,* and those who pull down, whilst we build up" that "there is a point beyond which you cannot go with impunity; that nothing will deter us from the prosecution of our purpose, whether it be our open enemies in the front, or the hidden and less respectable enemy in our midst; for the latter of whom, we take this occasion to express our most hearty scorn and contempt."[37]

The Texas Brigade passed their resolutions on January 24, 1865. Their public statement, as they hoped, appeared in newspapers across the South. Other units passed similar resolutions—Humphrey's Mississippi Brigade, the Fifty-Seventh Virginia, the Ninth Virginia, five Georgia brigades, and even individual companies.³⁸ While often viewed as a measure to boost military morale in early 1865, these resolutions are actually more reflective of homefront morale. The men's statements are too public to fairly gauge their determination or their frustrations. They certainly had complaints of their own. Indeed, only a week earlier, a Texas Brigade soldier's letter revealed some of their frustrations in the *Richmond Examiner* that men like Seaborn Dominey had express privately. The man asked: "Why is it that we are not paid our small pittance of wages, four months of which are now due us? We do not want the money for itself, but for the few comforts we could purchase. We were permitted a hundred dollar bond on the first of October. Why hasn't it been paid?" The letter was signed simply, "Texas Brigade."³⁹

The resolutions, however, received far more press than a solitary letter to the editor or private letters home. They served, as their authors intended, like a massive broadside that challenged citizens to show the same determination as those who had been risking everything they held dear—their families at home and their lives in battle—for nearly four long years. One could argue, though, that the problem at home was not one of will or the lack thereof, at least not for Texas Brigade families. It was a matter of debilitating inflation, the collapse of the Texas economy, and the inability of middling-class and impoverished Texans to feed their families and themselves.

Texans fared better than other southern states that both armies had ravaged, but by the middle of 1864, inflation was nearly out of control in the Lone Star State. Nearly 900 soldiers and women were registered on the indigent list in Howdy Martin's Henderson County in 1864. More than 700 families registered in Grimes County, and in Seaborn Dominey's Trinity County, Chief Justice William Rogers submitted the names of 668 soldiers and families in need.⁴⁰ By late fall, the Texas legislature abandoned efforts to allocate funds to counties to care for the indigent and impoverished soldier families and reverted to barter as they supplied cloth and thread produced at the state penitentiary that county leaders could use to trade for necessary food and supplies.⁴¹

It was not only the soldiers' families who suffered, but they received the most attention because their situation seemed so unjust compared to that of their contemporaries. Their suffering revealed a violation of the agreement made between a citizen-soldier and his community. He volunteered to protect the community's larger freedoms with the understanding that his neighbors would, if needed, help support his family in his absence.⁴² Texas, like most Confederate states, had tried to respond to these needs.

In 1863, everyone from the legislature to the county government to private citizens organized to support families at home and soldiers at the front. Newspapers were packed with announcements about fund-raiser balls and tableaux. Even the sisters of the Ursuline Convent in Galveston hosted a ball, teasing the local paper as they asked, "In making an appeal to the 'Ladies of Texas,' to second you in your charitable designs of relieving the destitution of the 'Texas Brigade' Hospital, in Virginia, you did not, I am certain, think of the Nuns ... down here in Galveston." The sisters had little personal wealth to share, but they challenged Texas women to model themselves after "the Roman Dames of old" to "part with our most precious jewels to alleviate the intense sufferings of those heroes who have achieved deeds of valor for their country."[43] Not to be outdone, the ladies of Crockett raised $525 in March, and they were matched and surpassed by the women of Seguin, Jefferson, Livingston, and in communities all across the state.[44]

The problem by late 1864 and early 1865 was that communities were either less willing or unable to give, and rural families had enough to do to simply survive. Their focus on the war was waning. Late in the war, Texas divorcée Ann Raney Coleman admitted that when the women in Lavaca County, Texas, did not receive their rations, they walked into the distribution office, "pistol in hand," and just like that "we got our rations." Coleman recalled, too, that when a Baptist Church collapsed after a storm hit their community, she and her daughter, whose husband was serving in the Confederate army, went out in the middle of the night to gather the splintered wood for their fires. As the women worked, more arrived to join them in securing firewood. When the guard who had been placed at the church tried to stop the women, "We told him there were enough of us to whip him, so he had as well say nothing.... He laughed at us for spunk. We threatened to tie him hand and foot if he should resist us."[45]

Coleman recalled that corn shortages led to similar results. Several of the poor women went to the local miller to request a small portion of what he was preparing for the wealthier families of the county. When he refused, some of the women guarded the man while others filled all of their sacks. They threatened to burn down the entire mill if he tried to stop them. "Be assured," Coleman scowled, "that it was the women that protected themselves in this war and not the men."[46]

Of course, not everyone suffered, and not everyone was convinced that the poverty was real. In Walker County, from which Fifth Texans William T.

Hill, Robert M. Powell, and Mark Smither hailed, an anonymous citizen complained: "The majority of them [soldiers' families], in this portion of the State, at all events, are bountifully supplied with all the necessaries, and to a great extent, with all the luxuries of life at present obtainable in the markets of the country. Several families of soldiers, in this country, within the writer's ken, live better, are better clad, and live in greater idleness than when their 'heads' were at home."[47]

Despite his claims, by 1865, things were dire indeed. The entire state had struggled to alleviate the suffering, but nothing seemed to work anymore. Counties distributed cotton and wool cards to aid destitute families with their home production of cloth. This helped, but no matter how much the state produced, they could not keep up with civilian demands, especially when Texas also needed to produce for military needs. Before the war, none of the cards were made in the South, so southerners had played a catch-up game over the last four years to increase card production to increase cloth production to increase uniform and clothing production. As is usually the case, they never quite caught up.

In Austin, the state legislature worked desperately to help soldiers' families. State legislators set aside $1 million each for 1864 and 1865, and another $500,000 to be provided each six months to the county courts based on the needs requested in their communities. The money could be used to purchase "necessary supplies" for soldiers' families. It helped a great deal, but, again, Texas could not keep up with its citizens' demands and with inflation. Complaints of women stealing cotton cards, government corn, and other food items, sometimes at gunpoint, surfaced in Galveston, Hardin, and Marion Counties and elsewhere throughout the state in 1864.[48]

Soldiers' complaints poured into the governor's office, too. One of the last of the war came from Calhoun County on April 4, 1865: "At the outbreak of this war," it began, "when the first call for volunteers was made by the Governor of this State, Indianola, then a town of about 900 inhabitants, furnished a company of artillery, 250 strong" for units including Hood's Texas Brigade. "When we enlisted, we were promised that our families never should suffer for want of life's necessary's; how this promise has been fulfilled the following will show. During the first year of the war, the families received for about 6 months corn and money, when suddenly it stopped altogether until July last year, when they were furnished with cornmeal" that was so fine it hardly baked into anything. The other problem was that the boats the women and townspeople used to gather driftwood for fires were pressed into service by local Confederate forces. Indeed, it seemed that every loose scrap of wood in town—including fences and outbuildings—was burned as civilians and soldiers alike struggled to survive the last winter of the war.[49] It is significant, however, that of all the petitions and complaints that came to the governor's office, almost none of them came from Texas Brigade families.[50]

As word of Texas difficulties traveled east, Confederate senator Louis T. Wigfall, on a trip home to Texas, expressed his concerns that such negative accounts were breaking soldiers' morale. He called on women across the state "to refrain from writing their husbands, sons and sweethearts, now in the army, to come home," and to abandon their "doleful accounts of their little troubles at home, which had produced so much uneasiness in the army and caused so much desertion and its consequences." Wigfall asked Texas women to abandon all such talk and instead to "stimulate" their soldiers "in every possible manner to stick to their posts of duty, and either die like heroes or come home at the end of the war covered with glory."[51]

It is significant to note, however, that in the hundreds of Texas Brigade letters to home and dozens from home, there are only a few that encourage their loved one to quit the fight and none from letters that exist from late in the war.[52] There are complaints to be sure. But of the wealth of southern letters from home that encourage men to desert or beg them to come home to save the farm, these do not exist for Texas Brigade soldiers. Part of the reason for this may be tied to the fact that Texas Brigade families were as motivated as their men who served in Virginia.

An event that spring captured that home-front support and shared determination. In early February, Robert E. Lee received a package from a "young lady in Texas" that contained stars made of gold "too precious for ordinary use." She asked that they be awarded to the nine bravest soldiers of the Texas Brigade. Senator Wigfall personally delivered the stars to the Texans and Arkansans in camp. In a fascinating demonstration of democracy, neither Bass, General Lee, nor any commanding officer selected the nine recipients. The men of the Texas Brigade put it to a vote—two recipients for each regiment except the Fourth Texas, which had three. In the First Texas the stars went to Pvts. William Durham and Josephus Knight; in the Fourth Texas, Cpl. James Burke, Sgt. James Patterson, and Cpl. W. C. May. In the Fifth Texas, the recipients were Sgt. C. Welborn and Sgt. Jacob Hemphill. The Third Arkansas recognized the bravery of Pvts. J. D. Staples and J. W. Cook.[53]

It is significant that three of these men (Knight, Burke, and Cook) were later enlistees who joined the Texas Brigade in the spring of 1862. By February 1865, it did not seem to matter if a man had volunteered amid the rush to arms following Fort Sumter or remained at home until the following spring. It is also notable that most of these men were not members of the planter elite who led the home communities in which Texas Brigade companies were raised. The majority of the Gold Star recipients came from middle-class farming families, some of whom were serving alongside multiple members of their family. In the case of Josephus Knight, he and his three brothers all enlisted in March 1862. Both Andrew and William left the First Texas within about a year due to chronic illness. Brother John had left his twenty-two-year-old wife, Sarah, at home to raise their two sons, both under the age of two, and run their profitable farm with the help of family. Sarah died six months after John left, but still he remained with the Texas Brigade, a twenty-eight-year-old widower who counted on his family to care for his children until he felt he could return.[54]

While the identity of the woman who donated the stars was never revealed, several of the Texans later suspected that it was a Miss Fuller of Houston, which means she was likely connected to another key home-front supporter of the Texas Brigade, Matilda Jane (Maude Jeannie) Fuller Young.[55] It might have been Young herself who sent the stars, or perhaps one of her younger sisters. They all lived in their parents' home before, during, and after the war, and their brother, Blucher Pulaski "Pugh" Fuller, had been serving in the Texas Brigade for four years. He was a lawyer who rose from private to second lieutenant in command of Company A of the Fifth Texas. Maude Young's only son was in the unit, too. He joined in 1864 at the age of sixteen. They were all part of the prominent Fuller family of Houston, where Maude's father, Nathan Fuller, earned a fortune before the war as a railroad agent. She had expanded the Fullers' reach in February 1847, when she married Dr. Samuel O. Young of an equally prominent Houston family. They were on the cusp of a bright future together when Samuel died suddenly that November. Seven weeks later their only child was born and named S. O. Young for the father he would never meet. By the final spring of 1865, Maude Young was a widow in her early thirties.[56]

Back in 1862, Maude Young made the Fifth Texas's flag, which General Hood had selected as the brigade's official flag at Gettysburg. She also raised $30,000 (about $413,000 in today's economy) to support the construction of the Texas Hospital in Richmond during the war. Few Texans did more to help the Texas Brigade throughout the entire conflict.[57] Late in 1864, the men of the Fifth Texas returned the flag to Young because it was so tattered from their many battles.[58]

As honored as Young was to receive it, she was worried, too. "You bid me 'hang the flag upon the outer walls' to strike terror to the hearts of the cowards skulking at home. Ah! my noble brothers of the 5th! if the sable-clad forms of mourning women and children, if the numberless maimed soldiers who greet us at every turn," she asked, "if the form of our Confederacy, beleaguered by foes and bleeding at every vein, strike no remorse, and inspire to no patriotic deeds, think you this flag will? They are joined to their idols—money making and selfish ease." But one day, she said, "you shall return and scourge them from the land. If honor or peace or safety were depending upon them, we would long ago have worn the Yankee yoke and ate the bread of slaves."[59]

Though written in November 1864, Young's letter to the Fifth Texas was published, at their request, in the *Richmond Whig* on January 17, 1865. That means it appeared in papers about two or three weeks before the Texas Brigade's and other units' famous resolutions appeared in print. And if inflation, lack of support, supply, and sustenance were breaking Texans down that final spring, Maude Young was going to fight that. As late as June 1865, she was still fighting.

The Texas Brigade loved Maude Young's loyalty and passion, but even they had their suspicions about victory in 1865. In late February, Rufus Felder's mood fluctuated between determination and doubt. He warned his sister that the reports of Sherman's campaign through South Carolina were true. Both Felders were born there, and he feared that "the insolent foe" had "committed depredations on the property, if not on the persons of our dear, but unfortunate relatives there." Rufus Felder had served more than three years in Company E of the Fifth Texas Infantry. "Our cause looks gloomy indeed," he admitted. "We have met with many recent & severe reverses, but I trust that the tide of battle will soon turn." Still, he advised that "you must all prepare your minds to see your negroes freed, at least a portion of them. Congress is preparing a bill to make soldiers of them.... [T]hey will have to be freed.... [A]ll the soldiers are in favor of it."[60]

Samuel S. Watson of the First Texas revealed similar vacillations in his mood. In February, he told a correspondent on the home front, Harriet C. Lewis, that the recent prisoner exchange "will make our Armies considerable stronger." It also meant Lewis's husband was likely on his way home "if he is

Still living." He had heard that Confederate leaders were "going to put in two hundred Thousand buck Negros" and believed "that will also help Sum." Watson had "a notion of applying for a command among them I dont know that I shall but I think of doing so." This was the same man who noted, after the fight against the Federal Third Brigade of USCTs at Fort Harrison, that "the boys litterley coverd the ground with Dead Nigs." By the spring of 1865, his concern over Confederate defeat had expanded Watson's willingness to consider arming slaves and free blacks, so long as they fought for the Confederacy. Watson believed Lee's army would "be able to hold Va.," but then he added, "I hope so, at least." Indeed, Watson admitted, "I will Say to you that Evry thing looks Sad and gloomy at this time in and a round Richmond, great many people has become dispondant and Sum disertion Sum dissatisfaction in difrant ways Sum for putting in the Negroes . . . to fight." Watson wished "they will all stop thare foolishness and let the men go home."[61]

Despite the concern sweeping through the ranks, Willis J. Watts of Company G of the First Texas Infantry remained unwaveringly and unusually optimistic that spring. Watts was twenty-three years old when he enlisted in Palestine, Texas, in April 1862. Wounded at Chickamauga and the Wilderness, he had also survived small injuries that did not require care, or at least not official treatment. On March 11, 1865, Watts told his cousin that he was "in the enjoyment of excellent health and Spirits." Watts had "undergone a great many hardships & privations Since I left Texas," and he expected "to undergo many more before I get back, at least I fear So." He remained confident, however, in Confederate victory. "Although we have Sufferd So much & So heavily, we are all in high Spirits, and more determine[d] on gaining our Independance than when we first enterd the army. I hear of no depondency in the army, but on the other hand they are all determining on our independence," Watts explained. There was some grumbling from other states, he admitted, but not from the Texans.[62] Whether optimistic or just stubborn, Hood's Texans still refused to give up the fight that spring.

The problem, though, was that the Army of Northern Virginia could barely operate in the field by April. There were too few weapons, too few men, too few supplies, and they were cut off from support. As Dugat Williams looked at his fellow Fifth Texans, his thoughts may have wandered to Pvt. Darius Rachal, who had tried so hard to rejoin Company F the previous September. He and Rachal had been part of the same mess in that first winter of the war along the Potomac River. Williams's mind may have wandered back to the image of his messmates that he had painted for Laura during his winter on the Potomac River in January 1862. Capt. King Bryan had been smoking in a badly made chair crafted by Peter Mallory. Pryor Bryan's laughter had been the loudest and the happiest. Around them, huddled with blankets and coats pulled tight, had sat Williams, Lts. J. E. Cobb and R. J. McKinnon, Sergeant J. F. Church, and Pvts. Charles Brashear and Darius Rachal.

Nearly three years to the day of writing that description, Williams was the only one left. Pryor Bryan had died from disease on the retreat from Yorktown, and no one was sure what had happened to Charley Brashear, but they thought he had been killed at Gettysburg.[63] He might have been captured, they hoped, like J. E. Cobb was. He was being held at the Federal prison at Johnson Island, Ohio. King Bryan, Cobb, McKinnon, Williams, and Rachal had remained in 1864, but then Rachal went home on furlough and could not get back to Virginia. Bryan spent the year in and out of hospitals due to lingering problems from his wounds from Gettysburg and the Wilderness. Ohio-born Peter Mallory, the enthusiastic carpenter, was killed in the fight at Darbytown Road in early October.[64]

A spent round hit R. J. McKinnon between the eyes at the fight at Williamsburg Road in late October.[65] In January 1865, word arrived that McKinnon was dying, and Williams sneaked into Richmond, refusing to wait on the two-day delay to secure a pass. Williams was at his friend's side when McKinnon died.[66] The next month, King Bryan received a medical discharge, much to his outrage. He had tried for months to convince doctors that the lingering numbness in his hand would not impede his ability to lead the Fifth Texas, but they disagreed.[67] By April 1865, Watson Dugat Williams was the only man left from his original mess. He was a captain now and in command of Company F, Liberty County's "Company Invincibles," which had only 12 men.[68]

WAGING PEACE
Texas Brigade Veterans and Families in Reconstruction and Beyond

On April 12, 1865, the 617 men of the Texas Brigade surrendered their weapons at Appomattox Court House, Virginia, along with the rest of Robert E. Lee's Army of Northern Virginia. Although Lee's was the best known of the Confederate armies, his surrender did not bring the war to an immediate close, but it signified that the end was near. After stacking their arms and receiving their paroles—which were key to protection from Federal arrest and to Federal assistance with the journey home—Texas Brigade soldiers would start their trek west as quickly as possible. Maj. "Howdy" Martin and Capt. W. T. Hill, volunteer officers of the Fourth and Fifth Texas respectively, would lead home anyone who wanted to travel with them. A good portion of the brigade accepted this offer, though it is impossible to know exactly how many. Some of the men chose to travel in smaller groups, and others broke off after traveling a few days with Hill and Martin.

Despite their different routes, two themes surfaced as the men made their way home. First, none of them spoke at the time or years later of joining other Confederate armies fighting farther south and west. Their paths went within close proximity to these forces, yet none of the Texans or Arkansans mentioned the possibility of joining them or of even considering this despite having brothers, cousins, and friends—men they respected—in these armies. The sources are silent on their precise motivations, but it is quite likely that, believing they were the best brigade of the best army in the Confederacy, Hood's Texans concluded that once Robert E. Lee and the Army of Northern Virginia were defeated, it was pointless to fight with anyone else.[1]

A second pattern that emerged from their journey home was their tendency to travel as a unit, ranging from a few men of one company to multiple companies and even much of a regiment. Some of this is not surprising—

companies raised in towns and counties contained soldiers who were returning to those same areas and thus would travel together. But these traveling companions maintained close connections well into the postwar era. They became business partners and supported each other's postwar efforts because of their shared brigade service, not just because of geographic proximity or antebellum familial connections. They traveled with soldiers from their company or regiment because of the success and security they felt as a brigade. This would echo through the postwar period as Hood's Texans waged the peace of Reconstruction together, just as they had waged their war for independence.

On the morning of April 9, Fifth Texan W. T. Hill and the Texas Brigade occupied a defensive position just southwest of Appomattox Court House, Virginia. The Brigade, commanded by Col. Powell, had fallen back from Richmond to Petersburg on April 2, but Lee's army lacked the strength to hold either city. The Texas Brigade had then served as the rear guard as Lee's men marched west toward Amelia Court House, and then on toward Danville. But Federal cavalry prevented them from reaching Danville, so Lee shifted to the west and led the men toward Appomattox Court House. There the Texans and Arkansans formed into a crescent-shaped line that straddled a stagecoach road, defended by breastworks built hastily from any material they could find. All around them were signs of the heavy marches both armies had made over those final days. "Cannons, wagons and ambulances in large numbers had been abandoned by the troops ahead of us," Hill noted, "for lack of teams strong enough to pull them. Horses already dead, and many others fast dying from exhaustion and for lack of feed, lay in the mud, in and by the side of the road."[2] Hill was the original first lieutenant of Company D. He was in his early twenties when the war began, working on his father's plantation in Waverly, Texas. With a combined property and personal wealth of nearly $214,000 that included more than twenty slaves, the Hills ranked among the wealthiest planters in Texas.[3] W. T. Hill received his promotion to captain just before the Battle of Second Manassas. He was well liked by the men and remembered for the prayer meetings he held throughout the war.[4] Wounded in the foot at Gettysburg, Hill had returned in time for the opening of the 1864 campaign season only to be slightly wounded again, this time in the arm in the Wilderness. He remained with the Fifth Texas through the rest of their fighting that year and was in command of the entire regiment, though only a captain, by the spring of 1865. They numbered just 149 men.

Fighting resumed briefly on April 9 as morning's light revealed their positions, but Hill knew there was little they could do. Our "line of retreat was blocked." Then, "suddenly, everything came to a death-like stillness." The men stopped working, "hunger stayed its gnawing, and expectant of evil tidings, but yet unprepared for the worst, faces grew grave and serious, and men when they talked at all spoke in whispers."[5] Teamsters walking through their lines later that day announced that Gen. Robert E. Lee had surrendered the Army of Northern Virginia, but the Texans refused to believe it.[6] When Lee's farewell address was read to the men the following day, though, Hill knew the end had come.[7]

Just down the line from W. T. Hill stood "Howdy" Martin of the Fourth Texas, motionless, trying to process what this meant. Lee had surrendered his army, surrendered them. Like Hill, Martin had commanded, advised, mourned, and loved the men of Company K since 1861. He had led them through that first disease-filled winter along the Potomac. Through bloody fights, often charging far in advance of the men, never slowing down because he knew the men needed him. Martin had even remained at their head when his brother Robert fell mortally wounded at Chickamauga, and Howdy also stayed despite his own wound at Darbytown Road in late 1864. Martin was the personification of a Civil War commander. After years of determined fighting, marching, digging, and dying, he realized that it was all over. Tears rolled down Martin's weathered face, and his body shook with sobs.[8] That night, despite Grant's promise to feed Lee's army, the men's stomachs remained empty. The Federals were hungry, too. The armies had outstretched their supplies, and spring rains kept the food stacked at the depot from reaching anyone that night. Some hardtack and coffee made it through to the Confederates, but not much. As if to compound their discomfort, as the Texans fell into a fitful sleep, a chilling rain began to fall.[9]

On the morning of April 12, some of the Fifth Texans had accepted defeat but refused to surrender their weapons. At least not while they were still usable, they explained. Captain Hill watched in quiet frustration as the men took turns placing their barrels in the fork of a red oak and then wrenched until the weapon was useless. Hill walked quietly toward the angry rebels and, calm as ever, reminded them that "General Grant would not grant a parole to any soldier who did not present his gun in good condition." The parole was their ticket home to Texas and protection from arrest by Union forces along the way. Some of the Virginians or North Carolinians might be close enough to walk off without paroles, but the Texans and Arkansans had a long journey home. The men nodded at Hill, informing him, "If that be the case we will straighten them back." Hill walked away, smiling at the "sublime failure" of their efforts.[10]

The regimental officers called the Texans into formation. The Army of the Potomac's corps' printing presses had worked around the clock for the last few days printing thirty thousand parole slips to be distributed to the surrendering Confederates.[11] On command, the Texans took their place in the line of Confederates, moving forward in their familiar cadence, rifles resting on their shoulders. The regiments were small—many had fewer than 200 men—but Field's division, in which the Texans served, remained Lee's largest.[12] As each regiment approached their mark, officers dressed the lines and the men stacked arms in fours, with the remaining men leaning their rifles on the stack as they went by or laying them on the ground. Faces gaunt, bellies empty, the men slipped off their belts and dropped their cartridge boxes in a pile by the weapons. It was, Basil Crow Brashear of the Fifth Texas recalled, "the hardest thing I had to do during the whole war." That was a powerful statement for a man who was discharged for chronic rheumatism in November 1861 but recruited again the following March 1862. Wounded twice at Gaines's Mill and Darbytown Road, Brashear had lost many friends over the last four years, including his brother, Charles, at Gettysburg.[13] But the surrender at Appomattox was his hardest day.

Not far from Brashear, John David Murray felt similar despair as he moved along with the line of Texans and Arkansans. Murray led Company F of the Fourth Texas Infantry even though he was only a color sergeant. He was the highest-ranking man left. He was also the last of the Murray brothers in the Texas Brigade. Four years earlier the Mustang Grays, as Company F was known, had marched out of Bexar County, sunshine soldiers warmed by the support of family and friends. John David and his brother, Robert Washington, were with them. Their younger brother James joined them as an 1862 recruit the following spring. The Murray boys came from a typical Fourth Texas background. Their father had moved the family from North Carolina in the 1850s, trying their luck first in Missouri, before settling in Bexar County, Texas, by the end of the decade. Owen Murray, his wife, Sarah, and two daughters had continued to work their hog farm in Guadalupe as best they could after three sons left for Virginia and their eldest, Asa, served in the Eighth Texas Cavalry in the West. By the summer of 1863, word arrived home that James had been killed during the Battle of Gettysburg. Compounding the tragedy was the fact that it had likely been friendly fire from his own company. Not quite a year later, Robert fell at the Battle of Wilderness. He survived the wound but lost a leg.

By April 1865, John David was the last Murray boy left in Company F. He was one of the last soldiers, period. Of the 120 men who mustered in with the company in 1861, only 7 remained at the surrender. As he made his way toward the stacked arms and pile of cartridge boxes, it was Murray's unhappy task to pause before the entire Fourth Texas and lay their furled battle flag atop the intertwined bayonets. Years later, after a lifetime of hardship, John Murray reflected on that somber April day and declared it "the saddest in his life."[14]

The First Texans had lost their battle flag to a Federal cavalryman just a few days earlier, and the Fifth Texans were never clear on whether they surrendered their colors or not. Most insisted that the tattered flag they returned to its creator, Maude Young, in the fall of 1864 was the last flag they had carried into battle. But the Arkansans had to surrender theirs. Like Murray, the color-bearer stepped forward and laid their colors across the stacked arms. Dangling from the staff was a note, a parting blow: "Mr. Yankee, You will please return this staff and shoulder belt over to the 9th Maine. [It] was captured at [Ft.] Gilmore on the 29th October 1864 by the . . . 3rd [Arkansas] Regt. Vols." The man had simply signed his name, "Big Rebel."[15]

Only 617 men were left in the Texas Brigade that April. More than 7,000 had served in the unit since 1861. Companies A and F of the First Texas had only two men to surrender. Company B had none. In the Fifth Texas, Company D could boast nine men, one of them Pvt. John T. Allison, whose brother Arthur had been captured at Gettysburg and heard of Lee's surrender at Fort McHenry Prison in Maryland. Their other brother, Andrew Jackson Allison, had enlisted with them in the Leon Hunters in the summer of 1861, but Andrew never made it out of Texas. Too sick to travel, he died at the training camp six months into the war.[16] One company after another, each bearing scars similar to those of the Allison and Murray families, passed through the surrender point and accepted their parole. Then the Arkansans and Texans made their way back to their encampment. "It was a sad, sad day for General Lee's army," Hill recalled.[17]

The paroles granted the men safe passage home in exchange for their pledge to not return to the fight. It also guaranteed free passage on any Federal train or vessel, as well as access to Federal food stores.[18] Most of the Arkansans decided to take their own route home via Chattanooga and Memphis, while the

Texans debated an overland versus a water route to the Lone Star State. Captain Hill and Major Martin offered to lead home whomever wished to follow them. Other men, like A. B. Green of the Fifth Texas, chose "to go our own way" along the roads, rivers, and rails to Texas, while Dugat Williams and a few men from the Fifth Texas relied on Williams's prewar occupation as a steamboat captain and followed him to West Point, Virginia. By late morning on April 13, all of the paroles had been distributed, and the brigade was on the march within the hour. They could not leave Appomattox quickly enough. As they walked, Robert Lowery of the Third Arkansas, ever the farmer, observed that the "trees are budding out." Maybe he could get home in time to plant a crop.[19]

The main force of Texans headed south toward North Carolina.[20] As they passed through Charlotte, the men ran into former Confederate postmaster and fellow Texan John Reagan, as well as President Jefferson Davis, members of Davis's cabinet, and the original Texas Brigade commander, Senator Louis T. Wigfall. Howdy Martin stopped to talk with John Reagan and shared extra blank paroles that Senator Wigfall later used to escape through Federal lines toward Confederate general E. Kirby Smith's army. Wigfall removed all signs of rank, shaved his beard, and renamed himself Pvt. J. A. White of Company M, First Texas Infantry. In a disguise he would use well into the postwar period, Louis T. Wigfall headed west for Texas, following the route he had taken years earlier as a young man on the rise.[21]

Most of the men reached their Texas and Arkansas homes in June 1865. Others, like Thomas Jewett Goree, did not arrive until late summer because he elected to escort his commander, Gen. James Longstreet, home. Others still, like Thomas's brother Ed Goree, lingered in Virginia until they were healthy enough to travel. Then Ed strapped his badly wounded and now shrunken leg behind him and, with the help of a crutch, walked and rode on a long, slow journey home. He spent Christmas 1865 in Huntsville, Alabama, with cousins and finally reached his family's home in Texas the following summer.[22]

There are several significant trends that surface in the multiple paths taken by the Texas Brigade after Appomattox. Most of the men took the less stable route from Virginia through the Carolinas and Georgia, which took them toward Sherman's army. None of the diarists mention joining General Johnston's army, nor do the postwar writers. Indeed, there is no mention of Johnston's army at all except to note when Hood's Texans are passing it. After the surrender at Appomattox Court House, the Texans seem convinced that they had completed the service they had promised, and they were likely un-

Texas Brigade Journeys Home, 1865

convinced that any army but theirs could win the war. Indeed, Fourth Texan Paul Ripley had explained just that back in September 1864, when he told his brother-in-law, "When we give up Virginia, we give up all hope of gaining our independence."[23]

They also made no mention of the assassination of President Abraham Lincoln. John Wilkes Booth shot Lincoln on the evening of April 14, and word spread quickly across the North and the South. Most of the Texas Brigade veterans had not even reached Danville, Virginia, by that point, and yet no one references the assassination or any mistreatment by Federal soldiers reflecting anger over Lincoln's murder, and none mentions hearing comments about Lincoln by civilians on their journey home. It is likely that they were focused on one goal: getting home. It is also possible that they avoided any mention of Lincoln in their diaries for fear that if Federals stopped and searched the men, they could fall suspect.

Regardless of which path they took, the journey home took about eight weeks. The majority of men stopped along the way to visit extended family and to check on the widows and parents of dead comrades. Some of them, like A. B. Green, John Calvert, Dennis Rowe, and John Wesley Smith (all veterans of Company K of the Fifth Texas), traveled miles out of their way to avoid contact with Federal forces. Others, like William A. Nabors and C. P. Nance, both of Company G of the Fifth Texas, did not mind interaction with Union forces and actually utilized their support and protection when some Federal cavalrymen, who were later apprehended, robbed the Texans.[24] Most of the groups, exhausted, stopped around Mississippi and rested for several weeks, often staying with relatives or the families of fellow soldiers. After resuming the journey, several barely made it home before sickness and fatigue forced them to pause again. A. B. Green and his group got lost in the swamps of southwest Arkansas, which was suffering from flooding that spring, and Green battled a fever for the final week of his journey. When he, Smith, Rowe, and Calvert finally reached their families in Moscow, Texas, Green made a final notation on July 11, 1865: "Stayed."[25]

At home in Texas and Arkansas, the men did not see as much of the physical damage that had scarred Virginia, the Carolinas, Georgia, and Mississippi. They did, however, face crippling financial losses. Dugat Williams captured their situation best in 1866. "Upon returning home from the war I found myself broke in every sense of the word. Broke pecuniarily, flat broke, and if I was not broke physically and mentally, I was wonderfully bent. The war's insatiable appetitive consumed all my little worldly possessions and gnawed ravenously at my once good constitution," Williams mused. He did not, however, "say this complainingly [sic], but rather with pride, as it treated most every confederate soldier with the same impartial generosity . . . proud to know all went in such a cause; and if I occasionally comb a gray hair out, it is flattering to believe it grew gray in the army."[26] The pride that Williams referenced shaped the connections the brigade maintained as they rebuilt their lives. It also fueled their determination to resist the socioeconomic reforms of Reconstruction that they had fought against for years and, despite their surrender, still hoped to defeat.

Hood's Texas Brigade waged the rocky peace that defined the postwar South just as they waged the Civil War. They maintained their bonds as a unit, they supported each other, and they worked steadfastly to secure the futures that the war had failed to provide. Much of their wealth and that of their communities was tied up in the men, women, and children they enslaved and everything those slaves produced. Emancipation destroyed the majority of the brigade's prewar wealth, just as it did throughout the largest slave-owning sections of the South. By maintaining their ties to their fellow Texas Brigade veterans and families, however, many of Hood's veterans found success in the New South.

When Dugat Williams left Liberty, Texas, in 1861, he was the stereotype of what his contemporaries celebrated as a self-made man. He was born amid scandal two decades earlier to a father who sided with Mexico during the Texas Revolution and spent most of Williams's life on the run, finally abandoning Williams, his mother, and his two siblings.[27] But by the time the Civil War began, Dugat Williams ranked among the Texas elite, living in Liberty as a steamboat captain with an estate valued at $22,000 that included a dozen adult slaves.[28]

The question in 1865, however, was how much of that wealth was left. Prewar Liberty, Texas, had a diversified economy that included cotton, sugarcane, tobacco, indigo, lumber, and cattle.[29] By 1870, however, the county had lost over 80 percent of its wealth, and, personally, Dugat Williams lost 96 percent.[30] He would struggle to provide a livelihood for himself and his wife, Laura Bryan Williams, whom he married in December 1865.[31] Indeed, an informal look at the best-known Texas Brigade veterans indicate similar losses.

Maj. "Howdy" Martin, the Athens, Texas, lawyer who closed the war commanding the Fourth Texas, suffered about the same losses as Dugat Williams between 1860 and 1870. Capt. William T. Hill of Walker County commanded the Fourth Texas when the brigade surrendered. He came from one of the wealthiest planter families in Texas, but by 1870, the Hills' wealth had shrunk by 99 percent. Hill's mother had died a few weeks before he arrived home in the summer of 1865, and his once influential father, whose wealth required him to make a personal appeal for amnesty to President Andrew Johnson, was an aging widower in Captain Hill's home with $250 to his name.[32]

A. B. Green of the Fifth Texas lived with his father, a Polk County blacksmith, when the war began. Far from rich, the Greens enjoyed a middle-class life in the community of Moscow in a home that was valued, along with the land and their personal effects, at $2,330. By 1870, Sergeant Green was twenty-eight years old, and he and his wife, Amanda, had a nine-month-old son and $100 to their names.[33]

A comparison of the total wealth of Texas counties that were home to Texas Brigade volunteers in 1860 with those counties' total wealth in 1870 reveals that, on average, they lost 67 percent of their wealth.[34] Thus, while Texas was not as physically scarred as the rest of the South, this challenges the impression that Texas was relatively stable compared to the rest of the former Confederacy in the postwar period.[35]

Although much remains unknown about how specific communities faired in the immediate postwar period, a close look at Texas Brigade veterans in the three Texas regiments, as well as the Third Arkansas, reveals debilitating financial personal losses between 1860 and 1870. Seventy percent of Texas Brigade veterans from Texas and Arkansas suffered financial loss between 1860 and 1870, and 80 percent of that group lost 65 percent or more of their 1860 wealth. This would include men like Willis Landrum, who joined the Porter Guards in the summer of 1861, which mustered into Confederate service as Company H of the Fourth Texas Infantry. Willis was eighteen when he enlisted along with his brother, Zach, who was twenty-two. They left comfortable lives in Montgomery County, Texas, on a farm north of Houston, where they lived with their mother and stepfather, Nancy and Appleton Gay, whose wealth ranked them in Texas's upper class. In addition, the Landrum brothers and their elder sister, Melissa, all had their own personal property, likely inherited from their late father. After the war, Zach and Willis Landrum eventually returned to Montgomery County, Texas, where Zach still bore the scars from a leg wound from the Battle of Gettysburg that left him permanently disabled. In 1868, he died from "disease." Willis married and had children but had lost all of his 1860s wealth.[36]

In the early twentieth century, Willis Landrum applied for a Confederate pension on three separate occasions, finally learning in 1923, with only his property to his name and no means of earning an income, that he was denied his pension because he was listed as a deserter on the rolls. Technically, Willis Landrum did desert in 1864, but it was not to rush home or away from war but to follow his brother, Zach, from one hospital to another after his Gettysburg wound. Indeed, Zach did not leave Virginia until he received his parole near Richmond in April 1865. But the pension board did not find those details, or the endorsement from fellow Texas Brigade veterans, sufficient.[37]

Despite all of this suffering, when Texas Brigade veterans' losses are compared with those of their communities as a whole, significant patterns surface. Geographically, there is no indication that those who stayed in East Texas did worse or better than those who settled around Austin in the west or Dallas County in the north. The majority of the men came from East Texas communities before the war and returned to these afterward. There is insufficient data to know if certain occupations fared better than others since most of the men, like heads of households across the country, were farmers. Slightly older men—those in their late thirties—tended to do better economically in the postwar period compared to those who suffered losses, but that difference is small.[38]

Significantly, in nearly two-thirds of cases, Hood's Texas Brigade veterans' losses were less than those suffered in their county as a whole between 1860 and 1870.[39] One possible reason for this was the determination Hood's Texas Brigade veterans displayed in maintaining ties with their fellow soldiers and supporting each other throughout the postwar period. They waged the peace of Reconstruction and the Jim Crow South as a brigade, just as they had waged the war.

Historians have been challenging for some time the theory that Civil War veterans entered a period of "hibernation" after the war, where they simply wanted to resume their peacetime lives and hesitated to discuss a conflict that was far more brutal and less ideologically influenced than their civilian families remembered.[40] This is certainly not true of Hood's Texas Brigade, where, as early as the summer of 1865, veterans worked to maintain their ties from the second they returned home.

In some ways, that was easy. It was impossible for veterans to isolate themselves from memories of the war. The Union army occupied postwar Texas and served as a constant reminder of what they had fought against. Every time a veteran farmer went to town to sell crops or buy supplies, he saw friends and neighbors with whom he had served in the war. Recruited from the same towns and counties and under military occupation, Confederate veterans could not avoid images and memories of the war.

That was certainly true of the Berryman brothers in Cherokee County, Texas, whose properties connected with the farm owned by the parents of Mort Murphy, their friend and fellow volunteer in the First Texas who was killed at Gettysburg. A similar inability to escape the war surfaced in 1865, when Dugat Williams was walking through Liberty, Texas, and ran into a fellow veteran. Williams discovered that his friend Charlie Brashear had, indeed, died at Gettysburg. Williams and the other men of Company F, including Brashear's brother Crow, always held out hope that he had been captured and would return one day. In their small communities, veterans crossed paths through marriage as well, as was the case of Amanda Day, once closely tied to Peter Mallory, who asked Dugat Williams to give Mallory's ring to Day as he lay dying at Darbytown Road. She became engaged to their fellow Company F volunteer W. L. McCary in late 1865. In Polk County, Fifth Texas veterans A. B. Green and Dennis Rowe married sisters Amanda and Angie Magee.[41] Texas Brigade veterans could not help but interact with their fellow soldiers and veteran families in the postwar period.[42]

More telling about the Texas Brigade, however, is how determined they were to maintain their ties with each other. An early example of this surfaced in June 1865, when Col. Robert "Mike" Powell, who commanded the Texas Brigade when they surrendered, wrote to *Houston Tri-Weekly Telegraph*'s editor Edward Cushing, offering Powell's thoughts on how the next few months and years would play out, and how white Texans of their middle-class backgrounds could take the lead to peacefully restore the old social and racial order. Powell refused to revisit "past calamities and present humiliation and injustice" and offered instead "the benefit of my observations upon affairs generally."[43]

The thirty-nine-year-old Powell saw President Andrew Johnson as an ally. His roots in the Democratic Party guaranteed his loyalty to "the high interests of the county," Powell argued, and inspired the president "to disregard the narrow and prejudiced ideas" of the Radical Republicans on his cabinet left over from President Lincoln. Johnson was under attack by "a large and powerful party in the North," Powell explained, and the South must "resurrect" the Democratic Party, "join its Northern wing, and do battle for the common good." Former Confederates may be "subjugated and coerced subjects of the government," but they had "rights and interests," he insisted, and they would "be recreant to both if we lapse into abject submission."

Powell was not calling for armed resistance. "Our cause is forever gone," he argued. "The Confederacy is gone ... acts of personal violence now is madness and invites the inexcusable acts of cruel tyranny which our masters are capable of." Instead, "the South," by which Powell meant the white, middle-class and elite men who led southern communities, "must seek to defend itself by the exercise of political power.... Let her organize and sustain the President and all will be done that is possible to save her from further distress and desolation." Readers across the eastern portion of the state knew that Powell had been one of the first to volunteer, that he rejoined the Texas Brigade after he was exchanged after being wounded and captured at the Battle of Gettysburg, and that he commanded the brigade when it surrendered.

Mike Powell saw no path to peace through emancipation. He believed that "there will be no morning until the African race has passed away" and been replaced by a white labor force in a solidly white South. Until then, Powell advised readers on what a fair wage was for freedmen field hands—"five dollars per month, and they furnish their clothes and pay their doctor's bill." In closing, Powell asked to be remembered to all members "of the old 'Texas Brigade'" and then tacked on a postscript, noting that a number of former Confederate congressmen had applied for pardons, received them "graciously, and revived their interest again in the Eagle."[44] Colonel Powell's advice for postwar Texas would restore the old order through the appearance of obedience but focus their strongest, peaceful efforts on cooperation with their presidential ally.

Brigade connections surfaced that summer as the men launched businesses and resumed their civilian lives. In July 1865, Robert Burns, an original private of the Fifth Texas who rose to major before the war ended, launched a business with Charles Merriman, who had served with Burns in the Fifth Texas's Company A, the "Bayou City Guards," and their mutual friend, C. A. Darling. The threesome reopened their Houston store—Darling, Merriman, & Company—at the corner of Main and Congress. After listing the wealth of sales experience and outstanding reputations enjoyed by the men, they reminded *Houston Tri-Weekly Telegraph* readers that "We need not add that any member of the old Texas Brigade who visits the city will always be made at home in this store."[45]

Later that month, Houstonians learned that Dr. R. J. Breckenridge, "a gentleman well known to the old Texas Brigade," had opened his practice in the city.⁴⁶ Breckenridge began the war as regimental surgeon for the Fifth Texas and by 1865 worked as headquarters surgeon for the Army of Northern Virginia, serving as the chief medical inspector. Despite such credentials, none of this was mentioned in his 1865 advertisement. The only endorsement Breckenridge seemed to need for his new practice was that he was "well known to the old Texas Brigade," which he was. Time and again, when Texas Brigade soldiers were wounded, they sought Breckenridge for treatment. But Breckenridge did not mention that, and he did not secure some key endorsements from the host of Confederates who benefited from his care. He also made no mention of his connections with Lee or the Army of Northern Virginia. All that mattered to Breckenridge, and to much of his East Texas client base presumably, was that Breckenridge had the support of "the old Texas Brigade."

In late October 1865, another ad appeared featuring Capt. D. C. Farmer, an original third lieutenant of Company A, Fifth Texas Infantry. Farmer had been wounded at Gettysburg and again at the Battle of the Wilderness, where he served as acting lieutenant colonel of the regiment. The ad boasted Farmer's "spirit of both business and mental energy" in opening a night school and reminded readers that he was "of the old Texas Brigade in Virginia."⁴⁷ Again, the endorsement made no mention of Farmer's experience as a teacher or his educational background. What mattered to East Texans were Farmer's ties to the Texas Brigade.

In the immediate postwar years, Texas Brigade veterans struggled to care for their fellow soldiers and families, and they focused their attention first on one of the most famous Confederate commanders of the war, Gen. John Bell Hood. Hood was a controversial figure in much of the Confederacy, especially after his failed leadership contributed to the fall of Atlanta and to the disastrous southern losses at the Battles of Franklin and Nashville in 1864. But for Texans, he was the best commander of the Texas Brigade. He led them at their great victories at Gaines's Mill and through countless other battles that secured their fame. A number of men commanded the unit over the course of the war, with Hood leading the brigade only from March through October 1862. But the brigade veterans and their contemporaries always referred to themselves as members of Hood's Texas Brigade. That loyalty inspired the men to action just months after the war ended to raise funds to provide a home for Hood when the war left him financially ruined. The *Houston Tri-Weekly Telegraph* captured the sentiments of Hood's men when the editors argued that Hood's "name is familiar in every household and his fame is identified with that of Texas forever! To thousands of your sons and brothers, he has been personally well known, as their commander upon many a bloody field, their companion in many a comfortless camp, and their friend everywhere."[48]

While the Freedmen's Bureau worked to provide for freedmen and loyal white citizens in the immediate postwar period, the Texas Brigade's middle-class businessmen and planters started the process of reclaiming their antebellum role as the paternalistic protectors of their communities.[49] They followed the advice Colonel Powell had given months earlier, pledging their loyalty to the Union and receiving amnesty in ever-increasing numbers in an effort to solidify their claims to their land and businesses and resume their leadership positions. Dugat Williams was among the first one hundred men in Liberty to swear his loyalty to the Union and its laws, signing an Amnesty Oath in July 1865.[50] Thomas J. Goree waited until nearly five thousand other men had done so, finally taking his oath in early November.[51]

It is unclear why Williams did not immediately return to work as a steamboat captain. Both he and Goree listed themselves as farmers in Liberty and Polk Counties, respectively. Other brigade veterans, like Fifth Texan Mark Smither of Huntsville, returned to their businesses and mercantile shops. Searching for a larger clientele, Smither took out ads in papers as far away as Memphis, Tennessee, to attract business to the area. Just as his compatriots had, Smither used his four years of service with Hood's Brigade as his endorsement with the public and added that he was one of only four remaining survivors of his company. Smither assured readers that "affairs are not as bad in Texas as is generally represented, and that the condition of the country is much better than one would suppose, after the great drain upon her active population."[52] East Texas, he promised, was open and ready for business.

For Smither, compared with his fellow brigade veterans, the postwar period was unusually profitable. He had worked as a clerk in his stepfather's store when the war began. Erasmus Wynne Farmer had a combined wealth in 1860 of $83,000, while Mark Smither's mother retained a separate estate valued at $67,000. The family suffered some setbacks, but by 1870, Mark Smither had married and was the father of two children, and his widowed mother lived with them in Huntsville. Somehow Smither retained an estate valued at $80,000 in 1870, perhaps through some of his mother's holdings or perhaps inherited from his stepfather.[53]

Most of Hood's veterans, however, were not doing as well as the Smithers. Indiana-born Mary Tiner was an extreme example of the poverty some of them endured. She had been a thirty-eight-year-old mother with four children under the age of eight when her husband, James, accepted a bounty in March

1862 and joined the First Texas Infantry. They had $200 to their names and owned no land in Jefferson County, Texas. James survived 1862 unscathed, but he was wounded at the Battles of Gettysburg and Chickamauga. He healed and was back in the fight for the 1864 campaign season until he was badly wounded at the Battle of Spotsylvania Court House. Doctors had to amputate his leg to save James's life, but he survived and returned home at the end of the war.

It is unclear when he took the Amnesty Oath, but like many of his fellow Texas Brigade veterans, Tiner registered to vote in 1867 to begin the process of reasserting his place in East Texas society, low though it may have been. Two years later, though, he died of his wounds. Over the next three decades, Mary depended on friends and her community to help raise her children and keep food on the table and a roof over their heads. She never remarried. In 1899, almost seventy-eight years old, Mary Tiner went before a Jefferson County judge to seek a pension that James's service provided. When asked, "Where is [your husband]?" she answered, "His soul is in Heaven and his body is lying on Magnolia Hill, and has been there thirty years now.... I have no means to support within myself," Mary Tiner explained. "I am too blind to work and have been for two years now. If I could see I could work. I don't own any property now. Don't own a homestead. The community and my friends have done the rest. I don't own a foot of land except enough to lay my body down on on the hill and I guess I won't be robbed of that."[54]

It was the plight of Texas Brigade widows like Mary Tiner that inspired the veterans to organize as early as 1866 to "provide for the widows and orphans of their fallen comrades; and to render suitable honors to the dead." They gathered in Galveston and later, on July 14, in Houston, and notices about the effort spread across the state, appearing in the *Dallas Weekly Herald* that summer. The organizers argued that their plan was nothing short of "a duty, an obligation, which the *people of Texas* all should promptly discharge, but it is appropriate that the men who were with them through battle, wounds, and death should take the initiative."[55] Their efforts did not get far, however. Gen. Philip Sheridan, who headed the Military District of the Southwest, made it clear that all organizations of ex-Confederates formed must be disbanded.[56] Texas Brigade veterans asked for clarification and delayed as long as possible, but Sheridan, disgusted by white Texans' continued resistance and suspicious of their full motivations, refused all requests.[57]

Sheridan kept Confederate veterans from organizing, but it was nearly impossible to thwart their efforts to rebuild their postwar lives as an echo, if not an exact replica, of the antebellum social order they preferred. By 1869,

Thomas Jewett Goree had married and moved his family to the town of Midway in Madison County, Texas, "having failed in my farming operations, like every one else in the same section of the State." Midway was "in a more prosperous condition" than Walker County, where Goree's family had lived at his mother's Raven Hill plantation. Goree opened a mercantile business, and though he was confident of success, his wife, Eliza T. "Tommie" Nolley Goree, "insist[ed] on teaching school to help us along. I do not like the idea at all," he confessed to her father, "but my protest is unavailing."[58]

The Gorees found gradual success in Midway, where they took in boarders while Thomas continued to work at his shop and Tommie taught forty pupils at the school she started. Times had certainly changed from the lives they had enjoyed before the war, but Thomas Goree was hopeful for the future, despite the recent turn in state politics. "It is true that Texas has disgraced herself in the Election of a radical Governor," he wrote, referring to the defeat of Unionist Democratic candidate A. J. Hamilton. Hamilton was a native of Huntsville, Alabama, like the Gorees, and had been a Unionist throughout the war. An early supporter of black suffrage and briefly a Radical Republican (though he would later reverse his position on suffrage and return to the Democratic Party), Hamilton was President Johnson's choice as provisional governor of Texas in 1865. After resigning from office in 1867, Hamilton ran again in 1869, only to lose to former Union general and Radical Republican Edmund J. Davis.[59]

Thomas Goree liked Hamilton and saw him as a moderate solution for a state that needed to accept the end of slavery but, in Goree's opinion, maintain white leadership. Not as radical as the Republicans or as the conservative Democrats, Hamilton represented what educated elites like Goree wanted for Texas, and Davis was just the opposite. "Texas has disgraced herself in the Election of a radical Governor," Goree wrote, "and I can but feel humiliated from the fact that the white people of the State are to blame for it. We had a large majority in the Registration and could have elected Hamilton by 40,000 majority, if the registered voters had gone to the polls. There are, no doubt, 10 or 15,000 whites who could have registered and did not do so." Still, Goree insisted, "Texas possesses this advantage, it is a white man's country. Already the whites have a tremendous majority, which is being constantly and steadily increased by the arrival of hundreds of immigrants daily. As soon as political quiet again prevails, Capital will seek investment here." He believed that "the many projected railroads across the length and breadth of the State will be built, besides, many others not now thought of and we will then have a country unsurpassed by any on the Continent." Thomas Jewett Goree, like many well-educated Texans who had enjoyed middle-class or elite wealth before the war, remained confident that the state could rebuild if moderate white Texans managed to reassert their antebellum influence.[60]

What writings exist from Hood's Texans in postwar Texas and Arkansas reveal the same racial sentiments they expressed during the war. They wanted white men running their communities and maintaining a white-controlled social order. They did not all agree on who should lead them, and some were clearly more radical than others. But they almost universally opposed black suffrage and the influence of African American men in their social, political, and economic affairs. A few men, like William Hamman, were furious about such changes. He served in Company C of the Fourth Texas and spent much of the early war in the commissary department until he was transferred to the Trans-Mississippi West at his request in 1863. When the war ended, Hamman refused to believe the new order of Robertson County, Texas, could be permanent. "The question is not one of dollars and cents," Hamman argued, "but whether the noblest, the proudest, the most chivalrous, the most moral and christian people will suffer themselves to be dragged down to the level with the negro, and then still lower to keep pace with the negro in his retrogradation in his liberate state, until finally our rich, prosperous, and happy land shall present the condition of Hayti, Mexico, and the Central American states." Hamman never believed the Confederacy had been wrong: "I am fully persuaded of the correctness of our cause, and that we had the men and means when we began the contest to have made it successful. But we committed many outrageous errors and we lost our liberties."[61]

There is some evidence of difficulties with the occupying U.S. forces in the years that followed the war and with the Freedmen's Bureau, but most of it is anecdotal. Edwin Sue Goree remembered the time her "Uncle Ed"—Edwin King Goree, the Fifth Texas brother badly wounded in the Wilderness who spent the rest of his life with his withered leg bound up behind him while utilizing the support of a wooden peg—was arrested by "Yankee Soldiers from Huntsville." Ed Goree had been helping his sister-in-law Tommie with an end-of-the-year play she hosted at her school in Midland. During the show, he drew back the curtains that were decorated with a Confederate sword hung in the middle. When the curtains stuck, Goree grabbed hold of the sword to balance himself. "Standing there between half-drawn curtains, resting on a wooden leg and grasping the sword, he must have made an appealing picture of the returned soldier of the Confederacy," his niece noted. The audience laughed and clapped, and they enticed Goree to sing a few songs. He favored them with "Bonnie Blue Flag" and a few other selections before ending with "I'm a Good Ol' Rebel," which closed with the lyrics, "I hate this old Republic—the Yankee Nation, too, And I don't want a pardon for anything I do." That was likely the moment, Sue Goree believed, that inspired his arrest by Federal soldiers.[62]

Edwin Sue Goree claimed that her father, Robert, who had served in the Sixth Texas Cavalry, belonged to the Ku Klux Klan, and she suspected his brothers, who fought in Hood's Texas Brigade, did, too. By the time of her writing, Sue Goree's family had taught her that the Klan "was a dangerous thing," though "made necessary by the lack of legal redress open to the Confederate soldier" right after the war.[63] While many of the specifics of Hood's Texans' postwar lives remain unclear, racial violence became an increasingly common problem as Reconstruction evolved in the Lone Star State. In 1871, Madison, Grimes, and some Hill Country counties all witnessed spikes in attacks on African Americans, including death threats against black members of the Texas State Police and the murder of at least two freedmen. At the same time in Walker County, just north of Houston, Capt. Leander H. McNelly of the state police, a former Confederate officer, arrested four men for the murder of freedman Sam Jenkins. Three of the men were convicted. But locals managed to arm the men, who shot their way out of the courthouse. When McNelly, who was wounded in the gun battle, tried to deputize men to capture the fugitives, only two citizens would help. Walker County fell under martial law by Governor Edmund J. Davis's order, for the next sixty days, but violence continued to ravage the region. When one of the fugitives, Nat Outlaw, was captured and sentenced to five years in prison for Jenkins's murder, he appealed his conviction, and Governor Davis reviewed and released Outlaw, who was later awarded $20,000 in damages for false imprisonment.[64] Reconstruction began in the Lone Star State with Governor Hamilton railing against those who would argue that "this is and was intended to be 'a White man's Gov't. It is and was intended to be 'a *free* man's Gov't" for blacks and whites.[65] By the early 1870s, however, Hamilton's dreams were failing as Texans struggled through a stubborn economic recession. As late as 1879, Fifth Texas veteran T. J. Newman complained: "Everything is cheap everywhere but there is no money in this country to buy with. We raised a pretty grand crop here the past season but cotton has been so low that it brought but little money." Much of the problem, he insisted, was due to the "terrible mixed population" of African Americans and German Americans, who "controls our local politics in a way that I don't like. With one or two exceptions we have a full set of radical officers in this county," and there were, Newman noted, "two negroes gone to the Legislature from this county."[66]

Just as Goree abandoned farming for a mercantile business, supported by his wife's school enterprise, J. R. Loughridge maintained his cotton business but considered accepting a position with the Red River Real Estate Company in 1871. This opportunity required travel from home, however, and Loughridge was uneasy about the idea of his wife, Felicia, having to handle matters with him gone. He also worried that she was uneasy without him. A possible solution, he suggested, would be for his fellow Fourth Texas officer C. M. Winkler to help her in Loughridge's absence.[67]

The strongest example of this mutual support was the organization of the Hood's Texas Brigade Veterans' Association in 1872. The men came together annually as a social organization, to collect their history, correct errors in their military record (especially of friends wrongly listed as deserters when they were unable to cross the Mississippi and rejoin the brigade), and "to succor the needy among its members."[68] Hood attended the first meeting in Houston, as did their former commander, J. B. Robertson, along with more than sixty other members of the brigade.[69] This was one of the earliest units to organize as veterans, further reflection of the ties Hood's Texans had never relinquished.

The brigade was busy raising funds for a monument when word arrived from New Orleans that John Bell Hood's wife, Maria, had died of yellow fever on August 24, 1879. Her loss reminded the Texas Brigade, they told Hood, of all of the "sufferings and sorrows of the ill-fated past. When we were but as your children and comrades in arms, you guarded our well being and honor," they explained. "Your old comrades share your poignant grief." Hood adored his children, but he confessed to a close friend that "he'd rather God had taken every one of his children in one day than to have lost his wife." Then Hood became ill, as did two of his daughters.[70] In his final moments, Hood likely worried about what would become of the eleven children he and Maria had brought into the world. Accounts claim that he asked that his children be placed in the care of the Hood's Texas Brigade Association veterans, though this responsibility was actually awarded to his mother-in-law, Eleanor R. Hennen. When word arrived of Hood's death along with that of his eldest daughter, Lydia, on August 30, his old soldiers rallied immediately. Fund raising began, and despite the lingering economic hardships that many of their families faced, Hood's Texas Brigade veterans contributed more than $3,100 by the summer of 1880 to the "Hood Relief Committee."[71]

For years afterward, Hood's Texas Brigade Association continued to contribute to the care of the Hood children and debate their proper care. At their 1884 reunion, on the twentieth anniversary of the Battle of the Wilderness, Maj. "Howdy" Martin delivered an impassioned speech declaring his concern that Hood's children were being educated in Europe and in the northern United States rather than in Texas, which was "one hundred years ahead of Europe in high education, in morals, Christianity, and the training of children for greatness," an idea that received thunderous applause from Hood's men.[72] They failed in this endeavor, but the association appointed committees to help secure appointments for two of Hood's sons to the U.S. Military Academy at West Point, New York. They continued to raise money for their support, too, even after being informed that the Hood children were all amply provided for, and years later they welcomed Hood's children and grandchildren at their reunions.[73]

As the nineteenth century came to a close, Hood's Texas Brigade veterans continued their efforts to support each other and ensure that the memory of their service was preserved. They played a key role in the opening of the Texas Confederate Veterans Home in Austin in 1889, which provided shelter and care to scores of Texas Brigade veterans. These men ranged from Col. F. S. Bass of the First Texas who briefly commanded the brigade during the war, to his fellow First Texas soldier Thomas J. Calhoun, a physician who fell on hard times. While the members of the Third Arkansas were often underrepresented at the reunions and in submitting materials for the brigade history, several of them, including William Berryman and H. C. Ivey, reunited with fellow Texas Brigade residents at the Confederate Home in Austin. Many of the Texas Brigade veterans who found their way there had previously secured pensions with the help of the Hood's Texas Brigade Association leadership, including advocates like Joe Polley and Frank Chilton. Other fellow Texas Brigade veterans served as the person of contact should anything happen to a Confederate Home resident, as in the case of lawyer W. F. M. Eringhaus, who listed his fellow member of Company D of the Fourth Texas Infantry and fellow Seguin, Texas, resident, Alexander Erskine, who still lived in Seguin near his brother's widow, Ann.

This was not unusual; veterans across the country sought out support from fellow soldiers to verify that they had served honorably throughout their term of service when applying for state or federal (in the case of Union veterans) aid. What was different about the Texas Brigade's actions was their lack of emphasis on loyal Confederate service in general, which they replaced with a focus on the Texas Brigade. To them, their loyalty and sacrifice was far different and greater than the average soldier's, and the brigade veterans worked tirelessly to ensure that their fellow Texas Brigade soldiers were cared for as they aged.[74]

This was the case with Pulaski Smith, a Fourth Texas private wounded at the Battle of Gettysburg. When J. M. Polk and W. G. Jackson heard that Smith was struggling to care for himself, they hurried to help him gain admittance to the Texas Confederate Home for Men in Austin, which Jackson entered in 1907. This facility was, Jackson explained "all that an old Confederate could ask and more than I expected." The only challenge, he joked, was getting "used to living with the old ugly... bald-headed crippled and feverish old fellows and do nothing but eat and sleep or run around town over the woods or go fishing in the Colorado River close by, play cards or dominoes."[75]

In a similar situation in 1909, Dr. A. C. Oliver testified to the service of his elder brother, S. W. Oliver. They, along with three other brothers, had served in Company D of the First Texas. H. B. and John Oliver died of pneumonia in the spring of 1862, and William H. died in 1863 from the wound he suffered at Chickamauga.[76] As S. W. entered his late seventies, A. C. Oliver, who had been a doctor before and after the war and served as a first lieutenant in the First Texas, testified to his brother's dedicated service. A. C. never mentioned their familial connection, perhaps because the interviewer was already aware of it, or perhaps because Oliver became impatient with the questions. When asked about the length of S. W. Oliver's service, A. C. explained that S. W. enlisted in 1861 and fought all four years, only surrendering at Appomattox Court House "because he had nothing to live on & the yanks had six men to our one and it seemed a ____ fool to fight any longer." After verifying that S. W. was badly wounded at Gettysburg, A. C. Oliver was asked to explain how well he knew the applicant during the war. Frustrated, Oliver explained that he "knew him from childhood, saw him enlist saw him sworn in saw him march and starve for bread saw him at night slept with him and eat with him and fought in the same battles with him and surrendered with him and came back to Texas with him."[77]

Support also came from the soldiers' old friends Gus and Mollie Bailey, who reopened their circus in Arkansas after the war and eventually moved to Dallas, Texas. They ran "A Texas Show for Texas People," which quickly became a favorite of Texas Brigade veterans who remembered the Baileys from their Hood's Minstrels days. Fifth Texan Edwin King Goree, who was left for dead at the Battle of the Wilderness, enjoyed back-to-back shows just before Christmas 1898 and noted what a favorite it was among his friends.[78] Gus and Mollie admitted the poor and veterans (Union and Confederate) free of charge and were known for family-friendly entertainment that delighted small towns across the state. When Gus retired in 1890, it became "The Mollie A. Bailey Show," and she continued to run their circus successfully for twenty years after his death in 1896. She managed more than 150 animals, numerous employees, almost three dozen wagons of equipment and supplies and was aided by her children, who participated in nearly every show.[79]

As the association continued to age, Texas Brigade veterans grew increasingly determined to erect a monument in the Texas capital of Austin. They wanted a lasting reminder of what they had sacrificed in their effort to preserve and support their antebellum successes and freedoms. It took years of fund raising and exhausting debates over what the monument should look like and what it should say. In the end, Joe Polley won his argument that it should feature an individual Confederate soldier and make no reference to Jefferson Davis or the Confederate government. It had to be about the brigade, about *their* sacrifice alone, he argued. "If a medallion of Davis appears on the monument at all, it is bound to have the central and most conspicuous place, and the men and women who when we are dead and gone look at it, will accept it as a monument to Davis and the cause he represented, and never give a thought to the brave men to whose memory alone it should be dedicated," Polley explained.[80] They had spent decades working to meet their 1872 objective to "collect and perpetuate all incidents, anecdotes, history and everything connected therewith." By 1906, they were still pushing to get "complete rosters of their original companies together with the fate of each man during the war and up to the present time."[81] If they were going to have a monument, it had to reflect the objectives that had guided them for nearly four decades.

On a warm October day in 1910, a crowd assembled in Austin to celebrate their accomplishments and to dedicate a monument to the soldiers of the Texas Brigade. William Hamby, president of Hood's Texas Brigade Association and former private in the Fourth Texas Infantry, took the stage. Looking out on the capitol grounds, Hamby reminded his audience:

> It was on Southern soil where the first declaration of civil and religious liberty was ever proclaimed in America. It was on Southern soil where the first

written constitution ever framed in America was adopted. It was a Southern man who wrote the Declaration of Independence. It was a Southern man who led the rebels of 1776 to victory. It was a Southern man who led the American army to victory again in 1815. It was a Southern man who led the American army to victory upon foreign soil in 1846. It was a Southern man who proclaimed that distinctive American idea known as the "Monroe Doctrine," which is respected and obeyed by every foreign power. It was under the administration of Southern men as Presidents of the United States that were added more than three-4ths of all the territory that now comprises the States of the American Union.[82]

Fellow Fourth Texan Joe Polley was sitting on the stage near Hamby and likely raised his brows at several inaccuracies in Hamby's speech. Governor Thomas Campbell, however, did not seem to think Hamby went far enough. In his lengthy speech, in which he used artistic license to make his case, Campbell reminded the men, women, and children who covered the statehouse grounds and stood in doorways or sat on open windowsills in the capitol building of the tremendous cost of the Civil War: "Six hundred thousand of the best men of the South opposed 2,500,000 of the Federal army and fought with them the 2,250 battles of the war.... At the end, 437,000 men were not there to answer 'here' to the last roll call; they had fallen in the fight, while 485,700 men of the Northern troops were slain." Looking out at his audience, Campbell closed his speech with a smile. "The men of the South," he argued, "did not surrender because they were whipped, for they never were, but they surrendered because they were tired of victory."[83]

The irony of Campbell's and Hamby's speeches is that the Texas Brigade veterans themselves rarely displayed that level of vitriol, perhaps because they thought their war record spoke for itself. Sitting on the stage with his prosthetic foot, Joe Polley was one of the most devoted members of Hood's Texas Brigade Association, but he regularly rejected such hyperbole. It was he who proposed that the association abandon their practice of adopting unmarried daughters of veteran members as "daughters of the brigade," a title the woman lost when she married. The practice had spawned recognition of the "Baby of the Brigade," "Song Bird of the Brigade," "Child Orator of the Brigade," and a host of other titles before Polley had had enough and proposed at the 1902 reunion that they welcome all of the veterans' children of the brigade as a sponsor and drop such titles. The association adopted his resolution immediately.[84]

Joe Polley was famous, by that point, for his distrust of ceremony and hypocrisy. In 1908, fed up with the Democratic Party, Polley informed his friend and fellow Texas Brigade veteran Frank Chilton of his frustrations with Texas politics and threatened to vote for Republican gubernatorial candidate John Nicholas Simpson (also a Confederate veteran). His speech accepting his party's nomination, Polley wrote, rang "so clear and true even to my Confederate ears" that Polley pledged to "do all I can to elect him to the governorship." Polley fought in the Fourth Texas from the summer of 1861 through the fall of 1864, when he had a foot amputated after his wounding at the Battle of Darbytown Road. He was a well-known contributor to the *Confederate Veteran* and anything but an apologist for the cause to which he had given so much. For him, though, the war had been fought nearly fifty years earlier; this was modern politics and a matter of principle and practicality. "I know it is to the interest of my district to have a Republican representative," Polley continued, adding that he was shifting parties in the presidential race as well. "I have decided to vote for Taft. I am tired of helping demagogues to office where they swindle the people at every turn and chance."

At this point, his fellow leader of the Hood's Texas Brigade Association, Frank Chilton, nearly had a fit in ink on paper. A shocked Chilton drew a finger in the margin of the letter, pointing at this section and wrote "awful," but Polley was still fuming: "The only characteristics of my daddy that he was able to impress upon me was his religion and politics; In all other matters, I have thought and acted for myself. . . . Though it is now rather late to make any change in either politics or religion, I am going to be as independent in one as in the other." And then, to make certain he was utterly clear on this point, Polley summarized his position: "In short, I do not intend any longer to let my memory of the war and reconstruction days dictate to and control my judgment."[85]

Like Polley, William B. "Bill" Fletcher of the Fifth Texas rejected ceremony and found success in the postwar South. When a wound at Chickamauga left him unfit for infantry service in the Texas Brigade, he joined Terry's Texas Rangers and ended the war when Confederate general Joseph E. Johnston surrendered his Army of Tennessee to William Tecumseh Sherman on April 26, 1865. The days that followed passed in a blur. "The thought of returning home, defeated," Fletcher remembered, "seemed to be depicted on each face, and for a few days I don't think I saw a smile." Fletcher recalled those "few days as the blankest part of my existence."

On the journey home, however, Fletcher adjusted rapidly to defeat. He recalled southern cavalry and infantry passing along a sunken country road one night, the infantrymen leaning against the road bank, letting the horse soldiers ride by. After a brief exchange between the forces, a North Carolinian called out, "Boys, have you got any bacon?" The cavalrymen answered that they did, and the North Carolina man responded, then "Grease and slide back into the Union." Fletcher did just that, and with astonishing effectiveness. He worked well with occupying Union forces in post–Civil War East Texas and became a successful timber giant, largely through fulfilling the role of the old southern patriarch employing poor whites and poor blacks.[86]

Fletcher's memoir is almost totally devoid of the "moonlight and magnolias" tone that ripples through the poems and songs authored by subsequent generations. After the war, Fletcher became known for befriending Union occupiers and drinking with them. Fletcher explained that they were "nice, jovial young fellows, [even] if they were born North of Mason and Dixon's line." Plus, "the boys were well equipped with cash, and liberal." Then, almost repeating Polley's pledge, Fletcher added, "after going through with a four years' experience," he "had learned something about individuality, so, if it did not hurt our pride to take a drink with the Yanks, we had committed no crime, and it was none of the other fellow's business." Echoing Polley's sentiments, Fletcher reminded his readers that "the war is over." Fletcher took pride in his service, but he shared a pragmatism about his service that may have been rooted in the Texas Brigade's reputation as one of the best brigades in the entire war. Its veterans had nothing to prove in the postwar period and felt that they shared none of the blame for defeat.[87]

Some of these sentiments changed over the years, and veterans could abandon moderate positions when they reached their final years. But Fletcher and Polley expressed their views, the former publicly and the latter privately, quite late in their lives. Perhaps the last to express such opinions was Texas Brigade veteran William Edgar Copeland. An original member of Company H of the Fourth Texas Infantry, Copeland fell early in the war at Gaines's Mill and left the brigade in the summer of 1862, when his foot was amputated. Like Polley and Fletcher, Copeland revealed an independence of mind that may have been tied to the fact that he need not express his patriotism; his wound did so for him. Writing in 1917, Copeland informed Hood's Texas Brigade Association secretary Frank Chilton that Copeland would very much like to see his old comrades at a reunion but that he rarely attended the gatherings because all he really wanted was the companionship of his fellow veterans. "I have no interest whatever in bloody-shirt speeches, such as I have often been compelled to listen to, (present company always excepted)," Copeland insisted. "As soon as I have seen and greeted them, I am ready to return home."[88]

The wives of the brigade responded differently in the postwar period. Some, like Felicia Loughridge, were not particularly active in public, but she wrote poems about the Civil War, and war in general, in private. Stanzas in poems celebrating her husband's bravery in 1863, such as "The Wounded Soldier" and "Chickamauga," have been credited to her. During the war, Felicia tracked the Texas Brigade closely and asked her husband for more information on the armies. "Love could you send me a map of the battle ground of Mannasses showing the position of the two armies on the 18 and 21st[?]," she asked in 1862.[89] Decades later, when Charles "Chinese" Gordon was killed in the Sudan, Felicia Loughridge was still fascinated by conflict and wrote a poem titled "General Gordon at Kartoum."[90]

Maude Fuller Young also reflected on the war in the postwar period. Like Tommie Goree, Young supplemented her family's diminished wealth by teaching school, and she published accounts on the war like *The Legend of Sour Lake*, which highlighted the rise and fall of the Confederacy.[91] Celebrated for her passionate support of the brigade during and after the war, Hood's Texas Brigade Association elected Young "Mother of the Brigade" at their 1877 reunion in Waco. Year after year, her veteran son would return to the reunions, called on by the men to pull out the tattered battle flag his mother had sewn for them and preserved when they returned it to her care.[92]

Much of her postwar work with the brigade, however, was done quietly and with her typical efficiency and thoroughness. This was the case with T. W. Fitzgerald, a private and former newspaperman in Company A of the Fifth Texas recruited out of Houston in 1861. He served as regimental color sergeant and was wounded in the knee and captured at the Battle of Gettysburg. He was one of the hundreds of men who made their way back to the Texas Brigade for the 1864 campaign season until Fitzgerald was wounded again at the Battle of Cold Harbor.

By the 1880s, the physical toll of the war had nearly broken Fitzgerald. He had been living in New York with his wife and son when he contacted his old friend Theodore Fowler, an editor with the *Houston Daily Post*. He also reached out to Maude Young, hoping she or Fowler could help him return to Texas. Doctors told Fitzgerald that a warmer climate would ease his rheumatism, but he could only raise enough money to get to Baltimore. He was certain a Confederate organization there could help him secure funds to reach Texas, but the Society of the Army and Navy of the Confederate States refused his plea, Fitzgerald explained, because, "its President informed me [it] was organized for historical purposes. I wonder how it would read to future generations," Fitzgerald asked, "the fact that a worthy comrade who helped make that history they are organized to perpetuate was permitted to suffer privations which a very little effort on their part—less historical, but more charitable—would have alleviated."[93]

Penniless and often bedridden with pain, Fitzgerald and his wife exchanged letters with Young and Fowler, who in turn worked to help the Fitzgeralds travel to Houston. Indeed, one of the last things Maude Young did before her death in 1882 was send funds to help cover his daily expenses and for a ticket home. Her support of the Fifth Texans, from their organization until her death, astonished Fitzgerald. "I cannot express to you how deeply the death of that estimable lady affected me. Her kindness of heart and disinterested efforts in my behalf will cause her memory to be ever gratefully revered."[94]

When fellow newspaper editor Thomas D. Sultzer of the *Baltimore Sun* tracked Fitzgerald down, likely at Fowler's request, Sultzer was stunned by what he found. The man once strong enough to lead his company as color sergeant "looked more like Rip Van Winkle, except dark hair, than anything I can imagine," Sultzer noted. Once a fellow newspaperman, Fitzgerald had become "so completely isolated as to be almost in entire ignorance of what is going on in the world" by the summer of 1882. "I found him in the most pitiable condition," Sultzer explained. "He is living with a woman reputed to be his wife. He is suffering with inflammatory rheumatism, and has not been out of bed for the past six months" and that was only possible if someone could lift Fitzgerald to his feet. Sultzer bought medicine and brought in a "first-class physician," but there was little anyone could do. Fitzgerald's spirits were decent, if only because he was "as proud as Lucifer—one who would suffer death rather than beg." He and Sultzer discussed the chances that "Fitz," as Sultzer came to call him, could renew his newspaper "card" and return to work, but Sultzer did not think he ever would. Fitzgerald's battlefield wounds were not the issue. Instead, the "worst kind of rheumatism" was slowly destroying the veteran's body. Still, Sultzer promised, "Anything I can do for him in my limited way you can rest assured shall be done."[95]

Tom Fitzgerald died three days later, in the early-morning hours of June 23, 1882. At the end, his fellow newspapermen assured that the veteran had "the best medical attendance, but he was too far gone, and naught could save him."

Fitzgerald died penniless, leaving behind a wife and six-year-old son. His illness and poverty had left him unable to work, which led to a lapse in his Union membership. He was ineligible for the fifty dollars in funeral benefits their members enjoyed. Sultzer and some friends in Baltimore pooled their resources, however, and ensured that these costs were covered and that Fitzgerald was buried with full rites in a local Catholic church. "I can assure you, under all the circumstances, he's much better off than in the suffering condition I found him in," Sultzer promised Fowler, trying to find comfort in the failure to reach an old friend and Texas Brigade veteran before it was too late.[96]

Less is known about the fate of women like Third Arkansas widow Ann Paulman, but she, too, struggled to make her way in the postwar South. Her husband, Henry Paulman, avoided military service as long as possible due to the responsibilities of caring for their ten children and his pacifist beliefs. Community pressures, however, drove him to enlist in Company I of the Third Arkansas in March 1863, and Ann received only a few letters before Henry was captured after suffering a wound during the fight for Rose Woods and Devil's Den at the Battle of Gettysburg. He was sent to Fort Delaware, where Henry died of typhoid fever on September 1, 1863. Accounts argue that when Ann died in 1908, she never knew what had happened to Henry Paulman; he simply never came home. Considering her approval for a widow's pension in the 1890s, it is more likely that Ann discovered his fate, perhaps from fellow Third Arkansas soldiers in her community. Whether that brought her peace or not is unknown. Like Tom Fitzgerald's widow, Ann Paulman would have to find a way forward without her husband.[97]

While veterans like Tom Fitzgerald and widows like Mary Tiner and Ann Paulman struggled tremendously in the postwar period, it is significant to note that other members of the Texas Brigade and their families adjusted to their postwar lives successfully. Few of them enjoyed the wealth that Mark Smither did, but Ann Johnson Erskine and her six children faced tremendous hardships in 1862 when she lost her father-in-law (whose properties and livestock Ann and her husband, Andrew, managed), her brother at Second Manassas, and Andrew at Antietam. By 1870, however, it appears that she was doing quite well. The cash value of their farm had decreased from $100,000 to $25,000, but countless families experienced far greater loss across the state. In the five years after the war, Ann tripled the number of horses they broke and sold, tripled their hog production, and held on to nearly all of the land they owned before the war. She also had enough wealth to employ three African American house servants and an Irish-born hostler to help her eldest son, Blucher, with the horses and livestock.[98]

In San Antonio, George Brackenridge's heart likely ached when he reflected on the life Ann Erskine had been left to face. The Indiana-born banker moved to Texas with his family in 1853, where he became a surveyor in Jackson County. His three brothers fought for the Confederacy, and his best friends, Thomas Ignatius Johnson and Andrew Erskine, served in Company D of the Fourth Texas Infantry. But George Brackenridge refused to fight. He helped expand his family's wealth in the wartime Matamoros cotton trade until 1863, when Brackenridge's openly pro-Union stance forced him to flee strongly pro-Confederate Texas. After the war, he returned to the state, became a Republican, and used his success to support growth in higher education around the state, but especially in the Austin area.

In the early twentieth century, Hood's Texas Brigade Association leader Frank Chilton reached out to Brackenridge as a respected Texas philanthropist who might want to support their work considering his close personal ties with several Texas Brigade veterans. Responding just after the Christmas celebrations of 1908, Brackenridge explained that he had no wish to remember his "warm personal friend[ship]" with Erskine and Johnson "in connection with the Confederacy." Brackenridge believed "they were perfectly honest, enthusiastic supporters of the Southern cause," but "I felt then, and have not changed my views, that it was a great mistake. While I should be pleased to have their memory perpetuated for what they were outside of and aside from their connection with the Confederacy, and in spite of it, I do not wish to have them remembered for what should never have been," Brackenridge explained.[99]

As the years passed and more veterans had died than remained, the Hood's Texas Brigade Association annual meetings were run by Katie Daffan, daughter of Fourth Texas veteran Lawrence Daffan. The organization still met, as they had nearly every year, on the anniversary of their first great victory, the Battle of Gaines's Mill. Elected "Daughter of the Brigade" before Joe Polley abolished such things, Katie Daffan served as secretary-treasurer for the association for its final twenty years. As her father's generation aged, it was Daffan and her peers who stepped up, having absorbed the veterans' lesson that their service must not be forgotten. By the early 1930s, Daffan was conducting the Texas Brigade reunion meetings for the last remaining men, some of whom were so weak by the time they arrived in town that they could not direct the brigade association business themselves. In June 1933, Daffan oversaw the final reunion, which had just two members of the brigade in attendance: E. W. B. Leach and S. O. Moodie. The following year, on the anniversary of the Texas Brigade's rise to fame at the Battle of Gaines's Mill, Daffan returned to the La Salle Hotel in Bryan, Texas, their host for their last several gatherings. In the late afternoon, right about the time the Texas Brigade had been rushing to strengthen the Confederate lines north of Boatswain's Creek, she held a quiet memorial service for the brigade and called the roll one last time, though no one was there to answer.[100]

Despite their overwhelming personal and financial losses, Hood's Texans survived the postwar period by maintaining their ties as a brigade. They helped each other open businesses and promote new ventures. They used the reputation they had earned in the war as their strongest endorsement of honesty, integrity, and dependability. Indeed, they cited connections with the brigade more often than the professional skills they needed for their postwar careers.

As the brigade veterans aged, they maintained their connections, helping each other secure pensions and endure the hardships that their service and age inflicted. A similar internal focus and call for outward attention led to the creation of their veterans' organization and the placement of the Hood's Texas Brigade monument in Austin. What success they found after the Civil War came through their loyalty to each other. They used the strength they found in war to navigate the equally difficult challenges of peace.

CONCLUSION

In Huntsville, Texas, in June 1865, Robert Campbell hand-wrote a 241-page history of his service in Hood's Texas Brigade. He wanted to put his memories to page before time blurred events, and he noted with care the purpose behind the combat injuries that had scarred his head, legs, arm, chest, and lungs. Campbell served in the Fifth Texas for three long years not for glory or simply being called a Confederate, he argued, "but because I felt it to be a duty." He had "loved not the dangers and hardship, the noise and confusion of battle." Rather, it was anger that drove him back to Hood's Brigade after multiple wounds and difficult recoveries: "I hated, I despised, I *loathed*, with my whole heart, that Govt who sought to oppress and afflict my southern home." Campbell took comfort in his Christian faith and felt pride in the successes of Hood's Brigade and "all of the 'Virginia Army.'" But he despaired for his future and that of his community: "The Confederate States are no more.... [Gen. Robert E.] Lee and a host of others now occupy felons cells, awaiting the decision of the tyrant at the 'Whitehouse.' I for one shall never boast of being a Southerner, though never deny my army—for the present, I have no country, no home, since I with all others lie at the feet of a tyrant."[1]

Campbell completed his memoir on June 18, 1865, just weeks after Confederate forces in Texas surrendered, along with the rest of the Trans-Mississippi West. He captured the extreme ideological motivations that inspired so many of Hood's Texans to serve in Virginia and to identify powerfully with fellow brigade members and with Robert E. Lee and his Army of Northern Virginia. That was the meaning behind his pledge to no longer "boast of being a Southerner, though never deny my army." Campbell also embodied the tremendous emotional, physical, and financial cost of that loyalty to Texas Brigade soldiers and their families. Their swift identification with and faith in the Confederate nation, their company-grade officers, and Robert E. Lee kept these men in the ranks when so many others in Lee's army deserted. As southern families grew frustrated amid the hardships at home, Texas Brigade families found ways to support themselves, each other, and the war. While fellow white southerners worried about the effects of emancipation in 1862 and 1863, Hood's Texans remained confident in the Confederate victory that would ensure that the enslaved labor that had fueled so much of their antebellum success would continue. Texas Brigade soldiers were confident, too, that the threats they saw in Republican Party policy would not touch them in their new nation, where they would thrive under a system led by southern white leaders who echoed the traditions of Thomas Jefferson, Henry Clay, and John C. Calhoun. In the end, when all their faith proved futile, Hood's Texans still stood together, firm in their convictions and determined to navigate the challenges of defeat and the changes of Reconstruction as a unit, just as they had fought the war. Hood's Texans and their families reveal the complex currents that flow through a "democracy at war." The Texas Brigade may be an exceptional unit, but these soldiers and their families are essential to achieving a full understanding of how and why men fought in the Civil War and the lasting effect this had on their communities and their nation.

NOTES

INTRODUCTION

1. Robert Campbell, *Lone Star Confederate: A Gallant and Good Soldier of the Fifth Texas Infantry*, ed. George Skoch and Mark W. Perkins (College Station: Texas A&M University Press, 2003), 6–7.

2. *Houston Tri-Weekly Telegraph*, January 20, 1865.

3. Campbell, *Lone Star Confederate*, xvii–xix, 114–15.

4. There is a growing body of scholarship on the southern middle class or middling class in mid-nineteenth-century America (see Jonathan Daniel Wells, *The Origins of the Southern Middle Class, 1800–1861* [Chapel Hill: University of North Carolina Press, 2004]; Jonathan Daniel Wells and Jennifer R. Green, eds., *The Southern Middle Class in the Long Nineteenth Century* [Baton Rouge: Louisiana State University Press, 2011]; Jennifer R. Green, *Military Education and the Emerging Middle Class in the Old South* [New York: Cambridge University Press, 2008]; Andrew L. Slap and Frank Towers, eds., *Confederate Cities: The Urban South during the Civil War Era* [Chicago: University of Chicago Press, 2015]; and Frank Byrne, *Becoming Bourgeois: Merchant Culture in the Antebellum and Confederate South* [Lexington: University Press of Kentucky, 2006]). For more on yeoman and self-farming antebellum southerners, see Stephanie McCurry, *Masters of Small Worlds: Yeoman Households, Gender Relations, and the Political Culture of the Antebellum South Carolina Low Country* (New York: Oxford University Press, 1995); Steven Hahn, *The Roots of Southern Populism: Yeoman Farmers and the Transformation of the Georgia Upcountry, 1850–1890* (New York: Oxford University Press, 1983); Randolph B. Campbell and Richard G. Lowe, *Wealth and Power in Antebellum Texas* (College Station: Texas A&M University Press, 1977); and Bradley G. Bond, *Political Culture in the Nineteenth-Century South: Mississippi, 1830–1900* (Baton Rouge: Louisiana State University Press, 1995). For a recent study that characterized household wealth by stated wealth but used narrower terms and covered a far larger geographic range, see Joseph T. Glatthaar, *Soldiering in the Army of Northern Virginia: A Statistical Portrait of the Troops Who Served under Robert E. Lee* (Chapel Hill: University of North Carolina Press, 2011), 7. Special thanks to Frank Towers, Andrew Slap, and Jon Wells for our discussions and your advice on Hood's Texans' middle-class character.

5. *Navarro Express* (Corsicana, Tex.), June 2, 1860; qtd. in Donald E. Reynolds, *Editors Make War: Southern Newspapers in the Secession Crisis* Reprint (Carbondale: Southern Illinois University Press, 2006), 57–58.

6. These ranges were set by Campbell and Lowe and used by Charles Brooks in "The Social and Cultural Dynamics of Soldiering in Hood's Texas Brigade," *Journal of Southern History* 67 (August 2001): 538.

7. Ibid., 538–40. Evidence documenting the connections between nonslaveholding soldiers in the Army of Northern Virginia to slaveholding households can be found in Joseph T. Glatthaar, *General Lee's Army: From Victory to Collapse* (New York: Free Press, 2008), 19–20.

8. As historian Colin Edward Woodward argues, late into the conflict "Confederate troops continued to believe slavery was worth defending, and more so, that they *could* defend it.... Despite the changes wrought by war, men did not abandon their proslavery views. They believed that African Americans ... were best kept in bondage" (see Woodward, *Marching Masters: Slavery, Race, and the Confederate Army during the Civil War* [Charlottesville: University of Virginia Press, 2014], 9–10, 13, 206–7). See also Lacy Ford's arguments about the paternalism and increased efforts toward racial control in the antebellum lower South in *Deliver Us from Evil: The Slavery Question in the Old South* (New York: Oxford University Press, 2009), 7–8, 76–77, 299–301.

9. See Drew Gilpin Faust, *Mothers of Invention: Women of the Slaveholding South in the American Civil War* (Chapel Hill: University of North Carolina Press, 1996), 243; and Drew Gilpin Faust, "Altars of Sacrifice: Confederate Women and the Narratives of War," in *Divided Houses: Gender and the Civil War,* ed. Catherine Clinton and Nina Silber (New York: Oxford University Press, 1992), 171–99. For an analysis of Confederates struggling with a desire to secure victory and sacrifice honorably while also desperately wanting the war to end, see Anne Sarah Rubin, *A Shattered Nation: The Rise and Fall of the Confederacy, 1861–1868* (Chapel Hill: University of North Carolina Press, 2005), 75–79; see also Stephanie McCurry, *Confederate Reckoning: Power and Politics in the Civil War South* (Chapel Hill: University of North Carolina Press, 2011), 198–202. For two of the best discussions of Confederate soldier motivation that pertain to this study, including such exceptional levels of devotion to the Confederate nation, see Jason Phillips *Diehard Rebels: The Confederate Culture of Invincibility* (Athens: University of Georgia Press, 2007); and Glatthaar, *General Lee's Army.*

10. R. E. Lee, Genl., Head Quarters, Army of Northern Virginia near Martinsburg [Virginia], to Genl. Louis T. Wigfall, September 21, 1862, Irenus Watson Landingham Collection, RG 552, Auburn University Special Collections & Archives Department, Auburn, Ala.

11. Angelina V. Winkler, *The Confederate Capital and Hood's Texas Brigade* (Austin, Tex.: Eugene von Boeckmann, 1894), 156.

12. Robert K. Krick, "'Lee to the Rear,' the Texans Cried," in *The Wilderness Campaign,* ed. Gary W. Gallagher (Chapel Hill: University of North Carolina Press, 1997), 179–80.

13. Donald E. Everett, *Chaplain Davis and Hood's Texas Brigade* (Baton Rouge: Louisiana State University Press, 1999), 63.

14. M. Le Comte De Paris, *Histoire de la Guerre Civile en Amerique,* 7 vols. (Paris: Michel, Levy, Freras, 1875), 179–80, qtd. in Harold B. Simpson, *Hood's Texas Brigade: Lee's Grenadier Guard,* 4th printing (Fort Worth, Tex.: Landmark, 1999), 109; William H. Hassler, "Dorsey Pender," *Civil War Times Illustrated* 1 (October 1962): 19.

15. Jefferson Davis to Frank Chilton, April 6, 1889, qtd. in Simpson, *Hood's Texas Brigade,* 408; Alexander Hunter, "The Rebel Yell," *Confederate Veteran* 21 (May 1913): 219.

16. These ideological connections to Lee and his army are central arguments in Gary W. Gallagher, *The Confederate War* (Cambridge: Harvard University Press, 1997), 58.

17. An excellent analysis of this exchange among company-grade officers and their men is found in Andrew S. Bledsoe, *Citizen-Officers: The Union and Confederate Volunteer Junior Officer Corps in the American Civil War* (Baton Rouge: Louisiana State University Press, 2015).

18. T. Harry Williams qtd. in Alan T. Nolan, *The Iron Brigade: A Military History* (1961; repr., Bloomington: Indiana University Press, 1994), xiv.

19. To name but a few, see Simpson, *Hood's Texas Brigade*, as well as Robert E. L. Krick, "'The Men Who Carried This Position Were Soldiers Indeed': The Decisive Charge of Whiting's Division at Gaines's Mill," in *The Richmond Campaign of 1862: The Peninsula & the Seven Days*, ed. Gary W. Gallagher (Chapel Hill: University of North Carolina Press, 2000); and Robert K. Krick, "'Lee to the Rear,' the Texans Cried." The Texas Brigade is also featured in the battle and campaign analyses of top military historians including Thomas G. Clemens, D. Scott Hartwig, Joseph Harsh, John Hennessy, William Marvel, Harry W. Pfanz, David A. Powell, Carol Reardon, Gordon Rhea, and Noah Andrew Trudeau, among others. A more extensive list of relevant works of traditional military history relating to the Texas Brigade can be found in the selected bibliography at the end of this book.

20. The broad Confederate response to Federal emancipation appears in numerous books, including Glatthaar, *General Lee's Army*, 305; and Chandra Manning, *What This Cruel War Was Over: Soldiers, Slavery, and the Civil War* (New York: Vintage, 2007), 106–9.

21. For a discussion of the "Anti-War," or "Dark Turn," in Civil War historiography, see Yael A. Sternhell, "Revisionism Reinvented? The Antiwar Turn in Civil War Scholarship," *Journal of the Civil War Era* 3 (June 2013): 239–56; see also Gary W. Gallagher and Kathryn Shively Meier, "Coming to Terms with Civil War Military History," *Journal of the Civil War Era* 4 (December 2014): 487–508. In her study of the Texas State Lunatic Asylum, Professor of Psychology Sarah Stitton noted that during the 1860s many of the causes listed for that facility's patients' insanity were "the war," "fright from soldiers," and "marauding soldiers." I was not able to ascertain, however, which, if any, residents were Texas Brigade veterans and what their ailments were (see Stitton, *Life at the Texas State Lunatic Asylum, 1857–1997* [College Station: Texas A&M University Press, 1999], 24). John A. Casey Jr. offers a fascinating look at how Civil War veterans' status and image evolved in the late nineteenth and early twentieth centuries, and though many of his arguments do not fit Hood's Texas Brigade, Casey's observation that Civil War service made soldiers into "New Men" does apply to this unit (see Casey, *New Men: Reconstructing the Image of the Veteran in Late-Nineteenth-Century American Literature and Culture* [New York: Fordham University Press, 2015]).

22. Robert Maberry Jr., *Texas Flags* (College Station: Texas A&M University Press, 2001), 83.

CHAPTER ONE

1. Edward S. Cooper, *Louis Trezevant Wigfall: The Disintegration of the Union and Collapse of the Confederacy* (Madison, N.J.: Fairleigh Dickinson University Press, 2012), xiv. The friend was Edward Pollard, newspaper editor and author of *The Lost Cause*.

2. Ibid., 36.

3. Ibid., 30.

4. Pryor to Marshall, July 16, 1860, *Texas State Gazette* (Austin), August 4, 1860, in Donald E.

Reynolds, *Texas Terror: The Slave Insurrection Panic of 1860 and the Secession of the Lower South* (Baton Rouge: Louisiana State University Press, 2007), 35.

5. Walter L. Buenger, "Secession," *Handbook of Texas Online*, www.tshaonline.org/handbook/online/articles/mgs02; see also Robin E. Baker and Dale Baum, "The Texas Voter and the Crisis of Union, 1859–1861," *Journal of Southern History* 53 (August 1987): 395–420.

6. John B. Walker, Round Rock, Texas, to "Brother & family," April 24, 1861, Philpott Texana Collection, 1844–1879, Dolph Briscoe Center for American History, University of Texas at Austin.

7. *Prairie Blade* (Corsicana, Tex.), November 17, 1855.

8. James Rodgers Loughridge, [location unstated but context indicates near Dumfries, Virginia, on the Potomac Blockade], to Felicia Loughridge, December 16, 1861, Loughridge Collection, Pearce Civil War Archives, Navarro College, Corsicana, Tex. Hereafter cited as Loughridge Collection.

9. *Navarro Express* (Corsicana, Tex.), May 8, 1861.

10. *Texas Republican* (Marshall), May 11, 1861.

11. *Houston Weekly Telegraph*, May 14, 1861.

12. This *Centerville Times* report was covered in the *Galveston Civilian and Gazette*, June 4, 1861.

13. *Houston Weekly Telegraph*, May 18, 1861.

14. *Corpus Christi (Tex.) Ranchero*, June 19, 1861; *Houston Tri-Weekly Telegraph*, May 28, 1861; Cooper K. Ragan, "Tyler County Goes to War," *Texas Military History* 1 (November 1961): 3.

15. *Austin (Tex.) State Gazette*, June 1, 1861.

16. *Houston Weekly Telegraph*, June 12, 1861, p. 1, col. 9.

17. *Dallas Herald*, July 17, 1861, p. 1, col. 3.

18. Charles Schadt, Galveston, Texas, to Caroline Schadt, Highland Bayou, Galveston, Texas, July 29, 1861, Schadt Family Papers, 1861–1957, Rosenberg Library, Galveston, Tex. Hereafter cited as Schadt Family Papers.

19. *Houston Telegraph* and *Texas Register*, August 19, 1837. See also Robert S. Shelton, "On Empire's Shore: Free and Unfree Workers in Galveston, Texas, 1840–1860," *Journal of Social History* (Spring 2007): 718.

20. William A. Fletcher, *Rebel Private: Front and Rear: Memoirs of a Confederate Soldier* (New York: Dutton/Penguin, 1995), 2–4.

21. Ibid., 5.

22. Camilla Davis Trammell, *Seven Pines: Its Occupants and Their Letters, 1825–1872* (Houston: Southern Methodist University Press, 1986), 122–23.

23. Judith N. McArthur and Orville Vernon Burton, eds., *A Gentleman and an Officer: A Military and Social History of James B. Griffin's Civil War* (New York: Oxford University Press, 1996), 10–11.

24. Ibid., 22–24.

25. Ibid., 17.

26. Ibid., 43.

27. Ibid., 45.

28. For more on this, see Charles E. Brooks, "The Social and Cultural Dynamics of Hood's Texas Brigade," *Journal of Southern History* 67 (August 2001): 539–42. For arguments on ties between slaveholders and nonslaveholders in the Army of Northern Virginia, see Glatthaar, *General Lee's Army*, 19–21.

29. Jacques D. Bagur, *Antebellum Jefferson, Texas: Everyday Life in an East Texas Town* (Denton: University of North Texas Press, 2012); sheep advertised for sale in *Clarksville Standard* of June 10, 1854; September 5, 1857, *Clarksville Standard* article on beef packing in Jefferson. Special thanks to Mr. Weldon Nash, Jefferson, Texas, for his assistance in tracking down the Black brothers, particularly H. H. Black, in the 1850s and 1860s. See also George T. Todd, Jefferson, Texas, to Mrs. W. M. Peal, November 18, 1895, United Confederate Veterans Collection, Haley Memorial Library and History Center, Midland, Tex. See also 1860 U.S. Federal Census, Jefferson, Marion, Texas, Roll: M653_1300, Page: 479, Image: 383, Family History Library Film: 805300.

30. *Houston Telegraph*, May 14, 1861.

31. D. D. Moore's Livingston Guards from Polk County (which became Company B) mustered in that same day in New Orleans.

32. *Shreveport Daily News*, May 2, 1861.

33. The original Texans in Company C, First Texas, largely came from Rusk, Harrison, Bowie, and Titus Counties, as well as from farther south in Washington and Polk Counties (see George Edward Otott Jr., *The 1st Texans: Antebellum Social Characteristics of the Officers and Men in the 1st Texas Infantry, CSA* [Irvine, Calif.: privately printed, 2004], 13–14).

34. This is based on a statistical sample created for this project of all the men who ever served in the Texas Brigade. The sample includes 1,335 men (1,212 enlisted men, 70 line officers, 31 Headquarters officers, 22 Headquarters enlisted). The sample adjusted for the length of time each company and regiment was in the Texas Brigade, drawing more heavily from those units that were in the brigade for a longer period of time. The sample itself was drawn from Harold B. Simpson, *Hood's Texas Brigade: A Compendium*, 2nd ed. (Fort Worth, Tex.: Landmark, 1999), which lists the name, rank, unit, and brief description of service for each man who served in the Texas Brigade between 1861 and 1865. Within that sample, 90 men were listed as deserters, but 10 of them were also identified as "term of service had ended," so they were removed from the desertion category. Even then, Company C of the First Texas continued to have the highest percentage of desertions, just over 8 percent. Admittedly, that is still low for a Civil War unit. Still, it is worth noting this problem within the Texas Brigade.

35. For a detailed description of each man who served in Company C, First Texas Volunteer Infantry Regiment, see Simpson, *Compendium*, 24–31. The desertions numbers could be higher than estimated here, but I am not including those for whom the record states, "No record of arriving in Virginia from Texas" or "No record after that date" or "may have resigned after 1 yr. enlmnt. expired" because that information is inconclusive due to the limited records.

36. Randolph B. Campbell, "Harrison County," *Handbook of Texas Online*, www.tshaonline.org/handbook/online/articles/hch08. Published by the Texas State Historical Association. See also F. S. Bass obituary clipped from July 9, 1897, *Marshall Morning Star* or *Marshall Morning News* in the James McCowan Scrapbook, p. 74, Harrison County Historical Museum (copy in the F. S. Bass Folder, Hood's Texas Brigade Collection, Texas Heritage Museum, Hill College, Hillsboro). For more biographical details, see *Austin (Tex.) Weekly Statesman*, vol. 26, 1st ed., Thursday, July 15, 1897.

37. *Texas Republican* (Marshall), June 8, 1861. For information on Swanson's Landing, see V. H. Hackney, "Swanson's Landing," *Handbook of Texas Online*, www.tshaonline.org/handbook/online/articles/hvsfc.

38. James H. Hendrick to "Ma," June 5, 1861, New Orleans, Louisiana, and July 7, 1861, Rich-

mond, Virginia, James H. Hendrick Letters, Texas Heritage Museum, Hill College, Hillsboro. Hereafter cited as James Hendrick Letters.

39. *Southern Confederacy* (Atlanta, Ga.), June 8, 1861, p. 1, col. 2.

40. Rainey's real estate was valued at $1,000, and his personal wealth estimated at $20,000 in 1860 U.S. Federal Census, Palestine, Anderson, Texas, Roll: M653_1287, Page: 7, Image: 17, Family History Library Film: 805287.

41. Alexis T. Rainey, Shreveport, Louisiana, to Ann Quarles Rainey, July 5, 1861, Alexis T. Rainey Letters, Historical Research Center, Texas Heritage Museum, Hill College, Hillsboro. Hereafter cited as Alexis T. Rainey Letters.

42. R. H. Gaston and W. H. Gaston, On Red River near Alexandria, Louisiana, July 6, 1861, to "Pa and Ma" [Colonel and Mrs. R. K. Gaston], Tyler, Texas, in Robert W. Glover, ed., *"Tyler to Sharpsburg": Robert H. and William H. Gaston (Their War Letters, 1861–62* (Waco, Tex.: W. M. Morrison, 1960), 5.

43. Alexis T. Rainey, New Orleans, Louisiana, to Ann Quarles Rainey, July 11, 1861, Alexis T. Rainey Letters.

CHAPTER TWO

1. Capt. J. T. Hunter, "When Texas Seceded," *Confederate Veteran* 25 (1917): 362–63.

2. *New York Times,* April 5, 1853.

3. Dr. John Warren Smith, "Hunter, Captain James Thomas," vertical file, Confederate records, Johnnie Jo Sowell Dickenson Genealogy Room, Huntsville Public Library, Huntsville, Tex.

4. Hunter listed his real estate wealth at $1,405 and personal wealth at $2,210 (1860 U.S. Federal Census, 1860, Walker, Texas, Roll: M653_1307, Page: 105, Image: 217, Family History Library Film: 805307).

5. B. F. Benton, San Augustine, Texas, to "His Excellency Edward Clark, Governor of Texas," 22 April 1861, Edward Clark Papers, 1842–1910, 1946, Dolph Briscoe Center for American History, University of Texas at Austin. Hereafter cited as Clark Papers.

6. Captain B. F. Carter to Governor Edward Clark, April 25, 1861, Clark Papers.

7. R. M. Powell to Governor Edward Clark, April 26, 1861, Clark Papers.

8. Larry Jay Gage, "The Texas Road to Secession and War: John Marshall and the Texas State Gazette 1860–1861," *Southwestern Historical Quarterly* 62, no. 2 (October 1958): 216.

9. John Marshall, Richmond, Virginia, to Governor Edward Clark, Austin, Texas, June 14, 1861, Clark Papers.

10. Captain King Bryan, Liberty, Texas, to Governor Edward Clark, Austin, Texas, July 19, 1861, Clark Papers.

11. *Navarro Express* (Corsicana, Tex.), July 17, 1861. Similar complaints came in from Jerome B. Robertson, whose recruiting efforts had also been forgotten. The original oversight of Robertson's company may have been tied to a note from his first lieutenant, Tacitus T. Clay, a few months earlier. In response to a query on the status of the company Robertson was raising, Clay had explained that it was "not yet fully organized nor will we be until the return of the Dr [Robertson] who is our Captain. He has gone to Montgomery and probably to Charleston or Fort Pickens, he will probably be back in ten days from this." Clay was doing his duty and clarifying honorably that the Texas Aides would not move without their company commander. Clark's staff, however,

may have noted the time involved in traveling to South Carolina and back and filed the Aides as unavailable in time for Virginia service. To be clear, though, this is all speculation (see Tacitus T. Clay, Independence, Texas, to Adjutant General William Byrd, Austin, Texas, May 29, 1861, Clark Papers). For Robertson's letter to Clark, see Jerome B. Robertson, Independence, Texas, to Governor Edward Clark, Austin, August 21, 1861, Clark Papers.

12. William H. Martin, Athens, Texas, to Governor Edward Clark, Austin, Texas, May 23, 1861. See also Martin to Clark, May 20, 1861, Clark Papers.

13. "The Confederate Governors of Texas," in *The Seventh Star of the Confederacy: Texas during the Civil War*, ed. Kenneth W. Howell (Denton: University of North Texas Press, 2009), 228–32.

14. *Texas Republican* (Marshall), July 27, 1861

15. *Colorado Citizen* (Columbus, Tex.), August 3, 1861.

16. *Houston Weekly Telegraph*, August 7, 1861.

17. Ibid., August 14, 1861, "Camp Van Dorn" letter dated August 7, 1861.

18. *Houston Weekly Telegraph*, August 14, 1861, "Camp Van Dorn" letter dated August 7, 1861.

19. Patrick Penn, Confederate Camp near Harrisburg, to Lizzie Menefee [Penn's sister], Oso, Texas, August 1, 1861, in Shelton B. McAnelly, "Penn Letters, 1860–1865," *Louisiana Genealogical Register* 27 (December 1970): 390.

20. Sullivan was right; Lubbock won the election later that month. McAnelly, "Penn Letters," *Louisiana Genealogical Register* 27 (December 1970): 390. Robert Sullivan's letter, August 3, 1861. Both men were writing to Patrick's older sister (Robert's cousin), Mrs. Mary Elizabeth Penn Menefee. For more on the Texas governor's race of 1861, see Ralph A. Wooster, "Texas," in *The Confederate Governors*, ed. Wilfred Buck Yearns (Athens: University of Georgia Press, 1910), 200.

21. "Civil War Reminiscences of William Burke," *Flatonia (Tex.) Argus*, February 8, 1923. Burke recalled Flatonia as "wide open, affording the very finest grazing both winter and summer for the thousands of horses that roved the broad expanse of prairies." Special thanks to Jane Gillette Riggs of Baytown, Texas, for sharing a wealth of information and family papers on the Penns, Sullivans, Crocketts, and Menefees. Thanks, too, to Judy Pate of the E. A. Arnim Archives & Museum of Flatonia, Texas, for her help with information on Oso, Texas, as well as larger Flatonia County and the *Flatonia Argus* newspapers.

22. "Oso: A Reminiscence by Mrs. J. R. Crockett," *Flatonia (Tex.) Argus*, May 30, 1912.

23. Jeff Carroll, "OSO, TX," *Handbook of Texas Online*, www.tshaonline.org/handbook/online/articles/hvo38.

24. William Heard Sullivan, "By Gone Days," *Flatonia (Tex.) Argus*, August 4, 1921. Pine Springs School opened in 1859.

25. Penn's father estimated his combined property and personal wealth in 1860 at more than $35,000, and the Sullivans were not far behind the Penns with a combined wealth of $21,000, much of it invested in livestock as well as the eleven slaves owned by Robert's father, John (Green W. Penn, 1860 U.S. Federal Census, Fayette, Texas, Roll: M653_1294, Page: 353, Image: 195, Family History Library Film: 805294. John Sullivan, 1860 U.S. Federal Census, Census Place: Fayette, Texas; Roll: M653_1294; Page: 332; Image: 154; Family History Library Film: 805294).

26. The Menefee brothers had a combined wealth of about $15,000 (Quinn M. Menefee, 1860 U.S. Federal Census, 1860; Fayette, Texas; Roll: M653_1294; Page: 353; Image: 196; Family History Library Film: 805294).

27. Edward R. Crockett, 1860 U.S. Federal Census, Fayette, Texas; Roll: M653_1294; Page: 353; Image: 195; Family History Library Film: 805294.

28. Patrick Penn, Richmond, Virginia, to "My Dear Sister" [Mary Elizabeth Penn Menefee], Oso, Texas, September 23, 1861, in McAnelly, "Penn Letters," *Louisiana Genealogical Register* 18 (June 1871): 100.

29. Robert Sullivan, Camp of the 4th Texas Regiment (near Richmond), to Mrs. Lizzie Menefee, Oso, Texas, November 25, 1861, in McAnelly, "Penn Letters," *Louisiana Genealogical Register* 18 (June 1871): 103.

30. Robert Sullivan, Tupelo, Miss., to "My Dear Mother" [Lucy Morton Sullivan], Oso, Texas, January 16, 1861. Shared with me by Sullivan descendant Jane Gillette Riggs, Baytown, Tex.

31. Charles David Grear, *Why Texans Fought in the Civil War* (College Station: Texas A&M University Press, 2010), 14–15.

32. Brooks, "Social Dynamics," 539–41.

33. Robert Sullivan, Richmond, Va., to "My Dear Cousin Lizzie" [Mary Elizabeth Menefee], Oso, Texas, September 23, 1861, in McAnelly, "Penn Letters," *Louisiana Genealogical Register* 27 (December 1970): 391.

34. Samuel Tine Owen, Harrisburg, Texas, to "Father and Mother," Athens, Texas, August 3, 1861, Samuel Tine Owen Papers, Texas Heritage Museum, Hill College, Hillsboro. Hereafter cited as Samuel Tine Owen Papers. Note that transcription of Owen letter of August 3, 1861, is missing a line that is clarified in news article in file titled "Letters of a Teen-Age Soldiers . . .," unknown author, date, publication location, Samuel Tine Owen Papers.

35. As Brooks notes, 26.6 percent of the original privates of the First Texas were poor, 66.8 percent were middle class, and 6.6 percent were wealthy. In the Fourth Texas, 29.3 percent were poor, 63.8 percent were middle class, and 6.9 percent were wealthy. In the Fifth Texas, 37.9 percent were poor, 43.9 percent were middle class, and 18.2 percent were wealthy (see Brooks, "Soldiering in Hood's Texas Brigade," 539–40).

36. John Owen was listed as a blacksmith in Alabama with no declared real estate wealth in 1850 (1850 U.S. Federal Census, Beat 15, Randolph, Alabama; Roll: M432_14; Page: 398A; Image: 236). He valued his real estate at $800 in 1860 and his personal estate at $450 (1860 U.S. Federal Census, Beat 3, Henderson, Texas; Roll: M653_1297; Page: 42; Image: 92; Family History Library Film: 805297). See similar complaints in *Houston Weekly Telegraph,* August 14, 1861. The letter titled "Camp near Harrisburg" was written on August 6, 1861 (Samuel Tine Owen Papers).

37. *Houston Weekly Telegraph,* August 21, 1861.

38. Martin listed his real estate property at $4,800 and personal property at $600 in the 1860 U.S. Federal Census (Athens, Henderson, Texas; Roll: M653_1297; Page: 17; Image: 39; Family History Library Film: 805297).

39. L. J. Faulk, *History of Henderson County* (Athens, Tex.: Athens Review Printing, 1929), 129; Martin family history; Martha E. Martin, "Sketch of Major W. H. Martin," *Biographies of Eminent Citizens and Historical Sketches of Henderson County,* vol. 2 (Athens, Tex.: Directory of Athens City, 1904), 24–25.

40. *Houston Weekly Telegraph,* August 28, 1861, Letter "Camp Earl Van Dorn," written August 19, 1861.

41. Sullivan to Lizzie Menefee, August 3, 1861, in McAnelly, "Penn Letters," *Louisiana Genealogical Register* 27 (December 1970): 390–91.

42. G. S. Boyton, "Letter to Editors Express," August 3, 1861, *Navarro Express* (Corsicana, Tex.), August 15, 1861.

43. Thomas J. Selman Diary, August 18, 1861, Thomas J. Selman Papers, Hood's Texas Brigade Collection, Historical Research Center, Hill College, Hillsboro, Tex. Hereafter cited as Selman Papers.

44. "Dear Brother," *Colorado Citizen* (Columbus, Tex.), September 28, 1861.

45. Robert Sullivan, Richmond, Va., to Lizzie [Menefee], Sept 23rd, 1861, in McAnelly, "Penn Letters," *Louisiana Genealogical Register* 27 (December 1970): 391–92.

46. Ibid.

47. Captain James T. Hunter, "When Texas Seceded," *Confederate Veteran* 25 (1917): 363; Zach Landrum, Richmond, Virginia, September 21, 1861, Zach Landrum Letters, Hood's Texas Brigade Collection, Historical Research Center, Hill College, Hillsboro, Tex.; hereafter cited as Landrum Letters; 1860 United States Federal Census, Ancestry.com (database online); Montgomery, Texas; Roll: M653_1301; Page: 89; Family History Library Film: 805301 (Ancestry.com Operations, Inc., 2009). Images reproduced by FamilySearch.

48. J. R. Loughridge, Milican's Depot, Brazos Co., Texas, to Felicia Loughridge, Falls County, Texas, July 29th 1861, Loughridge Collection.

49. Watson Dugat Williams, Camp in New Orleans, to Laura Bryan, Liberty, Texas, Sept 13th 1861, Watson Dugat Williams Letters, Texas Heritage Museum, Liberty. Hereafter cited as Watson Dugat Williams Letters.

CHAPTER THREE

1. J. Marquis Smither, Richmond, Virginia, to "Mother," Huntsville, Texas, September 12, 1861, Smither Papers, John W. Thomason Reading Room, Newton Gresham Library, Sam Houston State University, Huntsville, Tex. Hereafter cited as Smither Papers.

2. Ibid.

3. Reid Mitchell, *Civil War Soldiers: Their Expectations and Their Experiences* (New York: Viking Penguin, 1988): 240. See note 57: "One occasionally gets the sense that Texans, who had their own unique history with its own patriotic symbols, were the least Confederate of Southerners—although they did not have the strong identification with the generation of 1776 that many Virginians felt."

4. The record is a bit unclear on whether or not Elizabeth Wynne owned slaves, but there is an Elizabeth A. Wynne in Walker County in 1860 who owned twenty slaves. She appears nowhere else in the record. Elizabeth E. Wynne does; it is she who married Erasmus Wynne on April 29, 1858. Working against this slave ownership of Elizabeth E. Wynne theory is the fact that she is not listed anywhere near her husband, Erasmus Wynne, in the slave schedule; they are about thirty pages apart. Erasmus Wynne was born in Georgia and moved to Alabama, where most of his children were born, before the family moved on to Texas, where his combined wealth in 1860 surpassed $80,000, which included fifty-three slaves (see Robert and Elizabeth Smither in the 1850 U.S. Federal Census; Erasmus and Elizabeth Wynne in the 1860 U.S. Federal Census). Erasmus Wynne listed his personal wealth in 1860 at $54,600; he valued his real estate at $26,200. Elizabeth Wynne listed her personal wealth at $56,000 and real estate holdings totaling $11,000. For more on the Smither family history, see "Smither, Robert," Vertical File, Huntsville Public Library, Huntsville, Tex. See also 1860 U.S. Federal Census, Huntsville, Walker, Texas; Roll: M653_1307; Page: 95; Image: 197; Family History Library Film: 805307.

5. Brooks, "Social Dynamics," 538–42.

6. Like much of the First Texas, these Alabamians had rushed to Virginia that spring and mustered into Confederate service at Lynchburg on June 25, joining the First Texas as Company K. Covington's Alabamians were ordered to join Wigfall's Texas Battalion, as it was then known, on August 14, 1861, via Special Orders No. 250. See report of Adjt. and Insp. General's Office, Richmond, Virginia in U.S. War Department, *The War of the Rebellion: A Compilation of the Official Records of the Union and Confederate Armies*, 128 vols. (Washington: Government Printing Office, 1880–1901), ser. I, vol. 51, pt. II, p. 231. Hereafter cited as *O.R.*

7. Charles Schadt, Manassas, Virginia, to "Fred," [location unknown but likely in Galveston, Tex.], Sept. 1, 1861, Schadt Family Papers.

8. Thomas W. Cutrer, "McLeod, Hugh," *Handbook of Texas Online*, www.tshaonline.org/handbook/online/articles/fmc90.

9. Charles Schadt, Manassas, Virginia, to "Fred," [location unknown but likely in Galveston, Tex.], Sept. 1, 1861, Schadt Family Papers.

10. Ibid.

11. Selman Diary, September 20–21, 1861, Selman Papers.

12. Winkler, *The Confederate Capital and Hood's Texas Brigade*, 33.

13. *Dallas Herald*, August 21, 1861.

14. Irenus Watson Landingham, Camp Bragg, near Richmond, Virginia, to "Dear Mother," Texas, November 1, 1861, Irenus Watson Landingham Collection, RG 552, Auburn University Special Collections & Archives Department, Auburn, Ala.

15. Mark Smither, Camp Neabsco, Prince William County, Virginia, to "Aunt," January 17, 1862, Smither Papers.

16. Selman Diary, September 14, 1861; September 20–21, 1861; September 25, 1861, Selman Papers.

17. Robert Sullivan, Richmond, Va., to "My Dear Cousin Lizzie" [Mary Elizabeth Menefee], Oso, Texas, September 23, 1861, in McAnelly, "Penn Letters," *Louisiana Genealogical Register* 27 (December 1970): 391.

18. W. B. Campbell, Richmond, Virginia, to "Aunt" [Mrs. E. A. Woods], Danville, Montgomery County, Texas, September 20, 1861, W. B. Campbell Papers, 1861–1863, Pearce Civil War Collection, Navarro College, Corsicana, Tex.

19. *O.R.*, ser. I, vol. 5, p. 215.

20. Everett, *Chaplain Davis and Hood's Texas Brigade*, 17.

21. Watson Dugat Williams, Camp Bragg near Richmond, to "Dear Laura," Oct. 7, 1861, Watson Dugat Williams Letters.

22. Tacitus T. Clay to Mrs. Bettie Clay, October 6, 1861, emphasis original, Tacitus T. Clay Letters, Special Collections Department, Mississippi State University Libraries. Special thanks to Clay descendant Finney Mack Clay for sharing his research with me and discussing the Clay family history.

23. Mary W. Schaller and Marin N. Schaller, eds., *Soldiering for Glory: The Civil War Letters of Colonel Frank Schaller, Twenty-Second Mississippi Infantry* (Columbia: University of South Carolina Press, 2007), ix–x, 1–3, 52–55.

24. Watson Dugat Williams, Camp Bragg, near Richmond, Virginia, to Laura Bryan, Liberty, Texas, October 7, 1861, Watson Dugat Williams Letters.

25. Schaller and Schaller, *Soldiering for Glory*, 57. See also Everett, *Chaplain Davis and Hood's Texas Brigade* (Baton Rouge: Louisiana State University Press, 1999), 45–46.

26. W. A. Nabours, "Reminiscences," in *Reminiscences of the Boys in Gray, 1861–1865*, ed. Mamie Yeary (McGregor, Tex., 1912; repr., Dayton, Ohio: Morningside Books, 1986), 560.

27. Williams to Laura Bryan, October 7, 1861, Watson Dugat Williams Letters.

28. Simpson, *Lee's Grenadier Guard*, 61–62. Original source: Foster B. Womack, *An Account of the Womack Family* (Waco, Tex.: privately printed, 1937), 11.

29. William Henry Foster, Camp near Dumfries, Virginia, to "Dear Sister Eliza," January 17, 1862, William Henry Foster Papers, Hood's Texas Brigade Collection, Historical Research Center, Hill College, Hillsboro, Tex. Hereafter cited as Foster Papers.

30. William P. Townsend, 5 miles from Richmond [Virginia], to "My Dearest Wife," October 3, 1861, William P. Townsend Letters, Texas Heritage Museum, Hill College, Hillsboro, Tex. Hereafter cited as Townsend Letters.

31. Robert V. Foster, Camp near Richmond, to "Dear Father and Mother," November 7, 1861, Foster Papers.

32. Val C. Giles, *Rags and Hope: The Recollections of Val C. Giles, Four Years with Hood's Brigade, Fourth Texas Infantry*, ed. Mary Lasswell (New York: Coward-McCann, 1961), 44–45.

33. Ibid., 49–50.

34. J. B. Polley, *A Soldier's Letters to Charming Nellie: The Correspondence of Joseph B. Polley, Hood's Texas Brigade*, ed. Richard B. McCaslin (Knoxville: University of Tennessee Press, 2008), 208–11.

35. Giles, *Rags and Hope*, 47–48.

36. Winkler, *The Confederate Capital and Hood's Texas Brigade*, 36.

37. See, for example, Patrick Penn, Richmond, Va., to "My Dear Sister" [Mary Elizabeth Penn Menefee], Oso, Texas, September 23, 1861, in McAnelly, "Penn Letters," *Louisiana Genealogical Register* 18 (June 1971): 100. Penn writes: "I have just taken a look at the statues of Washington, Henry, Mason, and Jefferson and a bust of LaFayette. The statues are magnificent." See also Charles Brooks, "Popular Sovereignty in the Confederate Army"; he spells out the correlation between the Founding Fathers' arguments and the Texans' arguments in pages 205–6.

38. *Houston Telegraph*, July 3, 1861.

39. *Dallas Herald*, July 17, 1861.

40. For more on this exchange among Civil War company-grade officers and their men, see Bledsoe, *Citizen-Officers: The Union and Confederate Volunteer Junior Officer Corps in the American Civil War*.

41. *O.R.*, ser. I, vol. 5, pp. 913–14, 960–61, 1030.

42. Everett, *Chaplain Davis and Hood's Texas Brigade*, 48.

43. Ibid.

44. J. B. Polley, *Hood's Texas Brigade: Its Marches, Its Battles, Its Achievements* (New York: Neale, 1910; rpt., Dayton, Ohio: Press of Morningside Bookshop, 1976), 15–16.

45. Thomas W. Cutrer, ed. *Longstreet's Aide: The Civil War Letters of Major Thomas J. Goree* (Charlottesville: University Press of Virginia, 1995), 53.

46. James H. Hendrick, Richmond [Virginia], to "Dear Mother," August 6, 1861, James Hendrick Letters.

47. Polley, *A Soldier's Letters to Charming Nellie*, 10 (letter dated January 3, 1862).

48. Polley, *Hood's Texas Brigade*, 16.

49. Eugene O. Perry, Camp Quantico, Troops near Dumfries, to "Dear Pa," December 7, 1861, in Harold B. Simpson, ed., "Whip the Devil and His Hosts: The Civil War Letters of Eugene O. Perry," *Chronicles of Smith County, Texas* 6 (Fall 1967): 34–35.

CHAPTER FOUR

1. James Lile Lemon, *Feed Them the Steel! Being the Wartime Recollections of Captain James Lile Lemon, Co. A, 18th Georgia Infantry, C.S.A.*, ed. Mark H. Lemon (privately published by Lemon, 2013), 18.

2. Thomas Dowtin, Camp near Dumfries, Virginia, to "My Dear Sister," November 28, 1861, Confederate Miscellany, 1B, Box 20, Special Collections and Archives, Robert W. Woodruff Library, Emory University, Atlanta, Ga.

3. Author signed himself "Friend Gilbert," *The Spirit of '61* (camp newspaper of the Eighteenth Georgia Infantry) 1, no. 1, December 25, 1861, Confederate Miscellany, 1B, Box 20, Special Collections and Archives, Robert W. Woodruff Library, Emory University, Atlanta, Ga.

4. Lemon, *Feed Them the Steel!*, 19.

5. Mary Alice Wills, *The Confederate Blockade of Washington, D.C.* (Parsons, W.V.: McClain Printing, 1975), 6. One of the best semi-specific descriptions of the Texas Brigade's position that winter comes from Whiting's report to Confederate secretary of war Judah P. Benjamin in March 1862. In it, Whiting explains that the three Texas regiments "were posted on Telegraph road, between and upon Neabsco and Powell's Runs, with one battery. The 1st Texas at Talbot's Hill, on the Quantico, to cover the left of the Evansport Battery" (see *O.R.*, ser. I, vol. 5, p. 529).

6. George Todd mentions at least one trip as far north as Cockpit point in George T. Todd, *1st Texas Regiment* (Waco, Tex.: Texian Press, 1963), 3. For a detailed analysis of a possible location of the First Texas's winter quarters, see Robert H. C. Alton, "The Lost Camp," *North South Trader's Civil War* 33 (2008): 30–37, 58–60. For a detailed discussion of the construction and location of the batteries, see the report by Jan Townsend, Archeologist for Prince William County, Virginia, in "Freestone Point Battery, DHL No. 76–264," National Register of Historic Places Registration Form, United States Department of the Interior, National Park Service, May 1989. Although General Whiting refers to the First Texas on Talbot's Hill in his spring 1862 report, there is no firm agreement today on where exactly Talbot's Hill was located in 1861, though research conducted by Mr. Donald L. Wilson, Virginiana Librarian, Prince William Public Library System, indicated that it could have been near Possum Nose, where the Quantico River feeds into the Potomac. Lt. Col. Ron Smith's long research of the area, however, indicates that the First Texas may have camped on the southern bank of the Quantico, whereas Robert Alton's research places them on the northern bank. There's also a possibility that the wooden winter quarters were not constructed in precisely the same area where the men established their temporary tent quarters when they first arrived north of Dumfries. Howard R. Crouch, in *Relic Hunter: The Field Account of Civil War Sites, Artifacts, and Hunting* (1978; repr., Oakpark, Va.: SCS, 2006), offers a sketched map that places the Fourth Texas as the northernmost unit camped between Neabsco Creek and Powell's Run, and the Fifth Texas south of Powell's Run. The Fifth Texas camp was located between Neabsco Creek and Powell's Run—Col. James Archer described the unit (quoted below) to his brother in Decem-

ber 1861 in extremely precise terms (C. A. Porter Hopkins, ed., "The James J. Archer Letters: A Marylander in the Civil War, Part I," *Maryland Historical Magazine* 56 [March 1961]: 93). This was supported as well by letters from Fifth Texans like Lt. Watson Dugat Williams, who referred to their camp as "Camp Neabsco" in many of his late 1861 and early 1862 letters (see Watson Dugat Williams Letters). Despite this, the only firm location that can be offered is that the Texas Brigade spent the winter of 1861-62 in camps northeast of Dumfries, Virginia, that ran from Quantico Creek north to Neabsco Creek, and west to east from Telegraph Road to the Potomac River. I would like to thank Col. John Favors, USMC, ret., Lt. Col. Rick Eiserman, USA, ret., Lt. Col. Ron Smith, USMC, ret., and Mr. Robert H. C. Alton for their assistance in researching and debating the historical record, and walking the ground of these camps over several trips to Dumfries and Quantico. Thanks, too, to Dr. Richard DiNardo and Mrs. Rita DiNardo for their hospitality during those visits.

7. C. A. Porter Hopkins, ed., "The James J. Archer Letters: A Marylander in the Civil War, Part I," *Maryland Historical Magazine* 56, no. 2 (June 1961): 125.

8. Ibid., 93. This description is from a letter to Archer's brother dated December 18, 1861. Copies of Archer's original letters and transcriptions of these are in the James J. Archer File, Hood's Texas Brigade Collection, Texas Heritage Museum, Hill College, Hillsboro.

9. *O.R.*, ser. I, vol. 5, pp. 913-14. General Orders 15 specifically refers to one Louisiana regiment joining the three Texas regiments in forming the Fifth Brigade under Brig. Gen. Louis T. Wigfall. Beyond this, however, there is limited evidence to indicate that Louisianans served with the Texas that fall and winter.

10. *O.R.*, ser. I, vol. 51, pt. II, p. 231. On August 14, 1861, Special Order No. 250 from the Adjutant and Inspector General's Office in Richmond assigned the Alabama Company, popularly known as the Daniel Boone Rifles, to Wigfall's Texas Battalion. On March 8, 1862, Special Order No. 54, from that same office, transferred Company K (formerly the Daniel Boone Rifles), commanded by Lt. J. Farley, to Capt. A. S. Vandergraff's battalion of Alabama volunteers.

11. *Southern Confederacy* (Seguin, Tex.), October 11, 1861.

12. *Houston Weekly Telegraph*, October 30, 1861.

13. *Houston Tri-Weekly Telegraph*, December 4, 1861. Original letter written on November 8, 1861.

14. *Austin State Gazette*, December 14, 1861.

15. *Richmond Daily Dispatch*, January 17, 1862.

16. *Richmond Whig*, December 29, 1862. Special thanks to Mr. Mike Gormann for insights and source material (see www.mdgorman.com) on the establishment and workings of Texas Hospital, Richmond, Va.

17. Mark Smither, Headquarters 5th Regiment Texas Volunteers, Camp Neabsco near Dumfries, Virginia, to "Brother," January 18, 1862, Smither Papers.

18. A. T. Rainey, Manassas, Virginia, to "My Own Dear Little Wife," Alexis T. Rainey Letters. Special thanks to Rainey descendant Dolly S. Jeffus of Palestine, Texas, for sharing copies of the original letters and insights into Rainey.

19. On several occasions, E. O. Perry, though camped closest to Dumfries with the First Texas, commented on being undersupplied with food and necessities. See November 16, 1861, letter: "Our regiment has been very scant of provisions for the last two weeks." On December 7, 1861: "Our company gets along exceedingly well, considering we do not draw half rations." On January 9,

1862: "Pork is very high here very scarce. Bacon government prices 25 cts only get it once in ten days" (in Simpson, ed., "Whip the Devil and His Hosts," 34–39). North along the Neabsco, Mark Smither noted that they had been surviving on "flour and beef," in a letter dated February 27, 1862 (Smither Papers).

20. C. A. Porter Hopkins, ed., "The James J. Archer Letters: A Marylander in the Civil War, Part I," *Maryland Historical Magazine* 56 (March 1961): 92.

21. W. J. Tannehill, Camp near Richmond, to "Dear Father," October 22, 1861, William J. Tannehill Letters, Hood's Texas Brigade Collection, Texas Heritage Museum, Hill College, Hillsboro, Tex. Hereafter cited as Tannehill Letters.

22. W. J. Tannehill, Richmond, Va., to "Dear Father," December 17, 1861, Tannehill Letters.

23. James Lile Lemon, *Feed Them the Steel!*, 19.

24. Colonel Hugh McLeod, Compiled Service Record, 1st Texas Infantry, commander.

25. Eugene O. Perry, Winter Quarters, Troops near Dumfries, to "Dear Will," January 9, 1862, in Simpson, ed., "Whip the Devil and His Hosts," 37–39.

26. Simpson, *Compendium*, 558. See similar complaints about the high disease rates in Watson Dugat Williams, Camp "Neabsco" on the Potomac, 4 miles north of Dumfries, Prince William County, Virginia, to "My Dear Laura" [Bryan], December 20, 1861, Watson Dugat Williams Letters.

27. Glatthaar, *General Lee's Army*, 69.

28. For an excellent discussion of camp layout and the sanitary ignorance of soldiers that winter among the units that would form R. E. Lee's Army of Northern Virginia, see Glatthaar, *General Lee's Army*, 70–77.

29. One of the best descriptions of one of these evenings comes from Watson Dugat Williams, Camp "Neabsco" on the Potomac, Four miles north of Dumfries, Prince Williams County, Virginia, to unknown [but context indicates Laura Bryan], Liberty, Texas, January 4, 1862, Watson Dugat Williams Letters.

30. W. S. Shockley to Eliza, 23 November [1861], W. S. Shockley Letters, 1861–1864, David M. Rubenstein Rare Book & Manuscript Library, Duke University; Thomas Dowtin, Camp near Dumfries, Virginia, to "My Dear Sister," November 28, 1861, Confederate Miscellany, 1B, Box 20, Special Collections and Archives, Robert W. Woodruff Library, Emory University, Atlanta, Ga.

31. George W. Maddox, near Dumfries, to "Dear Pa," November 29, 1861, Book 59, Lewis Leigh Collection, U.S. Army Heritage and Education Center, Carlisle, Pa.

32. Polley, *A Soldier's Letters to Charming Nellie*, 10–11.

33. Watson Dugat Williams, Camp "Neabsco" on the Potomac, 4 miles north of Dumfries, Prince William County, Virginia, to "My Dear Laura" [Bryan], Liberty, Texas, December 24, 1861, Watson Dugat Williams Letters.

34. "An Observer," *The Spirit of 1861* (Eighteenth Georgia camp newspaper) 1, no. 1 December 25, 1861, Confederate Miscellany, 1B, Box 20, Special Collections and Archives, Robert W. Woodruff Library, Emory University, Atlanta, Ga.

35. Mark Smither, Camp Neabsco, Prince William County, Virginia, to "Aunt," January 17, 1862, Smither Papers.

36. W. S. Shockley to Eliza, 23 November [1861], W. S. Shockley Letters, 1861–1864, David M. Rubenstein Rare Book & Manuscript Library, Duke University.

37. *O.R.*, ser. I, vol. 5, pp. 998–99. Dunnington refers to the First Texas as the Second Texas, which they were briefly listed as until Wigfall used his political might to convince Confederate

authorities that the original Texans who mustered into service in Virginia must receive the honored ranking of First Texas Infantry.

38. *Texas Republican* (Marshall), February 15, 1862. Letter written by William B. Ochiltree while waiting outside the Military Committee Room, Richmond, Virginia, January 29, 1862. Ochiltree was a first sergeant in Company E, First Texas Infantry.

39. W. D. Pritchard, "War Reminiscences," *Crocket (Tex.) Courier*, November 5, 1897.

40. Mark Smither, Headquarters 5th Regiment Texas Volunteers, Camp Neabsco near Dumfries, Virginia, to "Brother," January 18, 1862, Smither Papers; W. S. Shockley to "Eliza," 23 November [1861], W. S. Shockley Letters, 1861–1864, David M. Rubenstein Rare Book & Manuscript Library, Duke University.

41. Polley, *A Soldier's Letters to Charming Nellie*, 7–9.

42. Giles, *Rags and Hope*, 52.

43. *O.R.*, ser. I, vol. 5, pp. 971–72.

44. First quote on building fortifications from Thomas Dowtin, Camp near Dumfries, Virginia, to "My Dear Sister," November 28, 1861, Confederate Miscellany, 1B, Box 20, Special Collections and Archives, Robert W. Woodruff Library, Emory University, Atlanta, Ga.; second quote referencing felling trees from George W. Maddox, near Dumfries, to "Dear Pa," November 29, 1861, Book 59, Lewis Leigh Collection, U.S. Army Heritage and Education Center, Carlisle, Pa.

45. *O.R.*, ser. I, vol. 5, p. 928.

46. Ibid., p. 950.

47. Ibid., p. 982.

48. Ibid., pp. 949–50.

49. Ibid., p. 961.

50. Ibid., p. 47. See a discussion of this in chapters 4 and 5 of Peter D. Skirbunt, "Washington Secured: Breaking the Confederate Blockade of the Potomac, 1861–1862" (master's thesis, Ohio State University, 1975), 141–78.

51. Wills, *The Confederate Blockade*, 86.

52. Winkler, *The Confederate Capital and Hood's Texas Brigade*, 42. See also E. O. Perry, Camp Quantico, Troops near Dumfries, to "Dear Pa," December 7, 1861, in Simpson, ed., "Whip the Devil and His Hosts," 34–35.

53. E. O. Perry, Camp Quantico, Troops near Dumfries, to "Dear Pa," December 7, 1861, in Simpson, ed., "Whip the Devil and His Hosts," 34–35.

54. J. H. Hendrick, Army of the Potomac, Camp Quantico, Virginia, to "Dear Mother," December 31, 1861, James H. Hendrick Papers, Texas Heritage Museum, Hill College, Hillsboro. See also a letter signed "Matt" and dated December 4, 1861, that was sent to *Houston Tri-Weekly Telegraph* editor E. H. Cushing from Dumfries that comments the Texans' ability to see Federal camp fires every night and their frustrations and attempts to shoot down the Federal observation balloon (*Houston Tri-Weekly Telegraph*, January 1, 1862).

55. Polley, *Hood's Texas Brigade*, 16.

56. The nine men were Cpl. Samuel T. Watson, Charles Mills, John Burke, Stephen Webb, Berry Webb, Adam Hope, James P. Spratting, Thomas Willingham, and James M. Burroughs (*Texas Republican* [Marshall], February 22, 1862).

57. Ochiltree's letter dated February 6, 1862, Richmond, Va., appeared in the *Texas Republican* (Marshall), February 22, 1862. Whiting's special order, dated January 30, 1862, appeared in the

Richmond Daily Dispatch, February 6, 1862. Northern accounts, most of which focused on Heintzleman's report, appeared in a number of papers including the *Washington, D.C., Evening Star*, January 29, 1862, *Washington, D.C., Daily National Intelligencer*, January 31, 1862, and *Harper's Weekly*, February 15, 1862, as well as the *Richmond Daily Dispatch*, February 3, 1862, which, it appears, their February 6 account was designed to correct. Judith N. McArthur, "'Those Texians Are Number One Men': A New Confederate Account of the Affair at Lee's House, Virginia," *Southwestern Historical Quarterly* (April 1992): 488–96, offers a detailed analysis of the event.

58. *O.R.*, ser. I, vol. 5, p. 993.
59. Glatthaar, *General Lee's Army*, 84.
60. Ibid., 84–85.
61. Simpson, *Lee's Grenadier Guard*, 85n46.
62. Eugene O. Perry, Winter Quarters, Troops near Dumfries, to "Dear Will" [likely his eldest brother], January 9, 1862, in Simpson, ed., "Whip the Devil and His Hosts," 37–39.
63. Mintie Price, San Augustine, to "My Dear Frank," January 5, 1862, in Jimmy L. Bryan, Jr., ed., "'Whip Them Like the Mischief': The Civil War Letters of Frank and Mintie Price," *East Texas Historical Association* 36, no. 2 (1998): 70.
64. Ibid., 71–72.
65. James Rodgers Loughridge, Richmond, VA, to "My dear Little Mary & Ella," January 14, 1862, James Rodgers Loughridge Letters, Loughridge Collection.
66. James Rodgers Loughridge, Camp Hood, 4th Texas Vol near Dumphries, VA, to "My dear Mother," January 24, 1862, Loughridge Collection.
67. Mary Felicia Loughridge, Falls County, Texas, to "My Dear Noble Husband," February 20, 1862, Loughridge Collection.
68. Cutrer, ed., *Longstreet's Aide*, 77–78.
69. In the U.S. Census of 1860, Sarah Kittrell Goree listed a personal wealth of $12,060 and real estate wealth of $30,000 (see 1860 U.S. Federal Census, Precinct 2, Polk, Texas; Roll: M653_1303; Page: 11; Image: 25; Family History Library Film: 805303). In the 1860 federal slave schedule, she is listed as owning thirty-one enslaved men, women, and children (see 1860 U.S. Federal Census—Slave Schedules, Ancestry.com [database online] [Ancestry.com Operations, Inc., 2010]).
70. Cutrer, ed., *Longstreet's Aide*, 76. Pleasant "Scrap" Goree joined his brothers in Virginia when he enlisted in Company H, Fifth Texas Infantry, on August 11, 1863, in Polk County, Texas (Compiled Service Record, Pleasant K. Goree, 5th Texas Infantry, Fold3.com).
71. See Knight brothers' Compiled Service Records, 1st Texas, Fold3.com.
72. See Erskine brothers' Compiled Service Records, 4th Texas Infantry, Fold3.com.
73. Campbell, *Lone Star Confederate*, 7.
74. For an analysis of this, see Francelle Pruitt, "'We've Got to Fight or Die': Early Texas Reaction to the Confederate Draft, 1862," *East Texas Historical Association Journal* 3 (1998): 3–17.
75. *Texas State Gazette* (Austin), March 29, 1862.
76. *Houston Tri-Weekly Telegraph*, April 16, 1862; *Texas Republican* (Marshall), March 1, 1862.
77. Louis T. Wigfall left the Texas Brigade in the spring of 1862, when Texans elected him to the Confederate Senate. He actually introduced the conscription bill in the Senate and argued that it ensured that all citizens contributed to the war effort and that it received their full attention and support. His fellow Texas senator, William S. Oldham, disagreed. Oldham worried that conscription recruited unpatriotic soldiers, who were less effective (see Pruit, "We've Got to Fight or Die," 12–13; see also William Simpson Oldham, "Speech of W. S. Oldham, of Texas, upon the bill

to amend the conscript law, made in the Senate, September 4, 1862," Emory University Digital Library Publications Program, https://archive.org/details/19154655.3711.emory.edu).

78. Compiled Service Records for William and Jasper Barron, 5th Texas Infantry, Fold3.com.

79. G. R. Thornwell, Camp Butler, to "Dear Jennie," November 30, 1861; G. R. Thornwell Letter, "South Carolina" no. 5, Bound Volume 88, Richmond National Battlefield Park, Richmond, Va.

80. *Houston Tri-Weekly Telegraph,* April 4, 1862. Letter written by Fifth Texan Virginius Petty, "Neabsco," Virginia, March 4, 1862. See also Thomas S. Terrell, *The Boys from Brenham: The Original Letters of Virginius E. Petty, Co. E, 5th Texas Regiment, Hood's Brigade, Army of Northern Virginia* (Kerrville, Tex.: privately published by Terrell, 2006). Texans made carvings of their own, though usually just their initials and unit, at Aquia Church near them, which rested along Telegraph Road. These can still be seen today in Stafford County, Virginia. For analysis of the graffiti, see Eric Mink's three-part essay, "If These Signatures Could Talk: Aquia Church Graffiti," at https://npsfrsp.wordpress.com/2011/12/07/if-these-signatures-could-talk-aquia-church-graffiti-part-1/.

81. William Gaffney, Compiled Service Record, 5th Texas, Fold3.com

82. Samuel Tine Owen, State of Virginia, Prince William County, to "Dear Father and Mother," February 5, 1862, Samuel Tine Owen Papers.

83. John Wade Owen served as a sergeant in Company E, later Company F, of the Twentieth Texas Cavalry Regiment. He survived the war (Compiled Service Record, M227 roll 28, U.S. National Archives). John Owen valued his real estate at $800 in 1860 and his personal estate at $450 (1860 U.S. Federal Census, Beat 3, Henderson, Texas; Roll: M653_1297; Page: 42; Image: 92; Family History Library Film: 805297).

84. McArthur, "Those Texians Are Number One Men," 495.

CHAPTER FIVE

1. Samuel Tine Owen, State of Virginia, to "Dear Father and Mother," March 16, 1862, Samuel Tine Owen Papers.

2. John Marquis Smither, 5th Texas Regiment, Camp Archer near Dumfries on the Potomac, February 27, 1862, Smither Papers.

3. John Marquis Smither, 5th Texas Regiment, Camp Archer near Dumfries on the Potomac, February 27, 1862, Smither Papers.

4. Cutrer, *Longstreet's Aide,* 79.

5. J. R. Loughridge, 4th Texas Regiment Army of the Potomac, to "Dear Wife" [Mary Felicia Loughridge], February 24, 1862, Loughridge Collection.

6. *O.R.,* ser. I, vol. 5, pp. 527–34.

7. Ibid.

8. Warren H. Cudworth, Chaplain, First Massachusetts, *History of the First Regiment (Massachusetts Infantry) from the 25th of May, 1861, to the 25th of May, 1864: Including Brief References to the Operations of the Army of the Potomac* (Boston: Walker, Fuller, & Co., 1866), 127.

9. "Mac," Camp Hooker, to "Friend Harry," March 13, 1862, "Mac" Letters of an unidentified enlisted man, November 7, 1861–March 13, 1862, Lewis Leigh Collection, Book 33A, Book 34, Box 10, U.S. Army Heritage and Education Center, Carlisle, Pa.

10. Charles C. Perkins Diary, Monday, March 10, 1862; Charles C. Perkins, 1st Massachusetts

Infantry Regiment Diaries, May 24, 1861–July 4, 1862, Civil War Times Illustrated Collection of Civil War Papers, Box 19, U.S. Army Heritage and Education Center, Carlisle, Pa.

11. Cudworth, *History of the First Regiment*, 129–30.

12. Ibid., 132.

13. *O.R.*, ser. I, vol. 5, p. 1097.

14. John Bell Hood, *Advance and Retreat: Personal Experiences in the United States and Confederate Armies* (Secaucus, N.J.: Blue and Grey Press, 1985), 20.

15. Hopkins, "The James J. Archer Letters," 133; *Galveston Weekly News*, July 24, 1862.

16. Josiah G. Duke, Camp Texas near Richmond, Virginia, to his maternal grandmother, Rebecca Cheek Philips of Rutherford County, Tennessee (or "Jourdan Valley Tennessee," as Duke noted on the letter), letter undated, but context indicates fall 1861 or early spring 1862, Josiah G. Duke File, Hood's Texas Brigade Collection, Texas Heritage Museum, Hill College, Hillsboro.

17. Winkler, *The Confederate Capital and Hood's Texas Brigade*, 59.

18. Hood, *Advance and Retreat*, 19.

19. Qtd. in Brooks, "Popular Sovereignty," 214, and cited as J. B. Polley Diary, Texas Heritage Museum, Hill College, Hillsboro, 51–51, 38.

20. J. Roderick Heller III and Carolynn Ayres Heller, eds., *The Confederacy Is on Her Way up the Spout: Letters to South Carolina, 1861–1864* (Columbia: University of South Carolina Press, 1998), 55.

21. Everett, *Chaplain Davis and Hood's Texas Brigade*, 54–55; see also Selman Diary, April 4, 1862, Selman Papers.

22. Glatthaar, *General Lee's Army*, 104–6.

23. Selman Diary, March 25, 1862, Selman Papers.

24. Ibid., April 8, 1862, Selman Papers.

25. Robert Gaston, Richmond, Virginia, to "Dear Pa & Ma," April 26, 1862, in Robert W. Glover, ed., *"Tyler to Sharpsburg,"* 14.

26. Selman Diary, April 8, 1862, Selman Papers.

27. Giles, *Rags and Hope*, 67–68.

28. Mark Smither, Camp near Yorktown, to "Dear Sister," April 19, 1862, Smither Papers.

29. Everett, *Chaplain Davis and Hood's Texas Brigade*, 57.

30. Giles, *Rags and Hope*, 43.

31. Simpson, *Lee's Grenadier Guard*, 97–99.

32. Ibid.

33. *O.R.*, ser. I, vol. 11, pt. I, p. 627; Winkler, *The Confederate Capital and Hood's Texas Brigade*, 60.

34. Winkler, *The Confederate Capital and Hood's Texas Brigade*, 60.

35. George T. Todd, Jefferson, Texas, to Mrs. W. M. Peal, November 18, 1895, United Confederate Veterans Collection, Haley Memorial Library and History Center, Midland, Tex.; see also Giles, *Rags and Hope*, 97–98.

36. William Schadt, Camp near Richmond, Virginia, to "Dear Sister" [Caroline Schadt], May 17, 1862, Schadt Family Papers.

37. Simpson, *Lee's Grenadier Guard*, 101. See also Jerome B. Robertson, comp., *Touched with Valor: The Civil War Papers and Casualty Reports of Hood's Texas Brigade*, ed. Harold B. Simpson (Hillsboro, Tex.: Hill Junior College Press, 1964), 85–86.

38. *New York Times,* May 14, 1862.

39. Mark Smither, Camp Wigfall near Fredericksburg, to "Dear Brother," April 6, 1862, Smither Papers. Smither refers to the two scouts in Hutcheson's company as "Dickie and Barker." It is unclear who "Dickie" was, but "Barker" was likely James C. Barker, assigned as a scout all winter on the Occoquan. He received a medical discharge for asthma in October 1862. Simpson, *Compendium,* 139.

40. Thomas J. Selman, Head Quarters, Camp near Richmond, Virginia, to J. F. Davis, Esq [brother-in-law], Saturday, May 24, 1862, Selman Papers.

41. Simpson, *Compendium,* 212. On 1862 volunteers, see Glatthaar, *General Lee's Army,* 202.

42. Watson Dugat Williams, Richmond, Virginia, to "My Dear Lollie" [Laura Bryan], April 17, 1862, Watson Dugat Williams Letters. See also Simpson, *Compendium,* 214.

43. Unpublished Erskine family history and transcription, "Civil War Commentary and Letters," 103. Hereafter cited as Erskine Collection. Special thanks to Erskine family descendants Melissa Lingwall and Melinda Kilian for sharing letters, photographs, and other information on the Erskine family history. Glatthaar, *General Lee's Army,* 202–3.

44. Andrew Nelson Erskine, Monroe, Louisiana, to "My dear wife" [Ann Johnson Erskine], Monday morning, May 19, 1862, Erskine Collection.

45. Watson Dugat Williams, Richmond, Virginia, to "My Own Laura" [Bryan], May 6, 1862, Watson Dugat Williams Letters, emphasis original.

46. Joseph Dugas [*sic*] and Marie Celanie Breaux had a number of children who included Margaretta Dugat (Watson Dugat Williams's mother), Eurlarian Dugat (Beasley Dugat's father), and Jean Joseph Dugat (Albert G. Dugat, who enlisted with Dugat Williams and would be killed at the Battle of Second Manassas). See Dugat family history, www.jcsisle.com/dugat.html. See also Margaretta Dugat Stanwood. See also Eurlarian Dugat in 1860 U.S. Federal Census, Chambers, Texas; Roll: M653_1291; Page: 11; Image: 26; Family History Library Film: 805291. See also Joseph Dugas in the 1860 U.S. Federal Census, Liberty, Texas; Roll: M653_1300; Page: 299; Image: 20; Family History Library Film: 805300.

47. Watson Dugat Williams, Camp near Richmond, Virginia, to "My Dear Laura" [Bryan], July 21, 1862, Watson Dugat Williams Letters.

48. Heller and Heller, *The Confederacy Is on Her Way up the Spout,* 54.

49. Andrew Nelson Erskine, Camp near Richmond, Virginia, to "My dear wife" [Ann Johnson Erskine], June 12, 1862, Erskine Collection.

50. O. Lee Sturkey, *Hampton Legion Infantry, C.S.A.: The South Carolina Roster Set* (Wilmington, N.C.: Broadfoot, 2008), 18.

51. Polley, *Hood's Texas Brigade,* 19.

52. McArthur and Burton, eds., *A Gentleman and an Officer,* 82.

53. See commentary on each company's formation throughout Simpson, *Compendium*.

54. All First Texas companies, including those who had mustered in "for the war," were part of the regimental reorganization on May 18, 1862.

55. McArthur and Burton, eds., *A Gentleman and an Officer,* 199–200.

56. Simpson, ed., "Whip the Devil and His Hosts," 40.

57. Ibid., 40, 59–60n.

58. McArthur and Burton, eds., *A Gentleman and an Officer,* 242–43. When Wade Hampton was promoted to brigadier general later that summer, Hampton's Legion voted Griffin as their new

colonel. He received another appointment, though, that would place him in state service closer to home. After great deliberation, Griffin chose to remain in South Carolina in the Reserves.

59. Robert E. L. Krick, "The Men Who Carried This Position Were Soldiers Indeed," 186. This account by Krick is one of the best studies available of Whiting's division at Gaines's Mill. I would like to thank Mr. Krick for hiking the Texas Brigade's positions on that field with me, answering countless questions, providing access to the archival holdings of the Richmond National Battlefield Park, and critiquing portions of this manuscript.

60. *Richmond Daily Whig,* August 4, 1862.

61. Bennett Wood account in Yeary, *Reminiscences of the Boys in Gray,* 815.

62. *Richmond Daily Whig,* August 4, 1862.

63. Unpublished memoir of R. A. Brantley Sr., Somerville, Tex., "The 5th Texas, Seven Days Battle around Richmond, Beginning June 27, 1862 at Gains Mill," bound volume 121, "Texas," Richmond National Battlefield Park.

64. Campbell, *Lone Star Confederate,* 39–41.

65. McAnelly, "Penn Letters," *Louisiana Genealogical Register* (September 1971): 266.

66. James Rogers Loughridge, location unknown, to "My dear wife" [Mary Felicia Loughridge], June 22, 1862, Loughridge Collection.

67. Lemon, *Feed Them the Steel!,* 22–23.

68. Robert E. L. Krick, "The Men Who Carried This Position Were Soldiers Indeed," 192; Hood, *Advance and Retreat,* 25–28.

69. Robert E. L. Krick, "The Men Who Carried This Position Were Soldiers Indeed," 192.

70. William R. Hamby, "4th Texas in Battle of Gaines's Mill," in *Texans Who Wore the Grey,* ed. Sidney S. Johnson (Tyler, Tex.: self-published, 1907), 390; Robert E. L. Krick, "The Men Who Carried This Position Were Soldiers Indeed," 192.

71. Lemon, *Feed Them the Steel!,* 23.

72. Ibid., 23–24.

73. Hamby, "4th Texas in Battle of Gaines's Mill," 391.

74. Polley, *A Soldier's Letters to Charming Nellie,* 38.

75. Andrew N. Erskine, Camp on the Battle Field, to "My dear Wife," June 28, 1862, Erskine Collection.

76. Giles, *Rags and Hope,* 111.

77. Lemon, *Feed Them the Steel!,* 25.

78. McAnelly, "Penn Letters," *Louisiana Genealogical Register* (December 1971): 341. Quinn Menefee was one of the 1862 recruits from Oso, Texas.

79. Robert E. L. Krick, "The Men Who Carried This Position Were Soldiers Indeed," 203.

80. Campbell, *Lone Star Confederate,* 41–42.

81. Robert E. L. Krick, "The Men Who Carried This Position Were Soldiers Indeed," 204; Everett, *Chaplain Davis and Hood's Texas Brigade,* 91; see also the official report of J. B. Hood, *O.R.,* ser. I, vol. 11, pt. II, pp. 568–69.

82. John Reagan, *John Reagan Memoirs with Special Reference to Secession and the Civil War* (New York: Neale, 1906), 145; Hood, *Advance and Retreat,* 28; *O.R.,* ser. 1, vol. 11, pt. II, p. 556; Robert E. L. Krick, "The Men Who Carried This Position Were Soldiers Indeed," 204–7.

83. Examples of this appear in the *Galveston Weekly News,* July 24, 1862, and July 29, 1862; *Houston (Tex.) Tri-Weekly News,* July 29, 1862, August 11, 1862, August 18, 1862, October 18, 1862;

Austin (Tex.) State Gazette, August 7 1862, September 3, 1862, August 14, 1862, and August 29, 1862.

84. *Galveston Weekly News,* July 24, 1862, emphasis original.

85. *Charleston (S.C.) Mercury,* July 9, 1862.

86. *Macon (Ga.) Telegraph,* August 1, 1862.

87. *Cincinnati (Ohio) Commercial Tribune,* July 14, 1862; *Philadelphia Inquirer,* July 12, 1862; *Richmond (Va.) Dispatch,* June 30, 1862.

88. *San Antonio (Tex.) Semi-Weekly,* August 11, 1862.

89. William Martin to Mrs. Roxey Edwards, August 13, 1862, William Martin File, Hood's Texas Brigade Collection, Historical Research Center, Hill College, Hillsboro, Tex.

90. Joseph B. Polley, Texas Depot–Richmond, to "Dear Father," July 15, 1862, unpublished letter shared with me by Polley historian Richard B. McCaslin via Katherine A. H. Goldberg, Henderson's great-great-great-granddaughter. I would like to thank both Dr. McCaslin and Ms. Goldberg for sharing the letter and family history.

91. Connally and Susan Henderson, 1860 U.S. Federal Census, Wilson, Bexar, Texas; Roll: M653_1288; Page: 441; Image: 409; Family History Library Film: 805288.

92. See notations by Katherine A. H. Goldberg that accompany letter and Find-a-grave listing for Conley Finley Henderson Tiner, born December 7, 1862. Special thanks to Conley Finley Henderson Tiner descendent Tammy Tiner, and her husband, Kenn Harding, and daughter Laura Harding of College Station, Texas, who have shared Polley and Henderson family stories and hiked this battlefield and others with me.

93. Lucy Morton Sullivan unpublished diary, June 1870, June 1871, June 1879, June 1880. Transcribed diary shared by Sullivan descendant Jane Gillette Riggs, Baytown, Tex.

94. Cecelia Morse, "Civil War Diary of Cecelia Morse," July 6–August 2, 1862, unpublished, transcribed by Janet K. Wagner. Special thanks to Mr. Dan Worrell for sharing a copy of the diary, which he is in the process of getting published, and detailed research and preservation efforts for the Morse-Bragg Cemetery, Houston, Tex.

95. Andrew N. Erskine, Camp on the Battle Field [Gaines's Mill], Virginia, to "My dear Wife" [Ann Johnson Erskine], June 28, 1862. See also Andrew N. Erskine, In Camp near Richmond, to "My dearest Wife" [Ann Johnson Erskine], July 17, 1862, Erskine Collection.

96. Details from Andrew N. Erskine letters July 8, 1862, through August 14, 1862, Erskine Collection.

97. Andrew N. Erskine, Camp on the Battle Field [Gaines's Mill], Virginia, to "My dear Wife" [Ann Johnson Erskine], June 28, 1862, Erskine Collection.

98. Simpson, *Lee's Grenadier Guard,* 124. The Eighteenth Georgia lost 14 killed, 128 wounded, and 3 missing; Hampton's Legion lost 2 killed, 65 wounded; First Texas lost 13 killed, 65 wounded; Fourth Texas suffered 44 killed, 208 wounded, 1 missing; Fifth Texas had 13 killed, 62 wounded.

99. William P. Townsend, Richmond, Virginia, recipient unknown, though from context it is his wife, Almira Jennings Townsend, July 16, 1862, Townsend Letters.

100. Winkler, *The Confederate Capital and Hood's Texas Brigade,* 84–85.

101. Selman Diary, July 10–13, 1862, Selman Papers.

102. For the connections between Confederate morale and Robert E. Lee's army, see Gallagher, *The Confederate War,* 58.

CHAPTER SIX

1. Gary W. Gallagher, ed. *Fighting for the Confederacy: The Personal Recollections of General Edward Porter Alexander* (Chapel Hill: University of North Carolina Press, 1989), 139.

2. Scott Patchan, *Second Manassas: Longstreet's Attack and the Struggle for Chinn Ridge* (Washington, D.C.: Potomac Books, 2011), 19; Simpson, *Lee's Grenadier Guard*, 140–41; John F. Schmutz, *"The Bloody 5th": The 5th Texas Infantry Regiment, Hood's Texas Brigade, Army of Northern Virginia*, vol. 1: *Secession to the Suffolk Campaign* (Eldorado Hills, Calif.: Savas Beatie, 2016), 155–57.

3. John J. Hennessy, *Return to Bull Run: The Campaign and Battle of Second Manassas* (New York: Simon and Schuster, 1993), 289–92; Simpson, *Lee's Grenadier Guard*, 134–44.

4. Hennessy, *Return to Bull Run*, 292–94.

5. Ibid., 294–96.

6. Ibid., 294–97; J. J. O'Neill, "Membership Record of Miss Leni L. O'Neill; Being a Brief History of the Military Career of Her Father, J. J. O'Neill, 18th Ga. Inf, Acworth Inf, Co. A," (Postwar account written by Eighteenth Georgia veteran J. J. O'Neill), J. J. O'Neill File, Hood's Texas Brigade Collection, Historical Research Center, Hill College, Hillsboro, Tex. For O'Neill family wealth, see 1860 U.S. Federal Census, Acworth, Cobb County, Georgia, Roll: M653_117; Page: 351; Image: 351; Family History Library Film: 803117; *O.R.*, ser. I, vol. 12, part II, p. 609; Giles, *Rags and Hope*, 125; Reverend Penfield Doll, "Facts, Incidents, and Casualties of Late Battles," *Richmond (Va.) Enquirer*, November 3, 1862; and Schmutz, *"The Bloody 5th,"* 161–64.

7. Hennessy's well-researched book and Hood's memoirs indicate that Hood pulled back around midnight or shortly after that. Andrew Erskine's (4th Texas, Co. D) letter of September 2, however, indicates that they "engaged with the enemy on Friday evening just at dark and drove them from their position, and we slept on the ground until nearly day, when we were withdrawn and brought back" (Hennessy, *Return to Bull Run*, 297–302; Hood, *Attack and Retreat*, 34–35; Andrew N. Erskine, On the Winchester and Alexandria Turnpike—20 miles from Washington City, to "My dear beloved Wife" [Ann Johnson Erskine], September 2, 1862, Erskine Collection).

8. Hennessy, *Return to Bull Run*, 297–302. Hood, *Attack and Retreat*, 34–35.

9. Giles, *Rags and Hope*, 127–28.

10. Alexander Madison Erskine, Camp on the Winchester & Alexandria, McAdamson Road, 5 miles from Fairfax C[ourt] H[ouse], to "My dear Bettie" [Maney Erskine], September 2, 1862, Alexander M. Erskine Letter, 1862, Pearce Civil War Collection, Navarro College, Corsicana, Tex.

11. Patchan, *Second Manassas*, 22; Hennessy, *Return to Bull Run*, 369–71.

12. Hennessy, *Return to Bull Run*, 369–71.

13. Ibid., 368–69.

14. Brian C. Pohanka, *Vortex of Hell: A History of the 5th New York Volunteer Infantry, Duryée's Zouaves, 1861–1863* (Lynchburg, Va.: Schroeder, 2012), 329; Hennessy, *Return to Bull Run*, 369–71.

15. Pleasant B. Watson Diary, August 30, 1862, Hood's Texas Brigade Collection, Historical Research Center, Hill College, Hillsboro, Tex. Hereafter cited as Pleasant Watson Diary. Pleasant Watson does not appear in Simpson's *Compendium*, but references throughout the diary clearly place him in Company E of the Fifth Texas Infantry. A copy of the diary is also in the Texas State Archives and in the past has been misidentified as a First Texas diary.

16. Campbell, *Lone Star Confederate*, 74–75; Schmutz, *"The Bloody 5th,"* 168–76.

17. Joe N. Smith, Red Rock, Texas, to Frank B. Chilton, Houston, Texas, May 31, 1911, Frank B. Chilton Papers, Texas Collection, Baylor University, Waco, Tex.

18. George A. Mitchell, Camp on Ball's Hill, to "My dear Parents," September 5, 1862, George A. Mitchell Letters, 1861–1863, New-York Historical Society.

19. Hennessy, *Return to Bull Run*, 373.

20. Ibid., 378; see also Pleasant Watson Diary, August 30, 1862.

21. Alexander Madison Erskine, Camp on the Winchester & Alexandria, McAdamson Road, 5 miles from Fairfax C[ourt] H[ouse], to "My dear Bettie" [Maney Erskine], September 2, 1862, Alexander M. Erskine Letter, 1862, Pearce Civil War Collection, Navarro College, Corsicana, Tex.

22. Polley, *Hood's Texas Brigade*, 88; Polley, *A Soldier's Letters to Charming Nellie*, 50; Hennessy, *Return to Bull Run*, 378; "Reminiscences of Mrs. Sue Monroe," *Confederate Veteran* 4 (1896): 379; Schmutz, *"The Bloody 5th,"* 178–79; some accounts note Texans' unwillingness to help Federal wounded, and other accounts document the opposite (see Pohanka, *Vortex of Hell*, 342–43).

23. Hennessy, *Return to Bull Run*, 379–96.

24. Rufus King Felder, Camp near Winchester, to "Dear Sister" [Emma Felder Adaline], October 1, 1862, Rufus King Felder Letters, Historical Research Center, Hill College, Hillsboro, Tex. Hereafter cited as Rufus King Felder Letters. Simpson, *Lee's Grenadier Guard*, 153–55.

25. Captain Ed. Cunningham, Head Quarters 4th Texas Reg near [Draymuth?], September 3, 1862, 4th TX Rg., letter, E. H. Cunningham from near Draymuth, TCM94.7.183– Box 4, General Files, Texas Confederate Museum Collection, United Confederate Veteran Collection, Nita Stewart Haley Memorial Library, Midland, Tex.

26. Patchan, *Second Manassas*, 118–20.

27. Rufus King Felder, Camp near Winchester, to "Dear Sister" [Emma Felder Adaline], October 1, 1862, Rufus King Felder Letters.

28. Pleasant Watson Diary, August 30, 1862.

29. Terrell, *The Boys of Brenham*, 213–15.

30. Andrew N. Erskine, On the Winchester and Alexandria Turnpike—20 miles from Washington City, to "My dear beloved Wife" [Ann Johnson Erskine], September 2, 1862, Erskine Collection.

31. Alexander Madison Erskine, Camp on the Winchester & Alexandria, McAdamson Road, 5 miles from Fairfax C[ourt] H[ouse], to "My dear Bettie" [Maney Erskine], September 2, 1862, Alexander M. Erskine Letter, 1862, Pearce Civil War Collection, Navarro College, Corsicana, Tex.

32. Andrew N. Erskine, In camp three miles from Frederick City, Maryland, to "My dear beloved Wife" [Ann Johnson Erskine], September 9, 1862, Erskine Collection.

33. Alexander Madison Erskine, Camp on the Winchester & Alexandria, McAdamson Road, 5 miles from Fairfax C[ourt] H[ouse], to "My dear Bettie" [Maney Erskine], September 2, 1862, Alexander M. Erskine Letter, 1862, Pearce Civil War Collection, Navarro College, Corsicana, Tex.

34. Ann Johnson Erskine, At Home [Seguin, Texas] to "Dear Husband" [Andrew Nelson Erskine], September 7 and September 9, 1862, Erskine Collection.

35. Polley, *A Soldier's Letters to Charming Nellie*, 214.

36. Watson Dugat William, Camp near Frederick City, Maryland, to "My dear Laura" [Bryan], September 9, 1862, Watson Dugat Williams Letters.

37. Simpson, *Lee's Grenadier Guard*, 161–62; Hood, *Advance and Retreat*, 38–39.

38. D. Scott Hartwig, *To Antietam Creek: The Maryland Campaign of September 1862* (Baltimore: Johns Hopkins University Press, 2012), 109–10; Simpson, *Lee's Grenadier Guard*, 160.

39. Rufus King Felder, Camp near Winchester, to "Dear Sister" [Emma Felder Adaline], October 1, 1862, Rufus King Felder Letters.

40. Watson Dugat William, Texas Depot, Richmond, Virginia, to "My dear Laura" [Bryan], October 2, 1862, Watson Dugat Williams Letters; Simpson, *Lee's Grenadier Guard*, 162.

41. Glatthaar, *General Lee's Army*, 166–68; Hartwig, *To Antietam Creek*, 120–21; Simpson, *Lee's Grenadier Guard*, 162–64.

42. Joseph L. Harsh, *Sounding the Shallows: A Confederate Companion for the Maryland Campaign of 1862* (Kent, Ohio: Kent State University Press, 2000), 170–75; Hartwig, *To Antietam Creek*, 297. Special thanks to Tom Clemens for walking this ground with me and editing this portion of the manuscript, along with Scott Hartwig.

43. Glatthaar, *General Lee's Army*, 166–68; Hartwig, *To Antietam Creek*, 297–99, 338–39; Jerry W. Holsworth, "Uncommon Valor: Hood's Texas Brigade in the Maryland Campaign," *Blue & Gray Magazine* 13 (August 1996): 11.

44. Polley, *A Soldier's Letters to Charming Nellie*, 55–56.

45. Hartwig, *To Antietam Creek*, 361–62; Hood, *Advance and Retreat*, 39–40.

46. Hartwig, *To Antietam Creek*, 364–65; Holsworth, "Uncommon Valor," 12; *O.R.*, ser. I, vol. 19, pt. I, p. 922

47. Holsworth, "Uncommon Valor," 13.

48. Ibid.

49. Joseph L. Harsh, *Taken at the Flood: Robert E. Lee and Confederate Strategy in the Maryland Campaign of 1862* (Kent, Ohio: Kent State University Press, 1999), 358–59; Holsworth, "Uncommon Valor," 13–14.

50. Ezra A. Carman, *The Maryland Campaign of September 1862*, vol. 2: *Antietam*, ed. Thomas G. Clemens (El Dorado Hills, Calif.: Savas Beatie, 2012), 31–32.

51. *O.R.*, ser. I, vol. 19, pt. I, pp. 268–69; John W. Stevens, *Reminiscences of the Civil War* (Hillsboro, Tex.: Hillsboro Mirror Print, 1902), 72; Hartwig, *To Antietam Creek*, 645–46; Holsworth, "Uncommon Valor," 14; Lemon, *Let Them Eat Steel!*, 33–34.

52. P. A. Work, Kountze, Texas, to Major Robert Hurns, Houston, Teas, February 13, 189, Folder: Hood's Division—Hood's Brigade, Col. W. T. Wofford, Box: Carman Confederate Hood's Division, Longstreet's Reserve Artillery, Evan's Independent Brigade, Antietam National Battlefield, Sharpsburg, Md.; *O.R.*, ser. I, vol. 19, pt. I, p. 923.

53. Carman, *The Maryland Campaign of September 1862*, vol. 2: *Antietam*, 88; Harsh, *Taken at the Flood*, 332, 362; Harsh, *Sounding the Shallows*, 193–94.

54. W. E. Barry, Navasota, Texas, to Major J. M. Gould, Portland, Maine, March 12, 1891, Folder: Hood's Division—Hood's Brigade, Colonel W. T. Wofford, Box: Carman, Confederate, Hood's Div., Longstreet's Reserve Arty., Evans Indp. Brig., Antietam National Battlefield, Sharpsburg, Md.; J. M. Polk, *The Confederate Soldier and Ten Years in South America* (Austin, Tex.: Von Boeckmann-Jones, 1910), 18; Holsworth, "Uncommon Valor," 16–17; Carman, *The Maryland Campaign of 1862*, vol. 2: *Antietam*, 88.

55. Hood, *Advance and Retreat*, 43; Holsworth, "Uncommon Valor," 17.

56. J. M. Polk, *The Confederate Soldier*, 18.

57. Carman, *The Maryland Campaign of 1862*, vol. 2: *Antietam*, 89; see also W. T. Hill

to J. M. Gould, July 21, 1891, Antietam Collection, John J. Gould, Dartmouth College Library, Hanover, N.H.

58. Carman, *The Maryland Campaign of 1862*, vol. 2: *Antietam*, 89; see also W. T. Hill to J. M. Gould, July 21, 1891, Antietam Collection, John J. Gould, Dartmouth College Library, Hanover, N.H.; and *O.R.*, ser. I, vol. 19, pt. I, p. 924.

59. *O.R.*, ser. I, vol. 19, pt. I, p. 931.

60. Simpson, *Compendium*, 243; Holsworth, "Uncommon Valor," 16–18; Polley, *Hood's Texas Brigade*, 123. Polley described Turner as being "as laconic in his [official] report [following the battle of Antietam] as he was brave in action."

61. Holsworth, "Uncommon Valor," 20; Hood, *Advance and Retreat*, 43.

62. D. Scott Hartwig, "'I Dread the Thought of the Place': The Iron Brigade at Antietam," in *Giants in Their Tall Black Hats: Essays on the Iron Brigade*, ed. Alan T. Nolan and Sharon Eggleston Vipond (Bloomington: Indiana University Press, 1998), 44.

63. Lemon, *Feed Them the Steel!*, 34.

64. Holsworth, "Uncommon Valor," 20.

65. Haywood Brahan, Sugar Land, Texas, to John M. Gould, January 25, 1891, Antietam Collection, John J. Gould, Dartmouth College Library, Hanover, N.H.

66. Lemon, *Feed Them the Steel!*, 34–35.

67. John Gibbon, *Personal Reflections of the Civil War* (New York: Putnam's Sons, 1928), 83–84; Holsworth, "Uncommon Valor," 52; Nolan, *The Iron Brigade*, 141; Lance J. Herdegen, *The Men Stood Like Iron: How the Iron Brigade Won Its Name* (Bloomington: Indiana University Press, 1997), 177.

68. *O.R.*, ser. I, vol. 19, pt. I, pp. 930–31; Holsworth, "Uncommon Valor," 50.

69. Carman, *The Maryland Campaign of 1862*, vol. 2: *Antietam*, 102.

70. William B. Wall, Crockett, Texas, to J. M. Gould, May 28, 1894, Antietam Collection, John J. Gould, Dartmouth College Library, Hanover, N.H.; W. A. Bedell, Bright Helmston, Maryland, to "Dear Mother," October 29, 1862, published in the *Galveston Tri-Weekly News*, February 9, 1863.

71. *O.R.*, ser. I, vol. 19, pt. I, pp. 932–34.

72. Ibid., pp. 931–34; P. A. Work, "The 1st Texas Regiment of the Texas Brigade of the Army of Northern Virginia at the Battles of Boonsboro Pass or Gap and Sharpsburg or Antietam, MD in September 1862," typed 1907 manuscript, Phillip A. Work Papers, Hood's Texas Brigade Collection, Historical Research Center, Hill College, Hillsboro, Tex. Hereafter cited as P. A. Work Papers.

73. P. A. Work, "The 1st Texas Regiment of the Texas Brigade of the Army of Northern Virginia at the Battles of Boonsboro Pass or Gap and Sharpsburg or Antietam, Md. in September 1862," P. A. Work Papers. See also P. A. Work, Kountze, Texas, to Major Robert Burns, Houston, Texas, February 13, 1891, Folder: Hood's Division—Hood's Brigade, Colonel W. T. Wofford, Box: Carman, Confederate, Hood's Div., Longstreet's Reserve Arty., Evans Indp. Brig., Antietam National Battlefield, Sharpsburg, Md.

74. John Hanson, James Day, Charles H. Kingsley, and James K. Malone, Compiled Service Records, 1st Texas Infantry, Fold3.com.

75. William Barry, Navasota, Texas, to John M. Gould, March 12, 1891, Antietam Collection, John J. Gould, Dartmouth College Library, Hanover, N.H.; Holsworth, "Uncommon Valor," 53; Robert Gaston, Richmond, Virginia, to Pa and Ma, Tyler, Texas, July 21, 1861; Glover, "*Tyler to Sharpsburg*," 5.

76. *O.R.*, ser. I, vol. 19, pt. I, p. 933.

77. P. A. Work, "The 1st Texas Regiment of the Texas Brigade of the Army of Northern Virginia at the Battles of Boonsboro Pass or Gap and Sharpsburg or Antietam, Md. in September 1862," P. A. Work Papers. See also P. A. Work, Kountze, Texas to Major Robert Burns, Houston, Texas, February 13, 1891, Folder: Hood's Division—Hood's Brigade, Colonel W. T. Wofford, Box: Carman, Confederate, Hood's Div., Longstreet's Reserve Arty., Evans Indp. Brig., Antietam Military Park, Sharpsburg, Md.; and Carman, *The Maryland Campaign of September 1862*, vol. 2: *Antietam*, 109.

78. *O.R.*, ser. 1, vol. 19, pt. I, pp. 1043–44.

79. John Marquis Smither, Huntsville, Texas, to Major J. M. Gould, March 24, 1891, Antietam Collection, John J. Gould, Dartmouth College Library, Hanover, N.H.

80. *O.R.*, ser. 1, vol. 19, pt. I, pp. 936–37.

81. P. A. Work, Kountze, Texas to Major Robert Burns, Houston, Texas, February 13, 1891, Folder: Hood's Division—Hood's Brigade, Colonel W. T. Wofford, Box: Carman, Confederate, Hood's Div., Longstreet's Reserve Arty., Evans Indp. Brig., Antietam Military Park, Sharpsburg, Md. In this letter, Work explains that about 15 of the men he detailed to roast corn on the night of September 16 did not rejoin the unit before it went into battle on September 17. Therefore, the First Texas went in with about 15 fewer men than what appeared in his official report, thus the total number of 211 with losses of 182 (per his original report and restated in postwar accounts), or 86.25 percent casualties. Polly, *Hood's Texas Brigade*, 134; Carman, *The Maryland Campaign of 1862*, vol. 2: *Antietam*, 102–3; Holsworth, "Uncommon Valor," 54.

82. Cecelia Morse, *Civil War Diary of Cecelia Morse*, September 8–October 12, 1862.

83. Patrick Penn, Winchester, Virginia, to "My Dear Sister" [Mary Elizabeth Penn Menefee, Oso, Texas], September 25, 1862, in McAnelly, "Penn Letters, 1860–1865," *Louisiana Genealogical Register* (March 1972): 109.

84. Patrick Penn, Camp of the 4th Texas Regiment, to "My Dear Sister" [Mary Elizabeth Penn Menefee, Oso, Texas], June 24, 1862, in McAnelly, "Penn Letters, 1860–1865," *Louisiana Genealogical Register* (December 1941): 340.

85. Robert A. Sullivan, Camp of Texas Brigade, Virginia, to Mrs. Lizzie Menefee, Oso, Texas, May 19, 1862, in McAnelly, "Penn Letters, 1860–1865," *Louisiana Genealogical Register* (December 1971): 340.

86. Quin M. Menefee, Camp 2 miles from Richmond, Virginia, to "Dear Lizzie" [Mary Elizabeth Penn Menefee], Oso, Texas, August 4, 1862, in McAnelly, "Penn Letters," *Louisiana Genealogical Register* (December 1971): 341–42.

87. Quin M. Menefee, Camp 2 miles from Richmond, Virginia, to "My Dear Willie" [William Penn Menefee], Oso, Texas, August 7, 1862, in McAnelly, "Penn Letters," *Louisiana Genealogical Register* (March 1972): 108.

88. 1850 U.S. Federal Census, Russell, Alabama; Roll: M432_14; Page: 70B; Image: 402; 1860 U.S. Federal Census, Gonzales, Texas; Roll: M653_1295; Page: 100; Image: 203; Family History Library Film: 805295.

89. 1860 U.S. Federal Census—Slave Schedules, Ancestry.com (database online), Alex Kindred, Gonzales, Texas; original data: United States of America, Bureau of the Census, Eighth Census of the United States, 1860 (Washington, D.C.: National Archives and Records Administration, 1860), M653, 1,438 rolls.

90. Simpson, *Compendium*, 131–34.

91. Alexander M. Erskine, Shepherdstown, Virginia, to Ann T. Erskine, Home Mill Point, Seguin, Texas, September 18, 1862, Erskine Collection.

92. W. H. Gaston, Fredericksburg, Virginia, to Pa [Col. R. K. Gaston], Tyler, Texas, November 28, 1862; Glover, *"Tyler to Sharpsburg,"* 21.

93. Henry Travis, Richmond, Virginia, to "Dear Sister" [Mary Quigley], September 25, 1862, Henry Travis Letter, Hood's Texas Brigade Collection, Historical Research Center, Hill College, Hillsboro, Tex.

94. R. E. Lee, Genl., Head Quarters, Army Northern Virginia near Martinsburg [Virginia], to Genl. Louis T. Wigfall, September 21, 1862, Irenus Watson Landingham Collection, RG 552, Auburn University Special Collections & Archives Department, Auburn, Ala.

95. Louis T. Wigfall, Richmond [Virginia] to "Dear Genl" [Robert E. Lee], September 26, 1862, Irenus Watson Landingham Collection, RG 552, Auburn University Special Collections & Archives Department, Auburn, Ala.

96. Simpson, *Compendium,* 535.

97. William P. Townsend, Camp near Richmond [Virginia], to "Dearest" [wife], August 7, 1862, Townsend Letters.

98. William P. Townsend, Warrenton, Virginia, to "My Dear Wife," October 10, 1862, Townsend Letters.

99. Hugh Perkins, Camp on the Battlefield, Maryland, to "My Friend" [Herbert E. Frisbie], September 21, 1862, Hugh Perkins Letters, private collection of D. Scott Hartwig, shared by descendant, also named Hugh Perkins, in 1980. Hereafter cited as Hugh Perkins Letters. Special thanks to Scott Hartwig for sharing transcriptions of the letters.

100. Ibid. See also 1860 U.S. Federal Census, Leon, Waushara, Wisconsin; Roll: M653_1435; Page: 837; Image: 87; Family History Library Film: 805435.

101. Hugh Perkins, Camp on the Battlefield, Maryland, to "My Friend" [Herbert E. Frisbie], September 21, 1862, Hugh Perkins Letters.

102. Hugh Perkins, Camp on the battle of Antietam, to "Dear Friend Herbert" [E. Frisbie], September 26, 1862, Hugh Perkins Letters.

103. Hugh Perkins, Camp on the Battlefield, Maryland, to "My Friend" [Herbert E. Frisbie], September 21, 1862, Hugh Perkins Letters.

104. Hugh Perkins, Camp on the Battle of Antietam, to "Dear Friend Herbert" [E. Frisbie], September 26, 1862, Hugh Perkins Letters.

105. Ibid.

106. W. A. Bedell, Bright Helmston, Maryland, to "Dear Mother," October 29, 1862, published in the *Galveston Tri-Weekly News,* February 9, 1863; Simpson, *Compendium,* 78; confirmed, William A. Bedell, Compiled Service Record, 1st Texas, Fold3.com.

CHAPTER SEVEN

1. *O.R.,* ser. I, vol. 19, pt. I, p. 936.
2. Ibid., p. 929.
3. Ibid., p. 923.
4. Ibid., p. 934.

5. D. K. Rice, Martinsburg, to "Dear Uncle" [William M. Rice], September 21, 1862, given to the *Houston Tri-Weekly Telegraph* by William Rice for publication; it appeared on October 15, 1862.

6. Polley, *Hood's Texas Brigade*, 239.

7. D. K. Rice, Martinsburg, to "Dear Uncle" [William M. Rice], September 21, 1862, given to the Houston *Tri-Weekly Telegraph* by William Rice for publication; it appeared on the October 15, 1862.

8. Cutrer, *Longstreet's Aide*, 99.

9. Numerous accounts describe the men's condition. See Col. M. W. Gary and Lt. Col. B. F. Carter's reports in *O.R.*, ser. I, vol. 19, pt. I, pp. 931, 936. See also Polley, *Hood's Texas Brigade*, 136; and Selman Diary, October 5–8, 1862, Selman Papers.

10. Selman Diary, October 21, 1862, Selman Papers.

11. For a discussion of these supply problems and Confederate attempts to address them, see Keith S. Bohannon, "Dirty, Ragged, and Ill-Provided For: Confederate Logistical Problems in the 1862 Maryland Campaign and Their Solutions," in *The Antietam Campaign*, ed. Gary W. Gallagher (Chapel Hill: University of North Carolina Press, 1999), 121, 126–27.

12. Selman Diary, November 15, 1862, Selman Papers.

13. *O.R.*, ser. I, vol. 19, pt. II, pp. 718–19; see also Simpson, *Lee's Grenadier Guard*, 189–90. The only unit to receive strong praise from Harvie was James Reilly's battery, which was often used in support of the brigade.

14. Selman Diary, October 20–21, 1862, Selman Papers.

15. Cutrer, *Longstreet's Aide*, 100.

16. Rufus King Felder, Camp near Winchester, to "Dear Sister" [Emma Felder Adaline], October 1, 1862, Rufus King Felder Letters.

17. Waters Berryman, Camp near Fredericksburg, Virginia, to "My Dear Ma," December 21, 1862, Waters Berryman Letters, Hood's Texas Brigade Collection, Historical Research Center, Hill College, Hillsboro, Tex. Hereafter cited as Waters Berryman Letters. Berryman was most likely referring to Captain Doty and Lieutenant Wolfe when he told his mother to "Tell them I have killed more Yankees here in a week than they will kill during the war where they are." He most likely meant Capt. O. S. Doty and 3rd Lt. S. G. Wolfe of the Twenty-First Texas Cavalry, originally known as the First Texas Lancers. They enlisted in this unit in Alto, Cherokee County, Texas, where both men lived near the Berryman family (Texas, Muster Roll Index Cards, 1838–1900, Ancestry.com [database online] [Ancestry.com Operations, Inc., 2011]).

18. Selman Diary, November 26, 1862, Selman Papers.

19. Polley, *Hood's Texas Brigade*, 142. Hood's Texans became famous during the war for their scavenging of food and uniforms from Federal soldiers and civilians and, on occasion, from fellow Confederates. One of the most colorful of these accounts appears ibid., 148.

20. Selman Diary, December 2–6, 1862, Selman Papers.

21. Polley, *Hood's Texas Brigade*, 205.

22. Polley, *A Soldier's Letters to Charming Nellie*, 66.

23. Davis's plea appeared in the *Richmond Whig*, November 5, 1862, and the *Richmond Enquirer*, November 29, 1862. Everett, *Chaplain Davis and Hood's Texas Brigade*, 177–79.

24. Everett, *Chaplain Davis and Hood's Texas Brigade*, 179.

25. Nemo, "Theatricals in Camp," in *The Civil War Reader*, ed. Richard B. Harwell (New York: Smithmark, 1994), 272–75; Martha Hartzog, "Mollie Bailey: Circus Entrepreneur," in *Legendary Ladies of Texas*, ed. Francis Edward Abernathy, Publications of the Texas Folklore Society, no.

43 (Denton: University of North Texas Press, 994), 107–14; Simpson, *Hood's Texas Brigade,* 450.

26. *Richmond Whig,* December 29, 1862; Winkler, *The Confederate Capital and Hood's Texas Brigade,* 87–88; Everett, *Chaplain Davis and Hood's Texas Brigade,* 87–88; Simpson, *Hood's Texas Brigade,* 131. The *Whig,* Davis, and Simpson all indicate that Texas Hospital opened in Richmond in the summer of 1862. It appears, however, that Chaplain Davis's diligent efforts, supported by Varina Davis, the YMCA, and others, actually led to construction, as Davis himself explains, of a "ward at the infirmary St. Francis De Sales." Texas Hospital did not officially open as a Texas-focused facility with three hundred beds until December 1862. See references to Texas hospital as a new facility in the *Richmond Whig,* December 29, 1862, and the *Houston Tri-Weekly Telegraph,* March 23, 1863. Special thanks to Michael Gorman (civilwarrichmond.com) and Robert E. L. Krick for their assistance with the riddle of the origins of Texas Hospital and data on the care Texas Brigade soldiers received in Richmond.

27. John Marquis Smither, Camp "Defiance," near Fredericksburg, Virginia, to "Dear Mother," December 28, 1862, Smither Papers.

28. Watson Dugat Williams, Texas Depot, Richmond, Virginia, to "My Own Laura" [Bryan], January 22, 1863, Watson Dugat Williams Letters.

29. Watson Dugat Williams, Camp near Fredericksburg, Virginia, to "My Dear Laura" [Bryan], January 26, 1863, Watson Dugat Williams Letters.

30. Ibid.

31. For some of the best examples of this, see the letters of J. R. and Felicia Loughridge, Waters Berryman, and Watson Dugat Williams.

32. H. W. Berryman, 1st Texas near Richmond, Virginia, to "My Dear Ma" [Helena Dill Waterman], February 25, 1863, Waters Berryman Letters.

33. Watson Dugat Williams, Knoxville, Tennessee, to "My Dear Laura" [Bryan], January 18, 1863, Watson Dugat Williams Letters.

34. Watson Dugat Williams, Camp near Richmond, to "My Own Dear Laura" [Bryan], February 23, 1863, Watson Dugat Williams Letters.

35. *O.R.,* ser. I, vol. 18, pp. 325–26, 942; Simpson, *Lee's Grenadier Guard,* 224.

36. Samuel H. Emerson, *History of the War of the Confederacy, '61 to '65* (Malvern, Ark.: privately printed, 1918), 39; H. W. Berryman, near Suffolk, Virginia, to "My Own Dear Mother" [Helena Dill Waterman], April 18, 1863, Waters Berryman Letters.

37. John Marquis Smither, Camp near Frederick Hall, Virginia, to "Dear Mother," May 12, 1863, Smither Papers.

38. *Countryman* (Turnwold, Ga.), April 28, 1863.

39. Stevens, *Reminiscences of the Civil War* (Hillsboro, Tex.: Hillsboro Mirror Print, 1902), 99.

40. Watson Dugat Williams, In front of Suffolk, Virginia, to "My Dear Lollie" [Laura Bryan], May 2, 1863, Watson Dugat Williams Letters.

41. Stevens, *Reminiscences,* 99.

42. John Marquis Smither, Camp near Frederick Hall, Virginia, to "Dear Mother," May 12, 1863, Smither Papers.

43. *O.R.,* ser. I, vol. 18, p. 1032.

44. Simpson, *Lee's Grenadier Guard,* 234.

45. Watson Dugat Williams, Camp on the Rapidan River near Sommerville's Ford, to "My Own Dear Laura" [Bryan], May 30, 1863, Watson Dugat Williams Letters.

46. Ibid.

47. John Marquis Smither, Camp near Frederick Hall, Virginia, to "Dear Mother," May 12, 1863, Smither Papers.

48. 1860 U.S. Federal Census, Huntsville, Walker, Texas; Roll: M653_1307; Page: 95; Image: 197; Family History Library Film: 805307. Erasmus Wynn listed nearly $80,000 in combined wealth in 1860, and Elizabeth Smither Wynne claimed nearly $70,000 in her own combined wealth.

49. John Marquis Smither, In Camp near Rapidan River, Virginia, to "Dear Mother," May 30, 1863, Smither Papers. Wisely suspicious historians might suspect that Smither adopted an optimistic tone when writing to his mother that was not a true measurement of his mood. The flaw in this theory, however, is revealed by his equally optimistic letters to his uncle and other male friends throughout the war.

50. Simpson, *Lee's Grenadier Guard*, 244–49.

51. Giles, *Rags and Hope*, 176.

52. Ibid., 176–77.

53. J. R. Loughridge, Headquarters 4th Texas Regiment, Culpeper Courthouse, Virginia, to Mrs. Mary F. Loughridge, June 16, 1863, Loughridge Collection.

54. Stephen W. Sears, *Gettysburg* (New York: Houghton Mifflin, 2003), 107.

55. John Marquis Smither, Camp near Chambersburg, Pennsylvania, to "Dear Mother," June 28, 1863, Mark Smither Letters.

56. James H. Hendrick, Chambersburg, Pennsylvania, June 28, 1863, signed "your son," James H. Hendrick Papers, Texas Heritage Museum, Hill College, Hillsboro.

57. Coddington, *The Gettysburg Campaign*, 369–70. See also Adelman and Smith, *The Battle for Devil's Den*, 17.

58. Albert Cuthburt "Cubb" Sims, Company F, 1st Texas, in *Jasper (Tex.) News-Boy*, May 17, 1911, copy in A. C. Sims Diary, "Texas First Infantry Regiment" Folder, Box 9 of 21: North Carolina–Texas, Confederate Units/Confederate Officers, "The Gettysburg Campaign," Robert L. Brake Collection, U.S. Army Heritage and Education Center, Carlisle, Pa. Hereafter cited as Brake Collection.

59. Coddington, *The Gettysburg Campaign*, 374–75; Harry W. Pfanz, *Gettysburg: The Second Day* (Chapel Hill: University of North Carolina Press, 1987), 106–7; Thomas J. Ryan, "The Intelligence Battle, July 2: Longstreet's Assault," *Gettysburg: Historical Articles of Lasting Interest* 43 (July 2010): 75–88).

60. Pfanz, *Gettysburg*, 119–23.

61. Thomas L. McCarty, "Battle of Gettysburg, July 1st– 2nd & 3d 1863," Public Address, Folder: Texas 1st Inf Reg, "The Gettysburg Campaign," Confederate Units, Confederate Officers, North Carolina–Texas, Box 9 of 21, Brake Collection. Hereafter cited as McCarty Address.

62. Thomas A. Courtney, "Mount St. Mary's and the American Civil War," *Analecta: Selected Studies in the History of Mount St. Mary's College and Seminary* 1 (2004): 11–12.

63. Emerson, *History of the War of the Confederacy*, 42; Calvin L. Collier, *"They'll Do to Tie To!": The Story of the Third Regiment, Arkansas Infantry, C.S.A.* (Jacksonville, Ark.: privately published, 1959), 139.

64. Polley, *Hood's Texas Brigade*, 176.

65. John C. West, *A Texan in Search of a Fight* (Waco: Hill, 1901; repr., Waco: Texian Press, 1969); Vivian Elizabeth Smyrl, "West, John Camden, Jr.," *Handbook of Texas Online*, www.tshaonline.org/handbook/online/articles/fwe50.

66. Qtd. in Pfanz, *Gettysburg,* 163.

67. Manning Official Report, *O.R.,* ser. I, vol. 27, pt. II, pp. 407–8. For an overview of the Third Arkansas's fight at Gettysburg, see Mauriel P. Joslyn, "'For Ninety Years or the War': The Story of the 3rd Arkansas at Gettysburg," *Gettysburg Magazine: Historical Articles of Lasting Interest* 14 (January 1996): 52–63.

68. *O.R.,* ser. 1, vol. 27, pt. II, pp. 404, 407.

69. Robertson to Bachelder, Bachelder Papers, 1:477.

70. *O.R.,* ser. 1, vol. 27, pt. II, p. 404.

71. Adelman and Smith, *The Battle for Devil's Den,* 28; *O.R.,* ser. 1, vol. 27, pt. II, p. 393. Law never explained why he did this, but Col. William F. Perry (Forty-Fourth Alabama) mentions it in his report.

72. Adelman and Smith, *The Battle for Devil's Den,* 28–29.

73. Ibid., 26–28; Hood, *Advance and Retreat,* 59; Pfanz, *Gettysburg,* 172–73.

74. H. W. Berryman, Hagerstown, Maryland, to "My Dear Mother, Sister and Family," July 9, 1863, Waters Berryman Letters.

75. A. C. Sims, "Recollections of the Civil War," 11.

76. John A. Wilkerson, "Experiences of 'Seven Pines' at Gettysburg, Diary of John A. Wilkerson, Co. H, 3rd Arkansas Infantry, Hood's Brigade, Longstreet's Corps, Army of Northern Virginia, unpublished transcribed manuscript. 7-Ar3, 3rd Arkansas Infantry Regiment Folder, Gettysburg National Military Park.

77. Frank Whittemore, near Gettysburg, Pennsylvania, to "Dear Parents," July 5, 1863, Franklin Whittemore, Civil War Miscellaneous Collection (Sgt. letter re: action of regt. June 3– July 5, 1863), U.S. Army Heritage & Education Center, Carlisle, Pa.

78. Adelman and Smith, *The Battle for Devil's Den,* 29.

79. *O.R.,* ser. 1, vol. 27, pt. II, p. 410.

80. Ibid.

81. For detailed analysis of the 124th New York's defense at Devil's Den, see Charles R. Bowery Jr., "Encounter at the Triangular Field: The 124th New York and the 1st Texas at Gettysburg, July 2, 1863," *Gettysburg: Historical Articles of Lasting Interest* 30 (2004): 49–62.

82. Carol Reardon and Tom Vossler, *A Field Guide to Gettysburg: Experiencing the Battlefield through Its History, Places, and People* (Chapel Hill: University of North Carolina Press, 2013), 222–23.

83. Sims, "Recollections of the Civil War," 12.

84. Zach Landrum, Winchester, Virginia, to "Dear Mother," July 15, 1863, Landrum Letters.

85. Giles, *Rags and Hope,* 181–82.

86. Landrum Letters, July 15, 1863.

87. John Marquis Smither, Camp 5th Texas, Culpeper Court House, Virginia, to "Dear Mother," July 29, 1863, John Marquis Smither Letters.

88. Giles, *Rags and Hope,* 181–82.

89. Jeremiah D. Caddell, Richmond, Virginia, to Andrew Caddell, July 23, 1863, J. D. Caddell Letters, Hood's Texas Brigade Collection, Historical Research Center, Hill College, Hillsboro, Tex.

90. Charles H. Salter, Bivouac 16 Michigan Regiment, to Isabella Duffield, July 12, 1863, 8pm, Salter, Charles H. 1st Lt. Co. B, 16th Michigan, Gettysburg, Michigan–New Jersey, Box 12 of 21, Brake Collection.

91. Ziba B. Graham, "On to Gettysburg: Ten Days from My Diary of 1863," paper read before

the Commandery of the State of Michigan, Military Order of the Loyal Legion of the U.S. (Detroit, Mich.: Winn & Hammond, Printers and Binders, 1893), 10.

92. William H. Brown, Company D, 44th New York at Gettysburg, New York–Ohio, Box 13 of 21, Brake Collection; original letter in William H. Brown Papers, 1861–1865, Brown University Library.

93. Transcription, "From the 140th—The Battle of Gettysburg," *Rochester (N.Y.) Evening Express,* July 8, 1863. File 6-NY140—140th New York Infantry Regiment, Gettysburg National Military Park; Account of Charles N. Smith, *New York Times,* July 3, 1913, New York–Ohio, Box 13 of 21, Brake Collection; Account of Civil War experiences of William H. Clarke, April 24, 1924, Greece, New York, File 6-NY140–140th New York Infantry Regiment, Gettysburg National Military Park.

94. Giles, *Rags and Hope,* 181, 183.

95. *O.R.,* ser. 1, vol. 27, pt. II, p. 409.

96. Sims, "Recollections," 12–13.

97. Harold A. Klingensmith, "A Cavalry Regiment's First Campaign: The 18th Pennsylvania at Gettysburg," *Gettysburg: Historical Articles of Lasting Interest* 20 (1998): 65; McCarty Address.

98. McCarty Address.

99. James H. Hendricks, Camp near Haggerstown, Maryland, to "Dear Mother," July 8, 1863, James Hendricks Letters.

100. Waters Berryman, Hagerstown, Maryland, to "My Dear Mother, Sister, and Family," July 9, 1863; Waters Berryman, Burkley County, Virginia, between Winchester and Martinsburg, to "Dear Ma, Sister, and family," July 19, 1863; Waters Berryman, Camp near Fredericksburg, Va., to "My Dear Friend, Mr. C. H. Roark," August 16, 1863, Waters Berryman Letters. Berryman insisted that the Federal cavalrymen were drunk and that he saw Farnsworth kill himself, but this claim remains unresolved by historians. For an analysis of the charges of Farnsworth's suicide among the men at the charge, see Eric Wittenberg, "The Great Controversy: Did Elon Farnsworth Shoot Himself?," *Gettysburg's Forgotten Cavalry Actions* (Eldorado Hills, Calif.: Savas Beatie, 2011), 78–91. For an analysis of the charge itself, see Wittenberg, "Farnsworth Charge," in *Gettysburg's Forgotten Cavalry Actions* (Eldorado Hills, Calif.: Savas Beatie, 2011), 39–77; see also Paul M. Shevchuk, "The 1st Texas Infantry and the Repulse of Farnsworth's Charge," *Gettysburg Magazine: Historical Articles of Lasting Interest* 2 (January 1990): 81–90; Steven A. Cunningham and Beth A. White, "'The Ground Trembled as They Came': The 1st West Virginia Cavalry in the Gettysburg Campaign," *Civil War Regiments: A Journal of the American Civil War* 6, no. 3 (1999): 59–88; Sgt. Horace K. Ide, "The First Vermont Cavalry in the Gettysburg Campaign," ed. Dr. Elliot W. Hoffman, *The Gettysburg Magazine: Historical Articles of Lasting Interest* 14 (January 1996): 7–26; Harold A. Klingensmith, "A Cavalry Regiment's First Campaign: The 18th Pennsylvania at Gettysburg," *Gettysburg: Historical Articles of Lasting Interest* 20 (1998): 61–69; Andie Custer, "The Kilpatrick-Farnsworth Argument That Never Happened," *Gettysburg Magazine: Historical Articles of Lasting Interest* 28 (2003): 100–116; Andie Custer, "John Hammond's 'Mis-stake': How a Misplaced Wooden Stake Altered the History of the Farnsworth Charge at Gettysburg," *Gettysburg Magazine: Historical Articles of Lasting Interest* 30 (2004): 98–113. Special thanks to the following for assistance with answering questions, providing sources, editing writing, and/or hiking the July 2 and 3 Texas Brigade positions with me: Carol Reardon, D. Scott Hartwig, Rick Eiserman, Jeffery S. Prushankin, Mark Snell, Beth White, Andie Custer, Charles Bowery, and David Ward.

101. For an overview of the Texas Brigade's fight at Gettysburg and an argument that the key to turning the battle was Longstreet's attack on July 2, not the famous Pickett-Pittigrew-Trimble charge of July 3, see Daniel M. Laney, "Wasted Gallantry: Hood's Texas Brigade at Gettysburg," *Gettysburg Magazine: Historical Articles of Lasting Interest* 16 (1997): 27–45.

102. James Rodgers Loughridge, Camp 4th Texas, to "Dearest Love" [Mary Felicia Loughridge], July 26, 1863, Loughridge Collection.

103. Waters Berryman, Burkley County, Virginia, between Winchester and Martinsburg, to "Dear Ma, Sister, and family," July 19, 1863, Waters Berryman Letters.

104. James Rodgers Loughridge, Camp 4th Texas, to "Dearest Love" [Mary Felicia Loughridge], July 26, 1863, Loughridge Collection.

105. West, "A Texan in Search of a Fight," 101.

106. Louise Wigfall Wright, *A Southern Girl in '61: The War-time Memories of a Confederate Senator's Daughter, 1861–1865* (Gansevoort, N.Y.: Corner House Historical Publications, 2000), 141.

107. *Houston Tri-Weekly Telegraph,* August 19, 1863.

108. Zach Landrum, Richmond, Virginia, to "Dear Mother," August 4, 1863, Landrum Letters.

109. Eric J. Wittenberg, J. Davis Petruzzi, and Michael Nugent, *One Continuous Fight: The Retreat from Gettysburg and the Pursuit of Lee's Army of Northern Virginia, July 4–14, 1863* (Eldorado Hills, Calif.: Savas Beatie, 2011), 14.

110. Wittenberg, Petruzzi, and Nugent, *One Continuous Fight,* 14–15; Gregory A. Coco, *A Strange and Blighted Land: Gettysburg: After the Battle* (Gettysburg, Pa.: Thomas, 1995), 268.

111. "Memories of the Gettysburg Campaign by John Lewis Tarkington and recorded by the Reverend D. W. Jackson," year unknown. Jerry Carl Beetz of Pearland, Texas, shared the transcription with me. My thanks to Mr. Beetz for sharing this and displaying the bone fragment from Tarkington's leg wound that was preserved by his daughter Mary Elizabeth Tarkington (Mamie Young) that she gave to her grandson, Mr. Beetz. Tarkington did surrender with the Fifth Texas at Appomattox, as he stated (see Polley, *Hood's Texas Brigade,* 342).

112. Letter of J. R. Loughridge, near Fredericksburg, Virginia, to Mary Felicia Loughridge, August 7, 1863, published in *Navarro (Tex.) Express,* October 1, 1863, Loughridge Collection.

113. John Marquis Smither, Camp 5th Texas, Culpeper Court House, Virginia, to "Dear Mother," July 29, 1863, John Marquis Smither Letters; "Memoirs of Campbell Wood, lieutenant and adjutant, Hood's Texas Brigade, CSA," 1908, typescript shared with Bell I. Wiley, Emory University, 7-TX5–5th Texas Infantry Regiment, Gettysburg National Military Park.

CHAPTER EIGHT

1. Longstreet, *From Manassas to Appomattox,* 434–36.

2. Robert Campbell [writing under the pseudonym Joe Joskins], "A Sketch of Hood's Texas Brigade," 133–34; unpublished manuscript, written at Huntsville, Texas, 1865, University of Texas, San Antonio Library, R. H. Porter Civil War Collection, digitized version: http://digital.utsa.edu/cdm/ref/collection/p15125c01110/id/8440. On November 15, 2013, in Huntsville, Texas, Lt. Col. Rick Eiserman (U.S. Army, ret. and Hood's Texas Brigade Association Reactivated [HTBAR] historian) presented his findings at the annual meeting of HTBAR that proved conclusively that the manuscript that has been known only as "A Sketch of Hood's Texas Brigade" by "Joe Joskins" was

actually written by Fifth Texas private and later Texas Brigade courier Robert Campbell of Huntsville, Texas (see Eiserman's brief presentation at the HTBAR annual meeting in October 2010 as well as final report on this project, "Will the Real Pvt. Joe Joskins, 5th TX, Please Step Forward?," unpublished manuscript, HTBAR annual meeting in November 2013).

3. *Wilmington (N.C.) Journal*, September 17, 1863.

4. Polley, *Hood's Texas Brigade*, 199. In 1918, W. H. Jenkins testified in Georgie S. Brietz's pension application, as the widow of Judge A. C. Brietz, that Jenkins served in the Eighth Texas Cavalry and that he saw Brietz at the Battle of Chickamauga (no. 35090, Mrs. Georgie S. Bietz, Confederate pension applications, Texas Comptroller's Office claims records. Archives and Information Services Division, Texas State Library and Archives Commission, Austin). For an account of the brief visit between men of the First Texas Infantry and the Seventh Texas Infantry, see William Thomas Ford, before Chattanooga, Tennessee, to "Dear Wife" [Dorcas M. Ford], October 12, 1863, Civil War Collection, Jefferson Historical Museum, Jefferson, Tex. Special thanks for Mr. Weldon Nash Jr. for sharing this with me.

5. In his resignation letter, Work claims to be suffering from syphilis. Considering that his father was a regimental surgeon, it is possible that this was an accurate diagnosis, but there were no blood tests at the time (see Phillip A. Work, Selma, Alabama, to J. A. Seddon, Secretary of War, November 12, 1863, in Phillip A. Work, Compiled Service Record, 1st Texas Infantry, Fold3.com). J. B. Robertson erroneously listed D. K. Rice as the commander of the First Texas at Chickamauga. R. J. Harding corrected this with the Hood's Texas Brigade Association in the postwar period (see Simpson, *Lee's Grenadier Guard*, 321n75; and *Dallas [Tex.] Morning News*, October 14, 1915). For a discussion of Work's frustrations regarding Rainey and command of the First Texas, see H. A. Hooks, M.D., *Lt. Col. Phillip A. Work: General Without a Star* (Waco, Tex.: Texian Press, 2003).

6. Richard J. Harding, Compiled Service Record, 1st Texas Infantry, Fold3.com.

7. David A. Powell, *The Chickamauga Campaign: A Mad Irregular Battle: From the Crossing of the Tennessee River through the Second Day, August 22–September 19, 1863* (Eldorado Hills, Calif.: Savas Beatie, 2014), 453.

8. Ibid., 440–41.

9. Ibid., 453; David A. Powell, *The Maps of Chickamauga: An Atlas of the Chickamauga Campaign, Including the Tullahoma Operations, June 22–September 23, 1863* (El Dorado Hills, Calif.: Savas Beatie, 2015), 98.

10. B. I. Franklin, near Chattanooga, Tenn. to "Dear Mary," October 2, 1863, Benjamin I. Franklin Papers, 1863–1968, Pearce Civil War Collection, Pearce Museum, Navarro College, Corsicana, Tex. Hereafter cited as Benjamin I. Franklin Papers.

11. *O.R.*, ser. I, vol. 30, pt. II, pp. 510–16.

12. "Account of P. L. Hubbard, 8th Indiana Light Battery, Cloverdale, Indiana," Viniard Family Folder, Chickamauga/Chattanooga National Military Park, Fort Oglethorpe, Ga.

13. *O.R.*, ser. I, vol. 30, pt. II, p. 511.

14. David A. Powell, *The Chickamauga Campaign: Glory or the Grave: The Breakthrough, the Union Collapse, and the Defense of Horseshoe Ridge, September 20, 1863* (Eldorado Hills, Calif.: Savas Beatie, 2015), 44–46.

15. Ibid., 356–60; Powell, *The Maps of Chickamauga*, 198.

16. Giles, *Rags and Hope*, 203.

17. Powell, *The Chickamauga Campaign: Glory or the Grave*, 362–63; Powell, *The Maps of Chickamauga*, 200.

18. Hood, *Advance and Retreat*, 64.

19. Polley, *A Soldier's Letters to Charming Nellie*, 96–97.

20. Waters Berryman, Bivouac near Chattanooga, Tennessee, to "My Dear Ma," October 12, 1863, Waters Berryman Letters.

21. Watson Dugat Williams, Camp near Chattanooga, to "My Dear Laura," October 2, 1863, Watson Dugat Williams Letters.

22. Waters Berryman, Bivouac near Chattanooga, Tennessee, to "My Dear Ma," October 12, 1863, Waters Berryman Letters.

23. Ibid.

24. T. A. Hamilton, near Chattanooga, Tennessee, addressee unknown, but possibly to Gen. John Bell Hood, November 3, 1863, Loughridge Collection.

25. John Daniel Staples, Camp near Chattanooga, Tennessee, to "My Dear Brother" [P. M. Staples], October 24, 1863, "Confederate" Bound Volume 378, Fredericksburg National Military Park, Fredericksburg, Va.

26. C. S. Worsham, Camp 4th Texas Regt. near Chattanooga, Tenn., to "My Dear Mother," Sept 24, 1863, C.S. Worsham Letters, Hood's Texas Brigade Collection, Historical Research Center, Hill College, Hillsboro, Tex.

27. B. I. Franklin, near Chattanooga, Tenn., to "Dear Mary," October 2, 1863, Benjamin I. Franklin Papers.

28. Polley, *Hood's Texas Brigade*, 217.

29. Jerome B. Robertson, Headquarters Texas Brigade, to R. M. Sims, Assistant Adjutant General, Longstreet's Corps, November 2, 1863, in Simpson, ed., *Touched with Valor*, 48.

30. Polley, *Hood's Texas Brigade*, 222–27.

31. Muster Rolls, Co. E, 4th Texas Infantry, Dec. 31, 1863–Feb. 29, 1864; Muster Rolls all Texas Brigade companies, Dec. 31, 1863–Feb. 29, 1864, detailed in Simpson, *Lee's Grenadier Guard*, 377.

32. Jack A. Bunch, *Roster of the Courts-Martial in the Confederate State Army* (Shippensburg, Pa.: White Maine, 2001).

33. Ibid., 40–41. Robertson's court included Maj. Gen. Simon B. Buckner (president), and Brig. Gen. Charles W. Field, James L. Kemper, John Gregg, Francis T. Nicholls, George T. Anderson, and Benjamin G. Humphreys. Maj. Garnett Andrews served as judge advocate. Micah Jenkins was prosecutor.

34. Simpson, *Touched with Valor*, 64.

35. Polley, *A Soldier's Letters*, 218.

36. West, *A Texian in Search of a Fight*, 140–41.

37. Watson Dugat Williams, Winter Quarters near Morristown, Tennessee, to "My Dear Laura" [Bryan], January 6, 1864, Watson Dugat Williams Letters.

38. Ibid.; West, *A Texian in Search of a Fight*, 139.

39. Watson Dugat Williams, Camp 5th Texas, Bull's Gap, Tennessee, to Laura Bryan, Liberty, Texas, March 3 and 4, 1864, Watson Dugat Williams Letters.

40. West, *A Texian in Search of a Fight*, 139; Robert Campbell [writing under the pseudonym Joe Joskins], "A Sketch of Hood's Texas Brigade," 152–53, unpublished manuscript, written at Huntsville, Texas, 1865, University of Texas, San Antonio Library, R. H. Porter Civil War Collec-

tion Digitized version: http://digital.utsa.edu/cdm/ref/collection/p15125c01110/id/8440; D. H. Hamilton, *History of Company M, 1st Texas Volunteer Infantry, Hood's Brigade, Longstreet's Corps, Army of the Confederate States of America* (1925; repr., Waco, Tex.: W. M. Morrison, 1962), 40–41; Leila Reeves Eads, *Defenders: A Confederate History of Henderson County, Texas* (Athens, Tex.: Henderson County Historical Survey Committee, 1969), 21.

41. Glatthaar, *General Lee's Army*, 356.

42. Robertson, *Touched with Valor*, 52–54.

43. *O.R.*, series I, vol. 32, pt. II, pp. 640–41.

44. Glatthaar, *General Lee's Army*, 408; Glatthaar, *Soldiering in the Army of Northern Virginia*, 13–18.

45. This is based on a statistical sample created for this project of all the men who ever served in the Texas Brigade. The sample includes 1,335 men (1,212 enlisted men, 70 line officers, 31 Headquarters officers, 22 Headquarters enlisted). The sample adjusted for the length of time each company and regiment was in the Texas Brigade, drawing more heavily from those units that were in the brigade for a longer period of time. The sample itself was drawn from Harold B. Simpson's *Hood's Texas Brigade: A Compendium*, which lists the name, rank, unit, and brief description of service for each man who served in the Texas Brigade between 1861 and 1865. Within that sample, 90 men were listed as deserters, but 10 of them were also identified as "term of service had ended" or they were found to have been unable to rejoin the unit after the fall of Vicksburg, and some of those enlisted in another Confederate force in the Trans-Mississippi West. In such situations of falsely accused deserters, those names were removed from the desertion category.

46. Glatthaar, *General Lee's Army*, 408–10. Note that Glatthaar also reports that men who enlisted in 1863 and 1864 were even more likely to desert, but only one of the 1863–64 deserters discussed here who enlisted in 1864 deserted—and he left two days after he signed up.

47. Of the 27 deserters that winter, 17 were volunteers of 1861, and 8 enlisted in the spring of 1862. One man, John Norwood, Company G, Fifth Texas Infantry, enlisted on February 2, 1864, in Morristown, Tennessee. He deserted two days later.

48. Elite units like the Texas Brigade remind scholars that our sweeping conclusions about Civil War soldiers' motivations for service need to be tested at the unit level. Historian Ken Noe has shown that Confederate enlistees who joined the army after the initial rush to arms in 1861 were not more likely to desert or poor soldiers. His broadly drawn sample of men were, however, more motivated by kinship ties to a small circle of men in their unit and less ideologically motivated overall (see Kenneth W. Noe, *Reluctant Rebels: The Confederates Who Joined the Army after 1861* [Chapel Hill: University of North Carolina Press, 2010]).

49. Thomas Jewett Goree, Morristown, Tennessee, February 8, 1864 to Sarah Williams Kittrell Goree [his mother], Huntsville, Texas, in Cutrer, *Longstreet's Aide*, 117.

50. Brigadier General John Gregg to "My dear friend" [possibly Col. Frank B. Sexton] May 25, 1864, Frank B. Sexton Papers, Sam Houston State University, Huntsville, Tex.

51. This appears to have been a key motivator for Deep South men throughout Longstreet's corps that winter (see Glatthaar, *Soldiering in the Army of Northern Virginia*, 13).

52. Felicia Loughridge, Corsicana, Texas, to "My Dear Husband" [James Rodgers Loughridge], September 29, 1863, Loughridge Collection.

53. L. W. Kemp, ed., "Early Days in Milam County: Reminiscences of Susan Turnham McCown," *Southwestern Historical Quarterly* 50 (January 1947): 376; Joshua Wilson McCown Jr.

served as director of transportation in the Trans-Mississippi West (see *History of Texas, Together with a Biographical History of Milam, Williamson, Bastrop, Travis, Lee and Burleson Counties* [Chicago: Lewis, 1893], 481–85).

54. Kemp, "Early Days," 376.

55. Leila Reeves Eads, *Defenders: A Confederate History of Henderson County, Texas* (Athens, Tex.: Henderson County Historical Survey Committee, 1969), 21.

56. Arwerd Max Moellering, "A History of Guadalupe County, Texas" (master's thesis, University of Texas, Austin, 1938), 135–36.

57. In February 1863, the Navarro County Court issued bonds totaling $7,000 to "support the families of soldiers in the service of the [Navarro] county." By January 1864, they were allocating $384 to ship cotton and wool cards to the county (see *County Commissioner's Report, 1861–1865*, Book C, Navarro County, Texas, Corsicana, Navarro County Courthouse, excerpts online at www.rootsweb.ancestry.com/~txnavarr/war/civil_war/commissioners_report/book_c.htm).

58. Alva Taylor, "The Diary of Jacob Eliot," *Navarro County Scroll*, 1965; reprinted online, Navarro County Historical Society, www.rootsweb.ancestry.com/~txnavarr/biographies/e/eliot_jacob.htm). As historians Deborah M. Liles and Angela Boswell argue, Texas women did not suffer the same hardships as women in other war-torn Confederate states, but the war certainly forced them to confront unique challenges (see Liles and Boswell, eds., *Women in Civil War Texas: Diversity and Dissidence in the Trans-Mississippi* [Denton: University of North Texas Press, 2016]; see also the essay in this collection by Brittany Bounds, "Finding Joy through Hard Times: Texas Women's Recreation during the Civil War," 77–98).

59. Brigadier General John Gregg to "My dear friend" [possibly Col. Frank B. Sexton], May 25, 1864, Frank B. Sexton Papers, Sam Houston State University, Huntsville, Tex.

60. Cutrer, *Longstreet's Aide*, 118.

61. Watson Dugat Williams, Camp 5th Texas near Strawberry Plains [Tennessee], to Laura Bryan, Liberty, Texas, February 20, 1864, Watson Dugat Williams Letters.

CHAPTER NINE

1. Examples of this sentiment run throughout J. Tracy Power, *Lee's Miserables: Life in the Army of Northern Virginia from the Wilderness to Appomattox* (Chapel Hill: University of North Carolina Press, 2002).

2. Winkler, *The Confederate Capital and Hood's Texas Brigade*, 156.

3. James H. Manahan, Virginia, to Miss Willie Thomason, Waco, Texas, 28 February 1864, James H. Manahan Letters, Center for American History, University of Texas at Austin. Williametta Thomason's father was a middle-class merchant in Waco with a combined wealth of more than $8,000 in 1860. He and a number of Williametta's siblings would be living with her in 1870, after Williametta married James in 1866. He clerked in her father's store (1860 U. S. Federal Census, McLennan, Texas; Roll: M653_1300; Page: 387; Image: 197; Film: 805300; see also marriage record of Williametta Thomason and James H. Manahan, September 24, 1866, Cherokee County, Texas [Ancestry.com (database online)], Texas, Select County Marriage Index, 1837–1965 [Ancestry.com Operations, Inc., 2014]).

4. Cutrer, *Longstreet's Aide*, 122.

5. Of the men who served in the Texas Brigade from 1861 through 1865, 66 percent joined in 1861, and 23 percent joined in 1862. Only 4 percent of the men volunteered in 1863, and a miniscule .02 percent of recruits showed up in Virginia in 1864. These findings are based on my sample of 1,335 members of the Texas Brigade (1,212 enlisted men, 70 line officers, 31 Headquarters officers, 22 Headquarters enlisted). The sample adjusted for the length of time each company and regiment was in the Texas Brigade, drawing more heavily from those units that were in the brigade longer. The sample itself was drawn from Harold B. Simpson's *Hood's Texas Brigade: A Compendium*, which lists the name, rank, unit, and brief description of service for each man who served in the Texas Brigade between 1861 and 1865.

6. *Houston Tri-Weekly Gazette*, July 30, 1863.

7. For broad studies of the Battle of the Wilderness, see Gordon C. Rhea, *The Battle of the Wilderness, May 5-6, 1864* (Baton Rouge: Louisiana State University Press, 1994); Gary W. Gallagher, ed., *The Wilderness Campaign* (Chapel Hill: University of North Carolina Press, 1997); and Noah Andre Trudeau, "Lee's Struggle in the Wilderness," *America's Civil War* 13 (September 2000): 26-32, 80.

8. Robert K. Krick, "'Lee to the Rear,' the Texans Cried," 162-63.

9. Ibid., 164-65.

10. Evander M. Law, "From the Wilderness to Cold Harbor," in *Battles and Leaders of the Civil War*, ed. Robert Underwood Johnson and Clarence Clough Buel, 4 vols. (New York: Century, 1887-88), 4:124.

11. Polley, *Hood's Texas Brigade*, 230-31; Robert K. Krick, "'Lee to the Rear,' the Texans Cried," 173, 176.

12. Robert K. Krick, "'Lee to the Rear,' the Texans Cried," 170-71.

13. Ibid., 171-72.

14. Ibid., 172.

15. Ibid., 166-69.

16. Gordon C. Rhea, *The Battle of the Wilderness*, 292-95.

17. Brigadier General John Gregg Letter to "My dear friend" [possibly Col. Frank B. Sexton], May 25, 1864, Frank B. Sexton Papers, Sam Houston State University, Huntsville, Tex.

18. Robert K. Krick, "'Lee to the Rear,' the Texans Cried," 180.

19. Solomon T. "Tom" Blessing, near the Chickahominy, Virginia, to "Dear Sister," May 29, 1864, published in the *Galveston (Tex.) Weekly News*, July 27, 1864.

20. Robert K. Krick, "'Lee to the Rear,' the Texans Cried," 182.

21. Mark Smither, Virginia, likely to his mother, Huntsville, Texas. Letter undated and without address with the first several pages missing, but context and death references all date the letter to May 1864 (John Marquis Smither Letters). "Huntsville Item," Walker County Historical Markers, www.walkercountyhistory.org/markers/dispMarker.php?mid=50.

22. Simpson, *Compendium*, 41-42.

23. Edwin Sue Goree, *A Family Mosaic* (Coolidge, Ariz.: J. D. Goree, 1961; published thirty years after compiled), 17-18; Cutrer, *Longstreet's Aide*, 127-30.

24. Samuel Bailey, Compiled Service Record, 5th Texas Infantry, Fold3.com.

25. Mark Smither, Virginia, likely to his mother, Huntsville, Texas, letter undated with the first several pages missing, but context and death references all date the letter to May 1864, John Marquis Smither Letters.

26. Watson Dugat Williams, Headquarters, 5th Texas Breastworks, near Spotsylvania Court House, Virginia, May 18, 1864, Watson Dugat Williams Letters.

27. Solomon T. "Tom" Blessing, near the Chickahominy, Virginia, to "Dear Sister," May 29, 1864, published in the *Galveston (Tex.) Weekly News*, July 27, 1864.

28. Polley, *Hood's Texas Brigade*, 242.

29. Emerson, *History of the War of the Confederacy*, 69.

30. George Butler, Morristown, Tennessee, to "My Dear Sister Emma" [Butler, Tulip, Arkansas], January 21, 1864, in Elizabeth Paisley Huckaby and Ethel C. Simpson, eds., *Tulip Evermore: Emma Butler and William Paisley, Their Lives in Letters, 1857–1887* (Fayetteville: University of Arkansas Press, 1985), 40–41.

31. George Butler, near Richmond, to Emma Butler, June 9, 1864, in *Tulip Evermore*, 43.

32. Denson, *The Life and Times of Reverend N. C. Denson*, 25; confirmed in N. C. Denson, Compiled Service Record, 3rd Arkansas, Fold3.com.

33. Robert Lowery Diary, July 17, 1864, Hood's Texas Brigade Collection, History Research Center, Hill College, Hillsboro, Tex. Hereafter cited as Robert Lowery Diary.

34. This is based on a spreadsheet of all men on Texas Brigade rolls for 1864, based on muster rolls of that year. Compiled and expanded upon by Alfred C. Young for his book *Lee's Army during the Overland Campaign: A Numerical Study* (Baton Rouge: Louisiana State University Press, 2013). Special thanks to Alfred Young for his willingness to share his data on the Texas Brigade and discuss it in detail.

35. Simpson, *Lee's Grenadier Guard*, 430.

36. Richard J. Sommers, *Richmond Redeemed: The Siege of Petersburg, The Battles of Chaffin's Bluff and Poplar Spring Church, September 29–October 2, 1864* (1984; repr., El Dorado Hills, Calif.: Savas Beatie, 2014), 30–32.

37. Mulholland, Military Order Congress Medal of Honor, 517; see also James S. Price, *Battle of New Market Heights: Freedom Will Be Theirs by the Sword* (Charleston, S.C.: History Press, 2011).

38. Sommers, *Richmond Redeemed*, 31–33.

39. Samuel S. Watson, Camp 1st Texas, Virginia, to "Dear Friend Harriet," October 21, 1864, Samuel S. Watson Letters, Hood's Texas Brigade Collection, History Research Center, Hill College, Hillsboro, Tex.

40. Robert E. Fitzgerald Diary, transcribed by Kevin Jones from private donor, September 29, 1864. Contextual remarks indicate that the diary was edited in the postwar period. Special thanks to Kevin Jones for sharing the Fitzgerald Diary, which covers the period from June 1, 1864, through October 27, 1864.

41. Polley, *A Soldier's Letters to Charming Nellie*, 165.

42. Emerson, *History of the War of the Confederacy*, 76.

43. Hamilton, *History of Company M*, 61–62.

44. J. D. Pickens, "Fort Harrison," *Confederate Veteran* 21 (1913): 484; Sommers, *Richmond Redeemed*, 35.

45. Sig Synnestvedt, "The Earth Shook and Quivered," *Civil War Times Illustrated* 11, no. 12 (December 1972): 37.

46. Sommers, *Richmond Redeemed*, 33–36.

47. Rufus King Felder, Camp near Chaffins Bluff, to "Dear Sister," September 18, 1864, Rufus King Felder Letters.

48. Hampton Newsome, *Richmond Must Fall: The Richmond–Petersburg Campaign, October 1864* (Kent, Ohio: Kent State University Press, 2013), 28–58.

49. Polley, *Hood's Texas Brigade*, 257.

50. Newsome, *Richmond Must Fall*, 53.

51. Ibid., 59–60. See also Noah Andre Trudeau, "That 'Unerring Volcanic Firearm,'" *Military History Quarterly* 7 (Summer 1995): 49–51.

52. Winkler, *The Confederate Capital and Hood's Texas Brigade*, 196.

53. Ibid.; Polley, *Hood's Texas Brigade*, 258–59.

54. J. P. O'Rear account in Yeary, *Reminiscences of the Boys in Gray*, 580–82.

55. Watson Dugat Williams, On Darbytown Road, 6 miles from Richmond, Head Quarters 5th Texas, to "My Dear Laura," October 13, 1864, Watson Dugat Williams Letters.

56. Winkler, *The Confederate Capital and Hood's Texas Brigade*, 196; *Richmond Sentinel*, October 10, 1864; *Richmond Whig*, October 10, 1864.

CHAPTER TEN

1. D. C. Rachal Parole, Houston, Texas, June 3, 1865. Darius Cyriaque Rachal, Compiled Service Record, 5th Texas Infantry; letter requesting return to Texas Brigade to unknown individual/office, September 6, 1864; both in Fold3.com. For information on Rachal's family, who owned a farm in Liberty, Texas, with a combined value of $7,000, see 1860 U.S. Federal Census, Liberty, Texas; Roll: M653_1300; Page: 312; Image: 46; Family History Library Film:805300.

2. Their return rates also reflected improvements that surgeons and Gen. Robert E. Lee had made in the Army of Northern Virginia through better medical care and logistics. The men benefited from the implementation of "Sanitary Camps" or quarantine sections in camp for returning men who still carried contagious diseases. The return rates also reflected the army's increased number of qualified surgeons and the creation of the Reserve Surgical Corps (see Glatthaar, *General Lee's Army*, 394–96).

3. The number of returnees was compiled from muster rolls and compiled service record data of Hood's Texas Brigade shared by Alfred Young, *Lee's Army on the Overland Campaign: A Numerical Study* (Baton Rouge: Louisiana State University Press, 2013). Specifically, 77 men returned from Gettysburg wounds or capture, and 89 men returned from Chickamauga wounds or capture. Ten men returned from wounds at both battles.

4. Glatthaar, *General Lee's Army*, 394–96.

5. Felder to "Dear Sister," Camp near Chaffins Bluff, [Virginia], September 18, 1864, Rufus King Felder Letters.

6. Rufus King Felder to "Dear Sister," Camp near Winchester, [Virginia], October 1, 1862, Rufus King Felder Letters.

7. Stephen Chicoine, ed., "... Willing Never to Go in Another Fight": The Civil War Correspondence of Rufus King Felder of Chappell Hill," *Southwestern Historical Quarterly* 106 (April 2003): 575. See also the 1860 U.S. Federal Census, where Felder's mother is listed as head of household with real estate valued at over $11,000 and personal wealth at over $37,000 (1860 U.S. Federal Census, Census Place: Washington, Texas; Roll: M653_1307; Page: 216; Image: 441; Family History Library Film: 805307).

8. Felder to "Dear Sister," Camp near Chaffins Bluff, [Virginia], September 18, 1864, Rufus King Felder Letters.

9. W. J. Terry, Camp near Chaffins Farm, Virginia, to Mrs. J. S. Terry, August 13, 1864, Terry (William J.) and Beal (D. R.) Papers, 1864, Pearce Civil War Collection, Navarro College, Corsicana, Tex.

10. W. J. Terry, Camp near Chaffins Farm, Virginia, to J. S. Terry, August 5, 1864, W. J. Terry Letters, Texas Brigade Collection, Historical Research Center, Hill College, Hillsboro, Tex.

11. Sidney E. Moseley to Dr. Alfred Mercer, Hampton Hospital Prisoners' Ward, Hampton, VA, December 5, 1864, Sidney E. Moseley Letters, Hood's Texas Brigade Letter Collection, Historical Research Center, Hill College, Hillsboro, Tex. See also Charles D. Grear, ed., "Debating the Rebellion: A Texan and a New Yorker Discuss Secession and the Civil War," *Military History of the West* 39 (December 2009): 41–58.

12. Grear, "Debating the Rebellion," 41–58.

13. Ibid.

14. Circular, Headquarters, Army of Northern Virginia, October 9, 1864, Folder 18 of the T. L. Clingman Papers, no. 157, Southern Historical Collection, Wilson Library, University of North Carolina at Chapel Hill, available online at: http://blogs.lib.unc.edu/civilwar/index.php/2014/10/09/9-october-1864/#sthash.nHp5S9s6.dpuf.

15. "A Bill to Be Entitled an Act to Authorize the Consolidation of Companies, Battalions, and Regiments," November 8, 1864, Confederate States of America (Richmond: C. S. A., 1864), original at Duke University; available through HathiTrust: http://hdl.handle.net/2027/du11.ark:/13960/t5bc4rg0z.

16. For discussions of consolidation and morale, see Glatthaar, *General Lee's Army*, 436; and Power, *Lee's Miserable*, 239–40.

17. Longstreet to Lee, January 10, 1865, in *O.R.*, ser. I, vol. 46, pt. II, p. 1033.

18. Rufus King Felder to "Dear Mother," Camp near Richmond, [Virginia], December 18, 1864, Rufus King Felder Letters.

19. Seaborn Dominey to Caroline Dominey, On Charles City Road near Richmond, Va., November 11, 1864; see also Seaborn Dominey to Caroline Dominey, On the Charles City Road near Richmond, Va., December 14, 1864, Seaborn Dominey Letters, Hood's Texas Brigade Letter Collection, Historical Research Center, Hill College, Hillsboro, Tex. Hereafter cited as Seaborn Dominey Letters.

20. Seaborn Dominey to Caroline Dominey, On the Charles City Road near Richmond, Va., December 14, 1864, Seaborn Dominey Letters.

21. Seaborn Dominey to "Dear Sister" [Miss Eliza Davis], Camp near Richmond, Va., December 20, 1864, Seaborn Dominey Letters.

22. Winkler, *The Confederate Capital and Hood's Texas Brigade*, 207.

23. Littlefield letter dated December 18, 1864, in Winkler, *The Confederate Capital and Hood's Texas Brigade*, 207.

24. Asbury Lawson, Compiled Military Service Record, 5th Texas, Fold3.com.

25. Edwin B. Searle, Compiled Service Record, 1st Texas, Fold3.com.

26. Henry F. Bradley, Compiled Service Record, 1st Texas, Fold3.com.

27. Joseph C. Chiles and C. M. Mixon, Compiled Service Record, 1st Texas, Fold3.com.

28. Winkler, *The Confederate Capital and Hood's Texas Brigade*, 208.

29. James I. Robertson Jr., *The Stonewall Brigade* (1963; repr., Baton Rouge: Louisiana State University Press, 1991), 226. See also *O.R.*, ser. 1, vol. 36, pt. II, p. 1001.

30. Claude H. Hall, "Congressman William H. 'Howdy' Martin," paper presented at the East Texas Historical Association Annual Meeting, October 7, 1967, Nacogdoches, Tex.; Mildred Martin Bond and George Doherty Bond, *Alexander Carswell and Isabella Brown: Their Ancestors and Descendants: Genealogy and History of Carswell, Brown, Gordon, Ruthven and the John Martin–Jane Hutchinson Family* (Chipley, Fla.: Carswell Foundation, 1977), 344–46. See also Kenneth W. Howell, *An Antebellum History: Henderson County, Texas, 1846–1861* (Austin, Tex.: Eakin, 1999), 75–76.

31. Martha E. Martin, "Sketch of Major W. H. Martin," *Biographies of Eminent Citizens and Historical Sketches of Henderson County*, vol. 2 (Athens, Tex.: Directory of Athens City, 1904), 24–25. Martin's widow, Martha E. Gallemore Martin, noted that the physical description of Martin that has been picked up by numerous historians and best captured in art by John W. Thomason Jr., nephew of the Goree brothers of the Fifth Texas and Longstreet's staff, came from Judge John Steven's address in Athens about his fellow Texas Brigade veteran.

32. Winkler, *The Confederate Capital and Hood's Texas Brigade*, 108–9. The physical description comes from Martin's Compiled Service Record, which states that he was forty-one at the end of the war, with gray eyes, brown hair, florid complexion, and five feet eleven inches tall (Compiled Service Record, H. William Martin, 4th Texas Infantry. Fold3.com).

33. Robert K. Krick, *Civil War Weather in Virginia* (Tuscaloosa: University of Alabama Press, 2007), 147–49.

34. "Resolutions of the Texas Brigade," January 24, 1865, Confederate Imprints. Box 2, C669, Special Collections, McCain Library and Archives, University of Southern Mississippi, University of Southern Mississippi Digital Collections, http://digilib.usm.edu/cdm/ref/collection/rarebook/id/2546.

35. Ibid.

36. Ibid.

37. Ibid.

38. For a discussion of these resolutions in the spring of 1865, see Jason Phillips, *Diehard Rebels: The Confederate Culture of Invincibility* (Athens: University of Georgia Press, 2007), 7, 22, 161–63.

39. Letter reprinted from the *Richmond Examiner* in the *Houston Tri-Weekly Telegraph*, January 18, 1865.

40. Linda Mears, transcription, *Confederate Indigent Families Lists of Texas, 1863–1865* (San Marcos, Tex.: privately published, 1995), 181, 210, 385.

41. Vicki Betts, "'A Sacred Charge upon Our Hands': Assisting the Families of Confederate Soldiers in Texas, 1861–1865," in *The Seventh Star of the Confederacy: Texas during the Civil War*, ed. Kenneth W. Howell (Denton: University of North Texas, 2009), 259.

42. For more on this version of the social contract, see McCurry, *Confederate Reckoning*, 198–202.

43. *Triweekly News*, February 24, 1863.

44. This type of response is not unique to Texas. See a discussion of how white women across the Confederacy responded to these appeals in Rubin, *A Shattered Nation*, 54–67.

45. Betts, "A Sacred Charge upon Our Hands," 258. For the original Coleman quotes, see C.

Richard King, ed., *Victorian Lady on the Texas Frontier: The Journal of Ann Raney Coleman* (Norman: University of Oklahoma Press, 1971), 153–55.

46. Betts, "A Sacred Charge upon Our Hands," 258.

47. Ibid., 256.

48. Ibid., 258–59.

49. Petition from citizens and soldiers in Indianola, Calhoun County, Texas, to Governor Pendleton Murrah, April 4, 1865, Governor Pendleton Murrah Records, 1863–1865, Box 2014/022-4, Folder 112, Texas State Library and Archives, Austin. Hereafter cited as Murrah Papers.

50. This conclusion is based on a careful search of citizens' petitions, protests, and exception requests sent to the Texas governor's office. This includes approximately eighty such items to submitted to Governor Lubbock and fifteen items submitted to Governor Murrah between 1861 and 1865 (see Murrah Papers; see also Governor Francis Richard Lubbock Records, 1861–1904, undated, bulk 1861–1863, Texas State Library & Archives, Austin).

51. *Dallas (Tex.) Herald,* September 7, 1864, taken from an August 20, 1864, address by Wigfall in Marshall, Texas.

52. In January 1862, Mintie Price, daughter of the largest slaveholder in San Augustine, Texas, and wife of 1st Lt. Frank Price, Company K, First Texas Infantry, wrote: "I think it would be wise in [sic] you to come home pretty soon. I think you are risking too much by staying there and so much sickness around you. Oh! Frank you must come. There is no use of your staying there" (Bryan, "Whip Them Like the Mischief," 71). In all likelihood, there were other letters like Mintie's that have not been located but remain highly rare when compared with the number of letters calling men home that came in to other Confederate units who lacked the Texas Brigade's unusually strong dedication to the war effort (shown by both the soldiers and their families) from the beginning to the bitter end of the war. For scholarship on fracturing Confederate morale and letters that encouraged men to resign commissions or desert and come home, see Faust, *Mothers of Invention,* 243; and Faust, "Altars of Sacrifice," 171–99. For an analysis of Confederates struggling with a desire to secure victory and sacrifice honorably while also desperately wanting the war to end, see Rubin, *A Shattered Nation,* 75–79.

53. Simpson, *Hood's Texas Brigade,* 451.

54. Details on the Knight brothers can be found in the 1860 U.S. Federal Census, Smith County, Texas. Sarah Knight's date of death, possibly from childbirth but the record is not clear on that, is found via the FindAGrave website for Sarah Elizabeth Shelton Knight at www.findagrave.com/cgi-bin/fg.cgi?page=gr&GRid=37514330&ref=acom.

55. Jacob Hemphill, in his short reminiscence of the war, noted that the stars were sent by "Miss Fuller of Houston, Texas" (Hemphill, "Reminiscences," in Yeary, *Reminiscences of the Boys in Gray,* 324).

56. Margaret Swett Henson, "Young, Matilda Jane Fuller," *Handbook of Texas Online,* www.tshaonline.org/handbook/online/articles/fy010.

57. See history of Fifth Texas Flag at the online exhibit, "Historic Flags of the Texas State Library and Archives," www.tsl.texas.gov/exhibits/flags/40475thTexas.html.

58. *Richmond Whig,* January 17, 1865.

59. Ibid.

60. Rufus King Felder, Camp near Richmond, to "My Dear Sister," February 23, 1865, Rufus King Felder Letters. The ellipses are due to a tear in the original letter.

61. Samuel S. Watson, "In the trenches North Side of the James," February [?], 1865 [no day listed], Samuel S. Watson Letters, Hood's Texas Brigade Collection, Historical Research Center, Hill College, Hillsboro, Tex.

62. W. J. Watts, Army of Northern Va. Camp 1st Texas Regt, to "Dear Cousin" [Mr. Philip Gathings], March 11, 1865. I thank descendants of Philip Gathings, HenryEtta Wilson, and John Stevens for sharing a copy of the original letter and transcription.

63. Williams ran into a fellow soldier shortly after the war who confirmed that Charley Brashear died at Gettysburg. See undated, unsigned letter in Williams collection, likely written shortly after the war (per context and reference to Williams's recent marriage), Watson Dugat Williams Letters.

64. Watson Dugat Williams, On Darbytown Road, 6 Miles from Richmond, Head Quarters 5th Texas, to "My Dear Laura" [Bryan], October 13, 1864, Watson Dugat Williams Letters; 1860 U.S. Federal Census, Liberty, Texas; Roll: M653_1300; Page: 318; Image: 59; Family History Library Film: 805300.

65. Watson Dugat Williams, Head Quarters 5th Texas near Richmond on Charles City Road, to "My Dear Laura" [Bryan], November 1, 1864, Watson Dugat Williams Letters.

66. Watson Dugat Williams, Texas Depot, Richmond, Virginia, to "My Own Dear Lollie" [Laura Bryan], January 3, 1865, Watson Dugat Williams Letters.

67. Simpson, *Compendium,* 167; Michael Dan Jones, *Lt. Col. King Bryan of Hood's Texas Brigade* (self-published, 2013), 170.

68. Polley, *Hood's Texas Brigade,* 300. A look at the names of the men in each company who surrendered in April 1865 indicates that this is representative of companies throughout the Texas Brigade when they surrendered.

CHAPTER ELEVEN

1. See Jason Philips, *Diehard Rebels,* 167–83, for a discussion of the shock and heartbreak throughout the Confederate armies as they surrendered in the spring and summer of 1865. Philips saw an acceptance of defeat among "diehard rebels," similar to what is described here for the Texas Brigade, and how they used their superb records to "overcome the humiliation of surrender" as discussed on page 182.

2. Hill's account in Polley, *Hood's Texas Brigade,* 277.

3. Hill Family, 1860 U.S. Federal Census, Walker, Texas; Roll: M653_1307; Page: 134; Image: 276; Family History Library Film: 805307.

4. Basil Crow Brashear, Gregory, Texas, to Frank B. Chilton, March 5, 1911, Basil Brashear Papers, Historical Research Center, Hill College, Hillsboro, Tex. Hereafter cited as Basil Brashear Papers.

5. Polley, *Hood's Texas Brigade,* 277.

6. W. T. Hill in Frank B. Chilton, *Unveiling and Dedication of monument to Hood's Texas brigade on the capitol grounds at Austin, Texas, Thursday, October twenty-seven, nineteen hundred and ten, and minutes of the thirty-ninth annual reunion of Hood's Texas brigade association held in Senate chamber at Austin, Texas, October twenty-six and twenty-seven, nineteen hundred and ten, together with a short monument and brigade association history and Confederate scrap book* (Houston, Tex.: self-published, 1911), 183.

7. Lee's Farewell Address, www.civilwar.org/education/history/primarysources/leefarewell.html.

8. Bond and Bond, *Alexander Carswell and Isabella Brown*, 346.

9. William Marvel, *A Place Called Appomattox* (Chapel Hill: University of North Carolina Press, 2000), 246.

10. Hill in Chilton, *Unveiling and Dedication*, 183.

11. "Paroling the Army of Northern Virginia," www.nps.gov/apco/learn/historyculture/paroling-the-army-of-northern-virginia.htm.

12. Marvel, *A Place Called Appomattox*, 259.

13. Basil Crow Brashear, Gregory, Texas, to Frank B. Chilton, March 5, 1911, Basil Brashear Papers.

14. Maberry, *Texas Flags*, 83; see also John D. Murray Papers, Hood's Texas Brigade Collection, Hill College, Hillsboro, Tex.; John D. Murray obituary, written by fellow Texas Brigade and Company F, Fourth Texas veteran J. B. Polley, *Floresville Chronicle-Journal*, March 3, 1916. Robert W. Murray, who lost a leg from a wound at the Wilderness, survived the war and lived to be one hundred years old (*Floresville Chronicle-Journal*, April 8, 1938). Special thanks to Dr. Richard McCaslin for sharing these articles.

15. Maberry, *Texas Flags*, 83.

16. "Arthur Butler Allison Biography," aaallison.com/download/i/mark_dl/u/4005219886/45 19284496/bio.

17. Hill in Chilton, *Unveiling and Dedication*, 184.

18. "Paroling the Army of Northern Virginia," www.nps.gov/apco/learn/historyculture/paroling-the-army-of-northern-virginia.htm. See also Marvel, *A Place Called Appomattox*, 252–53.

19. Robert Lowery Diary, April 13, 1865.

20. Hill in Polley, *Hood's Texas Brigade*, 279. Robert Lowery, who kept a diary during his journey home, appears to have been traveling with Hill and Martin, or in one of the smaller groups just ahead or behind them. Lowery passed through Charlotte on April 25, which would have been the day before Johnston surrendered, making it unlikely that any Texans from that army linked up with Hill and Martin's band. But, if Hill and Martin were a few days behind Lowery, it is possible.

21. Simpson, *Lee's Grenadier Guard*, 472–73; see also Reagan, *John Reagan Memoirs*, 206; Louise Wigfall Wright, *A Southern Girl in '61: The Wartime Memories of a Confederate Senator's Daughter* (Gansevoort, N.Y.: Corner House Historical Publications, 2000), 243. See also Confederate parole of Pvt. J. A. White, of Co. M, First Texas Infantry, in private collection of James and Marty Rogers, Statesville, North Carolina. Special thanks to Marty Rogers, Wigfall descendant, for sharing a copy of the fake parole.

22. Cutrer, *Longstreet's Aide*, 10.

23. Paul Ripley, Chaffin Farm, Virginia, to John Watkins, September 23, 1864, in *Hard Times, 1861–1865: A Collection of Confederate Letters, Court Minutes, Soldiers' Records, and Local Lore from Craig County, Virginia*, ed. Jane Echols Johnson (n.p.: Johnston and Williams, 1986), 207.

24. B. A. Nabours, "Active Service of a Texas Command," *Confederate Veteran* 24 (1916): 69–72.

25. A. B. Green Diary, entries for June 23 through July 11, 1865 (privately published, Hood's Texas Brigade Association Reactivated, 2015).

26. Undated letter to unknown recipient [context indicates letter written in 1866 and handwriting matches other Watson Dugat Williams letters], Watson Dugat Williams Letters.

27. Trammel, *Seven Pines*, 122–23. See also Margaret Swett Henson, "Williams, John A.," *Handbook of Texas Online*, www.tshaonline.org/handbook/online/articles/fwi27.

28. Williams listed his real estate at $2,000 and his personal estate at $20,000 (1860 U.S. Federal Census, Ancestry.com [online database], Liberty, Liberty County, Texas, "W. D. Williams"). See also 1860 U.S. Federal Census—Slave Schedules, Ancestry.com, Liberty, Liberty County, Texas, "W. D. Williams."

29. Diana J. Kleiner, "Liberty, TX (Liberty County)," *Handbook of Texas Online*, www.tshaonline.org/handbook/online/articles/HFL04.

30. Comparative Postwar Texas Brigade Sample. These numbers are grounded in a random 10 percent sample of the surviving members of the First, Fourth, and Fifth Texas and the Third Arkansas Infantry regiments that are part of my larger sample of all members of the Texas Brigade. Data for the statistical analysis of Texas Brigade veterans' counties comparing personal and real estate wealth came from the 1860 and 1870 U.S. Federal Censuses. See also NHGIS titles "NT23. True Value by Property Type" for 1860 and "NT37B. True Valuation of Real and Personal Estate" for 1870. Minnesota Population Center, *National Historical Geographic Information System: Version 2.0* (Minneapolis: University of Minnesota 2011), www.nhgis.org.

31. Watson Dugat Williams to unknown recipient, Galveston, Texas, January 1866, Watson Dugat Williams Letters.

32. John Hill application for Presidential Pardon, December 9, 1865; Hill family in 1860 U.S. Federal Census, Walker, Texas; Roll: M653_1307; Page: 134; Image: 276; Family History Library Film: 805307; 1870 U.S. Federal Census, Precinct 4, Walker, Texas; Roll: M593_1607; Page: 376A; Image: 266414; Family History Library Film: 553106.

33. Comparisons between personal and real estate values registered for William Martin (Henderson County, Tex.), William T. Hill (Walker County, Tex.), and A. B. Green (Polk County, Texas) from the 1860 and 1870 U.S. Federal Censuses, accessed on Ancestry.com.

34. Comparative Postwar Texas Brigade Sample.

35. Carl H. Moneyhon, *Texas after the Civil War: The Struggle of Reconstruction* (College Station: Texas A&M University Press, 2004), 9. For more on Texas financial challenges in the final years of the war, see Vicki Betts, "'A Sacred Charge upon Our Hands': Assisting the Families of Confederate Soldiers in Texas, 1861–1865," in *The Seventh Star of the Confederacy: Texas during the Civil War*, ed. Kenneth W. Howell (Denton: University of North Texas, 2009), 259.

36. Zach Landrum's cause of death and burial is noted at his FindAGrave website at www.findagrave.com/cgi-bin/fg.cgi?page=gr&GRid=16640485. Familial wealth of the Landrums is located in the U.S. Federal Census of 1860 and 1870 for Montgomery County, Texas. In 1860, the personal wealth for the Landrum children was Zach, $2,500; Willis, $3,000; Melissa, $5,000. Appleton Gay had an estate valued at $26,000.

37. Willis Landrum, Compiled Service Record, 4th Texas Infantry Regiment, Fold3.com.

38. The average age of the 15 percent of Texas Brigade veterans in the sample who saw any kind of financial improvement between 1860 and 1870 is thirty-seven, whereas the average age of those who showed losses is thirty-two (Comparative Postwar Texas Brigade Sample).

39. I did not simply compare Texas and Arkansas veterans with each other because this would not result in useful data—what happened to a veteran in Galveston will not tell us much when compared with another in Bowie County in the far northeastern corner of the state. Considering the size of Texas and the diversity of its economy, the more telling data came from comparing the

men with the rest of their home county. Since the 1860 and 1870 censuses did not break down real and personal wealth at the county level but rather offered total numbers by county, this comparison had to be made as a comparable percentage loss or gain of total wealth between 1860 and 1870.

40. Gerald Linderman, *Embattled Courage: The Experience of Combat in the American Civil War* (New York: Free Press, 1987), 267–75. One of the best arguments against Linderman is Brian Matthew Jordan's study of Union veterans in the postwar period, *Marching Home: Union Veterans and Their Unending Civil War* (New York: Liveright, 2014), 68–69. Here Jordan writes, "The many obstacles that Union veterans encountered returning to civilian life could *only be surmounted together*" (emphasis mine).

41. Ruth Peebles, "Summary and Commentary, The Diary of A. B. Green, 1865," unpublished, Polk County Memorial Museum. Details confirmed in 1860 and 1870 U.S. Federal Censuses for Polk County, Texas. Amanda Magee married A. B. Green, and Angie Magee married Dennis Rowe.

42. In 1870, Newton Berryman's farm was next to Jerry Murphy's, Mort Murphy's widower father. Waters Berryman's farm was two doors down from Newt's (see 1870 U.S. Federal Census, Beat 1, Cherokee, Texas; Roll: M593_1578; Page: 174B; Image: 201056; Family History Library Film: 553077; see also unaddressed letter by Watson Dugat Williams, Galveston, Texas, January 1866, Watson Dugat Williams Letters).

43. "Letter from Col. Mike Powell," *Houston Tri-Weekly Telegraph,* July 12, 1865.

44. Ibid.

45. *Houston Tri-Weekly Telegraph,* July 5, 1865.

46. Ibid., July 28, 1865.

47. Ibid., October 27, 1865.

48. Ibid., August 28, 1865.

49. William Lee Richter, *Overreached on All Sides: The Freedmen's Bureau Administrators in Texas, 1865–1868* (College Station: Texas A&M University Press, 1991), 4.

50. Watson Dugat William Amnesty Oath No. 96, July 19, 1865, Watson Dugat Williams Letters.

51. Thomas J. Goree, Amnesty Oath No. 4784, November 4, 1865, Confederate Amnesty Papers, Fold3.com.

52. *Memphis Daily Avalanche,* May 8, 1866.

53. Erasmus Wynne Household, 1860 U.S. Federal Census, Huntsville, Walker, Texas; Roll: M653_1307; Page: 95; Image: 197; Family History Library Film: 805307; J. M. Smither Household 1870 U.S. Federal Census, Huntsville, Walker, Texas; Roll: M593_1607; Page: 414A; Image: 269321; Family History Library Film: 553106.

54. 1860 U.S. Federal Census, Concord, Hardin, Texas; Roll: M653_1296; Page: 341; Image: 126; Family History Library Film: 805296; #02279 Mrs. Mary A. Tiner Pension Application, August 14, 1899, Jefferson County, Texas, Confederate pension applications, Texas Comptroller's Office.

55. *Dallas Weekly Herald,* June 30, 1866. A brief report on the Houston meeting, led by D. C. Farmer, can be found at W. A. Leonard, comp., *Houston City Directory, for 1867–68* (Houston: Gray, Smallwood & Co., 1867), 123–24, available online at: http://digital.houstonlibrary.org/pdfs/HCDir-1867-68.pdf.

56. See Joseph G. Dawson, *Army Generals and Reconstruction: Louisiana, 1862–1877* (Baton Rouge: Louisiana State University Press, 1982).

57. Leonard, comp., *Houston City Directory,* 124.

58. Thomas J. Goree, Galveston, Texas, to Colonel E. D. Nolley, Durant, Mississippi, February 20, 1869, Nolley Family Papers, Special Collections, Sam Houston State University, Huntsville, Tex. Hereafter cited as Nolley Family Papers.

59. Thomas J. Goree, Midway, Madison Co, Texas, to Colonel E. D. Nolley, Durant, Mississippi, June 2, 1869, Nolley Family Papers.

60. Thomas J. Goree, no location, no date; context indicates late 1869 or 1870, just after Hamilton-Davis gubernatorial race, to Edward D. Nolley, Durant, Mississippi, Nolley Family Papers.

61. William H. Hamman biography with letter excerpts. Hood's Texas Brigade Collection, Historical Research Center, Hill College, Hillsboro, Tex.

62. Goree, *Family Mosaic*, 19.

63. Ibid., 20.

64. Otis A. Singletary, "The Texas Militia during Reconstruction," *Southwestern Historical Quarterly* 60 (July 1956–April 1957): 28–29.

65. Haminto qtd. in William L. Richter, *Overreached on All Sides: The Freedmen's Bureau Administrators in Texas, 1865–1868* (College Station: Texas A&M University Press, 1991), 12.

66. T. J. Newman, Brenham, Texas, to Captain B. I. Franklin, Saundersville, Tennessee, January 7, 1879, B. I. Franklin Papers, Hood's Texas Brigade Collection, Historical Research Center, Hill College, Hillsboro, Tex.

67. J. R. Loughridge, Kosse, Texas, to Mrs. Mary Felicia Loughridge, April 28, 1871, Loughridge Collection.

68. Hood's Texas Brigade Minutes, Houston, May 14, 1872, Minutes of Hood's Texas Brigade Association Meetings, 1872–1896, Hood's Texas Brigade Collection, Historical Research Center, Hill College, Hillsboro, Tex.

69. Simpson, *Hood's Texas Brigade: In Reunion and Memory* (Hillsboro, Tex.: Hill College Press, 1974), 15–19.

70. Brian Craig Miller, *John Bell Hood and the Fight for Civil War Memory* (Knoxville: University of Tennessee Press, 2010), 220.

71. Simpson, *Reunion and Memory*, 162–70.

72. *Dallas Weekly Herald*, July 3, 1884.

73. Simpson, *Reunion and Memory*, 157–73; see also Brian Craig Miller, *John Bell Hood*, 226–37.

74. Katherine Hooper Davis, Linda Erickson Devereaux, Carolyn Reeves Ericson, comp., *Texas Confederate Home Roster* (Nacogdoches, Tex.: Ericson, 2003); Amy Sue Kirchenbauer, "The Texas Confederate Home for Men, 1884–1970" (master's thesis, University of North Texas, 2011); Giles, *Rags and Hope*, 7–8. Fourth Texas veteran Val Giles and his wife, Lou, worked tirelessly in their efforts to raise funds for the men's home and the women's home that opened in 1908. Lou Barnhart Giles later served as the first superintendent.

75. W. G. Jackson, Confederate Home, Austin, Texas to Pulaski Smith, Lafayette, Upsher County, Texas, May 15, 1908, Pulaski Smith Papers, Hood's Texas Brigade Collection, Historical Research Center, Hill College, Hillsboro, Tex.; Pulaski Smith Confederate Pension Application, State of Texas, August 1909, Pulaski Smith Papers, Hood's Texas Brigade Collection, Historical Research Center, Hill College, Hillsboro, Tex.

76. Simpson, *Compendium*, 33–36.

77. Oliver, S. W. (Dallas County), Rejected Confederate pension applications, 1910 and 1913.

Texas Comptroller's Office claims records, Archives and Information Services Division, Texas State Library and Archives Commission.

78. Edwin King Goree to "Dear Mother" [Sarah Williams Kittrell Goree], December 22, 1898, Box 4, Folder 5: Edwin King (E. K.) Goree Letters, 1891–1900, Goree Family Papers, 1833–1996, SHSU Special Collections, Newton Gresham Library, Sam Houston State University, Huntsville.

79. Hartzog, "Mollie Bailey: Circus Entrepreneur," 108–12; Simpson, *Hood's Texas Brigade in Poetry and Song*, 208–9.

80. J. B. Polley, Floresville, Wilson County, Texas, to Col. B. F. Chilton, Angleton, Texas, July 18, 1908, F. B. Chilton Papers, Texas Collection, Baylor University, Waco, Tex.

81. Chilton, *Unveiling and Dedication of Monument to Hood's Texas Brigade on the Capitol Grounds at Austin, Texas*, 79–80, 195–96.

82. Ibid., 20.

83. Ibid., 40.

84. Simpson, *Reunion and Memory*, 38.

85. Joseph B. Polley, Floresville, Texas to Frank B. Chilton, Angleton, Texas, September 13, 1908, F. B. Chilton Papers, Texas Collection, Baylor University, Waco, Tex. See also "Simpson, John Nicholas," *Handbook of Texas Online*, www.tshaonline.org/handbook/online/articles/SS/fsi22.html.

86. Fletcher, *Rebel Private*, 195.

87. Ibid., 212.

88. William Edgar Copeland, Rockdale, Texas, to Frank B. Chilton, Houston, Texas, April 19, 1917, F. B. Chilton Papers, Texas Collection, Baylor University, Waco, Tex.

89. Mary Felicia Loughridge, Falls County, Texas, to "My Dear Noble Husband" [James Rodgers Loughridge], February 6, 1862, Loughridge Letters.

90. Mary Felicia Loughridge, "Gen Gordon at Kartoum," Loughridge Collection.

91. Ida Raymond, *Southland Writers: Biographical and Critical Sketches of the Living Female Writers of the South* (Philadelphia: Claxton, Remsen & Haffelinger, 1870), 953.

92. See Harold B. Simpson, *Hood's Texas Brigade in Poetry and Song* (Hillsboro, Tex.: Hill Junior College Press, 1968), 226; see also Simpson, *Hood's Texas Brigade in Reunion and Memory* (Hillsboro, Tex.: Hill Junior College Press, 1974), 141.

93. T. W. Fitzgerald, Baltimore, Maryland, to Theodore A. Fowler, Houston, Texas, November 15, 1881, S. O. Young Collection (MSS 10), Box 4, folder 4, Houston, Texas, Metropolitan Research Center. Hereafter cited as S. O. Young Collection.

94. T. W. Fitzgerald, Baltimore, Maryland, to Theodore A. Fowler, Houston, Texas, January 9, 1882, and June 2, 1882, S. O. Young Collection.

95. Thomas D. Sultzer, Baltimore, Maryland, to Theodore A. Fowler, Houston, Texas, June 20, 1882, S. O. Young Collection.

96. Thomas D. Sultzer, Baltimore, Maryland, to Theodore A. Fowler, Houston, Texas, June 23, 1882, S. O. Young Collection.

97. James Southerland Upton, "Life of Henry Antone Paulman," *Arkansas Family Historian* 7 (January/February/March 1969): 5–8; "Arkansas Ex-Confederate Pension Records, 1891–1939," database with images, *FamilySearch* (https://familysearch.org/ark:/61903/1:1:Q2ST-5F6W, April 2016), L. A. Paulman, 1893–1905; citing Calhoun, Arkansas, United States, State Auditor's Office, Little Rock; FHL microfilm 2,209,370. See also "Arkansas Ex-Confederate Pension Records, 1891–

1939," database with images, *FamilySearch* (https://familysearch.org/ark:/61903/1:1:Q2ST-RRH6 : 28 April 2016), L. A. Paulman, 03 Sep 1894; Arkansas, United States, State Auditor's Office, Little Rock; FHL microfilm 2,209,370.

98. 1860 U.S. Selected Federal Census Non-Population, 1850–1880, Andrew Erskine, Agriculture, Seguin, Texas; 1870 U.S. Schedule Federal Census Non-Population, 1850–1880, Ann Erskine, Agriculture, Seguin, Texas; 1870 U.S. Federal Census, Precinct 1, Guadalupe, Texas; Roll: M593_1589; Page: 382B; Image: 297027; Family History Library Film: 553088.

99. George W. Brackenridge, San Antonio, Texas, to Frank Chilton, Angleton, Texas, December 29, 1908, F. B. Chilton Papers, Texas Collection, Baylor University, Waco, Tex. See also "Brackenridge, George Washington," *Handbook of Texas Online,* https://tshaonline.org/handbook/online/articles/fbr02.

100. Simpson, *Reunion and Memory,* 213–14.

CONCLUSION

1. Robert Campbell [writing under the pseudonym Joe Joskins], "A Sketch of Hood's Texas Brigade," 228, 237, 240, emphasis original, unpublished manuscript, written at Huntsville, Texas, 1865, University of Texas, San Antonio Library, R. H. Porter Civil War Collection Digitized version: http://digital.utsa.edu/cdm/ref/collection/p15125c01110/id/8440.

SELECTED BIBLIOGRAPHY

PRIMARY SOURCES

Manuscripts

Alabama
Auburn University Special Collections & Archives Department
    Irenus Watson Landingham Collection, RG 552

Georgia
Special Collections and Archives, Robert W. Woodruff Library, Emory University, Atlanta
    Confederate Miscellany, 1B, Box 20
        Thomas Dowtin Letter
        The Spirit of 1861 (Eighteenth Georgia camp newspaper)

Maryland
Antietam National Park, Sharpsburg
    Carman Confederate Hood's Division, Longstreet's Reserve Artillery, Evan's Independent Brigade
        W. E. Barry
        P. A. Work
    Ezra Carman Manuscript

Mississippi
Special Collections Department, Mississippi State University Libraries, Starkville
    Tacitus T. Clay Letters

New Hampshire
Dartmouth College Library, Hanover

Antietam Collection, John J. Gould
    J. E. Anderson Letter
    Benjamin Baker Letters
    Haywood Brahan Letter
    John C. Cox Letter
    Stephen Darden Letter
    W. T. Hill Letters
    C. J. Jackson
    J. H. Littlefield Letter
    Odin W. Putnam Letter
    Angelina Winkler Letter

New York
New-York Historical Society, New York City
    George A. Mitchell Letters, 1861–1863

North Carolina
David M. Rubenstein Rare Book & Manuscript Library, Duke University, Durham
    Moses Warren Kenyon Papers, 1849–1870
    W. S. Shockley Letters, 1861–1864

Southern Historical Collection, Wilson Library, University of North Carolina at Chapel Hill
    T. L. Clingman Papers

Pennsylvania
Gettysburg National Military Park, Gettysburg
    First Texas Infantry Regiment
        H. W. Berryman Letter
        James Henry Hendrick Letter
        Thomas L. McCarty Speech
        George T. Todd Letter
        Unknown Diary, July 1–August (?), 1863
        Unknown Diary, July 3, 1863
        P. A. Work Letter
    Third Arkansas Infantry Regiment
        Henry Antone Paulman Letters
        John A. Wilkerson Diary
    Fourth Texas Infantry Regiment
        Decimus et Ultimus Barziza Diary
        William H. Hamman Papers

Zack Landrum Letters
John M. Pinckney Account, in *U.S. Congressional Record,* 1906
J. M. Polk Account
Fifth Texas Infantry Regiment
Rufus King Felder Letters
M. A. Hubert Diary
Robert M. Powell Letters
Jerome B. Robertson Letters
J. Mark Smither Letter
Campbell Wood Memoirs
Sixteenth Michigan Infantry Regiment
Ziba B. Graham Papers
Twentieth Indiana
William Gilbraith Papers
Forty-Fourth New York Infantry Regiment
Edward Bennett Papers
140th New York Infantry Regiment
William H. Clark Account

U.S. Army Heritage & Education Center, Carlisle
Robert L. Brake Collection
First Texas File
H. W. Berryman Letter
James Henry Henrick Letter
Thomas L. McCarty Address
A. C. Sims Recollections
Third Arkansas File
Robert J. Lowry Diary
Fourth Texas File
L.A. Daffan Autobiography
Val C. Giles Papers
J. J. Haynes Account
Zack Landrum Letters
John M. Pinckney
Fifth Texas File
Rufus K. Felder Letter
M. A. Hubert Diary
A. B. Masterson Account
J. Mark Smither Letter
Sixteenth Michigan File
Charles H. Slater Letter

Twentieth Indiana File
    Erasmus Gilbreath Memoir
Forty-Fourth New York File
    William H. Brown Letter
140th New York File
    Charles N. Smith Account

Civil War Miscellaneous Collection
  John W. Baker Papers
  Peter L. Foust Letter
  John Gregg Papers
  Oliver Norton Letter
  Frederick Pechin Collection
  Miles Smith Reminiscences
  William R. Stone Letter
  Charles Henry Veil Memoirs
  Franklin Whittemore Letter

Civil War Times Illustrated Collection of Civil War Papers
  John Berry Account
  Fletcher B. Moore Account
  Henry Ruffner Morrison Account
  Charles C. Perkins Diaries
  Andrew Jackson Read Papers

Harrisburg Civil War Roundtable Collection
  William Hall Clarke

Johnson Family Papers
  Philo Conklin Letter

Lewis Leigh Collection
  A. H. Dalton Letters
  Daniel Gookin Journal
  R. E. Horn Letter
  "Mac" Letters
  George W. Maddox Letter
  E. O. Perry Letter

Jay Luvaas Collection
  Lt. Robert Taggart Diary

Thomas R. Stone Collection
    Hugh C. Perkins Letters

Tennessee
Chickamauga/Chattanooga National Military Park, Fort Oglethorpe
    First Texas Folder
        John Massey Sketch
    Fourth Texas Folder
        N. A. Davis Collection
    Eighth Indiana Light Battery Folder
        Luther P. Bradley Memoir
    Viniard Family Folder
        Lewis Day (101st Ohio) Reminiscence
        Judge Charles W. Lusk Account
        Seventy-Second Indiana Descriptions
        Viniard Family Genealogy & Photos

Texas
Archives and Information Services Division, Texas State Library and Archives Commission, Austin
    William Harvey Beeman, Papers, Correspondence, 1851–1874
    Frank B. Chilton Scrapbook
    Governor Edward Clark Records, 1861
    Nicholas A. Davis Papers
    Governor Francis Richard Lubbock Records, 1861–1904
    Governor Pendleton Murrah Records, 1863–1865
    James C. Murray Letters, 1862–1863
    Texas Comptroller's Office Claims Records
        Rejected Confederate pension applications, 1910 and 1913
        Willis Landrum
        S. W. Oliver
    Confederate Pension Applications
        A. A. Aldrich
        Colin Aldrich
        Ida Arnwine
        Williams Arnwine
        Jasper Barron
        Mrs. Jasper Barron
        Louis Barry
        Oliver Barton
        James Bass

Robert H. Bassett
H. D. Boozer
Georgia S. Brietz
Samuel R. Briley
Sarah R. Bullock
Thad W. Bullock
John G. Burden
William Henry Burgess
Benjamin Burke
Robert Burns
J. B. Bussy
J. A. Cameron
A. W. Colley
Sarah J. Cramer
Agnes Mercer Crockett
Edward R. Crockett
J. T. Cross
Fannie C. Cunningham
John W. Deel
Sue Derden
Joseph Dabney Dewall
Martha C. Dewall
James Downey
David Crockett Dunlap
Ella Ezell
William Goodloe
Margaret A. Grogard
Elizabeth Ann Hamby
Marshall Hamby
Serand Hardoin
Henry Haynes
Jacob Hemphill
Nathan Hollingsworth
W. A. Jernigan
M. E. Joyce
Robert Franklin Joyce
W. Zed Kerr
John A. Knight
William H. Knight
J. E. Landes
Alfred Llewellyn

M. E. Llewellyn
Theodore Lubbock
Sims L. Mathews
A. E. McCarter
Reuben McClanahan
Ephrom McCorquodale
George Merk
J. B. Milam
Belle A. Murray
John D. Murray
Robert Murray
E. A. Noble
J. W. Norford
Joseph Benjamin Polley
Mattie L. Polley
Mary E. Powell
Lelia L. Quarles
Jacob C. Quick
Mary Ann Quick
T. D. Rock
H. R. Rodgers
J. C. Rodgers
Peter M. Saloi
Lucretia Sellers
William H. Sellers
Joseph C. Sheldon
Mary Elizabeth Shropshire
Hiram Simpson
Pulaski Smith
Jasper Snowden
James A. Stallings
Thomas B. Stanfield
B. B. Stedman
J. P. Surratt
Mollie Riddle Surratt
Jack Sutherland
Mary A. Tiner
Sallie Torbett
Sam Torbett
Martin B. Turrentine
W. W. Wofford

Mary E. Wood
C. S. Worsham

Texas State Lunatic Asylum Records
Report of Superintendent 1863

Dolph Briscoe Center for American History, University of Texas at Austin
Burges-Jefferson Family Papers, 1836 (1857–1892) 1960
Governor Edward Clark Papers, 1842–1910, 1946
James Travis and William H. Cleveland Papers, 1850–1864
Edward Richardson Crockett Diary, 1864–1865
Annie B. Giles Papers, 1858–1963
James H. Manahan Letters, 1861–1864
Thomas L. McCarty Papers
Thomas Peck Ochiltree Papers, 1882–1897
Philpott Texana Collection, 1844–1879
Nicholas Pomeroy Reminiscences, 1861–1865, 1908–1911
Henry Oldham Robertson Papers, 1863–1864, and undated
Robert Anderson Sullivan Papers, 1856–1887

Daughters of the Republic of Texas Library, San Antonio
John and William Short Letters

Johnnie Jo Sowell Dickenson Genealogy Room, Huntsville Public Library, Huntsville
"Hunter, Captain James Thomas," vertical file, Confederate records

The Nita Stewart Haley Memorial Library and History Center, Midland
General Files
E. H. Cunningham Letter
Hood's Texas Brigade Monument Dedication History
Hood's Texas Brigade Monument Unveiling
Hood's Texas Brigade Records, 1912–1927
Hood's Texas Brigade Roster, 1905, 1913–1914, 1920–1934
John H. Roberts Letter

Jefferson Historical Society and Museum
William Thomas Ford Letter
George C. Sorell Letter

Metropolitan Research Center, Houston
T. S. O. Young Collection (MSS 10)

Navarro County Courthouse, Corsicana
    County Commissioner's Report, 1861–1865, Book C www.rootsweb.ancestry
    .com/~txnavarr/war/civil_war/commissioners_report/book_c.htm

Pearce Civil War Archives, Navarro College, Corsicana
    W. B. Campbell Papers, 1861–1863
    Alexander M. Erskine Letter, 1862
    Benjamin I. Franklin Papers, 1863–1968
    James Rodgers Loughridge Papers, pre-1838–1972
        Terry (William J.) and Beal (D. R.) Papers, 1864

Rosenberg Library, Galveston
    Schadt Family Papers, 1861–1957

SHSU Special Collections, Newton Gresham Library, Sam Houston State University, Huntsville
    Goree Family Papers, 1833–1996
    Pleasant Williams Kittrell Correspondence, 1805–1867
    Andrew Todd McKinney Papers, 1833–1989
    Frank B. Sexton Papers, 1844–1985
    J. Mark Smither Civil War Letters, 1861–1881
    Robert M. Powell Correspondence, 1827–1916

Special Collections, University of Texas at San Antonio Libraries, San Antonio
    R. H. Porter Civil War Collection
        Robert Campbell, "Joe Joskins, A Sketch of Hood's Texas Brigade"

Texas Heritage Museum, Hill College, Hillsboro
    Hood's Texas Brigade Collection
        Richmond Acker Papers
        Jack Adam Letters
        James J. Archer Letters
        John White Baker Autobiography
        Frederick S. Bass Papers
        John J. Bass Sketch
        E. M. Bean Sketch
        H. Waters Berryman Letters
        I. M. Bookman Letter
        R. A. Brantley Account
        Basil Brashear Letters
        Jack Burke Letter

J. B. Bussy Letters
Jeremiah D. Caddell Letters
Camp Newspaper, 1861 (18th Georgia)
Robert Campbell Collection
Frank Chilton Letters
Tacitus T. Clay Letters
Albert G. Cloptin Papers
Coffield Brothers Collection
Stephen R. Compton Letter
John P. Copeland Papers
Katie Daffan Papers
L. A. Daffan Papers
Matthew Dale Papers
Fannie Dardin Papers
Seaborn Dominey Letters
Oscar J. Downs
Josiah G. Duke Letters
John T. Dulaney Papers
Tim Dunklin Diary
W. L. Edwards Papers
J. D. Enlowe Letter
Rufus King Felder Letters
William Fletcher Sketch
Robert V. Foster Papers
William H. Foster Papers
B. I. Franklin Papers
G. L. Gage Letter
Robert H. and William H. Gaston Letters
Goree Brothers Papers
Thomas J. Goree Letters
A. B. Green Diary
Grimes County Greys Collection
W. R. Hamby Papers
D. H. Hamilton History
William H. Hamman Papers
O. T. Hanks History
Henry M. Haynie Papers
J. N. Hemphill Collection
George Henderson Papers
J. N. Henderson Papers
James H. Hendrick Collection

R. A. Higgason Papers
Silas M. Hines Papers
A. B. Hood Papers
John Bell Hood Papers
John Bell Hood, Jr. Papers
John Bell Hood, III Papers
Hood's Brigade Buried in Hollywood, Stonewall
Hood's Brigade Prisoners Who Died in Forst Delaware Prison, 1863–1865
Mark A. Hubert Diary
Robert W. Hubert Papers
James T. Hunter Letter
Joe Joskins/Robert Campbell Memoirs
Zach Landrum Letters
Robert E. Lee Letter
W. R. Lott Memoir
Robert Lowery Diary
John Percy Maloney Papers
Van H. Manning Papers
William H. Martin Biography
Fred L. Mathee Papers
John F. McGehee biography
John F. McKee Papers
Minutes of Hood's Texas Brigade Association Meetings, 1872–1896
Sidney E. Moseley Letters
Henry E. Moss Papers
Jim C. Murray Letters
John D. Murray Sketch
Robert W. Murray Papers
Navarro Rifles History
J. J. O'Neil Papers
Samuel Tine Owen Letters
William Paine Papers
Madison D. Parker Papers
E. O. Perry Papers
Joseph B. Polley Papers
Robert M. Powell Papers
William P. Powell Papers
R. Quickley Letters
Alexis T. Rainey Letters
Malachiah Reeves Memoir
James D. Roberdeau Account

A. S. A. Roberts Papers
Frank Robertson Letter
J. B. Robertson Collection
William H. Sellers Papers
Thomas J. Selman Papers
William Anson Sharp Letter
Miles V. Smith Reminiscence
Pulaski Smith Papers
W. R. & J. W. Smith Papers
Thomas B. Stanfield Papers
John D. Staples Papers
William J. Tannehill Letters
Henry Leonidas Taylor Letters
S. B. Terrell Letter
W. J. Terry Papers
George T. Todd Papers
William P. Townsend Letters
Isaac "Ike" Turner Letters
Henry Travis Letter
T. G. Wallingford Sketch
John Waltermays Sketch
Paul Watkins Letters
Pleasant B. Watson Diary
Samuel S. Watson Letters
John C. West Collection
August F. Wiggs Papers
Watson Dugat Williams Letters
John N. Wilson Papers
Robert Wilson Papers
Clinton M. Winkler Collection
Mark S. Womack Papers
Campbell Wood Reminiscence
John G. Wood Papers
William J. Woodson Papers
Phillip A. Work Papers
C. S. Worsham Testimony
E. L. Worsham Letters
Texas Collection, Baylor University, Waco
Frank B. Chilton Papers

United Confederate Veterans Collection
    Harvey H. Black Letter
    Ed Cunningham Letter
    Fourth Texas Infantry Muster Roll
    George Jones Letter
    George T. Todd Letter
    John C. Upton Letter

United Daughters of the Confederacy Collection
    Chester M. Bisbee Letter
    Edward H. Cunningham Letter
    Fifth Texas Infantry, Company G. Muster Roll
    G. A. Grant Medical Discharge
    George Jones Letter
    J. B. Orphans' Fund Records
    John H. Roberts Letter
    J. M. Snider Letter
    Jasper M. Stallcup Letter
    George T. Todd Letter

Virginia
Eleanor S. Brockenbrough Archives (formerly of the Museum of the Confederacy), Virginia Historical Society, Richmond
    B. L. Aycock Papers
    Confederate States of America "Roll of Honour"
    Andrew N. Erskine Papers
    Robert G. Holloway Diary
    T. M. Logan Papers
    H. W. Marchant Papers

Fredericksburg & Spotsylvania National Military Park, Fredericksburg
    "Confederate" Bound Volume 378
        John Daniel and William Jason Staples Letters

Richmond National Battlefield Park, Richmond
    R. A. Brantley Memoir
    James Campbell Letters
    William B. Campbell Letter
    Seaborn Dominey Letters
    Robert E. Fitzgerald Diary
    B. I. Franklin Letter

Paul Ripley Letters
Franklin Robertson Letter
Solon Z. Ruff Letter
W. J. Terry Letter
S. S. Watson Letters

Washington, D. C.
U.S. National Archives and Records Administration
    Letters Received by the C.S. Adjutant and Inspector General's Office, 2061-B-1863
        R. H. Bassett Letter
        B. F. Perry Letter

Private Collections
Jerry Carl Beetz, Pearland, Texas
    Memories of John Lewis Tarkington
HenryEtta McKinley Wilson, New Smyrna Beach, Florida, and John Stevens, Fresno, Texas
    W. J. Watts Letters
Katherine A. H. Goldberg, Richmond, Texas
    Joseph B. Polley Letter
D. Scott Hartwig, Gettysburg, Pennsylvania
    Hugh Perkins Letters
Melinda Laird Kilian, Austin, Texas, and Melissa Laird Lingwall, Cedar Hill, Texas
    Andrew N. Erskine Civil War Commentary and Letters
Weldon Nash Jr., Dallas, Texas
    H. H. Black tintype
Mary Lou Percy and Joanne Watson Percy, Georgetown, Texas
    Landrum Family Photo
Jane Gillette Riggs, Baytown, Texas
    Sullivan Family Papers
    Lucy Morton Sullivan Diaries
James and Marty Rogers, Statesville, North Carolina
    Private J. A. White (Louis T. Wigfall) Parole, Co. M, 1st Texas Infantry
Dan Worrell Private Collection, Houston, Texas
    Cecelia Morse Civil War Diary

Digital Collections
Arkansas Ex-Confederate Pension Records, 1891–1939, FamilySearch.org
    L. Ann Paulman
Confederate Amnesty Papers, Fold3.com
    Thomas J. Goree

Confederate Compiled Service Records, Fold3.com
    First Texas Infantry
        William A. Bedell
        Henry F. Bradley
        Joseph C. Chiles
        James Day
        John Hanson
        Richard J. Harding
        Charles H. Kingsley
        Andrew Knight
        John Knight
        Joseph Knight
        William Knight
        James K. Malone
        Hugh McLeod
        C. M. Mixon
        Edwin B. Searle
        Phillip A. Work
    Third Arkansas Infantry
        Nicholas C. Denson
    Fourth Texas Infantry
        Alexander M. Erskine
        Andrew N. Erskine
        Willis Landrum
        H. William Martin
    Fifth Texas Infantry
        Samuel Bailey
        Jasper Barron
        William Barron
        William Gaffney
        Pleasant K. Goree
        Asbury Lawson
        Darius Cyriaque Rachal
    Twentieth Texas Cavalry
        John Wade Owen
Rare Books Collection, University of Southern Mississippi Digital Collections, Hattiesburg
    "Resolutions of the Texas Brigade," January 24, 1865
United States Federal Census, Ancestry.com
    1850 United States Federal Census. Ancestry.com Operations, Inc., 2009
    1850 U.S. Federal Census–Slave Schedules. Ancestry.com Operations, Inc., 2004

1860 United States Federal Census. Ancestry.com Operations, Inc., 2009
1860 U.S. Federal Census—Slave Schedules. Ancestry.com Operations, Inc., 2010
1870 United States Federal Census. Ancestry.com Operations, Inc., 2009

Newspapers

Athens (Ga.) Southern Banner
Atlanta (Ga.) Southern Confederacy
Austin (Tex.) State Gazette
Austin (Tex.) Weekly Statesman
Bryan (Tex.) Daily Eagle
Charleston (S.C.) Mercury
Cincinnati Commercial Tribune
Clarksville (Tex.) Standard
Colorado Citizen (Columbus, Tex.)
Corpus Christi (Tex.) Ranchero
Countryman (Turnwold, Ga.)
Crocket (Tex.) Courier
Daily National Intelligencer (Washington, D.C.)
Dallas Herald
Dallas Morning News
Dallas Weekly Herald
Flatonia (Tex.) Argus
Floresville (Tex.) Chronicle-Journal
Galveston (Tex.) Civilian and Gazette
Galveston (Tex.) Tri-Weekly News
Galveston (Tex.) Weekly News
Greensborough (N.C.) Patriot
Harper's Weekly
Houston Daily Telegraph
Houston Tri-Weekly Telegraph
Houston Weekly Telegraph
Jasper (Tex.) News-Boy
Macon (Ga.) Telegraph
Marshall (Tex.) Morning News
Marshall (Tex.) Morning Star
Memphis (Tenn.) Daily Avalanche
Navarro Express (Corsicana, Tex.)
New Orleans Times
New Orleans Times-Picayune

New York Times
Philadelphia Inquirer
Prairie Blade (Corsicana, Tex.)
Richmond (Va.) Daily Dispatch
Richmond (Va.) Enquirer
Richmond (Va.) Examiner
Richmond (Va.) Whig
Rochester (N.Y.) Evening Express
San Antonio (Tex.) Semi-Weekly
Shreveport (La.) Daily News
Texas Republican (Marshall)
Texas State Gazette (Austin)
Wilmington (N.C.) Journal

Other Published Primary Sources

Barziza, Decimus et Ultimus. *The Adventures of a Prisoner of War, 1863–1864*. Austin: University of Texas Press, 1964.

"A Bill to Be Entitled an Act to Authorize the Consolidation of Companies, Battalions, and Regiments." November 8, 1864. Confederate States of America. Richmond: C.S.A., 1864. http://hdl.handle.net/2027/du11.ark:/13960/t5bc4rg0z.

Bond, Mildred Martin, and George Doherty Bond. *Alexander Carswell and Isabella Brown: Their Ancestors and Descendants: Genealogy and History of Carswell, Brown, Gordon, Ruthven and the John Martin–Jane Hutchinson Family*. Chipley, Fla.: Carswell Foundation, 1977.

Bryan, Jimmy L., Jr., ed. "'Whip Them Like the Mischief': The Civil War Letters of Frank and Mintie Price." *East Texas Historical Association* 36, no. 2 (1998): 68–84.

Campbell, Robert. *Lone Star Confederate: A Gallant and Good Soldier of the 5th Texas Infantry*. Edited by George Skoch and Mark W. Perkins. College Station: Texas A&M University Press, 2003.

Carman, Ezra A. *The Maryland Campaign of September 1862*. Vol. 2: *Antietam*, edited by Thomas G. Clemens. El Dorado Hills, Calif.: Savas Beatie, 2012.

Chicoine, Stephen, ed. "... Willing Never to Go in Another Fight": The Civil War Correspondence of Rufus King Felder of Chappell Hill." *Southwestern Historical Quarterly* 106 (April 2003): 574–97.

Chilton, Frank B. *Unveiling and Dedication of Monument to Hood's Texas Brigade on the Capitol Grounds at Austin, Texas, Thursday, October Twenty-Seven, Nineteen Hundred and Ten, and Minutes of the Thirty-ninth Annual Reunion of Hood's Texas Brigade Association held in Senate Chamber at Austin, Texas, October Twenty-Six and Twenty-Seven, Nineteen Hundred and Ten, Together with a Short Monument* and Brigade Association History and Confederate Scrap Book. Houston, Tex.: self-published, 1911.

Compiled Service Records, Confederate. Fold3.com.

Corbin, Richard Washington. *Letters of a Confederate Officer to His Family in Europe, during the Last Year of the War of Secession.* Baltimore: Butternut and Blue, 1993.

Cudworth, Warren H., Chaplain, First Massachusetts, *History of the First Regiment (Massachusetts Infantry) from the 25th of May, 1861, to the 25th of May, 1864: Including Brief References to the Operations of the Army of the Potomac.* Boston: Walker, Fuller, & Co., 1866.

Cutrer, Thomas W., ed. *Longstreet's Aide: The Civil War Letters of Major Thomas J. Goree.* Charlottesville: University Press of Virginia, 1995.

Davis, Katherine Hooper, Linda Erickson Devereaux, Carolyn Reeves Ericson, comps. *Texas Confederate Home Roster.* Nacogdoches, Tex.: Ericson, 2003.

Denson, Dillard, M.D. *The Life and Times of Reverend N. C. Denson: Reminiscences of a Confederate Soldier, Dedicated Minister, and Arkansas Leader.* Privately published, 2014.

Emerson, Samuel H. *History of the War of the Confederacy, '61 to '65.* Malvern, Ark.: privately printed, 1918.

Estill, Mary S., and F. B. Sexton, ed. "Diary of a Confederate Congressman, 1862–1863, Part I." *Southwestern Historical Quarterly* 38 (April 1935): 270–301.

———. "Diary of a Confederate Congressman, 1862–1863, Part II." *Southwestern Historical Quarterly* 39 (July 1935): 33–65.

Everett, Donald E. *Chaplain Davis and Hood's Texas Brigade.* Baton Rouge: Louisiana State University Press, 1999.

Faulk, L. J. *History of Henderson County.* Athens, Tex.: Athens Review Printing, 1929.

Fletcher, William A. *Rebel Private: Front and Rear: Memoirs of a Confederate Soldier.* New York: Dutton/Penguin, 1995.

Gallagher, Gary W., ed. *Fighting for the Confederacy: The Personal Recollections of General Edward Porter Alexander.* Chapel Hill: University of North Carolina Press, 1989.

Gibbon, John. *Personal Reflections of the Civil War.* New York: Putnam's Sons, 1928.

Giles, Val. C. *Rags and Hope. The Recollections of Val C. Giles, Four Years with Hood's Brigade, Fourth Texas Infantry.* Edited by Mary Lasswell. New York: Coward-McCann, 1961.

Glaze, Peyton, and John Glaze. *Lincoln to Linden: Correspondence of the Glaze Family.* Edited by R. G. Hopkins. N.p., 1992.

Glover, ed., Robert W. *"Tyler to Sharpsburg": Robert H. And William H. Gaston (Their War Letters, 1861–62.* Waco, Tex.: W. M. Morrison, 1960.

Goree, Edwin Sue. *A Family Mosaic.* Coolidge, Ariz.: J. D. Goree, 1961.

Graham, Ziba B. "On to Gettysburg: Ten Days from My Diary of 1863." *A Paper Read before the Commandery of the State of Michigan, Military Order of the Loyal Legion of the U.S.* Detroit: Winn & Hammond, Printers and Binders, 1893.

A. B. Green Diary, 1865. Austin: Hood's Texas Brigade Association Reactivated, 2015.

Greene, A. Wilson. *Civil War Petersburg: Confederate City in the Crucible of War.* Charlottesville: University of Virginia Press, 2006.

———. *The Final Battles of the Petersburg Campaign: Breaking the Backbone of the Rebellion.* 2nd ed. Knoxville: University of Tennessee Press, 2012.

Hamby, William R. "4th Texas in Battle of Gaines's Mill." In *Texans Who Wore the Grey,* ed. Sidney S. Johnson. Tyler, Tex.: self-published, 1907.

Hamilton, D. H. *History of Company M, 1st Texas Volunteer Infantry, Hood's Brigade, Longstreet's Corps, Army of the Confederate States of America.* 1925. Reprint, Waco, Tex.: W. M. Morrison, 1962.

Heller, J. Roderick, III, and Carolynn Ayres Heller, eds. *The Confederacy Is on Her Way up the Spout: Letters to South Carolina, 1861–1864.* Columbia: University of South Carolina Press, 1998.

History of Texas, Together with a Biographical History of Milam, Williamson, Bastrop, Travis, Lee and Burleson Counties. Chicago: Lewis, 1893.

Hood, John Bell. *Advance and Retreat: Personal Experiences in the United States and Confederate Armies.* Secaucus, N.J.: Blue and Grey Press, 1985.

Hood, Jonathan D. "A Yellow Rose in Old Dominion: The Civil War Reminiscences of Orlando T. Hanks." Master's thesis, Stephen F. Austin University, 1997.

Hood, Stephen M. *The Lost Papers of Confederate General John Bell Hood.* El Dorado Hills, Calif.: Savas Beatie, 2015.

Hopkins, C. A. Porter, ed. "The James J. Archer Letters: A Marylander in the Civil War, Part I." *Maryland Historical Magazine* 56 (March 1961): 125–49.

Huckaby, Elizabeth Paisley, and Ethel C. Simpson, eds. *Tulip Evermore: Emma Butler and William Paisley, Their Lives in Letters, 1857–1887.* Fayetteville: University of Arkansas Press, 1985.k

Hunter, Alexander. "The Rebel Yell." *Confederate Veteran* 21 (May 1913): 219.

Ide, Sgt. Horace K. "The First Vermont Cavalry in the Gettysburg Campaign." Edited by Dr. Elliot W. Hoffman. *Gettysburg Magazine: Historical Articles of Lasting Interest* 14 (January 1996): 7–26.

Johnson, Jane Echols, ed. *Hard Times, 1861–1865: A Collection of Confederate Letters, Court Minutes, Soldiers' Records, and Local Lore from Craig County, Virginia.* N.p.: Johnston and Williams, 1986.

Kemp, L. W., ed. "Early Days in Milam County: Reminiscences of Susan Turnham McCown." *Southwestern Historical Quarterly* 50 (January 1947): 367–76.

King, C. Richard, ed. *Victorian Lady on the Texas Frontier: The Journal of Ann Raney Coleman.* Norman: University of Oklahoma Press, 1971.

Law, Evander M. "From the Wilderness to Cold Harbor." In *Battles and Leaders of the Civil War,* edited by Robert Underwood Johnson and Clarence Clough Buel, 4 vols. New York: Century, 1887–88.

Lemon, Captain James Lile. *Feed them the Steel! Being the Wartime Recollections of Captain James Lile Lemon, Co. A, 18th Georgia Infantry, C.S.A.* Edited by Mark H. Lemon. Privately published, 2013.

Leonard, W. A., comp. *Houston City Directory, for 1867–68.* Houston: Gray, Smallwood & Co., 1867.

Longstreet, James. *From Manassas to Appomattox: Memoirs of the Civil War in America.* Philadelphia: Lippincott, 1895. Reprint, New York: Da Capo, 1992.

Martin, Martha E. "Sketch of Major W. H. Martin." In *Biographies of Eminent Citizens and Historical Sketches of Henderson County,* edited by J. L. Fault, vol. 2. Athens, Tex.: Directory of Athens City, 1904.

———. "Sketch of Major W. H. Martin." In *Biographies of Eminent Citizens and Historical Sketches of Henderson County,* edited by J. L. Fault, vol. 2. Athens, Tex.: Directory of Athens City, 1904.

McAnelly, Shelton B. "Penn Letters, 1860–1865." *Louisiana Genealogical Register* 27 (December 1970): 352, 389–94.

———. "Penn Letters, 1860–1865." *Louisiana Genealogical Register* 18 (June 1971): 100–105.

———. "Penn Letters, 1860–1865." *Louisiana Genealogical Register* 18 (September 1971): 262–67.

———. "Penn Letters, 1860–1865." *Louisiana Genealogical Register* 18 (December 1971): 338–42.

———. "Penn Letters, 1860–1865." *Louisiana Genealogical Register* 19 (March 1972): 108–11.

McArthur, Judith N., and Orville Vernon Burton, eds. *A Gentleman and an Officer: A Military and Social History of James B. Griffin's Civil War.* New York: Oxford University Press, 1996.

Mulholland, St. Clair A. *Military Order Congress Medal of Honor Legion of the United States.* Philadelphia: Town Printing, 1905.

Nabours, B. A. "Active Service of a Texas Command." *Confederate Veteran* 24 (1916): 69–72.

Oldham, William Simpson. "Speech of W.S. Oldham, of Texas, upon the bill to amend the conscript law, made in the Senate, September 4, 1862." Richmond, Va.: Crandall, M. L. Confederate imprints, 1862, Emory University Digital Library Publications Program, https://archive.org/details/19154655.3711.emory.edu.

Palmer, William A., Jr. "'Good Bye Dear Sister': The Unhappy War of a Texan Who Was the Last to Enlist and the First to Fall." *Civil War Times,* October 2016, 55–59.

Parker, Eddy R. *Touched by Fire: Letters from Company D, 5th Texas Infantry, Hood's Brigade, Army of Northern Virginia, 1862–1865.* Hillsboro, Tex.: Hill College Press, 2000.

Pickens, J. D. "Fort Harrison." *Confederate Veteran* 21 (1913): 484.

Polk, J. M. *The Confederate Soldier and Ten Years in South America.* Austin, Tex.: Von Boeckmann-Jones, 1910.

Polley, Joseph B. *Hood's Texas Brigade: Its Marches, Its Battles, Its Achievements.* New York: Neale, 1910. Reprint, Dayton, Ohio: Press of Morningside Bookshop, 1976.

———. *A Soldier's Letters to Charming Nellie: The Correspondence of Joseph B. Polley, Hood's Texas Brigade.* Edited by Richard B. McCaslin. Knoxville: University of Tennessee Press, 2008.

Powell, Robert M. *Recollections of a Texas Colonel at Gettysburg.* Gettysburg, Pa.: Thomas Publications, 1990.

Raymond, Ida. *Southland Writers: Biographical and Critical Sketches of the Living Female Writers of the South.* Philadelphia: Claxton, Remsen & Haffelinger, 1870.

Reagan, John. *John Reagan Memoirs with Special Reference to Secession and the Civil War.* New York: Neale, 1906.

Robertson, Jerome B., comp. *Touched with Valor: The Civil War Papers and Casualty Reports of Hood's Texas Brigade.* Edited by Harold B. Simpson. Hillsboro, Tex.: Hill Junior College Press, 1964.

Schaller, Mary W., and Marin N. Schaller, eds. *Soldiering for Glory: The Civil War Letters of Colonel Frank Schaller, Twenty-Second Mississippi Infantry.* Columbia: University of South Carolina Press, 2007.

Scroggs, Joseph J. "The Earth Shook and Quivered." Edited by Sig Synnestvedt. *Civil War Times Illustrated* 11, no. 12 (December 1972): 30–37.

Simpson, Harold B., ed. "Whip the Devil and His Hosts: The Civil War Letters of Eugene O. Perry." *Chronicles of Smith County, Texas* 6 (Fall 1967): 10–15, 33–44.

Skoch, George. "The Bloody Fifth." *Civil War Times Illustrated* 30 (December 1991): 36–43.

Stevens, John W. *Reminiscences of the Civil War.* Hillsboro, Tex.: Hillsboro Mirror Print, 1902.

Taylor, Alva. "The Diary of Jacob Eliot." *Navarro County Scroll*, 1965. Reprinted online, Navarro County Historical Society, www.rootsweb.ancestry.com/~txnavarr/biographies/e/eliot_jacob.htm.

Terrell, Thomas S. *The Boys from Brenham: The Original Letters of Virginius E. Petty, Co. E, 5th Texas Regiment, Hood's Brigade, Army of Northern Virginia.* Kerrville, Tex.: privately published by Terrell, 2006.

Thomason, John W. *Lone Star Preacher: Being a Chronicle of the Acts of Praxitales Swan, M.E. Church South, Sometime Captain, 5th Texas Regiment, Confederate States Provisional Army.* New York: Scribner's, 1941.

Todd, George T. *1st Texas Regiment.* Waco, Tex.: Texian Press, 1963.

Upton, James Southerland. "The Life of Henry Antone Paulman." *Arkansas Family Historian* 7 (January/February/March 1969): 4–8.

———. "The Life of Henry Antone Paulman." *Arkansas Family Historian* 7 (October/November/December 1969): 119–21.

U.S. War Department. *The War of the Rebellion: A Compilation of the Official Records of the Union and Confederate Armies.* 128 vols. Washington: Government Printing Office, 1880–1901. Cited as *O.R.*

West, John C. *A Texan in Search of a Fight.* Waco, Tex.: Hill, 1901. Reprint, Waco, Tex.: Texian Press, 1969.

Winkler, Angelina V. *The Confederate Capital and Hood's Texas Brigade.* Austin, Tex.: Eugene von Boeckmann, 1894.

Womack, Foster B. *An Account of the Womack Family.* Waco, Tex.: privately printed, 1937.

Wright, Louise Wigfall. *A Southern Girl in '61: The War-time Memories of a Confederate Senator's Daughter, 1861–1865.* Gansevoort, N.Y.: Corner House Historical Publications, 2000.

Yeary, Mamie. *Reminiscences of the Boys in Gray.* Reprint ed. Dayton, Ohio: Morningside Books, 1986.

SECONDARY SOURCES

Adelman, Garry E., and Timothy H. Smith. *Devil's Den: A History and a Guide.* Gettysburg, Pa.: Thomas Publications, 1997.

Alton, Robert H. C. "The Lost Camp." *North South Trader's Civil War* 33 (2008): 30–37, 58–60.

Ashcraft, Allan C. "Confederate Beef Packing at Jefferson, Texas." *Southwestern Historical Quarterly* 68 (October 1964): 259–70.

Bagur, Jacques D. *Antebellum Jefferson, Texas: Everyday Life in an East Texas Town.* Denton: University of North Texas Press, 2012.

Baker, Robin E., and Dale Baum. "The Texas Voter and the Crisis of Union, 1859–1861." *Journal of Southern History* 53 (August 1987): 395–420.

Betts, Vicki. "'A Sacred Charge upon Our Hands': Assisting the Families of Confederate Soldiers in Texas, 1861–1865." In *The Seventh Star of the Confederacy: Texas during the Civil War,* edited by Kenneth W. Howell. Denton: University of North Texas Press, 2009.

Bledsoe, Andrew Scott. *Citizen-Officers: The Union and Confederate Volunteer Junior Officer Corps in the American Civil War.* Baton Rouge: Louisiana State University Press, 2015.

———. "The Homecircle: Kinship and Community in the Third Arkansas Infantry, Texas Brigade, 1861–1865." *Arkansas Historical Quarterly* 71 (Spring 2012): 22–43.

Bohannon, Keith S. "Dirty, Ragged, and Ill-Provided For: Confederate Logistical Problems in the 1862 Maryland Campaign and Their Solutions." In *The Antietam Campaign,* edited by Gary W. Gallagher. Chapel Hill: University of North Carolina Press, 1999.

Bond, Bradley G. *Political Culture in the Nineteenth-Century South: Mississippi, 1830–1900.* Baton Rouge: Louisiana State University Press, 1995.

Bowery, Charles R., Jr. "Encounter at the Triangular Field: The 124th New York and the 1st Texas at Gettysburg, July 2, 1863." *Gettysburg: Historical Articles of Lasting Interest* 30 (2004): 49–62.

Brooks, Charles E. "Popular Sovereignty in the Confederate Army: The Case of Colonel John Marshall and the Fourth Texas Infantry Regiment." In *The View from the Ground: Experiences of Civil War Soldiers*, edited by Aaron Sheehan-Dean. Lexington: University of Kentucky Press, 2007.

———. "The Social and Cultural Dynamics of Hood's Texas Brigade." *Journal of Southern History* 67 (August 2001): 535–72.

Bunch, Jack A. *Roster of the Courts-Martial in the Confederate State Army*. Shippensburg, Pa.: White Maine, 2001.

Byrne, Frank. *Becoming Bourgeois: Merchant Culture in the Antebellum and Confederate South*. Lexington: University Press of Kentucky, 2006.

Campbell, Randolph B. *A Southern Community in Crisis: Harrison County, Texas, 1850–1880*. Austin: Texas State Historical Association, 1983.

Campbell, Randolph B., and Richard G. Lowe. *Wealth and Power in Antebellum Texas*. College Station: Texas A&M University Press, 1977.

Cetina, Judith Gladys. "A History of Veterans' Homes in the United States, 1811–1930." Ph.D. diss., Case Western Reserve University, 1977.

Chicoine, Stephen. *The Confederates of Chappell Hill, Texas: Prosperity, Civil War, and Decline*. Jefferson, N.C.: McFarland, 2005.

Coco, Gregory A. *A Strange and Blighted Land: Gettysburg: After the Battle*. Gettysburg, Pa.: Thomas, 1995.

Coddington, Edwin B. *The Gettysburg Campaign: A Study in Command*. 1968. Reprint, New York: Scribner's Sons, 1984.

Collier, Calvin L. *"They'll Do to Tie To!": The Story of the Third Regiment, Arkansas Infantry, C.S.A.* Jacksonville, Ark.: privately published, 1959.

Cooper, Edward S. *Louis Trezevant Wigfall: The Disintegration of the Union and Collapse of the Confederacy*. Madison, N.J.: Fairleigh Dickinson University Press, 2012.

Courtney, Thomas A. "Mount St. Mary's and the American Civil War." *Analecta: Selected Studies in the History of Mount St. Mary's College and Seminary* 1 (2004): 2–20.

Crews, D'Anne McAdams, ed. *Huntsville and Walker County, Texas: A Bicentennial History*. Huntsville: Sam Houston State University, 1976.

Crouch, Howard R. *Relic Hunter: The Field Account of Civil War Sites, Artifacts, and Hunting*. 1978. Fifth reprint with supplement. Oakpark, Va.: SCS, 2006.

Cunningham, Steve, and Beth A. White. "'The Ground Trembled as They Came': The 1st West Virginia Cavalry in the Gettysburg Campaign." *Civil War Regiments: A Journal of the American Civil War* 6, no. 3 (1999): 59–88.

Custer, Andie. "John Hammond's 'Mis-stake': How a Misplaced Wooden Stake Altered the History of the Farnsworth Charge at Gettysburg." *Gettysburg Magazine: Historical Articles of Lasting Interest* 30 (2004): 98–113.

———. "The Kilpatrick-Farnsworth Argument that Never Happened." *Gettysburg Magazine: Historical Articles of Lasting Interest* 28 (2003): 100–116.

Dawson, Joseph G. *Army Generals and Reconstruction: Louisiana, 1862–1877.* Baton Rouge: Louisiana State University Press, 1982.

Eads, Leila Reeves. *Defenders: A Confederate History of Henderson County, Texas.* Athens, Tex.: Henderson County Historical Survey Committee, 1969.

Faust, Drew Gilpin. "Altars of Sacrifice: Confederate Women and the Narratives of War." In *Divided Houses: Gender and the Civil War,* edited by Catherine Clinton and Nina Silber. New York: Oxford University Press, 1992.

———. *Mothers of Invention: Women of the Slaveholding South in the American Civil War.* Chapel Hill: University of North Carolina Press, 1996.

Gage, Larry Jay. "The Texas Road to Secession and War: John Marshall and the Texas State Gazette 1860–1861." *Southwestern Historical Quarterly* 62, no. 2 (October 1958): 191–226.

Gallagher, Gary W. *The Confederate War.* Cambridge: Harvard University Press, 1997.

Gallagher, Gary W., and Kathryn Shively Meier. "Coming to Terms with Civil War Military History." *Journal of the Civil War Era* 4 (December 2014): 487–508.

Glatthaar, Joseph T. *General Lee's Army: From Victory to Collapse.* New York: Free Press, 2008.

———. *Soldiering in the Army of Northern Virginia: A Statistical Portrait of the Troops Who Served under Robert E. Lee.* Chapel Hill: University of North Carolina Press, 2011.

Gluba, Gregory. "Five Hundred Acres of History: Freestone Point, Virginia, in the Civil War." *Prologue: Quarterly of the National Archives and Records Administration* 31 (Fall 1999): 191–201.

Gordon, Lesley J. *A Broken Regiment: The 16th Connecticut's Civil War.* Baton Rouge: Louisiana State University Press, 2014.

Grear, Charles D., ed. "Debating the Rebellion: A Texan and a New Yorker Discuss Secession and the Civil War." *Military History of the West* 39 (December 2009): 41–58.

———. *The Fate of Texas: The Civil War and the Lone Star State.* Fayetteville: University of Arkansas Press, 2008.

———. *Why Texans Fought in the Civil War.* College Station: Texas A&M University Press, 2010.

Green, Jennifer R. *Military Education and the Emerging Middle Class in the Old South.* New York: Cambridge University Press, 2008.

Hahn, Steven. *The Roots of Southern Populism: Yeoman Farmers and the Transformation of the Georgia Upcountry, 1850–1890.* New York: Oxford University Press, 1983.

Hall, Claude H. "Congressman William H. 'Howdy' Martin." Paper presented at the East Texas Historical Association Annual Meeting, October 7, 1967, Nacogdoches.

Harrison, Kathleen R. Georg. "'Our Principal Loss Was in This Place': Action at the Slaughter Pen and at the South End of Houck's Ridge Gettysburg, Pennsylvania, 2 July 1863." *Morningside Notes.* Morningside House, 1984.

Harsh, Joseph L. *Sounding the Shallows: A Confederate Companion for the Maryland Campaign of 1862*. Kent, Ohio: Kent State University Press, 2000.

———. *Taken at the Flood: Robert E. Lee and Confederate Strategy in the Maryland Campaign of 1862*. Kent, Ohio: Kent State University Press, 1999.

Hartwig, D. Scott. "'I Dread the Thought of the Place': The Iron Brigade at Antietam." In *Giants in Their Tall Black Hats: Essays on the Iron Brigade*, edited by Alan T. Nolan and Sharon Eggleston Vipond. Bloomington: Indiana University Press, 1998.

———. *To Antietam Creek: The Maryland Campaign of September 1862*. Baltimore: Johns Hopkins University Press, 2012.

Hennessy, John J. *Return to Bull Run: The Campaign and Battle of Second Manassas*. New York: Simon and Schuster, 1993.

Herdegen, Lance J. *The Men Stood Like Iron: How the Iron Brigade Won Its Name*. Bloomington: Indiana University Press, 1997.

Holsworth, Jerry W. "Uncommon Valor: Hood's Texas Brigade in the Maryland Campaign." *Blue & Gray Magazine* 13 (August 1996): 6–20.

Hood, Stephen M. *John Bell Hood: The Rise, Fall, and Resurrection of a Confederate General*. El Dorado Hills, Calif.: Savas Beatie, 2013.

Hooks, H. A., M.D. *Lt. Col. Phillip A. Work: General without a Star*. Waco, Tex.: Texian Press, 2003.

Howell, Kenneth W. *An Antebellum History: Henderson County, Texas, 1846–1861*. Austin, Tex.: Eakin, 1999.

"Huntsville Item." Walker County Historical Markers, Walker County, Tex. www.walkercountyhistory.org/markers/dispMarker.php?mid=50.

Jones, Michael Dan. *Lt. Col. King Bryan of Hood's Texas Brigade*. Self-published, 2013.

Jordan, Brian Matthew. *Marching Home: Union Veterans and Their Unending Civil War*. New York: Liveright, 2014.

Joslyn, Mauriel P. "'For Ninety Years or the War': The Story of the 3rd Arkansas at Gettysburg." *Gettysburg Magazine: Historical Articles of Lasting Interest* 14 (January 1996): 52–63.

Kirchenbauer, Amy Sue. "The Texas Confederate Home for Men, 1884–1970." Master's thesis, University of North Texas, 2011.

Klingensmith, Harold A. "A Cavalry Regiment's First Campaign: The 18th Pennsylvania at Gettysburg." *Gettysburg: Historical Articles of Lasting Interest* 20 (1998): 51–74.

Krick, Robert E. L. "'The Men Who Carried This Position Were Soldiers Indeed': The Decisive Charge of Whiting's Division at Gaines's Mill." In *The Richmond Campaign of 1862: The Peninsula & the Seven Days*, edited by Gary W. Gallagher. Chapel Hill: University of North Carolina Press, 2000.

Krick, Robert K. *Civil War Weather in Virginia*. Tuscaloosa: University of Alabama Press, 2007.

———. "'Lee to the Rear,' the Texans Cried." In *The Wilderness Campaign*, edited by Gary W. Gallagher. Chapel Hill: University of North Carolina Press, 1997.

———. "A Lone Star in Virginia." *Civil War Times* 39 (December 2000): 34–46.

———. "A Texas Private's Long-Forgotten Account of Robert E. Lee's Brush with Death at the Battle of the Wilderness." *Civil War Times* 50 (February 2011): 44–47.

Ladd, Kevin. *Chambers County, Texas in the War Between the States*. Baltimore: Gateway, 1994.

Laney, Daniel M. "Wasted Gallantry: Hood's Texas Brigade at Gettysburg." *Gettysburg Magazine: Historical Articles of Lasting Interest* 16 (1997): 27–45.

Latschar, Terry. "'My Brave Texans, Forward and Take Those Heights!' Jerome Bonaparte Robertson and the Texas Brigade." In *I Ordered No Man to Go When I Would Not Go Myself: Leadership in the Campaign and Battle of Gettysburg*. Papers of the Ninth Gettysburg National Military Park Seminar. Gettysburg National Military Park: National Park Service, 2002.

Liles, Deborah M., and Angela Boswell. *Women in Civil War Texas: Diversity and Dissidence in the Trans-Mississippi*. Denton: University of North Texas Press, 2016.

Linderman, Gerald. *Embattled Courage: The Experience of Combat in the American Civil War*. New York: Free Press, 1987.

Maberry, Robert, Jr. *Texas Flags*. College Station: Texas A&M University Press, 2001.

Manning, Chandra. *What This Cruel War Was Over: Soldiers, Slavery, and the Civil War*. New York: Vintage, 2007.

Marten, James. *Sing Not War: The Lives of Union and Confederate Veterans in Gilded Age America*. Chapel Hill: University of North Carolina Press, 2011.

Marvel, William. *A Place Called Appomattox*. Chapel Hill: University of North Carolina Press, 2000.

McArthur, Judith N. "'Those Texians Are Number One Men': A New Confederate Account of the Affair at Lee's House, Virginia." *Southwestern Historical Quarterly* 95 (April 1992): 488–96.

McCurry, Stephanie. *Confederate Reckoning: Power and Politics in the Civil War South*. Chapel Hill: University of North Carolina Press, 2011.

———. *Masters of Small Worlds: Yeoman Households, Gender Relations, and the Political Culture of the Antebellum South Carolina Low Country*. New York: Oxford University Press, 1995.

Mears, Linda, trans. *Confederate Indigent Families Lists of Texas, 1863–1865*. San Marcos, Tex.: privately published, 1995.

Miller, Brian Craig. *John Bell Hood and the Fight for Civil War Memory*. Knoxville: University of Tennessee Press, 2010.

Mink, Eric. "If These Signatures Could Talk: Aquia Church Graffiti." https://npsfrsp.wordpress.com/2011/12/07/if-these-signatures-could-talk-aquia-church-graffiti-part-1/.

Minnesota Population Center. *National Historical Geographic Information System: Version 2.0*. Minneapolis: University of Minnesota, 2011. www.nhgis.org.

Mitchell, Reid. *Civil War Soldiers: Their Expectations and Their Experiences*. New York: Viking Penguin, 1988.

Moellering, Arwerd Max. *A History of Guadalupe County, Texas*. Master's thesis, University of Texas, Austin, 1938.

Moneyhon, Carl H. *Texas after the Civil War: The Struggle of Reconstruction*. College Station: Texas A&M University Press, 2004.

Moore, James O. "The Men of the Bayou City Guards (Company A, 5th Texas Infantry, Hood's Texas Brigade)." Master's thesis, University of Houston, Clear Lake, 1988.

Newsome, Hampton. *Richmond Must Fall: The Richmond-Petersburg Campaign, October 1864*. Kent, Ohio: Kent State University Press, 2013.

Nolan, Alan T. *The Iron Brigade: A Military History*. 1961. Bloomington: Indiana University Press, 1994.

Otott, George Edward, Jr. "Clash in the Cornfield: The 1st Texas Volunteer Infantry in the Maryland Campaign." *Civil War Regiments: A Journal of the American Civil War* 5 (1997): 73–123.

———. *The 1st Texans: Antebellum Social Characteristics of the Officers and Men in the 1st Texas Infantry, CSA*. Irvine, Calif.: privately printed, 2004.

Owen, Joseph L., and Randy S. Drais. *Texans at Gettysburg: Blood and Glory with Hood's Texas Brigade*. Charleston, S.C.: Fonthill Media, 2016.

Patchan, Scott. *Second Manassas: Longstreet's Attack and the Struggle for Chinn Ridge*. Washington, D.C.: Potomac, 2011.

Peebles, Ruth. "Summary and Commentary, The Diary of A. B. Green, 1865." Unpublished. Polk County Memorial Museum.

Pfanz, Harry W. *Gettysburg: The Second Day*. Chapel Hill: University of North Carolina Press, 1987.

Phillips, Jason. *Diehard Rebels: The Confederate Culture of Invincibility*. Athens: University of Georgia Press, 2007.

Pohanka, Brian C. *Vortex of Hell: A History of the 5th New York Volunteer Infantry, Duryée's Zouaves, 1861–1863*. Lynchburg, Va.: Schroeder, 2012.

Powell, David A. *The Chickamauga Campaign: A Mad Irregular Battle: From the Crossing of the Tennessee River through the Second Day, August 22–September 19, 1863*. El Dorado Hills, Calif.: Savas Beatie, 2014.

———. *The Chickamauga Campaign: Glory or the Grave: The Breakthrough, the Union Collapse, and the Defense of Horseshoe Ridge, September 20, 1863*. El Dorado Hills, Calif.: Savas Beatie, 2015.

———. *The Maps of Chickamauga: An Atlas of the Chickamauga Campaign, Including the Tullahoma Operations, June 22–September 23, 1863*. El Dorado Hills, Calif.: Savas Beatie, 2015.

Power, J. Tracy. *Lee's Miserables: Life in the Army of Northern Virginia from the Wilderness to Appomattox*. Chapel Hill: University of North Carolina Press, 2002.

Price, James S. *Battle of New Market Heights: Freedom Will Be Theirs by the Sword*. Charleston, S.C.: History Press, 2011.

Pruitt, Francelle. "'We've Got to Fight or Die': Early Texas Reaction to the Confederate Draft, 1862." *East Texas Historical Association Journal* 3 (1998): 3–17.

Reardon, Carol, and Tom Vossler. *A Field Guide to Gettysburg: Experiencing the Battlefield through Its History, Places, and People*. Chapel Hill: University of North Carolina Press, 2013.

Reynolds, Donald E. *Editors Make War: Southern Newspapers in the Secession Crisis*. Reprint, Carbondale: Southern Illinois University Press, 2006.

———. *Texas Terror: The Slave Insurrection Panic of 1860 and the Secession of the Lower South*. Baton Rouge: Louisiana State University Press, 2007.

Rhea, Gordon C. *The Battle of the Wilderness, May 5–6, 1864*. Baton Rouge: Louisiana State University Press, 1994.

Richter, William L. *The Army in Texas during Reconstruction, 1865–1870*. College Station: Texas A&M University Press, 1987.

———. *Overreached on All Sides: The Freedmen's Bureau Administrators in Texas, 1865–1868*. College Station: Texas A&M University Press, 1991.

Robertson, James I., Jr. *The Stonewall Brigade*. 1963. Reprint, Baton Rouge: Louisiana State University Press, 1991.

Rosenburg, R. B. *Living Monuments: Confederate Soldiers' Homes in the New South*. Chapel Hill: University of North Carolina Press, 2001.

Rubin, Anne Sarah. *A Shattered Nation: The Rise and Fall of the Confederacy*. Chapel Hill: University of North Carolina Press, 2005.

Ryan, Thomas J. "The Intelligence Battle, July 2: Longstreet's Assault." *Gettysburg: Historical Articles of Lasting Interest* 43 (July 2010): 75–88.

Schmutz, John F. *"The Bloody 5th": The 5th Texas Infantry Regiment, Hood's Texas Brigade, Army of Northern Virginia*. Vol. 1: *Secession to the Suffolk Campaign*. El Dorado Hills, Calif.: Savas Beatie, 2016.

Sears, Stephen W. *Gettysburg*. New York: Houghton Mifflin, 2003.

Shelton, Robert S. "On Empire's Shore: Free and Unfree Workers in Galveston, Texas, 1840–1860." *Journal of Social History* (Spring 2007): 717–30.

Shevchuk, Paul M. "The 1st Texas Infantry and the Repulse of Farnsworth's Charge." *Gettysburg Magazine: Historical Articles of Lasting Interest* 2 (January 1990): 81–90.

Shuffler, R. Henderson. "Decimus et Ultimus Barziza." *Southwestern Historical Quarterly* 66 (April 1963): 501–12.

Simpson, Harold B. *Hood's Texas Brigade: Lee's Grenadier Guard*. Waco, Tex.: Texian Press, 1970. Reprint, Fort Worth, Tex.: Landmark, 1999.

———. *Hood's Texas Brigade in Poetry and Song*. Hillsboro, Tex.: Hill Junior College Press, 1968.

———. *Hood's Texas Brigade: A Compendium*. 2nd ed. Fort Worth, Tex.: Landmark, 1999.

———. *Hood's Texas Brigade: In Reunion and Memory*. Hillsboro, Tex.: Hill College Press, 1974.

———. "The Recruiting, Training, and Camp Life of a Company of Hood's Brigade in Texas, 1861." *Texas Military History* 2 (August 1962): 171–92.

Singletary, Otis A. "The Texas Militia during Reconstruction." *Southwestern Historical Quarterly* 60 (July 1956–April 1957): 23–35.

Skirbunt, Peter D. "Washington Secured: Breaking the Confederate Blockade of the Potomac, 1861–1862." Master's thesis, Ohio State University, 1975.

Slap, Andrew L., and Frank Towers, eds. *Confederate Cities: The Urban South during the Civil War Era*. Chicago: University of Chicago Press, 2015.

Sommers, Richard J. *Richmond Redeemed: The Siege of Petersburg, The Battles of Chaffin's Bluff and Poplar Spring Church, September 29–October 2, 1864*. 1984. Reprint, El Dorado Hills, Calif.: Savas Beatie, 2014.

Spender, John W. *From Corsicana to Appomattox: The Story of the Corsicana Invincibles and the Navarro Rifles*. Corsicana, Tex.: Texas Press, 1984.

Sternhell, Yael A. "Revisionism Reinvented? The Antiwar Turn in Civil War Scholarship." *Journal of the Civil War Era* 3 (June 2013): 239–56.

Stitton, Sarah C. *Life at the Texas State Lunatic Asylum, 1857–1997*. College Station: Texas A&M University Press, 1999.

Stocklin, Barbara Ann. "The Texas Confederate Woman's Home: A Case Study in Historic Preservation and Neighborhood Conservation Planning." Master's thesis, University of Texas at Austin, 1991.

Sturkey, O. Lee. *Hampton Legion Infantry, C.S.A.: The South Carolina Roster Set*. Wilmington, N.C.: Broadfoot, 2008.

Townsend, Jan. "Freestone Point Battery, DHL No. 76-264," National Register of Historic Places Registration Form, United States Department of the Interior, National Park Service, May 1989.

Townsend, Stephen A. *The Yankee Invasion of Texas*. College Station: Texas A&M University Press, 2006.

Trammel, Camilla Davis. *Seven Pines: Its Occupants and Their Letters, 1825–1872*. Houston: Southern Methodist University Press, 1986.

Trudeau, Noah Andre. "Costly Union Reconnaissance." *America's Civil War* 7 (July 1994): 42–48, 82.

———. "Lee's Struggle in the Wilderness." *America's Civil War* 13 (September 2000): 26–32, 80.

———. "No Brilliant Victory to Record." *America's Civil War* (May 1996): 34–40, 82.

———. "That 'Unerring Volcanic Firearm.'" *Military History Quarterly* 7 (Summer 1995): 44–53.

Wells, Jonathan Daniel. *The Origins of the Southern Middle Class, 1800–1861*. Chapel Hill: University of North Carolina Press, 2004.

Wells, Jonathan Daniel, and Jennifer R. Green, eds. *The Southern Middle Class in the Long Nineteenth Century*. Baton Rouge: Louisiana State University Press, 2011.

Williams, Edward B. *Hood's Texas Brigade in the Civil War*. Jefferson, N.C.: McFarland, 2012.

Wills, Mary Alice. *The Confederate Blockade of Washington, D.C.* Parsons, W.V.: McClain Printing, 1975.

Wittenberg, Eric. *Gettysburg's Forgotten Cavalry Actions*. El Dorado Hills, Calif.: Savas Beatie, 2011.

Wittenberg, Eric J., J. Davis Petruzzi, and Michael Nugent. *One Continuous Fight: The Retreat from Gettysburg and the Pursuit of Lee's Army of Northern Virginia, July 4–14, 1863*. El Dorado Hills, Calif.: Savas Beatie, 2011.

Woodward, Colin Edward. *Marching Masters: Slavery, Race, and the Confederate Army during the Civil War*. Charlottesville: University of Virginia Press, 2014.

Wooster, Ralph A., ed. *Lone Star Blue and Gray: Essays on Texas in the Civil War*. Austin: Texas State Historical Association, 1995.

———. *Texas and Texans in the Civil War*. Austin: Eakin, 1995.

Yearns, Wilfred Buck. *The Confederate Governors*. Athens: University of Georgia Press, 1910.

Young, Alfred C. *Lee's Army during the Overland Campaign: A Numerical Study*. Baton Rouge: Louisiana State University Press, 2013.

INDEX

Note: Italic page numbers refer to illustrations.

abolitionism, 12, 234
African Americans: attacks on, 268; Hood's Texas Brigade soldiers' views of, 3; political power of, 268–69; Mike Powell on, 262; and southern paternalism, 23; suffrage of, 4, 266, 267
African American Union soldiers: attack on Hood's Texas Brigade, 4; and Battle of New Market Heights, 221, 222–23, 225, 226, 227; combat roles of, 143; Hood's Texas Brigade soldiers' views of, 241, 247, 248
Alexander, E. Porter, 104, 152, 183–84
Allen, J. G., 142
Allen, Lafayette, 153
Allen, R. T. P., 38, 50–51, 52, 53, 79
Allison, Andrew Jackson, 254
Allison, Arthur B., *169*, 254
Allison, John T., 254
Alton, Robert H. C., 294–95*n*6
Alversen, John, 213
Anderson, G. T., 208
Anderson, Richard H., 216, 220, 227
Anderson, Robert, 125–26
Archer, James J.: as commander of Hood's Texas Brigade, 48–49, 53, 77, 78; and Potomac Blockade, 61, 63, 64, 295*n*8
Arkansas: Texas compared with, 328–29*n*39. *See also* Third Arkansas Infantry
Army of Northern Virginia: and Battle of Antietam, 117, 118; and Battle of Gettysburg, 165, 168; and Battle of Second Manassas, 112; defeat of, 10; and desertions, 199; Hood's Texas Brigade's contributions to, 4, 5, 6, 8, 55, 61, 104, 132, 271; Hood's Texas Brigade's reuniting with, 202, 205–6, 231; Hood's Texas Brigade's separation from, 9, 183, 195, 205; and medical care, 232, 263, 322*n*2; organization of, 139, 147–48; supplies of, 137, 138, 145, 198, 248; surrender at Appomattox Court House, 250, 251, 252
Army of Tennessee, 185, 195
Army of the Potomac: and Battle of Antietam, 117, 118; and Battle of Gaines's Mill, 90; and Ulysses S. Grant, 204; and George McClellan, 114; and Potomac Blockade, 74, 76; and surrender at Appomattox Court House, 253
Austin City Light Infantry, 32
Austin College, 30–31
Austin State Gazette, 12, 16

Bailey, Gus, 141–42, 271–72
Bailey, Mollie, 141–42, 271–72
Bailey, Sam, 216–17
Baker, Ben, 34, 39
Baldwin, Ben, 194
Ball, William Watts, 22
Ballinger, William Pitt, 17
Baltimore Sun, 277
Bane, J. P., 185, 188
Banks, Nathaniel T., 207

Barbee, Wilson, 158
Barker, James C., 301n39
Barney, Ewing, 76
Barrett, Milton, 80, 88
Barron, Jasper, 73
Barron, William, 73
Barry, William E., 120, 126
Barziza, Decimus et Ultimus: and Battle of Gaines's Mill, 90, 91, 95, 96; and Battle of Gettysburg, 153; and Fourth Texas, 52, 53, 57
Bass, Frederick S.: and Battle of Darbytown Road, 229; and Battle of New Market Heights, 222, 225, 226; and campaign season of 1865, 235; and election of officers in First Texas, 89; and honorary Gold Stars for Hood's Texas Brigade, 245; and journey to Virginia, 26–27; and Potomac Blockade, 69; and Texas Confederate Veterans Home, 270
Bassett, Robert H., 188
Battle of Antietam: casualties of, 124, 125–31, 133, 134–35, 137, 142, 214, 308n81; Hood's Texas Brigade's contributions to, 4, 9, 75, 104, 116–21, 123–32, 135, 136–37, 138, 139, 145, 212, 214; map of, *122*
Battle of Chancellorsville, 146, 158
Battle of Chickamauga: Robert Campbell in, 1; casualties of, 183, 188–89, 191, 192, 193–94, 232, 322n3; Hood's Texas Brigade's contributions to, 183, 184–85, 187–94; map of, *186*
Battle of Cold Harbor, 219, 276
Battle of Darbytown Road: Robert Campbell in, 1–2, 229; casualties of, 229, 230; Hood's Texas Brigade's contributions to, 226–27, 229; map of, *228*
Battle of Eltham's Landing, 5, 83–85
Battle of First Manassas, 7
Battle of Fredericksburg, 139
Battle of Freeman's Ford, 104
Battle of Gaines's Mill: anniversaries of, 279, 280; casualties of, 97, 98, 99, 100–102, 111, 113, 128, 129, 303n98; Hood's Texas Brigade's contributions to, 5, 8, 30, 75, 90–91, 93–102, 103, 111, 113, 133, 214, 302n59; map of, *92*
Battle of Gettysburg: casualties of, 153, 155, 161, 164, 165–67, 232, 322n3; Hood's Texas Brigade's contributions to, 8, 148, 149–55, 157–68; map of, *156*
Battle of Murfreesboro, 144
Battle of New Market Heights: Hood's Texas Brigade contributions to, 221–23, 225–26; map of, *224*
Battle of Second Manassas: Robert Campbell in, 1; casualties of, 111–13, 116, 121, 166, 206, 233, 301n46; Hood's Texas Brigade's contributions to, 30, 75, 104–7, 109–11, 132, 133, 304n7; map of, *108*
Battle of Seven Pines, 85–86
Battle of Spotsylvania Courthouse, 216–18, 220, 238
Battle of the Alamo, 42, 46
Battle of the Wilderness: anniversary of, 270; casualties of, 212–15; Hood's Texas Brigade's contributions to, 1, 5, 135, 202, 203, 207–9, 211–14, 218; map of, *210*
Battle of Wauhatchie, 194, 196
Battle of Williamsburg Road, 232
Bayou City Guards, 34, 73, 74, 262
Bedell, William A., 125, 135, 212
Beetz, Jerry Carl, 315n111
Benjamin, Judah P., 54, 294n5
Benning, Henry L. "Rock": and Battle of Chickamauga, 184, 187, 189, 190; and Battle of Gettysburg, 159, 160; and Battle of the Wilderness, 211–12, 213, 214
Benton, Benjamin F., 14–15, 32, 71
Bermuda Hundred, 220
Berryman, Helena Dill, 144
Berryman, Newt, 163, 261, 329n42
Berryman, Waters: and Battle of Gettysburg, 155, 158, 163–65, 314n100; and campaign season of 1863, 192, 310n17; farm of, 329n42; on Suffolk, 145; on Trans-Mississippi West, 139; as veteran, 261
Berryman, William, 270
Birney, David G., 157
Black, Albert, 23–24
Black, Harvey Hannibal, 23–25, 26, 84, *169*
Black, Isaac, 50
black suffrage, 4, 266, 267. *See also* African Americans
Blessing, Samuel "Tom," 212, 213, 214, 217–19

Bookman, J. M., 83, 188
Booth, John Wilkes, 257
Boswell, Angela, 319n58
Bowles, Pinckey, 226, 227
Boyton, G. S., 39
Brackenridge, George, 279
Bradfield, James O., 159
Bradley, Henry, 238
Bragg, Braxton, 183–84, 191, 192, 194–95, 200
Brahan, Haywood, 123–24, 239–40
Brantley, Robert, 91
Brashear, Charlie, 86, 249, 253, 261, 326n63
Brashear, Crow, 86, 253, 261
Bratton, John, 227
Breckenridge, R. J., 215, 262–63
Breckinridge, John C., 26
Breckinridge, Robert H., 168
Brietz, A. C., 316n4
Brietz, Georgie S., 316n4
Brooks, Charles, 2, 290n35
Brown, John, 22
Brown, Joseph E., 106
Brown, William, 162
Bryan, Kindallis "Dallis," 86, 87
Bryan, Kindallis "King": and Battle of Gettysburg, 160, 161, 164, 168, 185; and Battle of Second Manassas, 111; and Battle of the Wilderness, 213; as commander of Hood's Texas Brigade, 196, 200; Company Invincibles organized by, 19, 33; and Fifth Texas, 86, 88; health of, 249; on journey to Virginia, 41
Bryan, Laura. *See* Williams, Laura Bryan
Bryan, Pryor, 50, 88, 249
Burditt, W. B., 207
Burges, William H., 240
Burke, James, 245, 246
Burke, John, 297n56
Burke, William, 289n21
Burnett, A. F., 59
Burns, Robert, 262
Burnside, Ambrose, 195
Burroughs, James M., 297n56
Burroughs, J. J., 15
Buster, J. C., 112
Butler, Benjamin F., 221, 225
Butler, George, 219–20

Butler, Parson, 102
Buxton, P. C., 19

Caddell, J. D., 161, 167
Caddos, 45
Calhoun, John C., 282
Calhoun, Thomas J., 270
Calvert, John, 257
Campbell, Robert: and Battle of Chickamauga, 1; and Battle of Darbytown Road, 1–2, 229; and Battle of Gaines's Mill, 91, 93, 97, 100; and Battle of Second Manassas, 109; as courier, 1; infantry service of, 1; injuries of, 1–2; recruitment of, 73; "A Sketch of Hood's Texas Brigade," 281–82, 315–16n2; on supplies, 198
Campbell, Thomas, 273
Campbell, William, 47
Camp Bragg, 47, 54
Camp Clark, San Marcos, 34, 51
Camp Texas, Richmond, 240
Camp Van Dorn, Harrisburg, 33, 34–35, 37, 40–42, 44, 45, 51
Carrington, Bernard, 76
Carter, Benjamin Franklin: and Austin City Light Infantry, 32; and Battle of Antietam, 121, 123, 124, 127–28; and Battle of Gettysburg, 160, 161, 164, 166, 167, 185; and Battle of Second Manassas, 105, 107, 111; as junior officer in Hood's Texas Brigade, 30, 102
Cartwright, E. W. "Ras," 40
Cartwright, James, 40
Cartwright, Lemuel, 40
Cater, Thomas, 207
Centerville Times, 15
Chambers, Thomas Jefferson, 35
Cherokee, 45
Chiles, Joseph, 238
Chilton, Frank, 270, 274, 275, 279
Choate, Pryor, 213
Church, J. F., 249
citizenship, concepts of, 54
citizen-soldier volunteers: Confederates' reliance on, 73; John Hood's leadership of, 79, 80; in Hood's Texas Brigade, 6, 7; individual freedoms of, 33, 240; and Marshall Guards,

citizen-soldier volunteers (*continued*) 27; and William Martin, 38; men's development as, 7–8, 54; and military life, 47, 51, 70, 82; power exchange with officers, 54; and selection of officers, 89; and social class, 41
Clark, Edward, 13, 31–34, 45, 288–89n11
Clarke, W. H., 162
Clay, Henry, 282
Clay, Tacitus T., 49, 188, 288n11
Clemens, Thomas G., 285n19
Cleveland, John C., 85, 189
Cloptin, Albert Gallatin, 26–27
Cobb, J. E., 249
Cole, Fred, 214
Coleman, Ann Raney, 243
Coleman, N. D., 25
Colorado Citizen, 34, 39
Colquitt, A. H., 127
Comanches, 13, 20
communities at war, and Hood's Texas Brigade, 6, 10, 48, 79, 282
Company Invincibles, 19, 33, 40–41, 249
Confederacy: Hood's Texas Brigade's ideological dedication to, 2, 4, 5, 6, 8–9, 10, 11, 69, 73–74, 112, 113–14, 132–33, 143, 146, 202–3, 231, 233–37, 239–42, 247–48, 281; Robert E. Lee on, 198–99; on projected length of Civil War, 13; request that Texas defend own state, 13, 15, 23, 30; Texans' ideological dedication to, 4, 5, 6, 8–9, 10, 11, 15; troop levies of, 27, 38; Union prisoners of, 46
Confederate Camp, Richmond, 42
Confederate Congress, 70, 89, 235, 240
Confederate independence: Hood's Texas Brigade soldiers' views of, 1, 3–4, 8–9, 11, 58–59, 71, 75, 76, 86, 131, 132–33, 144, 166, 167, 233, 248; James Loughridge on, 14, 71–72, 76, 167; and surrender at Appomattox Court House, 257
Confederate Veteran, 274
Confederate War Department: and Potomac Blockade, 67; and selection of officers, 48, 53–54
conscription, 70, 73, 89, 113, 298n77
Consolidation Bill, 235–37, 238
Cook, J. W., 245, 246

Cooke, Philip St. George, 96
Cooper, Samuel, 67, 70
Copal, Octave, 213
Copeland, William Edgar, 275–76
Cortina War, 31
cotton production, 21–22
Covington, Albert, 44, 292n6
Crabtree, William, 193
Crockett, Agnes, 36
Crockett, Edward, 36, 128, 129
Crockett, Ellen, 35–36
Cromwell, James, 158–59
Crouch, Howard R., 294–95n6
Cudworth, Warren, 77–78
Cunningham, Edward, 111–12
Cushing, Edward H., 261, 297n54

Daffan, Katie, 279
Daffan, Lawrence, 279
Dale, Matt, 125
Dallas, Texas, fire in, 12
Dallas Herald, 12
Dallas Weekly Herald, 265
Daniel Boone Rifles, 44
Darby, Willie, 200
Darling, C. A., 262
Davenport, Marcus, 124, 135
Davenport, William, 124, 135
Davis, Edmund J., 266, 268
Davis, Elisa, 236
Davis, Jefferson: appointment of officers to Texas regiments, 47–48, 49, 51, 53–54, 56, 79; and campaign season of 1862, 81; and Confederate desertions, 199; and Consolidation Bill, 238–39; on Hood's Texas Brigade, 5, 8, 84, 98, 192; and Hood's Texas Brigade's resolution, 240; and Joseph Johnston, 76–77; June levy of troops, 38; and Mexican War, 133; pardons of, 238; on Texas regiments, 15, 16, 30, 46; and John West, 153
Davis, Nicholas: on disease of Potomac Blockade, 62; and Dumfries, 55; fund-raising efforts of, 141, 142, 310n23; and St. Francis de Sales hospital, 142; and selection of officers, 48, 50, 51; and Texas Hospital, 311n26; and Earl Van Dorn, 39

Davis, Varina, 142, 311n26
Dawes, Rufus, 123
Day, James, 126
Deal, John, 83
Dean, Sam, 112
Democratic Party: and Andrew Jackson, 52, 261; Mike Powell on resurrection of, 261–62; and slavery, 133
Denson, Nicholas, 220
desertion: in Company C, First Texas, 25–26, 287n34, 287n35; from Hood's Texas Brigade, 9, 25, 74, 87, 183, 195–96, 198–99, 200, 236, 237–38, 260, 269, 287n34, 318n45; Hood's Texas Brigade's divergence from Confederate desertions, 4, 6, 183; increases in, 9, 104, 198–99; and Palmer Guards, 25; statistics on, 318n45, 318n46, 318n47
Dickinson, Albert Glassel, 25, 27–28
Dickinson, Susan Marshall Coleman, 25, 28
Dingle, J. H., Jr., 124
disease: deaths in combat compared to, 132; and Potomac Blockade, 8, 61–64, 67, 69, 70; yellow fever, 17, 28, 31, 43, 85, 269
Doll, Penfield, 106
Dominey, Caroline, 235–36
Dominey, Seaborn, 235–36, 237, 242
Doty, O. S., 310n17
Doubleday, Abner, 105, 124, 125
Dowtin, Thomas, 58, 64
Draper, Alonzo G., 225
Drayton, Thomas F., 118
DuBose, Dudley, 227
Dugat, Albert Germilia, 86, 116, 301n46
Dugat, Beasley, 86, 87, 88, 301n46
Dugat, Eurlarian, 301n46
Dugat, Margaretta, 19, 301n46
Duke, Josiah, 79
Duncan, Samuel, 222, 225, 227
Dunnington, C. W. C., 65–66, 296–97n37
Durham, William, 245
Duryée, Abram, 59, 109

Edey, Arthur, 128, 142
Edgerton, Nathan, 222
Edwards, Roxey, 99
Edwards, William, 99

Ehringhaus, William, 87
Eighteenth Georgia Infantry Regiment: and Battle of Antietam, 119–20, 121, 123, 124, 127, 128, 134; and Battle of Gaines's Mill, 91, 93–94, 96–97, 98, 303n98; and Battle of Second Manassas, 105, 107, 109, 110, 111; and campaign season of 1862, 83; Company A of, 58–59; Company C of, 64, 66; Company G of, 64; Company K of, 64; departure from Hood's Texas Brigade, 8, 139; enlistment period of, 88–89; joining Hood's Texas Brigade, 8, 55, 58–59, 80; and Potomac Blockade, 61, 63, 64, 65–66, 67; and respect for locals' property, 65–66
Eighth Indiana, 188
Eighth Texas Cavalry, 184, 316n4
Eighty-Sixth New York, 157, 158
Eiserman, Rick, 295n6, 315–16n2
Eleventh Mississippi, 96, 97
Eleventh Pennsylvania, 110
Eliot, Jacob, 202
Elliott, John B., 152
Ellis, A. Van Horne, 158–59
emancipation, 3–4, 6, 262, 282
Emancipation Proclamation, 6, 8, 143, 144, 202
Emerson, Samuel H., 145, 153, 219, 223
Eringhaus, W. F. M., 270
Erkel, Josh, 101, 115
Erksine, Blucher, 101
Erksine, Eddie, 101
Erskine, Agnes Haynes, 20
Erskine, Alexander: arrival in Virginia, 87; and Battle of Antietam, 130–31, 135; and Battle of Gaines's Mill, 101; and Battle of Second Manassas, 107, 113; and First Texas, 73; and Hood's Texas Brigade Association, 270; and ideological dedication to Confederacy, 113, 114, 131; Texas transfer of, 131
Erskine, Andrew: arrival in Virginia, 87, 88; and Battle of Antietam, 130–31; and Battle of Gaines's Mill, 95, 100–102; and Battle of Second Manassas, 113, 304n7; death of, 130–31; and First Texas, 73; and ideological dedication to Confederacy, 113, 114; marriage of, 20–21, 87; portrait of, *170*

Erskine, Ann Theresa Johnson: and Battle of Gaines's Mill, 100–102; and death of brother, 113; and death of husband, 130–31; marriage of, 20–21, 87, 113; portrait of, *170;* and postwar adjustment, 278–79; responsibility for running farm, 114–15, 131
Erskine, Bettie, 114
Erskine, Blucher, 279
Erskine, Michael, 20, 21, 101, 115, 131
Erskine, Powell, 87, 101, 115
Estes, James, 124
Evans, Nathan G. "Shanks": and Battle of Antietam, 118; and Battle of Second Manassas, 105, 106, 111; and John Hood, 116, 117, 118
Ewell, Richard S., 91, 93, 147, 150, 207, 216
Excelsior Brigade, 59, 80

families of Hood's Texas Brigade: and Battle of Antietam, 128; and Battle of Chickamauga, 194; and Battle of Eltham's Landing, 84–85; and Battle of Gaines's Mill, 98, 99–102; and Battle of Gettysburg, 165; on black suffrage, 4; and casualties, 88; challenges of, 243–45, 319n58; communities of, 6; correspondence of, 201; and disease of Potomac Blockade, 61–62; economic stability of, 200; and Emancipation Proclamation, 144; and Federal operations in Texas, 207; funding of volunteers of Hood's Texas Brigade, 7; fundraising efforts of, 141, 243, 246–47, 324n44; ideological dedication to Confederacy, 2, 4, 6, 7, 8, 72–73, 231–32, 247; on Robert E. Lee, 8; local tax funds for, 201–2, 319n57; morale of, 7, 241, 242, 245, 325n52; and mothers' fears, 37; motivations of, 6, 282; petitions to Texas governor's office, 325n50; and postwar adjustment, 6–7; and recruitment, 72–73, 75; and reputation of Texas regiments, 46, 65; as slave owners, 5, 7, 36, 37, 72, 114, 115, 130, 143–44, 147, 258, 298n69; and social class, 5, 20–21, 35–36, 37, 44, 73, 74, 147, 201, 206, 213, 231, 242, 246, 251, 258, 259, 289n25, 289n26, 291n4, 298n69, 312n48, 319n3, 322n7; southern connections of, 35–36, 40, 43, 87, 102, 202, 255, 257; state funds for, 244; support for troops, 9, 71,

75; work ethic of, 3
Farmer, D. C., 263
Farnsworth, Elon J., 163, 314n100
Favors, John, 295n6
Federal Loyalty Oath, 238
Felder, Gabriel, 233
Felder, Miers, *171*, 233
Felder, Rufus King: and Battle of Antietam, 119; and Battle of New Market Heights, 225–26; and Battle of Second Manassas, 111, 112, 116; on casualties, 139; morale of, 232–33, 247; portrait of, *171;* and recruitment, 235
Field, Charles W., 208, 211, 216, 227, 229, 253
Fifth Corps, 90–91
Fifth New York Zouaves, 59, 74, 109–10, 111
Fifth Texas Infantry Regiment: and Battle of Antietam, 119–20, 121, 123, 124, 127, 128, 136, 145; and Battle of Chickamauga, 185, 188, 190; and Battle of Darbytown Road, 227, 229, 230; and Battle of Gaines's Mill, 91, 93, 97, 98, 100, 303n98; and Battle of Gettysburg, 152, 154, 155, 160, 161, 162, 167; and Battle of Second Manassas, 105, 107, 109, 110, 111, 112, 116, 121, 304n15; and Battle of Spotsylvania Courthouse, 217; and Battle of the Wilderness, 211–12, 213, 215; and campaign season of 1862, 82, 83; and campaign season of 1864, 206; Robert Campbell in, 1; and Camp Bragg, 47, 54; casualties of, 121, 139; citizen-soldier volunteers of, 7, 30; Company A of, 46, 73, 93, 100, 216–17; Company B of, 66, 82; Company C of, 237; Company D of, 47, 167, 217, 251, 254; Company E of, 16, 112, 232, 247, 304n15; Company F of, 16, 48, 87–88, 230, 231, 249; Company G of, 200–201, 206, 257; Company H of, 85, 167; Company I of, 16, 223; Company K of, 64, 93, 121, 257; conditions of, 142; and disease at Potomac Blockade, 63, 64; and Dumfries, 55; and honorary Gold Stars for Hood's Texas Brigade, 245; and journey home following surrender, 255, 257; location of camp at Potomac Blockade, 61, 294–95n6; and middle-class values, 3; mustering of, 45; and Potomac Blockade, 68; and recruitment, 70, 86, 88–89, 204; reputation of, 46; and selec-

tion of officers, 47–50, 53, 196; social class of soldiers in, 37, 44, 290n35; supplies of, 138; and surrender at Appomattox Court House, 252, 253, 254; Maude Young making flag of, 246–47, 254

Fifty-Sixth Pennsylvania, 105

First Massachusetts, 77–78

First Texas Infantry Regiment: and Battle of Antietam, 119, 120, 121, 124–27, 128, 135, 136; and Battle of Chickamauga, 188; and Battle of Eltham's Landing, 84, 85; and Battle of Gaines's Mill, 91, 97, 303n98; and Battle of Gettysburg, 152, 154, 155, 157, 158–59, 162, 163–66; and Battle of Second Manassas, 105–6, 107, 111; and Battle of Spotsylvania Courthouse, 217–18; and Battle of the Wilderness, 211–12, 215; and campaign season of 1862, 83, 88–89; camping at Manassas Junction, 44, 45–46; in Camp near Quantico, Virginia, *172;* casualties of, 85, 125–26, 128, 188, 215, 303n98, 308n81; Company A of, 26, 128, 254; Company B of, 26, 185, 254; Company C of, 25–26, 27, 128, 237, 287n33, 287n34, 287n35; Company D of, 15, 26, 89; Company E of, 56, 69, 89, 128; Company F of, 128, 238, 254; Company G of, 88, 248; Company H of, 73, 126; Company I of, 66; Company K of, 58, 61, 71, 292n6; Company L of, 16, 212, 214; Company M of, 128; conditions of, 136–37; food rations of, 295–96n19; and honorary Gold Stars for Hood's Texas Brigade, 245; leadership of, 185; location of camp at Potomac Blockade, 61; and officer elections, 88–89; original volunteers of Hood's Texas Brigade forming, 7, 23, 25, 27, 30, 42, 54–55; and Potomac River defenses, 47, 55, 61, 68–69, 294–95n6; and recruitment, 70–71; reputation of, 68; and respect for locals' property, 65–66, 296–97n37; slave owners as captains of, 23; social class of volunteers, 290n35; supplies of, 138; and surrender at Appomattox Court House, 254; training regime of, 44–45

Fisher, Naomi, 166

Fisher, Samuel Reed, 166

Fitzgerald, Robert E., 223

Fitzgerald, T. W., 276–78

Flake, Ferdinand, 17

Fletcher, Alyeneth, 18

Fletcher, Margaret, 18

Fletcher, Thomas, 17–18, 19

Fletcher, William B. "Bill," 18–19, 274–75

Ford, John S. "Rip," 34

Fort Donelson, 76

Fort Henry, 76

Fort Sumter, 7, 18

Forty-Eighth Alabama, 155, 159, 160, 185

Forty-Fourth Alabama, 155, 159, 160

Foster, Bob, 52

Foster, William, 52

Fourteenth Georgia, 133

Fourth Maine, 157

Fourth New Jersey, 97

Fourth New York, 154, 157

Fourth Texas Infantry Regiment: and Battle of Antietam, 119–20, 121, 123–24, 127, 130–32, 133, 134; and Battle of Chickamauga, 185, 188, 190; and Battle of Darbytown Road, 229; and Battle of Gaines's Mill, 91, 93–94, 96–97, 98, 102, 113, 303n98; and Battle of Gettysburg, 152, 153, 154, 155, 159, 160, 162, 164, 167; and Battle of New Market Heights, 223; and Battle of Second Manassas, 105–6, 107, 110, 111, 113; and Battle of Spotsylvania Courthouse, 217; and Battle of the Wilderness, 208, 211–12, 213, 215; and Battle of Wauhatchie, 194; and campaign season of 1862, 76, 80, 81, 83, 86; and campaign season of 1863, 148; and Camp Bragg, 47, 54; casualties of, 97, 98, 102, 130, 133, 153, 193, 303n98; citizen-soldier volunteers of, 7, 30, 37; Company A of, 15; Company B of, 62; Company C of, 52; Company D of, 87; Company E of, 153; Company F of, 93, 130, 253–54; Company G of, 85; Company H of, 40, 103, 131–32, 166, 188, 259; Company I of, 79, 93, 123, 148, 161; Company K of, 119–20, 239, 252; and disease at Potomac Blockade, 62, 63; and Dumfries, 55; and honorary Gold Stars for Hood's Texas Brigade, 245; and John Hood as commander, 79; location of camp at Potomac Blockade, 61, 294n6; mustering of, 45;

Fourth Texas Infantry Regiment (*continued*) and permanent winter quarters at Potomac Blockade, 66; and Potomac Blockade, 61, 66, 68, 75, 294*n*6; and recruitment, 70, 88–89; reputation of, 46–47; and selection of officers, 47–48, 50–54, 56–57, 196; and Seven Days Battles, 103; social class of soldiers in, 37, 290*n*35; supplies of, 138; and surrender at Appomattox Court House, 254
Fourth U.S. artillery, 123
Fowler, Theodore, 276, 277, 278
Francis, Ed, 188
Franklin, B. I., 188, 193–94
Franklin, Mary, 193–94
Franklin, William, 83
Freedmen's Bureau, 264, 267
Fremantle, Arthur J. L., 148–49
French, S. G., 145
Frisbie, Herbert, 134, 135
Fugitive Slave Law, 234
fugitive slaves, 59
Fuller, Blucher Pulaski "Pugh," 246
Fuller, Nathan, 246

Gaffney, William, 74
Galveston, Texas, yellow fever in, 17
Galveston Weekly News, 214
Garland, Samuel, 127
Gary, Martin Witherspoon, 22, 105, 121, 124, 127, 226, 227
Gaston, Robert, 28–29, 81–82, 126, 131
Gaston, William, 28–29, 126, 131
Gay, Appleton, 259
Gay, Nancy, 259
Gee, Leonard, 212
George, Moses, 131
Gibbon, John, 123, 124, 135
Giffin, R. H., 213
Giles, Lou Barnhart, 330*n*74
Giles, Val: and Battle of Antietam, 119; and Battle of Chickamauga, 190, 191; and Battle of Gaines's Mill, 95–96; and Battle of Gettysburg, 160–61, 162; and Battle of Second Manassas, 106, 107; and campaign season of 1863, 148; on John Hood, 82, 83; and Hood's Texas Brigade Association, 330*n*74; portrait of, *172*; and selection of officers, 52, 53; and winter quarters at Potomac Blockade, 66–67
Glatthaar, Joseph T., 318*n*46
Goldthwaite, George, 15
Gordon, Charles "Chinese," 276
Goree, Edwin K.: arrest by Federal soldiers, 267–68; and Gus and Mollie Bailey, 272; and Battle of Antietam, 119, 138; and Battle of the Wilderness, 215–16; in Hood's Texas Brigade, 55–56, 72, 74, 199, 206; and journey home following surrender, 255; portrait of, *173*
Goree, Edwin Sue, 267–68
Goree, Eliza T. "Tommie" Nolley, 266, 267, 276
Goree, Langston, 55–56, 72, 74, 119, 138, 199, 206
Goree, Pleasant "Scrap," 72, *173*, 199, 202, 206–7, 298*n*70
Goree, Robert D., 72, 74, 119, *173*, 206, 268
Goree, Sarah Kittrell: correspondence with Thomas Goree, 74, 199–200, 202; and Edwin Goree, 215, 216; personal wealth of, 298*n*69; responsibilities for plantation, 72–73, 206
Goree, Thomas Jewett: as aide to James Longstreet, 55, 72, 76, 206, 255; and Amnesty Oath, 264; and Battle of Antietam, 119, 137; on casualties, 138; correspondence with Sarah Goree, 74, 199–200, 202; and Ed Goree, 215–16; and journey home following surrender, 255; on morale, 199–200, 202, 206; portrait of, *173*; postwar adjustment of, 266, 269; on social order, 266–67; on Louis Wigfall, 55–56
Gorman, Michael, 311*n*26
Graham, Ziba B., 161–62
Grant, Ulysses S.: and Battle of New Market Heights, 223; and Battle of Spotsylvania Courthouse, 218; and Battle of the Wilderness, 207, 218; and Braxton Bragg's withdrawal from Chattanooga, 195; and campaign season of 1864, 219, 220; as commander of Union forces, 204; parole for surrendered soldiers, 252–53, 254, 255; Richmond-Petersburg Campaign, 221

Graves, Junius, 194
Green, A. B., *174*, 255, 257, 259, 261
Green, Amanda, 259
Gregg, John: and Battle of Darbytown Road, 227, 229, 230; and Battle of New Market Heights, 222, 225; and Battle of the Wilderness, 202, 203, 212, 213, 214; as commander of Hood's Texas Brigade, 140, 196, 200, 202–3, 205; funeral of, 230
Griffin, Eliza "Leila" Harwood Burt, 21, 23, 88, 89
Griffin, James Benjamin, 21–23, 74, 88, 89, 301–2n58
Griffin, James Hampton, 88
Griffith, John, 160
Guadalupe Manufacturing Company, 201

Hamby, William, 94, 95, 96, 272–73
Hamilton, A. J., 266, 268
Hamilton, D. H., 198, 223, 225
Hamilton, Tilford A., 192–93
Hamman, William, 267
Hammond, James Henry, 21
Hampton, Wade, 23, 73, 83, 88, 121, 139, 301–2n58
Hampton's Legion: and Battle of Antietam, 119, 121, 123, 124, 133, 134; and Battle of Gaines's Mill, 91, 98, 303n98; and Battle of Second Manassas, 105, 107, 109, 110, 111; and campaign season of 1862, 83, 88–89; Company H of, 88; departure from Hood's Texas Brigade, 8, 139; joining Hood's Texas Brigade, 23, 73, 88; and officer elections, 88–89, 90, 301–2n58; supplies of, 138
Hancock, Winfield Scott, 207–9, 221
Hanks, Amos G., 125
Hanks, O. T., 197, 217–18
Hanson, John, 126
Hardin, Martin, 110
Harding, R. J., 185, 188, 316n5
Harker, Charles G., 190
Harriot, R. R., 86–87
Harris, J. Q., 167
Harris, Tom, 34
Harsh, Joseph, 285n19
Hartwig, D. Scott, 285n19

Harvie, Edwin J., 138, 141, 310n13
Hays, Jack Coffee, 20
Heg, Hans, 187
Heintzleman, Samuel P., 69
Hemphill, Jacob, 245, 325n55
Henderson, Conley, 99
Henderson, Connally Findlay, 99
Henderson, Susan, 99
Hendrick, James, 27, 56, 68, 149, 163
Hennen, Eleanor R., 269
Hennessey, John J., 304n7
Hennessy, John, 285n19
Heth, Henry, 209
Hicks (private), 125
Hill, A. P., 147, 150, 207–9
Hill, D. H., 117, 118, 127
Hill, William T.: and Battle of Darbytown Road, 227, 230; and Battle of Gettysburg, 168, 251; and Battle of Second Manassas, 251; and Battle of the Wilderness, 251; and journey home following surrender, 250, 255, 327n20; portrait of, *174*; postwar financial losses of, 258–59; on reputation of Hood's Texas Brigade, 121; and surrender at Appomattox Court House, 251, 252–53, 254
Hoke, Jacob, 166
Hoke, Robert, 226
Holloman, Tom, 102
Holmes, James, 194
Holmes, T. H., 70
Holmes, W. A., 194
home front. *See* families of Hood's Texas Brigade
Hood, John Bell: arrest of, 116, 117–18; and Battle of Antietam, 118, 119–21, 123, 124, 126–28, 136, 138; and Battle of Chickamauga, 184–85, 187, 189, 191; and Battle of Eltham's Landing, 83–84; and Battle of Gaines's Mill, 90–91, 93–95, 97, 98, 99, 133; and Battle of Gettysburg, 151, 152, 153, 155, 158, 164, 167; and Battle of Second Manassas, 104–7, 111, 112, 113, 304n7; brigades added to division, 139; as commander, 5, 8, 64, 78, 79–83, 104–5, 113, 137, 138, 140–41, 192, 263; as controversial figure, 263; death of, 269–70; and food rations, 137–38; and

Hood, John Bell (*continued*)
Hood Relief Committee, 270; and Hood's Texas Brigade veterans, 10, 269–70; portrait of, *175;* West Point training of, 79, 141; and whiskey rations, 148

Hood, Lydia, 269

Hood, Maria, 269

Hood's Minstrels shows, 141, 272

Hood's Texas Brigade: and campaign season of 1862, 75, 104–7, 132; and campaign season of 1863, 132, 140–46, 183–84, 191–92, 194, 205; and campaign season of 1864, 183, 202, 204, 205, 217–20, 230, 231–32; and campaign season of 1865, 235, 241; Robert Campbell in, 1–2; captured soldiers, 234, 254; casualties of, 8, 75, 82, 84, 85, 97, 98, 99, 100–102, 111–13, 128, 132, 133, 136, 139, 164, 188–89, 198, 199, 204, 213, 214, 232, 303n98; as community, 6, 10, 48, 148, 231, 251, 258, 282; and Confederate pensions, 260; and Consolidation bill, 235–37, 238; cultural connections of soldiers, 2, 3; and desertions, 9, 25, 74, 87, 183, 195–96, 198–99, 200, 236, 237–38, 260, 269, 287n34, 318n45, 318n47; discipline problems of, 195–96, 197; and Dumfries, 55, 58, 59, 67, 294n6; as elite unit, 7, 11, 30, 75; enlistment in, 7, 11, 15, 206–7, 320n5; enthusiasm of, 74; food rations of, 63, 70, 77, 120, 137, 140, 145–46, 183, 195, 197, 198, 202, 205–6, 237, 295–96n19, 310n19; ideological dedication to Confederacy, 2, 4, 5, 6, 8–9, 10, 11, 69, 73–74, 112, 113–16, 132–33, 143, 146, 202–3, 231, 233–37, 239–42, 247–48, 281; journey home following surrender, 250–51, 255, *256,* 257; junior officers of, 8, 9, 30, 40, 41, 52, 231; leadership of, 8, 9, 30, 40–41, 44–45, 53, 54, 64–65, 75, 79–80, 93, 117, 139, 140–43, 183–85, 187, 190, 194, 196, 197, 199–200, 202, 205, 241; location of camps in Potomac Blockade, 59, *60,* 294n5, 294–96n6; and middle class, 2–3, 5–6, 73, 74, 86, 114, 201, 290n35, 299n83; and military life, 58, 67, 69, 70, 74, 79, 80–84, 88, 129, 137, 142–43; morale of, 8, 88, 103, 104, 142–45, 148–49, 164, 168, 183, 190, 192, 195, 197–99, 206, 232–33, 235, 236–37, 242; motivations of, 6, 44, 75, 129, 143–44, 199, 250, 281, 318n48; payment of salaries, 197, 242; and postwar adjustment, 6–7, 9–10, 263–64, 266, 269, 274–75, 278; postwar financial losses of, 257–60, 328n30; rebuilding of, 139; reputation of, 4–6, 8, 10, 30, 65, 74, 85, 93, 98, 103, 104, 132–33, 136, 139, 147, 149, 184, 204, 230, 231, 239, 275, 280; resolutions of, 239–42; and return rates, 231, 232, 322n2, 322n3; and scouting, 68–69, 74, 85, 86, 98, 104, 116, 152; and selection of officers, 42, 47–54, 88–89, 117; self-identification as Texans, 5–6; semi-disciplined fighting style of, 7, 85, 98, 112, 121, 124–25, 126, 184, 192; as sharpshooters, 86, 145; studies on, 6, 285n19; supplies for, 137, 138, 139–40, 141, 142, 145–46, 158, 183, 195–96, 197, 198, 202, 205, 236, 310n19; surrender at Appomattox Court House, Virginia, 9, 250, 251, 252–54, 326n68; unique characteristics of, 2, 4; and winter of 1863–64, 195–99, 202, 205–6. *See also* families of Hood's Texas Brigade; *specific battles*

Hood's Texas Brigade Association, 270–76, 279–80, 316n5

Hood's Texas Brigade Association Reactivated (HTBAR), 315n2

Hood's Texas Brigade veterans: and Amnesty Oath, 264, 265; average age of, 328n38; on black suffrage, 4; business connections of, 262, 263, 264, 280; and Confederate pensions, 260; and doctors, 262–63; establishment of organization, 10, 269; maintaining ties with other veterans, 260–61, 269, 270–71, 275–76, 280; and marriage ties, 261; monument in Austin, 272–73, 280; and postwar financial losses, 260, 264–65, 268–69, 328n38; on war record, 273; widows of, 265, 278

Hood's Texas Brigade Veterans Association, 10, 269

Hooker, Joseph: and Battle of Antietam, 118, 119, 120; and campaign season of 1863, 144, 146; and Potomac Blockade, 67, 68

Hope, Adam, 297n56

Houghton, W. R., 189

Houston, Sam, 12, 72
Houston Telegraph, 24, 54
Houston Tri-Weekly Telegraph, 73, 128, 165, 261, 262, 263–64, 297n54
Houston Weekly Telegraph, 14, 34, 38
Hubbard, P. L., 188
Hunter, Alexander, 5
Hunter, George, 31
Hunter, James T.: and Battle of Chickamauga, 188, 190; and campaign season of 1862, 82; as junior office in Hood's Texas Brigade, 30, 40, 41; and recruitment, 31, 32, 33
Hunter, Tamar, 31
Huntsville Item, 213
Hutcheson, John, 85, 301n39
Hutchinson, Julien, 42, 112

Ivey, H. C., 270

Jackson, Andrew, 52
Jackson, Thomas Jonathan "Stonewall": and Battle of Gaines's Mill, 90, 98; and Battle of Second Manassas, 104–5; and campaign season of 1862, 90; death of, 147, 148; on Hood's Texas Brigade, 8, 98
Jackson, W. G., 271
Jefferson, Thomas, 282
Jenkins, Micah, 194, 196
Jenkins, Sam, 268
Jenkins, W. H., 316n4
Johnson, Andrew, 259, 261, 262, 266
Johnson, Bushrod, 184, 187
Johnson, Edward "Allegheny," 238
Johnson, Ignatius, 21
Johnson, Joseph F., 20
Johnson, Thomas Ignatius "Ig," 73, 87, 113, 114, 115, 131, 279
Johnston, Joseph E.: and Battle of Seven Pines, 85–86; and campaign season of 1862, 81, 83, 85–86; and campaign season of 1863, 195; and campaign season of 1864, 219; and Hood's Texas Brigade, 9, 55, 74; and Potomac Blockade, 67, 68; surrender of, 255, 274, 327n20; withdrawal from Potomac, 76, 78
Johnston, S. R., 151
Jones, A. C., 212

Jones, Austin, 102
Jones, David R. "Neighbor," 120
Jones, James, 62
Jones, J. K. P., 191
Jordan, Brian Matthew, 329n40
Joskins, Joe. *See* Campbell, Robert

Kautz, August Valentine, 226–27
Kemper, James, 111
Kerns, Mark, 110–11, 113, 166
Kershaw, Joseph B., 208, 211, 214, 220
Key, John C. G., 51, 102, 138, 154, 160, 164
Kickapoos, 45
Kilby, John, 193, 194
Killingsworth, Allen G., 188
Kilpatrick, Judson, 163
Kindred, Alexander, 130
Kindred, Elisha, 130
Kindred, James, 130
Kindred, John, 130
Kindred, Joseph, 130
Kindred, Joshua, 130
Kindred, Lucy Threadgill, 130
Kindred, Sarah, 130
Kingsley, Charles H., 126
Kirkland, Pauline, 141
Knight, Andrew, 73, 246
Knight, John, 246
Knight, Josephus, 73, 245, 246
Knight, Sarah, 246, 325n54
Knight, Thomas, 73
Knight, William, 73, 246
Krick, Robert E. L., 302n59, 311n26
Ku Klux Klan, 268

Landingham, Irenus Watson, 46
Landrum, Ann Elizabeth "Lizzie" Harris, *176*
Landrum, Nancy Lula, *176*
Landrum, Willis, 103, *176*, 259–60
Landrum, Zack, 40, 160, 165–66, 259, 260, 328n36
Latham, Alexander C., 152
Law, Evander M.: and Battle of Antietam, 119, 121, 123, 124, 127; and Battle of Chickamauga, 185, 187; and Battle of Darbytown Road, 226; and Battle of Gaines's Mill, 91,

Law, Evander M. (*continued*)
93, 94, 95, 96, 98; and Battle of Gettysburg, 150, 152, 154–55, 159, 160, 161, 162, 313n71; and Battle of Second Manassas, 105–6; and Battle of the Wilderness, 208, 212
Lawrence, Groce, 212
Lawson, Asbury, 237
Lawton, Alexander, 120–21
Leach, E. W. B., 280
Lee, Robert E.: and Battle of Antietam, 116–17, 118, 119, 128; and Battle of Darbytown Road, 226, 227, 229; and Battle of Gaines's Mill, 97, 98, 103; and Battle of Gettysburg, 149, 150–52, 154, 164–65, 167; and Battle of New Market Heights, 221–22; and Battle of Second Manassas, 105, 106, 107; and Battle of Spotsylvania Court House, 216, 218; and Battle of the Wilderness, 208, 209, 212, 213, 214; and campaign season of 1862, 81, 86, 90; and campaign season of 1864, 219–20, 221; on desertions, 198–99; farewell address of, 252; and food rations, 138; and honorary Gold Stars for Hood's Texas Brigade, 245; and John Hood, 116, 117–18, 128; on Hood's Texas Brigade, 4–5, 8, 137, 205, 209, 212, 214, 227, 236, 239; Hood's Texas Brigade's devotion to, 7, 8, 10, 113, 137, 147, 165, 168, 212, 214, 231, 281; and Hood's Texas Brigade's resolution, 240; Hood's Texas Brigade's reuniting with, 202, 205–6, 231; Hood's Texas Brigade's separation from, 9, 183, 195, 205; and Maryland invasion, 114; and medical care, 322n2; recall of men on detached duty, 235; on recruitment, 136; surrender at Appomattox Court House, 250, 251, 252
Lee, Stephen D., 119
Lemon, James, 58, 59, 94–95, 96, 120, 123, 124
Lewis, Harriet C., 247–48
Lewis, Jackson, 209
Lewis, William E., 213
Lewis, William H., 213
Liles, Deborah M., 319n58
Lincoln, Abraham: assassination of, 257; election of, 2, 11, 12, 14, 22, 24, 134; and Joseph Hooker, 144; and George McClellan, 78, 90, 114; and Radical Republicans, 261. *See also* Emancipation Proclamation
Littlefield, J. H., 237
Livingston Guards, 26
Lockhart, W. G., 212
Lone Star Guards, 46
Lone Star Rifles of Galveston, 14, 15–16, 17, 26, 44
Longstreet, James: and Battle of Antietam, 116, 117, 118; and Battle of Chickamauga, 183–85, 189; and Battle of Gaines's Mill, 91, 93; and Battle of Gettysburg, 149, 150–52; and Battle of Second Manassas, 104–7, 111, 112; and Battle of the Wilderness, 208, 211, 212, 216; and campaign season of 1863, 147–48, 183–84, 194–95; and campaign season of 1864, 202, 206, 220; on Consolidation Bill, 235; and Hood's Texas Brigade, 5, 55, 72, 76, 137; and journey home following surrender, 255; and J. B. Robertson, 194, 196; and Suffolk Campaign, 145; and supplies, 145, 146; and winter of 1863–64, 197, 199
Loughridge, Ella, 71–72, *177*
Loughridge, Felicia: correspondence of, 76, 164, 165, 167, 200; and husband's postwar adjustment, 269; ideological dedication to Confederacy, 14, 72; portrait of, *176*; reflections on war in postwar period, 276
Loughridge, James Rodgers: and Battle of Chickamauga, 192–93; and Battle of Gaines's Mill, 93, 102, 148; and Battle of Gettysburg, 161, 164–65, 167; dedication to Confederate independence, 14, 71–72, 76, 167; as junior officer in Hood's Texas Brigade, 30, 40, 41, 76; portrait of, *177*; postwar adjustment of, 269; on reenlistment, 71–72; on secession movement, 13–14; in state legislature, 203
Loughridge, Mary, 71–72, *177*
Louisiana, and Texas regiments' journey to Virginia, 39–41, 55, 56, 63
Louisiana regiments, 46, 47, 61, 295n9
Lowery, Robert, 220, 255, 327n20
Lubbock, Francis, 35, 289n20, 325n50
Lubbock, T. S., 15
Lunday, R. W., 142

McBride, J. J., 213
McCalister, W. H., 112
McCarty, Thomas, 155, 163
McCary, William L., 19, 261
McClellan, George B.: and Battle of Antietam, 117, 118, 135; and Battle of Gaines's Mill, 90, 98; and campaign season of 1862, 78, 81, 90, 104; on Hood's Texas Brigade, 5; and Peninsula campaign, 114; and Potomac Blockade, 68; and Seven Days Battles, 102
McCown, Joshua Wilson, Jr., 318–19n53
McCown, Susan Turnham, 201
McCulloch, Henry, 34
McDowell, Irvin, 110
McKeen, Alfred C., 45
McKinnon, R. J., 230, 232, 249
McLaws, Lafayette: and Battle of Chickamauga, 184–85; and Battle of Gettysburg, 149, 150, 151, 152; and campaign season of 1863, 183–84; John Hood on, 136
McLeod, Hugh, 45, 63–64
McNelly, Leander H., 268
McRae, D. K., 127
Maddox, George, 64
Magee, Amanda, 261
Magee, Angie, 261
Magruder, John, 81
Mallory, Peter, 230, 249, 261
Malone, James K., 126
Manahan, James, 205–6
Manahan, Williametta "Willie" Thomason, 206, 319n3
Manning, Van H.: and Battle of Chickamauga, 185, 187, 190; and Battle of Gettysburg, 152, 154, 157, 158, 159, 164; as commander of Third Arkansas, 139, 185; portraits of, 178
Mansfield, Joseph K. F., 127
Marion Rifles, 14, 24–25, 26
Marshall, John (Chief Justice), 25
Marshall, John F.: and Battle of Gaines's Mill, 93, 94, 102; as Fourth Texas commander, 51–53, 57, 80–81; as newspaper editor, 12, 51; and Texas volunteers, 15, 32
Marshall Guards, 26–27
Marshall University, 26
Martin, Martha E. Gallemore, 324n31

Martin, Robert, 252
Martin, William H. "Howdy": and Battle of Antietam, 119–20; and Battle of Chickamauga, 252; and Battle of Darbytown Road, 252; and Battle of Gaines's Mill, 99; and campaign season of 1863, 148; and Consolidation Bill, 238–39; and Hood's Texas Brigade Association, 270; journey home following surrender, 250, 255, 327n20; as junior officer in Hood's Texas Brigade, 30; leadership of, 41, 238–39, 252; physical descriptions of, 38, 324n31, 324n32; portrait of, 178; postwar financial losses of, 258; and Potomac Blockade, 252; property of, 290n38; in state senate, 33; and surrender at Appomattox Court House, 252
Marvel, William, 285n19
May, Thomas, 40
May, W. C., 245
Meade, George Gordon, 150, 165, 204, 221
Menefee, Mary Elizabeth Penn, 36, 97, 128, 129, 289n20
Menefee, Quinn, 36, 97, 128, 129, 130, 289n26
Menefee, T. W., 36, 289n26
Menefee, Willie, 129
Mercer, Alfred, 234–35
Merriman, Charles, 262
Mexican War, 42, 45, 133
Mexico, relations with Texas, 34
middle class: definition of, 3; and families of Hood's Texas Brigade, 5, 73, 74, 206, 231, 242, 246, 259, 319n3; and Hood's Texas Brigade, 2–3, 5–6, 73, 74, 86, 114, 201, 290n35, 299n83; and peaceful restoration of social and racial order, 261, 264; postwar power of, 262; and slave owners, 18, 23; and Texas regiments, 37, 38, 290n35
Military District of the Southwest, 265
Miller, David R., 119, 121, 126
Miller, M. Erskine, 87, 101
Millett, Alonzo, 102
Millican, E. B., 207
Mills, Charles, 297n56
Mitchell, George, 109–10
Mitchell, Reid, 291n3
Mixon, Charles, 238

Moncrief, Charley, 112
Moodie, S. O., 280
Moore, Albert Berkley, 115
Morris, William, 95
Morse, Cecelia, 100, 128
Morse, George, 100
Morse, Henry, 100, 128
Morse, William, 128
Mosely, Sidney E., 234–35
Mullins, Newton, 112
Murphy, Jerry, 329n42
Murphy, Mort, 155, 261, 329n42
Murrah, Pendleton, 325n50
Murray, Asa, 253
Murray, James, 253–54
Murray, John David, 253–54
Murray, Owen, 253
Murray, Robert Washington, 253, 254, 327n14
Murray, Sarah, 253
Mustang Grays, 35, 39, 130, 253
Myers, Abraham C., 138

Nabors, William A., 257
Nance, C. P., 257
Napoleon I (emperor of the French), 49
Navarro County Court, local funds for families of soldiers, 201–2, 319n57
Navarro Rifles, 33, 39, 40
Newman, T. J., 268–69
New Orleans, Louisiana, Texas regiments in, 24–29, 39, 40–41
New South, 258
New York Herald, 223
New York Times, 85
Nichols, Ebenezer B., 34
Nichols, George W., 191
Nineteenth Indiana, 123
Ninetieth Pennsylvania, 121
Ninety-Ninth Pennsylvania, 157, 159
Ninth Pennsylvania Reserves, 126
Noe, Kenneth W., 318n48
Norwood, John, 318n47

Ochiltree, Tom, 69
Ochiltree, William, 69
Oldham, William S., 298n77

Oliver, A. C., 89, 271
Oliver, John, 271
Oliver, S. W., 271
Oliver, William H., 271
101st Ohio, 187
124th New York, 157, 158–59
O'Neill, J. J., 106
O'Rear, John Pinkney "Pink," 229
O'Rourke, Patrick, 162
Outlaw, Nat, 268
Owen, Asenath, 74
Owen, Elizabeth, 74
Owen, John Wade, 74, 290n36, 299n83
Owen, Samuel Tine, 37, 39, 74, 75
Owen, Sarah, 74

Palmer Guards, 25, 26, 28
Panic of 1857, 24
paternalism, 3, 23, 225, 264
Patrick, Marsena, 123
Patterson, James, 245
Paulman, Ann, 278
Paulman, Henry, 278
Pender, Dorsey, 5, 8
Penn, Abe, 37
Penn, Patrick: and Battle of Antietam, 128–29, 130; and Battle of Gaines's Mill, 93, 96–97, 99, 100; and Camp Van Dorn, 35; family background of, 36–37, 289n20, 289n25; on Founding Fathers, 293n37; and journey to Virginia, 39–40; on Richmond, 47
Perkins, Chapman, 134
Perkins, Charles, 77
Perkins, Hugh, 134–35, 136
Perkins, Margaret, 134
Perry, Bose, 215
Perry, Clinton, 89, 215
Perry, Eugene O.: and Battle of Chickamauga, 187, 215; and Battle of the Wilderness, 214–15; on food rations, 295–96n19; and officer elections, 89; and Potomac Blockade, 64, 68; on recruitment, 71; on Louis Wigfall, 56
Perry, Howard, 215
Perry, William F., 155, 212, 213, 214, 313n71
Petty, Virginius, 112
Pfanz, Harry W., 285n19

Phelps, Walter, Jr., 121, 123
Philips, Jason, 326*n*1
Pickens, James D., 225
Pickett, George, 145, 220
Pickett-Pettigrew-Trimble charge, 163
Poague, William T., 209, 211–12, 214
Polk, J. M., 120, 121, 123, 271
Pollard, Edward, 285*n*1
Polley, Joseph B. "Joe": and Battle of Antietam, 119; and Battle of Cold Harbor, 219; and Battle of Darbytown Road, 229, 274; and Battle of Gaines's Mill, 93, 99; and Battle of New Market Heights, 223; and Battle of Second Manassas, 110–11; and Battle of the Wilderness, 208–9, 213; and Battle of Wauhatchie, 194; on campaign season of 1863, 140–41, 192, 195; on campaign season of 1864, 220–21; on food rations, 196; on Hampton's Legion, 88; on John Hood's leadership, 80, 93, 117, 140–41; and Hood's Texas Brigade Association, 270, 273–74; and Hood's Texas Brigade veterans' monument, 272, 273; and ideological dedication to Confederacy, 115–16; on journey to Virginia, 39; on John Marshall, 53; portrait of, *179;* and postwar adjustment, 274, 275, 279; and Potomac Blockade, 66, 68–69; on Jerome Robertson's leadership, 140–41, 194; on Texas regiments, 184; on Ike Turner, 307*n*60; on Louis Wigfall, 55, 56
Pope, John, 104, 105, 109, 111, 114
Poppenheim, D. P., 124
Porter, Fitz John, 90
Porter, Proctor, 31, 33
Porter Guards, 40, 188, 259
postwar adjustment, and Hood's Texas Brigade, 6–7, 9–10, 263–64, 266, 269, 274–75, 278
Potomac Blockade, Winter 1861–1862: and disease, 8, 61–64, 67, 69, 70; ending of, 78; and food rations, 63, 77; location of camps, 59, 60, 61, 64, 294–95*n*6; objectives of, 67–68, 297*n*54; and permanent winter quarters, 64–67, 69, 75, 77–78; and respect for locals' property, 65–66; retreat from, 75; and scouting raids, 68–69, 74; and Union/Confederate animosity, 74, 299*n*80

poverty: definition of, 2–3; of families of Hood's Texas Brigade, 242, 243–44
Powell, David A., 285*n*19
Powell, Robert M. "Mike": and Battle of Gettysburg, 154, 160–61, 164, 168, 185; on peaceful restoration of social and racial order, 261–62; and surrender at Appomattox Court House, 251; and Texas volunteers, 32, 33
Prairie Blade, 13–14
Price, Frank, 71, 325*n*52
Price, Mintie, 71, 325*n*52
Prichard, W. D., 66
Pridgen, John J., 217
Pry, Samuel, 119
Pryor, Charles R., 12

Quattlebaum, Paul J., 50, 53

Rachal, Anais, 231
Rachal, Cyriaque, 231
Rachal, Darius, 231, 232, 248, 249
racial superiority: Hood's Texas Brigade soldiers' views on, 4, 225–26; Hood's Texas Brigade veterans views on, 266–67
racial violence, 223, 225–26, 268. *See also* Battle of New Market Heights
Radical Republican Party, 4, 261, 266
Rainey, Alexis T., 28–29, 63, 84, 85, 102, 105, 185
Rainey, Ann, 28
Ramsey, F. M., 137–38
Randall, W. P., 214
Ransom, Dunbar, 125
Raven Hill Plantation, 72–73, 206, 266
Rawls, Tom, 97
Reagan, John, 98, 239, 255
Reagan Guards, 29
Reardon, Carol, 285*n*19
Reconstruction: and Hood's Texas Brigade, 6, 9, 10, 251, 258, 268, 282; and racial violence, 268; socioeconomic reforms of, 258
Red River Real Estate Company, 269
Reeves, Leila Ione, 201
Reeves, Malachiah, 198, 201
Régis de Trobriand, Philip, 157
Reilly, James, 152, 310*n*13

Republican Party, 2, 4, 261, 266
Republic of Texas, 45
Rhea, Gordon, 285n19
Rice, D. K., 136–37, 316n5
Richmond Examiner, 242
Richmond Whig, 141, 247, 310n23, 311n26
Ricketts, James B., 121, 123
Riggs, Jane Gillette, 289n21
Ripley, Paul, 257
Robertson, Jerome Bonaparte: and Battle of Chickamauga, 183, 184, 187, 188, 189, 190, 191, 196, 316n5; and Battle of Gettysburg, 153, 154, 162, 164, 185, 196; and Battle of Second Manassas, 105, 111, 112; court-martial of, 196, 200; and desertions, 199; and drilling, 140; and Hood's Texas Brigade Veterans' Association, 269; and leadership of Hood's Texas Brigade, 8, 9, 53, 139, 140–43, 183, 184, 185, 194, 196, 197, 200; nicknames of, 140; and recruitment, 288n11; transfer to Trans-Mississippi West, 196, 237
Rodes, Robert E., 118
Rogers, J. C., 161, 185, 188, 200–201
Rogers, William, 18–19, 242
Rosecrans, William S., 184, 189, 191
Rowe, Dennis, 257, 261
Ruff, Solon Z., 93–94, 121, 127, 128

St. Francis de Sales hospital, Richmond, 142, 311n26
Salter, Charles H., 161
San Antonio Semi-Weekly, 99
Sandy Point Mounted Rifles, 37–38
Santa Fe Expedition of 1841, 45
Schadt, Carl, 16–17
Schadt, Caroline, 16, 17, 84–85, 214
Schadt, Caroline Schaeffer, 16–17
Schadt, Charles, 16, 17, 44–45, 84–85
Schadt, William, 16, 17, 45, 84–85, 88, 214
Schaller, Frank, 3, 49–50, 53, 79
Scroggs, Joseph, 225
Searle, Edwin, 237–38
secession: and defense of rights as slave owners, 4; James Loughridge on, 13–14; in South Carolina, 22; in Texas, 13, 18, 19, 24, 26, 28; William Townsend on,' 133; Louis Wigfall on, 11–12
Second U.S. Sharpshooters, 123, 154
Second Wisconsin, 121, 123
Seddon, James, 145, 235, 236
Seguin, Texas, 20–21
self-made man, 3, 5, 50, 258
Sellers, W. H., 105, 112
Selman, Thomas: on Confederate independence, 86; on food rations, 137, 138, 140; on John Hood, 81–82; and journey to Virginia, 40; on John Marshall, 51; portrait of, *179;* and recruitment, 153; on Richmond, 46; on Jerome Robertson, 140; and Seven Days Battle, 103
Settle, Charles, 229
Seven Days Battles, 102–3
Seventeenth Maine, 157
Seventh Texas Infantry, 184
Seventh Wisconsin, 123, 134–35
Seventy-Sixth New York, 105, 106
Sevy, Albert, 76
Shaw, James, 213
Sheffield, James L., 185, 187, 189
Sheppard, Webb, 34
Sheridan, Philip, 221, 265
Sherman, William Tecumseh, 106, 219, 247, 255, 274
Shockley, William, 64, 65, 66
Short, Elvira, 194
Short, John, 193, 194
Short, William, 194
Shotwell, John, 229
Shropshire, J. Winkfield, 125
Sickles, Daniel, 59, 69, 80–81, 151, 157
Simmons, James, 12
Simpson, Harold B., 287n34, 311n26, 318n45, 320n5
Simpson, John Nicholas, 274
Sims, A. C., 149–50, 151, 155, 159–60, 162–63
Sims, Albert Hubert, 150
Sixteenth Michigan, 161–62
Sixth Texas Cavalry, 206
Sixth Wisconsin, 121, 123
slave conspiracies, 12

slave owners: families of Hood's Texas Brigade as, 5, 7, 36, 37, 72, 114, 115, 130, 143–44, 147, 258, 298n69; Hood's Texas Brigade officers as, 3, 4, 5, 133, 143–44; and middle class, 18, 23; paternalism of, 23; and secession, 4; Texas regiment soldiers as, 36, 37, 143–44
slave patrols, 22
slave rebellions, 18, 22
slavery: Confederate troops' views of, 284n8; economic wealth generated by, 37; Hood's Texas Brigade soldiers' views of, 3, 9, 133, 226, 241, 258; North's push for limits to expansion of, 133, 226; Republican Party's policies on, 2
Smilie, Jake, 97–98
Smilie, James, 91, 98
Smilie, William, 98
Smith, E. Kirby, 9, 55, 61, 231, 255
Smith, Gustavus A., 5
Smith, G. W., 84
Smith, James, 157, 158, 159, 160
Smith, Joe, 109
Smith, John Wesley, 257
Smith, Miles, 190, 216
Smith, Pulaski, 271
Smith, Ron, 294–95n6
Smither, Elizabeth E. Calmes, 43–44, 149
Smither, John Marquis "Mark": and Battle of Antietam, 119, 127; and Battle of Eltham's Landing, 85; and Battle of Gettysburg, 149, 151; and Battle of Spotsylvania Court House, 216–17; and Battle of the Wilderness, 213; and campaign season of 1862, 82; and campaign season of 1863, 142; on Stonewall Jackson, 147; optimism of, 147, 167–68, 312n49; postwar life of, 264, 278; and Potomac Blockade, 63, 65, 66, 75–76, 77, 296n19; on reputation of Texans, 42–43, 46; on Suffolk Campaign, 146; on Ike Turner, 145
Smither, Robert, 43–44
social class: and citizen-soldier volunteers, 41; and families of Hood's Texas Brigade, 5, 20–21, 35–36, 37, 44, 73, 74, 147, 201, 206, 213, 231, 242, 246, 251, 258, 259, 289n25, 289n26, 291n4, 298n69, 312n48, 319n3, 322n7; and Hood's Texas Brigade, 2–3, 36; and Texas regiments, 36, 37, 44, 290n35. *See also* middle class; poverty; upper class
social order: Hood's Texas Brigade soldiers' views on, 4; and Hood's Texas Brigade veterans' rebuilding antebellum social order, 265–67; Mike Powell's views on peaceful restoration of, 261–62, 264
Society of the Army and Navy of the Confederate States, 277
Soldiers' Aid Society of Guadalupe County, 201
Southern Confederacy, 61–62
Spirit of '61 (camp newsletter), 59
Spratting, James P., 297n56
Spratting, J. B., 69
Staples, Elizabeth, 193
Staples, J. D., 245
Staples, Jethro, 193
Staples, John, 193
Staples, William, 193
Stevens, John, 120, 145–46, 324n31
Stonewall Brigade, 238
Stuart, J. E. B., 117
Suffolk Campaign, 145, 146
Sullivan, Bettie, 40
Sullivan, Lucy Morton, 37, 99–100, *180*
Sullivan, Morton, 37, 40
Sullivan, Robert Anderson: and Battle of Gaines's Mill, 99–100, 128, 129; and Camp Van Dorn, 35; family background of, 36–37, 289n25; and journey to Virginia, 39–40; on Francis Lubbock, 35, 289n20; and military life, 39; portrait of, *180;* on Richmond, 47
Sullivan, Timothy, 105
Sullivan, William, 36
Sultzer, Thomas D., 277–78
Swinney, Ransom, 145

Taft, Howard, 274
Tannehill, William, 63
Tapp, Catharine, 208, 209, 211, 212, 214, 215
Tapp, Phenie, 209
Tarkington, John Lewis, 167, 315n111
Tarkington, Mary Elizabeth, 315n111

Templeman, Madison Monroe, 85
Tenth New York, 109
Terry, William, 233–34, 238
Terry's Texas Rangers, 184, 274
Texas: Arkansas compared with, 328–29n39; companies raised in, 14–19; defense of, 13, 15, 23, 30, 33–34, 39, 130, 131, 139, 144, 150, 207, 236; economy of, 242, 247, 258, 259, 264, 268, 328–29n39; immigrants in, 16–17; inflation in, 242, 247; possible Federal invasion of, 34; reputation of Texans, 42–43, 44, 46–50, 58, 65, 74, 80, 85, 291n3; secession in, 13, 18, 19, 24, 26, 28; total wealth of counties in 1860 compared to 1870, 259, 260; Unionists in, 12, 13, 17–18, 19, 266, 279; Union occupation of, 260–61, 275; volunteer rates in, 73
Texas Battalion, 29, 30, 45
Texas Confederate Home for Men, 271
Texas Confederate Veterans Home, 10, 270
Texas Guards, 28–29
Texas Hospital, Richmond, 62, 143, 167, 243, 246, 311n26
Texas Rangers, 20, 21, 31
Texas regiments: drilling of, 38, 44–45; and scouting duties, 58; and selection of officers, 42, 47–54, 56–57; and social class, 36, 37, 290n35; volunteering for fighting in Virginia, 14–19, 30, 34, 37, 38–40, 42, 46–47, 56. *See also* specific regiments
Texas Republican (Marshall), 27, 73
Texas Revolution, 258
Texas State Gazette (Austin), 73
Texas Troubles, 14
Third Arkansas Infantry: and Battle of Antietam, 139; and Battle of Chickamauga, 188, 190; and Battle of Gettysburg, 154, 155, 157, 158, 159, 162; and Battle of Spotsylvania Courthouse, 217; and Battle of the Wilderness, 211–12, 214; and Emancipation Proclamation, 143; and Hood's Texas Brigade Association, 270; horses of, 147; joining Hood's Texas Brigade, 8, 139; and journey home following surrender, 254–55; and Van Manning, 138, 185; and postwar financial losses, 259; reputation of, 139, 149; and selection of officers, 196; and surrender at Appomattox Court House, 254
Third Brigade of Texas Militia, 32
Thirteenth Pennsylvania Reserves, 119–20, 125–26
Thirteenth Texas Infantry Regiment, 150
Thirty-Eighth Illinois, 187
Thirty-Seventh New Yorkers, 69
Thomas, Howell G., 53–54
Thomason, John W., Jr., 324n31
Thompson, James, 121
Thompson, L. A., 15
Thompson, Leslie, 152
Thornwell, G. R., 73–74
Tilden, John Newel, 234
Tiner, James, 264–65
Tiner, Mary, 264–65, 278
Todd, George T., 84, 294n6
Tom Green Rifles, 62, 207
Townsend, Almira, 102, 132, 133
Townsend, Tom, 133
Townsend, William P., 52, 53, 57, 102, 105, 132–33
Trans-Mississippi West, 139, 185, 196, 207, 267, 281, 318n45
Travis, Henry, 131–32
Trudeau, Noah Andrew, 285n19
Turner, Ike: and Battle of Antietam, 12, 119–20, 123, 127–28, 136, 145, 307n60; and Potomac Blockade, 64; and Suffolk Campaign, 145
Twelfth Corps, 127
Twentieth Indiana, 157, 158
Twentieth Texas Cavalry, 74, 299n83
Twenty-First Ohio, 190
Twenty-First Texas Cavalry, 310n17
Twenty-Fourth New York, 106

Unionists, in Texas, 12, 13, 17–18, 19, 266, 279
U.S. Colored Troops (USCT), 222–23, 225, 226, 227, 248
upper class: definition of, 3; and families of Hood's Texas Brigade, 20–21, 35–36, 37, 147, 213, 246, 251, 259, 289n25, 289n26, 298n69,

312n48; and First Texas Infantry Regiment, 290n35; and Fourth Texas Infantry Regiment, 130, 147; postwar power of, 262
Upton, Ann, 112
Upton, John C.: and Battle of Gaines's Mill, 93, 97, 100; and Battle of Second Manassas, 111–12; as junior officer in Hood's Texas Brigade, 30, 34; as middle class, 3
Ursuline Convent, Galveston, 243

Van Dorn, Earl, 34, 38–39
Vicksburg, Mississippi, 146, 165, 168, 207, 318n45
Vincent, Strong, 162
Virginia: surrender at Appomattox Court House, 9, 250, 251, 252–54, 326n68; Texas regiments' journey to, 26–27, 39–40, 55, 56, 63; Texas regiments volunteering for fighting in, 14–19, 30, 34, 37, 38–40, 42, 46–47, 56. *See also specific battles*
Virginia Military Institute, 26, 185

Wadsworth, James S., 213
Walker, Elijah, 211
Walker, John, 13
Ward, John Henry Hobart, 157, 158
Warde, Jennette, 28
Warren, Gouverneur K., 207
Warwick, Bradfute, 94, 98, 102
Watson, Pleasant B., 109, 112, 304n15
Watson, Samuel S., 222–23, 247–48
Watson, Samuel T., 297n56
Watts, Willis J., 248
Waverley Confederates, 42, 47
Webb, Berry, 297n56
Webb, Stephen, 297n56
Welborn, C., 245
Wells, Lou, 52
West, Eliza, 153, 165
West, John, 153, 165, 167, 198
Wheeler, J. G., 212
Whig Party, 26
White, W. W., 59
Whiting, W. C. "Chase": and Battle of Gaines's Mill, 90, 91, 97, 98, 302n59; and campaign season of 1862, 83; on Hood's Texas Brigade, 8, 294n5, 294n6; illness of, 104; and officers of Hood's Texas Brigade, 78; and Potomac Blockade, 67, 69; on withdrawal from Potomac, 77
Whittemore, Frank, 157
Wigfall, Charlotte, 165
Wigfall, Louise, 165
Wigfall, Louis Trezevant: as commander of Texas Brigade, 11–12, 15, 23, 29, 44, 45, 54–56, 61, 64–65, 71, 84, 292n6, 295n9; and Confederate Senate, 77, 78, 298n77; and Consolidation Bill, 239; on cotton, 21; elite regiment raised by, 16; and honorary Gold Stars for Hood's Texas Brigade, 245; on Hood's Texas Brigade, 98; journey home following surrender, 255; and Mrs. Wigfall's flag, 126; and naming of First Texas Infantry Regiment, 296–97n37; portrait of, *181;* and Potomac Blockade, 69; and recruitment, 132; on slavery, 226; on soldiers' morale, 245; training regime of, 44–45
Wilcox, Cadmus M., 209, 221
Wilder, John T., 189
Wild Tiger Rifles, 47
Wilkerson, John, 157
Williams, Eugenia, 218
Williams, Laura Bryan: correspondence with King Bryan, 41; correspondence with Dugat Williams, 88, 116, 146, 192, 197, 249; engagement of, 142; marriage of, 258
Williams, T. D., 240
Williams, T. Harry, 6
Williams, Watson Dugat: and Amnesty Oath, 264; and Battle of Antietam, 119; and Battle of Chickamauga, 192; and Battle of Darbytown Road, 230; and Battle of Gettysburg, 151; and Battle of Spotsylvania Courthouse, 218; and Battle of the Wilderness, 214, 218; and campaign season of 1864, 219; on Company F, 87–88; on Confederate independence, 116; family background of, 19–20; family of, 301n46; on food rations, 145; and ideological dedication to Confederacy, 146; on isolation, 197; and journey home fol-

Williams, Watson Dugat (*continued*) lowing surrender, 255; journey to Virginia, 40–41; on mess mates, 248–49; and officer's role, 48–49; on postwar financial losses, 257–58; on Potomac Blockade, 65, 295n6, 296n29; and recruitment, 86–87, 116, 142, 144, 204; on relations with Union soldiers, 143; on returning furloughed men, 202; on Jerome Robertson, 143; on Frank Schaller, 50; as veteran, 261

Willingham, Thomas, 297n56

Wilson, Donald L., 294n6

Wilson, Herod, 124

Winckler, Angelina V. Smith, 102–3, 205, 230

Winkler, Clinton M.: and Battle of Darbytown Road, 229; and Battle of Gaines's Mill, 102; and Battle of Gettysburg, 192; and campaign season of 1864, 221; on John Hood as commander, 79; leadership of, 240; on Robert E. Lee, 205; and J. R. Loughridge, 269; and recruitment, 14, 33

Wofford, William T.: and Battle of Antietam, 119, 121, 136; and Battle of Gaines's Mill, 93; and Battle of Second Manassas, 105, 112; and leadership of Hood's Texas Brigade, 8, 64–65, 139

Wolfe, S. G., 310n17

Wollard, Andy, 46–47

Wolseley, Garnet, 136–37

Womack, Mark, 51

women: effects of war on Texas women, 243–45, 319n58; and fund-raising efforts, 243, 246–47, 324n44; as soldiers, 28, 46; as widows of Hood's Texas Brigade veterans, 265, 278

Wood, Bennett, 91

Wood, Campbell, 168

Wood, Thomas, 190

Woodville Rifles of Tyler County, 15

Woodward, Colin Edward, 284n8

Woodward, John M., 29, 125

Work, Philip A.: and Battle of Antietam, 120, 121, 124–27, 128, 136, 308n81; and Battle of Gettysburg, 154, 157, 158, 159, 162, 166; and Battle of Second Manassas, 105, 107; and Jefferson Davis, 15; health of, 185, 316n5

Worsham, C. S., 193

Worsham, Ned, 193

Wynne, Elizabeth Smither, 44, 147, 168, 264, 291n4, 312n48, 312n49

Wynne, Erasmus, 44, 147, 264, 291n4, 312n48

yellow fever, 17, 28, 31, 43, 85, 269

YMCA, 311n26

Young, Alfred C., 321n34, 322n3

Young, Maude Jeannie Fuller: and T. W. Fitzgerald, 276, 277; and flag for Fifth Texas, 246–47, 254, 276; fund-raising efforts of, 246–47, 277; honorary Gold Stars donated by, 246, 325n55; portrait of, *182;* reflections on war in postwar period, 276

Young, Samuel O., 246

www.ingramcontent.com/pod-product-compliance
Lightning Source LLC
Chambersburg PA
CBHW051249300426
44114CB00011B/952